Terms introduced with PSP1

PSP1 Project Plan Summary	
LOC/Hour	The total new and changed LOC developed to date divided by the hours required to develop them; LOC/Hour = 60*(N, To Date)/(Time in Phase, Total To Date)
Base LOC (B), Plan	When a previously developed program is to be enhanced, its total LOC are counted before start of development.
Deleted LOC (D), Plan	The LOC to be deleted from the base; estimated during project planning
Modified LOC (M), Plan	The base program LOC that are to be modified; estimated during project planning
Added LOC (A), Plan	The LOC to be added; calculated as $A = N - M$
Reused LOC (R), Plan	The previously developed program LOC to be reused without modification; additions are counted as New Reused LOC
New and Changed LOC (N), Actual	The code to be either added or modified during development; calculated on the Size Estimating Template: $N = \beta_0 + \beta_1(P + M)$
Total LOC (T), Plan	The planned total LOC for the finished program; calculated as $T = N + B - M - D + R$
New Reused LOC, Plan	The portion of the new and changed LOC planned for addition to the reuse library

Size Estimating Template	
Base Additions (BA)	Those LOC to be added to the base program
New Objects (NO)	The LOC of new objects to be developed
Projected LOC (P)	The projected LOC to be developed: $P = BA + NO$
M	The base LOC that are modified
LPI	lower prediction interval; LPI = N − Range
UPI	upper prediction interval; UPI = N + Range
N	New and changed lines of code (N): $N = \beta_0 + \beta_1(P + M)$
β_0, β_1	Linear regression parameters

(PSP1 terms continued inside back cover)

A Discipline for Software Engineering

Watts S. Humphrey
CARNEGIE MELLON UNIVERSITY

ADDISON-WESLEY PUBLISHING COMPANY

Reading, Massachusetts ■ Menlo Park, California ■ New York
Don Mills, Ontario ■ Wokingham, England ■ Amsterdam ■ Bonn
Sydney ■ Singapore ■ Tokyo ■ Madrid ■ San Juan ■ Milan ■ Paris

SOFTWARE ENGINEERING INSTITUTE
THE SEI SERIES IN SOFTWARE ENGINEERING

Associate Editors
Peter Freeman, *Georgia Institute of Technology*
John Musa, *AT&T Bell Laboratories*
Editorial Advisors
Roger Bate, *Software Engineering Institute*
Laszlo Belady, *Mitsubishi Electronic Research Laboratory*
Barry Boehm, *University of Southern California*
John Ellis, *Xerox Corporation*
Robert Goldberg, *IBM Corporate Technical Institutes*
Harlan D. Mills, *Software Engineering and Technology Institute*
William E. Riddle, *Software Design and Analysis, Inc.*
William A. Wulf, *University of Virginia*

Library of Congress Cataloging–in–Publication Data

Humphrey, Watts S.
    A discipline for software engineering / Watts S. Humphrey.
    p. cm. — (SEI series in software engineering)
    Includes bibliographical references and index.
    ISBN 0-201-54610-8
    1. Software engineering. I. Title. II. Series.
QA76.758.H857 1995
005.1—dc20   93-41673
                                                                    CIP

1 2 3 4 5 6 7 8 9 10-MA-9897969594

TO DR. JOHN E. YARNELLE

an inspiring teacher

CREDITS

Figures 1.1 and 1.2: Paulk et al, *Capability Maturity for Software*, Version 1.1, CMU/SEI-93-TR-24, February 1993. Reprinted with permission from the Software Engineering Institute.

Figure 11.2: Boehm, "A Spiral Model of Software Development and Enhancement," *IEEE Computer*, May 1988, p. 64, © 1988 IEEE. Reprinted with permission.

Table 5.3: Putnam/Myers, *Measures for Excellence: Reliable Software on Time, Within Budget*, © 1992, p. 77. Reprinted with permission of Prentice Hall, Englewood Cliffs, NJ.

Tables 5.4, 5.5, and quote on p. 109: Jones, *Applied Software Measurement: Assuring Productivity and Quality*, © 1991, NY: McGraw-Hill, Inc. Reprinted with permission.

Table 6.1: T. F. Winslow, Construction Industry Production Manual, © 1972, Carlsbad, CA: Craftsman Book Co., p. 49. Reprinted with permission.

Table 10.3: Denis De Champeaux, Douglas Lea and Penelope Faure, *Object-Oriented System Development*, © 1993 Hewlett-Packard Co., p. 186. Reprinted by permission of Addison-Wesley Publishing Co., Inc.

Table 12.2: From Mills, *Principles of Computer Programming*, © 1987 by Allyn and Bacon. Reprinted with permission.

Table 13.1: Feiler, *Software Process Development and Enactment: Concepts and Definitions*, CMU/SEI-92-TR-04, September 1992. Reprinted with permission from Software Engineering Institute.

Table 13.2: Horn, *Developing Procedures, Policies, and Documentation*, © 1991 R. E. Horn, p. 1. Reprinted with permission of Information Mapping, Inc., Waltham, Massachusetts.

Table A1: Donald B. Owen, Handbook of Statistical Tables, © 1962 Addison-Wesley Publishing Co., Inc., pp. 3–10. Reprinted with permission.

Table A2: From Table III of Fisher & Yates, *Statistical Tables for Biological, Agricultural and Medical Research*, published by Longman Group UK Ltd., 1974.

Table A3: Adapted from *Biometrika Tables for Statisticians*, Vol. 1, 3/E, Cambridge University Press, 1966, edited by E. S. Pearson and H. O. Hartley; and from H. L. Harter, "A new table of percentage points of the chi-square distribution," *Biometrika*, Vol. 1, 1964. Reprinted with permission of the Biometrika Trustees.

FOREWORD

This book presents a new approach to a problem that has bedeviled software engineering since its infancy. We have long known that by using standard engineering and scientific principles, we can improve our profession. What we have not known is how to introduce these principles in a way that will convince engineers to consistently practice them. In this book, Watts Humphrey introduces a disciplined way to do software engineering. By discipline, however, he does not mean constraining regimentation but rather the rapid and powerful learning that comes from a measured and structured working environment. By following the step-by-step exercises in this book, software engineers can learn how to use these methods. They can then see for themselves where the methods help and how they can use them for the greatest personal benefit.

These concepts, however, are not new. In any scientific and engineering discipline, improvement comes about in an evolutionary fashion:

- □ Through the definition of good processes
- □ Through experimentation with those processes in the domain in which they will be applied
- □ Through measurement of the effects of the processes on the product being built
- □ Through feedback of those effects to the designer of the processes
- □ And finally, through the further refinement of those processes based on the feedback

This experimentation, measurement, and feedback loop is not a one-pass algorithm but a way of doing business. It exemplifies continuous improvement and epitomizes evolutionary learning: planning, doing, learning, and using what we have learned to improve.

These evolutionary improvement concepts have been applied in manufacturing to improve all forms of production. People like Shewart, Deming, and Juran have demonstrated that the use of experimentation, measurement, and feedback loops, combined with statistical quality control, can dramatically improve the quality of manufactured goods.

In recent years, we have come to recognize that software development is an engineering process, and so we, too, must learn and improve through experimentation, measurement, and feedback. Several of us have worked on applying these evolutionary improvement concepts to the development domain rather than the production domain. For example, I personally have worked in the Software Engineering Laboratory (SEL) at NASA Goddard Space Flight Center to tailor these concepts for development at the organization level rather than the production level. That is, how does an organization learn and improve in an evolutionary manner?

There are two potential problems with applying these concepts to software development. First, we do not necessarily have the same number of data points that can be gathered from the manufacture of thousands of products. We can, however, still gather data, learn from the data, and use the feedback information for improvement. Second, software professionals generally have not developed the personal skills and disciplines needed to gather and use the data that are available to them. They are thus not aware of the great potential benefits of these methods.

With this book, Watts Humphrey has developed an evolutionary improvement paradigm, at the personal level, by providing a mechanism for learning through experience, measurement, and feedback. The mechanism enables individual engineers to understand their own strengths and weaknesses and improve their programming performance and abilities.

The book covers all the details and provides many examples, most of them personal experiences of the author, in a clear, step-by-step manner. It can be used by individuals or in a classroom setting and in fact has been successfully used in both ways. If we are to improve the processes of organizations, we first need to improve the processes of the individual and make the programmer cognizant of the various aspects of evolutionary improvement.

The approach should help software developers of all abilities to improve the way they develop software by improving their understanding of themselves and their activities, i.e., what they do, where they spend their time, and the kinds of mistakes they make. This improvement should take place for all programmers. It should affect how we teach programming, by showing them how to build their own feedback loops and therefore to think of programming as an iterative process that can be continually improved.

I would expect that engineers who take seriously the approach recommended in this book will learn more about their own personal software development processes and then be able to improve their personal performance in a measurable way.

Vic Basili
University of Maryland

PREFACE

Have you ever written what you thought would be a simple program but struggled for hours to get it to work? Even the best software engineers make many errors, and some of the defects they introduce can be unbelievably hard to find. Such personal difficulties, while inconvenient for individual engineers, can be a severe problem for the engineers' organizations. Software quality starts with the individual engineer. If even your smallest programs are not of the highest quality, they will be hard to test, take time to integrate into larger systems, and be cumbersome to use.

You have probably noticed that you can be highly productive when you write very small programs. Your productivity, however, falls off sharply when you develop larger programs. While some of this is due to the added tasks that come with larger projects, a significant part of the problem is caused by defects. As you write larger programs, the difficulty of finding and fixing problems increases exponentially. If you consistently wrote very high-quality small programs, you would not only produce better products but you also could substantially improve your own and your organization's productivity.

A disciplined software engineering process includes both effective defect management and comprehensive planning, tracking, and analysis methods. This book introduces these disciplines and shows you how to use them to do better development work on both small and large programs.

The Approach Taken by This Book

Software is now a critical element in many businesses, but all too often the work is late, over budget, or of poor quality. Society is now far too dependent on software products for us to continue with the craft-like practices of the past. It needs engineers who consistently use effective disciplines. For this to happen, they must be taught these disciplines and have an opportunity to practice and perfect them during their formal educations.

Today, when students start to program, they generally begin by learning a programming language. They practice on toy problems and develop the personal skills and techniques to deal with issues at this toy problem level. As they take more courses, they improve these methods and soon find they can develop fairly large programs relatively quickly. These programming-in-the-small skills, however, are inherently limited. While they may have sufficed on small-scale individual tasks, they do not provide an adequate foundation for solving the problems of large-scale multiperson projects.

This book follows a fundamentally different strategy. It scales down industrial software practices to fit the needs of small scale program development. It then walks you through a progressive sequence of software processes that provide a sound foundation for large scale software development. By doing the exercises and using the methods described in this book to analyze your results, you will learn how to use the methods for yourself. Once you have learned and used these practices on small programs, you will have a solid foundation on which to build a personal software engineering discipline.

The principal goal of this book is to guide you in developing the personal software engineering skills that you will need for large-scale software work. You will learn how to make accurate plans, how to estimate the accuracy of these plans, and how to track your performance against them. You will use defect management, design and code reviews, design templates, and process analysis. You will do this with a defined and measured personal software process. These measurement and analysis disciplines will then help you to evaluate your performance, to understand your strengths, and to see where you should try to improve. From all of this you will develop the tools to continue your personal improvement throughout your professional career.

This Book's Audience

This book was designed as a text for graduate and senior-level undergraduate university courses. It is also designed to help experienced engineers work through the material on their own. The book is self-contained, and no special preparation is required. While substantial use is made of statistics, the statistical methods are explained wherever they are needed.

As is true in most walks of life, the benefits you get will depend on the efforts you invest. You are urged to do the exercises at the end of each chapter. You should write at least 10 of these small- to modest-sized programs, gathering data on your work, analyzing these data, and producing project summary reports. Then use these results to make process improvements for the next exercise. Each exercise should take about 5 to 10 hours to complete, with some taking a little more or less time.

These programming examples involve developing (or enhancing) small programs. While writing small programs is not the only important aspect of software development, small programming exercises can be used to demonstrate many of the practices engineers should master during their educations. Small-scale program development also turns out to be the only significant aspect of the software life cycle that can be reduced to challenging individual-sized exercises. These exercises should thus be viewed as illustrations of various engineering methods. After learning these methods on these small programming exercises, you will better see how to use them on larger projects.

Whether you are a student or an experienced engineer, you will be exposed to an evolving software development process that introduces many of the practices you will need for large-scale software development. You will see the difference between being a programmer and being a professional software engineer. You will better appreciate which practices best suit which tasks. You will more thoroughly understand your own capabilities and be able to make commitments you can more consistently meet. All of this will enable you to be a more effective team member and to deal more responsibly with your peers and your managers. In sum, the methods and practices you learn from this book will help you to improve your personal performance as a software engineer.

FOR INSTRUCTORS WHO WANT TO USE THIS BOOK AS A TEXTBOOK

When using this book as a textbook for either a graduate or senior-level undergraduate course, you should work through the material from beginning to end, having the students do a programming project or process analysis exercise every week. Depending on the time available, you could assign from 10 to 19 of the programming exercises and the five process reports. While one assignment strategy is suggested in the book, many others are possible. Appendix D describes the interdependencies among the book chapters, the process levels, and the programming and report exercises. By reviewing this material, you can construct an assignment strategy to suit your particular needs.

Before taking this course, students should be reasonably adept with at least one programming language, understand basic design methods, and have been exposed to the rudiments of the software life cycle. To obtain maximum benefit from the material, they should be encouraged to use a programming language with which they are thoroughly familiar. Students who use this course to learn a new programming language will not see as clearly the benefits of their improving personal process.

It would also be helpful if the students had experience with object-oriented programming, although this is not essential. The examples in the book use a pseudocode that will be readily understood by anyone familiar with C, C++, Ada, Pascal, or a similar language. The students will also find that familiarity with logic notation and statistical methods is helpful but not essential.

POTENTIAL FOLLOW-ON COURSES

After completing a first course with this text, the students should be prepared for a variety of follow-on courses in which they could use their newly acquired personal process skills on larger projects. Such courses should deal with team dynamics, project management, requirements management, and configuration management.

Preferably software engineers will start their formal software education by following the disciplines they will need later. While some of this material could be used in an introductory software engineering course, the statistical topics would need revision. Students should also have been exposed to basic design concepts and an explanation of software life-cycle issues before they attempt this material. These adjustments should enable beginning students to easily grasp the process principles and concepts in the book.

SUPPLEMENTS

Both an Instructor's Guide and an Instructor's Diskette are available free of charge for use by instructors in courses where *A Discipline for Software Engineering* has been adopted as a required text. The Instructor's Guide includes lecture and grading suggestions, as well as forms that can be copied for student use. The Instructor's Diskette contains electronic copies of the forms, lecture overheads, and spreadsheets to help with reviewing and analyzing student data.

In this book are provided seven versions of the personal software process (PSP) and exercises to demonstrate their use. To assist individual readers in doing these exercises and in producing the required analyses and reports, a Support Diskette is available from the publisher. This diskette contains copies of the forms illustrated in the book, as well as data analysis spreadsheets for the exercises.

Ordering information appears on the last page of this book.

Industrial Strategies

Industrial organizations are generally interested in the personal process because they see it as an efficient way to bring process improvement benefits to small projects and organizations. Other groups see it as a way to avoid much of the cost and the organizational disruption of a major process improvement effort. While the PSP can greatly facilitate process improvement in both large and small organizations, it should not be viewed as a replacement for an organizational process improvement effort. The two, in fact, are quite complementary. However, organizations near the CMM process maturity level 2—the repeatable level—or above are likely to be most successful in introducing the PSP.[1]

There are many ways to introduce the PSP into industrial software organizations. You may find the following guidelines helpful:

1. PSP introduction should follow organizational process improvement and should generally be deferred until the organization is at or near CMM level 2.[2]

2. While most engineers are intrigued by the idea of a personal process and are willing to try it, their managers generally will not want them to participate unless the managers see direct and immediate benefits. Even though this material will quickly help engineers in their work, such benefits hard to prove in advance.

3. When senior managers clearly demonstrate their support for this work, the project managers will generally support it as well.

4. While management's visible support is essential, each engineer's participation must be voluntary.

5. Attempts to substitute project programs for the problems in the text will not be successful. Business pressures will interfere and the time required to get feedback from most projects is far too long to support effective learning.

---

[1]For an explanation of CMM process maturity levels, see Watts S. Humphrey, *Managing the Software Process* (Reading, MA: Addison-Wesley, 1989).

2[Paulk] M. C. Paulk, Bill Curtis, M. B. Chrisis, and Charles V. Weber, "Capability Maturity Model for Software, Version 1.1," *Software Engineering Institute Technical Report*, CMU/SEI-93-TR-24 (February 1993).

Attempts by engineers to learn these PSP methods by reading this book and then trying to apply the techniques on their projects have not worked. Until they have practiced these methods and seen their effectiveness for themselves, they are not likely to apply them on the job. The most effective learning technique is for the engineers to work the problems in the book as they read the chapters. On average the problems take about four hours each with about 80 percent of the students finishing in under seven hours. The proper way for management to support a PSP effort is to allow the engineers a full day a week to do the assignments. This should continue for the entire four months required for the course. While this is a substantial investment, it should pay immediate dividends in improved organizational performance. This will occur, however, only if learning the PSP is part of the engineers' jobs. The most effective way to ensure this is to have the engineers' immediate managers take the course with them.

Book Overview

The book summarizes the costs and benefits of a personal software process (PSP). It describes why a PSP is needed and where it fits and does not fit. It provides the framework for a statistically managed software engineering discipline and shows how you can develop and use a PSP in your work. Each chapter introduces a new concept or method supported by examples and exercises. After reading each chapter, you should use the new concept or method to write at least one exercise program. To guide you in doing this, Appendix D describes the PSP exercises, relates them to the process levels defined in Appendix C, and shows how they support the book chapters.

While you could write any of the programs with any given process level, you should use the most advanced process consistent with the chapters you have completed. You should also complete the programs in numerical order. For example, if you plan to write 10 programs, write 1A, then 2A, then 3A, and so on. If you plan to write 19, however, write 1A, then 1B, then 2A, then 2B, and so on. For an intermediate number of programs, write all the A programs in order and add the B programs in sequence where appropriate. Appendix D provides the criteria for making such choices.

This book takes a phased approach to introducing personal process discipline. You will use process measurements and apply refined planning techniques. You will use defect measurements, design and code reviews, coding standards, and design templates. These will help you to improve the quality and productivity of your work.

When you have finished reading this book and doing the exercises, you will have mastered the basic material needed to apply process discipline to the management and improvement of your own work. While you will have learned a great deal, you should recognize that this is just a beginning. Your next challenge is to use these disciplines as the foundation for continuous learning and personal improvement.

How to Read This Book

After finishing the Preface, read Chapters 1 and 2. Then, before you do any of the exercises, read the opening sections of Appendixes C and D in order to obtain an overview of these appendixes and help you to identify the parts of them you need to do the exercises. Before doing each exercise, read about that program or report in Appendix D and read about the process you will use in Appendix C. Appendix C includes examples of completed process forms and an explanation of the new process elements. The process methods are explained in the chapters, however, so Appendix C is not a substitute for the book's chapters.

After you have completed Chapter 4, read Chapters 5 and 6, which introduce a series of statistical topics that are used in the rest of the book's exercises. If you are not generally familiar with statistics or statistical methods, you should read the opening sections of Appendix A. Appendix A contains a concise summary of the statistical methods used in the book, together with examples of the methods used in the software exercises. Before doing each exercise, read the appropriate sections of Appendix A that deal with that exercise. These sections are referenced by the problem descriptions in Appendix D.

The suggested strategy for reading the book thus is to read each chapter, decide which exercises you will do, and read the pertinent sections of Appendices C and D. If the exercises involve statistical methods that are new to you, also read the pertinent sections of Appendix A.

Acknowledgements

This book is the culmination of many years of observation and study and a few years of intense work. I have long been interested in the application of process principles to small software teams and to the work of individual software professionals. While I have spent many years thinking about and studying this subject, my duties at the Software Engineering Institute (SEI) did not permit me time to pursue the subject in depth. When I relinquished my SEI management role, SEI Director Larry Druffle kindly nominated me as an Institute Fellow. Being an SEI

Fellow has enabled me to pursue my long-term interest in applying process principles to personal work. It also made this book possible. I especially thank Larry for his support and encouragement.

I have also been blessed with many supportive associates, both at the SEI and throughout the software community. They have encouraged my work and offered many helpful suggestions and ideas. While the list of reviewers is long, I want to include every one. I want to particularly thank those who read and commented on almost the entire manuscript. These hardy souls are Jim Armitage, Ed Averill, Peter Malpass, Judah Mogilensky, Marie Silverthorn, and Peter Spool. Judy Bamberger was particularly helpful, offering detailed comments and insightful suggestions on almost every manuscript page. Many others read selected parts and provided valuable help and advice on one or more chapters. These people are Daniel Ash, Dean Brisco, Maribeth Carpenter, Jack Harding, Linda Ibrahim, Paul Oman, Dan Roy, Roger VonScoy, Eileen Takach, and James Wells. My special thanks to Clyde Chittister and Capers Jones for the time they took from their busy schedules to comment on the parts that dealt with their special areas of interest. I also especially thank Neil Brenner and Michael Mullaney for their advice and comments on the statistical material in Appendix A. All these people provided valuable comments, suggestions, and encouragement. For that I am most grateful. Finally, both Julia Mullaney and Howie Dow reviewed the entire book twice. They first reviewed the manuscript draft and then the rewritten manuscript. Their highly informed reviews were a great help in spotting oversights and inconsistencies. I deeply appreciate their help.

Several people used early copies of the book manuscript as a text for graduate software engineering courses. These faculty members are Howie Dow at the University of Massachusetts at Lowell, Soheil Khajenoori at Embry Riddle Aeronautical University, John McAlpin at Bradley University, and Nazim Madhavji at McGill University. Their advice, comments, and encouragement have been invaluable, both in suggesting improvements and in providing data on their classroom experiences.

Several industrial groups have also experimentally used parts of the book in their work. Their questions, issues, and experiences have been most helpful in ensuring that the end results are suitable for industrial use. While I cannot recognize all the involved people in these organizations, I want to particularly thank Girish Seshagiri and Pat Ferguson at Advanced Information Services, Inc. (AIS). Girish has provided the leadership and support and Pat has given the management and guidance to introduce these methods in their company. Tom Murphy and Peter Spool at Siemens Corporate Research were also early supporters. Through the support and enthusiasm of Howie Dow, Howard Hayakawa, and Glenn Rosander, several projects at the Digital Equipment Corporation are also using these methods. Finally, Sue Stetak, Tony Engberg, Paul Primmer, and James Wells at Hewlett Packard have led the introduction of these techniques in

Hewlett Packard. I thank them all for their interest and support and for their willingness to be pioneers in the early industrial use of these methods.

Another group of pioneers who deserve special thanks is my first graduate class at the School of Computer Science at Carnegie Mellon University. They were Peter Abowd, Jim Armitage, Eduardo Frias, Jim Gallagher, Jose Galmes, Mark Magee, Julia Mullaney, Paul Rehnet, Neal Reizer, Erik Riedal, Dan Roy, Kent Sarff, Francis Trunchon, Hung-Ming Wang, Todd Webb, and Rob Wojcik. Their comments and suggestions were invaluable, and I particularly appreciate their letting me use some of their data in this text.

The mechanics of producing a book can be daunting. Here I want to thank Peter Gordon, Helen Goldstein, and Helen Wythe of Addison-Wesley and their able staffs. The advice and guidance of Addison-Wesley's reviewers was also most helpful. They were Robert Lechner, William Lively, C. V. Ramamoorthy, James Tomayko, Laurie Honour Werth, and Marvin Zelkowitz. My special thanks to them. The help of my secretary, Dorothy Josephson, has been invaluable. She has made and distributed manuscript copies, reproduced lecture notes, and handled the myriad of correspondence and other matters that accompany a work of this kind. For that I am most grateful.

I also want to thank my wife, Barbara, for her continued patience through yet another book. Her encouragement, support, and continued good humor have been of immense help. Again, my deepest thanks.

Finally, I have dedicated this book to Dr. John E. Yarnelle. He was my first mathematics teacher and the joy he imparted to the subject has been a lifelong inspiration. He had a remarkable ability to make mathematics and science both enjoyable and interesting. I was fortunate to have had such an inspiring teacher at an early age.

Watts S. Humphrey
Sarasota Florida

TABLE OF CONTENTS

1

The Personal Software
Process Strategy

The *personal software process* (PSP) is a self-improvement process designed to help you control, manage, and improve the way you work. It is a structured framework of forms, guidelines, and procedures for developing software. Properly used, the PSP provides the historical data you need to better make and meet commitments and it makes the routine elements of your job more predictable and more efficient.

Note that any predefined process must be an approximation, so some of the exercises in this book may be more helpful to you than others. After you have practiced them all, you will be able to decide which to use and when. Apply the PSP principles where you feel they will help. As you become more familiar with them, you will begin to understand how to define, measure, and analyze your own processes. With increased experience, you will be able to enhance your processes to take advantage of new technology, tools, and methods. Above all, it enables you to understand your own performance and to see where and how to improve it.

This chapter describes some common software engineering problems and the logic for the PSP. It introduces process concepts and describes the role of process in software development. It relates the problems of industrial software development to the issues of professional discipline and describes how you can use disciplined methods to improve your personal performance as a software engineer.

1

The PSP's Purpose

The PSP's sole purpose is to help you be a better software engineer. It is a powerful tool you can use in many ways, for example, to manage your work, assess your talents, and/or build your skills. It can help you plan better, track your performance precisely, and measure the quality of your products. Whether you design programs, develop requirements, write documentation, or maintain existing software, the PSP can help you to do better work.

Rather than using one approach for every job, software engineers need a sophisticated array of tools and methods and the knowledge to use them appropriately. The PSP gives the data and analysis techniques you can use to determine which technologies to adopt and which methods work best for you.

It gives you a framework for understanding why you make errors and how best to find them. You can determine the quality of your reviews, the error types you miss, and the methods that are most effective for you.

Any predefined process must be an approximation; therefore you will find some of the exercises in this book are more helpful than others. After you have practiced them all, you will be able to decide which to use and when. As you study and use them, you will soon know how to define, measure, and analyze your own processes. Over the years, as you gain experience and as technology evolves, you can then enhance your processes to take advantage of new tools and methods.

The PSP is not a magic answer to all your software engineering problems. Although it can suggest where and how you can improve, you must make the improvements yourself.

1.1   The Logic for a Software Engineering Discipline

Software has become a critical issue in modern society. Everyone seems to need more and better software faster and cheaper. Many development projects are now so large and complex that a few brilliant specialists can no longer handle them. Unfortunately, there is no sign of a magic new technology to solve these problems. The alternatives are to improve the performance of practicing software engineers while encouraging more people to enter the field.

The intuitive software development methods generally used today are acceptable only because there are no alternatives. The current practice is nearer a craft than an engineering discipline. Professionals generally develop their own private methods and techniques. Some of these professionals are outstandingly creative; a few do really poor work. Most finished software products usually can be made to work, but only after extensive testing and repair. From a scientific viewpoint, the process is distressingly unpredictable. It is much like the Brownian motion of particles in a gas. Here, physicists cannot predict what any individual particle will do, but they can statistically characterize the behavior of an entire volume of particles. This analogy suggests that large-scale software development should be treated as a problem of crowd control: Don't worry about what each individual does as long as the crowd behaves predictably.

This approach, while generally tolerated, has been expensive. An intuitive software process leaves the quality of each individual's work a matter of blind luck. There are no disciplined frameworks, no sets of acceptable standards, no coaching systems, and no conducted rehearsals. Even agreement on what would characterize "good" professional performance in software engineering is lacking. Software engineers are left to figure out their own working methods and standards without the guidance and support that professionals find essential, for example, in sports, the arts, or medicine.

This situation becomes critical when each individual's contribution is uniquely important. A symphony orchestra best illustrates this idea. While the orchestra's overall performance is a careful blend of many instruments, each musician is a highly competent and disciplined contributor. Individual performers occasionally stand out, but the entire orchestra is far more than the sum of these parts, and a single sour note by any individual could damage the entire performance.

Unlike the musician, the software engineer must be part composer as well as performer. Like an orchestral performance, however, the performance of a software system can be damaged by almost any defective part. Because computers today possess extraordinary computational power, one badly handled interrupt or pointer could sooner or later cause an entire system to crash.

As our products become larger and are used in increasingly critical applications, the potential of damaging errors will almost certainly increase; just about any software engineer could commit one. The software industry has responded to this threat by resorting to increasingly rigorous and time-consuming tests. However, this testing strategy has not been totally effective, as demonstrated by the Thorac disaster that killed two patients or the telephone switching-system failure that shut down large segments of the United States. [Armour] The only responsible choice left is to improve the working disciplines of software professionals.

In most professions, competency requires demonstrated proficiency with established methods. It is not a question of creativity versus skill because often creative work simply is not possible until one has mastered the basic techniques. Well-founded disciplines encapsulate years of knowledge and experience. Beginning professionals, such as in the performing arts, high-energy physics, and brain surgery, must demonstrate proficiency with many techniques before they are allowed to perform even the most routine procedures. Flawless skill, once acquired, enhances creativity. A skilled professional in a field can outperform even the most brilliant but untrained layman.

A disciplined software engineering organization will have well-defined practices. Its professionals will use those practices, monitor and strive to improve their performances, and hold themselves responsible for quality control. In addition, they will have the confidence and data required to resist unreasonable commitment demands.

Practiced disciplines have the further benefit of making software engineering more fun. Writing programs can be highly rewarding. Getting some clever routine to work is an achievement. And it is enormously satisfying to see a sophisticated program do what you intended. This satisfaction, however, is often diluted by the treadmill of debugging and the constant embarrassment of missing commitments. It is not fun to make the same mistakes over and over or to produce a poor-quality result. Even though you worked hard, nobody appreciates a late, over-budget, or poorly-performing product.

While engineers are initially nervous about the structure and discipline of the PSP, they soon find it helpful. They quickly learn to make better plans and to meet them. They find they can do things they never thought possible. Their reaction is like one student who wrote on his homework: "Wow, I never did this before!" He had just written a program having several hundred lines of code that compiled and tested without a single defect. The PSP can help to make software engineering the fun it should be.

1.2   What Is a Software Process

Some organizations have addressed the problem of developing large-scale software systems by adopting the concept, taken from the manufacturing community, of a defined and managed process. [Deming, Humphrey 89] By properly managing the software process at the project and laboratory level, these organizations have successfully improved the capabilities of their development groups. [Cohen, Dion, Humphrey 91, Kolkhorst, Wohlwend]

The *software process* is the sequence of steps required to develop or maintain software. A *software process definition* is a description of this process. When properly designed and presented, the definition guides software engineers as they work. A team that follows different processes, or more commonly, uses no defined process at all, is like a ball team with some team members playing soccer, some baseball, and others football. Under these conditions, even the best individual players will form a poor team. In contrast, a team that follows the same process definition can better coordinate the work of individual members and more precisely track their progress.

More specifically, the software process sets out the technical and management framework for applying methods, tools, and people to the software task, while the process definition identifies roles and specifies tasks. The definition further establishes measures and provides exit and entry criteria for every major step. An effectively designed definition helps to ensure that every work item is properly assigned and its status is tracked. It also provides an orderly mechanism for learning. As better methods are found, they are incorporated into the organization's official process definitions. A defined process thus permits each new project to build on its own experiences as well as its predecessors'.

Defined processes are what Deming calls *operational definitions*: something everyone can communicate about and work toward. [Deming] They provide the following benefits: [Kellner]

- They enable effective communication about the process among users, developers, managers, customers, and researchers.

- They enhance management's understanding, provide a precise basis for process automation, and facilitate personnel mobility.

- They facilitate process reuse. Process development is time consuming and expensive. Few project teams can afford the time or resources to fully define the way they will work. They can save both by using the standard reusable elements a defined process provides.

- They support process evolution by providing an effective means for process learning and a solid foundation for process improvement.

- They aid process management. Effective management requires clear plans and a precise, quantified way to measure status against them. Defined processes provide such a framework.

Not surprisingly, organizations that effectively communicate, evolve, and manage their processes are more efficient. A well-defined process also is easier to improve. For example, problems may result if some steps are not followed or if the process itself is faulty. Or the definition may not be clear, communication may be poor, or engineers may not be motivated to properly use it. Corrections can then be made to address the identified causes. The process, its definition, and its supporting infrastructure thus evolve with experience.

1.3   Process Maturity

Processes are like habits: hard to establish and even harder to break. Merely defining a good set of methods and practices is rarely sufficient. Software engineers must be convinced of the need to change, shown what changes to make, and supported while they learn and practice the new processes. [Humphrey 87]

The processes for large-scale software development can themselves be quite large and complex. Thus they often are hard to define, hard to comprehend, and even harder to introduce. This is why the *software process maturity framework* was developed. [Humphrey, 89] This framework is an orderly way for organizations to determine the capabilities of their current processes and to establish priorities for improvement. It does this by establishing and defining five levels of progressively more-mature process capability: [Paulk]

"**1.** Initial: The software process is characterized as ad hoc and occasionally even chaotic. Few processes are defined, and success depends on individual effort.

2. Repeatable: Basic project management processes are established to track cost, schedule, and functionality. The necessary process discipline is in place to repeat earlier successes on projects with similar applications.

3. Defined: The software process for both management and engineering activities is documented, standardized, and integrated into a standard software process for the organization. All projects use an approved, tailored version of the organization's standard software process for developing and maintaining software.

4. Managed: Detailed measures of software process and product quality are collected. Both the software process and products are quantitatively understood and controlled.

5. Optimizing: Continuous process improvement is enabled by quantitative feedback from the process and from piloting innovative ideas and technologies."

The Software Engineering Institute (SEI), working with leading U.S. software organizations, has refined these level definitions and their practices into the Capability Maturity Model (CMM) for Software. [Paulk] At each level, key process areas (KPAs) provide goals and example practices (see Fig. 1.1). The CMM has been reviewed and refined by many specialists and represents their best current judgment of the most effective methods for achieving the objectives of each maturity level.

The CMM is the best available description of the goals, methods, and practices needed for the industrial practice of software engineering. You need to understand the CMM and know how to apply its principles. The question is how to do this in a classroom or laboratory environment? That is the role of the PSP.

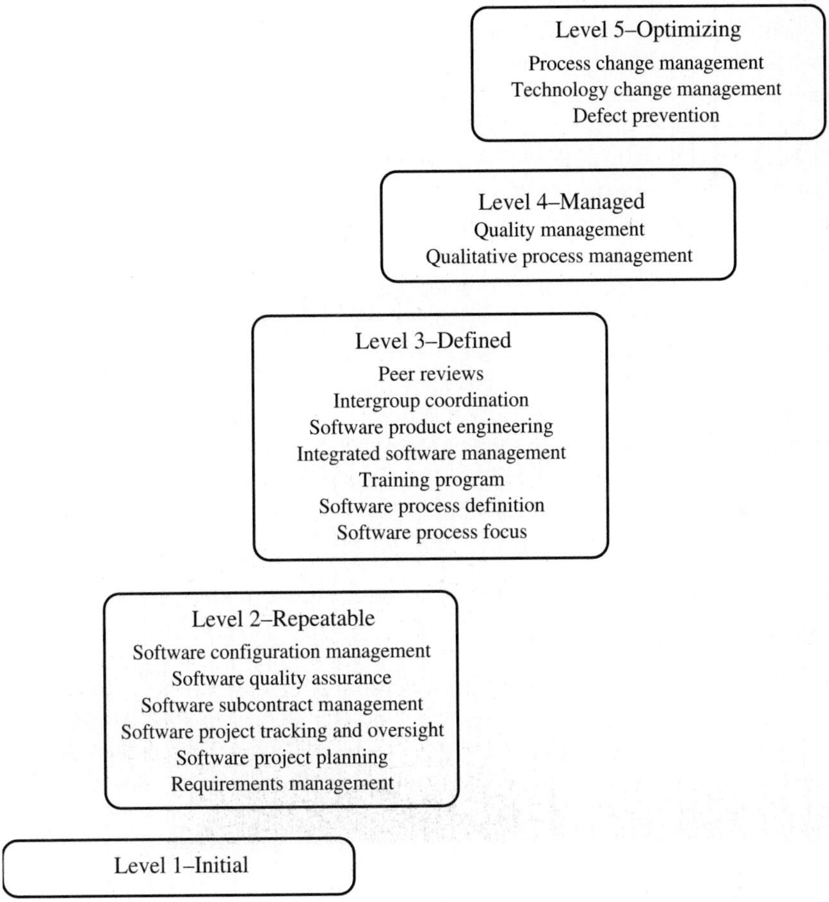

Level 5–Optimizing

Process change management
Technology change management
Defect prevention

Level 4–Managed
Quality management
Qualitative process management

Level 3–Defined

Peer reviews
Intergroup coordination
Software product engineering
Integrated software management
Training program
Software process definition
Software process focus

Level 2–Repeatable

Software configuration management
Software quality assurance
Software subcontract management
Software project tracking and oversight
Software project planning
Requirements management

Level 1–Initial

FIGURE 1.1
The Capability Maturity Model (CMM) Key Process AREAS (KPAs)

1.4 Your Personal Responsibilities

We each have responsibilities to others and to ourselves. We need to understand our own abilities, to apply them to our assigned tasks, to manage our weaknesses, and to build on our strengths. While we should do this as part of our everyday work, it is also our responsibility to ourselves. We are each blessed with unique talents and opportunities. We need to decide what to do with them.

PERSONAL EXCELLENCE

Consistent high performance takes persistent effort, an understanding of your own abilities, and a dedication to personal excellence. World-class runners know their best time for a mile, and they know the world record. They know it would make no sense to strive for a 3:00 mile but that 3:40 may soon be achievable. Decades ago, the 4:00 mile was thought beyond human capability. Roger Bannister proved that wrong in 1954. While beating a world record is more challenging than ever before, people keep doing it. They don't do it blindly, however. They develop aggressive personal goals and work ceaselessly to achieve them. When they achieve them, they then pick more aggressive goals and start all over again.

Not everyone can or should strive to be a world champion. As professionals, however, we should be aware of our own capabilities and learn how best to apply them and to improve them. This requires an understanding of your personal strengths and limitations and a realistic appreciation of what it means to be human. What you seek is not some arbitrary goal but a very personal one. What does excellence mean for you and how can you achieve it? The drive for personal excellence is challenging and demanding but intensely rewarding.

PERSONAL MOTIVATION

The PSP is a self-improvement process. Mastering it requires research, study, and a lot of work. But the PSP is not for everyone. Recall that the PSP is designed to help you be a better software engineer. Some people are perfectly happy just getting by on their jobs. The PSP is for people who strive for personal achievement and relish meeting a demanding challenge.

Even highly motivated people might properly question whether they should pursue the PSP. If you feel this way, you should review it and decide for yourself. Personal improvement involves many hours of effort and many years of gradual improvement. The PSP can be highly rewarding; at times it also can be frustrating. A long-term PSP program is a major undertaking that should not be approached tentatively. Take a course, review available material, and consider the costs and benefits. Once you decide to proceed, however, stick with it long enough to see the benefits. And you will see some early benefits. You also will encounter frustrating blocks and regressions. At times, you may conclude that your data doesn't properly reflect how your process is working. Know and understand the data but listen to your intuition. While your data will not lie, it will always fluctuate. If a process feels wrong, analyze the data, try to understand what is wrong, and experiment with variants until you feel more comfortable.

You must want to improve the way you work. If you can be objective about your performance and have the persistence and the dedication to stick with it, the PSP will pay off.

1.5 The Personal Software Process (PSP) Strategy

The following is the approach taken by the PSP:

- □ Identify those large-system software methods and practices that can be used by individuals.
- □ Define the subset of these methods and practices that can be applied while developing small programs.
- □ Structure these methods and practices so they can be gradually introduced.
- □ Provide exercises suitable for practicing these methods in an educational setting.

The PSP has a maturity framework much like that of the CMM. Figure 1.2 shows the CMM again, in this case with those KPAs that are at least partially addressed by the PSP shown in bold italics and noted with an asterisk. Some CMM items are excluded for the following reasons:

- □ Software subcontract management and Intergroup coordination: These cannot be practiced at the individual level.
- □ Requirements management and Software configuration management: These can be usefully practiced by individuals but their implications are better demonstrated in a small-team environment. While both are critical, they should be addressed immediately after the initial PSP steps described in this text.
- □ Software quality assurance and Training program: These relate more directly to broader organizational issues. While the capabilities you learn with the PSP are relevant to these areas, useful exercises to demonstrate them at an individual level are difficult or impossible to develop.

The PSP progression is shown in Fig. 1.3. Each process improvement phase is described in the following section.

PSP0: THE BASELINE PROCESS

The first step in the PSP is to establish a baseline that includes some basic measurements and a reporting format. This baseline provides a consistent basis for measuring progress and a defined foundation on which to improve. PSP0 should be the process you currently use to write software, but enhanced to provide measurements. If you have not written many programs and do not have a regular process, then your PSP0 should be the design, code, compile, and test phases done in whatever way you feel is most appropriate. While you can use input from your peers, your programming textbooks, or your instructor, you will find that the simple programs in this text do not require a sophisticated definition for these phases.

PSP0 is enhanced to PSP0.1 by adding a coding standard, size measurement and the *process improvement proposal* (PIP). The PIP is a form that provides a structured way to record process problems, experiences and improvement suggestions.

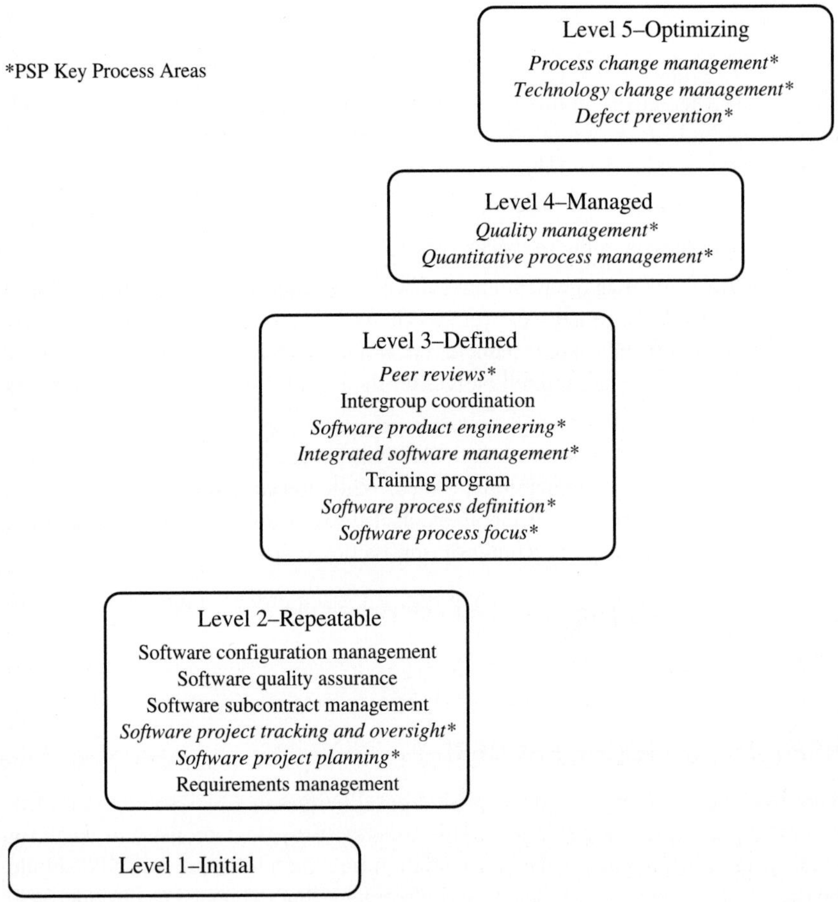

*PSP Key Process Areas

Level 5–Optimizing
Process change management*
Technology change management*
Defect prevention*

Level 4–Managed
Quality management*
Quantitative process management*

Level 3–Defined
Peer reviews*
Intergroup coordination
Software product engineering*
Integrated software management*
Training program
Software process definition*
Software process focus*

Level 2–Repeatable
Software configuration management
Software quality assurance
Software subcontract management
Software project tracking and oversight*
Software project planning*
Requirements management

Level 1–Initial

FIGURE 1.2
The CMM and the PSP

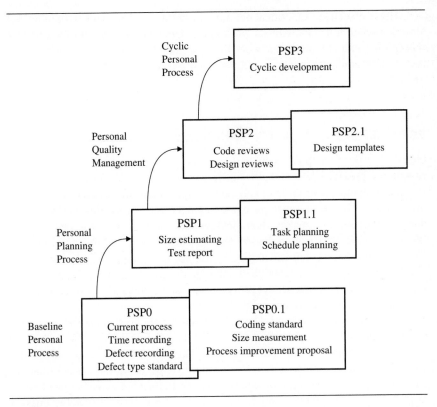

FIGURE 1.3
The PSP Evolution

PSP1: THE PERSONAL PLANNING PROCESS

PSP1 adds planning steps to PSP0. The initial increment adds a test report and size and resource estimation. In PSP1.1, task and schedule planning are introduced.

You want to make explicit, documented plans for your work for the following reasons:

- □ To help you understand the relation between the size of the programs you develop and the time you take to develop them
- □ To help you to make commitments you can meet
- □ To give you an orderly plan for doing the work
- □ To give you a framework for determining the status of your work

These objectives are critical not only for large projects but also for individuals, even when those individuals work alone. Once you know your own performance rate, you can plan your work more accurately, make commitments more realistically, and meet those commitments more consistently.

PSP2: PERSONAL QUALITY MANAGEMENT PROCESS

One PSP goal is to help you learn early on how to deal realistically and objectively with the program defects that result from your errors. While it is nonsense to feel guilty about being fallible, software engineers are often embarrassed about their errors.[1] That most errors are typographical errors, oversights, and just plain dumb mistakes only makes them feel worse. Beizer calls this "bug guilt." [Beizer] Trying harder often doesn't help because just as with touch typing, the key factor is inherent skill and ability. So, the focus should be on improving your abilities to do quality work and then doing quality work naturally. To paraphrase Pirsig, the way to write a perfect program is to make yourself a perfect programmer and then just program naturally. [Pirsig]

Defect data gathered on both students and experienced engineers show that typically the number of compile and unit test defects falls between 50 to 200 per one thousand lines of code (KLOC). This range is for uninspected and unreviewed programs. With comprehensive code reviews, fewer defects are found in compile and test; however, more are found overall, then the range is more like 75 to 200 defects per KLOC. This is one defect for every five to twelve lines of code. A few experienced software engineers will have lower rates, and many will occasionally do better for small programs. Not surprisingly, beginning programmers generally have higher error rates. While many people will quote numbers like 10 to 20 defects per KLOC, they do not usually count the defects they find in desk-checking, compiling, or even unit test.

To manage your defects, you must know how many you make. PSP2 adds review techniques to PSP1 to help you find defects early when they are least expensive to fix. You do this by gathering and analyzing the defects found in compile and test for your earlier programs. With these data, you can establish review checklists and make your own process quality assessments.

PSP2.1 addresses the design process. However, this is done in a nontraditional way. The PSP does not tell you how to design but rather how to complete a design. That is, after you have finished the design, what must you have? PSP2.1 establishes design completeness criteria and examines various design verification and consistency techniques.

---

[1]A definition note: Software engineers make **errors** or **mistakes** that result in program **defects** or **faults**.

Note that while the design phase is used here as an example of completeness criteria, you can use the same approach with many process phases, including requirements specification, documentation development, and test development. Phase completion criteria are important because without them, you cannot do an effective review of the work done in that phase.

PSP3: A CYCLIC PERSONAL PROCESS

Until now, the PSP has concentrated on a simple linear process for building small programs. While this works well for the smallest projects, it does not easily scale up to larger ones. For example, a program of 10,000 lines of code (LOC) is too big to write and debug and code review using PSP2. Even with well-commented code, you can quickly lose track of a program's logic, forcing you to retrace the logic from the beginning. You would also probably spend a lot of time trying to test the entire program as a single unit.

Instead of PSP2, you should use the abstraction principle embodied in PSP3, not just in program design but in the PSP itself. The strategy is to subdivide a larger program into PSP2-sized pieces. The first build is a base module or kernel that you enhance in iterative cycles. In each iteration, you do a complete PSP2, including design, code, compile, and test. Each enhancement builds on the previously completed increments, so PSP3 is suitable for programs of up to several thousand LOC (KLOC).

The cyclic PSP3 process effectively scales up to large programs only as long as each successive increment is high quality. If this is the case, you concentrate on verifying the quality for the latest increment without worrying about the earlier ones. But if a prior increment has poor quality, testing will be much more complex and the scale-up benefits will be largely lost. This is why design and code reviews are emphasized in the earlier PSP steps. The test report also is important because with it you can rerun earlier tests to verify that the new increment did not cause problems with previously working functions. Such problems are called *regressions*. Regression testing is a very important part of most large-system development processes.

TSP: THE TEAM SOFTWARE PROCESS

Using PSP3, you can build programs with over 10 KLOC. There are, however, two problems typical to large programs. First, as the size grows, so do the time and effort required. This can be a particular problem if you are the only engineer on the project. Second, most engineers have trouble visualizing all the important facets of even moderately sized programs. There are so many details and interrelationships that they may overlook some logical dependencies, timing interactions, or exception conditions. This problem is compounded by what is called habituation, or self-hypnosis, which causes them to see not the actual design on the page or screen, but rather their mental images of the design. Thus they tend to miss "obvious" mistakes not because the mistakes are too complex but because the engineers cannot see them.

There are many possible answers to these problems. One of the most powerful, however, is the team software process (TSP) where you call on the support of your peers. When several people cooperate on a common project, they can finish sooner. They also can address the habituation problem by reviewing each other's work. This review is only partially effective because teams too can suffer from habituation. This can be countered by periodically including an outsider in design reviews. The outsider's role is to ask the "dumb" questions. A surprising percentage of these "dumb" questions will identify fundamental issues that have been assumed for so long they have been forgotten.

Beyond this brief discussion, this book does not address TSP. It does, however, provide you with the basic disciplines and methods you will need to be a more effective member of a software team.

1.6   The Logic for the PSP

Growing evidence shows that the PSP works, but it has not been proven to be suitable for everyone. While the PSP is still new and undoubtedly will grow and evolve over time, it has derived from proven principles in other fields. The logic for the PSP is as follows:

- □ Software professionals will better understand what they do if they define, measure, and track their work.
- □ They will then have a defined process structure and measurable criteria for evaluating and learning from their own and others' experiences.
- □ With this knowledge and experience, they can select those methods and practices that best suit their particular tasks and abilities.
- □ By using a customized set of orderly, consistently practiced, and high-quality personal practices, they will be more effective members of their development teams and projects.

This logic is based on five principles. These principles and some of the evidence to support them are summarized here and discussed further in the following sections.

1. A defined and structured process can improve working efficiency.

2. Defined personal processes should conveniently fit the individual skills and preferences of each software engineer.

3. For professionals to be comfortable with a defined process, they should be involved in its definition.

4. As the professionals' skills and abilities evolve, their processes should do the same.

5. Continuous process improvement is enhanced by rapid and explicit feedback.

EFFICIENCY THROUGH A DEFINED AND STRUCTURED PROCESS

There is no question that a well-ordered and structured process can greatly improve the efficiency and effectiveness of purely routine tasks. There also is little disagreement that order and structure will generally inhibit the kind of free-wheeling mental processes required for high creativity. It is, in fact, this dichotomy that led to the Hawthorne studies in the 1920s and 1930s and that fueled the management debates between authoritarian (theory X) and participative (theory Y) management. [Hersey, Humphrey 87, Taylor] The Hawthorne studies' principal discovery was that routine factory workers did substantially better work when they were treated as thinking and feeling human beings rather than as animate machines. However, there is considerable debate about the benefits of defined processes for work that is partly creative and partly routine.

When dealing with software, we are structuring, creating, and managing extraordinarily complex logical entities. Large-scale software engineering involves volumes of challenging tasks that must be flawlessly performed. While we cannot hope to standardize and control the creative part of this work, we can address the problem of determining where creativity is required. Few will debate, for example, that parts of the planning and tracking activities of the software process can be made routine. Design work, however, often is viewed as entirely creative. As systems grow larger, the number of parts increases and their relations become increasingly complex. The problem then is to ensure that nothing is forgotten, no issue is overlooked, and all the pieces fit properly. The demands for accuracy, precision, and completeness soon exceed informal methods and more orderly approaches are needed. This then requires some systematic framework to ensure all details are properly handled. Such systematic frameworks are ideal candidates for process definition.

That key parts of the software design task are creative is no reason for treating them all that way. Thomas Alva Edison once remarked that "invention is 99 percent perspiration and 1 percent inspiration." [Evans] The key is to treat the creative and the routine differently. Once the creative tasks have been identified and bounded, the routine work often can be made more accurate and efficient.

Much process improvement comes from recognizing that many routine tasks are frequently repetitive. When those tasks are supported by forms, procedures, and historical data, their quality can be improved and made more efficient. Engineers then can spend more time on the truly creative parts of their jobs.

PERSONAL PROCESSES NEED TO FIT INDIVIDUAL PREFERENCES

While it is generally desirable to adapt a process to the whims and desires of its users, doing this is particularly important for intellectual disciplines like software development and maintenance. No one can be forced to do intellectual work in a particular way. If you want to do it one way, you will and most likely nobody will ever know. So you must be convinced of the value of using a process and must have a specific process that you want to use. The process thus must fit your personal needs and preferences.

SOFTWARE PROFESSIONALS SHOULD DEFINE THEIR OWN PROCESSES

Professionals must participate in process definition to help ensure the processes fit their personal needs as closely as possible. You best know which methods are most effective for you and which improvements are currently most important to you. On the basis of your prior experiences, you know the adjustments you need to make. After you next use the process and note its problems, you then can make further improvements. This improvement process should never end, but you will soon achieve a reasonably convenient process. You then should start to use the PIP described in Appendix C and schedule monthly or quarterly personal process improvement cycles.

While I know of no scientific studies that demonstrate that this participative principle works, its effectiveness is obvious to anyone who has worked on software process improvement. This principle also is the basis for many methods used in industrial quality management, the best early example of which was the quality circle, where every employee is treated as an asset with potentially useful process improvement ideas. [Amsden, Juran 80, Juran 88] It also is a primary tenet of the Malcolm Baldrige National Quality Award Criteria. [MBNQA]

THE PROCESS SHOULD EVOLVE WITH USERS

Like many accepted truths, the evolutionary principle is hard to prove. Experimental verification would be quite difficult, so I resort to the following logic:

1. The software industry is new and rapidly evolving.

2. The functions and characteristics of software products are changing at the same rate.

3. The software development task is also evolving as fast or faster.

4. Consequently, software engineers can expect their jobs to become more challenging every year.

5. Software engineers' skills and abilities must thus evolve with their jobs.

6. If their processes do not evolve in response to these challenges, those processes will cease to be useful.

7. As a result, the processes will not be used.

The truth of this logic is supported by my personal experience. Some of the worst-performing software organizations I have worked with had documented practices to govern how the software job was to be done. In none of these, however, were these practices followed regularly.

FEEDBACK ENHANCES PROCESS IMPROVEMENT

Reinforcement is an accepted teaching principle. Students given clear and timely feedback on successes and failures are more motivated to continue learning. Unfortunately, many positive software engineering actions such as walkthroughs and inspections can generate negative short-term feedback. The long-term benefits of improved product quality and reduced testing are unquestionable. [Humphrey 89] The short-term consequences, however, are delayed start of coding, early resource needs, and often a lot of rework. The long-term feedback cycle is generally months, while the short-term cycle is days or weeks, so most software organizations skip walkthroughs and inspections. For these steps to be used consistently, it is essential to establish ways to generate positive short-term feedback.

One example of the benefits of rapid and explicit feedback is Gregg Upp's experiences at the AIS Corporation of Peoria, Illinois. As a newly hired engineer, Upp was first assigned to translate a number of SAS programs into COBOL. Following the PSP principles, he first defined a nine-step process to do the work. He next designed some estimating and recording forms. He initially had no idea how long the project would take, so he decided not to make an estimate but merely to measure his first use of the process, including the time he spent by phase, the defects he found, and the size of the product he produced.

From this experience, he calculated how many COBOL LOC were required for each SAS line and how long he spent on each phase of the translation project. He then made a size and resource estimate for the second project and measured it. Using the results of these two projects, he planned the next ones. The results of his work are shown with the plan and actual data in Figs. 1.4 and 1.5. While his

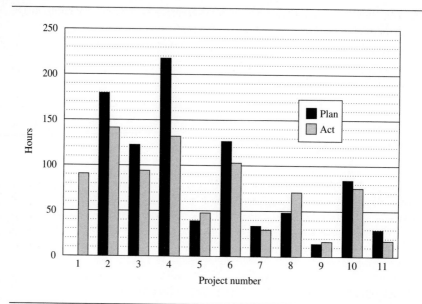

FIGURE 1.4
Plan versus Actual Time

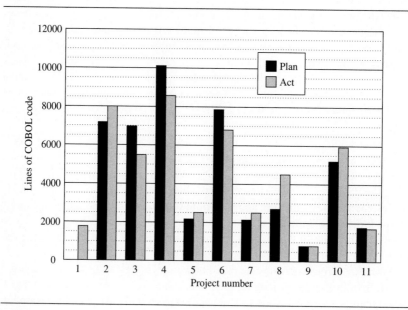

FIGURE 1.5
Plan versus Actual Size

size estimates became quite accurate, his development times were often better than planned. He attributed this to his improved productivity resulting from experience. He now has a clear understanding of the time such projects take and a stable and predictable process for planning and doing the work.

1.7 Productivity and the PSP

When you first use the PSP to write a small program, odds are your productivity will appear to decline. This is because the PSP involves many tasks that are not normally a part of developing small programs. It introduces planning, measurement, and analysis steps for building the skills you need to produce larger-scale programs. As you gain PSP experience, however, you will find your productivity improving, possibly beyond where you started.

TWO STUDENT EXAMPLES

Not all small programs are the same. The number of hours required to develop a small program is only one measure of the quality of the work that was done. Consider the following example. Student 1 is a systems engineer who has been writing programs for over 13 years, but has written only about 20 KLOC of programs. Student 2 is a software engineer with 11 years of experience who has written over 100 KLOC. Student 1 uses C and student 2 uses Ada. Neither has written many programs in these languages.

Both are given identical specifications for the ten programs in the A problem series in this text. As you can see from Fig. 1.6, their development times differed significantly. Because student 1 took much longer than student 2, you might be tempted to say that student 2 is the better engineer. Before deciding, however, look at the sizes of their programs. The programs are in different languages, so LOC measurement comparisons are not entirely accurate. But they do give some indication of the amount of development work involved. As Fig. 1.7 shows, student 2's programs are either substantially smaller or about the same size as student 1's. These size data imply that student 2 was able to do the same job with a lot less code than could student 1. However, examine the programs more closely and you will see that the students took significantly different approaches, explained as follows:

□ Student 1 called for the user to enter file names: Student 2 hard-coded the file name; doing this will force the user to change the source code in order to use a different file.

□ Student 1 echoed the input back to the user to ensure it was correct; student 2 did not.

□ In performing calculations on input data, student 1 constructed a linked list and then did the calculations. Student 2 did the calculations on the input data as they were entered, which could make program enhancement more difficult.

□ Student 1 provided extensive user messages; student 2 did not.

Student 1 also produced extensive comments, including a description of how the program is to be used and how it was designed; student 2 included no comments. If you could not read student 2's source code, you would not be able to figure out what the program does. Further, student 1 added a design description for each program; student 2 included one only for programs nine and ten.

You could extend your examination by considering, for example, how the two students' levels of productivity compared. As shown in Fig. 1.8, student 1 produced between 8 and 22 LOC per hour, while student 2's productivity fluctuated much more widely. Notice, however, that as the students learned how to use the PSP process more consistently, their levels of productivity began to converge.

Some of student 2's productivity fluctuation resulted from wide swings in the number of defects found in test (see Fig. 1.9). Student 1 had fewer test defects, implying that the finished code will have fewer defects. This, of course, cannot be verified without further testing.

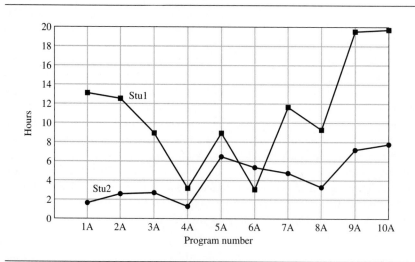

FIGURE 1.6
Student Development Times

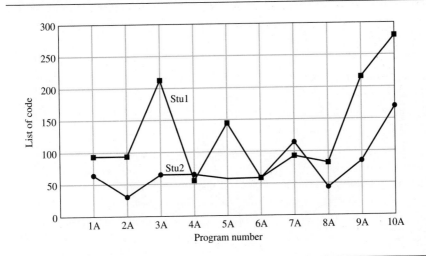

FIGURE 1.7
Student Program Sizes

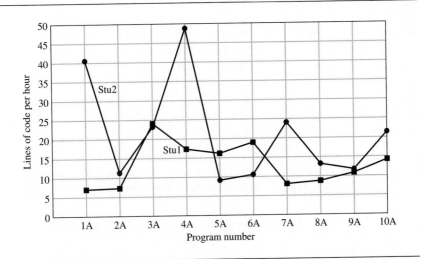

FIGURE 1.8
Student Development Productivity

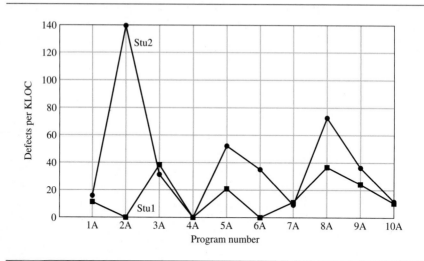

FIGURE 1.9
Student Test Defects per KLOC

PRODUCTIVITY JUDGMENTS

Clearly, even when given identical functional descriptions, the students produced totally different programs. Depending on the program's intended use, either could be considered the better. Student 1 produced extensive comments and documentation to help the user, but lost time and productivity by doing so. Student 2 used far less code than student 1 did. This student deserves credit for producing much smaller products—in some conditions, this could be important. However, the resulting programs were much less flexible and usable. Although the issue here is not which program is right or wrong, generally, student 1's programs would be judged to be substantially better.

The following facts are clear from these data:

□ Productivity is directly affected by the size of the product to be produced. A larger program will take proportionately more time to design, implement, and test.

□ When additional commenting or documentation is included, the amount of work will increase and productivity will decline.

□ When the number of defects entering test fluctuates widely, the test time will do the same, thus further affecting productivity.

Obviously, including many activities that are not directly related to producing and testing the code reduces productivity. Conversely, the design approach can significantly affect productivity, as can the quality of the engineer's processes.

PRODUCTIVITY VARIATIONS

Even with all other factors equal, productivity differences will still exist among individuals. Just as some people can run faster, type more accurately, or hammer more nails per hour, some are more adept at programming than others. These skill differences will remain regardless of the processes used. Because cost is important, however, productivity comparisons cannot be avoided.

Productivity can be examined in one way by considering the degree of variation among individual engineers. Boehm in his COCOMO model, assigns a weight of 4.18 to variations in the average capabilities of the individuals or software teams. [Boehm] Average language experience, for example, gets a weight of only 1.20. While the 4.18 capability weight for capability variation is the highest in the COCOMO model, this would imply that the variation from the most to the least competent team is only about four times.

While productivity factors can be useful for statistically controlled populations, they generally are meaningless when applied to uncontrolled populations. This is because those populations could have members who are incapable of satisfactorily completing the project. For example, notice from Fig. 1.10 the times 25 graduate students took to write program 1A. The times range from 53 to 1080 minutes. Cumulatively, 50 percent of the students took fewer than 145 minutes and 72 percent took fewer than 236. Overall, there is more than a 20 to 1 ratio between the fastest and the slowest times. When you consider that some of these programs probably still had defects and thus would not work properly, the true range is probably wider.

This degree of variation is among students who were told they had to be able to write programs in at least one language before they could register for the PSP course. An examination of their data shows that some were marginally competent while others were highly adept. From data on their education and experience, however, there is no simple, objective way to select the most competent from the least competent. All reported knowledge of at least two programming languages and had each written their first program more than three years earlier. Even the lifetime total LOC they had written to date is not a useful indicator. While the student with the longest time had written the fewest lines—only 300—the one who had the second shortest time had also written the second smallest amount of code—2000. The five programmers who each had written lifetime totals of over 100,000 LOC placed randomly between the twentieth and seventy-sixth per-

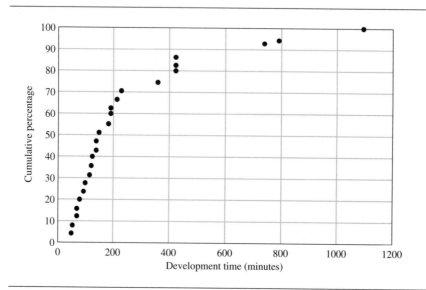

FIGURE 1.10
Student Variation

centiles. The students with the smallest lifetime totals were somewhat more heavily represented in the longer development times.

In the broader population, productivity variations for any challenging task are infinite. At one extreme, many people will not be able to do the task at all. From the point at which people become marginally competent, productivity measurement is more useful. Any discussion of productivity distribution, however, is useful only if you establish criteria for membership in the sample. Any discussion of variation thus must concern the range between an arbitrary membership criterion and the fastest achievable performance. Even measures of the fastest possible time to perform a software project, however, involve many questions of precise project definitions. As we saw with students 1 and 2 in the earlier example, however, individual performance measures are essentially meaningless without such precise project definitions.

Despite these complications, productivity determines the degree to which individuals and organizations can compete. Productivity variations are thus important. The operative questions are then the degree to which society is demanding programming skills and the premium it is willing to pay for them.

1.8   Caveats

As you use the PSP, keep the following points in mind:

☐ This book concentrates on the design, code, and test phases of software development; however, these phases are only examples. The PSP applies not only to them but also to almost any other aspect of the software process, including requirements specification, product maintenance, test planning, and documentation development.

☐ This book does not describe the possible tools that could be used to support the PSP. You should learn these methods first before attempting to automate them. You then will be in a better position to identify and evaluate the tools that could help you most.

These points are discussed further in the following sections.

CONCENTRATION ON DESIGN, CODE, AND TEST

As presented in this book, the PSP concentrates on the detailed design, code, and unit test phases of the software process. These phases are suitable for reasonably challenging classroom exercises, and they provide an objective basis for evaluating both product and process quality issues. They also are critical parts of the software development process. According to Boehm, they consume from 59 percent to 68 percent of the development costs in most software organizations. [Boehm, 91] Further they also are the part of the process that produces the running product. This does not mean that nothing else is important, only that these phases must be done well or the rest will not matter.

Focussing on code development does not mean this phase is the most critical part of software development. The requirements, documentation, and installation planning work also must be done properly or products will not be successful. An interesting IBM incident some years ago demonstrates this. IBM shipped product code to customers even though not all the required documentation was ready. So the customers had to pay for products for which they did not have the necessary information. Some irate customers even said they viewed the documentation as the product and the code as incidental. They recommended that if the company did not have the documentation ready, it should ship nothing until it did. After some heated debates among the engineers and marketing people, IBM followed that recommendation. This change made it clear to the software developers that the documentation could not be deferred until the code was done. They realized that late documentation would delay shipment of their precious code.

Schedule, cost, and quality problems of code development typically cost organizations a lot. While testing costs are obvious, documentation and installation costs are not as clearly related to code quality. For many products, much of the documentation is required either because the product is hard to understand or install or for later product repair or enhancement. Much of this documentation would not be needed if the code were initially of high quality. So both the developing organization and the user organization could be helped by improved code quality.

TOOLS TO SUPPORT THE PSP

Tools can be enormously helpful, but they alone will not fully solve software engineering's problems. Neither will process alone. Both are needed to obtain a balanced result. Improved tools, in fact, are needed in most aspects of the software process. They can improve productivity, reduce errors, simplify routine tasks, and free engineers for more creative work.

Tool support can make the methods described in this book more efficient and easier to use. Such standard aids as word processors, spreadsheets, and statistical packages provide an adequate base initially, but ultimately CASE environments are needed that embody the PSP methods in engineering workstations, in addition to all the other tools generally available. CASE facilities that automatically log time, track defects, maintain data, and do statistical calculations will make the PSP methods easier to introduce and use. While this will be a big step forward, engineers still must understand the principles and methods behind their working environments. So they will still need to become skillful PSP users.

1.9   Summary

Society is demanding more and better software faster and cheaper. The intuitive software development methods currently in general use will work only as long as society can tolerate the degree of unpredictability they entail. Basically, our development practices are those of individual craftsmen. As our products become larger and are used in increasingly critical applications, such uncertainty will no longer be acceptable. In many cases, competent work is not possible unless the professionals know the basic methods of their fields and practice them with discipline. It is not a question of creativity versus discipline; creative work is simply not possible without discipline.

When writing programs, we are creating, structuring, and managing extraordinarily complex logical products. While we cannot hope to standardize and control the creative part of this work, we must determine where creativity is required, and where it is not. That some elements of the software task are creative is no reason to treat them all as such. The Personal Software Process (PSP) recognizes that even the most challenging tasks are not totally creative. Once we identify and bound the creative tasks, we can often make the routine work more accurate and efficient.

The PSP teaches you how to measure your work. It also can help you to learn from your performance variations and then to incorporate these lessons into a growing body of documented practices. Defined processes are widely recognized as necessary for large projects, but it is not so generally understood that they can help small teams and even individuals. A defined process identifies and simplifies routine tasks and helps you to think more precisely about your work. Once your process is defined and measured, you can more readily change and enhance it. You also can accurately project your performance.

SEI's Capability Maturity Model (CMM) for Software sets out the principal practices for managing large-scale software development. Many of these practices also can be used by teams and even by individual software engineers. This book follows the CMM progression from project planning through defect and quality management to continuous process improvement. By applying the techniques defined herein, you will see how to define, measure, and analyze your own processes. As you gain experience and as technology evolves, you will likely add new tools and methods. You might even invent some of your own.

References

[Amsden] R. T. Amsden, and D. M. Amsden, eds. QC Circles Applications, Tools, and Theory, ASQC, 310 West Wisconsin Ave., Milwaukee, WI 53203.

[Armour] Jody Armour and W. S. Humphrey, "Software Product Liability," Software Engineering Institute Technical Report, CMU/SEI-93-TR-13 (August, 1993).

[Beizer] B. Beizer, *Software Testing Techniques* (New York: Van Nostrand Reinhold, 1983).

[Boehm, 81] Barry W. Boehm, *Software Engineering Economics* (Englewood Cliffs, NJ: Prentice-Hall, 1981).

[Cohen] I. Cohen, "Using SEI Maturity Model to Improve the Software Process," Proceedings of the Sixth Israel Conference on Computer Systems and Software Engineering, June 2–3, 1002, Herzliya, Israel.

[Deming] W. Edwards Deming, *Out of the Crisis*, MIT Center for Advanced Engineering Study, Cambridge, MA (1982).

[Dion] Raymond Dion, "Process Improvement and the Corporate Balance Sheet," *IEEE Software* (July 1993): 28–35.

[Evans] Bergen Evans, *Dictionary of Quotations* (New York: Bonanza Books, 1966): 266:17.

[Hersey] Paul Hersey and Kenneth Blanchard, *Management of Organizational Behavior, 3rd ed.* (Englewood Cliffs, N.J.: Prentice-Hall, Inc., 1977).

[Humphrey 87] W. S. Humphrey, *Managing for Innovation, Leading Technical People* (Englewood Cliffs, NJ: Prentice-Hall, 1987).

[Humphrey 89] W. S. Humphrey, *Managing the Software Process* (Reading, MA: Addison-Wesley, 1989).

[Humphrey 91] W. S. Humphrey, T. R. Snyder, and R. R. Willis, "Software Process Improvement at Hughes Aircraft," *IEEE Software* (July 1991): 11–23.

[Juran 80] J. M. Juran, "International Significance of the QC Circle," *Quality Progress,* vol. 13, no. 11 (Nov. 1980): 18–22.

[Juran 88] J. M. Juran and Frank M. Gryna, *Juran's Quality Control Handbook, 4th ed.* (New York: McGraw-Hill Book Company, 1988).

[Kellner] M. I. Kellner, "Representation Formalisms for Software Process Modeling," Proceedings of the 4th International Software Process Workshop, ACM Press, (1988): 93–96.

[Kolkhorst 88] B. G. Kolkhorst and A. J. Macina, "Developing Error-free Software," *Proceedings of Computer Assurance COMPASS '88,* NIST, IEEE (July 1988).

[MBNQA] *Malcolm Baldrige National Quality Award Criteria*, United States Department of Commerce, National Institute of Standards and Technology, Gaithersburg, MD 20899-0001

[Paulk] M. C. Paulk, Bill Curtis, and M. B. Chrisis, "Capability Maturity Model for Software, Version 1.1," Software Engineering Institute Technical Report, CMU/SEI-93-TR (February 24, 1993).

[Pirsig] Robert M. Pirsig, *Zen and the Art of Motorcycle Maintenance: An Inquiry into Values* (New York, NY: Bantum Classics Spectra, 1984).

[Random] *The Random House Dictionary of the English Language, 2nd Edition* (New York, NY: Random House, 1983).

[Taylor] Frederick Winslow Taylor, *The Principles of Scientific Management* (New York: Harper and Row, Publishers, Inc., 1911).

[Wohlwend] Harvey Wohlwend, "Software Improvements in an International Company," 15th International Conference on Software Engineering, Baltimore, Maryland (May 17–21, 1993).

2

The Baseline
Personal Process

This chapter defines the initial process you will use in doing the first exercises in this book. This process is enhanced with new techniques and methods for the exercises in each succeeding chapter.

Defined processes help in managing large projects, they help small teams, and they can help you when you work alone. Such a process will help in the following ways:

- □ When you define the process for doing a job, you identify its principal activities.
- □ This in turn helps you to separate its routine from its complex elements.
- □ It also helps you to establish precise criteria for the entry and exit of each process phase.
- □ A defined and measured process helps you to understand your performance.
- □ This in turn helps you to estimate when tasks will be completed.
- □ With sufficient historical data, you can even judge the accuracy of these projections.
- □ Process data helps you to identify those process phases that cause you the most trouble.
- □ This in turn helps you to see how to improve your work and to plan these improvements.

When you define your personal process, you begin to think in its terms. Abstract tasks become structured and subject to rational analysis. Until you define the tasks you perform in sufficient detail, however, you will have difficulty improving them. For example, when you think of design as a vague category of work, it is difficult to reason about. Once you separate it into elements, you can better understand its subtasks and how they relate. You have a framework for measurement and a focus for improvement. Much like professional body builders, you no longer think about just building muscle; you think in terms of arms, legs, and torsos. With more experience, you start to think of building specific muscles: for example, the biceps, the triceps, and the deltoids. The clearer the focus, the better you can improve in each area.

2.1   The Baseline Process

The PSP0 is the foundation for the process enhancements introduced in Chapters 4, 5, 6, 8, 10, and 11. Its principal objective is to provide the framework for gathering your initial process data. By gathering data on your own work, you will build a quantitative understanding of each step and will soon see how process methods can help you to improve the quality and productivity of your work.

The PSP0 process is shown in simplified form in Fig. 2.1. The scripts guide you through the process steps, the logs help you record process data, and the plan summary provides a convenient way to record and report your results. If you already use a defined process, you will find the PSP0 sufficiently general to adopt with little change. Note, however, that if you wanted to adapt the PSP0 to your particular working habits, you would have to redesign all the scripts, forms, and logs in this book to conform to your process. You would then have to submit these revised definitions with your homework assignments. Before you do so, you should read Section 2.9, Customizing the Initial Process.

The PSP0 process provides

☐ a convenient structure for doing small-scale tasks,

☐ a framework for measuring these tasks, and

☐ a foundation for process improvement.

Each of these items is discussed in the following sections.

A CONVENIENT WORKING STRUCTURE

A defined process provides a consistent and proven structure for doing a job. When you perform any but the most trivial task, you always face the question of

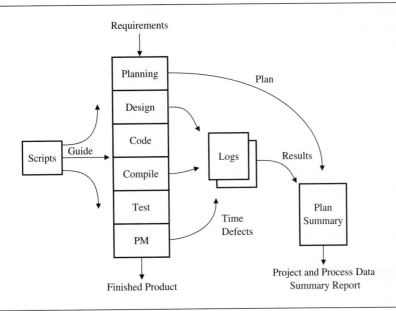

FIGURE 2.1
PSP0 Process Flow

how to attack it. What do you do first, second, and so on? Even when you do this properly, such planning takes time. When you attack the job in an inefficient or suboptimal way, however, it could take you much longer to do.

The PSP has been carefully designed and tested with many users, so there is no question that it works. In this book, you will thus use a predefined process. The intent, however, is not to force everyone into some common mold but to give you the knowledge and experience to see how processes are designed and how they can help you. You then can define and improve your processes so that they truly fit your personal needs.

While a defined process may sound restrictive, it is not. In fact, if you find your personal process inconvenient or uncomfortable, you should adjust it to fit your needs. The process is your servant. If it does not help you, you must change it. While organization or team processes generally have constraints, the personal process is your private property. It is much like your education or your health. If you don't manage it yourself, nobody else will.

MEASUREMENT FRAMEWORK

A defined process permits you to gather data on the time you spend on each software task and to track the numbers of defects you introduce and remove in each process step. These data then help you to analyze your process, to understand its faults, and to improve it.

By defining the steps in a process, you give the process measurements explicit meaning. When you define the coding phase, for instance, measures of coding time or of injected defects are clear and specific. To produce a definition of the coding phase, of course, you must have explicit criteria for entry to and exit from the coding step. With the PSP0 process, some of the entry and exit criteria are explicit and others are not. As this process is progressively refined in subsequent chapters, however, many of these criteria are made more precise.

With the small program examples in this book, it is not necessary to use sophisticated processes. As the PSP is enhanced, however, it will provide you an improved basis for establishing your personal role in larger-scale projects. When you know how you work, you can better relate to your teammates and to the other activities of a larger project.

FOUNDATION FOR IMPROVEMENT

If you don't know what you are doing, it is hard to improve it. While most software professionals would argue that they know how they develop software, they can rarely describe what they do in any detail. When you follow a defined process, you are more aware of your actions. You observe your own work, and you quickly see how to refine each larger step into smaller elements. Over time, as you build a more refined understanding, your improvement ideas become more refined as well. This will help you to focus on those precise steps that you find most time consuming or troublesome.

2.2   Why Forms Are Helpful

The PSP uses a lot of forms. While you could view this as a disadvantage, you will find that it can be an enormous help. Consider, for example, how forms could help in planning your work. First, any reasonably challenging job involves a series of steps. To do the job, you must thus

- □ determine what is to be done,
- □ decide how to do it,
- □ do it,
- □ check to make sure it is correct,
- □ fix any problems, and
- □ deliver the final result.

Even for relatively simple tasks, these steps can take time. Suppose, for example, you were asked to produce a plan for the next program you were to write. If you had never made such a plan, it would probably take you some time to figure out what a plan should contain and how to produce it. Then you would have to decide on the plan format. Finally, you would make the plan. When you finished, however, you would have to do several checks. First, did you leave out anything important? Second, was the information correct? Finally, does the format and content meet the requirements?

Suppose, instead, that you had a planning form. Now you don't need to decide what to do; the form tells you. All you do is fill in the blanks. The form may even provide guidance on how to do the required calculations. When you are through, you have to check to ensure you did the work properly, but you can easily check to see if you left out any data. When you use an approved standard form, you also can be confident that you have provided the desired data. Properly designed forms thus improve the efficiency of your work and help to ensure that you have produced a complete and correct result.

Good forms, however, are hard to develop, and they must be periodically reviewed and revised to ensure they meet the current needs of the project. It is particularly important to ensure that all the forms supporting a process are designed and maintained as a coherent whole. If they are not, some may call for duplicate information, terminology may be inconsistent, or formats may have confusing variations. The result may be inefficiency and errors. When the same data show up in two or more places, there is a problem if the values differ. While automated data recording systems can solve this problem, it is far simpler and easier to avoid the problem with proper forms' design.

2.3   The PSP Process Elements

The PSP0 process is shown in Fig. 2.2. First, in the planning step, you produce a plan to do the work. Next, you do the software development. At the end, in the postmortem step, you compare your actual performance with your plan, record the process data, and produce a summary report. While these planning and postmortem steps may not seem necessary when writing small programs, they are essential to building a disciplined personal process. You will use them to produce a plan and to do a postmortem for every program you write with the PSP. If the program is so simple that a plan seems pointless, the plan should be trivial to produce. Frequently, however, these trivial programs hold surprises that a plan could help you to anticipate.

A process may be simple or complex. Large defined processes, for example, will have many elements or phases, each of which can also be viewed as defined processes. At the lowest level, the process phases will be composed of steps that

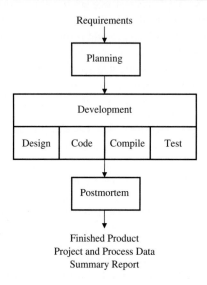

Requirements

Planning

Development

| Design | Code | Compile | Test |

Postmortem

Finished Product
Project and Process Data
Summary Report

FIGURE 2.2
The PSP0 Process

have no further defined substructure. [Feiler] For a large process, for example, each phase would itself have a process definition. In the case of PSP0, the planning, development, and postmortem phases have process definitions but design, code, compile, and test are named as unrefined steps. When a process element has a definition and a structure, I call it a phase. When it has no defined structure, I call it a step or a task. In general terms, I talk about the parts of a process as its phases even when some of them are defined and some are not.

THE PLANNING PHASE

As you produce and document your plan, a planning form guides your work and provides a consistent format for your results. While your initial PSP0 plans will not be very complex, they will help you to practice project planning on these small programs.

THE POSTMORTEM PHASE

The postmortem phase is equally important. When you have completed even a small project, you have potentially a large amount of useful data. Unless you promptly record these data in a convenient and retrievable form, however, they will likely be lost. When you try to enter your data in a database, use them in a spreadsheet, or enter them in one of your programs, you will appreciate the value of using forms. Data that are not gathered in a structured and defined format are almost impossible to later find and use. Even if you wait only a week to produce the summary report, you will waste a lot of time searching for all the data and ensuring they are complete and accurate.

By learning and practicing these planning and reporting methods on small programming exercises, you will build your project planning and data management skills. In a controlled classroom environment, you will also quickly see how these methods can work and how they help you to improve your performance. Experience with the small exercises in this book will help you develop the habits you will need to plan, track, and manage the larger-scale work you will likely do in the future.

2.4   The PSP0 Process

The PSP script guides you through a process. The principal elements of this script are its purpose, the entry criteria, the phases (or steps) to be performed, and the exit criteria. In more sophisticated processes, data are also generally needed on responsibilities, the sources for the inputs, and required approvals. For the PSPs, however, you will need only the most basic of script contents.

The PSP0 Process Script is shown in Table 2.1. It describes in words the simple process structure shown in Fig. 2.2. A second PSP0 script, the Planning Script, is shown in Table 2.2. It briefly summarizes the simple planning steps required in PSP0. With a simple process like PSP0, you may not need to look at the script very often, but with a more complex process, it would be wise to consult the script at least at the beginning and end of every process phase.

The planning and postmortem phases are quite clear from the scripts in Tables 2.2 and 2.3, but the development phase in Table 2.4 has four steps: design, code, compile, and test. Until these steps have explicit entry and exit criteria, there is no way to tell when each starts or ends. One common confusion, for example, concerns the distinction between code and compile. While the compiler is first run, that is clearly compile time, but how do you count the time spent making the necessary coding changes to fix the defects found during compilation? In this book, I suggest you count the time spent correcting compile defects as compile time. Similarly, the time spent correcting and compiling test defects is counted as test time. Until all the entry and exit criteria are precisely defined, however, the measurements of these steps must also be recognized as imprecise. The reason you take such measurements with the PSP is to learn how to better define

TABLE 2.1   PSP0 PROCESS SCRIPT

Phase Number	Purpose	To guide you in developing module-level programs
	Inputs Required	• Problem description • PSP0 Project Plan Summary form • Time and Defect Recording Logs • Defect Type Standard • Stop watch (optional)
1	Planning	• Produce or obtain a requirements statement. • Estimate the required development time. • Enter the plan data in the Project Plan Summary form. • Complete the Time Recording Log.
2	Development	• Design the program. • Implement the design. • Compile the program and fix and log all defects found. • Test the program and fix and log all defects found. • Complete the Time Recording Log.
3	Postmortem	Complete the Project Plan Summary form with actual time, defect, and size data.
	Exit Criteria	• A thoroughly tested program • Completed Project Plan Summary with estimated and actual data • Completed Defect and Time Recording Logs

TABLE 2.2   PSP0 PLANNING SCRIPT

Phase Number	Purpose	To guide the PSP planning process
	Entry Criteria	• Problem description • Project Plan Summary form • Time Recording Log
1	Program Requirements	• Produce or obtain a requirements statement for the program. • Ensure the requirements statement is clear and unambiguous. • Resolve any questions.
2	Estimate Resources	• Make your best estimate of the time required to develop this program.
	Exit Criteria	• A documented requirements statement • A completed Project Plan Summary with estimated development time data • Completed Time Recording Log

TABLE 2.3 PSP0 POSTMORTEM SCRIPT

Phase Number	Purpose	To guide the PSP postmortem process
	Entry Criteria	• Problem description and requirements statement • Project Plan Summary with planned development time • Completed Time Recording Log • Completed Defect Recording Log • A tested and running program
1	Defects Injected	• Determine from the Defect Recording Log the number of defects injected in each PSP0 phase. • Enter this number under Defects Injected—Actual on the Project Plan Summary.
2	Defects Removed	• Determine from the Defect Recording Log the number of defects removed in each PSP0 phase. • Enter this number under Defects Removed—Actual on the Project Plan Summary.
3	Time	• Review the completed Time Recording Log. • Enter the total time spent in each PSP0 phase under Actual on the Project Plan Summary form.
	Exit Criteria	• A fully tested program • Completed Project Plan Summary form • Completed Defect and Time Recording Logs

and measure your process. You thus start with imprecise measurements and use them to help make the process and its measures more precise.

While defining such straightforward and obvious tasks as design, code, compile, and test may seem unnecessary, it is important to understand how you perform even simple tasks. When you make a preliminary definition for a process phase and then gather data while you perform it, you learn a great deal about it. You gain new insight into how you spend your time and see what parts of the phase caused you the most trouble. You are then better able to improve your process. PSP0 is a first step in this direction.

2.5 PSP0 Measures

The PSP0 has two measures:

- ☐ The time spent per phase
- ☐ The defects found per phase

TABLE 2.4 PSP0 DEVELOPMENT SCRIPT

Phase Number	Purpose	To guide the development of small programs
	Entry Criteria	• Requirements statement • Project Plan Summary with planned development time • Time and Defect Recording Logs • Defect Type Standard
1	Design	• Review the requirements and produce a design to meet them. • Record time in Time Recording Log.
2	Code	• Implement the design. • Record in the Defect Recording Log any requirements or design defects found. • Record time in Time Recording Log.
3	Compile	• Compile the program until error free. • Fix all defects found. • Record defects in Defect Recording Log. • Record time in Time Recording Log.
4	Test	• Test until all tests run without error. • Fix all defects found. • Record defects in Defect Recording Log. • Record time in Time Recording Log.
	Exit Criteria	• A thoroughly tested program • Completed Defect Recording Log • Completed Time Recording Log

The time spent per phase is a simple record of the clock time you spend in each part of the PSP process. Your objective is to determine where you spend the bulk of your time and how that distribution changes as you change your process. You thus should record your time with sufficient precision to permit you to analyze trends and ratios. While there is no theoretical reason to pick any particular unit, for the PSP you should record your time in minutes. Actually, once you decide to use a clock to measure your time the units do not make much difference. You will probably find it easier to record 38 minutes than to record 0.633 hours. The PSP0 Time Recording Log is discussed in Section 2.6.

Recording defect data is a little trickier. Here, at a minimum, you should record data on every defect you find during compile and test. A defect is counted every time you make a program change. The change could be one character, or it could be multiple statements. As long as the changes all pertain to the same compile or test problem, they constitute one defect. Note that you determine the defect count by what you change in the program. Some compilers, for example, generate multiple error messages for a single defect. If these were all connected to one problem, then you would merely count it as one defect. You should also count defects in your test procedures. In these cases, however, you should make a note that it was a test case defect. The Defect Recording Log is discussed in Section 2.7.

The reason for gathering both time and defect data is to give you the basis for planning your future projects. They give you a baseline against which to measure your performance, show where you spend your time, and indicate where you make and find the most defects. They will also help you to see how these distributions change as your process evolves. You can then decide for yourself how the process changes affected the productivity and quality of your work.

2.6 Time Recording Log

Table 2.5 shows the PSP Time Recording Log, and Table 2.6 contains the instructions for completing it. While I have found this format convenient, you should experiment with it and draw your own conclusions. If you wish to expand or add a field or change some headings, for example, you should feel free to do so. However, you will use this form without any subsequent changes throughout the PSP, so it is important that you be comfortable with it. Your only objective is to promptly and accurately collect all the specified data.

Before you start the planning phase, enter your name, the date, the instructor's name and the program or other assignment number at the top of the log. Also enter the date and the time you started the planning phase. Enter some designation like PLN, for planning, under Phase and write "planning phase" under Comments. You will probably finish planning your first project in a few minutes, so the entries for the planning phase will likely take only a single row of the log. When you finish planning, enter the time you finished under Stop and the difference between the start and stop times in the Delta Time column. If you were interrupted during this phase, either enter the times you stopped and restarted or note the interruption time in the Interruption Time column. Table 2.7 shows an example of a completed time log. These data are for the time one student spent writing program 1A.

With phases that take several hours, you will often be interrupted, for example, if you get a phone call or someone stops by to ask you a question. You will want to keep track of time lost to interruptions. If you consistently ignore the time such interruptions take, you will not have an accurate idea of the time you spent on various tasks. Unfortunately, with most interruptions, it is impossible to

TABLE 2.5   TIME RECORDING LOG

Student _____   Date _____

Instructor _____   Program # _____

Date	Start	Stop	Interruption Time	Delta Time	Phase	Comments

TABLE 2.6   TIME RECORDING LOG INSTRUCTIONS

Purpose	This form is for recording the time spent in each project phase. These data are used to complete the Project Plan Summary.
General	• Record all the time you spend on the project. • Record the time in minutes. • Be as accurate as possible. If you need additional space, use another copy of the form.
Header	Enter the following: • Your name • Today's date • The instructor's name • The number of the program • If you are working on a nonprogramming task, enter a job description in the Program # field.
Date	Enter the date when the entry is made.
Example	10/18/93
Start	Enter the time when you start working on a task.
Example	8:20
Stop	Enter the time when you stop working on that task.
Example	10:56
Interruption Time	Record any interruption time that was not spent on the task and the reason for the interruption. If you have several interruptions, enter their total time.
Example	37—took a break
Delta Time	Enter the clock time you actually spent working on the task, less the interruption time.
Example	From 8:20 to 10:56, 156 minutes less 37 minutes, or 119 minutes.
Phase	Enter the name or other designation of the phase or step being worked on.
Example	planning, code, test, and so on
Comments	Enter any other pertinent comments that may later remind you of any unusual circumstances regarding this activity.
Example	Had a compiler problem and had to get help.
Important	It is important to record all worked time. If you forget to record the starting, stopping, or interruption time for a task, promptly enter your best estimate of the time.

TABLE 2.7   TIME RECORDING LOG EXAMPLE

Student   Student 3 _____   Date   1/19/94 _____

Instructor   Humphrey _____   Program #   1A _____

Date	Start	Stop	Interruption Time	Delta Time	Phase	Comments
1/19	16:25	16:30	0	5	plann'g	
	16:35	17:05	0	30	design	
	17:05	17:40	3	32	code	phone call
	17:40	17:55	0	15	compile	
	17:55	18:00	0	5	test	
1/21	9:25	9:30	0	5	pm	
1/24	15:40	15:55	0	15	pm	
	17:15	17:25	0	10	pm	

tell at the outset how long they will take. You can note, possibly in the Comments column, when the interruption started and can determine the lost time when the interruption is over. For an 18-minute interruption, for example, you would enter 18 in the Interruption Time column. This means you should subtract 18 minutes from the elapsed time when you stop or suspend work on that phase.

Often, you will forget to record the start time or the stop time of a phase or of an interruption. You should then make your best estimate of the time involved. If you make this estimate promptly, it will likely be fairly accurate. Another way to handle unplanned interruptions is to keep a stop watch at hand and start it when you are interrupted. While this may seem inconvenient, it is actually easier to start and stop a stop watch than to make notations in the time log. At the end of the phase, you can then note the accumulated interruption time in the Interruption Time column. Again, when you occasionally forget to start or to stop the stop watch, you will have to make your best estimate. While you might prefer to have an automated timer as part of your support system, this turns out to be almost exactly like a stop watch. You will still have to start it and stop it and you will also occasionally forget to do so.

As a result of keeping such a log, you will likely discover that you are frequently interrupted. Each interruption breaks your train of thought and is a potential source of error, so reducing interruption frequency and duration can pay big dividends. Having the data can help you to see the problem and to figure out ways to address it. Particularly in an industrial environment, this process can also help you to get help in addressing the problem.

Another problem you will likely have is deciding when a step starts or ends. With design, for example, you may find yourself doing design in the middle of coding. If, for example, you feel you can implement a simple program without completing a formal design step, you can enter 0 for the design time and go directly to implementation. While this is never good practice and you may feel guilty about doing it, if that is what you do you should record it that way on your time recording log. As you complete implementation, however, you may discover that a more thorough design would have been helpful. If you actually stop implementation and go back to the design phase and start over, you should count this next effort as design time even though it comes after the coding you have already done. If, however, you do the design "on-the-fly," while completing coding, count this time as coding.

Compile is another example of the confusion about phase boundaries. The time you should enter for compile is the time you spend getting your program to compile completely the first time. As you fix the defects you find in test, however, these changes must also be compiled. This time should be entered as part of the test phase and not as part of compile. Compile ended with the first successful compile. With some interpretative and fourth-generation systems, of course, there is no compile time. In this case, you would drop this phase and go directly from code to test.

Until the entry and exit criteria for each step are explicit, you must use your judgment on what you were really doing. The rule is to enter what seems most appropriate to you. If you conclude that you really did switch back to a design phase, enter your time that way. If, however, you are designing as part of fixing a defect or struggling with an implementation problem, record your time in the phase in which you found and fixed the problem.

2.7   Defect Recording Log

The Defect Recording Log and its instructions are shown in Tables 2.8 and 2.9. The example in Table 2.10 shows how one student completed his defect log for program 1A. First complete the header information on a blank form before you start the compile phase. Then keep this form on hand during compile and test. When you encounter a defect in compile, for example, enter a defect number at the next blank entry in the log. In the example, the student started with 1.

When you finish fixing the defect, note the type from the Defect Type Standard shown in Table 2.11. This standard was modeled on the work of Chillarege at IBM Research, and it should be sufficiently general to cover most of your needs. [Chillarege] If you prefer to use a different standard, you can do so, but you should wait until you have enough defect data to do a competent job. You should also keep your defect type list small until you have a good idea of your personal problem areas and can be explicit about the types that most concern you. When you make a new standard, however, you should do it with care because standards changes can invalidate your historical data. If you use a different standard, you must define it and submit a copy of that definition with each assignment.

To the extent you know the phase or step in which a defect was injected, you should note that phase under Inject. If you don't know, enter your best estimate. In the example in Table 2.10, the student judged that all but two of the defects injected were made in the coding phase.

Next, enter under Remove the phase or step in which the defect was found. If, as in the example, defect 1 was found and fixed in the compile phase, then enter Compile. If, for some reason, you fix a defect in a different phase than that in which you found it, enter the phase in which it was *found* and make a note in the Description section on where it was *fixed*.

FIX TIME

Fix time is a bit more of a problem. Most compile problems will likely be fixed in a minute or so, therefore you can generally enter 1 under Fix Time. In some

```
Defect Types
10  Documentation   60  Checking
20  Syntax          70  Data
30  Build, Package   80  Function
40  Assignment       90  System
50  Interface       100  Environment
```

TABLE 2.8   DEFECT RECORDING LOG

Student _____   Date _____
Instructor _____   Program # _____

Date	Number	Type	Inject	Remove	Fix Time	Fix Defect

Description: _____

Date	Number	Type	Inject	Remove	Fix Time	Fix Defect

Description: _____

Date	Number	Type	Inject	Remove	Fix Time	Fix Defect

Description: _____

Date	Number	Type	Inject	Remove	Fix Time	Fix Defect

Description: _____

Date	Number	Type	Inject	Remove	Fix Time	Fix Defect

Description: _____

Date	Number	Type	Inject	Remove	Fix Time	Fix Defect

Description: _____

Date	Number	Type	Inject	Remove	Fix Time	Fix Defect

Description: _____

Date	Number	Type	Inject	Remove	Fix Time	Fix Defect

Description: _____

Date	Number	Type	Inject	Remove	Fix Time	Fix Defect

Description: _____

cases, you may think you can fix a problem in a minute but find it takes a lot longer. If you do not use a stop watch to track fix time, enter your best estimate. In test, however, it is easy to lose track of how long you spend on each defect. In this case, it is generally wise to use a stop watch or to record the time you start and stop working on a fix.

TABLE 2.9   DEFECT RECORDING LOG INSTRUCTIONS

Purpose	This form holds the data on each defect as you find and correct it. You use these data to complete the Project Plan Summary.
General	• Record in this log all defects found in review, compile, and test. • Record each defect separately and completely. If you need additional space, use another copy of the form.
Header	Enter the following: • Your name • Today's date • The instructor's name • The number of the program
Date	Enter the date when the defect was found.
Number	Enter the defect number. For each program, this should be a sequential number starting with, for example, 1 or 001.
Type	Enter the defect type from the defect type list in Table C20 (also summarized in the top left corner of the log form). Use your best judgment in selecting which type applies.
Inject	Enter the phase during which this defect was injected. Use your best judgment.
Remove	Enter the phase during which the defect was removed. This would generally be the phase during which you found the defect.
Fix Time	Enter your best judgment of the time you took to fix the defect. This time can be determined by using a stop watch or your judgment.
Fix Defect	If you injected this defect while fixing another defect, record the number of the improperly fixed defect. If you cannot identify the defect number, enter an X in the Fix Defect box.
Description	Write a succinct description of the defect that is clear enough to later remind you about the error and help you to remember why you made it.

Defect Types
10 Documentation	60 Checking
20 Syntax	70 Data
30 Build, Package	80 Function
40 Assignment	90 System
50 Interface	100 Environment

TABLE 2.10   DEFECT RECORDING LOG EXAMPLE

Student ___Student 3_____   Date ___1/19/94___
Instructor ___Humphrey_____   Program # ___1A___

Date	Number	Type	Inject	Remove	Fix Time	Fix Defect
1/19	1	20	code	compile	1 min	

Description: ___missing semicolon___

Date	Number	Type	Inject	Remove	Fix Time	Fix Defect
	2	20	code	compile	1 min	

Description: ___missing semicolon___

Date	Number	Type	Inject	Remove	Fix Time	Fix Defect
	3	40	design	compile	1 min	

Description: ___wrong type on RHS of binary operator, must cast integers as float___

Date	Number	Type	Inject	Remove	Fix Time	Fix Defect
	4	40	code	compile	1	

Description: ___wrong type on RHS, constant literal should be 0.0 not 0___

Date	Number	Type	Inject	Remove	Fix Time	Fix Defect
	5	40	code	compile	1	

Description: ___wrong type on RHS, had to cast an integer as a float___

Date	Number	Type	Inject	Remove	Fix Time	Fix Defect
	6	40	design	compile	7	

Description: ___exponent must be an integer, researched and used math lib for sqrt.
integral is not calculated correctly.

Date	Number	Type	Inject	Remove	Fix Time	Fix Defect
	7	80	code	test	1	

Description: ___answer (std. dev.) incorrect - equn not coded properly, subtracted when I
should have divided.

Date	Number	Type	Inject	Remove	Fix Time	Fix Defect

Description: _____

Date	Number	Type	Inject	Remove	Fix Time	Fix Defect

Description: _____

THE MULTIPLE-DEFECT PROBLEM

One problem you will likely encounter concerns multiple-defects—while fixing one defect, you encounter and fix another. You should separately record each defect and its fix time. If you spent a few minutes fixing compile defect 18 while working on a complex test defect (defect 17), deduct the fix time for defect 18 from the total fix time for defect 17. The example shown in Fig. 2.3 illustrates this.

- ☐ Defect 17 is a logic defect you encountered in test at 11:06. After 41 minutes, you had a fix ready to compile.

- ☐ While compiling the fix for defect 17, you encountered defect 18—a typographical error you made while fixing defect 17. You found it at 11:47 and fixed it in 1 minute.

- ☐ While fixing defect 18, you noticed defect 19 and started to fix it at 11:48. It was a wrong name that was introduced in coding. It took 2 minutes to fix.

- ☐ After fixing defect 19, you spent 6 more minutes compiling and testing the fix to defect 17 before you were convinced you had fixed it. Your total elapsed time was 50 minutes but the actual fix time for defect 17 was only 47 minutes.

- ☐ A little later in testing you find defect 20. It is a logic error that you injected while fixing defect 17. It took 26 minutes to fix.

TABLE 2.11   DEFECT TYPE STANDARD

Type Number	Type Name	Description
10	Documentation	comments, messages
20	Syntax	spelling, punctuation, typos, instruction formats
30	Build, package	change management, library, version control
40	Assignment	declaration, duplicate names, scope, limits
50	Interface	procedure calls and references, I/O, user formats
60	Checking	error messages, inadequate checks
70	Data	structure, content
80	Function	logic, pointers, loops, recursion, computation, function defects
90	System	configuration, timing, memory
100	Environment	design, compile, test, or other support system problems

Here, the total elapsed time for all this fix activity was 76 minutes, with 12 minutes of intervening test time between the end of defect 17 and the start of defect 20. You presumably stopped the clock on defect 17 at 50 minutes when you thought you had it fixed. Subsequent testing, however, showed that you introduced defect 20 while fixing defect 17. This defect took another 26 minutes to fix. Here, defects 18 and 20 are both noted in the Defect Recording Log in Table 2.12 as injected during test. The fact that these were fix errors is noted with an entry in the Fix Defect box. You will find this is helpful when you later analyze these data. Only the times for defects 18 and 19 are deducted from the elapsed time of 50 minutes to give the fix time of 47 minutes for defect 17. Your Defect Recording Log now has four new defects, as shown in Table 2.12.

It is important to note that these data are only to be used by you in deciding where you can improve your process. While numerical precision is not critical,

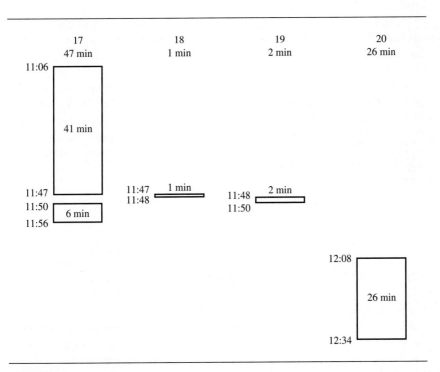

FIGURE 2.3
Defect Fix Time Example

the fix times do help to identify the time you save as you improve your process. Experience has shown that fix times for the identical defect types are 5 to 10 or more times longer in the test phases than earlier in the process. These fix time data will help you to see the value of striving for high-quality work early in your process. They will also help you to evaluate the cost and schedule consequences of your personal process improvements.

You should describe each defect well enough so you can later figure out how to prevent it or how you could have found it earlier. That is the role of the Description section in the defect log. A simple description, often a single character, is generally adequate. For a more complex defect, however, you may have to write a more complete description. Make enough of a notation to indicate what the defect was and to suggest how it may have been found earlier or even prevented. Because you will later be using these data to help improve your process, you need to keep good records now. If this takes more lines than are available in the three-line description space, use more rows in the log.

It is important to describe the defect when you first complete the log entry. If you do not, you will likely not remember it later. After you spend an hour or more fixing a defect, its details will begin to merge with all the others. In any but the smallest programs, there are generally so many defects, they are easily confused.

The only reason for recording the date you find a defect is to help in cross checking. You need enter the date only for the first defect found on any given day. Until you enter a new value, the previous date is assumed to repeat. You could also follow this practice with the phase removed entry, but this is not a good practice. While doing so would not likely cause you problems with the PSP, more sophisticated processes are more dynamic. A consistent practice of entering the phase when each defect is removed is essential, or much of your defect data will be incomplete and much less useful. A point to remember is that if you do not intend to gather the data carefully enough to be useful for later analysis, you should not bother to gather it at all.

2.8   PSP0 Project Plan Summary

The PSP0 Project Plan Summary and its instructions are shown in Tables 2.13 and 2.14. First, fill in the header information: Enter your name, the date you start the project, the name you give the program if any, and the program number. For the homework assignments, the program number should be the numbers 1A, 1B, 2A, 2B, and so on, given in the program descriptions in Appendix D. Also enter the instructor's name and the language you used to write the program.

```
Defect Types
10  Documentation  60  Checking
20  Syntax          70  Data
30  Build, Package  80  Function
40  Assignment      90  System
50  Interface      100  Environment
```

TABLE 2.12 A MULTIPLE-DEFECT EXAMPLE

Student	John Doe				Date	1/10/94
Instructor					Program #	5A

Date	Number	Type	Inject	Remove	Fix Time	Fix Defect
1/10/94	17	80	Design	Test	47	

Description: StepPointer advanced an extra step when CycleCounter loop exceeded
its limit.

Date	Number	Type	Inject	Remove	Fix Time	Fix Defect
	18	20	Test	Test	1	17

Description: Misspelled Step-counter while correcting #17

Date	Number	Type	Inject	Remove	Fix Time	Fix Defect
	19	50	Code	Test	2	

Description: Noticed that the input SummaryFile was improperly referenced. Should
have been TotalsFile.

Date	Number	Type	Inject	Remove	Fix Time	Fix Defect
	20	80	Test	Test	26	17

Description: While fixing 17, corrected the StepPointer advancing but forgot to adjust
the SyncPointer at the same time.

Date	Number	Type	Inject	Remove	Fix Time	Fix Defect

Description:

Date	Number	Type	Inject	Remove	Fix Time	Fix Defect

Description:

Date	Number	Type	Inject	Remove	Fix Time	Fix Defect

Description:

Date	Number	Type	Inject	Remove	Fix Time	Fix Defect

Description:

Date	Number	Type	Inject	Remove	Fix Time	Fix Defect

Description:

TABLE 2.13 PSP0 PROJECT PLAN SUMMARY

Student   _____   Date   _____

Program   _____   Program #   _____

Instructor   _____   Language   _____

Time in Phase (min.)	Plan	Actual	To Date	To Date%
Planning		_____	_____	_____
Design		_____	_____	_____
Code		_____	_____	_____
Compile		_____	_____	_____
Test		_____	_____	_____
Postmortem		_____	_____	_____
Total	_____	_____	_____	_____
Defects Injected		**Actual**	**To Date**	**To Date%**
Planning		_____	_____	_____
Design		_____	_____	_____
Code		_____	_____	_____
Compile		_____	_____	_____
Test		_____	_____	_____
Total Development		_____	_____	_____
Defects Removed		**Actual**	**To Date**	**To Date%**
Planning		_____	_____	_____
Design		_____	_____	_____
Code		_____	_____	_____
Compile		_____	_____	_____
Test		_____	_____	_____
Total Development		_____	_____	_____
After Development		_____	_____	

In planning the job, estimate in whatever way you can how much total time it will take you to write the program. If you don't have a better way, you will have to make a guess. Then enter this number in the total time row under Plan. You may subdivide this into the time you expect to spend for each phase, but this is not necessary with PSP0. Until you have data on the actual distribution of your development time, you will probably not be able to allocate your total time among the phases.

During the postmortem or when you complete each phase, enter the total time you spent in that phase in the Actual time column. Beside Design, for example, you enter the time you spent doing the design work. When you have completed the project, calculate the total time for each phase from your Time Recording Log and enter this total in the actual time column in the plan form. Also, from your Defect Recording Log, count the defects you found in compile and the defects you found in test and enter them in the Compile and Test positions, respectively. An example Project Plan Summary is shown in Table 2.15. It includes the data from the examples in Tables 2.7 and 2.10.

TABLE 2.14   PSP0 PROJECT PLAN SUMMARY INSTRUCTIONS

Purpose	This form holds the estimated and actual project data in a convenient and readily retrievable form.
Header	Enter the following: • Your name and today's date • The program name and number • The instructor's name • The language you used to write the program
Time in Phase	• Under Plan, enter your original estimate of the total development time. • Under Actual, enter the actual time in minutes spent in each development phase. • Under To Date, enter the sum of the actual time and the To Date time from your most recently developed program. • Under To Date %, enter the percentage of To Date time in each phase.
Defects Injected	• Under Actual, enter the number of defects injected in each phase. • Under To Date, enter the sum of the actual numbers of defects injected in each phase and the To Date values from the most recently developed program. • Under To Date %, enter the percentage of To Date defects injected by phase.
Defects Removed	• Under Actual, enter the number of defects removed in each phase. • Under To Date, enter the sum of the actual number of defects removed in each phase and the To Date value from the most recently developed program. • Under To Date %, enter the percentage of the To Date defects removed by phase. • After development, record any defects later found during program use, reuse, or modification.

2.9   Customizing the Initial Process

If you have a particular way to design software that does not fit this PSP0 structure, you can adjust PSP0 to fit what you do. For example, if you now do design reviews or code reviews you might find that the PSP2 process described in Appendix C is a better fit. You would then use the PSP2 forms and scripts for doing the exercises.

Because it would likely cause you a great deal of extra work, I suggest you do not modify the PSP. While most of us in the programming business have a natural desire to do things our own way, you would be wise to restrain yourself and

TABLE 2.15 PSP0 PROJECT PLAN SUMMARY EXAMPLE

Student	Student 3		Date	1/19/94
Program	Standard Deviation		Program #	1A
Instructor	Humphrey		Language	Ada

Time in Phase (min.)	Plan	Actual	To Date	To Date%
Planning		5	5	4.3
Design		30	30	25.6
Code		32	32	27.4
Compile		15	15	12.8
Test		5	5	4.3
Postmortem		30	30	25.6
Total	180	117	117	100.0

Defects Injected		Actual	To Date	To Date%
Planning		0	0	0.0
Design		2	2	28.6
Code		5	5	71.4
Compile		0	0	0.0
Test		0	0	0.0
Total Development		7	7	100.0

Defects Removed		Actual	To Date	To Date%
Planning		0	0	0.0
Design		0	0	0.0
Code		0	0	0.0
Compile		6	6	85.7
Test		1	1	14.3
Total Development		7	7	100.0
After Development		0	0	

focus on learning from what is here. When you have finished the book, then you can change whatever you want. If, however, you feel you must change the PSP, you must complete all the definition elements for your new process and submit them with your homework assignments. You will then have to revise and update this modified process for each assignment in the book. If you decide to make such process adaptations, you should keep the following points in mind:

□ Write down the process and give it a version number.

□ Keep it simple!!! For example, if the process has more than seven to nine steps, it is too big. Either eliminate steps or make them defined subprocesses.

□ Include a planning and a postmortem phase in every process.

□ Gather at least the basic data called for in PSP0. While you may want to gather more, at a minimum include the time per phase and the compile and test defects.

□ The data you gather for every defect should include the defect type, the phase injected, the phase removed, and the time to fix.

□ Use forms and logs for gathering and recording data.

□ Use whatever format seems most convenient to you.

□ With each PSP enhancement, make sure your process includes all the new PSP items.

While this approach is theoretically possible, the people I know who have attempted to do this during the early work on the PSP soon gave up. They decided it would be far easier to use the processes in this book for these exercises. Once they finished the book, they then adapted the PSP2.1 or PSP3 process to meet their needs in whatever way they found most helpful. In short, you should use the PSP processes as they are currently defined to do the exercises in this book. Feel free to adopt or modify the PSP in any way you want but wait until you have finished the book to do so.

2.10   Summary

A defined process can help you to understand your performance as a software engineer and to see where and how to improve it. This chapter introduces the PSP0 process as a foundation for your personal process improvement. You will use PSP0 to complete the initial programming assignments in the text.

PSP0 measures the time you spend in each development phase and the defects you inject and find per phase. You use standard formats for defect and time recording. You will then use these data in later chapters to help you to make better plans and to guide you as you improve your process.

If you have a particular way to design software that does not fit this PSP0 structure, you should examine the processes in Appendix C and see if some other PSP is a better fit. In this book, it is suggested that you use the PSP as a learning vehicle and refrain from modifying it until you have completed the book.

2.11   Exercises

The standard assignment for this chapter uses PSP0 to write program 1A. The specifications for program 1A are given in Appendix D and the PSP0 process is described in Appendix C. In completing this assignment, you should faithfully follow the report submission format specified for PSP0 in Appendix C.

For other assignment options, consult Appendix D.

References

[Chillarege] Ram Chillarege, Inderpal S. Bhandari, Jarir K. Chaar, Michael J. Halliday, Diane S. Moebus, Bonnie K. Ray, and Man-Yuen Wong, "Orthogonal Defect Classification—A Concept for In-Process Measurements," *IEEE Transactions on Software Engineering,* vol. 18, no. 11 (November 1992): pp 943–956.

[Feiler] P. H. Feiler and W. S. Humphrey, "Software Process Development and Enactment: Concepts and Definitions," SEI Technical Report CMU/SEI-92-TR-04 (September 1992).

3

Planning I—The Planning Process

Planning is the first step in the PSP for three reasons. First, without good plans you cannot effectively manage even modestly sized software projects. Second, planning is a skill that you can learn and improve with practice. Third, good planning skills will help you to do better software work.

This chapter introduces software planning and provides a general overview of the planning process. It discusses what a plan is and what it should contain. It reviews the reasons why planning is important and the elements of an effective planning process. It then discusses plan quality and how your work with the PSP will help you do better work and be a more effective team and project member. Chapters 4–6 show you how to measure software size, how to estimate the size of a program before you develop it, and how to make resource and schedule plans.

The planning methods described in this and the next three chapters are for your personal work. The planning skills you develop with the PSP will help you in planning all your future projects.

3.1 Why Make Plans

In software engineering as in other fields, the role of engineers is to devise economical and timely solutions to their employer's needs. Engineers must thus consider costs and schedules. The connection between cost, schedule, and the planning process can best be illustrated by an example. Suppose you want to put an addition on your home. After deciding what you want and getting several bids, most of which are around $14,000, you pick a builder who offers to do the job in two months for $10,000. While this is a lot of money, you need the extra space and can arrange for a home-equity loan. You then sign an agreement, and the builder starts the work. After about a month into the job, the builder comes to you and explains that because of problems the job will take an extra month and cost an additional $4000.

This presents you with several problems. First, you badly need the space and another month of delay is a real inconvenience. Second, you have already arranged for the loan and don't know where you can get the extra $4000. Third, if you get a lawyer and decide to fight the builder in court, all work on the job will stop for many months while the case is decided. Fourth, it would take a great deal of time and probably cost even more to switch to a new builder in the middle of the job.

On exploration, you conclude that the real problem is that the builder did a sloppy job of planning. While you have not been told what went wrong, you conclude that the builder forgot to include some major costs like the labor or materials to do the woodwork or the final plastering and painting. You can endlessly debate what the job should cost, but essentially the problem is caused by poor planning. If you had originally been given the $14,000 price, you could have decided then whether to proceed with that builder and how to finance the work. The odds are that at this point, you will try to negotiate a lower price but will continue with the current builder. Because the other bids were close to $14,000, you know this is a pretty fair price. You would not use this builder again, however, and would probably not recommend the company to anyone else.

This is the essential issue of the planning process: being able to make plans that accurately represent what you can do. Businesses operate on commitments, and commitments require plans. To be successful, businesses must make commitments they can fulfill at a profit. Often, when they contract to do the work for a fixed price, they are stuck with any mistakes or omissions. If their costs come in above what was planned, the difference comes out of profit. While you may not think a software project that comes in over cost is that big a deal, there is usually someone in management who is seriously concerned. If you do this often, you could end up with some very upset managers. That may not worry you too much, but it should. These are the people who decide who gets raises, who gets promoted, and who gets fired. For software engineers, good planning will be an increasingly important part of their job security.

While personal planning is important to project planning, it is only a part of the process. Many more issues are involved in producing a complete plan for a large project. These larger project plans, however, are more likely to be realistic when they are composed of multiple personal plans made by the individuals or teams who will do the work. As the accuracy and completeness of these elemental plans improves, their composite will then also be higher quality. Conversely, if the individual plans are poorly done, they will provide a poor foundation for the overall project.

Well-thought-out plans provide leverage. They help you to make commitments you can meet and to accurately track and report your progress. If you want such leverage, you need to be able to plan. You should thus prepare for these future planning needs. Identify your major tasks, keep track of the size of the products you produce, and note how long they took to develop. Record these data in a summary report and build a permanent file. Such data are gold, and your summary report file is your personal Fort Knox. Guard it accordingly.

Planning is serious business. It defines commitments and supports business decisions. You thus need to treat planning as an important skill that you can develop, practice, and hone. As you practice the methods described in this and the next three chapters, you will quickly learn how to make competent plans.

3.2   What Is a Plan

"The project plan defines the work and how it will be done. It provides a definition of each major task, an estimate of the time and resources required, and a framework for management review and control. The project plan is also a powerful learning vehicle. When properly documented, it is a benchmark to compare with actual performance. This comparison permits the planners to see their estimating errors and to improve their estimating accuracy." [Humphrey 89] A plan is thus many things. In mature software organizations, plans typically are used as

☐ a basis for agreeing on the cost and schedule for a job,

☐ an organizing structure for doing the work,

☐ a framework for obtaining the required resources, and

☐ a record of what was initially committed.

The connection between plans and commitments is thus extremely important. Every project starts as a new endeavor. At the outset, the project must be created out of thin air. New projects typically start with no staff. Some manager, user, or customer must commit funds, and some workers and suppliers must be convinced to participate in the work.

When you start a major project, you are all alone. You must assemble a planning and proposal team and produce an overall plan. This helps you to get funding, hire the staff, and arrange for all the facilities, supplies, and other support you will need. Without a clear and convincing plan, however, these steps are almost impossible to achieve. Nobody wants to pay for an undefined job, and few people will work on a project that has unclear objectives. You could not describe the required space, machines and tools, or support services. With a plan, you can negotiate with people and convince some of them to give your needs priority over their other existing commitments. In short, a plan is the essential first step in creating a project.

In software development, plans have often been incomplete and inaccurate. Once, when we at IBM needed a critical new function for the OS/360 programming system, the engineering estimate was $175,000. Naively, that is all the funding I requested. Some months later, the engineers found the work would cost $525,000. It turned out that they had omitted many tasks from their original plan. They had forgotten documentation, testing, and quality assurance. Sure enough, however, the coding and unit test costs were about $175,000. They had made a pretty good estimate, but their plan was unacceptably incomplete. The problem is that few software organizations have a planning process that ensures that plans are complete, thoroughly reviewed, and properly approved.

3.3   Contents of a Software Plan

Because there are many good books on software project planning, I will not try to summarize them here. [Boehm 81, Rakos, Zells] In this book, the focus is on the PSP planning process and the products it must produce. While I will occasionally relate the individual planning process to the larger topics of project planning and project management, the emphasis here is on learning and practicing planning for your personal software projects.

In deciding what a plan should contain, you must think first about the plan's users and what they will want from it. Your PSP plans have two users: you and your customers. Your and your customers' interests differ, so it is important to explore your needs separately. For your own work, you need four general things from a plan:

  □ Job sizing: How big is this job, and how long do you expect it to take?

  □ Job structure: How are you going to do the work? What will you do first, second, and so on?

☐ Job status: How do you know where you are? Are you going to finish on time and are the costs under control?

☐ Assessment: How good was your plan? Did you make any obvious errors, what mistakes should you avoid in the future, and how can you do a better job next time?

Your customers might be your course instructor, your coworkers, your manager, or an end user. These people also want four general things from your plan.

☐ What is the commitment? Specifically, what is to be delivered, when, and at what cost?

☐ How good is this product likely to be? Is it what they wanted? Is the right work planned to assure that the product fits their needs? Are there provisions for them to make interim checks on product quality? Are there provisions for resolving issues?

☐ Is there some way to monitor progress? Will they have early warning of cost, schedule, or quality problems? If so, how early can they detect problems and what can they do about them?

☐ Will they be able to later evaluate how well the job was done? Can they separate the problems caused by poor planning from those caused by poor management? Will the impact of scope changes be clear and identifiable?

These issues will not be very complex when you develop the small programs described in this text, but they are still important. In doing an assignment, you will want some idea of the size of the job. Can you start work a day before the assignment is due or should you allow a week or more? As work progresses, do you need a crash effort to finish on time or can you take a break to watch a movie or ball game?

Different customers will have different questions. Users and coworkers will want to know if they can count on the results when they need them and whether they need backup provisions. Everyone will be evaluating you. Your instructor will grade your work and everyone else will be considering whether they want to deal with you in the future.

When you examine the plan in the context of these questions, several things are clear:

1. The plan must be based on doing a defined piece of work. Otherwise, there is no way to make an accurate plan, and you could even build the wrong product.

2. The work should involve multiple steps that are clearly defined and measurable. This provides a framework for your plan and a basis for tracking your progress.

3. You will often want some way to check the plan with the user before you start work. This is always a good idea, and it is essential for any but the smallest tasks.

4. You will need to make periodic progress statements to your customers. Again, for any but the shortest projects such communications dispel uninformed fears and help to build an attitude of trust and partnership.

When estimating for a project rather than for your own personal work, you will need to plan for the way that project will be conducted rather than how you would do it or how you think it should be done. When your estimate differs from the final result, that is a planning problem. While there may have been many development problems, your job as a planner was to estimate the cost and schedule for the job that was actually done, and you did not do that. The saving grace in all this is that at the PSP level, projects are both simpler and a great deal more consistent. Thus, while gross data on large projects may not be very helpful for planning, PSP data are. You also have the advantage of estimating your own work. This is the ideal case: You decide how to do the work, produce a plan, and then do the job. When you are done, you can then see how good your plan was.

3.4   Planning a Software Project

The following steps will help you to build a stable and effective estimating process:

- □ Start with an explicit statement of the work to be done and check to ensure that it is what your customer expects. The ways in which projects can differ are endless, and there is no standard plan framework that will fit all or even most projects in an organization. It is thus important that you think through what is required for this particular project and how it will be done.

- □ For projects that take more than a few days' work, break them into multiple smaller tasks and estimate each task separately. The added detail will improve the precision of your plan and will likely improve your accuracy as well.

- □ Base your estimates on comparing this job with the historical data on your prior work.

- □ Record your estimates and later compare them with your actual results.

With every estimate, you need to ensure that the historical data you use are still appropriate. An actual case will make this clear. In estimating the work required to define a series of functional requirement statements, a software professional used historical data from a previous project. Part way through, he found he was spending three times longer than he had estimated. While the numbers of items had increased modestly, it was taking him a great deal longer to do each item than it did on the previous project. On examination, he found that the current requirements dealt with system-wide issues, while the requirements in the previous project concerned a small, stand-alone application. The central nature of this new work required that he deal with many more people to resolve system issues and to get the requirements approved. By tracking and analyzing his work as he was doing it, he was able to see this problem early enough to identify it and resolve it with his management and customer.

USE PLANNING TOOLS

Tools are an important part of planning. For the small programs in this book, you will not need any automated tools. As you work through the chapters, however, some of the programs produced in the exercises can be used as tools to help plan the later exercises. A spreadsheet will also help you to do the calculations, and a database would be useful for analyzing your defect data. Beyond these, however, no other planning tools are needed for this book.

When you go beyond the small programs in this book, two kinds of tools will be useful: PERT planning systems and cost models.

PERT is a critical-path scheduling system for analyzing a job that contains multiple, interdependent tasks. Because each task takes time to perform and some tasks must be completed before others can be started, the order in which you do them can be important. PERT systems analyze all the project data and identify the arrangement of the tasks that will produce the shortest over-all schedule.

PERT planning tools are thus helpful when you are deciding how to do the work. For even moderately complex software projects, there are many interdependent tasks that must be completed in order. With this minimum schedule, you then have some tasks that are on what is called the critical path. If any of these tasks takes longer than planned, the total project schedule is delayed.

Tasks not on the critical path have what is called slack time, that is, they can be delayed by the amount of this slack time before they become critical. Because these relationships can be very complex and because the task structure can change substantially with even minor schedule changes, PERT planning tools can be extremely helpful in making and updating software development plans.

Cost models, such as COCOMO and PriceS, produce standardized planning projections based on their built-in historical data. [Boehm, Park, Putnam] They spread labor hours over project phases and provide projected dates for standard project milestones. The designers of these cost models analyzed the data on a family of historical projects and produced a series of factors to relate resources to estimated product size. They could then provide typical resource time profiles.

Because these cost models were based on large volumes of data, the designers could even consider the impact of various project characteristics on resource needs. For example, when you are working on a very tight schedule or a constrained hardware configuration, the costs are generally higher per unit of program size.

These models start with a size estimate that is fed to the model as input. They must be used responsibly, however, for they can easily be misused. For example, if the resulting schedule is too long or the costs too high, it is easy for the uninformed user to make a "more accurate" size estimate and try again. After a few tries, you can get a very impressive pseudo-plan that will convince any but the most skeptical that you have thoughtfully produced a detailed plan.

THE PLANNING FRAMEWORK

The PSP planning framework is shown in Fig. 3.1. The tasks you perform are shown in the rectangles and the various data, reports, and products are shown in the ovals. Here, starting with a customer need, you define the requirements. Next, because many possible products could conceivably be built from a single requirement, you produce a conceptual design, which in turn helps you to relate your planning estimate to the actual product you intend to build.

With this conceptual design and historical data on products you have previously built, you can estimate the likely size of the new product. With this size estimate, you can use your historical productivity data to estimate how many hours the work is likely to take. Finally, you allocate these hours on a calendar to get the project schedule. With these data and with a presumed starting date, you can now estimate the date when you will finish.

With the plan in hand, and assuming you have all the information and facilities you need, you start development. Both during development and at project completion, you record the time you spent and the size of the product you produced. You use these data to produce periodic tracking reports and to make process analyses. These analyses provide the size and productivity data you will use to make future plans.

3.5   Producing a Quality Plan

As you build your planning skills, you need to think about plan quality. What constitutes a good plan? How do your plans measure up and what can you do to

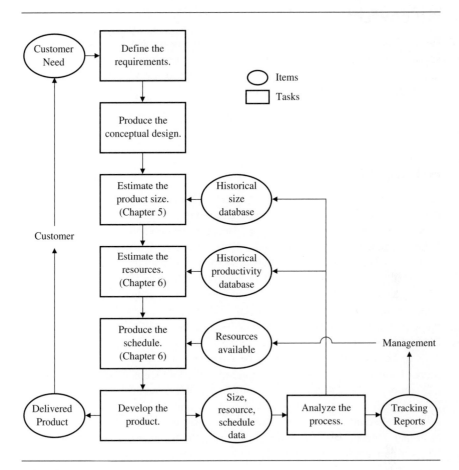

FIGURE 3.1
Project Planning Framework

improve your planning skills? The six key questions to ask about your plan are
the following:

1. Is it complete?
2. Is it accessible?
3. Is it clear?
4. Is it specific?
5. Is it precise?
6. Is it accurate?

These topics are discussed in the following sections.

IS IT COMPLETE

Here is where your defined process can be most helpful. Do you have a form that specifies what is needed? Is it filled out? Have you left any blanks? While there are many ways to ensure your plans are complete, using well-designed forms is among the most convenient and economical.

IS IT ACCESSIBLE

Accessibility is best illustrated by the case of a company that was fighting a major lawsuit. At one point, they were required to provide all the historical documents that related to a particular topic. Because the company was large, this material was scattered among thousands of files. The cost of searching all those files would have been prohibitive, so they gave the plaintiff all the files that could possibly contain any of the desired data. Even though these files undoubtedly contained material the company didn't want released, they judged this problem to be minor compared to the costs of a detailed document review. While the plaintiff knew that what he wanted was somewhere in the many thousands of pages of files, he might as well not have had it. In practical terms, it was inaccessible.

To be accessible, a plan must be where you can find it, it must be in the proper format, and it must not be cluttered with extraneous material. While having complete plans is important, voluminous plans are unwieldy. You need to know what is in the plan and where it is. You should be able to find quickly the original schedule and all the subsequent revisions. The defect data should be clear and the program size data must be available for every program version. To be most convenient, these data should be in a prescribed order and in a known, consistent, and nonredundant format.

IS IT CLEAR

It is surprising how many students turn in homework that is absolutely unintelligible. Some entries are scrawled, others are scratched out. Incomprehensible notes are jotted in the margins. Some spaces are blank, or two or three items are inscribed in a space in which one belongs. Such work is not data and should be rejected. Of all the things this book teaches, the most fundamental is the importance of quality data. If the entries on the forms are not unmistakably clear, they cannot be used with confidence. If they cannot be used with confidence, there is no point in entering them at all.

IS IT SPECIFIC

A specific plan says what will be done, when, by whom, and at what costs. If these items are not absolutely clear, the plan is not specific. For the initial PSP, the plans you produce with the Project Plan Summaries specifically answer these questions. You will write the numbered program by the following week and for the cost of your total estimated time.

IS IT PRECISE

Precision is a matter of relating the unit of measure to the total magnitude of the measurement. If, for example, you analyzed a project that took 14 programmer years, you would not be interested in units of minutes, hours, or probably even days. In fact, programmer weeks would probably be the finest level of detail you could usefully consider.

For a PSP job that takes five hours, units of days or weeks would be useless. On the other hand, units of seconds would be far too detailed. Here you are probably interested in time measured in minutes.

To determine an appropriate level of precision, consider the error introduced by a difference of one in the smallest unit of measure. A project that is planned to take 14 programmer years would require 168 programmer months. An uncertainty of one month would contribute an error of at most 0.6 percent. In light of normal planning errors, this is small enough to be quite acceptable. For a five-hour project, an uncertainty of one minute would contribute a maximum error of about 0.33 percent. A unit of measure of one minute would thus introduce tolerable errors, while units of an hour or even a tenth of an hour would probably be too gross.

IS IT ACCURATE

While the other five points are all important, accuracy is crucial. The principal topics of the next three chapters are the means to measure, predict, and improve planning accuracy.

As you learn to plan your PSP work, you should not be too concerned about the errors in your small task plans as long as they appear to be random. That is, you want to have about as many overestimates as underestimates. As you work on larger projects or participate on development teams, these small-scale errors will balance each other and the combined total will be more accurate. The next several chapters provide methods to help you produce unbiased plans.

3.6   Summary

Planning is the first step in the PSP for three reasons. First, without good plans you cannot effectively manage even modestly sized software projects. Second, planning is a skill that you can learn and improve with practice. Third, good planning skills will help you to do better software work.

In software engineering as in other fields, the role of engineers is to devise economical and timely solutions to their employer's needs. This is the essential issue of the planning process: being able to make plans that accurately represent what you can do. This in turn will help you to better manage your personal work and to be a more effective team and project member.

While personal planning is an important part of project planning, it is only a part. Many more issues are involved in producing a complete plan for a large project. These larger project plans, however, are more likely to be realistic when they are composed of multiple personal plans made by the individuals or teams who will do the work. As the accuracy and completeness of these elemental plans improves, their composite will then also be higher quality. Conversely, if the individual plans are poorly done, they will provide a poor foundation for the overall project.

3.7   Exercises

There is no standard assignment for this chapter. For various assignment options, consult Appendix D. If you choose to do an exercise at this point, you should use PSP0. The specifications for the PSP0 process are in Appendix C. In completing an assignment with PSP0, you should faithfully follow the specified report submission format.

References

[Boehm 81] Barry W. Boehm, *Software Engineering Economics* (Englewood Cliffs, NJ: Prentice-Hall, 1981).

[Humphrey 89] W. S. Humphrey, *Managing the Software Process* (Reading, MA: Addison-Wesley, 1989).

[Park 89] Robert E. Park, "The Central Equations of the PRICE Software Cost Model," Proceedings, National Estimating Society Conference, McLean, VA (June 1989).

[Putnam] L. H. Putnam and W. Myers, *Measures for Excellence* (Englewood Cliffs, NJ: Yourdon Press, 1992).

[Rakos] John J. Rakos, *Software Project Management for Small to Medium-Sized Projects* (Englewood Cliffs, NJ: Prentice Hall, 1990).

[Zells] Lois Zells, *Managing Software Projects* (Wellesley, MA: QED Information Sciences, Inc., 1990).

4

Planning II—Measuring
Software Size

The software planning process starts with an estimate of job size. By estimating the size of the product you plan to build, you can better judge the amount of work required to build it. Before you can estimate software size, however, you need a consistent and repeatable way to describe a product's size. This chapter describes the various ways to measure this size and how and when those ways should be used. Chapter 5 then deals with software size estimating, while Chapter 6 deals with estimating resources and schedules. The planning process, however, starts with size estimates, which require size measures.

4.1 Size Measures

In selecting software size measures, you primarily must ensure that the selected measures are useful for planning and are precise. That is, when several people independently measure the same product, will they consistently get identical results? Because manual counting is time consuming and error prone, you also want a measure that is automatically countable. These three topics—usefulness for planning, precision, and automated counting—are discussed in the following sections.

USEFULNESS FOR PLANNING

Not surprisingly, studies show that more resources are required to develop large programs than small ones. [Boehm 81] While most such studies are of large development projects, this relationship also holds for small programs and can be described in terms of their correlation. **Correlation** is the degree to which two sets of data are related. The correlation value, r, varies from -1.0 to $+1.0$. To be useful for estimating and planning purposes, the value of r^2 should be greater than 0.5. How the correlation coefficient, r, is calculated, is described in Section A3 of Appendix A.

The degree to which a correlation measure is meaningful is also important. It is indicated by what is called *significance*, essentially, the probability that you could have gotten this result by chance. Thus a significance of 0.25 says that one quarter of the time this result could have occurred as the result of random fluctuations. On the other hand, a significance of 0.005 says that this result would likely occur at random only once in about 200 times. That is a very high significance. A significance of 0.05 is considered good; one of 0.20 is considered poor. The significance calculation is described in Appendix A, Section A4.

With a small number of points, you can get a high correlation, but it is not very significant. With a large number of points, you generally get high significance even with a low correlation. In evaluating size measures, you are interested in the correlation between the size measure and the development hours and in the significance of this correlation.

Figures 4.1 and 4.2 show data for the development times of two students on 10 of the exercise programs in this book. Each program is represented by one circle. While there is some dispersion in these data, there is a strong linear rela-

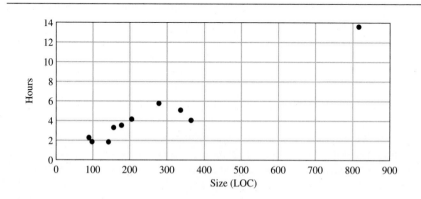

FIGURE 4.1
Size versus Development Time—Student 6

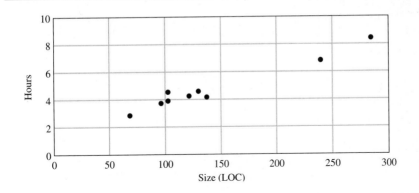

FIGURE 4.2
Size versus Development Time—Student 14

tionship between program size and development time. At least for these students, their development times were essentially a linear function of program size. Thus, if you could estimate the size of a new product and if the sizes of your programs correlated reasonably well with your development times, you should be able to make a pretty good estimate of how long this new development would take.

On large projects, there are usually many kinds of products. In addition to the code, there may be documents, databases, or other support packages. Because these products all require development effort, you will also need to plan the resources they require. It is thus important to find several different types of size measures. Examples would be documentation pages, test scenarios, or database records. To be useful for planning, such measures of product size should reasonably well correlate with the hours you need to develop them. You should also be able to estimate the sizes of these products.

Figure 4.3 shows the hours I took to write each chapter of my previous book, *Managing the Software Process*, as a function of the number of pages in each chapter. While there is a general relationship, it is far from perfect. Here, the correlation is a moderately good 0.78, with a very high significance of better than 0.005. Because $r^2 = (0.78)^2 = 0.61 > 0.5$, the correlation is suitable for planning purposes.

A different case is shown in Fig. 4.4. These data are for the hours several software engineers took to develop and test menu screens as a function of the number of LOC in each screen. These screens were developed in a fourth-generation language that generated the screen code. They were used in a business application to enter data, make menu selections, or enter inquiries. Clearly, as Fig. 4.4 shows, the number of generated LOC is not a good indicator of the development time. Not surprisingly, the correlation is a somewhat lower 0.66, but

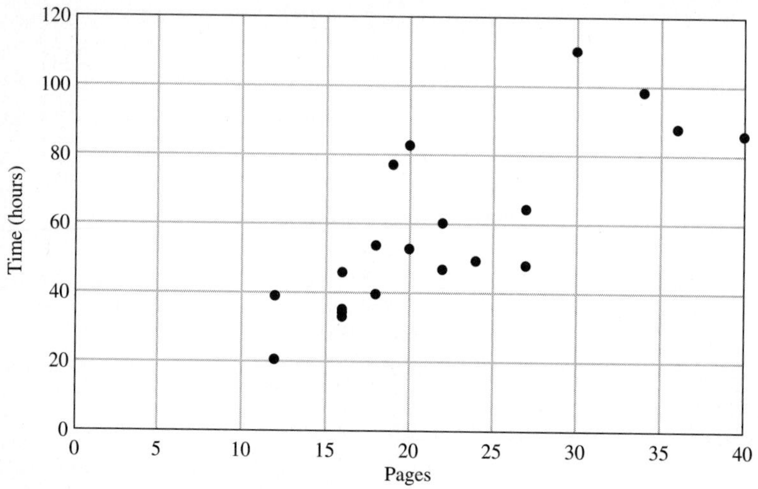

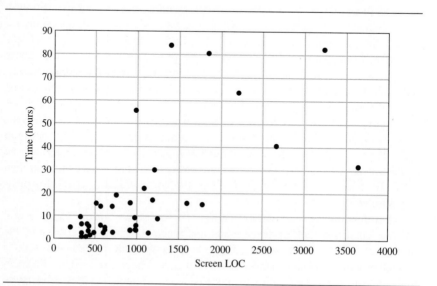

FIGURE 4.3
Chapter Pages versus Development Time

FIGURE 4.4
Screen LOC versus Development Time

the significance is still very high at better than 0.005. Here, with an r^2 of 0.436 (or less than 0.5), the relationship between screen LOC and development time is not suitable for planning.

In all cases, the critical test is whether the required development effort is reasonably correlated with the size as measured. If it is, then that measure will likely be useful for planning purposes. If it is not, then either the process being used is unstable, you need a different measure, or you cannot use a size-based estimating method. Many engineers, when they first use the PSP, find that their productivity fluctuates widely from one program to the next. This can be caused by lack of experience or by a changing development process. Because your process will be changing throughout this book, the correlation between size and development hours for the book's exercises may not be very good. As your process improves, however, your performance should stabilize and you will be able to make more accurate estimates and plans. This means that you need to periodically reexamine your estimating methods. You may find that measures that had not previously been very helpful become much more useful. If, however, you cannot find any usable size measures for the work you plan to do, then you will have to estimate development hours directly without bothering with a size estimate.

Because source LOC (sometimes called SLOC) are a common size measure and have been shown to correlate quite well with development effort, this book uses LOC as the basic size measurement. However, the same estimating and planning approach would apply equally well to such other size measures as document pages, screens, files, or function points.

PRECISION

There is an important distinction between accuracy and precision. Suppose you scheduled an appointment for 8:16 A.M. next Tuesday. That would be a very precise appointment. If, however, you arrived at 9:06 A.M., it would not have been an exceptionally accurate appointment. A much less precise but more accurate statement would have been that you would be there around nine A.M. Precision thus deals with the granularity or level of detail in your measure. Accuracy, however, concerns the relation between an assertion (when you said you would be there) and the actual fact (when you arrived).

With size measures, the principal precision issue concerns the degree to which the measure is completely defined. As is shown in Section 4.3, there are many possible ways to define software LOC. They concern the programming constructs that you count, the treatment of comments and blanks, the handling of reused code, and so forth.

LOC can be defined in so many ways that it is easy to get confused. It is such a conceptually simple measure that people often treat the subject superficially. Because of the many possible LOC definitions, the proper use of size measures depends on the care with which you specify and apply the measure. When usage specifications are not precise, different LOC measures of identical products often vary so widely that the measures are useless. Flaherty, for example, found productivity variations of 56 to one, largely due to differences in LOC definitions. [Flaherty]

AUTOMATED COUNTING

Once you have selected a precise size measure, you will need automated means to ensure it is accurately and economically counted. As you shall see, this information is essential if you are to develop an effective estimating and planning system. Manually counting the instructions in even small programs is tedious, time consuming, and inaccurate. For large programs, it is practically impossible. In the late 1980s, IBM had an inventory of over 30,000,000 LOC and shipped several million new LOC every year. It used a single standard automated counter to ensure that every laboratory produced consistent and accurate size measurement data.

4.2 A Size Measurement Framework

The Software Process Measurement Project at the SEI has developed a framework for describing software size measurements. The two principal criteria for this work were the following: [Park 92]

□ "**Communication**: If someone uses our methods to define a measure or describe a measurement result, will others know precisely what has been measured and what has been included and excluded?"

□ "**Repeatability**: Would someone else be able to repeat the measurement and get the same result?"

In meeting these objectives, the SEI established a framework for precisely defining the LOC metric. A simplified version of the form they developed is shown in Table 4.1. When specifying a LOC counting standard, you can use this form to describe the important items. The meanings and uses of the various entries in this table are as follows:

□ Definition Name: The name you give the standard

□ Language: The language you are using, such as C, C++, or Ada

□ Author: Your name

□ Date: The date you produced the standard

- Count Type: Here, your choices are logical or physical. Logical LOC counts language elements; physical LOC counts text lines. This subject is discussed further in Section 4.3.
- Statement Type:
  - Executable: You will generally include executable statements in the manner described in Table 4.1 under "Clarifications."
  - Declarations: Here, you have many choices. Even when you decide to include declarations, you must decide how to count them. For example, when a single **var** statement declares two variables, do you count that as one or two LOC? Also, how do you count headers and do you include procedure declarations in header statements and also in the implementation section? I count every declared variable and every procedure declaration every time it is given.
  - Compiler Directives: There is no industry consensus on the best way to count compiler directives. You must, however, decide whether to count them. I count them.
  - Comments: Whether you count logical or physical LOC, it is not general practice to include comments in the LOC counts. When they appear on the same line with executable source code, you count the source code as if the comments were not there.
  - Blank Lines: Again, it is general industry practice not to count blank lines.
- Clarifications: A fully defined standard will generally require many notes and comments in the clarifications section.

As part of generating a LOC counting standard, you will find it a good idea to manually check your standard with a few example programs. When doing this, you should assume you are writing a program to do the counting and step through an example program one line at a time to ensure your standard clearly defines the counting action to be taken.

In generating your personal counting practices, use a LOC specification format like that shown in Table 4.1. Complete a copy for every counting practice and for every language that you use. As examples, the rules I use for counting Object Pascal and C++ are shown in Tables 4.2 and 4.3, respectively.

4.3 Establishing a Counting Standard

When you use the form in Table 4.1, you will have to make a great many decisions. Rather than making each individually, you should establish a

TABLE 4.1   LOC COUNTING STANDARD TEMPLATE

Definition Name: _____   Language: _____
Author: _____   Date: _____

Count Type	Type	Comments
Physical/Logical		

Statement Type	Included	Comments
Executable		
Nonexecutable:		
Declarations		
Compiler directives		
Comments		
On own lines		
With source		
Banners		
Blank lines		

Clarifications		Examples/Cases
Nulls		continues, no-ops, . . .
Empty statements		";", lone ;'s, etc.
Generic instantiators		
Begin. . .end		when executable
Begin. . .end		when not executable
Test conditions		
Expression evaluation		when used as sub program arguments
End symbols		when terminating executable statements
End symbols		when terminating declarations or bodies
Then, else, otherwise		
Elseif		
Keywords		procedure division, interface, implementation
Labels		branch destinations when on separate lines

TABLE 4.2   EXAMPLE PASCAL LOC COUNTING STANDARD

Definition Name: _____ Example Pascal LOC Std. _____   Language: _____ Pascal _____

Author: _____ W. S. Humphrey _____   Date: _____ 12/20/93 _____

Count Type	Type	Comments
Physical/Logical	Logical	
Statement Type	**Included**	**Comments**
Executable	yes	
Nonexecutable:		
Declarations	yes	
Compiler directives	yes	
Comments	no	
On own lines	no	
With source	no	
Banners	no	
Blank lines	no	
Clarifications		**Examples/Cases**
Nulls	yes	continues, no-ops, . . .
Empty statements	yes	";", lone ;'s, etc.
Generic instantiators		
Begin. . .end	note 1	when executable
Begin. . .end	note 1	when not executable
Test conditions	yes	
Expression evaluation	yes	when used as sub program arguments
End symbols	notes 1,2	when terminating executable statements
End symbols	notes 1,2	when terminating declarations or bodies
Then, else, otherwise	note 1	
Elseif	note 1	
Keywords	notes 1,3	procedure division, interface, implementation
Labels	yes	branch destinations when on separate lines

TABLE 4.2   (continued)

Clarifications		Examples/Cases
note 1		unless followed by ; or. or included in {}, count the following keywords once: BEGIN, CASE, DO, ELSE, END, IF, RECORD, REPEAT, THEN, UNTIL
note 2		count every ; and . that is not within a {} or ()
note 3		count each , between USES and the next ; or between VAR and the next ;

general strategy. You could take a rather large-scale view of logic statements, treating each logical construct as a single countable line. Then, for example,

```
if A>B
      then A-B
      else A+B;
```

would be one statement. Similarly, it would still be one statement if you wrote it as

```
if A>B
      then
                begin
                        A-B
                end
      else
                begin
                        A+B
                end;
```

You could, on the other hand, count selected keywords such as **if, then, else, begin**, and **end** as well as assignment statements. Your counts in these two cases would be five and nine, respectively. While many of your choices are arbitrary, you must make them explicit and use them consistently.

When defining LOC for my work, I have adopted the following general approach:

□ Count logical statements as, for example, every semicolon and selected keywords.

□ Count all statements except blank lines and comment lines.

□ Count and record each language separately.

The reasons for these choices are discussed in the following sections.

TABLE 4.3   EXAMPLE C++ LOC COUNTING STANDARD

Definition Name: _____Example C++ LOC Std._____   Language: ___C++___

Author: _____W. S. Humphrey_____   Date: ___12/20/93___

Count Type	Type	Comments
Physical/Logical	Logical	
Statement Type	**Included**	**Comments**
Executable	yes	
Nonexecutable:		
Declarations	yes, notes 3,4	
Compiler directives	yes, note 4	
Comments	no	
On own lines	no	
With source	no	
Banners	no	
Blank lines	no	
Clarifications		**Examples/Cases**
Nulls		
Empty statements	yes	";;", lone ;'s, etc.
Generic instantiators		
Begin. . .end	note 1	when executable
Begin. . .end	note 1	when not executable
Test conditions	yes	
Expression evaluation	yes	when used as sub program arguments
End symbols	notes 1, 2	when terminating executable statements
End symbols	notes 1, 2	when terminating declarations or bodies
Then, else, otherwise	note 1	
Elseif	yes	
Keywords	yes	procedure division, interface, implementation
Labels	yes	branch destinations when on separate lines

TABLE 4.3   (continued)

Clarifications		Examples/Cases
note 1		count once every occurrence of the following key words: CASE, DO, ELSE ENUM, FOR, IF, PRIVATE, PUBLIC, STRUCT, SWITCH, UNION, WHILE
note 2		count once every occurrence of the following: ; , { } or };
note 3		count each variable and parameter declaration
note 4		count once each #define, #ifdef, #include, etc. statement

COUNT LOGICAL STATEMENTS

The general objective in counting LOC is to obtain data that you can use to estimate the size of future programs. Other reasons would be to characterize the relative numbers of defects or to calculate development productivity. For these purposes, it is important that your measure relate to the program's logical content rather than its format. It is the program logic that generally determines the development labor and defect content, not the number of pages or text lines. If, for example, you were to run the program through some printing utility that reformatted the program so that it required 50 percent more text lines but did not change its logic, you would not want its LOC count to change. This is possible only if the size count is determined by the program's logical statements.

OMIT BLANKS AND COMMENTS

The decision to omit blanks and comments naturally follows from the decision to count logical statements. To ensure your programs have adequate comments, however, you should establish a coding standard that covers your commenting practices.

COUNT AND RECORD EACH LANGUAGE SEPARATELY

This is absolutely essential. Your development productivity could be quite different for each language, so you should separately count and record the size data for each language you use.

COUNTING ANOMALIES

These counting practices can lead to some anomalies. With my C++ counting standard, for example, the word **main** would be counted as one statement, as would a compound statement like

```
ThisPage.PrintL(MyList.GetString(ThisData, 1));
```

Clearly, a lot more programming effort is required to develop the latter statement. You will find, however, that the mix of statement types you use will be relatively standard as long as you work in the same general application area. Your historical productivity data will then compensate for these statement type variations.

4.4   Using LOC Counts

Line of code counts can easily be misinterpreted and misused. Their definitions should thus be precise, and the specific items covered should be noted when they are used. It would make no sense, for example, to combine assembler LOC and C++ LOC. It would similarly be poor practice to mingle LOC counts for test code, support code, and product code. When you produce substantial support or test code, you should separately count and record their size data.

You should also be careful about using LOC counts to compare your work with that of other engineers. In an example of two engineers who each wrote the 10 A-series programs in this book, engineer 1 produced a total of 1322 LOC and engineer 2 wrote 743 LOC. These two sets of programs were quite different in many respects, even though they were based on the same requirements. In most cases, the larger programs of engineer 1 were far more readable and had more functionality. On the other hand, engineer 2 took much less time and produced on average about 50 percent more LOC per hour. Even though more LOC imply more function, this does not necessarily mean it is a better program. Excess functions cost time and money and expose the program to unnecessary defects. On the other hand, too-small a program could mean that the function provided was inconvenient or inadequate. Unless you carefully analyzed these two products to determine how well they met the requirements, these numbers would provide no basis for judging which did the better job.

The issue, of course, is which attributes of each program are important for which purposes. In counting LOC, you want to use program size typically for one of the following reasons:

- □ To deal with the program's packaging
- □ To measure, evaluate, or predict work on the product

□ To assess the program's quality

These topics are discussed in the following sections.

PACKAGING

While product packaging and shipment might seem incidental, the total packaging and shipping costs for widely distributed software products often exceed their development costs. Because these handling costs are generally most closely related to physical product volume, you would want size counts of all the physical lines in the source program, including comments and blanks. Here, the pages of documentation are also a critical size measure.

Another packaging issue concerns the physical memory space required to hold a running program. This again can be critical in some applications. Here, the relevant size measure would be bytes of object code rather than lines of source code. While such packaging issues can be important, they are not discussed further in this book.

EVALUATING DEVELOPMENT WORK

In evaluating development work, you are generally interested in relating the amount of product produced to the development effort expended. You could also be interested in various product categories or process phases. Suppose, for example, you wanted to determine development status. If you had unit tested and integrated 4823 LOC out of an estimated 15,000 LOC and had used three of the planned four months of test time, you would probably conclude that your schedule was exposed. For these comparisons, you are most likely interested in counting the new and changed LOC.

Another example would be to estimate the labor required to develop a program based on historical productivity data. That is, if you plan to develop a program that you estimate will require 1170 LOC and your development records show that you have produced an average of 15 LOC per working hour, you could expect this job to take you about 78 hours. Here, the simplest and most commonly used approach is not to consider unmodified reused code in the product LOC count.

In making productivity evaluations, you are most concerned with counting the amount of source code to be produced. This means that for imported code, you would count only the code you modify and not the deletions or unmodified includes. If, however, you felt that the volume of reuse and modification work was so great that it should be considered, you should gather data for several projects and see what counts give the best correlation between size and development hours. Then you could make an intelligent decision. You should keep the counting approach as simple as you can, however, at least until you have a substantial amount of supporting data.

There is no magic answer that fits all cases, so you may want to use a different counting approach for the different kinds of work. For example, with new development, you may count only new and changed LOC. For small modifications or repairs to large existing programs, you could decide to count every LOC that is added, deleted, or changed. You must examine each situation on its own merits. The statistical methods for making these analyses are multiple regression and correlation. These are discussed in subsequent chapters and in Appendix A. If you use several different types of productivity calculations, you must, of course, be careful to use them in precisely the same way when you do your productivity analyses and when you use these data to make development plans.

ASSESSING PROGRAM QUALITY

In judging the quality of a program, you will typically want to reduce the defect counts to a standard form for cross-project or cross-product comparisons. When you divide the total defects found in a program by that program's LOC, you get the program's defect density. This normalization, at least to some degree, compensates for the size differences among your programs. The principal reasons you would do this are as follows:

- To help determine the quality of all or some part of your development process
- To determine the relative defect content of some parts or versions of large programs
- To judge the future maintenance and support workload for a program

In making such analyses, software engineers most commonly count the LOC added and modified during the development process. When considering the relative quality of several finished programs, however, you would be wisest to consider their total finished LOC. While I know of no published data on this point, my experiences at IBM suggest that total program size correlated most closely with product service costs. While this may seem strange, it is more logical when you realize that defect-related costs are only a small part of total service costs for any but very poor-quality products. Here, the total number of service calls is likely to be more closely related to the total functional content of the program than to the new LOC content in a given release. You can also test this assumption for your products if you have sufficient data and use the methods discussed in later chapters and in Appendix A.

Every counting choice has advantages and disadvantages. The use of total LOC in quality measures would suggest that small modifications to large programs are not a significant quality concern. This has historically not been the case. There is evidence that small code changes, on a defects per changed LOC basis, are nearly 40 times as error prone as new development. [Humphrey 89] Conversely, counting only new and changed lines tends to ignore the quality of the large inventory of reused code. If this code had any significant defect content, your maintenance cost estimates would then likely be too low. In determining the relative quality of several releases of a single program, one is likely interested in both of these measures. The defects per KLOC in the new and changed code is probably the best indicator of the quality of the development and test phases, while the defects per KLOC of the total program is likely the best indicator of customer problems, maintenance costs, and service calls. Again, when in doubt or if substantial amounts of money are involved, get the data and do the analyses to see what works best for you.

For the purposes of the PSP, your principal focus is on the quality of your personal development process. Here, you will use the lines of new and changed code for all the analyses called for in this book. You will also, however, keep track of the lines of reused, added, deleted, and modified code.

4.5   Reuse Considerations

In addition to the issues of packaging, development evaluation, and quality, there is a serious question about how to motivate engineers to reuse previously developed programs rather than developing them again. In programming, you can either write new code or reuse code you obtain from elsewhere. Actually, you can also reuse someone else's design and do the coding yourself. The possibilities in fact are almost endless. You may be called on to convert existing code into a new language or operating environment, to copy sections of code from another program, or to modify existing code. When you include many previously produced source lines in a new program, you need to decide how to count them. If you treat them in the same way as newly developed code, the productivity numbers you use in planning your development must reflect this practice.

On the one hand, it is important to motivate software engineers to use existing reusable code. On the other hand, once you are assured of the reusable programs' function and quality, the effort required to incorporate it is substantially less, per LOC, than writing a new program. If you include two or more types of code that require significantly different amounts of development time, you risk destroying the correlation between size and development resources. Regardless of how logical such choices might seem, they destroy the effectiveness of size measures as a planning tool.

The debates about how to treat reused code can become heated. Because different counting approaches are appropriate for different purposes, there is no single best answer. Some argue that counting only new and changed LOC could motivate engineers to write excessively long programs just to get better productivity numbers. This is a possible danger, particularly where the programmers' personal productivity numbers are closely monitored by management.

A more realistic concern is that counting only new and changed LOC does not properly motivate engineers to reuse existing code. While this is certainly true, the problems most organizations have with increasing the volume of reuse is caused by more than just lack of engineer motivation. Reusing code that someone else has produced does take a good deal of work. You must find code that fits your needs, learn how to use it, assure yourself of its quality, and verify that it complies with all your standards and conventions. Until organizations recognize that reusable programs are products that must be managed, marketed, and supported and until there are a sufficient number of suitably supported reusable software components, reuse will not be widely practiced. Software engineers have learned that attempting to achieve significant volumes of reuse of anything but the simplest standard routines is not a productive way to spend their time.

Lest this sound too negative, I want to add that reuse is the only currently available technology that shows promise of order of magnitude improvements in software development quality and productivity. One of the principal reasons the PSP spends so much time addressing quality issues is to help you to produce code that is of suitable quality for inclusion in a reuse library. It may initially be your own private reuse library, but at least that would be a useful start.

4.6 Line of Code Accounting

When you develop or enhance programs, you need some way to track all the additions, deletions, and changes. By periodically counting a program during its several development versions, you could get the problem illustrated in Fig. 4.5. Starting with version 0, which has a counted size of 350 LOC, you add or change a total of 125 LOC. Thus you expect to have a finished Version 1 of 475 LOC. When you count Version 1, however, it has only 450 LOC. Where did the 25 LOC go?

This can best be understood by the LOC accounting format shown in Table 4.4. Here, starting with a new program base of zero LOC you develop 350 new LOC to give a total of 350 LOC in Version 0. This 350 LOC is then the base on which you develop Version 1. In developing Version 1, you add 100 LOC and

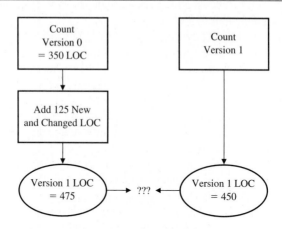

FIGURE 4.5
The LOC Accounting Problem

modify 25 LOC. The 125 new and changed LOC is thus made up of 100 LOC new and 25 LOC changed. Notice, however, that the 100 LOC are shown only in the Added column on the left of Table 4.4, but the 25 LOC are shown in both the Added and Subtracted columns. The reason for this is that a modified LOC must be counted as if it were a one-line deletion accompanied by a one-line addition. Version 1 (or Version 2 base) now is shown to contain 450 LOC, just as the counter indicated.

Table 4.4 works as follows:

1. Every version starts with some base number of LOC that are carried over from the prior version. Version 0 thus starts with a base of 0, and the Version 1 base is the finished size of Version 0, or 350 LOC.

2. All the additions to this version are entered in the marked spaces in the Added column. These are the reused, added, and modified LOC.

3. All the subtractions are entered in the marked spaces in the Subtracted column. These are the modified and the deleted lines.

4. Sum the amounts for each version in the Added and Subtracted columns.

5. Enter the added total minus the subtracted total in the Net Change column.

6. Add this net change to the version base to give the version total.

7. Copy this version total under the Base column as the base for the next version or the total for the finished product.

All the items in Table 4.4 must be counted for every version or the totals will not be proper. One nice feature of this LOC accounting structure is that it is additive. That is, for several versions you can add up the corresponding numbers in each cell to get totals that give the combined effect of several versions. This is shown in Table 4.5 for the three versions given in Table 4.4. For example, the Reused entry in Table 4.5 is the sum of the three Reused entries in Table 4.4, or $0 + 0 + 600 = 600$. Also, the Added entry in Table 4.5 is the total of the three Added entries in Table 4.4, or $350 + 100 + 50 = 500$. Similarly, the two Modified entries are $0 + 25 + 75 = 100$, and the Net Change total is $350 + 100 + 450 = 900$. Notice that you do not add up the entries in the Base column.

Note also from Table 4.5 that if the number of modified lines were not subtracted along with the deleted lines, the final total would be 100 LOC bigger than the counted size of the final program. Similarly, the deleted lines must also be subtracted or the totals will be incorrect.

The way these various elements combine and produce a final total of 900 LOC in the finished Version 2 can also be seen in Fig. 4.6. Starting with zero, you can see that the added code initially brings the product size up to 500 LOC. After 200 LOC are deleted, only 300 remain. Of these, 100 are modified, leaving the total product LOC count unchanged at 300. The reused 600 LOC then bring the total to 900 LOC.

While this may seem a little complex, after a number of releases you will need to count the finished product and know how you got that total. This accounting scheme permits you to check your figures. It also gives you a way to track development through a large number of releases and to account precisely for all the changes.

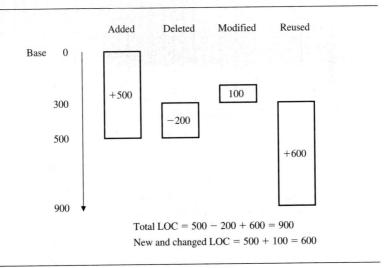

Total LOC = 500 − 200 + 600 = 900
New and changed LOC = 500 + 100 = 600

FIGURE 4.6
LOC Accounting Example

TABLE 4.4 LOC ACCOUNTING EXAMPLE

	Added	Subtracted	Net Change	Base
Base V0				0
Deleted		0		
Modified	0	0		
Added	350			
Reused	0			
Totals V0	350 −	0 =	350 +	= 350
Base V1				350
Deleted		0		
Modified	25	25		
Added	100			
Reused	0			
Totals V1	125 −	25 =	100 +	= 450
Base V2				450
Deleted		200		
Modified	75	75		
Added	50			
Reused	600			
Totals V2	725 −	275 =	450 +	= 900
Final Product				900

4.7   Calculating Productivity

When calculating productivity, you divide the amount of product produced by the hours you spent. This gives the volume of product you produced per hour. For programming, for example, if you developed a 600-LOC program in 60 hours, your productivity would be 10 LOC per hour. While this may seem simple enough, there are a great many choices on how to pick the LOC and the hours to use in the calculations.

For example, various combinations of the numbers used in the LOC accounting example in Table 4.5 are shown in Table 4.6. There is some basis for arguing that any one of these six numbers should be used to measure development productivity. Assuming you spent a total of 60 hours developing this program,

TABLE 4.5 LOC ACCOUNTING—COMBINED VERSIONS

	Added	Subtracted	Net Change	Base
Base V0				0
Reused	600			
Added	500			
Modified	100	100		
Deleted		200		
Totals V0	+ 1200	− 300 =	900 +	= 900
Final Product				900

TABLE 4.6 VARIATIONS IN LOC PRODUCTIVITY

Option	LOC	Productivity (LOC/hour)
Added	500	8.33
Added + Modified	600	10.00
Added + Modified + Deleted	800	13.33
Added + Modified + Reused	1200	20.00
Added + Modified + Deleted + Reused	1400	23.33
Total Finished Product	900	15.00

your various productivity options could differ by factors of three or more times. This variation is caused solely by your choice of how to count LOC. It is small compared to what you could get if you combined different languages in the same counts or if you considered documentation. The point is that you can get almost any numbers you want by changing the way you count LOC. That is why comparisons of productivity numbers between organizations or even among individuals are rarely useful. Without a great deal of careful analysis, the odds are that the counting methods will be different.

While you can select how you want to count LOC from among these or other options, you should consider the amount of work involved in each case. If, for example, you assumed that both a reused and a modified LOC would take the same development effort, your productivity numbers would probably not be useful across a very wide range of projects. The reason is that it generally takes a great deal more time to add or modify a LOC than to reuse one. For example, if in the case of a 1000-LOC product you expected 10 percent reuse and 90 percent new development and in another case you planned for 75 percent reuse and 25 percent added code, the new and changed LOC would be 900 LOC in case 1 and 250 in case 2. Assuming you used the same productivity numbers in both cases, you would likely seriously underestimate the first project or overestimate the second, or both.

For most new software development, added plus modified LOC is probably most appropriate for calculating productivity. For small modifications of large programs, the issue is much more complex. The reason is that the productivity of software modification is substantially lower than that for new development. [Flaherty] You should, however, start on the PSP by using only new and changed LOC for the productivity calculations. By gathering data on the time you spent, the sizes of the changes, and the fraction of the base program you modified, you will likely find that small changes in large programs are relatively much more difficult than either new development or large modifications. You should study your own data and see what categories provide the best correlations with your development effort. Again, the methods discussed later in this book on multiple regression and correlation can help you to arrive at appropriate productivity figures.

4.8   LOC Counters

LOC counters can be designed to count physical lines, logical lines, or logical lines by using a coding standard and a physical LOC counter. While all three methods are discussed next, the PSP uses the third to produce a simple LOC counter to count the programs you develop with the PSP.

PHYSICAL LOC COUNTERS

The simplest type of counter counts physical LOC. Here, you either ignore comments and blank lines or count them separately. Lines that have both comments and source code are counted as both code lines and comment lines. One reason to count comment lines would be to check on whether the commenting guidelines in the coding standards have been followed. This is not a very useful check, however, since you have no way of knowing if the comments are meaningful. The only effective check is to actually read the code and examine the quality of the comments.

In counting physical lines, it is normal to count all source lines in a given program unit. It is also often desirable to count the various program elements. For example, if you intend to reuse some of the newly developed procedures, you would want to know how many lines each contains. As you will see in Chapter 5, such counts can also help with size estimating.

If you plan to maintain separate counts for each procedure, you will need some method to determine where each procedure starts and ends. You will also need to recognize and retain the procedure name so that the counter can print it with its line count. In a counter I built for Object Pascal, for example, the logic for recognizing when a procedure declaration starts required recognizing the keywords **procedure**, **function**, **constructor**, and **destructor**. I also included the procedure header LOC as part of the procedure LOC.

To determine the end of procedure implementation in Object Pascal, I tracked **begin-end** pairs, adding one for each **begin** and subtracting one for each **end**. Starting with the value one at the first **begin**, the procedure counter stepped up one for every **begin** and down one for every **end**. The **begin-end** counter was stopped when it reached zero, indicating the end of that procedure implementation. For the declaration section, the counter started by recognizing the **procedure** keyword and stopped with the first **end**. The method for counting C++ procedures is similar but a little more complex. Rules for counting Ada are also quite similar.

LOGICAL LOC COUNTERS

Logical LOC counters work much like physical counters except that line-counter stepping is more complex. First, you must establish a logical line-count standard. While you can have endless debates about the best way to count, the details do not appear that important. The key is to be precise and absolutely consistent. In the example rules for counting Object Pascal and C++ in Tables 4.2 and 4.3, I counted every logical program statement. While some may argue that counting **begin** and **end** statements is not a good idea, this is a matter of personal preference. If you could show, however, that the hours you took to develop a program had a higher correlation with LOC if **begin-end** pairs were not counted than if they were, that would be a good reason not to use them. Doing this would also be the proper way to resolve almost any LOC counting definition questions.

Presently, there is no compelling evidence to support that one counting method is superior to any other. With good data, however, a study of the various alternatives could quickly show which if any was best. It may show, as is likely, that there are many different approaches that give roughly equivalent results. This means that the selection is arbitrary. The fact that it is arbitrary, however, does not mean that everyone should do it differently. If all the projects in an organization used the same counting standard, they could develop a single high-quality automated counter for everyone to use.

USING CODING STANDARDS AND A PHYSICAL LOC COUNTER

One simple way to count LOC is to use a coding standard and to count physical LOC, omitting comments and blanks. Here, you would write your source code to use a separate physical text line for every logical LOC. Then, when you count physical lines, omitting comments and blanks, you are also counting logical lines. This method requires that you carefully follow your coding standard. It also takes a lot more paper. If, at the same time, you also follow consistent indenting standards, you will get much more readable code. Note, however, that when you count LOC this way, you cannot reformat the code without changing the LOC counts. For any but your personal use, you should thus develop true LOC logical counters.

You may even want to enhance this approach to accommodate some special cases. For example, with a language like C++ you might prefer to write every { and } on a separate line with indentation so that you can readily match them up. This method would also be much like that of using a separate line for every **begin** and **end** in Pascal. A pure physical line counter would then count each of these brackets or **begin-end** pairs as two lines. If you did not want to do this, you could slightly enhance your physical line counter to treat all such lines as blanks.

One problem with this approach is caused by long instructions that take multiple text lines. Here, since your LOC counter will count each line as a single LOC, you will get too large a count. It is also often desirable to write complex instructions on multiple text lines to make them more readable. In all these cases, you must either scan the program for multiple-line instructions and make corrections or write a true logical LOC counting program. In no case should you compromise program function or readability to simplify LOC counting.

COUNTING DELETIONS AND MODIFICATIONS

One of the more difficult counting problems, while it seems simple in concept, is keeping track of the added, deleted, and changed LOC in multiversion programs. For small programs, you can identify these changes manually, but for larger programs, this is impractical. Even for small programs, such manual counts are almost impossible unless you do the counting during or immediately after you complete each modification.

One approach is to flag each program line separately with a special comment. A special LOC counter could then recognize these flags and count the added and deleted code. Although nice in theory, this approach is impractical. While modifying a program, you will find it almost impossible to remember to comment every addition and deletion. It is even more difficult to remember to do it when you are fixing defects in test.

A second alternative is both practical and convenient, but it involves a bit of programming. Here, you use a special program counter to compare each new program version with its immediate predecessor, as shown schematically in Fig. 4.7. This counter works as follows:

- □ The LOC counter receives the Version N source code as input and produces the Version N LOC as output.
- □ The comparitor counter has two inputs: the Version N source code and the previous, or Version N-1, source code.
- □ The counter comparitor makes a line-by-line comparison of these versions to determine their differences.
- □ Every line in Version N that is not in Version N-1 is counted as an added LOC.
- □ Every line in Version N-1 that is not in Version N is counted as a deletion.

This counter has no way of knowing whether a new line is a modification or an addition, so all modifications are counted as deletions and additions. This counting method, you will note, is exactly equivalent to the LOC accounting rules. If you retain every program version, then the comparitor counter can be run after every change. You can even count the LOC added and deleted for every defect fix.

One common practice is to build such a comparitor counter into the code control system. Every program update would then be analyzed and every line flagged with the date it was added. An even more convenient feature would be to designate every program fix, release, or version update with a change number.

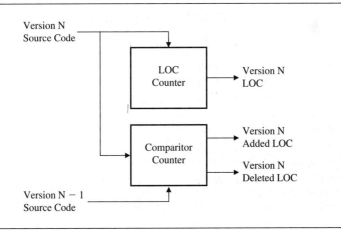

FIGURE 4.7
LOC Comparitor Counter

The code control system could then affix the change number and the date to every added line in each update. This would make it practical to determine when every change was made, when a defect was injected, or how much code was added and deleted with each change. As you will see in later chapters, these data are essential for the effective quality management of larger programs.

4.9   Summary

There are many reasons to measure software size. One of the most important is to help you in planning your software projects. The size measure you select should reasonably correlate to your development effort, should be precise, and should be automatically countable.

Since LOC counts can be misleading, they should be treated with some care. Use precise definitions and carefully note the types of program elements included. It is not a good idea to use LOC counts to compare projects or organizations because there are generally many differences that are not detectable from simple LOC data. Even at the PSP level, LOC counts are not a useful basis for comparing the productivity or effectiveness of individuals.

In measuring development productivity, software engineers usually count the number of source statements per development hour. For this purpose, you should count newly developed plus modified statements. It is also important to use precisely the same definitions in calculating development productivity and in project planning.

When comparing the defect rates among programs, engineers commonly use the defect rate per thousand lines of added and modified code. When estimating the likely maintenance workload for a program, however, you will find it most appropriate to consider the total finished-product LOC.

LOC counters can be designed to count physical lines or logical lines. A third method combines these two: counting logical lines by using a coding standard and a physical LOC counter. This is the approach used with the PSP.

Many useful LOC statistics can be obtained with properly designed tools. For each program modification, for example, you will want to know how many LOC were added and deleted. A practical way to get such data is with a program that compares each new program version with its immediate predecessor. This comparitor then identifies and counts every added or deleted line.

The key to effective software size measures is ensuring they fit your personal needs. Understand your purpose for using the measure and gather historical data on your work and on the proposed measure. Then make sure your measurement data significantly correlate with your intended purpose for the measure.

4.10 Exercises

The standard assignment for this chapter includes exercises R1 and R2 and uses PSP0.1 to write program 2A. The specifications for program 2A and the two exercises are given in Appendix D. In completing this assignment, you should review and become familiar with the PSP0.1 process described in Appendix C and faithfully follow the report submission format that it specifies.

For other assignment options, consult Appendix D.

References

[Boehm 81] Barry W. Boehm, *Software Engineering Economics* (Englewood Cliffs, NJ: Prentice-Hall, 1981).

[Flaherty] M. J. Flaherty, "Programming Process Productivity Measurement System for System/370," *IBM Systems Journal*, vol. 24, no. 2 (1985), pp 168–175.

[Humphrey 89] W. S. Humphrey, *Managing the Software Process* (Reading, MA: Addison-Wesley, 1989).

[Park 92] Robert E. Park, "Software Size Measurement: A Framework for Counting Source Statements," Software Engineering Institute Technical Report, CMU/SEI-92-TR-20 (September 1992).

5

Planning III—Estimating Software Size

This chapter first discusses the size estimating problem and then describes the PROBE estimating method used in this book. Several other size estimating methods are briefly described along with some of the issues you should consider in using them. Because the principal objective of size estimating is to get accurate size estimates, you should experiment with various estimating methods and use whatever works best for you. You should, however, use the PROBE method for the exercises in this book.

5.1 Background

The principal reason you should estimate the size of a software product is to help you to plan the product's development. The quality of a software development plan, in turn, generally depends on the quality of the size estimate. With a good plan, you have the basis for funding and staffing the work. You know what has to be done, when, and by whom. You also know how long it will take and understand the critical dependencies or other constraints. Poor software planning is one of the principal reasons software projects get into trouble. [Humphrey 89] A frequent cause of poor plans is a poor size estimate.

Accepted practice in engineering, manufacturing, and construction is to base development plans on product size estimates. Building construction provides a good example. Competent builders get detailed information about the kind of building you want before they give you a construction estimate. They then make materials and labor cost estimates based on their prior experiences. They use historical factors for such items as the costs per square foot for wiring, carpentry, plastering, and painting. Experienced builders can often estimate large projects to within one or two percent of the actual finished cost.

The degree to which you can accurately and precisely plan a job depends on what you know about it. At the earliest, or preproposal, stage, you have only a general idea of the product requirements. About the only way to make an estimate is by analogy to previous products. This situation is like that faced by a builder when a home buyer wants the price for a one-story ranch house with three bedrooms. An experienced builder could show the buyer several homes that fit this description and give their prices, but would not quote a price for such a general requirement.

After the preproposal phase, you know progressively more about the planned product. You can then make more-refined estimates of job size. Again, it is instructive to consider what builders do when they need a competitive estimate for a multi-million dollar construction job. They work with detailed architectural specifications and a group of proven subcontractors. They calculate the linear feet of interior and exterior walls, the square feet of floor and ceiling, and the square feet of concrete. They can then determine the number of studs and the amount of linear feet of finished lumber required, and the plumbing, wiring, and masonry costs. When they need an accurate estimate, they define the project in great detail.

Estimates for large software jobs can be handled in much the same way. To make an accurate estimate, you must start with a design specification. You then examine and estimate each part of the job. This estimate requires separate estimates for each software component, each major document, the test cases, installation planning, file conversion, and user training. The program components may have different subelements. If there are screens to develop, reports to generate, or functional logic to design, these must also be estimated. For large software products, there is a great deal of potentially useful detail. If you want to make accurate estimates, you will have to define all these details and consider each one in the estimate.

THE SIZE ESTIMATING FRAMEWORK

The generalized planning framework for software development was described in Chapter 3 and is shown again in Fig. 5.1. The tasks you perform are shown in the rectangles, and the various data, reports, and products are shown in the ovals. In estimating the size you first define the requirements and then produce a concep-

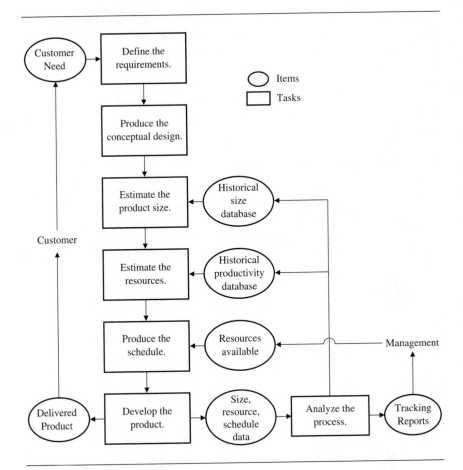

FIGURE 5.1
Project Planning Framework

tual design. You then compare the elements of this conceptual design with the
known sizes of program elements you have previously developed. This process
helps you to judge the size of the parts of the new product. The tricky part of software size estimating is in characterizing the product elements and relating them
to your historical experience.

THE SIZE-RESOURCE RELATIONSHIP

Size is an accurate predictor of the resources required to develop a product.
[Boehm] The relation between size and required resources has led to the development of a number of cost models such as COCOMO, PriceS, and SLIM. [Boehm,

Park 89, Putnam] While these models can be generally useful, they must be calibrated for each using organization. Each such organization must thus gather its own historical data and use them to set the factors in its cost models. The models also require a size estimate as input. Before you can use them, you must estimate the product size. The accuracy of the models is thus limited by the accuracy of the size estimates. So, even when you use an estimating model, you need an accurate size estimate.

SOME ESTIMATING EXPERIENCE

Hihn reports several studies that show size estimation errors as high as 100 percent. [Hihn] Size estimates that are seriously in error result in poor resource estimates and unrealistic project schedules. This is one reason why software groups get into trouble. They either had no initial estimate or the one they had was seriously in error. Under these conditions, projects often start in trouble and never recover.

Hihn reports on a Jet Propulsion Laboratory study that showed that only 22 percent of the surveyed professionals actually used size estimates in making cost estimates. He also showed that the people who were most accurate in size estimating had done it the most and had done it most recently. Size estimation is a skill that can be learned and improved.

The unknowns early in the software development process cause major cost-estimating inaccuracies. [Boehm] Boehm states that these inaccuracies range up to 400 percent in the early feasibility phases and up to 60 percent or more during the requirements phase. They only decline to 25 percent or less during and after detailed design. Clearly, if you make a development estimate too early, when you know less about the product to be built, your estimate will likely be less accurate.

SIZE ESTIMATING CRITERIA

A widely usable size estimating method should meet the following criteria:

- □ It should use structured and trainable methods. A structured method facilitates training and process improvement. It also permits you to track and improve the estimating method itself.

- □ It should be a method you can use during all phases of software development and maintenance. You use size estimates early in the development cycle to make realistic plans and commitments. During development, you may need to modify your plans to adjust for changes. On larger projects, it is also good practice to periodically reestimate the product size and needed resources at the end of every major phase. As these plans become more accurate, they provide a firmer basis for project management and tracking.

- It should be usable for all software product elements. It should handle not only the code, but also files, reports, screens, and documentation. It should also be suitable for the types of systems and applications you work on as well as for new product development, enhancement, and repair.

- It should be suitable for statistical analysis. A statistically based size estimating method will provide the means for you to adjust your estimating parameters based on your historical data.

- It should also be adaptable to the types of work you are likely to do in the future. As you build estimating data and experience, you will then be building an asset of continuing value.

- It should provide the means to judge the accuracy of your estimates.

You should always compare each estimate with the size of the actual resulting product. By reviewing these comparisons, you will often see the causes of your errors and be better able to adjust and improve your estimating method.

5.2   Popular Estimating Methods

This section covers four size estimating methods that have been described in the literature. It is followed by an extensive discussion of the PROBE estimating method that was developed specifically for the PSP.

Size estimating is a skill that must be learned, practiced, and maintained. Because it involves considerable judgment, the selection of an estimating method is also largely a matter of personal taste. You may find that the PROBE method described later in this chapter works well for you, or you might want to try other techniques to see if one is more effective. While you should use the PROBE method for the exercises in this book, you should review the four methods described in this section. Experiment with these methods and with the PROBE method to see how they work for you. Then decide what is most effective. You should, however, continually monitor your estimating performance and watch the literature for new and improved estimating methods.

Boehm has described the Wideband-Delphi method for using multiple experts' opinions. Putnam has defined the fuzzy-logic method and the standard-component method for judging the sizes of new products based on historical size data. Albrecht's function-point method uses standard factors for judging the relative importance of various functional requirements. These methods are important not only because they have each been found useful but also because their concepts form the foundation for the PROBE method used with the PSP.

WIDEBAND-DELPHI METHOD

The Wideband-Delphi estimating method was originated by the Rand Corporation and refined by Boehm. [Boehm] It calls for several engineers to individually produce estimates and it then uses a Delphi process to converge on a consensus estimate. The procedure is essentially as follows [Humphrey 89]:

1. A group of experts is each given the program's specifications and an estimation form.

2. They meet to discuss project goals, assumptions, and estimation issues.

3. They then each anonymously list project tasks and a size estimate.

4. The estimates are given to the estimate moderator, who tabulates the results and returns them to the experts, as illustrated in Fig. 5.2.

5. Only each expert's personal estimate is identified; all others are anonymous.

6. The experts meet to discuss the results. They each review the tasks they have defined but not their size estimates.

7. The cycle continues at step 3 until the estimates converge to within an acceptable range.

For reasonably large programs, the estimators make simultaneous estimates for several product components. At the end of the estimating process, these estimates are combined to produce the total final estimate.

The estimating process is run by a moderator who should always be careful never to reveal the source of any individual estimate. The appropriate attitude is that no one knows the right answer. Everyone has a partial view; the purpose of

---

Project: XYZ
Estimator: John Doe
Date: 4/1/94
Here is the range of estimates from the <u>1st</u> round:

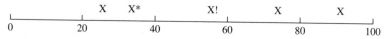

X – estimates
X* – your estimate
X! – median estimate

Please enter your estimate for the next round: ___ SLOC.
Please explain any rationale for your estimate.

FIGURE 5.2
Wideband-Delphi

the Delphi process is to share those views. By encouraging the participants to discuss the project tasks, a skilled moderator can facilitate very informative discussions. The person who made a particularly high or low estimate is sometimes willing to explain why that value was picked. The resulting discussions often shed light on the problem and surprisingly often convince the other engineers to change their estimates. While confidentiality will often become a non-issue, the decision to reveal any estimator's identity must be left up to that estimator. This method can produce quite accurate estimates. It also often provides a solid foundation from which to start the work as well as the commitment of the engineers to get the job done for the cost and time they put in the estimate.

FUZZY-LOGIC METHOD

Putnam describes the fuzzy-logic estimating method where estimators assess a planned product and roughly judge how its size compares with historical data on prior products. [Putnam] For example, you could break the sizes of all your organization's previously developed products into size categories, as shown in Table 5.1. With sufficient data, you could subdivide these gross size ranges into more detailed categories as shown in Table 5.2(a). To show how these ranges are constructed, Table 5.2(b) gives the logarithms of the ranges. As you can see, the size ranges are evenly spaced on a logarithmic scale. When, as shown here, each division is subdivided into five parts, the resulting 25 categories provide the basis for making reasonably precise estimates.

To show how you might divide a size range into categories, suppose your smallest program had 173 LOC and your largest 10,341. To divide this range into five equal sets on a logarithmic scale, take the base 10 logarithms of 173 and 10,341, giving 2.238 and 4.014, respectively. To get five categories, divide the 1.776 difference between these numbers by four, giving 0.444. This is the logarithmic increment between each category.

TABLE 5.1   FUZZY-LOGIC SIZE RANGES

Range	Size—LOC	Low—LOC	High—LOC
Very Small	2,000	1,000	4,000
Small	8,000	4,000	16,000
Medium	32,000	16,000	64,000
Large	128,000	64,000	256,000
Very Large	512,000	256,000	1,028,000

TABLE 5.2(A)   FUZZY-LOGIC SIZE RANGES—LOC

Subrange Gross Range	Very Small LOC	Small LOC	Medium LOC	Large LOC	Very Large LOC
Very Small	1,148	1,514	2,000	2,630	3,467
Small	4,570	6,025	8,000	10,471	13,804
Medium	18,197	23,988	32.000	41,687	54,954
Large	72,444	95,499	128,000	165,958	218,776
Very Large	288,403	380,189	512,000	660,693	870,964

TABLE 5.2(B)   FUZZY-LOGIC SIZE RANGES—LOG(LOC)

Subrange Gross Range	Very Small log(LOC)	Small log(LOC)	Medium log(LOC)	Large log(LOC)	Very Large log(LOC)
Very Small	3.06	3.18	3.30	3.42	3.54
Small	3.66	3.78	3.90	4.02	4.14
Medium	4.26	4.38	4.50	4.62	4.74
Large	4.86	4.98	5.10	5.22	5.34
Very Large	5.46	5.58	5.70	5.82	8.94

The lowest category is the 173 number you started with. The next category has a logarithm of 2.682 and a value of 481 LOC. Similarly, the other categories are 1338, 3719, and 10,341. If you also want to know the middle points between these numbers, the increment would be cut in half, to 0.222. You would now know the top points, bottom points, and midpoints of each of the five size ranges as follows:

Very small	104	173	288
Small	288	481	802
Medium	802	1,338	2,230
Large	2,230	3,719	6,202
Very large	6,202	10,341	17,243

To make an estimate, you would judge which of these categories the new project most closely resembles. You do this by first deciding into which gross size range it fits. Then, by comparing the new project with the known characteristics of the projects in this size range, you place it in a subrange.

While this estimating technique gives only a crude size judgment, it does provide an orderly way to compare the sizes of planned projects with the sizes of previously developed ones.

In using this method, several considerations are important:

□ Historical data are required on a large number of projects. Only then will you likely have a reasonable number of historical products in each size category. Until you have data on some products in every category, you will not have examples with which to compare all the new products you might have to estimate.

□ While you can use any number of size ranges, they should cover the entire span of expected project sizes. You should then extend these ranges up or down as you get further data. You should not change the existing ranges, however, because you will become adept at judging programs in terms of the ranges you have learned. When you change the ranges, your estimating accuracy will likely suffer, at least until you relearn the new ranges.

To provide a meaningful number of examples in each size range, you will need a considerable amount of historical data. If there is not at least a modest distribution in a given range, an estimator will have trouble judging the relative size of a new program. Until you have a large base of data, therefore, it is wisest to distribute your historical data into no more than about five major categories and make comparative judgments at this level. To do this properly, of course, you should be familiar with all the programs in the database.

One problem with the fuzzy logic method is that the size of major programming applications has historically grown by about an order of magnitude every 10 years. Reasonably accurate estimates of the very largest category are thus particularly important. Unfortunately, any gross sizing method will not likely be of much help in estimating a new program that is much larger than anything you have previously built. To handle this situation, you would have to subdivide the new product into smaller components and estimate each component.

STANDARD-COMPONENT METHOD

The standard-component estimating method is described by Putnam as a way to use an organization's historical data to make progressively more-refined program size estimates. [Putnam] You start by gathering data on the sizes of the various levels of program abstractions you use, for example, subsystems, modules, and screens. You then judge how many of these components will likely be in your new program. You also judge the largest number you could imagine being in the program as well as the smallest number. You combine these estimates by taking four times the most likely number and adding both the smallest and largest numbers. Then divide this total by six to give the likely number of that component. The standard deviation of the final estimate should be roughly one sixth of the difference between the smallest conceivable number and the largest conceivable number. In equation form, this procedure is

Estimated Number = [smallest conceivable number + 4*(likely number) + largest conceivable number]/6.

Some of the values Putnam uses for standard-component estimating are shown in an example in Table 5.3. [Putnam] This example includes several files, modules, screens, and reports. Here, the file components each average 2535 SLOC. In this application, the estimator was confident that there would be at least three file components; the largest number expected was 10, and the most likely number was about 6. Using the formula given above, you get an estimate of 6.17 file components. Because each is expected to contain the historical average of 2535 SLOC, you get a total of 15,633 SLOC. The other components' SLOCs are calculated in the same way and totaled to give the final estimate of 46,359 SLOC.

FUNCTION-POINT METHOD

The function-point method is probably the most popular for estimating the size of commercial software applications. Invented by Albrecht at IBM in 1979, it has attracted a growing number of users. Albrecht identified five basic functions that occur frequently in commercial software development and categorized them ac-

TABLE 5.3   EXAMPLE OF COMPONENT ESTIMATING

Standard Component	SLOC per Component	S	M	L	X = (S + 4*M + L)/6	SLOC
SLOC	1					
Object Instructions	0.28					
Files	2,535	3	6	10	6.17	15,633
Modules	932	11	18	22	17.5	16,310
Subsystems	8,175					
Screens	818	5	9	21	10.3	8,453
Reports	967	2	6	11	6.17	5,963
Interactive Programs	1,769					
Batch Programs	3,214					
Total						46,359

cording to their relative development complexities. [Albrecht] The definitions of these functions are as follows: [Jones]

1. *Inputs:* Inputs are screens or forms through which human users of an application or other programs add new data or update existing data. If an input screen is too large for a single normal display (usually 80 columns by 25 lines) and flows over onto a second screen, the set counts as 1 input. Inputs that require unique processing are what should be considered.

2. *Outputs:* Outputs are screens or reports that the application produces for human use or for other programs. Note that outputs requiring separate processing are the units to count; for example, in a payroll application, an output function that created, say, 100 checks would still count as one output.

3. *Inquiries:* Inquiries are screens that allow users to interrogate an application and ask for assistance or information, such as Help screens.

4. *Data files:* Data files are logical collections of records that the application modifies or updates. A file can be, for example, a flat file such as a tape file, one leg of a hierarchical database such as IMS, one table within a relational database, or one path through a CODASYL network database.

5. *Interface:* Interfaces are files shared with other applications and include incoming or outgoing tape files, shared databases, and parameter lists.

To make a function-point estimate, you review the requirements and count the numbers of each type of function the program will likely need. You then enter these numbers in the blanks in Table 5.4 and multiply them by the weights to produce the total numbers of function points in each category. Jones, in his definitive text on this subject, suggests that this function-point total be adjusted by the influence factors shown, with an example, in Tables 5.5 and 5.6. [Jones] The influence factor values are selected from 0 to 5, depending on the degree to which you judge that the particular factor falls between very simple to very complex or very

TABLE 5.4 FUNCTION-POINT CATEGORIES

Basic Counts	Function Types	Weights	Total
	Inputs	× 4	
	Outputs	× 5	
	Inquiries	× 4	
	Logical Files	×10	
	Interfaces	× 7	
	Unadjusted Total		

TABLE 5.5   AN EXAMPLE OF FUNCTION-POINT INFLUENCE FACTORS

Factor	Influence
Data communications	2
Distributed functions	0
Performance objectives	3
Heavily used configuration	3
Transaction rate	4
On line data entry	4
End-user efficiency	3
On line update	2
Complex processing	3
Reusability	2
Installation ease	3
Operational ease	4
Multiple sites	5
Facilitate change	3
Sum of influence factors =	41
0.65 + 0.01 * (Sum of Influence Factors) = Complexity Multiplier =	1.06
Function Points = Complexity Multiplier*Unadjusted Function Points =	143

low to very high, and so on. Because there are 14 factors in Table 5.5 and their values can each range from 0 to 5, the total of the influence factors then ranges from 0 to 70. From the formula at the bottom of Table 5.5, you can see that the total complexity multiplier varies from .65 to 1.35, or from minus to plus 35 percent.

For example, a count of an applications requirement statement might yield a total of 8 inputs, 12 outputs, 4 inquiries, 2 logical files, and 1 interface. As shown in Table 5.6, you multiply these numbers by the weights to give the values in the total column. The 8 inputs, for example, are multiplied by a weight of 4, giving a total of 32. The unadjusted function-point total would then be 135.

The influence factors you selected from Table 5.5 are used to calculate a function point adjustment of 1.06. When you multiply the unadjusted function-point total of 135 by this factor, you get a total of 143 function points.

As useful as they are, function points are not fully satisfactory for two reasons. First, they cannot be directly measured and second, they are not sensitive to implementation decisions. Jones addressed this first problem by producing a

TABLE 5.6 FUNCTION-POINT CATEGORY EXAMPLE

Basic Counts	Function Types	Weights	Total
8	Inputs	8 × 4	32
12	Outputs	12 × 5	60
4	Inquiries	4 × 4	16
2	Logical Files	2 ×10	20
1	Interfaces	1 × 7	7
	Unadjusted Total		135

number of function-point conversion factors that permit you to count LOC and calculate the program's likely function point content. [Jones]

The second issue, implementation independence, is more debatable. While implementation independence is an advantage in cross-language or cross-system comparisons, it is a disadvantage in development cost estimates. Development costs are typically sensitive to implementation language, design style, or application domain, so either the estimating method must consider them or some other allowance must be made.

The function-point method continues to be refined, so if you intend to use it you should obtain copies of the latest International Function Point Users Group (IFPUG) guidelines and standards. [Sprouls, Zwanzig] You should also review some of the techniques and practices people have found most helpful in applying function points. [Jones]

5.3 Proxy-based Estimating

In project planning, estimates are generally required before development can begin. At this early stage, the requirements may be understood but little is generally known about the product itself. The estimating problem is thus to predict the likely finished size of the required product. Because no one can know in advance how big a planned product will be, software size estimating will always be an uncertain process. The need, however, is to make as accurate an estimate as possible. In general, all estimating methods use data on previously developed similar programs to establish some basis for judging the size of the new program. This suggests a generalized estimating process as illustrated in Fig. 5.3.

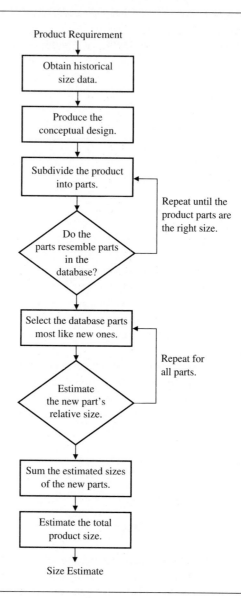

FIGURE 5.3
Size Estimating Overview

PROXIES

Consider again the example of construction. In home building, the number of square feet of living space provides a basis for estimating construction costs. Few people, however, can visualize the house they want in terms of square feet. We have the same problem with software. If we could accurately judge the numbers of LOC in a planned software product, we could make good development estimates. Unfortunately, few people can directly judge how many LOC it will take to meet a software requirement.

The need is for some proxy that relates product size to the functions the estimator can visualize and describe. A proxy is a substitute or a stand-in. Assuming it is easier for you to visualize the proxy than the size measure you are using, a proxy can help you judge product size. This section shows how proxies can be used to estimate a product's LOC. Examples of proxies are objects, screens, files, scripts, or function points.

SELECTING A PROXY

The criteria for a good proxy are as follows:

- □ The proxy size measurement should closely relate to the effort required to develop the product.
- □ The proxy content of a product should be automatically countable.
- □ The proxy should be easy to visualize at the beginning of a project.
- □ The proxy should be customizable to the special needs of using organizations.
- □ The proxy should be sensitive to any implementation variations that impact development costs or effort.

These points are discussed in the following sections.

Related to Development Effort.   A proxy, to be useful, must have a demonstrably close relationship to the resources required to develop the product. By estimating the size of the proxy, you can then accurately judge the size of the job. You determine the effectiveness of a proxy by obtaining historical data on a number of products you have developed and comparing the proxy values with the development costs. Using the correlation method described in Appendix A, section A3, you can then determine if this or some other proxy is a better predictor of product size or development effort. If the proxy does not pass this test, there is no point in using it. You can generally determine this quickly by examining the data in a scatter plot, like that in Fig. 5.4.

Automatically Countable Proxy Content.   Because historical proxy data are needed for making new estimates, it is desirable to have a large amount of proxy data. This requires that the data be automatically countable, which in turn suggests the proxy must be a physical entity that can be precisely defined and algorithmically identified. It need not be easy to identify as long as it meets the other

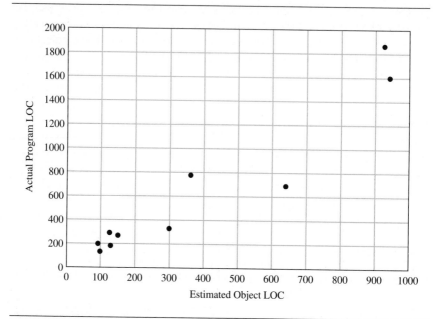

FIGURE 5.4
Object LOC versus Program LOC
10 Pascal Programs

proxy criteria. If you cannot automatically count the proxy content of a program, there is no convenient way to reliably obtain the statistical data you need to generate estimating factors customized for your particular development process and design style.

Easily Visualized at the Project's Beginning.   If the proxy is harder to visualize than the number of programmer hours required to do the development, you may as well estimate hours directly and not worry about the proxy. The usefulness of a proxy thus depends on the degree to which it helps you to visualize the size of the project to be done. This in turn depends on your background and preferences. So there will likely not be one best proxy for all purposes. With suitable historical data, you could even end up using several different proxies in one estimate. The multiple regression method described in Appendix A, section A9, can be helpful for this purpose.

Customizable to the Needs of the Using Organization.   Much of the difficulty organizations have with various estimating methods comes from their attempts to use data from one development group for planning developments by another group. While this is principally a problem with resource models, it also applies to the use of proxies. It is important, therefore, to gather and use data that are relevant to the particular project being estimated. This suggests that large organizations have size and resource databases for each major software product type. Similarly, you should gather and use data on your own PSP work. If you find that the PSP-selected proxies are not suitable for some of the work you do, then your data should help you to identify other more suitable proxies and their estimating factors.

Sensitive to Implementation Variations. This issue involves a difficult trade-off. The proxies that are most easily visualized at the beginning of a project are application entities, such as inputs, outputs, files, screens, and reports. Unfortunately, a good development estimate requires entities that closely relate to the product to be built and the labor to build it. This need also requires that data be available on proxy and product size for each implementation language, design style, and application category. Thus it is essential that the languages, design styles, and application categories to be used on a project be represented in the data used to calculate the estimating factors to be used.

POSSIBLE PROXIES

Many potential types of proxies could meet the previously outlined criteria. The function-point method is an obvious candidate because it is widely used. Many people have found function points to be helpful for resource estimating, so you should consider them. However, as noted earlier in this chapter, their principal disadvantage is that they are not directly countable in the finished product.

Other possible proxies are objects, screens, files, scripts, and document chapters. The data I gathered during the PSP research work on objects and document chapters show that, at least for my work, these elements generally meet the proxy criteria. I do not have sufficient data on screens, reports, and scripts to draw any general conclusions. It also appears that the usefulness of these proxies depends on the application and on the programming language. If your data indicate that any of these proxy types are suitable for your work, you should use them. You could even combine multiple proxies with the multiple proxy technique described in Chapter 6.

Objects as Proxies. The principles of object-oriented design suggest that objects would be good estimating proxies. During initial program analysis and design, application entities are used as the basis for selecting system objects. [Booch, Coad, Shlaer, Wirfs-Brock] Here, an application entity is something that exists in the application environment. For example, in an automobile registration system, entities might include automobiles, owners, registrations, titles, or insurance policies. In an object-based design, you select program objects that will model these real-world entities. This means that your highest-level product objects could be visualized during requirements analysis. Objects thus potentially meet one of the basic requirements for a proxy.

To determine whether objects are a good size proxy, you next examine historical data. Figure 5.4 shows the relation between estimated object LOC and actual total program LOC for a family of 10 small Object Pascal programs that I wrote during my PSP research. Figure 5.5 shows similar data for a family of 25 C++ programs. Figures 5.6 and 5.7 compare these estimated object LOC with the hours spent developing these same Pascal and C++ programs. In both cases, the correlation and significance are very high. Because total program LOC correlates to development hours and objects correlate highly with total program LOC, objects thus meet the requirement that they closely relate to development effort.

Finally, as discussed in Chapter 4, objects are physical entities that can be automatically counted. Assuming you use an object-oriented design methodology and implementation language and you gather size data on your objects, objects will meet all the criteria for a proxy.

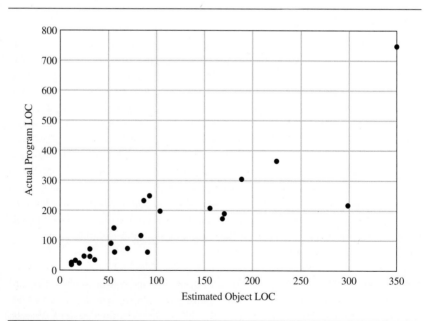

FIGURE 5.5
Object LOC versus program LOC
25 C++ programs

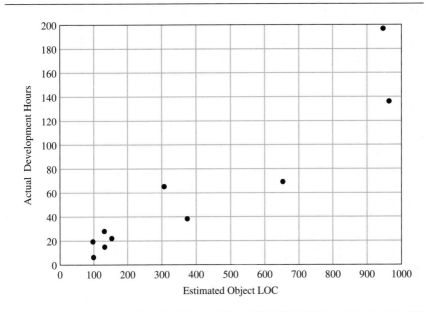

FIGURE 5.6
Pascal object LOC versus hours
correlation 0.934, significance < 0.005

To use objects as proxies, divide your historical object data into categories
and size ranges. The construction example illustrates why you do this. When estimating the square feet in a house, a builder needs to think about big rooms and
small rooms and about how many of each the buyer wants. It is even important
that the builder think about room categories; for example, a big bathroom would
likely be much smaller than even a small family room.

In estimating how many LOC objects contain, you should similarly first
group these objects into functional categories. You then make estimates by judging how many objects of each category you need for the new product and the relative size of each object in its category. Using Putnam's fuzzy-logic method, you
divide these object categories into ranges of very small, small, medium, large,
and very large objects. [Putnam] The Pascal and C++ categories used with the
PSP are shown in Table 5.7.

In the top part of Table 5.7, the C++ objects are listed in six categories.
These data show that a medium- or average-sized C++ object for mathematical
calculations would have about 11 LOC, while a very large calculation object
would have 54 LOC.

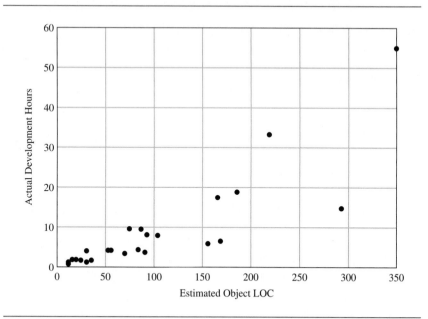

FIGURE 5.7
C++ Object LOC versus Hours
Correlation 0.980, Significance < 0.005

Object size is also a matter of style. Some people prefer to group many functions in a few objects; others prefer to create many objects of relatively few functions. The data used for estimating purposes should accurately reflect the languages and practices you use in developing software. Therefore, it is a good idea to use object size data on your own personal work. Because of the wide variations in the numbers of methods or procedures per object, I have also found it helpful to normalize objects by their numbers of methods (or procedures) and to judge object size on a per-method basis. The data in Table 5.7 are thus given in LOC per method. In Pascal terms, this would be LOC per procedure; for example, if you have a medium-sized Pascal text object that has four methods, it would average 16.48*4, or about 66, LOC.

In estimating LOC per object, you first decide which functional category of object you are considering, then judge how many methods it likely will contain, and finally determine whether it falls into the very small, small, medium, large, or very large size range. A method for calculating these estimating factors is described in Section 5.5.

5.4   The PROBE Size Estimating Method

The *PRO*xy-*B*ased *E*stimating (PROBE) method uses objects as proxies. A flow-chart of the PROBE size estimation procedure is shown in Fig. 5.8. These steps are also explained in the PROBE script in Appendix C (Table C36) and in the size estimating template instructions (Table C40). The following sections describe these steps and give an example.

THE CONCEPTUAL DESIGN

For the size estimate to properly reflect the product you plan to build, you must start with a conceptual design. This design establishes a preliminary design ap-

TABLE 5.7   OBJECT CATEGORY SIZES IN LOC
PER METHOD

C++ Object Size in LOC per Method					
Category	Very Small	Small	Medium	Large	Very Large
Calculation	2.34	5.13	11.25	24.66	54.04
Data	2.60	4.79	8.84	16.31	30.09
I/O	9.01	12.06	16.15	21.62	28.93
Logic	7.55	10.98	15.98	23.25	33.83
Set-up	3.88	5.04	6.56	8.53	11.09
Text	3.75	8.00	17.07	36.41	77.66

Object Pascal Object Size in LOC per Method					
Category	Very Small	Small	Medium	Large	Very Large
Control	4.24	8.68	17.79	36.46	74.71
Display	4.72	6.35	8.55	11.50	15.46
File	3.30	6.23	11.74	22.14	41.74
Logic	6.41	12.42	24.06	46.60	90.27
Print	3.38	5.86	10.15	17.59	30.49
Text	4.63	8.73	16.48	31.09	58.62

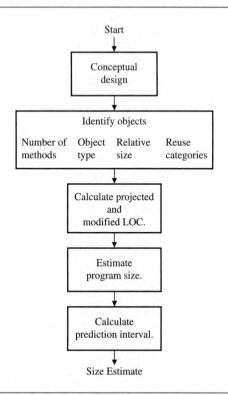

FIGURE 5.8
The PROBE Size Estimating Method

proach and names the expected product objects and their functions. Your intent here is not to do the complete design but to postulate the objects that will be needed and the functions they will perform. This is an abstraction process during which the estimator says, "If I had objects that did functions A, B, and C, I would know how to build this product."

Note, however, that you should not feel obliged to follow this early conceptual design. You produce it solely to make the size estimate. When you do the design, you may want to examine several alternate approaches, brainstorm design ideas with your associates, or examine the designs of previously developed products. A few minutes spent in such exploration can often reveal approaches that can reduce the development work by large factors. **Don't feel constrained to implement a design just because it is the first one you thought of**. While it is possible your first idea will turn out to be the best, you should always be suspicious of it until you have examined one or two alternatives and found that it is still best.

When you are estimating a large product, producing a conceptual design can be a significant task. While you may question the need to go into all this detail just to make an estimate, the issue is accuracy. If you need an accurate estimate, you must refine the conceptual design to the level of objects you know how to build. Even for fairly large programs, however, this need not take you more than a few days' work.

Large Product Conceptual Designs.   When you are estimating relatively small products, you can produce a conceptual design directly. For larger products, you will likely need a system or high-level design step for subdividing the product. If some or all of the resulting parts are still too large to permit a sufficiently detailed conceptual design, then you will have to refine each to a lower level. You continue this refinement process until you reach a level of detail at which you can describe the product's functions in terms of objects that are similar to your historical object data. You do this by working through the product requirements and deciding how you would likely build the product. Your intent is to define the mathematical or logical principles you will use and to establish an overall structural design concept. You name the major parts, identify the principal files, and perhaps specify the documentation, test, and support facilities. Your objective is to break each of the major product parts into elements that resemble those for which you have experience and data.

After you have subdivided the product into parts, you check to see if you have historical data on them. If a part does not resemble any element in your database, you reexamine it to see if you have refined it to the proper level. Assuming you have a reasonably complete and well-structured historical database, if a program element does not naturally fit a category you will likely find it to be a composite of several more basic parts. You should then refine it into those parts.

If an object is at the right level and does not belong to any of the existing categories, then you estimate its size as the first of a new category. You do this by relating it to other known objects in the database or by whatever other method seems most appropriate. You must then measure this new object once it is developed and enter the data into the database as the first of a new category.

DETERMINE OBJECT TYPE AND SIZE

You now have the conceptual design, have named each object, and have determined its category. You next find the objects in the database that each of these objects most closely resembles. For each new object, you judge how its size compares with those in the database in its category. On the basis of this judgment, you estimate roughly where the new object's size will fall.

Consider, for example, the estimate Student 12 made for the C++ program 10A shown in the estimating form in Table 5.8. Using the conceptual design, the

TABLE 5.8   SIZE ESTIMATING EXAMPLE

Student	Student 12		Date	5/1/94
Instructor	Humphrey		Program #	10A

BASE PROGRAM				LOC
BASE SIZE (B)	=> => => => => => => => => =>			695
LOC DELETED (D)	=> => => => => => => => => =>			0
LOC MODIFIED (M)	=> => => => => => => => => =>			5

PROJECTED LOC (P)

BASE ADDITIONS	TYPE	METHODS	RELATIVE SIZE	LOC
TOTAL BASE ADDITIONS (BA)=> => => => => => => =>				

NEW OBJECTS (NO)	TYPE[1]	METHODS	RELATIVE SIZE	LOC (New Reused*)
Matrix	Date	13	Medium	115
Linear System	Calc.	8	Large	197
Linked List	Data	3	Large	49*
TOTAL NEW OBJECTS (NO)=> => => => => => => =>				361

REUSED OBJECTS	LOC
Linked List	73
Data Entry	96
REUSED TOTAL (R) => => => => => => => => =>	169

Projected LOC (P):	$P = BA + NO$	361
Regression Parameter:	β_0	62
Regression Parameter:	β_1	1.3
Estimated New and Changed LOC (N):	$N = \beta_0 + \beta_1{}^*(P + M)$	538
Estimated Total LOC (T):	$T = N + B - D - M + R$	1397
Estimated Total New Reused (sum of * LOC):		49
Prediction Range:	Range	235
Upper Prediction Interval:	$UPI = N + Range$	773
Lower Prediction Interval:	$LPI = N - Range$	303
Prediction Interval Percent:		90%

[1]L=Logic, I=I/O, C=Calculation, T=Text, D=Data, S=Set-up

student named each new object and determined its type. The first object, Matrix, was of the Data type. The student next estimated how many methods or procedures this object would likely contain, in this example, 13. Next the student judged the relative size of this object to be medium and determined from the historical database for C++ objects in Table 5.7 that a medium Data object would have 8.84 LOC per method. Multiplying out the number of methods gave in this case 114.9 LOC. The student then repeated this procedure for each new object to give a total of 361 new-object LOC.

BASE PROGRAM

At the same time you are estimating the new objects, you also determine the size of the base program you are enhancing and any changes to it. Table 5.8 shows that Student 12 identified 695 LOC of base code, 5 of which he planned to modify.

REUSED OBJECTS

If you can find available objects or procedures that could provide the functions required by your conceptual design, you may be able to reuse them. You could save a significant amount of time doing this, provided the objects work as you intend and are of suitable quality. For any objects you plan to take from the reuse library, note their names and sizes in the reused line. In the example in Table 5.8, Student 12 identified two reused objects with a total of 169 LOC.

New Reused Objects. The PROBE method considers two kinds of reused objects. The first are the reused objects taken from the reuse library. The second, the new reused objects, are new objects you plan to develop, just like the other new objects you have already estimated. You identify them as new reused objects because you feel they are sufficiently general to be put in the reuse library. It is good practice to build a reuse library, so you will want to track the amount of code you add to it with each program you develop. In the example in Table 5.8, the LinkedList object had three methods added to it. These methods are to be added to the reuse library and so are noted with an asterisk beside their LOC estimates. The other LinkedList methods were taken from the reuse library, so they are included with the Reused Objects LOC.

CALCULATE PROJECTED AND MODIFIED LOC

Starting at the top of the example size estimating template in Table 5.8, enter the various totals. The Base (B) is 695 LOC, Deleted (D) is 0, and Modified (M) is 5.

The Base Additions (BA) are 0. There are three New Objects (NO) that total 361 LOC and 49 LOC of these are New Reused.

LINEAR REGRESSION

Once you have the object LOC, you need a way to calculate total program size. A simple way to do this is to look at your development history. For example, suppose your historical data show that the finished program is always 25 percent bigger than the total estimated sizes of the objects it contains. Once you have an estimate for the total size of the objects, you would then add 25 percent to get the estimate for the finished program. All that the linear regression calculations do is calculate a formula for making this conversion.

As is noted in Appendix A, Section A7, these calculations are a little more complex than taking simple averages. The linear regression method, however, does produce the statistically best fit, called the maximum likelihood fit, to your historical data. It produces two parameter values, β_0 and β_1, that you can use in Eq. (5.1) to calculate the estimated program size.[1]

When two sets of data are strongly related, it is often possible to use a linear regression procedure to model this relationship. [DeGroot] As Figs. 5.4 and 5.5 show, estimated object LOC and actual total program LOC are closely correlated. This means that linear regression is appropriate. The linear regression formula for making this calculation is

Program Size $= \beta_0 +$ Object Size $* \beta_1$.

Or, more generally,

$$y_k = \beta_0 + x_k \beta_1. \tag{5.1}$$

The estimating parameters β_0 and β_1 are calculated from your historical data using the following equations:

$$\beta_1 = \frac{\sum_{i=1}^{n} x_i y_i - n x_{avg} y_{avg}}{\sum_{i=1}^{n} x_i^2 - n(x_{avg})^2} \tag{5.2}$$

$$\beta_0 = y_{avg} - \beta_1 x_{avg}$$

Here, for example, x_1 would be the object size that you originally estimated for program 1 and y_1 would be the total finished program size of program 1. Simi-

---

[1] Note, to be statistically correct, you are not calculating the actual parameters but rather the best estimates of them. Statisticians often indicate this by using different characters or special identifying symbols for the βs.

larly, x_2 and y_2 would be these data for program 2, and so forth. Also, x_{avg} is the average of all the x_i terms and y_{avg} is the average of all the y_i terms.

Using Estimated Object LOC.   To make estimates, you want to base your linear regression calculations on the relation between your estimated object LOC and the actual new and changed LOC in the finished program. Doing this will enable you to better account for your historical estimating biases and also give you a basis for determining the accuracy of your estimates. The calculation of the β parameters and an example are given in Appendix A, Section A7.

While there are risks in using this method, it has the advantage of relating your estimating method to your personal data. Some of the principal cautions and risks of using it are described in Section 5.6 and in Appendix A, Section A7.4.

DETERMINE ESTIMATED PROGRAM SIZE

The finished product will contain more than the objects you have just estimated. Your object estimates, for example, do not include the main routine or the declaration and header code. For these, you apply some factor based on your historical experience. The PROBE method uses the linear regression parameters β_0 and β_1 to do this.

In the example in Table 5.8, the new object LOC are 361 and 5 LOC are modified, so 366 LOC is used in the regression calculations. The β_0 and β_1 regression parameters then adjust for the fact that finished programs have historically been somewhat larger than the projected LOC. In essence, this calculation adds 30 percent to the object LOC to account for this overhead ($\beta_1 = 1.0 + 30$ percent). It also adds another 62 LOC to compensate for a small estimating bias. These calculations result in a total of 538 estimated new and changed LOC. After adding the 695 LOC of base code, the 169 LOC of reused code, and subtracting the 5 LOC of modified code, you get a total estimate of 1397 LOC for the finished program. The modified LOC are subtracted, since they have been counted twice: once in the 695 LOC Base and again in the new and changed LOC (N). The purpose of the β_0 and β_1 regression parameters is to obtain the best fit of a straight line to the historical data such that the data have minimum variance from the regression line defined by Eq. (5.1).

PREDICTION INTERVAL

Once you have made an estimate, you need to assess its quality. Using historical data and something called the t, or Student's t, distribution, you can calculate the prediction interval. This interval gives you the range around your estimate within which the actual program size is likely to fall. The prediction interval is described in Appendix A, Section A8. If you are not familiar with it, you should read that section before proceeding here. The formula for the prediction interval is[2]

$$\text{Range} = t(\alpha/2, n-2)\sigma \sqrt{1 + \frac{1}{n} + \frac{\left(x_k - x_{avg}\right)^2}{\sum_{i=1}^{n}\left(x_i - x_{avg}\right)^2}}. \tag{5.3}$$

Here, the x_i terms are again the numbers of estimated object LOC in each program in your historical database. The x_{avg} term is the average of the estimated object LOC in these same programs. The x_k term is the estimated object LOC in the new program, and n is the number of programs in the database. $\alpha/2$ refers to the percentage used for the prediction interval, such as 70 percent or 90 percent. Note that standard statistical tables give the single-sided t distribution, while the range formula uses the two-sided value from the t distribution. The double-sided distribution is indicated by the $\alpha/2$ parameter in the t expression. The difference between the single- and double-sided distributions is described in Appendix A, section A1.8. In general, however, to find the t distribution value for an $\alpha/2$ of 70 percent, look in Table A2 under $p = 0.85$ and for 90 percent, under $p = 0.95$.

The σ term in Eq. (5.3) is the standard deviation of your data around the regression line. It is calculated as shown in Eq. (5.4) using the β_0 and β_1 parameters. An example of these calculations is given in Appendix A, Section A8.

$$\text{Variance} = \sigma^2 = \left(\frac{1}{n-2}\right)\sum_{i=1}^{n}\left(y_i - \beta_0 - \beta_1 x_i\right)^2 \tag{5.4}$$

$$\text{Standard Deviation} = \sqrt{Variance} = \sigma$$

You can now calculate the value of Range. The prediction interval is then the estimated value you calculated for the program LOC plus or minus this interval range. An example of this calculation is shown in Appendix A, Section A8.

Using data on prior programs and Eq. (5.3), Student 12 in Table 5.8 found the 90 percent range for program 10A to be 235 LOC. This means that roughly 90 percent of the time, the actual new and changed LOC in the program should fall between 303 ($538 - 235$) and 773 ($538 + 235$) LOC. In this case, the finished size of 482 LOC was slightly less than the midpoint of this range.

The Meaning of the Prediction Interval.   The quality of an estimate made with the PROBE method is a direct function of the quality of the data you use. It also depends on the degree to which these data correspond to the way you intend to develop the next program. For example, if your historical data have wild variations, prediction intervals will be large. A stable development process will thus

---

[2]Again, more precisely you are not using the standard deviation and variance in these calculations but rather the best estimates of them.

improve your estimating accuracy. It is also essential that the process you used for these historical programs resemble the one you intend to use with the new one. For example, if you changed your design method, built a much larger program, or developed a new class of applications, your historical data would not accurately represent what you intended to do. While you may still choose to use the PROBE method, you must recognize that the prediction interval is not a good indication of the error range of your estimate.

Another way to look at this is to consider every estimate as a game of chance. In essence, you throw darts at a target to get a number. Assume your historical database contains the data on 10 prior throws and that each prior throw or estimate has some error. The darts, for example, may have clustered around the value of 100 with a couple at 80 and one as far out as 60. Statistically, your new estimate is just another dart throw. The presumption then is that its likely value is best represented by the variation of all the previous throws. If, however, you decide this time to use a bow and arrow or to switch to a different-sized dart or to stand twice as far away, your previous data would not be very helpful in estimating the error of this new throw.

5.5   Object Categories

The PROBE estimating method requires that you have historical data on the sizes of the objects you have developed and that these data be divided into categories. Methods for dividing these data are described in the following sections.

OBJECT SIZE CATEGORIES

You need object size categories in order to give yourself a framework for judging the size of the new objects in your planned product. If, for example, you knew the sizes of all the text objects you previously developed you could better judge the likely size of a new text object. In my PSP research work, I produced a total of 13 Pascal text objects, as listed in Table 5.9. Note from this table that the objects range from 18 to 558 LOC, a spread of over 30 to 1. Also, the number of methods in each object varies from 3 to 10. Because you are primarily interested in the relative sizes of the objects based on your judgment of their functional complexity, it is helpful to normalize object size by dividing the total object LOC by the number of methods in each object. Now, if you have a complex object with one method it can be distinguished from a simple object with many methods.

After making this normalization, you have the data given in Table 5.10. The smallest number of object LOC per method is now 6 and the largest is 55.8.

TABLE 5.9 PASCAL TEXT OBJECT SIZES

Object Name	Number of Methods	Object LOC
each_line	3	31
each_char	3	18
list_clump	4	87
character	3	87
single_character	3	25
string_read	3	18
list_clp	4	89
char	3	85
single_char	3	37
converter	10	558
string_manager	4	82
string_builder	5	82
string_decrementer	10	230

While this is still nearly a 10 to 1 spread, it is somewhat more useful than the 30 to 1 spread you had without normalization. The value of knowing this range is clearer when you consider the extreme case. Say, for example, you knew that the size range for text objects would fall between 3 LOC and 3000 LOC. This does not provide a great deal of help when you try to pick a LOC value for the size of a new text object. Size ranges are thus most helpful if they are reasonably narrow.

You next seek a way to determine the size of an average text object. You would also like measures for very small text objects or large ones. Now you are faced with providing a structure for your intuitive sense of size. The view that some object will be a large object when compared with all other text objects is purely subjective. So we are seeking a way to take advantage of the way we intuitively compare things. For this purpose, we look at natural phenomena.

The *normal distribution* is a mathematical way to describe how many things, such as peoples' heights, are distributed. If you are not familiar with the normal distribution, you should now read the discussion in Appendix A, Section A1. Also, as is described in Appendix A, Section A2, the *standard deviation* is a measure of the "fatness," or the degree of spread, of the bell-shaped normal curve.

TABLE 5.10 PASCAL TEXT OBJECT LOC PER METHOD

Object Name	Number of Methods	Object LOC	LOC per Method
each_line	3	31	10.333
each_char	3	18	6.000
list_clump	4	87	21.750
character	3	87	29.000
single_character	3	25	8.333
string_read	3	18	6.000
list_clp	4	89	22.250
char	3	85	28.333
single_char	3	37	12.333
converter	10	558	55.800
string_manager	4	82	20.500
string_builder	5	82	16.400
string_decrementer	10	230	23.000

OBJECT SIZE RANGES

To judge the relative sizes of objects, we use standard deviations. Unfortunately, because size data are not normally distributed, the object size calculation is a bit more complicated than just measuring standard deviations above and below the mean. Before getting into this complication, however, we describe a simplified approach for picking the five size ranges very small, small, medium, large, and very large and then describe how to handle the complication. The approach is essentially the same as the fuzzy-logic estimating method used earlier. As described in Appendix A, Section A2, the variance and standard deviation are calculated by using the following formulas:

$$\text{Var} = \sigma^2 = (1/n) \sum_{i=1}^{n} \left(x_i - x_{avg}\right)^2$$

(5.5)

$$\text{StdDev} = \sqrt{Var} = \sigma$$

where n is the number of items. In the case of the Pascal text objects in Tables 5.10 and 5.11 and since there are 13 objects in the total population, use n rather than $n - 1$ in the variance calculation. Also, x_i is the LOC per method and x_{avg} is the average.

This standard deviation calculation is shown in Table 5.11. The standard deviation for the sizes of the 13 text objects turns out to be 12.839 LOC, which means the midpoints of the text size ranges are as follows:

Very Small (VS) = −5.68
Small (S) = 7.16
Medium (M) = 20.0
Large (L) = 32.84
Very Large (VL) = 45.68

These objects and range values are shown in sorted order in Table 5.12. The complication mentioned earlier is that this is not a very representative size range. First, regardless of how simple a function was, it could never have a negative number of LOC, as shown by the Very Small category. Further, even from only

TABLE 5.11   PASCAL TEXT OBJECT STANDARD DEVIATION

Object Name	LOC per Method	$(LOC\text{-}LOC_{avg})^2$
each_line	10.333	93.494
each_char	6.000	196.072
list_clump	21.750	3.054
character	29.000	80.954
single_character	8.333	136.171
string_read	6.000	196.072
list_clp	22.250	5.051
char	28.333	69.402
single_char	12.333	58.817
converter	55.800	1281.456
string_manager	20.500	0.247
string_builder	16.400	12.978
string_decrementer	23.000	8.985
Total	260.033	2142.753
Average	20.003	
Variance = Total/n = σ^2		164.827
Standard Deviation = $\sqrt{Variance} = \sigma$		12.839

TABLE 5.12 PASCAL TEXT OBJECTS AND SIZE RANGES

Size Ranges	Range Midpoint LOC	Object LOC/Method
VS	−5.68	
		6.000
		6.000
S	7.16	
		8.333
		10.333
		12.333
		16.400
M	20.00	
		20.500
		21.750
		22.250
		23.000
		28.333
		29.000
L	32.84	
VL	45.68	
		55.800

13 objects, one object is substantially larger than the Very Large category. These problems result from the fact that you are not dealing with a normally distributed set of data—for example, the data do not vary from minus to plus infinity. This is not normally a problem when the data values are all well above zero. The problem occurs when negative values are within three standard deviations of the mean or average of the data. With the object size distribution, zero is within two standard deviations of the mean.

Log-normal Object Size Ranges. A trick for handling this situation is to calculate the natural logarithms of the data, compute the standard deviations and range values on these logarithmic data, and then convert back to the antilogarithms. These calculations are shown in Table 5.13 for the 13 Pascal text objects. Briefly, you follow these steps:

TABLE 5.13 PASCAL TEXT OBJECT ln(LOC/METHOD)

Object Name	LOC per Method	ln(LOC per Method)	$(\ln LOC - \ln LOC_{avg})^2$
each_line	10.333	2.335	0.2173
each_char	6.000	1.792	1.0196
list_clump	21.750	3.080	0.0773
character	29.000	3.367	0.3201
single_character	8.333	2.120	0.4641
string_read	6.000	1.792	1.0196
list_clp	22.250	3.102	0.0905
char	28.333	3.344	0.2943
single_char	12.333	2.512	0.0836
converter	55.800	4.022	1.4890
string_manager	20.500	3.020	0.0479
string_builder	16.400	2.797	0.0000
string_decrementer	23.000	3.135	0.1115
Total	260.033	36.419	5.2348
Average	20.003	2.802	
Variance	164.827		0.4027
Standard Deviation	12.839		0.6346
lnVL = 2.802 + 1.269	4.071	$VL = e^{4.071} =$	58.62
lnL = 2.802 + .635	3.437	$L = e^{3.437} =$	31.09
lnM = 2.802	2.802	$M = e^{2.802} =$	16.48
lnS = 2.802 − .635	2.167	$S = e^{2.167} =$	8.73
lnVS = 2.802 − 1.269	1.533	$VS = e^{1.533} =$	4.63

1. Calculate the natural logarithm of the LOC per method value for each of the 13 objects. For example, the natural logarithm of the first object, **each_line**, 10.333, is 2.335.

2. Calculate the average of the logarithmic values. In this case, the average is 2.802.

3. Calculate the variance of the logarithmic values around their mean or average value. You do this as follows:

□ For each term, calculate the square of its distance from the mean; for example, for the first term,

$$\left[\ln 10.333 - (Lnx)_{avg}\right]^2 = (2.335 - 2.802)^2 = (.467)^2 = 0.2173.$$

Note that 2.802 is not the log of the average; it is the average of the logs.

□ Add all the squared values to give 5.2348.

□ Divide by the number of objects, 13, to give the variance as 0.4027.

□ Take the square root of the variance, 0.4027, to get the standard deviation, 0.6346.

4. Using these logarithmic values for the average and standard deviations, calculate the logarithms of the size range midpoints, as follows:

$\ln(\text{VL}) = avg_{\ln} + 2*\text{StdDev} = 2.802 + 1.269 = 4.071$

$\ln(\text{L}) = avg_{\ln} + 1*\text{StdDev} = 2.802 + 0.635 = 3.437$

$\ln(\text{M}) = avg_{\ln} = 2.802$

$\ln(\text{S}) = avg_{\ln} - 1*\text{StdDev} = 2.802 - 0.635 = 2.167$

$\ln(\text{VS}) = avg_{\ln} - 2*\text{StdDev} = 2.802 - 1.269 = 1.533$

5. Take the antilogarithms of these to get the object size range midpoints in LOC:

$e^{4.071} = 58.62$ LOC

$e^{3.437} = 31.09$ LOC

$e^{2.802} = 16.48$ LOC

$e^{2.167} = 8.73$ LOC

$e^{1.533} = 4.63$ LOC

When the logarithmic values are converted back to LOC terms, you get the ranges shown in Table 5.14. While these ranges represent a somewhat better balanced distribution than that shown in Table 5.12, it is clearly not perfect. Now, a very large text object would be 59 LOC and an average one would be 16 LOC. These are the values shown in Table 5.7 for Pascal text objects. This procedure for calculating size ranges is necessary for calculating the size ranges of objects for the PROBE method. It works because the log values of object sizes are more closely normally distributed than are the LOC size values.

Initially, you may have a limited amount of data and so may have to make these range calculations for all the objects or procedures in your database. As soon as you have enough data to produce a reasonable distribution for object categories, break them into groups that appear to be significantly different and do this analysis for each smaller category. That is, you would want to do this for I/O objects, for calculation objects, for logic objects, and so on. Six to eight object values are enough to give an initially useful range of values.

TABLE 5.14   PASCAL TEXT OBJECTS AND SIZE RANGES

Size Ranges	Range Midpoint LOC	Object LOC/Method
VS	4.63	
		6.000
		6.000
		8.333
S	8.73	
		10.333
		12.333
		16.400
M	16.48	
		20.500
		21.750
		22.250
		23.000
		28.333
		29.000
L	31.09	
		55.800
VL	58.62	

Note that for the C++ objects in the top section of Table 5.7, you can tell if objects should be in separate categories by examining their distributions. For example, even though set-up and calculation objects have similar sizes, their very large sizes differ significantly. It also appears from these data that the logic and I/O objects have a similar size distribution, at least for the objects in my database.

OBJECT SIZE DISTRIBUTION

You should also examine your size estimates to make sure they are reasonable. Suppose, for example, you estimated, using the PROBE method, that a new program would require 18 objects and all were either large or very large compared to your historical objects of these types. If you had a logical reason for these selections, this estimate might be reasonable; if not, you could be unconsciously compensating for some previous underestimate.

While there is no hard-and-fast rule, you should tend to balance your estimates so your size categories more or less conform to the normal distribution. For example, the percentage of objects that should fall in the medium range of the normal distribution is 38.3 percent. Figure 5.9 shows how this is determined. The medium range (M) is the area from −0.5 standard deviation to +0.5 standard deviation from the mean. For the normal distribution, the probability of values less than −0.5 standard deviation is around 0.3 (actually 0.3085). Also, the probability of a value less than +0.5 standard deviation is around 0.7 (0.6915). The number between −0.5 and +0.5 is thus the difference of these probabilities, or 0.383, or 38.3 percent. This is the likely number of objects that are within plus or minus 0.5 standard deviation of the average value. Using the PROBE method, assume that all the medium-sized objects have this medium number of LOC. Similarly, the percentages that are large would be 24.17 percent. This is the number that would fall between 0.5 and 1.5 standard deviations above the mean of the distribution. These normal ranges are shown in Fig. 5.9. The range values are as follows:

- □ 6.68 percent should be very small
- □ 24.17 percent should be small
- □ 38.3 percent should be medium
- □ 24.17 percent should be large
- □ 6.68 percent should be very large

If your estimate has such a distribution, it would be typical of the programs in your size estimation database. While you should use these numbers only as gen-

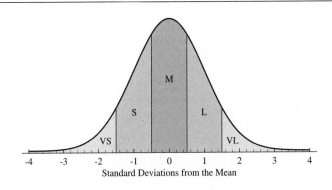

FIGURE 5.9
Normal Distribution with Size Ranges

eral guides, an estimate that has a significantly different distribution should be re-examined to ensure you did not make an error.

If your estimate distribution does not approximate this standard, you have four choices.

1. You could use the estimate without change. However, you should only do this after you carefully review the basis for your estimate and conclude that it is appropriate.

2. You could ask another estimator to make an independent estimate and then compare that estimate with yours. If the estimates differ, you may have to ask a third or even a fourth estimator to act as tie breaker. If you commonly use this approach, you might consider using the Wideband-Delphi estimating method to help obtain a consensus.

3. You could modify the estimate to make it more nearly match a normal distribution. This alternative could be a mistake if the original estimate included a number of very large parts that should really have been refined to a lower level. This is often the case when you are in a hurry and do not want to take the time and trouble to make a further refinement.

4. If it appears that some of the very complex objects in your estimate are composites of several lower-level functions, you should re-do the estimate, this time refining the conceptual design to the proper level.

5.6   Estimating Considerations

Estimating is a skill that you should develop and improve. Next, I discuss ways that can help you to do this.

PSP ESTIMATING OBJECTIVES

Because it is common to make fairly large errors in estimating either the development time or the size of small programs and because student error rates do not generally appear to improve in only the 10 exercises in this book, you may wonder why you should bother making estimates. The answer is that by tracking and analyzing your estimates, you can improve your overall estimating ability even though each estimate may still be substantially in error.

To see how this works, suppose you are estimating a large job as a single unit. The amount of fluctuation in your estimates can be measured by their standard deviation. The square of the standard deviation is called the *variance*. If you estimate the size of a program at 10,000 LOC and if the standard deviation between your estimates and the actual program sizes is 25 percent, or 2500 LOC, then about 65 percent of the time the actual program size for all such estimates would likely fall between 7500 and 12,500 LOC, or plus or minus one standard deviation.

However, this is not the entire story. Your estimate will have two general kinds of errors. First, your estimating accuracy will fluctuate around some mean or average, say plus or minus 25 percent. Second, your estimate may have some bias. That is, you may always tend to estimate about 25 percent too low. For example, if your estimates have a consistent negative bias of 25 percent, then for a 10,000 LOC program your estimates would fluctuate around 7500 LOC, not 10,000 LOC. The amount of bias depends on your estimating experience and your knowledge of the application. It also depends on how much design work you have done, your degree of optimism about the job, and your estimating ability. The amount of an estimator's bias will fluctuate over time, and it can be radically influenced by such factors as management pressure, personal commitment, or errors in previous estimates.

Next, suppose that before you estimate this 10,000 LOC program, you subdivide it into 100 parts. Now, however, assume that each part is independently estimated by 100 different estimators, all of whom estimate with the same relative estimating variance and bias as before. Each of the nominal 100 LOC programs would then be estimated with a bias of 25 LOC and a standard deviation of 25 LOC. Statistically speaking, the mean of the sum of these estimates is the sum of their means. The average program estimate would thus be 25 LOC too low, or about 75 LOC. When all these estimates were combined into one big estimate, the result would then be 100 times the average, or 7500 LOC for the actual 10,000-LOC program. That is, on average the bias of 25 LOC would impact every estimate and the resulting estimate for the total program would be around 7500 LOC.

The standard deviation, however, is a different matter. Assuming the individual estimates were all independently made, their variances, and not their standard deviations, would be summed. Because the variance of each estimate is the square of the 25 LOC error, or 625, the variance of the total estimate is the sum of the separate variances, or 62,500. The standard deviation of the total is thus the square root of this or 250 LOC. This means that about 65 percent of such estimates would be expected to fall between 7250 and 7750 LOC. That is, they would be within about plus or minus 250 LOC of the biased average estimate of 7500 LOC.

One might argue that this is a worse estimate than before, since the estimate upper limit does not reach the 10,000-LOC total program size. However, it actually is a much better estimate. The bias is likely to be a somewhat more consistent error that can be measured and at least partially compensated for, while the variance is not. If you were to gather data on many such estimates and calculate their biases and if these estimating processes were reasonably stable, then you should be able to make an accurate bias adjustment. That, in fact, is what the linear regression method does.

The objective with the PSP, however, is to improve your ability to make estimates. Some engineers' estimating errors swing quite widely between frequent large underestimates and large overestimates. As they learn to use historical size data and to track their estimating experience, their estimating quality should gradually improve. Even the most experienced estimators, however, occasionally make significant errors. By quantifying your estimating experience, you will gradually learn how to make better estimates and to compensate for your consistent biases. For example, if you always estimate too low, you will soon recognize this trend and begin to reduce your bias. Over time, then, your estimates will tend to fluctuate around zero. Even when you make reasonably unbiased estimates, however, you will still make occasional large errors. Your overall estimating ability, however, will be greatly improved.

The basic philosophy behind the PROBE method is to provide a procedure and the objective criteria for making estimates. The defined estimating procedure helps to produce more consistent results. With feedback from each estimate, you can then adjust your estimating process to gradually reduce your estimating biases.

ESTIMATING PRACTICE

While you are learning to make consistent estimates, your estimate quality will likely fluctuate widely and your β_0 and β_1 parameters will also change significantly from one project to the next. Over time, however, your estimates will tend to stabilize. When you see that your regression parameters begin to converge on reasonably stable values, you can stop recalculating them for every estimate. You should still keep track of your estimating data and periodically update your parameters, but you need not do it every time.

Also, over time, your process will tend to evolve. This means that as you gain experience, the data on some of the programs you previously planned and developed will no longer represent your current practices. You should then adjust your statistical calculations to drop these old data and include only the newer and more representative ones. You always want to retain your data, of course, but you should move your analysis database to those situations that represent how you currently operate.

ESTIMATING JUDGMENT

In using any statistical method, you may possibly get nonsensical results. For example, the β_0 and β_1 parameters calculated by the linear regression method are a straight-line fit to the relationship between your estimated object LOC and the new and changed LOC in the finished program. Because the total program size should be somewhat larger than the estimated object LOC, you would expect the β_1 parameter to be somewhat larger than 1.0. A β_1 of 1.25, for example, would mean that on average your total programs have a new and changed LOC content that is about 25 percent larger than the estimated object LOC.

If your data contain some wildly inaccurate estimates, however, it is possible to get almost anything for the β_0 and β_1 values. In fact, I have seen in student data β_1 values as low as 0.05 and as high as 4.0 or more. Negative β_1s are even possible. When the value of β_1 is this far from 1.0, the linear regression method is likely to give misleading results. This would also be the case if the value of β_0 were a large positive or negative number. A large β_0 value would be one that was either larger than the numbers of LOC in some of the smaller programs in your database or a significant fraction of the size of the program you are estimating.

When your linear regression parameters are obviously incorrect, you should use historical averages for your estimates. That is, you add up all your object LOC estimates and all the total new and changed LOC for these same programs. You then use the ratio of these totals to make your estimates.

For example, suppose you estimated a new program to contain 137 new-object LOC. Suppose also that you found the values of β_0 and β_1 to be 168 and 0.26, respectively. Because β_0 is quite large and β_1 is much less than 1.0, you decide to use an averaging method instead of linear regression. You then add up the object LOC estimates in your previous four programs for a total of 427 LOC. You also add up the final new and changed LOC for these same programs for a total of 583 LOC. The ratio of these gives you 1.365. When you multiply this value times your estimate of 137 object LOC for the new program, you get a total program new and changed LOC estimate of 187 LOC.

Whenever your linear regression parameters appear unreasonable, use average values for your estimates. Also, make a general practice of checking your linear regression estimates against an estimate made with average data. If the results are significantly different, check your calculations and reconsider the suitability of using linear regression.

USING LIMITED DATA

Another problem, particularly in the early stages of the PSP, is that you will have few historical data. To use the linear regression method, you must have at least three sets of historical data. This means that you cannot use the PROBE method as described here until you have data on at least three programs for which you have made object LOC estimates. Until you have this much history, you should calculate the β_0 and β_1 parameters from your actual object LOC and new and changed LOC data and use the averaging method to make your size estimates. I discuss this issue further in Chapter 6. The use of the PROBE estimating script for time estimates is also described in Appendix C (Table C36).

BIAS

You can reduce your estimating bias by obtaining feedback. By comparing the actual sizes of finished programs with their estimates, you will gradually learn how to make more consistently good estimates. This process is complicated, however, by another source of error. When you estimate the size of a new program before you have designed it, you will likely be uncertain about precisely how to build it. The only way to completely compensate for this would be to complete the design before you make the estimate. Of course, this method is impractical when you need an estimate and a plan before making a development commitment. In this case, you must make the best estimate you can, consult the available historical data, use a statistically sound estimating method, and utilize the judgment of any available experts.

A principal source of bias is lack of knowledge. While this lack will increase estimating variance, its most important impact is on estimating bias. Because bias is a natural consequence of early estimates, it is important that you learn as much about it as possible. One approach for doing this for large projects is to reestimate the program's size at several points during development. Assuming you made all the estimates yourself, they should get progressively more accurate as development progresses. Over time, as you gather such data on a number of projects, you will gradually learn which errors to expect at each phase. This would require that you gather separate data and calculate different regression parameters and prediction intervals for estimates made at each development phase.

On your larger projects, you should get in the habit of making a new size and resource estimate when you complete the design and again when you finish coding. Make sure you record the phases at which you make these estimates and then compare them during the project postmortem. This is not a useful exercise for the small program exercises in this book, but you should do it with your larger projects.

SELECTING AN ABSTRACTION LEVEL

In selecting an abstraction level, you need to pick a reasonably low level so that you will have a sufficient statistical sample. The smaller the abstraction, the more data points you can obtain from each project. Conversely, if you pick too small an abstraction you must consider a larger number of parts for each estimate. You could also have trouble visualizing these minute proxies while making an initial plan.

For example, if the typical object has methods averaging about 10 to 15 LOC each and there are 3 to 10 methods per object, then the objects will range from about 30 to 150 LOC each. When you later use the PROBE method to estimate a 50,000 LOC system, you would then have to identify, categorize, and rate for complexity about 400 to 600 objects. This could be a substantial job.

With adequate data and experience, you can learn to make size estimates for programs of up to 5000 LOC in less than an hour or two. Such programs would typically contain 50 or so objects. While an estimate for a 50,000-LOC program probably would take you more than 10 times as long to produce as would an estimate for a 5000-LOC program, it would probably take you less than 100 times as long. This means that using the PROBE method, you could make a detailed estimate for a 50,000-LOC program in under 100 hours. A 50,000-LOC program would probably take a good many programmer months to develop, so 100 hours spent in estimating should not seem excessive.

Large Systems.   For systems much larger than 50,000 LOC, it could be a major job to reduce the conceptual design to the level of program objects. It would thus seem desirable to use higher-level constructs as proxies. One approach would be to group sets of objects into classes and then estimate the classes. Doing this would require that the classes be normalized by the numbers of their objects and the objects normalized by the numbers of their methods. Data and estimating factors would then also be needed for these various categories of larger units.

For example, you might name the **text_class** to hold a large number of text objects. One object could be the **text_library** object that handles the book title, author, Library of Congress reference, copyright notice, and other such topics. The **text_book** object would include methods for counting and numbering chapters and inserting standard front matter. The **text_chapter** object may include custom methods for handling chapter headings, references, and chapter summaries. You could similarly have objects for page, paragraph, line, word, and even character, each with its own methods.

While it might seem attractive to make an estimate for a large system by naming one text class, one control class, three calculating classes, a file class, and an I/O class, doing so probably would not help you to make very good estimates. You would still have to estimate the contents of each class. The less you know about them, the less accurate your estimate would likely be. It would be like expecting a detailed estimate from a home builder when all you can tell him is that you want a two-story house with a two-car garage and three bedrooms. This level of detail may be sufficient for ballpark numbers but not for estimating.

Another problem with this approach is that high-level abstractions are generally much harder to categorize. This is because they generally contain mixes of several types of objects. Also, you would likely have data on a relatively few such large abstractions, so statistical analysis would not be practical. You would then find it hard to relate these abstractions to the characteristics of a new program. Thus using such larger components would tend to negate the statistical advantages of using a routine data-supported estimating procedure.

If these problems could be solved and if you could make reasonable complexity judgments at the class level, this approach could be practical. If, however, each object and method had to be considered individually, the end result would involve the same level of detail as required with objects.

A more practical approach is to break larger programs into several major parts. You then separately estimate each part, using the object abstraction level. While this approach would not reduce the total level of detail, it would separate the project into more manageable elements. It would also have the benefits that come with multiple, statistically independent estimates.

It is probably wisest to stick with the estimating level with which you have the most experience and to recognize that you should spend proportionately more time planning larger programs than smaller ones.

Unprecedented Products.   All of this assumes that you can produce a conceptual design fairly quickly and that you can readily reduce it to the object level. While this is generally no problem with products of types you have previously built, for new and unprecedented products it could be difficult or impossible to do a competent job. An *unprecedented product* is one whose size, complexity, performance, function, or some combination of these is so different from anything you have previously developed that you have no benchmarks to guide you in planning or development. The best answer in this case is to resist making firm estimates for unprecedented products until you have completed a feasibility study and built some prototypes, both of which will give you the knowledge to refine the conceptual design to the object level. If you can't do this, then you are no longer making an estimate—you are making a guess.

Over and Under Compensation.   One problem with a statistical view of estimation is that people do not behave consistently. While much of the variation from one estimate to the next is normal statistical fluctuation, you may find yourself feeling guilty about your errors and attempting to correct each one. Of course, you should be aware of your estimation accuracy and make adjustments if you are consistently off in one direction or the other. However, do this only after thoughtfully studying your historical trends. Remember, statistical fluctuation is normal. If you attempt to correct your process for each error, you could actually make the result much worse. The best approach is to consciously make small corrections and maintain them consistently for several estimates, even if they appear to overcorrect for the previously observed problems.

While you should attempt to follow a consistent estimating pattern and not worry about your prior errors, doing this is almost impossible. The estimation process involves so many judgments, it is easily biased. The only reliable protection is to use a defined method and historical data. When the methods for using these data are regularized and are repeatedly applied, the statistical aberrations will be reduced. While you must still make judgments, they can be checked to ensure they are reasonably balanced, provided they are statistically based.

5.7 Summary

The principal reason you estimate the size of a software product is to assist you in planning its development. The quality of software development plans, in turn, generally depends on the quality of the size estimates. Several methods were discussed for estimating software size. Boehm, for example, described the Wideband-Delphi method for using multiple experts' opinions and Putnam described the fuzzy-logic method and the standard-component method for judging the sizes of new products based on historical data. Albrecht's function-point method uses standard factors for judging the relative importance of various functional requirements.

In project planning, estimates are generally required before development can begin. At this early stage, the requirements may be understood but little is generally known about the product itself. A proxy is thus needed to relate product size to the required product functions. The criteria for a good proxy are that its size closely relates to the effort required to develop the product and that it can be automatically counted. It should also be easily visualized at the beginning of the project and be language, style, and design dependent.

The principles of object-oriented design suggest that objects are good estimating proxies. If, during initial analysis and design, you use application entities as the basis for selecting system objects, this will provide implementation proxies that you can easily visualize during requirements analysis. The PROBE method divides objects into size ranges and calculates estimating factors for each. The estimating process then starts with a conceptual product design. After all the objects have been estimated, the total object LOC is obtained by multiplying the LOC per method by the number of methods. These are then totaled to give the total estimated object LOC. With the total object LOC, you can then estimate the program size and prediction interval.

When a large job is estimated as a single unit, there are two sources of error. First, estimating accuracy will fluctuate around some mean or average. Second, the estimate will typically have some bias. If you were to gather data on many estimates and calculate their biases and if the estimating process were reasonably stable, you should be able to make an accurate bias adjustment. This, in fact, is what the PROBE method does.

Without training and experience with an estimating method, you will find that your estimates will be inconsistent and unpredictable. As you gain training and experience, you should better appreciate the statistical implications of your work and better understand the importance of gathering and using the historical data on which sound estimating factors are based.

5.8   Exercises

The standard course plan assumes that this chapter is covered in two lectures, so there are two exercises. The first assignment uses PSP0.1 to write program 3A. It also requires you to produce the Defect Analysis Report, R3. The second assignment uses PSP1 to write program 4A. The specifications for these programs and the report are given in Appendix D. The PSP0.1 and the PSP1 processes are described in Appendix C. You should review and become familiar with these processes and faithfully follow them and the report submission formats they specify.

For other assignment options, consult Appendix D.

References

[Albrecht] A. J. Albrecht and J. E. Gaffney, Jr., "Software Function, Source Lines of Code, and Development Effort Prediction: A Software Science Validation," IEEE Trans. on Software Eng. SE-9, 639–648 (1983).

[Boehm] Barry W. Boehm, *Software Engineering Economics* (Englewood Cliffs, NJ: Prentice-Hall, 1981).

[Booch] G. Booch, "What Is and What Isn't Object-Oriented Design?" *American Programmer*, vol. 2, no. 7–8 (Summer 1989): 14–21.

[Coad] Peter Coad and Edward Yourdon, *Object-Oriented Analysis* (Englewood Cliffs, NJ: Yourdon Press, 1991).

[DeGroot] Morris H. DeGroot, *Probability and Statistics* (Reading, MA: Addison-Wesley, 1989).

[Hihn] Jairus Hihn and Hamid Habib-agahi, "Cost Estimation of Software Intensive Projects: A Survey of Current Practices," 13th International Conference on Software Engineering (Cat. No. 91CH2982-7), Austin, TX, USA; (May, 1991): 13–16.

[Humphrey 89] W. S. Humphrey, *Managing the Software Process* (Reading, MA: Addison-Wesley, 1989).

[Jones] Capers Jones, *Applied Software Measurement: Assuring Productivity and Quality* (New York: McGraw-Hill, 1991).

[Park 89] Robert E. Park, "The Central Equations of the PRICE Software Cost Model," Proceedings, National Estimating Society Conference, McLean, VA (June 1989).

[Putnam] Lawrence H. Putnam and Ware Myers, *Measures for Excellence: Reliable Software on Time, within Budget* (Englewood Cliffs, NJ: Yourdon Press, 1992).

[Shlaer] S. Shlaer and S. J. Mellor, *Object-Oriented Analysis: Modeling the World in Data* (Englewood Cliffs, NJ: Yourdon Press, 1988).

[Sprouls] J. Sprouls, ed., *IFPUG Function Point Counting Practices Manual, Release 3.0 Ed.,* International Function Point Users Group, Westerville, Ohio (1990).

[Wirfs-Brock] R. Wirfs-Brock, B. Wilderson, and L. Wiener, *Designing Object-Oriented Software* (Englewood Cliffs, NJ: Prentice-Hall, 1990).

[Zwanzig] K. Zwanzig, ed., *Handbook for Estimating Using Function Points*, Project DP-1234, GUIDE International (1984).

6

Planning IV—Resource and Schedule Estimating

This chapter describes how to make plans for small programs and how to combine the plans for several small programs into larger composite plans. Schedule planning involves such topics as resource loading, resource utilization, and earned value tracking, all of which are covered.

The PSP can be applied to many kinds of work. The PSP resource planning process can be used for planning software development as well as almost any other task for which you have a process definition and historical data.

6.1 Resource Planning

In the PSP, the resource you plan is your own time—how much time do you expect to spend developing a program? Starting with a program size estimate, you use the methods described in this chapter to estimate the time the work will take, judge the accuracy of this estimate, and generate a schedule.

THE SOFTWARE PLANNING FRAMEWORK

The generalized software development planning framework was shown in Chapters 3 and 5 and is shown again in Fig. 6.1. The tasks to be performed are shown

145

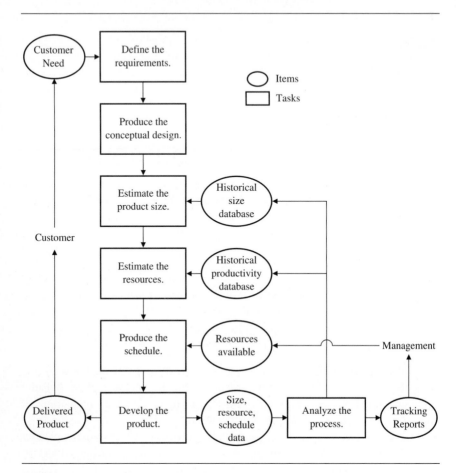

FIGURE 6.1
Project Planning Framework

in the rectangles, and the various data, reports, and products are shown in the ovals. Once you have made the size estimate, you need to estimate the resources and produce a schedule. You do this by relating the time you spent on prior projects to the estimated sizes of the programs you produced. Thus you must get data on the estimated sizes and the actual development times for several prior projects. If you develop programs in several different languages, you will need separate sets of data for each language. You should also have data for each major application domain as well as for any other special tools or methods you generally use. You want to be careful about your data because the accuracy of your plans depends on the degree to which the projects in your database are similar to the projects you plan to do.

PRODUCTIVITY

Productivity is generally measured as the labor hours required to do a unit of work. It is such a simple concept that people tend to think of productivity as a simple calculation. It is nothing of the sort. When calculating productivity, you must consider, for example, the unique conditions of each job and the quality of the resulting product. If you estimate the size of a new job and then use some global productivity factor to determine the total hours required, you will generally get a misleading result. It would be like always allowing for the average driving time when you go to the airport. You will miss a lot of flights around rush hour and do a lot of waiting the rest of the time.

Each project is different. If you lump all project activities into some global productivity number, you will eliminate much of the thought required to produce a good plan. DeMarco illustrates this in his book, *Controlling Software Projects*. [DeMarco] His illustration of the hours required to finish a concrete surface is reproduced in Table 6.1. An accurate estimate of this seemingly simple job requires breaking the work down into nine elemental steps, several of which have alternate methods. Depending on the specific characteristics of the job, different factors are used to estimate each step. Assuming all the steps are required in each case, the time to finish 1000 square feet of concrete could vary from 390 to 470 hours. Because software design and development is a vastly more complex task than is finishing concrete, the planning process for a software job obviously should be more comprehensive rather than less.

The basic approach in software resource planning is to gather data on your historical productivity for several prior jobs. For example, if your data show that on average you produce about 30 LOC every working hour, you would estimate that a 184-LOC project would take about 6.1 hours. Further, if your historical data showed that the normal fluctuation in your productivity was from 21 to 39 LOC per hour, then you could judge the likely range of your new job to be between 4.7 and 8.8 hours. While this might seem like a very wide range, it is an accurate projection based on your prior experience. You will likely be better off knowing this range than just assuming a simple average. Now you can at least establish contingency plans in case the project takes longer than you expect.

6.2 Estimating Development Time

When planning the time required to develop a small program with the PSP, follow the procedure shown in Fig. 6.2.

TABLE 6.1 LABOR HOURS REQUIRED FOR FINISHING CONCRETE
SURFACES

Steps	Type of Work	Labor Hours per 100 Square Feet
1	Troweling Floor, Sidewalks	2.0 to 3.0
	Troweling Plain Base and Cove	2.0 to 3.0
	Troweling Fancy Base and Cove	5.0
2	Carborundum Rubbing, Floor and Walls, Typical	7.0
	Carborundum Rubbing, Sill, Base, Cove, Typical	9.0
3	Machine Grinding, Typical	6.0
4	1-Inch Granolithic or Terrazzo Laid after Concrete Has Hardened, Incl. Mixing and Placing	11.0
	1-Inch Granolithic or Terrazzo Laid Integral with Concrete, Incl. Mixing and Placing	9.0
5	Removing Fins, Patching Rock Pockets	2.0 to 3.0
6	Scrubbing Surface	3.0
7	Washing Surface with Acid	3.0
8	Sand Blasting Surface	4.0
9	Cement or Other Kind of Surface Work, per Coat	3.0

Source: Tom DeMarco, *Controlling Software Projects* (1982): 7. Reprinted by permission, Addison-Wesley, Inc.

PLANNING DEVELOPMENT TIME

One of your first planning concerns is selecting the historical data to use. Basically, your choices are as follows:

□ A: Use data on estimated object LOC and total actual development hours.
This is your best choice because it represents the way the PROBE method produces the estimates. It will thus give you the most realistic prediction interval. To use this choice, you need at least three data points where the object LOC and actual development hours correlate with an $r^2 \geq 0.5$. (See Appendix A, Section A3.)

□ B: Use actual object LOC and actual development hours.
This is your choice if you do not have enough data for choice A. It requires

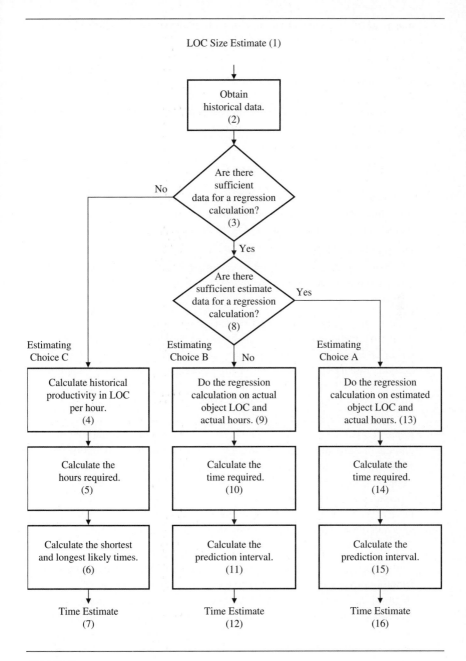

FIGURE 6.2
Planning Development Time

that you have data on actual development hours and actual object LOC for at least three projects and that the actual object LOC and actual development hours correlate with an $r^2 \geq 0.5$. (See Appendix A, Section A3.)

☐ C: Use data on actual total new and changed LOC and actual hours.
If you do not have at least three historical data points for either choice A or B, you must use choice C. This approach works even with data on only one prior project.

To select among these choices, follow the logic shown in Fig. 6.2. The numbers in the following description refer to the numbers in this figure:

1. **LOC Size Estimate**
   With the PROBE method, you should have an estimate for the object LOC and the total new and changed LOC in the new program.

2. **Obtain historical data.**
   Get whatever data you have on the estimated and actual sizes of your previously developed programs and the actual hours you spent developing these programs.

3. **Determine whether there are sufficient data for a regression calculation.**
   Your first decision is whether you must use choice C or whether you can use either choice A or B. Until you have at least three or more data points that demonstrate a reasonable relationship between size and development hours, you should not use the regression method. Even when you appear to have enough data, some of the points may be *outliers* that should be discarded. An outlier is a data point at which something unusual occurred. If all that happened is that you made a much larger than normal estimating error, you cannot discard that point. However, if something unusual happened, you should discard the point because it can cause the regression method to produce nonsensical results. Outliers are discussed further in Section A1.10 in Appendix A. The question now is, after you remove the outliers, do you have at least three points that show reasonable correlation between program size and development hours? Again, this means that $r^2 \geq 0.5$.

4. **Calculate your historical productivity in LOC per hour.**
   If your answer to step 3 is no, you must take choice C. At this point, your estimating process becomes a simple productivity extrapolation. You calculate the total new and changed LOC you produced for the programs in your database and the total hours you required. You then divide this total LOC by the total hours to get your average productivity in new and changed LOC per hour. For example, assume you had written two programs of 172 and 242 new and changed LOC and took 7.6 and 15.3 hours respectively to develop them. You would have produced a total of 414 LOC in 22.9 hours for a total rate of 18.07 LOC per hour.

5. Calculate the time required for the new program.
Continuing with choice C, estimate the time for the new program by dividing your estimated new and changed LOC size estimate by your historical productivity rate to give your new estimated time. For example, if your new size estimate is 156 LOC, the productivity rate of 18.07 would indicate a likely total development time of 8.63 hours.

6. Calculate the shortest and longest likely times.
Again, in choice C, your limited data will not provide reliable prediction intervals but you can get an idea of the likely range of your development times. You do this by calculating your shortest likely time using the best productivity you have historically achieved and your longest time by using your lowest historical productivity. In the example, your highest historical productivity was for 172 LOC in 7.6 hours, or 22.63 LOC per hour. This would suggest a shortest time of 6.9 hours for developing 156 LOC. Your lowest historical productivity was for 242 LOC in 15.3 hours, or 15.82 LOC per hour. This would suggest a longest development time of 9.86 hours for developing 156 LOC.

7. Determine the time estimate and range.
Your answer for choice C is thus 8.6 hours with a range of from 6.9 to 9.9 hours.

8. Determine whether there are sufficient estimate data available for a regression calculation.
If the answer to step 3 was yes, you now need to decide between choices A and B. Do you base this analysis on actual object LOC or on estimated object LOC? Do you have at least three cases of programs for which you have estimates for the object LOC and data for the actual development hours? Again, if you do, these data must correlate with at least $r^2 \geq 0.5$.

9. Do the regression calculation for total actual LOC and actual hours.
If the answer to step 8 is no, you must take estimate choice B and do the calculations based on the actual hours and the actual object LOC for the programs you have developed. Even though these programs may have been planned with different methods, you are not using the planning data, so that does not matter. Here, if you had the data shown in Table 6.2, you have estimated object LOC for only two programs. You thus must use the actual object LOC and actual hours data for the regression calculations.

10. Calculate the time required to develop the new program.
Continuing with choice B, use the regression method to calculate the estimated development time for the new program, using the data for actual object LOC and total development hours. That is, in Table 6.2, you would use the actual object LOC and the actual total hours for programs 1 through 5 to calculate the β_0 and β_1 parameters.

TABLE 6.2   EXAMPLE HISTORICAL DATA

Program Number	Estimated Object LOC	Actual Object LOC	Actual Total Hours
1		83	11.2
2		116	9.3
3		186	21.6
4	97	81	6.9
5	81	114	10.2
Totals	178	580	59.2

11. Calculate the prediction interval for this estimate.

To complete choice B, use the prediction interval calculation method described in Chapter 5 and in Section A8 of Appendix A to calculate the upper prediction interval (UPI) and lower prediction interval (LPI) for this estimate. Use the same data you used in the regression calculations in step 10 to make these calculations. Note that the prediction interval will not be a useful indicator of your estimating accuracy, since it does not account for your historical size estimating errors. Once you have enough data to use estimated object LOC, the prediction interval will be more useful.

12. Determine the time estimate and range.

The final estimate for choice B is the time calculated in step 10 and the prediction interval calculated in step 11.

13. Do the regression calculation on estimated LOC to development hours.

If the answer to step 8 was yes, you have enough historical data to use choice A. Here, you make your estimate based on actual hours and estimated object LOC. You now determine the β_0 and β_1 parameters from the data on the estimated object LOC and the actual development hours.

14. Calculate the time required for the new program.

Continuing with choice A, use the regression parameters to calculate the estimated development time for the new program.

15. Calculate the prediction interval for this estimate.

To complete choice A, calculate the prediction interval as described in Section A8 of Appendix A, using the same data used in step 13 to calculate the β parameters. Notice that this interval should be wider than that obtained in step 11 because your calculations now consider size estimating errors as well as productivity variations.

16. Determine the time estimate and range.

The answer for choice C is the time calculated in step 14 and the prediction interval calculated in step 15.

A Resource Calculation Example. The following example performs these calculations using the data in Table 6.2. The following steps are numbered as shown in Fig. 6.2.

1. You have an estimate of 114 object LOC for a new program.

2. You get the data shown in Table 6.2.

3. Because you have five historical cases, you have enough data to do the regression calculations.

8. You have estimated data for only two of the programs, so you check the correlation between actual object LOC and hours and find that $r^2 = 0.83$. You can then do the regression calculations for the actual object LOC and actual hours data.

9. Using the values shown in Table 6.3, calculate the regression parameters and hours as follows:

$$\beta_1 = \frac{\sum_{i=1}^{5} LOC_i * Hours_i - 5 * LOC_{avg} * Hours_{avg}}{\sum_{i=1}^{5} LOC_i^2 - 5 * LOC_{avg}^2} =$$

$$\frac{7747.7 - 5*116*11.84}{74498 - 5*116^2} = 0.121987$$

$$\beta_0 = Hours_{avg} - \beta_1 * LOC_{avg} = 11.84 - 0.121987 * 116 = -2.31046$$

TABLE 6.3 EXAMPLE REGRESSION CALCULATIONS

Program Number	Actual Object LOC	Actual Hours	LOC^2	LOC * Hours
1	83	11.2	6,889	929.6
2	116	9.3	13,456	1,078.8
3	186	21.6	34,596	4,017.6
4	81	6.9	6,561	558.9
5	114	10.2	12,996	1,162.8
Totals	580	59.2	74,498	7,747.7
Averages	116	11.84		

10. Using the β parameters calculated in step 9 and the total estimated 114 object LOC from step 1, calculate the estimated development time for the new program as follows:

    $$Time_t = \beta_0 + \beta_1 * Size_k = -2.31046 + 114*0.121987 = 11.596$$

11. Using the values in Table 6.4, calculate the 70 percent prediction interval as follows:

    $$\sigma^2 = \left(\frac{1}{n-2}\right) \sum_{i=1}^{5} (Hours_i - \beta_0 - \beta_1 * LOC_i)^2 = (1/3)*21.804 = 7.268$$

    $$\sigma = \sqrt{\sigma^2} = \sqrt{7.268} = 2.696$$

    $$t = 1.25$$

    You find the double-sided value of t for a 70 percent prediction interval by looking in Table A2 under 0.85 and 3 ($n - 2$) degrees of freedom. This gives a t value of 1.25.

    $$Range = t(\alpha/2, n-2)*\sigma* \sqrt{1 + \frac{1}{n} + \frac{(LOC_k - LOC_{avg})^2}{\sum_{i=1}^{n}(LOC_i - LOC_{avg})^2}} =$$

    $$1.25*2.696* \sqrt{1.2 + \frac{(114 - 116)^2}{7218}} = 3.69$$

    $$UPI = Hours_t + Range = 11.596 + 3.69 = 15.29$$

    $$LPI = Hours_t - Range = 11.596 - 3.69 = 7.90$$

TABLE 6.4   EXAMPLE PREDICTION INTERVAL CALCULATIONS

Program Number	LOC	Hours	$(Hours_i - \beta_0 - \beta_1 LOC_i)^2$	$(LOC_i - LOC_{avg})^2$
1	83	11.2	11.462	1,089
2	116	9.3	6.452	0
3	186	21.6	1.491	4,900
4	81	6.9	0.450	1,225
5	114	10.2	1.949	4
Totals	580	59.2	21.804	7,218

12. Your time estimate is thus 11.6 hours with a 70 percent prediction interval of 7.9 to 15.3 hours. Note, however, that in these calculations you used the actual object LOC historical data and you have estimated object LOC only for the new program. These calculations thus assume that your object LOC estimate is exactly correct. Because your size estimates will likely have some errors, you must recognize that your actual 70 percent range of prediction error will be much larger than the values you have calculated.

6.3   Estimating Task Time

Although most of the assignments in this book deal with planning and developing small programs, two require you to plan and produce reports. As you use your PSP in later software engineering courses or on other projects, you will also find many situations in which PSP methods can help you to plan, manage, and track many different kinds of work. In estimating the time you will need to do these tasks, refer to the decision tree in Fig. 6.3 that walks you through the logic of selecting an estimating method. When you are faced with a new task for which you do not have an established planning process, these are the decisions and actions you should take in deciding how to proceed. The following steps are numbered as shown in Fig. 6.3.

1. Ensure you have a clear statement of the requirements for the task to be done.

2. Do you have a defined process for the task? It is difficult to make an intelligent plan for an ill-defined task. It is also difficult to measure the work, track progress, or judge the quality of the result.

3. If your answer to step 2 is no, you should produce a simple process definition. This definition need not be very complex, but it must include planning and postmortem steps. It should also divide the work into elements that are between about 10 percent and 25 percent of the total job. With more experience and some historical data, you can then refine the process further.

4. Do you have defined process measures? You need measures both to plan your work and to record your results so that you can make better plans in the future.

5. If your answer to step 4 is no, you need to define at least size and resource measures. For PSP planning purposes, your interest is in the time taken by process step and the size of the product produced.

6. Do you have historical data? You need some quantitative historical basis for judging the size of the job and the effort required.

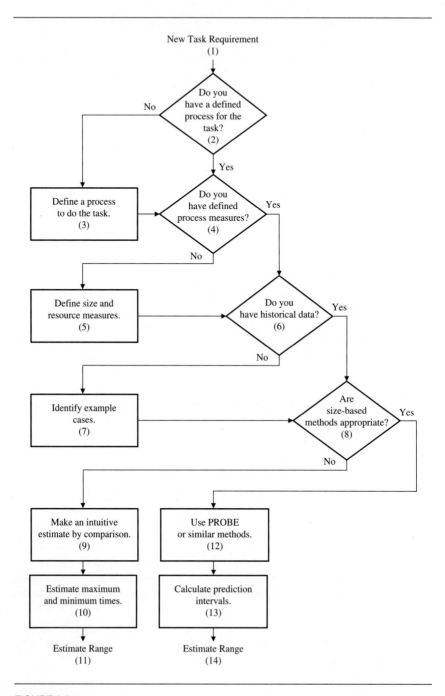

FIGURE 6.3
Estimating New Tasks

7. Even if your answer to step 6 is no, you can usually identify some similar jobs and judge how long they took. If you have never measured any of your previous work, your estimates for new work could be off by as much as six or more times. When they are in error by this much, they are also generally too low. That is why you should search for any relevant examples and try to judge the time they took. This will help you to reduce your initial planning errors.

8. Are sized-based resource estimates appropriate? You need to satisfy the following conditions before you can make size-based resource estimates:

   □ You must have an explicit size measure.

   □ This measure must have a correlation with resources with an $r^2 \geq 0.5$.

   □ You must have data on at least one similar historical case.

   □ You must know how to estimate size.

   If you can satisfy all these conditions, then you should use the size-based estimating methods discussed in Section 6.2. If you have enough data, you should use the PROBE method.

9. If the answer to step 8 is no, you must make an intuitive estimate based on comparison with other work. If you cannot use size-based estimating, you should consider the various alternate methods discussed in Chapter 5 and see if similar techniques will work for you. In many cases, the function-point method could be appropriate, or you might find the Wideband-Delphi, fuzzy-logic, or standard-component methods suitable. These are discussed in Chapter 5. In any event, you must use some technique to relate your available historical data to the new job and to judge the amount of time you will likely take.

10. Estimate the maximum and minimum times the job will likely require. This is an important step. Often you will find that your estimate is unconsciously the minimum time you feel the job could possibly take. By carefully assessing the job and estimating the time consequences of some of the things that could go wrong, you will end up with a more realistic plan that falls somewhere between the maximum and minimum times. If it is near either extreme, reexamine your estimate to ensure you are not being overly optimistic or overly pessimistic.

11. Determine the likely estimate range. Your estimate is the number produced in step 9 and the range is from the minimum to the maximum times determined in step 10.

12., 13., 14. Follow the PROBE method to produce the estimate and the prediction interval.

6.4   Combining Multiple Estimates

Suppose you are planning a job that has several parts. You are to develop some code, write a report, and produce a database. From the discussion in Sections 6.2 and 6.3, you know how to estimate each of these parts separately, but you need some way to combine them.

Assume you start with the separate estimates for the parts of this job as shown in Table 6.5. It is obvious that your total estimate should be 134.0 hours. It is not as clear, however, how to pick the prediction interval. You could, of course, just add up the separate prediction intervals for each part. For the upper limit, for example, this would give 195.2 hours. This number represents the case in which everything goes wrong simultaneously. That is, to get this limit, every part of the job would have to come in at its upper prediction limit simultaneously. While such extremes are possible, you are most interested in a 70 percent or 90 percent prediction interval and not in worst or best-case estimates.

These prediction intervals are combined as shown in Table 6.6. If you assume the individual tasks have 70 percent prediction intervals, the intervals represent about one standard deviation above and below the mean. In this case, because the estimate is not midway between the upper and lower limits, calculate the standard deviation as half the difference between the upper and lower prediction limits. For the develop program item, for example, this is $(98.3 - 49.2)/2 = 24.55$ hours.

In combining prediction intervals, you don't just add the standard deviations; you add the variances. Because the variance is the square of the standard deviation, the sum of the variances is 1107.69. The square root of this is 32.28, the standard deviation of the combined estimate. To get the UPI and LPI for the estimate, add and subtract this standard deviation from the mean between the upper and lower prediction limits shown in Table 6.5, or $(89.8 + 195.2)/2 =$

TABLE 6.5   EXAMPLE MULTI-PART ESTIMATE

Task	Estimated Hours	Lower Prediction Interval: LPI	Upper Prediction Interval: UPI	Prediction Interval—Mean: (UPI + LPI)/2
Develop program	63.8	49.2	98.3	73.8
Write report	28.3	21.2	34.6	27.9
Produce database	41.9	19.4	62.3	40.8
Totals	134.0	89.8	195.2	142.5

TABLE 6.6   EXAMPLE MULTI-PART ESTIMATE (continued)

Task	Estimated Hours	Lower Prediction Interval: LPI	Upper Prediction Interval: UPI	Standard Deviation: (UPI − LPI)/2	Variance: (UPI − LPI)^2/4
Develop program	63.8	49.2	98.3	24.55	602.70
Write report	28.3	21.2	34.6	6.70	44.89
Produce database	41.9	19.4	62.3	21.45	460.10
Total estimate	134.0	89.8	195.2	32.28	1107.69
Range		110.22	174.78		

142.5. You do this because the standard deviation is around the mean and not around whatever your estimate turns out to be. Thus the upper prediction interval is 142.5 + 32.28 = 174.78 and the lower prediction interval is 142.5 − 32.28 = 110.22.

Notice that the prediction interval range for the total job is much narrower than the sum of the ranges of the individual estimates. By just adding the limits, you have a spread of over 100 hours. By combining them properly, you get a prediction interval of only about 65 hours.

THE PREDICTION INTERVAL FOR COMBINED RESOURCE ESTIMATES

When you make several separate estimates for each part of a larger project, you end up with a set of hourly estimates, each of which has its own prediction interval. You may have made these estimates with the linear regression method discussed in Chapter 5, or you may have used some other method. If you have calculated a prediction interval for each case and if all these intervals were generated in the same way, you can treat them as standard deviations and combine them. Assuming your various estimates are a, b, c, and d, their respective hourly estimates are H_a, H_b, H_c, and H_d, and their standard deviations are σ_a, σ_b, σ_c, and σ_d, you calculate the total hourly estimate, H_t, and total standard deviation, σ_t, as follows:

$$H_t = H_a + H_b + H_c + H_d \tag{6.1}$$

$$\sigma_t = \sqrt{\sigma_a^2 + \sigma_b^2 + \sigma_c^2 + \sigma_d^2} \tag{6.2}$$

The upper and lower prediction intervals for this estimate are then

$$
\begin{aligned}
H_{upper} &= H_t + \sigma_t, \\
H_{lower} &= H_t - \sigma_t.
\end{aligned}
\tag{6.3}
$$

Note that this formula assumes these separate estimates are statistically independent. This assumption requires that the estimates were obtained independently and used separate databases for calculating the regression parameters. The variances of the individual estimates could be added as just described and the square root taken to yield the standard deviation. A 68 percent (or about 70 percent) prediction interval is then obtained by taking the estimate plus or minus one standard deviation. You would get 95 percent prediction intervals by using plus or minus two standard deviations.

Note also that the estimate should not have some common bias. A common bias could occur, for example, if the estimators all worked on a single project or for a common manager. Or they might all be equally motivated to win a competitive order or they could have a common misapprehension about a design approach. In any of these cases, you should use the prediction intervals with caution.

COMBINING PROBE-GENERATED PREDICTION INTERVALS

When the estimates and prediction intervals for several component programs have all been generated from a common set of data, the combined prediction interval calculation is a bit more complex. This could be the case, for example, if you used the methods described in Section 6.2 and the PROBE method described in Chapter 5 for all the programs. Here, you would get the same β_0 and β_1 regression parameters for each of the separate component estimates. You would still get the total estimate by adding the individual estimates, but you would use a different prediction interval calculation. In the case of estimating hours from LOC, you would start with n size values in your original database, which are called $Size_1$, $Size_2, \ldots, Size_n$. These would have an average value of $Size_{avg}$. You would also start with a total size estimate, $Size_k$, for the new program. $Size_k$ is the sum of each of the separate component size estimates. You now use these terms in the range calculation as follows:

$$
Range = t(\alpha/2, n - 2)\sigma\sqrt{1 + \frac{1}{n} + \frac{\left(Size_k - Size_{avg}\right)^2}{\sum_{i=1}^{n}\left(Size_i - Size_{avg}\right)^2}},
\tag{6.4}
$$

where n is the number of cases in your historical dataset, $Size_{avg}$ is the average of the LOC in this dataset, $Size_i$ represents each LOC value in this dataset, and $Size_k$ is the total estimated size of the new program. The value of the t distribution is found in Table A2. Note that the ½ indicates t must be the double-sided value of the t distribution. The value of σ, the standard deviation, is obtained by taking the square root of the variance, σ^2. The variance is calculated in the same way as in the example in Section 6.2:

$$\sigma^2 = \frac{1}{n-2} \sum_{i=1}^{n} (Hours_i - \beta_0 - Size_i\beta_1)^2, \tag{6.5}$$

where n is the number of items in your historical dataset and the β_0 and β_1 are the regression parameters.

An Example of Combining Multiple Estimates.   Suppose you have the data shown in Table 6.7. Also assume you estimate a new project in three parts as taking 144, 193, and 318 object LOC, respectively. From this dataset, you calculate the values of β_0 as -5.950 and β_1 as 0.1482, using the following formulas:

$$\beta_1 = \frac{\sum_{i=1}^{n} Size_i\, Hours_i - nSize_{avg}Hours_{avg}}{\sum_{i=1}^{n} Size_i^2 - nSize_{avg}^2} =$$

$$\frac{33,116.5 - 8*170.88*19.38}{278,327 - 8*170.88^2} = 0.1482$$

$$\beta_0 = Hours_{avg} - \beta_1 Size_{avg} = 19.38 - 0.1482*170.88 = -5.95$$

Next, calculate the hours for the total project, as follows:

$$Size_k = 144 + 193 + 318 = 655$$
$$Hours_t = \beta_0 + Size_k\beta_1 = -5.95 + 0.1482*655 = 91.13$$

The value of σ is calculated, as follows:

$$\sigma^2 = \frac{1}{n-2} \sum_{i=1}^{n} (Hours_i - \beta_0 - Size_i\beta_1)^2 = 194.24/6 = 32.37$$

and

$$\sigma = \sqrt{32.37} = 5.69.$$

To calculate the 70 percent prediction interval for this estimate, look up the two-sided t value in a table for the t distribution for 6 degrees of freedom and a p value of 0.85. From Table A2, this t value is 1.134. Next, using the values from Table 6.7, you get the range as follows:

$$Range = t(\alpha/2, n-2)\sigma\sqrt{1 + \frac{1}{n} + \frac{\left(Size_k - Size_{avg}\right)^2}{\sum_{i=1}^{n}\left(Size_i - Size_{avg}\right)^2}}$$

$$= 1.134*5.69*\sqrt{1 + \frac{1}{8} + \frac{\left(655 - 170.88\right)^2}{44740.88}} = 16.27$$

Using the 91.13 value for $Hours_t$ calculated earlier, the 70 percent prediction interval for this estimate is the following:

UPI = $Hours_t$ + Range = 91.13 + 16.27 = 107.40
LPI = $Hours_t$ − Range = 91.13 − 16.27 = 74.86

6.5 Using Multiple Regression

Suppose you are working on a program and estimate that it will have about 650 LOC of new code. You also plan to reuse about 3000 LOC of unmodified code from a previous program and to modify an additional 155 LOC from this same program. You have the historical data shown in Table 6.8. Unfortunately, this is all the detail you have. Thus you have no way to figure out how much time you spent developing new code, working on reusing the previous product, or making the modifications.

You can overcome this lack of data in one way by using the statistical technique called *multiple regression*, which enables you to estimate the relative contributions of the work on the new, reused, and modified code in the total development hours. This method is likely not as accurate as detailed data on the development time for each of these product categories; however, generally it would be impractical to separately track your development time for each. Thus, if you want to consider the relative contributions of these various types of work, you will have to use multiple regression.

THE MULTIPLE REGRESSION PARAMETERS

The regression equation with three variables and four β parameters is

$$Hours_t = \beta_0 + New_k\beta_1 + Reuse_k\beta_2 + Modify_k\beta_3. \tag{6.6}$$

Here, the t subscript indicates the total estimate and the k subscript indicates the newly estimated values. The estimates for the β parameters are obtained by

TABLE 6.7   EXAMPLE OF COMBINING MULTIPLE ESTIMATES

	Object LOC $Size_i$	Hours $Hours_i$	$(Size_i - Size_{avg})^2$	$Size_i^2$	$Size_i Hours_i$	$(Hours_i - B_0 - B_1 Size_i)^2$
1	123	14.2	2,292.02	15,129	1,746.6	3.69
2	86	9.6	7,203.77	7,396	825.6	7.86
3	321	46.1	22,537.52	103,041	14,798.1	20.03
4	214	31.4	1,859.77	45,796	6,719.6	31.74
5	186	13.8	228.77	34,596	2,566.8	61.10
6	98	11.3	5,310.77	9,604	1,107.4	7.43
7	118	9.4	2,795.77	13,924	1,109.2	4.57
8	221	19.2	2,512.52	48,841	4,243.2	57.81
Average	170.88	19.38				
Sum	1367	155	44,740.88	278,327	33,116.5	194.24

solving the simultaneous equations in Eq. 6.7. Here n is the number of cases in your database and i is an index that is summed from 1 to n. These equations are solved using standard algebraic techniques for simultaneous linear equations either by successive variable elimination or with determinants. Section A11 in Appendix A describes Gauss's method of solving such equations. This method has the advantage of providing an orderly procedure that you can use to write a simple program to solve the equations.

$$\beta_0 n + \beta_1 \sum New_i + \beta_2 \sum Reuse_i + \beta_3 \sum Modify_i = \sum Hours_i$$

$$\beta_0 \sum New_i + \beta_1 \sum New_i^2 + \beta_2 \sum New_i Reuse_i + \beta_3 \sum New_i Modify_i$$
$$= \sum New_i Hours_i$$

$$\beta_0 \sum Reuse_i + \beta_1 \sum New_i Reuse_i + \beta_2 \sum Reuse_i^2 + \beta_3 \sum Reuse_i Modify_i$$
$$= \sum Reuse_i Hours_i$$

$$\beta_0 \sum Modify_i + \beta_1 \sum New_i Modify_i + \beta_2 \sum Reuse_i Modify_i$$
$$+ \beta_3 \sum Modify_i^2 = \sum Modify_i Hours_i \tag{6.7}$$

A Multiple Regression Example.   To solve for the β parameters in Eq. (6.7), first evaluate the variable terms. For the example in Table 6.8, you do this by calculating the products of the various data columns and totaling them as shown in Table 6.9. The simultaneous linear equations with their actual numerical values are then as follows:

$$6\beta_0 + 4,863\beta_1 + 8,761\beta_2 + 654\beta_3 = 714$$
$$4,863\beta_0 + 4,521,899\beta_1 + 8,519,938\beta_2 + 620,707\beta_3 = 667,832$$
$$8,761\beta_0 + 8,519,938\beta_1 + 21,022,091\beta_2 + 905,925\beta_3 = 1,265,493$$
$$654\beta_0 + 620,707\beta_1 + 905,925\beta_2 + 137,902\beta_3 = 100,583$$

TABLE 6.8   MULTIPLE REGRESSION EXAMPLE DATA

Program Number	New LOC	Reuse LOC	Modified LOC	Hours
1	1,142	1,060	325	201
2	863	995	98	98
3	1,065	3,205	23	162
4	554	120	0	54
5	983	2,896	120	138
6	256	485	88	61
Totals	4,863	8,761	654	714
Averages	810.5	1460.17	109	119
Estimate	650	3,000	155	140.90

These equations are solved using standard algebraic methods. This example is worked out using Gauss's method, given in Appendix A. The resulting values for the β parameters are the solutions of these equations as follows:

$\beta_0 = 6.701$
$\beta_1 = 0.0784$
$\beta_2 = 0.0150$
$\beta_3 = 0.2461$

By using these values in the original equation, you can calculate the estimated value for the new project,140.902 hours, as follows:

Hours $= 6.71 + 0.0784*650 + 0.0150*3000 + 0.2461*155 = 140.902$

You can interpret the β parameters as follows:

☐ Every project has a constant overhead of 6.7 hours.

☐ It takes 0.0784 hours to develop a new LOC, which is 12.76 LOC per hour.

TABLE 6.9   MULTIPLE REGRESSION EXAMPLE CALCULATIONS

Program Number	New²	New * Reuse	New * Modified	New * Hours
1	1,304,164	1,210,520	371,150	229,542
2	744,769	858,685	84,574	84,574
3	1,134,225	3,413,325	24,495	172,530
4	306,916	66,480	0	29,916
5	966,289	2,846,768	117,960	135,654
6	65,536	124,160	22,528	15,616
Totals	4,521,899	8,519,938	620,707	667,832

Program Number	Reuse²	Reuse * Modified	Reuse * Hours	Modified²	Modified * Hours
1	1,123,600	344,500	213,060	105,625	65,325
2	990,025	97,510	97,510	9,604	9,604
3	10,272,025	73,715	519,210	529	3,726
4	14,400	0	6,480	0	0
5	8,386,816	347,520	399,648	14,400	16,560
6	235,225	42,680	29,585	7,744	5,368
Totals	21,022,091	905,925	1,265,493	137,902	100,583

- □ It takes 0.015 hours to reuse a line of previously developed LOC, or 66.48 LOC per hour.
- □ It takes 0.2461 hours to modify a LOC, or 4.06 LOC per hour.

While these numbers are hypothetical examples, in a real case you should examine these β parameters to see if they make sense. If they do not, you should read some of the cautions about the regression method in Appendix A and take some of the corrective actions suggested there.

MULTIPLE REGRESSION PREDICTION INTERVAL

The multiple regression prediction interval is calculated in much the same way as in the single regression case, but with a few more terms. First, calculate the estimate of the variance term as follows:

$$\sigma^2 = \left(\frac{1}{n-p} \right) \sum_{i=1}^{n} (Hours_i - \beta_0 - \beta_1 New_i - \beta_2 Reuse_i - \beta_3 Modify_i)^2 \quad (6.8)$$

This equation gives the mean square deviation of the linear regression line from the actual $Hours_i$ values. Clearly, a larger value of σ indicates a poorer linear regression fit to the actual data and thus a larger prediction interval.

Then calculate the interval value with the following equation:

$$Range = t(\alpha/2, n-p)\sigma \sqrt{1 + \frac{1}{n} + \frac{\left(New_k - New_{avg}\right)^2}{\sum\left(New_i - New_{avg}\right)^2} + \frac{\left(Reuse_k - Reuse_{avg}\right)^2}{\sum\left(Reuse_i - Reuse_{avg}\right)^2} + \frac{\left(Modify_k - Modify_{avg}\right)^2}{\sum\left(Modify_i - Modify_{avg}\right)^2}}$$

$$(6.9)$$

where the value of p is determined by the number of parameters that were estimated in the multiple regression calculations. For linear regression, you had two β parameters, so p was 2. That is why $n - 2$ was used when finding the value of the t distribution. Here, with four parameters being estimated by the βs, $p = 4$, so you would use $n - 4$. While this formula looks formidable, it is actually a simple extension of the formula for the single variable case given in Eq. (5.3) in Chapter 5.

Example of Calculating the Multiple Regression Prediction Interval.
Using the same example as in the previous section, calculate the multiple regression prediction interval from Eq. (6.9). The values of the terms needed for this calculation are given in Table 6.10. The variance value and standard deviation are then as follows:

$$\sigma^2 = 1{,}026.115/2 = 513.06$$

$$\sigma = \sqrt{\sigma^2} = \sqrt{513.06} = 22.65$$

TABLE 6.10   MULTIPLE REGRESSION PREDICTION INTERVAL CALCULATIONS

Program Number	$(Hours_i - \beta_0 - \beta_1 New_i - \beta_2 Reuse_i - \beta_3 Modify_i)^2$	$(New_i - New_{avg})^2$	$(Reuse_i - Reuse_{avg})^2$	$(Modified_i - Modified_{avg})^2$
1	79.077	109,892.25	160,133.4	46,656
2	237.495	2,756.25	216,380	121
3	322.995	64,770.25	3,044,443	7,396
4	4.322	65,792.25	1,796,047	11,881
5	354.253	29,765.25	2,061,617	121
6	27.973	307,470.25	950,950	441
Totals	1,026.115	580,437.50	8,229,571	66,616

$\beta_0 = 6.70134$
$\beta_1 = 0.07837$
$\beta_2 = 0.01504$
$\beta_3 = 0.24606$

Next, calculate the value of the t distribution term. Here, with four β parameters, look for the double-sided value of t in Table A2 under $n - 4$. In this case, $n = 6$, so look in the row for 2 degrees of freedom. For a 70 percent prediction interval, look in the table under the $p = 0.85$. The resulting value for t is 1.386.

Now, in evaluating the term under the square root, the k subscripted terms are the values for the desired estimate. That means that the three numerator terms are as follows:

$$\left(New_k - New_{avg}\right)^2 = (650 - 810.5)^2 = 25,760.25$$

$$\left(Reuse_k - Reuse_{avg}\right)^2 = (3,000 - 1,460.167)^2 = 2,371,085.668$$

$$\left(Modify_k - Modify_{avg}\right)^2 = (155 - 109)^2 = 2,116$$

The range calculation is then made as follows:

Range

$$= 1.386{*}22.65{*}\sqrt{1 + (1/6) + \frac{25,760.25}{580,437.5} + \frac{2,371,085.668}{8,229,571} + \frac{2,116}{66,616}}$$

$$= 38.84$$

The final answer is thus the original estimate of 140.902 hours plus or minus this range. The 70 percent prediction interval for this estimate is:

$$UPI = Hours_t + \text{Range} = 140.9 + 38.84 = 179.74,$$
$$LPI = Hours_t - \text{Range} = 140.9 - 38.84 = 102.06.$$

6.6   Schedule Estimating

Even with a good size estimate and reliable productivity data, the schedule is still a major unknown. And even with very good estimates, if you make incorrect assumptions about the amount of daily or weekly time you can spend on the job, your schedules can be seriously in error.

THE SCHEDULE ESTIMATING PROCESS

The schedule estimating process requires a detailed estimate of the hours needed to do the total job. You then allocate these hours to the various project phases. While you could use sophisticated statistical methods for doing this, it is generally adequate to use your historical time distribution on prior similar projects. An effective practice is to spread your total estimated hours across the planned project phases using the historical percentage of time spent on each phase. Then examine these times and adjust up or down to compensate for any special factors or issues you expect with this job.

Using this approach, you would now have an estimate for how many direct hours you expect to spend in each phase. While this is almost enough information to calculate the schedule, you still need to judge how much direct time you will spend each day or week. In most organizations, people spend their time on many indirect activities. They have vacations, are sick, participate on committees, go to classes, attend staff meetings, go to conferences, read mail, and so on. While there is convincing evidence that people are more productive if they spend a modest percentage of their time on activities that are not directly related to their projects, for planning purposes, you can consider only the direct hours. [Humphrey 87]

The need, therefore, is to account for this time difference. Unfortunately, organizational accounting systems are not designed to gather such data. Many people would resist reporting in the detail such a system would require, so you will have to build your own personal record. With the PSP, however, this turns out to be quite simple. When you keep track of your direct tasks, everything else is either overhead or time spent on other projects.

The importance of doing this can be seen by examining the available work hours in a year. A working year of 52 weeks of 40 hours each week has 2080 working hours. When you account for vacations, holidays, sickness, and personal time, the total working hours are cut by 10 to 15 percent. In addition, most engineers spend another 5 to 15 hours a week consulting on other projects, assisting some marketing effort, or performing any of the myriad other tasks they are typically asked to do. In a 40-hour work week, then, the actual working hours would be 20 to 30 hours. Many factors affect these hours and they vary substantially among individuals. When you take away all the "lost time," however, there will generally be a substantial reduction in available working time.

DIRECT PROJECT TIME

When writing some of the programs for the later chapters in this book, perform a simple test. Divide your week into what you consider to be your key activities. For the PSP work, use the project plans. For other activities, you might attend classes or meetings, assist coworkers else with their work, perform some special task, or have some personal commitments. For good measure, throw in some miscellaneous category like "other." The rule is that you must account for all your time. In an organization, you should also include categories for vacations, holidays, personal time, and sickness.

As you observe and track your time, you will learn a great deal about how you spend that time. The purpose of this exercise is twofold. First, you may find that you do some unnecessary things. By recognizing how much time you spend on casual interruptions and other diversions, you can see how to better manage your time. Second, you will better understand what percentage of your normal day is really available for working on what you had planned to do. Unless you are willing to gather these data, you will find it hard to make good schedules.

THE UNPLANNED TIME CUSHION

When you work in a software organization, you will find that the amount of time you can devote to direct work will fluctuate considerably. Except in times of crisis, people are generally able to spend between 50 and 75 percent of their time in direct work. If your data show you spend less than this, you are either trying to do too many things or you work in a nonproductive environment. If your time percentage is higher, you are either being wildly optimistic or you could be working at an unsustainably feverish pitch.

By using a realistic "unplanned time" cushion, you will be able to meet many of your schedules, even when your estimates are seriously off. When the crisis comes, you can defer all your other work and devote from 100 percent to 150 percent of your normal work time to the priority task. For a brief period, you won't answer your mail, go to meetings, do paperwork, or even take coffee breaks. You will do nothing but work. When you have estimated a 75 percent utilization factor and get into such a crunch, you can put in some extra hours and easily double your productive time. When you do this for any length of time, however, you will tire pretty quickly and the quality of your work will suffer.

In the long run, you will likely find that these periodic crunches help you to meet commitments, but they do not improve your overall productivity. While you will be very productive for a short period, your productivity will then drop sharply. Just as in the fable of the hare and the tortoise, over the long term, if you make steady and orderly progress, you will generally outperform those who work in feverish spurts. Try to make realistic plans that leave a reasonable allowance for the normal events of your daily life. This will then also provide an essential cushion for an occasional last-minute crunch.

MAKING THE SCHEDULE

The PSP schedule development procedure is shown in Fig. 6.4. While this complex a procedure is not needed for the small assignments in this text, it is a good idea to learn and practice these methods on any PSP project that you estimate will take several days' work. The following descriptions are keyed to the numbered items in Fig. 6.4:

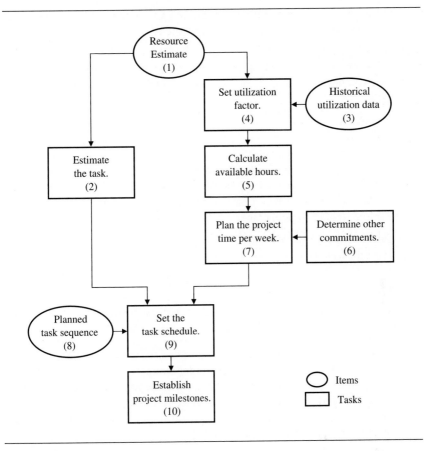

FIGURE 6.4
PSP Schedule Planning

1. **Resource Estimate**
   Start with a resource estimate. For the PSP, this is the total estimated hours for the project.

2. **Estimate the task hours.**
   For any but the smallest project, you need an estimate for the hours each project phase will likely require. That is, for a program development you would have the hours for the planning, implementation, and test phases. If you have made a detailed resource plan, you already know how many hours each task will take. If your estimated hours are for the total project, however, you will have to do a task breakdown. Here again, without data you are only guessing. Assuming these tasks are similar to your PSP projects, you

can use their percentage time distributions as a guide. Without such guidance, you will have to use your own judgment.

3. Historical utilization data

Based on your historical records, you will have a good idea of how much time you have been able to devote to planned projects on a daily or weekly basis.

4. Set utilization factor.

You need to estimate how much productive time you can expect to spend on this project. For the smallest PSP jobs, you will be most interested in how many productive hours you can spend per day. For larger projects, you would consider your weekly, and even monthly, rates. While the principles are the same regardless of time period used, the longer time periods tend to be more stable and predictable.

5. Calculate the available hours.

Enter the hours you expect to devote to project tasks for each calendar day or week. Unless you have a more detailed plan, you should calculate this as follows:

Available hours = Total working hours * Utilization factor

6. Determine your other commitments.

Before you can establish your planned hours for the new project, you need to project the hourly needs of your other commitments. For example, you may plan a vacation or expect to take a trip or have commitments for courses or other projects. Whatever the source, you need to think about all your commitments to determine when they will impact your schedule and how much time they will likely take.

7. Plan your available project time per week.

Take your available hours less the hours required by your other commitments and enter the net hours you can plan for this project each week. The schedule planning template in Table 6.11 is convenient for this purpose. Enter the Week No., the Date of the *Monday* starting that week, and the net Direct Hours you expect to have available that week. It is also helpful to keep a cumulative total of these hours. That is, for week 1, you may have 10 hours and for week 2, 8 hours. Your cumulative totals would then be 10 for week 1 and 18 for week 2. An example of a form with such data is shown in Table 6.12. The other columns on this form are explained later in the chapter as part of a complete example.

8. Plan the task sequence.

Before you can spread the required hours over the project tasks, you must account for the fact that some tasks have prerequisites. For both large and small projects, you thus need a time profile of the tasks. That is, what is the

TABLE 6.11   SCHEDULE PLANNING TEMPLATE

Student   _____   Date   _____

Project   _____   Instructor   _____

		Plan			Actual			
Week No.	Date (Monday)	Direct Hours	Cumulative Hours	Cumulative Planned Value	Direct Hours	Cumulative Hours	Cumulative Earned Value	Adjusted Earned Value

TABLE 6.12   SCHEDULE PLANNING—PRODUCTIVE TIME

Student   W.S. Humphrey   Date   3/12/93

Project   Book Manuscript Draft   Instructor

Week No.	Date (Monday)	Plan			Actual			Adjusted Earned Value
		Direct Hours	Cumulative Hours	Cumulative Planned Value	Direct Hours	Cumulative Hours	Cumulative Earned Value	
1	3/8	20	20					
2	3/15	20	40					
3	3/22	20	60					
4	3/29	10	70					
5	4/5	15	85					
6	4/12	15	100					
7	4/19	20	120					
8	4/26	15	135					
9	5/3	20	155					
10	5/10	15	170					
11	5/17	20	190					
12	5/24	20	210					
13	5/31	20	230					
14	6/7	20	250					
15	6/14	20	270					
16	6/21	20	290					
17	6/28	20	310					
18	7/5	20	330					
19	7/12	20	350					
20	7/19	20	370					
21	7/26	20	390					
22	8/2	20	410					
23	8/9	20	430					
24	8/16	20	450					

TABLE 6.12 (continued)

Week No.	Date (Monday)	Plan Direct Hours	Plan Cumulative Hours	Plan Cumulative Planned Value	Actual Direct Hours	Actual Cumulative Hours	Actual Cumulative Earned Value	Adjusted Earned Value
25	8/23	20	470					
26	8/30	20	490					
27	9/6	20	510					
28	9/13	20	530					
29	9/20	20	550					
30	9/27	20	570					
31	10/4	20	590					
32	10/11	0	590					
33	10/18	0	590					
34	10/25	10	600					
35	11/1	20	620					
36	11/8	20	640					
37	11/15	20	660					
38	11/22	20	680					
39	11/29	20	700					
40	12/6	20	720					
41	12/13	20	740					
42	12/20	20	760					
43	12/27	0	760					
44	1/3	10	770					
45	1/10	10	780					
46	1/17	10	790					
47	1/24	10	800					
48	1/31	10	810					

TABLE 6.13 TASK PLANNING TEMPLATE

Student _____   Date _____
Project _____   Instructor _____

Task		Plan					Actual	
#	Name	Hours	Planned Value	Cumulative Hours	Cumulative Planned Value	Date (Monday)	Date	Earned Value	Cumulative Earned Value

TABLE 6.13 (continued)

Task			Plan				Actual		
#	Name	Hours	Planned Value	Cumulative Hours	Cumulative Planned Value	Date (Monday)	Date	Earned Value	Cumulative Earned Value
Totals									

TABLE 6.14   TASK PLANNING EXAMPLE

Student ___W. S. Humphrey___ Date ___3/7/93___
Project ___Book Manuscript Draft___ Instructor _____

Task			Plan			Actual		
#	Name	Hours	Planned Value	Cumulative Hours	Cumulative Planned Value	Date (Monday)	Date	Earned Value	Cumulative Earned Value
1	Plan	15.10		15.10		3/8			
2	Preface	8.14		23.24		3/15			
3	Chapter 1 Draft	21.70		44.94		3/22			
4	Chapter 2 Draft	44.75		89.69		4/12			
5	Chapter 3 Draft	55.60		145.29		5/3			
6	Chapter 4 Draft	44.75		190.04		5/24			
7	Chapter 5 Draft	66.45		256.49		6/14			
8	Chapter 6 Draft	66.45		322.94		7/5			
9	Chapter 7 Draft	55.60		378.54		7/26			
10	Chapter 8 Draft	66.45		444.99		8/16			
11	Chapter 9 Draft	32.55		477.54		8/30			
12	Chapter 10 Draft	44.75		522.29		9/13			
13	Chapter 11 Draft	66.45		588.74		10/4			

TABLE 6.14 (continued)

Task			Plan				Actual		
#	Name	Hours	Planned Value	Cumulative Hours	Cumulative Planned Value	Date (Monday)	Date	Earned Value	Cumulative Earned Value
14	Chapter 12 Draft	66.45		655.19		11/15			
15	Chapter 13 Draft	55.60		710.79		12/6			
16	Chapter 14 Draft	44.75		755.54		12/20			
17	Chapter 15 Draft	44.75		800.29		1/31			
Totals		800.3							

order in which these tasks should start and end? There is also a critical path that determines the overall project schedule. For large projects, it is almost impossible to effectively plan the task sequence without using a critical path scheduling system like PERT. [Zells]

You must not view this initial task order as sacred, however, since projects change and new issues arise. To create this initial plan, just make some reasonable assumptions about task order. Once you do, you can calculate the dates when each task will start and end. A form like that shown in Table 6.13 can help. Five of the columns in the table are for the Plan data and three are for the Actual data. To complete this form, enter the task number and name and the planned hours for that task. Also enter the cumulative hours for these tasks in the Cumulative Hours column. Table 6.14 shows an example of these data using my plan for the manuscript draft for this book. The other columns are described later in the chapter as part of an example.

9. Set the task schedule.

With these data, you are now ready to set the schedule. Look at the first task to see how many cumulative hours it requires. In Table 6.14, this is 15.10 hours. From the schedule planning form in Table 6.12, you see that you will have spent more than 15 hours during week 1, starting March 8. You thus enter 3/8 for task 1 in the column headed plan - date. Note that your completion date could be at the end of this week, not on March 8. For task 2, the Preface, the cumulative hours were 23.24. These cumulative hours were exceeded in week 2, so the task 2 date is March 15. Continue this process until you have dates for all the tasks.

10. Establish project milestones.

Finally, identify those tasks that will be key indicators of your progress, then list their planned completion dates as project milestones and track progress against them.

You now have your plan. While these forms contain the typical information you will need for a small task, if you were developing a team or project schedule, you would also need data on key dependencies, task responsibilities, and principal checkpoints.

6.7 Earned Value Tracking

Earned value (EV) tracking is a way to evaluate project progress. [Boehm, Humphrey 89] It establishes a relative value for every task and credits that value when you complete the task. If you planned to do a project with many tasks and planned to complete them in a specific order, you would want a way to judge your progress even if you change this task order. If all tasks took an equal amount of time or if there were only a few of them, this might not be too difficult. With many tasks of differing sizes, however, this could become quite complex.

This status tracking problem is further complicated when you introduce new tasks or delete old ones. While this is a common problem with large software projects, it is even an important issue for the PSP because your plans generally change as you learn new things. You first make a plan when you know relatively little about the work to be done. As you do the work, you learn more about the tasks and often see better ways to do them.

Software engineering tasks can be as different as designing a module, writing a manual, or conducting a test, so you need a common measure you can use to judge progress. This is the purpose of the earned value system.

ESTABLISHING THE EARNED VALUE

The earned value system provides a common value scale for every task, regardless of the type of work involved. The total hours to do the entire project are estimated and every task is given an earned value based on its estimated percentage of this total. That is, for a project of 1000 hours, a 15-hour task would be given a planned value of 1.5. When this task is completed, it then contributes 1.5 percent to the cumulative earned value of the total project.

Note that partially completed tasks are not given partial credit. The earned value credit is given only when the task is completed. If the task is half done, it contributes nothing. If you have a task that is so big you want some intermediate measures, you have to break it into subtasks. In writing a larger program, some such tasks could be the following:

- □ The product specifications are documented, reviewed, and approved.
- □ The high-level design is completed and inspected, and corrections are made.
- □ Component A is designed, implemented, and tested as the first system baseline.
- □ Component B is designed, implemented, tested, and integrated to form the second system baseline.
- □ Component C is designed, implemented, tested, and integrated to form the third system baseline.
- □ The system is tested.
- □ The system is installed for customer trials.
- □ Acceptance tests are conducted.
- □ The customer accepts the system.

This fairly high-level project outline has many activities that could each be assigned a planned value. Depending on project size, you could also establish many similar steps within each of these phases. Requirements development, for example, has many potential subtasks, as do design, implementation, and test activities. The only requirement is that every task have explicit completion criteria. When these completion criteria are met, the earned value for that task is credited.

Depending on the project's size and its expected duration, you will want to plan to a level of detail that provides frequent status feedback. For example, for a 100-hour project that will stretch over two or three weeks, more than 10 or so checkpoints would probably be excessive. While you do want to see progress on a reasonably continuous basis, you don't want to track yourself to death. My rule of thumb is that regardless of project size, one checkpoint a week is not enough and one per day is too many. I prefer two to four a week.

An Earned Value Example.   Tables 6.15 and 6.16 show the actual task and schedule plans I used for writing the draft of this book. I had expected to spend a total of 800.29 hours to write this draft and, based on my planned available time, I expected to finish in late January 1994. As you can see, I had planned a vacation in October (weeks 32 and 33), during which I expected to accomplish nothing on the manuscript.

Based on my overall book plan, I calculated this draft would take 52.62 percent of the total book writing time of 1,520.89 hours. In Table 6.15, the planned completion dates for the chapters are listed, together with the planned value that each would contribute to the project.

The early progress on the manuscript is documented in Tables 6.17 and 6.18. Clearly, the book chapters were not written in the order originally planned. I wrote the Preface, then Chapter 11, then Chapter 6. Next were Chapters 1, 2, and 3, written in order. However, I finished Appendix A before Chapter 4.

There are several important messages here. First, even though this is my fourth book, my plan was not very accurate. I had originally planned to start the book with the material now in Chapter 13. As writing progressed, however, I realized that this was not the right way to start this book so I did a redesign. The earned value tracking system gave me credit for each chapter whenever I finished it, whether or not it was done in the original order.

Later, I also discovered that the statistical material covered in many of the chapters needed to be treated more completely in a separate appendix, a new Appendix A. Because the appendix was not in the original plan, the work on it would not earn any value unless I changed my plan. When I decided to plan for Appendix A, I judged it to require 41 draft pages, so I assigned it the same earned value as the 41-page Chapters (3, 7, and 13). Also, its total hours were not accounted for in the original resource and schedule plan. I could have reestimated and recalculated the entire plan, but that would have taken more time than I wanted to spend at that point. So I entered an adjusted earned value column on the right of Table 6.19.

The adjusted earned value was generated by reducing the total earned value of each of the other tasks to bring the total to 52.62 when Appendix A was included. Because the draft of a 41-page chapter was worth 3.66, all the cumulative planned value numbers were adjusted downward by this same ratio. The sum of the earned values for all the tasks up to manuscript completion was originally 52.62. Adding 3.66 to this gave 56.28. The ratio of 52.62/56.28 equals 0.93497. The actual earned value was then multiplied by this ratio to give the results in the Adjusted Earned Value column in Table 6.19. This new earned value track now reached 52.62 percent by the end of the manuscript draft and 100 percent at the end of the project with Appendix A included. Note that the addition of a new task actually reduced the earned value credit of all the other tasks. This adjustment was necessary so that the cumulative earned value at the end of the manuscript phase could be kept the same. Thus I could adjust my tracking system to allow for an additional task within the original schedule. Obviously, if I had changed the schedule, I would have had to make a new plan.

This approach provides an audit trail of your planning changes as well as a sound basis for judging progress against the original plan, even with several task adjustments. At manuscript completion time, when I produced a new plan, I incorporated Appendix A along with all the other changes. Even though I made further changes in the chapter order and contents when I produced the final manuscript, the earned value system allowed me to track my progress and readily project job completion.

Comments on the Earned Value Example.   This example identifies a couple of points that are worthy of comment. First, the checkpoint detail shown here is quite crude, with only a single checkpoint per manuscript chapter. Actually, this is a simplified picture because my writing process and plan have a total of 21 checkpoints for each chapter, with 10 of them for the time required to produce the draft manuscript. Hence I could track the project's progress approximately three times a week. This sense of steady progress is very helpful. Even when you are working productively, if your tracking system does not show progress, you are likely to get discouraged.

It is clear from Tables 6.18 and 6.19 and Fig. 6.5 that this plan was seriously off. At 14 weeks into the project, I had reached the 23-week earned value level, which meant I was 9 weeks ahead of schedule and would finish the manuscript four months ahead of plan. This of course assumed that I continued to work at the same rate and that nothing happened to change the tasks. To see how this could have happened, the Cumulative Hours column in Table 6.19 shows that I was spending 63 percent more hours than planned. That is, I had expected to expend 250 direct hours by week 14 but had actually expended 407.61. Also, in that 407 hours, I had done work that was projected to take 390 hours. Because the cumula-

TABLE 6.15 TASK PLANNING EXAMPLE

Student   W. S. Humphrey   Date   3/7/93
Project   Book Manuscript Draft   Instructor

	Task		Plan					Actual		
#	Name	Hours	Planned Value	Cumulative Hours	Cumulative Planned Value	Date (Monday)	Date	Earned Value	Cumulative Earned Value
1	Plan	15.10	.99	15.10	.99	3/8			
2	Preface	8.14	.53	23.24	1.52	3/15			
3	Chapter 1 Draft	21.70	1.43	44.94	2.95	3/22			
4	Chapter 2 Draft	44.75	2.94	89.69	5.89	4/12			
5	Chapter 3 Draft	55.60	3.66	145.29	9.55	5/3			
6	Chapter 4 Draft	44.75	2.94	190.04	12.49	5/24			
7	Chapter 5 Draft	66.45	4.37	256.49	16.86	6/14			
8	Chapter 6 Draft	66.45	4.37	322.94	21.23	7/5			
9	Chapter 7 Draft	55.60	3.66	378.54	24.89	7/26			
10	Chapter 8 Draft	66.45	4.37	444.99	29.26	8/16			
11	Chapter 9 Draft	32.55	2.14	477.54	31.40	8/30			
12	Chapter 10 Draft	44.75	2.94	522.29	34.34	9/13			
13	Chapter 11 Draft	66.45	4.37	588.74	38.71	10/4			

TABLE 6.15 (continued)

			Plan					Actual		
#	Name	Hours	Planned Value	Cumulative Hours	Cumulative Planned Value	Date (Monday)	Date	Earned Value	Cumulative Earned Value	
14	Chapter 12 Draft	66.45	4.37	655.19	43.08	11/15				
15	Chapter 13 Draft	55.60	3.66	710.79	46.74	12/6				
16	Chapter 14 Draft	44.75	2.94	755.54	49.68	12/20				
17	Chapter 15 Draft	44.75	2.94	800.29	52.62	1/31				
Totals		800.3	52.62							

TABLE 6.16   SCHEDULE PLANNING EXAMPLE

Student   W. S. Humphrey   Date   3/7/93

Project   Book Manuscript Draft   Instructor _____

		Plan			Actual			
Week No.	Date Monday	Direct Hours	Cumulative Hours	Cumulative Planned Value	Direct Hours	Cumulative Hours	Cumulative Earned Value	Adjusted Earned Value
1	3/8	20	20	.99				
2	3/15	20	40	1.52				
3	3/22	20	60	2.95				
4	3/29	10	70	2.95				
5	4/5	15	85	2.95				
6	4/12	15	100	5.89				
7	4/19	20	120	5.89				
8	4/26	15	135	5.89				
9	5/3	20	155	9.55				
10	5/10	15	170	9.55				
11	5/17	20	190	9.55				
12	5/24	20	210	12.49				
13	5/31	20	230	12.49				
14	6/7	20	250	12.49				
15	6/14	20	270	16.86				
16	6/21	20	290	16.86				
17	6/28	20	310	16.86				
18	7/5	20	330	21.23				
19	7/12	20	350	21.23				
20	7/19	20	370	21.23				
21	7/26	20	390	24.89				
22	8/2	20	410	24.89				
23	8/9	20	430	24.89				
24	8/16	20	450	29.26				

TABLE 6.16   (continued)

Week No.	Date Monday	Plan			Actual			Adjusted Earned Value
		Direct Hours	Cumulative Hours	Cumulative Planned Value	Direct Hours	Cumulative Hours	Cumulative Earned Value	
25	8/23	20	470	29.26				
26	8/30	20	490	31.40				
27	9/6	20	510	31.40				
28	9/13	20	530	34.34				
29	9/20	20	550	34.34				
30	9/27	20	570	34.34				
31	10/4	20	590	38.71				
32	10/11	0	590	38.71				
33	10/18	0	590	38.71				
34	10/25	10	600	38.71				
35	11/1	20	620	38.71				
36	11/8	20	640	38.71				
37	11/15	20	660	43.08				
38	11/22	20	680	43.08				
39	11/29	20	700	43.08				
40	12/6	20	720	46.74				
41	12/13	20	740	46.74				
42	12/20	20	760	49.68				
43	12/27	0	760	49.68				
44	1/3	10	770	49.68				
45	1/10	10	780	49.68				
46	1/17	10	790	49.68				
47	1/24	10	800	49.68				
48	1/31	10	810	52.62				

TABLE 6.17   SCHEDULE PLANNING EXAMPLE

Student	W. S. Humphrey	Date	6/16/93
Project	Book Manuscript Draft	Instructor	

		Plan			Actual			
Week No.	Date (Monday)	Direct Hours	Cumulative Hours	Cumulative Planned Value	Direct Hours	Cumulative Hours	Cumulative Earned Value	Adjusted Earned Value
1	3/8	20	20	.99	12.60	12.60	0	
2	3/15	20	40	1.52	33.47	46.07	.99	
3	3/22	20	60	2.95	25.70	71.77	1.52	
4	3/29	10	70	2.95	16.58	88.35	1.52	
5	4/5	15	85	2.95	22.05	110.40	5.89	
6	4/12	15	100	5.89	32.93	143.33	5.89	
7	4/19	20	120	5.89	32.08	175.42	10.26	
8	4/26	15	135	5.89	25.80	201.22	10.26	
9	5/3	20	155	9.55	34.58	235.80	10.26	
10	5/10	15	170	9.55	31.65	267.45	14.63	
11	5/17	20	190	9.55	29.65	297.10	14.63	
12	5/24	20	210	12.49	31.95	329.05	14.63	
13	5/31	20	230	12.49	46.68	375.73	21.95	
14	6/7	20	250	12.49	31.88	407.61	24.89	
15	6/14	20	270	16.86				
16	6/21	20	290	16.86				
17	6/28	20	310	16.86				
18	7/5	20	330	21.23				
19	7/12	20	350	21.23				
20	7/19	20	370	21.23				
21	7/26	20	390	24.89				
22	8/2	20	410	24.89				
23	8/9	20	430	24.89				
24	8/16	20	450	29.26				

TABLE 6.17   (continued)

Week No.	Date (Monday)	Plan			Actual			Adjusted Earned Value
		Direct Hours	Cumulative Hours	Cumulative Planned Value	Direct Hours	Cumulative Hours	Cumulative Earned Value	
25	8/23	20	470	29.26				
26	8/30	20	490	31.40				
27	9/6	20	510	31.40				
28	9/13	20	530	34.34				
29	9/20	20	550	34.34				
30	9/27	20	570	34.34				
31	10/4	20	590	38.71				
32	10/11	0	590	38.71				
33	10/18	0	590	38.71				
34	10/25	10	600	38.71				
35	11/1	20	620	38.71				
36	11/8	20	640	38.71				
37	11/15	20	660	43.08				
38	11/22	20	680	43.08				
39	11/29	20	700	43.08				
40	12/6	20	720	46.74				
41	12/13	20	740	46.74				
42	12/20	20	760	49.68				
43	12/27	0	760	49.68				
44	1/3	10	770	49.68				
45	1/10	10	780	49.68				
46	1/17	10	790	49.68				
47	1/24	10	800	49.68				
48	1/31	10	810	52.62				

TABLE 6.18 TASK PLANNING EXAMPLE

Student W. S. Humphrey   Date   6/16/93
Project Book Manuscript Draft   Instructor

#	Name	Plan					Actual		
		Hours	Planned Value	Cumulative Hours	Cumulative Planned Value	Date Monday	Date	Earned Value	Cumulative Earned Value
1	Plan	15.10	.99	15.10	.99	3/8	3/12	.99	.99
2	Preface	8.14	.53	23.24	1.52	3/15	3/19	.53	1.52
3	Chapter 1 Draft	21.70	1.43	44.94	2.95	3/22	5/4	1.43	11.69
4	Chapter 2 Draft	44.75	2.94	89.69	5.89	4/12	5/8	2.94	14.63
5	Chapter 3 Draft	55.60	3.66	145.29	9.55	5/3	5/28	3.66	18.29
6	Chapter 4 Draft	44.75	2.94	190.04	12.49	5/24	6/2	2.94	24.89
7	Chapter 5 Draft	66.45	4.37	256.49	16.86	6/14			
8	Chapter 6 Draft	66.45	4.37	322.94	21.23	7/5	4/17	4.37	10.26
9	Chapter 7 Draft	55.60	3.66	378.54	24.89	7/26			
10	Chapter 8 Draft	66.45	4.37	444.99	29.26	8/16			
11	Chapter 9 Draft	32.55	2.14	477.54	31.40	8/30			
12	Chapter 10 Draft	44.75	2.94	522.29	34.34	9/13			
13	Chapter 11 Draft	66.45	4.37	588.74	38.71	10/4	4/4	4.37	5.89

TABLE 6.18 (continued)

Task			Plan				Actual		
#	Name	Hours	Planned Value	Cumulative Hours	Cumulative Planned Value	Date (Monday)	Date	Earned Value	Cumulative Earned Value
14	Chapter 12 Draft	66.45	4.37	655.19	43.08	11/15			
15	Chapter 13 Draft	55.60	3.66	710.79	46.74	12/6			
16	Chapter 14 Draft	44.75	2.94	755.54	49.68	12/20			
17	Chapter 15 Draft	44.75	2.94	800.29	52.62	1/31			
18	Appendix A Draft	55.60	3.66	855.89	56.28		5/30	3.66	21.95
Totals		800.3	56.28						

TABLE 6.19   SCHEDULE ADJUSTMENT EXAMPLE

Student   W. S. Humphrey   Date   6/16/93

Project   Book Manuscript Draft   Instructor _____

		Plan			Actual			
Week No.	Date (Monday)	Direct Hours	Cumulative Hours	Cumulative Planned Value	Direct Hours	Cumulative Hours	Cumulative Earned Value	Adjusted Earned Value
1	3/8	20	20	.99	12.60	12.60	0	0
2	3/15	20	40	1.52	33.47	46.07	.99	.93
3	3/22	20	60	2.95	25.70	71.77	1.52	1.42
4	3/29	10	70	2.95	16.58	88.35	1.52	1.42
5	4/5	15	85	2.95	22.05	110.40	5.89	5.51
6	4/12	15	100	5.89	32.93	143.33	5.89	5.51
7	4/19	20	120	5.89	32.08	175.42	10.26	9.59
8	4/26	15	135	5.89	25.80	201.22	10.26	9.59
9	5/3	20	155	9.55	34.58	235.80	10.26	9.59
10	5/10	15	170	9.55	31.65	267.45	14.63	13.68
11	5/17	20	190	12.49	29.65	297.10	14.63	13.68
12	5/24	20	210	12.49	31.95	329.05	14.63	13.68
13	5/31	20	230	12.49	46.68	375.73	21.95	20.52
14	6/7	20	250	12.49	31.88	407.61	24.89	23.27
15	6/14	20	270	16.86				
16	6/21	20	290	16.86				
17	6/28	20	310	16.86				
18	7/5	20	330	21.23				
19	7/12	20	350	21.23				
20	7/19	20	370	21.23				
21	7/26	20	390	24.89				
22	8/2	20	410	24.89				
23	8/9	20	430	24.89				
24	8/16	20	450	29.26				

TABLE 6.19   (continued)

Week No.	Date Monday	Plan			Actual			Adjusted Earned Value
		Direct Hours	Cumulative Hours	Cumulative Planned Value	Direct Hours	Cumulative Hours	Cumulative Earned Value	
25	8/23	20	470	29.26				
26	8/30	20	490	31.40				
27	9/6	20	510	31.40				
28	9/13	20	530	34.34				
29	9/20	20	550	34.34				
30	9/27	20	570	34.34				
31	10/4	20	590	38.71				
32	10/11	0	590	38.71				
33	10/18	0	590	38.71				
34	10/25	10	600	38.71				
35	11/1	20	620	38.71				
36	11/8	20	640	38.71				
37	11/15	20	660	43.08				
38	11/22	20	680	43.08				
39	11/29	20	700	43.08				
40	12/6	20	720	46.74				
41	12/13	20	740	46.74				
42	12/20	20	760	49.68				
43	12/27	0	760	49.68				
44	1/3	10	770	49.68				
45	1/10	10	780	49.68				
46	1/17	10	790	49.68				
47	1/24	10	800	49.68				
48	1/31	10	810	52.62				

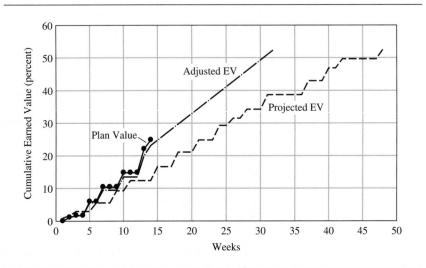

FIGURE 6.5
Earned Value Plan & Actual—Book Manuscript

tive manuscript pages at that point were running slightly under plan and my writing time per page was somewhat above plan, this result was not too surprising. You can see this in Table 6.19 by noting that the actual 407 hours had earned a value of 24.89. In the Cumulative Planned Value column, however, this 24.89 value should have been reached in 390 hours.

The big difference between planned and actual performance was that I spent many more than the planned 20 weekly hours. I had averaged 26 hours per week during manuscript preparation for my previous book, but I did not believe I could maintain that same rate on this new book. I thus used a more conservative 20 hours per week for this book. I actually averaged over 29 hours per week. This was not a planning system problem but an error in planning judgment.

A planning system based on historical data will project your future performance if everything continues to work as it has in the past. I had not expected to spend this many hours per week, but I was wrong. By using the earned value system, however, I recognized this planning error after only a few weeks. After the first month of a two-year project, I could see that I would finish the manuscript draft much earlier than originally planned. After the first 10 weeks, I had enough data to confidently commit to finishing the manuscript draft four months early, in September. That, in fact, is when I did finish.

It is interesting to note that I had the reverse problem with the final manuscript rewrite and cleanup. Because of this rapid early progress, I could offer the manuscript draft as a text for six university courses and could get a large number of technical reviews. This volume of feedback complicated the rewriting process, which took nearly two months longer than originally planned. Again, by using earned value tracking, I could quickly recognize and adjust for this eventuality. With all these changes, the final manuscript was sent to the publisher for final editing and publication in June 1994, exactly as planned a year and a half earlier.

ALERTING MANAGEMENT TO CHANGES

By carefully tracking your plans, you can better see where you are. This is particularly true on industrial projects. If you are ahead of plan and feel confident that your rate of progress will continue, you may want to provide early warning of the schedule improvement. Similarly, if you are falling behind, you can warn management and possibly even get some help. When you get behind, don't just hide your head; talk to your manager and see what can be done to hold the schedule. While Brooks's law says that adding staff late in a project will delay it, that is not always the case. [Brooks] When you see specific tasks that others could assist with, and if you can get capable support, added staffing can be a big help. Explain the alternatives to your management and help them to resolve the problems the schedule change creates. When you have such problems and particularly when you need help, use your managers. That is an important part of why they are there.

An example shows why doing this can often bring surprising results. Some years ago, before everybody had workstations, I was walking through the machine room of IBM's programming development laboratory late one night. I heard cursing in one corner and went over to check it out. This poor programmer had obviously been working for hours. He was late finishing test and was frustrated because the file subsystem hardware had just failed. He told me that this machine failed so often that he could not get his program tested. This was a new file system, and he was developing the file I/O software. The program was late, and he was under intense pressure to finish it.

The next morning, I called the vice president in charge of the file hardware and discovered that they had a warehouse full of these machines. They couldn't ship them until the program was ready. The VP committed to having four machines delivered to the machine room that morning with an engineer to keep them running. This move accelerated the testing, and the program was soon completed.

The point is, if you have a problem you can't handle, get help. Good schedule planning and tracking can often help you to do this in time to avoid broader business problems.

EARNED VALUE AND MOTIVATION

Maintaining your motivation can be a special problem with the earned value tracking system. Once you have established an earned value tracking system, you will tend to avoid starting tasks that do not earn credit. With this book, for example, I was reluctant to start work on Appendix A. When I finally decided that Appendix A was essential and adjusted my earned value plan to include it, I had no further problem. You should promptly assign earned value credit to essential new tasks. Conversely, if you find you have partially completed something that is no longer necessary, you should promptly drop it from your plan. Here you adjust the plan just as before except you remove the earned value for the entire deleted task and increase the value of everything else you have done. The work you have wasted, of course, earns no credit.

While using earned value tracking is very helpful, it also will affect your behavior. The key is to recognize that you are still in charge and that the earned value is only a measure. You can stay in control by modifying the total plan with new additions and deletions whenever you feel it necessary. Remember, however, that all additions dilute the value of everything you have already done. Because every project is unique, however, there are no general guidelines on when to change plans. You must use your best judgment. For small task changes, you can make plan adjustments as described in the earned value example. However, if you feel a task addition or deletion will significantly affect your schedule or impact your interactions with others, you should redo your entire plan.

6.8   Estimating Accuracy

Estimating is tricky business; it is part analysis, part design, part projection, and part calculated risk. Even when all your thoughtful analyses are absolutely correct, you may be unlucky. The best way to deal with this problem is to measure and track your planning process and then work to improve it. To do this, you need to establish measures. The most obvious measure is planning accuracy, that is, the degree to which the plan matches the actual result. By planning and tracking your work, you will gain insights that will help you to judge your planning performance. Do not get too concerned about your small task planning errors, however, as long as they are reasonably balanced around zero. That is, if you make about as many overestimates as underestimates, your plans will be reasonably balanced.

SOME EXAMPLE PLANNING DATA

The best way to determine plan quality is to wait until after the job is done, measure the time actually taken, and calculate the error between the actual and planned hours. Figures 6.6 and 6.7 show the planning performance of a 12-student class on the 10 A-series programs in this book. The amount of their planning error, in all cases, was calculated as follows:

Error% = 100*(Actual − Estimate)/Estimate

In Figs. 6.6 to 6.13, the class data are the combined estimates for the students, that is, the class estimate is the sum of the students' estimated hours. Similarly, the class actual time is the sum of the students' actual hours. As you can see in Figs. 6.6 and 6.7, the students' estimating performance fluctuated widely. Some underestimated and some overestimated the size and development times of every program. It is also clear that estimating accuracy is a highly individual trait. For example, Figs. 6.8 and 6.9 show that Student 11 fluctuated between over- and underestimates for both program size and development time. On balance, however, the student's size estimates were generally within plus or minus 20 percent. For both size and time estimates, however, there was overcompensation. This is a common problem that even experienced estimators frequently encounter. When they have overestimated one program, they tend to underestimate the next. The more they overcorrect, the wider the swings seem to get. While there is no uni-

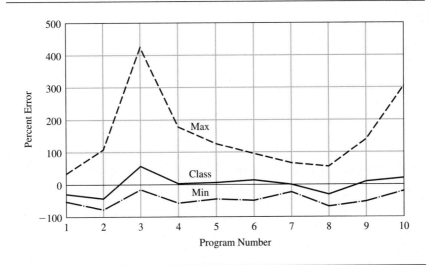

FIGURE 6.6
Students' Planning Errors—LOC

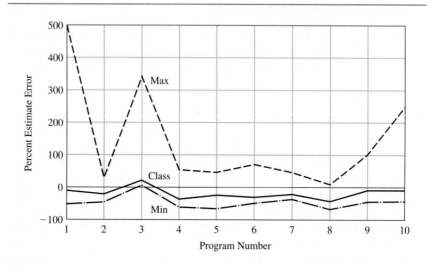

FIGURE 6.7
Class Time Estimating Accuracy

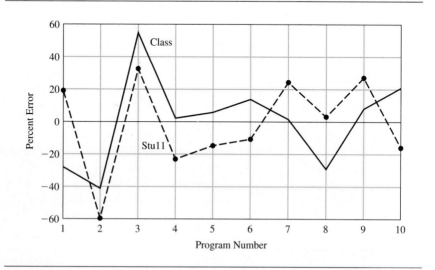

FIGURE 6.8
Size Estimating Error—Student 11

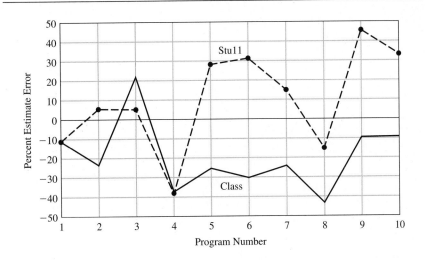

FIGURE 6.9
Time Estimating Accuracy—Student 11

versal answer to this, some approaches are discussed in the section on overcompensation later in this chapter.

An example of a student whose accuracy steadily improved is shown in Figs. 6.10 and 6.11. Here, both size and time estimates became quite accurate and reasonably balanced around zero. It is important to recognize, however, that all estimators will occasionally make a major error. Note from Figs. 6.12 and 6.13, Student 6 seemed to be achieving some stability with size and time estimates until the last program where the student made a serious size underestimate that resulted in a serious time underestimate. Estimators who have such problems must be careful to maintain a consistent estimating process and not overcompensate when planning the next few programs.

These data raise two questions: Is there a learning process and how long does it take? While these data do not prove that there is a learning process, the students assert there is. It is clear, however, that the amount of learning time required depends on the individual. While some students learn more quickly than others, the learning rate still appears to be quite slow and highly individualistic. It is also likely that even after you learn to make good estimates, you will occasionally make serious errors.

SMALL TASK ESTIMATING ERRORS

Estimates for small tasks generally have fairly large percentage errors. The reason is that most tasks are subject to considerable variation. Very few things, in

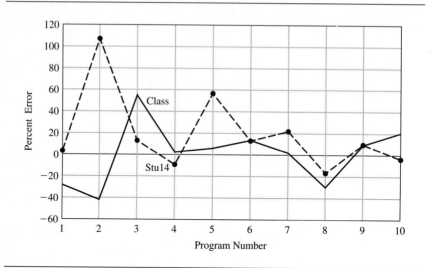

FIGURE 6.10
Size Estimating Error—Student 14

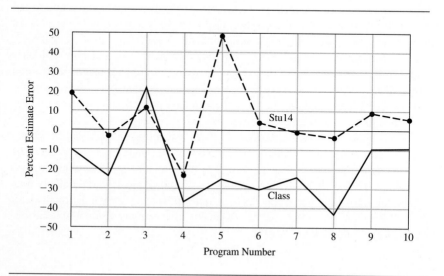

FIGURE 6.11
Time Estimating Accuracy—Student 14

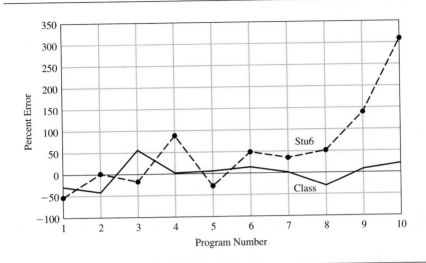

FIGURE 6.12
Size Estimating Error—Student 6

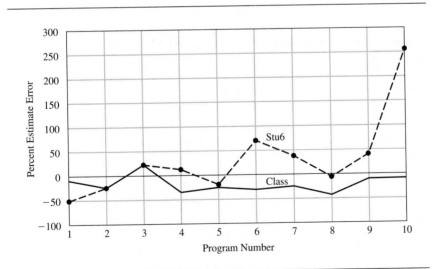

FIGURE 6.13
Time Estimating Accuracy—Student 6

fact, are so routine that you can project the time required to do them with great accuracy. If you were to reduce your work to microscopic tasks like recompiling a program, making a source update, reprinting a listing, or updating a database, you would see that each seemingly simple task has many possible complications. Surprises will also occasionally make seemingly trivial jobs stretch to an hour or more.

You will also find, however, that if you keep track of the time you spend on these tasks, the variations average out. The point is that minor interruptions and problems are a normal part of every task. While each case will vary about some norm, the average time will be fairly consistent. As explained earlier in this chapter, the regression method enables you to use these data both to make projections and to judge the accuracy of the projections.

While presumably it is possible to improve the planning process and while some people are undoubtedly better planners than are others, small task plans will generally have a high degree of variation. The need, therefore, is to understand as many of the causes of these variations as you can and to attempt to reduce them. You do this by following a consistent planning process, using historical data, and planning in detail.

COMPOSITE ESTIMATES

Even if several small estimates are seriously in error, their composite will likely be more accurate. If you estimate the job in many parts and if each estimate has a random error, the total will be much more accurate. This result assumes, of course, that the estimates were independently made and that they had no common biases. As noted in Chapter 5, when you make such independent estimates, estimating accuracy improves by the square root of the numbers of parts in the estimate.

This averaging phenomena is best illustrated with the estimating data from the 12-student class. Here, the error of the total class data is the error in the sums of their estimates. That is, in Fig. 6.6 the class data were calculated by adding all the students' LOC estimates and all the LOC actuals for each program and computing the percentage differences. As you can see, the composite appears to be more stable and more balanced around zero. The composite tendency to overestimate in Fig. 6.7 appears to result from the fact that the students' processes were evolving during the course. Because their productivity was gradually improving, the regression method was based on their average productivities rather than on their productivity trends. Thus their estimates always assumed a slightly lower productivity than they achieved and a slightly longer time than was actually required. This is a common problem when you use data from an evolving process. If your productivity is gradually changing, you may want to adjust your plans to reflect your most recent experience.

OVERCOMPENSATION

If you are consistently underestimating or overestimating jobs, you need to thoughtfully examine the way you make estimates. Look in more detail and see if the problem is in your size estimate, your resource estimates, or both. If the problem is principally with the size estimates, you may not be using appropriate historical data or you could be making too gross a conceptual design. Often, you can substantially improve your estimating by taking a bit more time to do a somewhat more complete high-level conceptual design. If the problem is principally in the hours calculation, you should examine the amount of variation between seemingly very similar tasks. Thus, if you estimate everything as an "average" project, you will be wrong almost all the time. As you more closely observe your work, you will better understand the factors that cause some tasks to take longer than others and will be better able to plan for them

If you are having a problem with alternately underestimating and overestimating, you need to seek some way to stabilize your estimating process. One problem you will likely encounter is the tendency to adjust all your estimates up or down to compensate for previous over- or underestimates. These intuitive adjustments are almost impossible to control and so should be avoided. You thus should try to make your adjustments in the data you use or the estimating methods you employ. The danger of trying to adjust your intuition is that you can lose your intuitive sense by attempting to treat it analytically.

If your estimating accuracy still continues to oscillate, you may find it helpful to seek outside help, for example, one or two teammates or classmates. Don't ask them to do the estimate but have them review it and raise issues and questions. You will likely find that by explaining your estimates, you will better see where and how they could be improved. Always do your own estimates but do not hesitate to have others review and comment on them.

ESTIMATING JUDGMENT

You also need to look at every estimate to ensure it is reasonable. The linear regression method is very useful, but it can occasionally give some strange results. For example, if you had historical data on a number of programs that were all approximately the same size, you could easily get small or negative β_1 parameter values. This could happen, for example, when the normal fluctuation in your data made it look as if larger programs took less time to develop than did smaller ones. This is clearly nonsense.

Another common problem is when the β_0 parameter is larger than many of your data points. A large, positive β_0 means the regression calculations indicate a relatively low effect of size on development time. Here, you will likely find that you make underestimates for large programs and overestimates for small ones. If β_0 were a fairly large, negative number, you would have the reverse problem.

These problems can generally result from any one or more of the following situations:

- ☐ Your historical data are clustered in a relatively close size range.
- ☐ You are making a new estimate either above or below the range for which you have historical data.
- ☐ You have included one or more outlier points.

When the regression parameters have any of these problems, you should disregard the regression method and use simple LOC per hour averages for the programs you have developed to date. For a more complete discussion of these issues, consult Section A7.4 in Appendix A on the limitations of the regression method.

6.9 Summary

By structuring your planning process, gathering historical data, and using effective methods, you can produce better plans in less time. As you gain planning experience, your confidence in your estimates will give you the conviction to defend and sell your plans. This improved planning ability will also improve your working relationships with your peers and managers and make you a more consistently effective software engineer.

You start the planning process by making a size estimate. Then you estimate the required resources and produce a schedule. You do this by relating the development hours used on prior projects to their size estimates. Because every project is different, if you lump all project activities into some global productivity number you will eliminate much of the thought required to produce a good plan. It is thus important to think through what is uniquely required for each project.

Before you can make a schedule, you need a detailed resource plan. Generally, this will be an estimate of how many direct hours you expect to spend on each task. You also need to project the total direct time you will have available. This projection must allow for your other commitments and the many ancillary activities that fill a normal working day. Engineers often find they spend only about 50 percent of their time on their direct project work.

With an estimate of your available direct time and a detailed resource plan, you can calculate when each task will start and end. You then set planning dates for the key project milestones. These dates provide a sound basis for making commitments.

Earned value tracking is a way to evaluate project progress. With it you establish a planned value for every task and credit an earned value when the task is completed. The earned value system provides a common value scale for every task, regardless of the type of work involved. You estimate the total hours to do the entire job and give every task a planning value based on its estimated percentage of this total. You then give earned value credit to this task when you complete it. Partially completed tasks get no credit.

6.10 Exercises

The standard course plan for this chapter uses PSP1.1 to write program 5A. The specification for this program is given in Appendix D and the PSP1.1 process is described in Appendix C. In completing this assignment, you should review and become familiar with PSP1.1 and faithfully follow the process and the report submission format that it specifies.

For other assignment options, consult Appendix D.

References

[Boehm 81] Barry W. Boehm, *Software Engineering Economics* (Englewood Cliffs, NJ: Prentice-Hall, 1981).

[Brooks] Frederick P. Brooks, *The Mythical Man-Month* (Reading, MA: Addison-Wesley, 1972).

[DeMarco] Tom DeMarco, *Controlling Software Projects* (Englewood Cliffs, NJ: Yourdon Press, 1982).

[Humphrey 87] W. S. Humphrey, *Managing for Innovation, Leading Technical People* (Englewood Cliffs, NJ: Prentice Hall, 1987).

[Humphrey 89] W. S. Humphrey, *Managing the Software Process* (Reading, MA: Addison-Wesley, 1989).

[Zells] Lois Zells, *Managing Software Projects*. Wellesley, MA: QED Information Sciences, Inc. (1990).

7

Measurements in the Personal Software Process

Gathering and using data is a fundamental part of the PSP. Because your sole reason for gathering data is to use them, these data must be accurate, must represent the processes you are measuring, and must cover the topics of greatest concern to you. This chapter outlines the principles of process measurement and describes the Goal-Question-Metric paradigm. [Basili] It also provides guidelines to help you measure your PSP.

7.1 Measurement Overview

Complex processes have many elements, and there are many potential ways to improve them. Without a quantitative understanding of the process steps, however, it is difficult to tell which ones are effective. Process measurements provide the data you need to objectively understand how your process works and to see what you can do to improve it.

You measure to get data, and you want data to help you with the following [Humphrey 89]:

□ Gain quantitative understanding

□ Evaluate a product, process, or organization

□ Control a product or a process

□ Make an estimate or a plan

The principal measurement categories are the following [Humphrey 89, SEL]:

□ Objective/subjective
Objective measures count things, and subjective measures involve human judgment.

□ Absolute/relative
Absolute measures are typically invariant to the addition of new items. The size of one program, for example, is an absolute measure and is independent of the sizes of other programs. Relative measures change, as with an average or a grading curve. Objective measures are often absolute, while subjective measures tend to be relative.

□ Explicit/derived
Explicit measures are taken directly, while derived measures are computed from other explicit or derived measures. An example of an explicit measure is programmer hours expended. An example of a derived measure is the number of LOC developed per programmer hour.

□ Dynamic/static
Dynamic measures have a time dimension, as with the earned value on your project to date. Here, the values tend to change depending on the measures you make. Assuming you made progress on your project, your earned value on July 1 would be different from that on June 1. Static measures remain invariant, as with program LOC, development hours, or total defects found.

□ Predictive/explanatory
Predictive measures can be obtained or generated in advance, while explanatory measures are produced after the fact.

To intelligently ask questions about your process, you need a *mental model*, that is, a defined process. For example, if you are developing a program and want to know whether you are on schedule, you need to understand your development process. With the PSP, you can see how much time you planned and what you have spent so far in each process phase. Having such a mental model helps you to determine your schedule status.

A mental model provides a defined context for gathering data. For example, if you are measuring the testing process, you might define testing as composed of unit test, integration test, component test, system test, and acceptance test. You can now measure each test phase to determine the defects found and the programmer hours spent. Once you have defined the test phases, you can define the data you want to gather and make plans to gather them. Because the software process definition provides the data gathering model, at least a basic process definition should always precede data gathering.

In measuring complex activities, you will often find it helpful to subdivide these activities into subtasks. Each subtask should then be defined with explicit entry and exit criteria. Even if you do not have a precise process definition, you can initially postulate a process model and use it to gather data. Doing this gives you a deeper understanding of the process and provides a more informed basis for refining the model. With this refined process definition, you can then gather more explicit data on the questions that most concern you.

This method could work with unit testing, for example, if you looked in more detail at how you conducted unit tests. You might have a test planning step followed by test development. You could then start by testing the program's functions. After you have gotten the functions to work, you may do some path tests to assure that all branches of your decision logic work properly. You could then conclude with exception testing for data values and user parameters.

While this level of definition would be excessive for the small programs in this book, it could provide useful data on larger projects. You could quickly see, for example, how long these tests take and the numbers of defects they typically expose. You would also have the data to later determine the yields of each test phase and the typical costs per defect found. By examining data on subsequent test phases, you could also determine whether an added investment in unit test would provide corresponding benefits in later phases. None of these data or analyses would be possible, however, without the mental model provided by your unit testing process definition.

7.2 Fundamental Process Measures

In establishing a measurement program, you will find it helpful to start by considering what objective, absolute, and explicit measures you can identify. You then use these measures as the foundation for a family of more useful derived measures. For the software process, the fundamental process measures fall in three categories: products, processes, and resources. [Fenton]

PRODUCT MEASURES

Product measures generally refer to the volume of product produced. They include LOC, pages of documentation, numbers of screens, numbers of files, and so on. These measures may be of various product elements, such as modules, components, or manuals. You can also measure by phase, such as the amount of code produced in the implementation phase or the LOC changed during unit test. Similarly, size may be related to process activity, as with the LOC changed while you were repairing a defect. Measures of other product attributes might include system throughput, memory capacity, cyclomatic complexity [Gill], module coupling [Card], and function points [Albrecht].

PROCESS MEASURES

Process measures quantify the behavior of your process. They are generally objective, absolute, explicit, and dynamic. They also provide the elements for a host of useful derived measures.

One general category of process measures is event counts. Here, you count things that happen, such as the numbers of defects found in test, requirements changes, or milestones met. Event categories, event properties, or process phases are often important. Examples of these are design defects injected while fixing defects in test or requirements defects found during design reviews.

Another general category concerns time measures. The time required to complete a project is often called *cycle time*. In highly competitive industrial work, cycle time is often more important than reducing development cost. Precise knowledge of the times required for various project tasks can help you to optimize your process around resources, around cycle time, or around some combination of the two. The major payoff comes from reducing waste and eliminating distractions. As explained in Chapter 6, process time measures can also help you to make better development plans.

RESOURCE MEASURES

Resource measures apply to labor hours, the principal software development resource. Here, the concerns are working hours, job categories, and task activities. While common resource measures are in programmer months or weeks, measures of personal time are not terribly useful if the unit is longer than minutes or fractions of an hour. It is almost impossible to devote an entire working day to any single activity. This means that any job you measure in days, weeks, or months will contain many unrelated activities. To identify, plan, and manage these unrelated activities, you will need finer-grained measures. Even hourly measures are too gross to permit detailed understanding of many processes. While gathering time in minutes might seem extreme, it is not difficult. Once you decide to track your time, the units don't make much difference.

By gathering detailed time data, you can identify many extraneous activities. Steps like having phones answered for you can improve your productivity by eliminating distracting interruptions. When you stop for a phone call that takes 45 minutes, should that time be counted as design time? While counting this time somewhere may be necessary, calling these diversions productive time is not very helpful. Administrative meetings, inadequate clerical service, and poorly supported computing facilities also waste time and reduce productivity.

Every interruption has three potential costs: the lost time, the added time it will take you to reconstruct where you were when interrupted, and the increased likelihood of error. A principal focus of any productivity or cycle-time improvement effort thus should be to identify and reduce these distractions. In many organizations, the quickest and least expensive way to improve productivity is to reduce the amount of time engineers spend on extraneous activities. This, by the way, cannot be done by simply telling people to stop wasting their time. It requires a study of where they spend their time and what could be done to reduce distractions. These items rarely take days of effort, or even hours, but they can take a lot of minutes. If you can properly manage your minutes, the hours will generally take care of themselves.

7.3 Goal-Question-Metric Paradigm

Basili has devised the Goal-Question-Metric (GQM) paradigm as a framework for guiding measurement efforts. [Basili] According to GQM, you:

- □ define the principal goals for your activity,
- □ construct a comprehensive set of questions to help you achieve these goals, and
- □ define and gather the data required to answer these questions.

DEFINING GOALS

In one organization, management launched a measurement program because they thought it was a good thing to do. However, the engineers who designed the measurement program knew of no business-connected reasons for gathering the data, so they started with the measures they could most easily find. Rather quickly they amassed what was essentially a write-only database; nobody had any reason to use it!

There are so many things you could measure about the software process that the odds of randomly selecting useful measures are remote. You should thus have clear goals of what you are trying to do before you start gathering data. This is often difficult to define without a context, so it is helpful to consider the goals hierarchy in Fig. 7.1. When you start to define a task's goals, you should always ask, "Why am I doing this?" If the answer is "because my manager told me to," your odds of success are reduced. While you should gather data when your man-

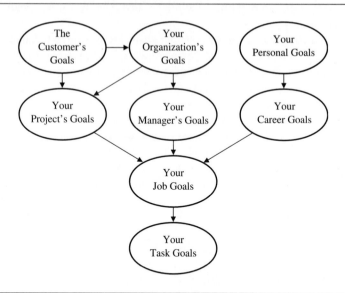

FIGURE 7.1
The Goals Hierarchy

ager tells you to, you should try to make the data useful. To do this, you need to know how the data are to be used.

In measuring your own process, you should think about what you are trying to achieve. This is principally related to your organization, project, and management goals. Hence, in defining your goals you will often find it helpful to consider the goals of those above you in the organization.

THE GOALS HIERARCHY

The goals hierarchy in Fig. 7.1 can help you to put your goals in proper context. Start by trying to connect your goals to your organization's goals. At a senior management level, these goals are probably quite stable and are often in broad-enough terms to be readily understandable. Understanding the connection between your goals and those above you will also help you to explain what you are doing in terms that are most meaningful to your management. When you can show a clear connection between what you are doing and what management is trying to achieve, you are most likely to get its support.

As logical as this sounds, you cannot always get people to explain their goals to you. Sometimes, they may not even know them themselves. You may have to infer their goals or at least postulate them as a basis for initial data gathering. Over time, you can test these assumed goals and gradually refine them based on what you observe and learn.

Even if you cannot get a clear picture of the goals hierarchy, you should explicitly establish goals for yourself. Here, your goals will deal with what, how, when, and how much. They should also deal with improvements such as lower defect rates or shorter schedules.

ROLE OF QUESTIONS

In GQM, questions should make your request for data explicit and ensure that the data you collect will meet a defined need. In general, you are starting with rather vague goals and must end up with useful numbers. The questions are intended to make a connection between these extremes. You do this by considering each goal and determining what you would like to know about it. Some typical metric-related questions could be the following:

- □ For each process goal, where did I start, where am I now, and where do I want to go?
- □ What is important about this goal?
- □ What is the best that has been achieved against this goal?
- □ Does improved performance against this goal have any absolute limit, and if so, what is it?

METRICS DEFINITION

Once you have established your goals and determined the key questions, you need to define specific measures. If other people are to gather these data, you must also specify what you want with sufficient precision so that their results are consistent with yours. Even if you are taking all the measurements yourself, you need explicit data definitions.

Producing precise data definitions involves a lot more effort than you may expect. There are many special cases and unique conditions in even simple processes. You will likely include some of these in your initial metrics definitions but will discover others when you start to gather the data. You will then have to stop to resolve these problems before you can gather more data. You may need to refine your data definitions several times before you have a set that covers all the important cases.

Another reason metrics definition takes time is forms design. To ensure the desired data are consistently gathered and are presented in an understandable and retrievable form, you should design forms for gathering the data. Well-designed forms can also reveal holes and inconsistencies in your metrics definitions. Forms can also improve the efficiency of data gathering, provide a convenient storage and communication medium, and facilitate checking for data accuracy and completeness.

7.4   General PSP Objectives, Goals, and Questions

One reason to study the PSP is to improve your effectiveness as a software engineer. Your overall PSP data gathering goals are thus

- □ to understand how the personal software development process works,
- □ to determine the steps you could take to improve product quality,
- □ to determine the impact of process changes on your productivity,
- □ to establish benchmarks to measure process improvement, and
- □ to assist you in making more-accurate plans.

Starting with these general goals, you should establish more explicit goals. You could, for example, set a goal to meet all your delivery commitments or to reduce your unit test defects to under two per KLOC. You could establish goals for productivity, planning accuracy, or product quality. Your initial problem will likely be that you do not have good measures of your current performance. If you have not established a productivity measure and have no historical data, you cannot set reasonable productivity goals. This is equally true of any other aspect of your process performance. You should thus establish an initial goal to learn about your process. In doing this, some questions you should consider are the following:

- □ What aspects of my performance are important?
- □ How would I measure these aspects?
- □ What is the best performance I have achieved?
- □ What can I learn from these achievements?
- □ What are other people achieving?
- □ What of their methods might help me to improve?

As you explore these questions and define the measures that relate to them, you can start to gather data. Over time, these data will permit you to set more informed goals. As you refine your process, you can progressively refine your goals, define new questions to address them, establish measures, and build a database to help you to set more meaningful goals in the future.

7.5   A GQM Example

The following example illustrates how you may use the GQM paradigm to improve your PSP process.

Goal: To produce programs that contain no defects.

Question: How can you produce software of such quality that no defects will be found in later testing or use?

In addressing this question, you need to determine how to judge, during development, whether a program is likely to be defect free.

PRODUCING DEFECT-FREE SOFTWARE

There is no way to guarantee that you have produced a defect-free program. With sufficient data and a suitably controlled process, however, you can improve the likelihood that your program is defect free. The critical development issue is to identify those current measures that will indicate the likely numbers of defects that will later be found in your program.

The PSP strategy for attacking this problem is shown in Fig. 7.2. Here, your PSP process is an alternating sequence of development and appraisal phases. After each development phase, you appraise the product in one or more appraisal phases. These appraisals might be design or code reviews, compilations, team inspections, or various types of tests. You gather defect data from each appraisal phase and correlate the defects found in that phase with those found in all preceding phases. You then use these data to help you decide if a program or program element is of high-enough quality to release, if it should be reappraised, or if it needs to be reengineered.

You should view each appraisal phase as a filter for removing defects. Thus the number of defects found in each phase is proportional to the number of defects entering that phase. Because every appraisal phase will find only a fraction of the total number of defects in the product at that point, the number of remaining defects also is proportional both to the numbers that entered that phase and to the number of defects found. By managing your process so that you improve the effectiveness or yield of each appraisal phase, you can be reasonably sure to improve the quality of the delivered product. Depending on the number of phases N and the yield of each phase, you can presumably reduce the likelihood of finding subsequent defects to whatever value you choose. A key constraint, however, is the amount of time and expense needed for all the appraisal steps. In practical terms, another limiting value to this process is the quality of the fix process itself.

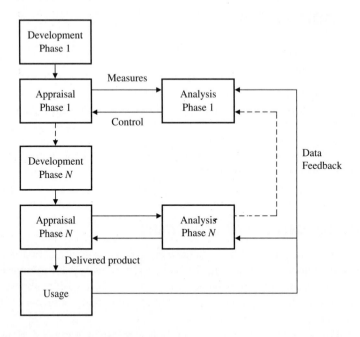

FIGURE 7.2
A Software Quality Strategy

When you frequently inject defects into the product while making fixes, it is much more difficult to achieve very high yields and thus harder to achieve very high product quality.

METRICS REQUIRED

This quality strategy now suggests the need for several kinds of data. You will want to know the numbers of defects found in every appraisal phase. You will also want data on the defects found during the post development use of your programs. These data might come from three sources:

□ Later use of the program in your PSP work. The use of program 3A, the LOC counter, is an example of this case.

□ Reuse of a program in the development of a later program. For example, you might use program 2A as the base on which you built program 3A.

□ Use of a program by someone else.

You could discover defects in a completed program in any of these cases. In recording these data, you should enter them in the Defect Recording Log for the program you are currently developing but clearly identify them so they are not counted in this program's totals. During the postmortem phase, you then enter them in the Project Plan Summaries of the appropriate programs and reference where they were found. You would record each of these defects in the "after development" row of the summary report for that program. If, for example, you find a defect in program 3A while using it to count the LOC for program 7A, you would update the Project Plan Summary for program 3A as shown in Table 7.1. You judge when this defect would likely have been injected and update the Defects Injected–Actual column as shown in Table 7.1. While this approach would be adequate for the PSP exercises in this book, in a software organization, you would need some more formal means to get data on the defects later found in your programs.

In addition to these defect data, you also need data on the cost effectiveness of each appraisal phase. The PSP provides for this as described in the subsequent chapters on design and code reviews and quality management.

As you gather these data and as your process stabilizes, you can then better judge the probable costs of producing programs that are likely free of defects.

7.6   Gathering Data

Several authors have described the issues of gathering and using software data. [Card 90, Grady, Humphrey 89, Putnam] Even though you are in complete control of your PSP data gathering, several issues will impact your work. In gathering PSP data, you generally will not have special data-gathering tools and so must gather the data manually. Thus you will create forms for recording the data, set up a place to keep the data, and keep an engineering notebook. These topics are discussed in the following sections.

MANUAL DATA GATHERING

It would be nice to have a tool to automatically gather the PSP data. Because judgment is involved in most personal process data, however, no such tool exists or is likely in the near future. Examples of the need for personal judgment in PSP data gathering are the following:

- It would be impossible for your computer to know what you were doing when you stopped using the keyboard. For example, were you thinking about the design or had you left to go to a meeting or to answer the phone?

TABLE 7.1   A PSP1 PROJECT PLAN SUMMARY WITH AN AFTER-DEVELOPMENT DEFECT

Student	Student 4		Date	2/7/94
Program	Humphrey		Language	C
Instructor	LOC Counter		Program #	3A

Summary	Plan	Actual	To Date
LOC/Hour	9.0	14.1	13.4

Program Size (LOC):	Plan	Actual	To Date
Base(B)	52	52	
	(Measured)	(Measured)	
Deleted (D)	7	6	
	(Estimated)	(Counted)	
Modified (M)	5	5	
	(Estimated)	(Counted)	
Added (A)	25	52	
	(N − M)	(T − B + D − R)	
Reused (R)	0	0	0
	(Estimated)	(Counted)	
Total New & Changed (N)	30	57	185
	(Estimated)	(A + M)	
Total LOC (T)	70	98	216
	(N + B − M − D + R)	(Measured)	
Total New Reuse	0	0	0

Time in Phase (min.)	Plan	Actual	To Date	To Date %
Planning	10	7	37	4.5
Design	30	50	130	15.6
Code	75	48	268	32.3
Compile	25	9	77	9.3
Test	40	115	283	34.1
Postmortem	20	13	36	4.3
Total	200	242	831	100.0

Defects Injected	Actual	To Date	To Date %
Planning	0	0	0.0
Design	1 + 1*	1 + 3	12.5
Code	6	20	83.3
Compile	0	0	0.0
Test	0	1	4.1
Total Development	7	24	100.0

TABLE 7.1 (continued)

Defects Removed	Actual	To Date	To Date %
Planning	0	0	0.0
Design	0	0	0.0
Code	0	0	0.0
Compile	4	13	54.2
Test	3	11	45.8
Total Development	7	24	100.0
After Development	1	1	

* Found in program 7A

- It would also be impossible to count defects automatically from code changes. For example, was the change made to correct a problem or did you think of a better way to do the job?
- Where in the process was this defect most likely injected?

For now, we must thus content ourselves with manual data gathering and hope that tools will be developed that will help make this work more accurate, complete, and efficient. Tools to assist in data gathering are feasible and could certainly help. They would probably not save a lot of time, but they could significantly improve data accuracy and completeness. If such tools were available as an integral part of your development environment, they could be a substantial help. Once the data are gathered and are in a database, many automatic analysis tools could assist in estimating, planning, and progress reporting. You might even visualize something analogous to a process instrument panel that would display your status and progress on this project compared to your plans and prior history on defects, development schedules, and productivity.

The tools required to manually gather, analyze, and summarize process data are logs, forms, databases, spreadsheets, and summary reports. While various statistical programs could also be helpful, the statistical techniques discussed in this book can be conveniently handled with databases, spreadsheets, or simple analysis programs.

FORMS AND TEMPLATES

Forms and templates are important tools for gathering and using data. Well-designed forms are helpful when you are generating estimates and plans and provide a convenient repository for the actual data at project completion. Your forms should thus provide space for both estimated and actual data.

Forms are used when the amount of data you are gathering is fixed, and templates are used when the volume of data is unpredictable. For example, you use a form when you estimate the time for each project phase. Here, you know the information required and can design a form with the required blank spaces. With a size estimate, however, you have an indeterminate amount of data. Because large programs could have from dozens to hundreds of objects, an expandable template is required to provide space for data on each object. The data needed for each object can be completely specified, however, so the template is just as explicit as the form except that it is of indeterminate length. Here, a convenient practice is to use separate sheets for each object category and enter their totals in the size estimating template. As long as you record the program number, object category, and attachment page numbers at the top of each sheet, you can use this template to estimate the size of almost any sized program.

As you incorporate new forms in your process, you will often need an early test and modification cycle to make them usable. Some items may seem poorly placed, inconvenient, or badly worded. Some measures could turn out to be unnecessary, and you may need to add new items. It is a good idea to dry run each new form with data from a completed project. If you find problems, redesign the form and do another dry run. When you finally get the form to a suitable level of quality, use it experimentally on a real project. You will again often find new problems. You did not see them earlier because your reactions when you copy data from one place to another differ from your reactions when you first generate the data.

THE DEFECT DATABASE

Table 7.2 gives an example of a defect database format suitable for use with the PSP. Here, data on four defects are shown with each record containing the raw data on one defect. These are four defects reported by a student on program 3A. The fields in this database are identical to those in the Defect Recording Log. By analyzing your defect data, you can generate a host of valuable analyses and reports. Several of these are described in more detail in subsequent chapters, but following are some examples:

- ☐ A table of the numbers of defects injected and removed by phase. While defects are easy to count for small programs, they are much more difficult for large programs. With a defect database, counting them is a simple matter.

- ☐ Data on the numbers and types of defects found in a specific phase.

- ☐ Data on the numbers of defects that were in the product at phase entry but not found during that phase. An example would be the number of defects missed in a code review. This is discussed in more detail in Chapters 8 and 9.

TABLE 7.2 DEFECT DATABASE EXAMPLE

Field	Data for Defect n	Data for Defect $n+1$	Data for Defect $n+2$	Data for Defect $n+3$
Program Number	3A	3A	3A	3A
Program Defect Number	6	7	8	9
Type	20	20	40	20
Phase injected[1]	40	40	20	40
Phase removed	60	60	70	70
Time-to-fix	1	1	30	1
Fix Error				

[1]Phase numbers: 10—planning
20—design
40—code
60—compile
70—test
80—postmortem

☐ The time required to fix a defect as a function of the phase in which it was removed. This subject is discussed further in Chapters 8 and 9.

You can obtain a great deal of useful information from a defect database. Because the amount of defect data can become very large, you will likely find it helpful to enter these data promptly after you complete developing each program. It is even a good idea to do this as part of the postmortem phase.

Because the PSP database requirements are relatively simple, you can use almost any commercially available database. You should check that it has convenient facilities for generating charts and reports and that it permits interchange of data with the spreadsheet you use for analyzing program data.

THE PSP SPREADSHEET

A spreadsheet layout suitable for PSP program data is shown in Table 7.3. This spreadsheet is used for recording the raw project and process data for each program. Depending on your preference, you can enter the field names down the left column and the program data in each column or vice versa. The categories shown in Table 7.3 provide for all the explicit data required on your summary project forms. The derived data can then be generated by spreadsheet programs when

TABLE 7.3 PROGRAM SPREADSHEET FIELDS

Category	Field Name	Program n	Program $n + 1$	Program $n + 2$
Program Number				
Summary	Estimated new and changed LOC			
	Actual new and changed LOC			
	Estimated time			
	Actual time			
	Estimated defects			
	Actual defects			
Size—estimated	Base			
	Reused			
	Added			
	Deleted			
	Total new and changed			
	Total			
Size—actual	Base			
	Reused			
	Added			
	Deleted			
	Total new and changed			

needed. Because some of your analyses will concern estimating accuracy, each data category has an estimated and an actual entry. The major categories in Table 7.3 are as follows:

□ Summary

Much of the analyses you do will concern total time, total LOC, or total de-

TABLE 7.3 (continued)

Category	Field Name	Program n	Program n + 1	Program n + 2
Time—estimated	Total			
	Requirements and Planning			
	Detailed design			
	Design review			
	Code			
	Code Review			
	Compile			
	Test			
	Postmortem			
Time—actual	Requirements and Planning			
	Detailed design			
	. . .			
Defects Injected—estimated	Requirements and Planning			
	Detailed design			
	. . .			
Defects Injected—actual	Requirements and Planning			
	Detailed design			
	. . .			

fects. It is thus convenient to accumulate all these data in one place on your spreadsheet.

☐ Size:

The size category contains the size elements in the Project Plan Summary. Both the estimated and actual data are entered for each value.

TABLE 7.3 (continued)

Category	Field Name	Program n	Program n + 1	Program n + 2
Defects Removed–estimated	Requirements and Planning			
	Detailed design			
	. . .			
Defects Removed–actual	Requirements and Planning			
	Detailed design			
	. . .			

☐ Time

The estimated and actual time per phase are entered here. During the course, you will use the actual phase times for several analyses. You will, however, use only the total estimated time. For larger projects, you will need to accurately project the development time for each project phase.

□ Defects
Because actual and estimated data are needed for the defects injected per phase and the defects removed per phase, there must be four defects sections in the spreadsheet.

Some of the analyses that can be made with these data are the following:

□ Regression calculations
The size and resource regression calculations can be readily made on a spreadsheet. Students generally find this method most convenient.

□ Yield
Various yield calculations are required in subsequent chapters. Yield is the percentage of defects in the program that are removed in a particular phase or group of phases. It can be calculated on the spreadsheet; the method is described in the subsequent chapters.

□ Productivity
You can use these data to calculate your development productivity. You can also calculate the rates at which you find defects in test, in compile, or in reviews. Many productivity analyses are possible using these data.

□ Charts
One great benefit of using a spreadsheet to make these calculations is that you can readily plot charts of your progress as you work through the PSP exercises.

The spreadsheet requirements for the PSP are not particularly sophisticated, so almost any general-purpose product will suffice. Chart facilities are essential. The capability to link multiple records and to link the spreadsheet to the database would also be helpful.

THE ENGINEERING NOTEBOOK

An engineering notebook is a convenient place in which to make notes, do calculations, or document exploratory designs. By recording experiments, test results, alternate designs, and other calculations and analyses in your notebook, you can easily find them if and when you later need them. Also, surprisingly, the discipline of recording your work improves the quality of your work. You are more explicit about your assumptions and conclusions when you document them. In some fields, the engineer's notebook is an important legal document. This is particularly true in cases of product liability and patent litigation. In industrial work, you should thus date every entry and have important events witnessed and signed by two colleagues. Examples of such events may be a patentable design idea or the analyses to support a critical design decision. You should also date and number each notebook so you can easily find old data. If your products are used in critical applications, it is increasingly likely you will someday need evidence that you followed a disciplined personal process in doing the work. In such situations, an engineering notebook could be a major help.

I keep my notebook and my Time Recording Log on hand always, so I have found it convenient to combine them. Because of the inconvenience of recording two kinds of data in one notebook and of having to search for where I made my time entries, I enter my time recording data from the back of the notebook, working forward. At the front of the notebook, I then leave a blank page for an index and important references. I also number each notebook page.

7.7   The Impact of Data Gathering

Data take time and effort to gather and analyze. Data gathering will also affect your behavior by increasing your awareness of your performance.

DATA GATHERING TAKES TIME

Data gathering can be time consuming and tedious. To be consistently effective in gathering data, you must be convinced of its value to you. If you do not intend to use the data, the odds are you will either not gather them or the data you gather will be incomplete or inaccurate. This is especially true for the PSP. Here, you gather data to improve your process. You should thus understand your data-gathering goals, the questions these data are intended to answer, and how you will use the data to get answers. While much of the process design work has been done for you with the PSP, you still need to relate these data to your personal objectives. By thinking through your process improvement goals and relating them to the PSP data gathering goals discussed in Section 7.4, you can decide how important these data are to you. This will provide a framework for deciding what aspects of the PSP you will continue to use and where you should make additions or changes. Unless you make a clear connection between your personal objectives and the PSP process, you are not likely to make effective use of the PSP.

THE DATA CAN AFFECT YOUR PERFORMANCE

The data you gather on your PSP will likely affect your performance. Try as we may, few of us can be totally objective about our work. We are embarrassed about our errors and are anxious to improve. The principal issue is whether the data you gather are for your personal use or for someone else's. If you are gathering data for someone who sets your pay or evaluates your work, you will likely be careful to show good results. If it is for your personal use, however, you can be more objective.

Once you have evidence that your process is improving, you may want to show your data to others. You should not show your data to others too quickly, however. Wait until you have enough data-gathering experience to understand your own performance.

The key point to remember is that data on your own performance are sensitive. For example, suppose you showed your classmates how long it took you to write a program and how many defects you found. If they in turn shared their data with you and you found that you had taken much longer and introduced many more defects than anyone else had, how would you feel? Conversely, your data might embarrass someone else. An important PSP lesson is learning to treat your personal data objectively.

To put this in perspective, think about comparing times for running 100 meters. If you were a cross-country runner, you may not be too concerned about your comparative time for sprinting. But even in your own event, there may be faster runners on your team and there are undoubtedly faster runners in the world. While you probably worked hard to win races, you did not quit the first time you did badly. Try to think about your personal data in these terms. Recognize that there is great satisfaction in doing competent work even if it is not a world's record. Every time you make a personal best, you are entitled to celebrate. Experiment with sharing some of your data and see how you and your associates react. Over time, you should learn to be objective about your personal performance.

7.8 Establishing a Baseline for Your Personal Process

As you use your personal process, you will probably want to know if your performance is improving. Unless the improvements are very substantial, it is almost impossible to answer this question without substantial data. Personal process results vary considerably and you may sometimes feel you are improving when you are not. You can often tell only by statistically examining a large-enough volume of data to get significant results. The 10 PSP programs in this book should provide enough data to give you an indication of the areas in which you have made significant improvement and those in which you need to make further effort.

This problem of judging your own performance has two complications: bolstering and clutching. *Bolstering* is your selectively remembering those results that reinforce what you want to believe. When we don't keep and analyze data on our work, we tend to forget the disasters and remember the successes. Over time, this builds a rosy impression that somehow things are getting better. A little data will soon dispel this illusion.

Clutching occurs when a result is so important that it affects your performance. It is caused by unconscious feedback. Here, when it is critical that a result turn out well, it often does not. My first experience with clutching was when I had gathered several years of data on a simple personal financial process. I had noted a consistent, improving trend and decided it was worth a brief technical paper. The very next month, the process results were a disaster, invalidating the paper I had already drafted. At first I was concerned that there was something wrong with my process. I have subsequently found the following general phenomenon: When consistent results are crucial, we unconsciously behave differently, often invalidating historical trends. This occurs because our statistics may not measure our behavior under similar high-pressure situations. If we had gathered data when we were under similar pressure to produce good results, we could expect more consistent performance.

The presence of pressure introduces unknown factors that change your behavior. This, however, is a matter of process maturity. As you gain experience, you will become more confident of your process. Your performance will be more stable and less influenced by transient emotional pressures. Achieving this takes time, however, so you should be careful when you publicly commit to an improvement trend. You could put more pressure on yourself than you are prepared to handle.

Finally, data on your personal performance can be discouraging. Your results will fluctuate, but despite all your attempts to do better, you may not see much change. Even when you know that just trying harder does not work, you will likely still try. To achieve a consistent improvement trend, you must make specific changes in your process so that you actually change your behavior. It is behavior changes that produce different results.

With a baselined process, you have a basis for analyzing future results and determining where and how your performance is improving. This helps you to plan your work and justifies your process improvement efforts.

7.9   Summary

We gather and analyze data to help us to understand and improve our processes. To intelligently ask questions about your process, you need a process model. This is why you define your software process before you start to gather extensive data.

The measures you use to gather data fall into three categories: product, process, and resource. Product measures refer to the volume of product produced. Process measures relate events to process phases. Resource measures primarily measure programmer time.

The Goal-Question-Metric (GQM) paradigm can help you design and implement a measurement program. You gather data to meet specific goals and to answer explicit questions. These data must also be precisely defined, consistently gathered, and properly used.

The aids required to manually gather, analyze, and use PSP data are forms, databases, spreadsheets, and summary reports. Automated tools can help to make this data gathering and analysis more convenient, timely, and accurate. Because judgment is involved in gathering most process data, however, tools to automatically gather these data are not probable in the near future.

Gathering data on your software process will impact your performance. It also can be time consuming and tedious. If you are not committed to gathering and using the data, the odds are you will either not collect it or that data will be incomplete and inaccurate.

As you start using your personal process, you will probably be curious about whether your performance is improving. While this is a valid concern, it is almost impossible to address without substantial data. You can tell if you are improving only by statistically examining a large volume of data. This problem of judging your own performance has two further complications: bolstering and clutching. Bolstering is when you selectively remember those results that reinforce what you want to believe. Clutching is caused by unconscious feedback, that is, when it is critical that we get good results, we often do not.

Data on your personal performance can be discouraging. Your results will fluctuate, and as you strive to do better, they may not show consistent improvement. Even when you know that just trying harder does not work, you will likely still try. To achieve a consistent improvement trend, you must make specific changes in your process.

With a baselined process, you have a basis for analyzing future results and determining where and how you are making progress. Doing this helps you to plan your work and justifies your process improvement efforts.

7.10 Exercises

The standard course plan for this chapter uses PSP1.1 to write program 6A. This is the same process you used for program 5A. The specification for this program is given in Appendix D, and the PSP1.1 process is described in Appendix C. In completing this assignment, you should review and become familiar with PSP1.1 and faithfully follow the process and the report submission format that it specifies.

For other assignment options, consult Appendix D.

References

[Albrecht] A. J. Albrecht and J. E. Gaffney, Jr., "Software Function, Source Lines of Code, and Development Effort Prediction: A Software Science Validation," *IEEE Transactions on Software Engineering* SE-9, 639–648 (1983).

[Basili] V. Basili and D. M. Weiss, "A Methodology for Collecting Valid Software Engineering Data," *IEEE Transactions on Software Engineering*, vol. SE-10, no. 6 (Nov. 1984): 728–738.

[Card 90] David N. Card and Robert L. Glass, *Measuring Software Design Quality* (Englewood Cliffs, NJ: Prentice-Hall, 1990).

[Fenton] N. Fenton, *Software Metrics: A Rigorous Approach* (Chapman and Hall, 1991).

[Gill] G. K. Gill and C. F. Kemerer, "Cyclomatic Complexity Density and Software Maintenance Productivity," *IEEE Transactions on Software Engineering*, vol. 17, no. 12 (Dec. 1991): 1284–1288.

[Grady] R. B. Grady, *Practical Software Metrics for Project Management and Process Improvement* (Englewood Cliffs, NJ: Prentice Hall, 1992).

[Humphrey 89] W. S. Humphrey, *Managing the Software Process* (Reading, MA: Addison-Wesley, 1989).

[Putnam] L. H. Putnam and W. Myers, *Measures for Excellence* (Englewood Cliffs, NJ: Yourdon Press, 1992).

[SEL] Software Engineering Laboratory Series, *Evaluation of Management Measures of Software Development, Volume 2: Data Description*, Goddard Space Flight Center, SEL-82-001 (September 1982).

8

Design and Code Reviews

By doing design and code reviews, you will see more improvement in the quality and productivity of your work than you will see from any other single change you make in your personal software process. On larger programs, it will pay you to review your requirements, your specifications, your designs, and your code. Review each program before you first compile it. Study it and understand it. Fix the defects, logic, structure, and clarity. When the program is unclear or confusing, add comments or, better yet, rewrite it to make it simpler. Make it easy to read and to understand. Produce something you would be proud to publish or to show your friends and associates. This chapter describes design and code reviews, why they are important, and how you can improve your skill at doing them.

8.1 What Are Reviews

Doing reviews is the most important step you can take to improve your software engineering performance. This section discusses the various review methods and the kinds of products you can review.

REVIEW METHODS

There are many ways to review software products. The principal ones are inspections, walk-throughs, and personal reviews.

An *inspection* is a structured procedure for the team review of a software product. Inspections were introduced by Fagan in 1976 and have become widely used. [Fagan 76, Fagan 86] Inspections have a formal structure, and each participant has a defined role. A typical inspection process has three phases:

1. Preparation,
2. Inspection meeting,
3. Repair and report.

The preparation phase starts with a kick-off meeting to ensure all participants understand the product to be reviewed, are informed of their roles in the inspection, and know how to perform those roles. The reviewers then separately prepare for the inspection by studying the program materials and noting any problems or questions. The inspection meeting phase involves the reviewers discussing their findings with the program author and with each other. The defects found are noted and resolution responsibility is assigned, usually to the program author. The repair and report phase calls for the repair of any product defects and the preparation and submission of an inspection report. To be most effective, inspections are measured, a report is produced, and the action items are tracked to closure.

A *walk-through* is a less formal process that usually follows a presentation format. A developer walks through how the program performs a typical application, while the audience raises issues and asks questions. When both users and developers are present, walk-throughs can be effective at discovering and resolving omissions and misunderstandings. They can also be used to educate users or staff members. Walk-throughs generally involve little in the way of advance preparation or follow-up.

A *personal review* is where you examine your own products. Your objective is to find and fix as many defects as possible before you implement, inspect, compile, or test the program. Some years ago, when programs had to be compiled and executed on large central computing systems, programmers had only one or two shots at the computer in a day. They could not afford to waste an entire day for a simple typo, so it was general practice to carefully review code before submitting it for the first compile. Many programmers became so skilled at reviewing that their programs often compiled correctly on the first try. With the general availability of personal workstations, however, this practice has seemed unnecessary. Instead of thoughtfully examining their work, programmers now generally try to compile and test their programs without checking them first. As the PSP data will show, a little time spent carefully reviewing your code can save the much longer amount of time that would have been spent debugging and fixing the program during compile and test.

REVIEW PRODUCTS

All software products can be examined by inspections, walk-throughs, or personal reviews. Because of the critical importance of the products of the earliest software phases to the entire design and development process, projects should usually put highest priority on reviewing them. Some form of requirements walk-through can identify and resolve problems before the engineers waste their time designing and building the wrong product. Design inspections and design reviews can similarly identify and fix problems early in the development process. These problems are easier and cheaper to fix during the design phase than they are later.

Other products besides code that can benefit from inspections, walk-throughs, and personal reviews are documentation, development plans, test cases, and test plans. You should ensure that every product and product change is reviewed at least once.

8.2   Why Review Programs

Reviewing a program is like reviewing a draft paper. While some people feel they can write a perfect first draft, professional writers will tell you that the secret to good writing is rewriting. Writing good programs is much the same. Some programmers feel they can write a high-quality program on the first try. However, they generally then struggle to compile and test a defect-prone first draft.

Many engineers who start using the PSP spend more than one third of their time in compiling and testing. Figure 8.1 shows the maximum, minimum, and average percentage of total development time that 12 students in one course spent compiling and testing the 10 A series programs in this book. Initially, the class averaged around 30 percent of their time in compile and test, with the percentage of their development time ranging from around 11 percent to over 50 percent. As they worked through the PSP exercises in this book, the quality of their programs improved substantially. For the last program, their average compile and test time dropped to around 10 percent, or about one third their time at the beginning of the course. The final range was 8 percent to 28 percent. By introducing reviews and being more aware of the defects they made, the students cut their average compile and test time by nearly three times. Nearly half the class, in fact, reduced the amount of time spent in compile and test to 10 percent or less of total development time. As shown in Fig. 8.2, the students' improvement in compile time was the most dramatic, with the average being from about 13 percent of development to about 3 percent. This improvement in compile and test performance saved the students time, made their development process more predictable, and resulted in better products.

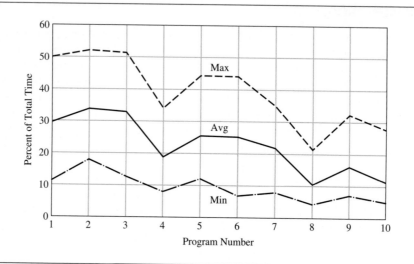

FIGURE 8.1
Compile and Test Time Range

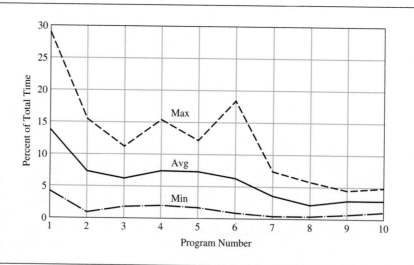

FIGURE 8.2
Compile Time Range

REVIEW EFFICIENCY

Perhaps your biggest single problem with reviews will be convincing yourself that the time they take is worth the effort. Somehow, manually searching through a program for defects seems slow and laborious when you have a powerful computer, a compiler, and a debugging facility waiting to be used. While you can read all that I or anyone else says on the subject, the only way to convince yourself is to measure your own reviews and see for yourself.

In my early PSP research work, I wrote over 70 Pascal and C++ programs. The relative fix times I measured are shown in Table 8.1. On average, I took eight times as long to find and fix a Pascal defect in test as in code review. The average code review time to find and fix a defect in both Pascal and C++ was between one and two minutes. The average time to find and fix defects in unit test was longer for both languages and was even longer after unit test. This fix time, however, was made up of a lot of fixes that took only a few minutes and a few that took much longer.

I also examined this fix time pattern by defect type and found that the ratios are essentially the same for most defect types. The principal exception was typographical defects where for both Pascal and C++, it took about five times as long to find and fix typographical defects in unit test as it did in code review.

Student review data. Figure 8.3 shows the defects the students found per hour in compile, design review, code review, and test. These data show the average time spent per defect; for example, a code review that took 30 minutes and uncovered five defects would result in a rate of 10 defects per hour. From these data, it is clear that code reviews are at least three to five times as efficient as testing in finding defects. Note that with the class data in Fig. 8.3, design reviews were not introduced until program 10A. The PSP has since been changed to introduce design reviews with program 7A.

TABLE 8.1 RELATIVE DEFECT FIX TIMES

The ratio of fix times in code review, unit test, and after unit test.

	Relative Code Review Time	Relative Unit Test Fix Time	Relative Postunit Test Fix Time
38 Pascal Programs	1	8	16
25 C++ Programs	1	12	60

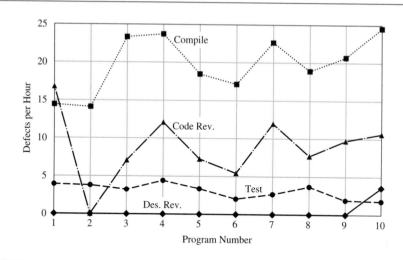

FIGURE 8.3
Defect Removal Rates—Class

CODE REVIEWS ARE MORE EFFICIENT THAN TESTING

In reviews, you find the defects directly; in testing, however, you get only symptoms. The time you spend to get from symptoms to defects is called debugging.
Debugging is the process of finding the actual defect in the program that caused it
to behave improperly. Some trivial defects can produce unbelievably complex
system behavior. You then can spend a lot of time figuring out what caused those
weird symptoms. The amount of debugging time will often bear little relation to
the sophistication of the defect.

It might seem surprising that the defect fix time difference between reviews
and testing could be so large. When you review a program, however, you know
where you are and the results its logic is supposed to produce. As you work
through the code, you establish logical relationships and gradually construct a
mental context of the program's behavior. When you see something you don't understand, it is because the program doesn't do what you thought it would. With
deeper study, you sometimes find the program is correct and sometimes conclude
there is a defect. You thus start with a potential problem and try to find its consequences. With experience, you learn to make such searches quite directly and
logically. You don't need to stumble into a lot of blind alleys to figure out what
could have caused an unexpected behavior. Because the review helps you to
build a mental picture of what the program does and why, you are also in a better
position to correctly fix any problems you find.

In debugging, the situation is quite different. You start with some unexpected system behavior. For example, the screen could go blank or the system may just hang, produce an incorrect result, or print out gibberish on the 87th iteration of a recursive loop. Some confirmed debuggers will argue that they can find defects more efficiently with a debugging tool than they can by inspecting the design or the code. While it is true that some defects can be traced quite quickly, others can be extraordinarily hard to find. In one operating system example, three experienced engineers worked for three months to find a subtle system defect that was causing persistent customer problems. At the time they found this defect, the same code was being inspected by a different team of five engineers. As an experiment, this inspection team was not told about the defect. Within two hours, this team found not only this defect, but also 71 others! Once found, the original defect was trivial to fix.

A debugger's principal advantage is that it helps you to step through the program logic and check the important parameter values. This process is effective, however, only if you know what the parameter values are supposed to be. You thus must have already worked through the program's logic. If you must go through all that trouble anyway, why not be a little more thorough and check the accuracy of the logic at the same time?

NEEDLE IN THE HAYSTACK

If there were only one or two defects in a one-KLOC program, you might question the wisdom of studying every line to ensure its correctness. Of course, whether you do study every line depends on how important it is that the program be defect free. PSP data show, however, that even experienced programmers typically make about 100 defects per KLOC. Four experienced software engineers who took this course produced a total of 1155 LOC for programs 1A, 2A, and 3A. Their total defects for these programs were 107, or 92.6 defects per KLOC. Of these, 58 were found in compile and 49 in test. On these three programs, the engineers' composite defect rate fluctuated between 73 and 113 defects per KLOC. Less experienced students have a much wider range of variation as well as a somewhat higher overall defect rate. In general, however, about half their defects are found in compile; they must find the rest in test.

This means that unless you are unusually talented, you will have to find around 50 defects per KLOC in test. The issue is not how much time you will likely waste looking for a rare defect, but what is the most effective way to find and fix lots of defects. The principal lesson of the PSP is that you have to measure your own work before you will believe how much more effective reviewing is than testing.

8.3   Personal Reviews

When you find engineers who regularly produce programs that run correctly the first time, ask them how they do it. You will find that they take pride in the quality of their products. They carefully review their programs before they first compile or test them. If you want a quality product, you must spend the time to personally engineer it, review it, and rework it until you are satisfied with its quality. Only then is it ready for compiling and testing.

Contrast this method with the more common approach where once the program is coded, the engineer immediately tries to compile it. The compiler then leads the engineer by the nose from one problem to the next. When the program finally compiles, the engineer is so relieved that the immediate desire is to see if it will run. One of the best clues that a shop follows this approach is complaints about how slow the compilers are.

It is interesting to note that there is some correlation between the number of defects found in compile and that found in test. As illustrated in Fig. 8.4, individual data can show a strong relationship between compile and test defects. While the data for groups of students are generally much more random, there is evidence that low compile defects are associated with low test defects.

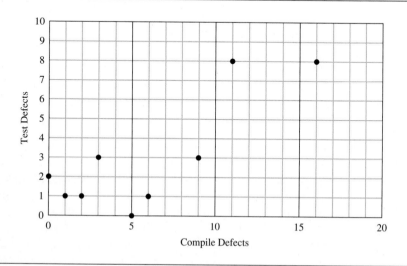

FIGURE 8.4
Compile vs Test Defects—Student 1

The PSP starts by recognizing that all humans are error prone. For a software product of any complexity, your programs will initially have many defects. It is not that you are incompetent, just that you are human. Once you see the data on the defect content of your programs, you can work to find and fix these defects in the most effective way. Following are the steps you should take to do this:

- Gather data on your reviews, your compilations, and your tests.
- Study these data to decide which defect removal methods work best for you.
- Adjust your process to use these defect removal methods.

Each person is different. Until you have data on your own performance, you cannot know how effective reviews will be for you. By using the PSP, however, you need not rely on opinion. You can study your own data and see for yourself. Try the methods that have worked for others and experiment with any ideas you think may be improvements. Learn from the facts, let the data talk, and use your best judgment. But be sure to give each method a fair trial and be guided by what the data tell you. Regardless of what I or anyone else says, if your data support some particular method, then that is probably right for you.

8.4 Review Principles

The basic principles of reviews are the following:

1. Establish defined review goals.
2. Follow a defined review process.
3. Measure and improve your review process.

ESTABLISH REVIEW GOALS

A PSP goal is to find and fix all defects before the first compile or test. By doing design and code reviews before you first compile, you will find many defects that the compiler would also have caught. You will also likely miss a lot. When engineers start doing reviews, their PSP data indicate that they find only about one third to one half of the defects in their programs. By analyzing the data on your reviews and making appropriate changes in your review process, you can significantly improve these rates. With care and practice, many students find they can catch 80 percent or more of their defects before their first compile.

While an 80 percent review yield may not seem bad, few engineers can consistently do that well. Even an 80 percent yield, however, leaves a lot of defects for compile and test. Engineers, however, vary widely in their ability to do reviews. After analyzing your defects and working hard to improve, you may conclude that reviewing is not your strong suit. However, even if your yield is only 50 percent or so you will still find that reviews pay.

Some people are much better at reviewing than are others. Some may even be able to consistently reach a 95 percent or better review yield. In general, however, such high review yields will require that you get help from your teammates or associates through some form of walk-through or inspection. There is nothing wrong with getting help with your work. While you must estimate, design, code, compile, and test your own programs, you are encouraged to use whatever methods you can to improve your review yield. You should, of course, adjust your process to include these methods, record the time you and your associates spend, and report the defects you find.

You may not ultimately set a personal goal of finding 100 percent of your defects before the first compile. However, that is the goal the PSP establishes. It is thus the goal you should pursue while doing the exercises in this book. From your own PSP data, you can then set a goal you feel is appropriate for you. In any event, you should set an explicit goal and strive to meet it. Doing this will require you to measure and track your review processes.

FOLLOW A DEFINED REVIEW PROCESS

The review process is much like other processes. It requires entry criteria, a set of tasks, and exit criteria. A typical code review script is shown in Table 8.2. The design review process is identical except that it has slightly different entry and exit criteria and uses a different checklist.

The principal code review entry criteria are the program design and a listing of the code to be reviewed. The design review entry criteria are similar, except they call for the requirements and specifications instead of the design. You should also have copies of the review checklist; the design, coding, and defect standards; and the Defect and Time Recording logs. Except for the code review checklist, the other items have been discussed in previous chapters. The checklist I have used for C++ programs is shown in Table 8.3.

A checklist is a script for use in the review process. You should use a copy of the checklist whenever you do a review. The completed checklist is then your record of the review. The checklist also disciplines your work and guides you through the detailed steps of your reviews. Because you will likely change your checklists as you improve your reviews, it is helpful to separate them from the review scripts. Doing this enables you to change the checklists without changing anything else. It also simplifies your review scripts.

TABLE 8.2 A TYPICAL CODE REVIEW SCRIPT

Phase No.	Purpose	To guide individuals in the code review of small programs
	Entry Criteria	Program design Source program listing Code review checklist Coding standard Defect type standard Time and defect log forms Stop watch (optional)
1	Review	Follow the code review checklist. Check off each item as it is completed. For multiple procedures or programs, complete a separate checklist for each.
2	Correct	Correct all defects. • If the correction cannot be completed, abort the review and return to the prior phase. Record for each defect: • Defect type (see standard) • Phase injected • Phase removed (code review) • Time to fix the defect
3	Check	Check each defect fix for correctness. Re-review all design changes. Record any fix defects as new defects and, where you have the defective fix number, enter it in the fix defect box. If you do not have a fix number, enter an * in the fix defect box.
	Exit Criteria	A fully reviewed source program One or more Code Review Guideline and Checklist with every line checked All identified defects fixed Completed defect and time logs

Defined review standards are also important. By reviewing against defined standards, you can ensure your programs comply with the established system interfaces, the reuse criteria, the commenting guidelines, the header formats, the naming conventions, and so on.

The exit criteria require that you have checked off every box in the checklist and fixed all identified defects. You should therefore be careful about the items you put on your checklist. If you believe the action should be taken on every review, then state it that way. However, if you believe that you need a review step only under certain conditions, you should carefully word it that way. For exam-

TABLE 8.3 C++ CODE REVIEW GUIDELINE AND CHECKLIST

Program Name and #:

Purpose	To guide you in conducting an effective code review				
General	As you complete each review step, check off that item in the box to the right. Complete the checklist for one program unit before you start to review the next.				
Complete	Verify that the code covers all the design.				
Includes	Verify that includes are complete.				
Initialization	Check variable and parameter initialization: • At program initiation • At start of every loop • At function/procedure entry				
Calls	Check function call formats: • Pointers • Parameters • Use of '&'				
Names	Check name spelling and use: • Is it consistent? • Is it within the declared scope? • Do all structures and classes use '.' reference?				
Strings	Check that all strings are • identified by pointers and • terminated in NULL.				
Pointers	Check that • pointers are initialized NULL, • pointers are deleted only after new, and • new pointers are always deleted after use.				
Output Format	Check the output format: • Line stepping is proper. • Spacing is proper.				
{} Pairs	Ensure the {} are proper and matched.				
Logic Operators	Verify the proper use of ==, =, ||, and so on. Check every logic function for proper ().				
Line-by-line Check	Check every line of code for • instruction syntax and • proper punctuation.				
Standards	Ensure the code conforms to the coding standards.				
File Open and Close	Verify that all files are • properly declared, • opened, and • closed.				

ple, suppose you decide to recheck the design of any loop constructs that had defects. Your checklist should explicitly say something like, "Recheck the design of every loop construct that was found to have a defect."

MEASURE AND IMPROVE YOUR REVIEW PROCESS

You measure your reviews in order to improve their quality. Generally, a high-quality review is one that finds the greatest number of defects in the least amount of time. To assess review quality, you must therefore measure the time you spend on your reviews and track all the defects you find, as well as track those you find later. You then use these data to improve the quality and efficiency of your reviews. Like other skills, however, reviewing takes time to learn and even longer to master. The principal review measures are discussed in Section 8.7.

8.5 Separate Design and Code Reviews

To get high-quality reviews, you should review your design separately from your code. The reasons for doing this are as follows:

☐ **To make designs more understandable**
One problem with attempting to decipher the program's logic from the source code is the volume of material you must review. Even simple source programs can involve several pages of documentation. A design represented in a condensed format is much easier to understand. To ensure design compactness, your design standards should encourage the use of pseudo code, precise mathematical notations, and standardized functional abstractions.

☐ **To save implementation time**
By reviewing the design before you code, you will save the time you would have spent coding incorrect logic. Doing this will also improve program quality because you are more likely to produce a clean implementation when you start with a high-quality design. When you implement an incorrect design and then later review it, you unconsciously try to minimize changes. You seek to correct the design problems in ways that will preserve as much of the existing code as possible. Because you no longer have the single priority of producing a quality design, design quality will likely suffer.

☐ **To avoid missing product defects**
You are more likely to miss product defects when you attempt to review too much material at one time. When you review source code for design defects,

you can easily be sidetracked by coding problems, which can be surprisingly distracting. These obvious errors seem to capture your attention, making it much more difficult for you to visualize the larger design issues. A focus on design while doing code reviews can also cause you to do a poorer job of finding coding problems.

□ **To spot possible design improvements**
By reviewing the design before you implement it, you are more likely to see possible design improvements and be more willing to incorporate them. This step can be important particularly if you design the way I do. When faced with a logic problem, I usually see some "obvious" way to solve it. Sometimes this way is sound, but occasionally it is not. With a little reflection, I will often see a neater solution that takes less code, has a cleaner structure, and is faster and easier to understand and to modify. If you design this way, and if you implement your designs before you review them, you will have made a large investment in this initial design. After implementation, you are thus more likely to stick with a poor but workable design, even if it does not cleanly fit the functional need. With each new problem, you will patch the design. Soon the program can get so complex that you will have trouble understanding it yourself. This type of situation is the source of many thickets of code that are impossible to modify or even to fix.

By reviewing your design before you implement it, you are more likely to examine design alternatives. You will both look for defects and seek ways to make the design neater and cleaner. Clean designs generally stay clean, even when modified. Patched-up designs generally get more complex with every change.

8.6   Design Review Principles

There are no hard and fast rules about the proper way to do design reviews. However, I have found the following guidelines helpful:

□ Produce designs that can be reviewed.

□ Follow an explicit review strategy.

□ Review the design in stages.

□ Verify that the logic correctly implements the requirements.

PRODUCE DESIGNS THAT CAN BE REVIEWED

It is almost impossible to pick up a random design and review it. There are not only questions about the design's context, but also questions about its completeness, representation, notations, standards, and conventions. These complications suggest you should consider review issues when you produce your design. Your goal should be to produce a design that is both correct and reviewable.

For a design to be reviewable, its purpose and function must be explicitly stated. Even when you are reviewing your own design, you should explicitly list the functions it must provide and the constraints and conditions it must satisfy. When you work in a development organization, you may have standards that all designs must meet and particular standards for each system or product. You should also have your own personal design standards. Without all these standards, you will have a poor basis for doing a design review. The presence of defined standards is the first essential condition of a reviewable design.

In addition, the design description must be complete and precise. In the discussion of design and verification issues in Chapters 10 and 12, various techniques are described to help you produce correct and precise designs. Several system issues are also often important: memory allocation, performance, usability, compatibility, expandability, maintainability, and reliability. To the extent that these topics have important design implications, they should be explicitly described and considered during your design reviews.

Finally, a reviewable design should be segmented into logical elements. That is, it must suit a review strategy that focuses on one limited design segment at a time. During the review, you need to build a mental picture of the entire design. My rule of thumb is that the design to be reviewed should be limited to one page of text. While you might prefer to review a larger design than this in one pass, there are no prizes for reviewing the most complex program. The goal is to find and correct all the defects.

Rather than debate the amount of design material you review at one time, you should gather data on your review process and see what works for you. We all have limitations on what we can visualize, and individual abilities to do this vary enormously. If your design reviews have high yield even up to several pages of logic, then feel free to review such designs. I suspect, however, that there is some size beyond which you will start missing design problems. Until you have a sense for what that size is, you would be wise to start with a single page of logic.

FOLLOW AN EXPLICIT DESIGN REVIEW STRATEGY

The review strategy dictates the order in which you examine the various elements of the design. Because this order depends on the structure of the product you are reviewing, your review strategy should be part of your development strategy.

You obviously can't review a design before you produce it. You will also want to review each design in conjunction with other related designs. Doing this will help you to build a review context and to improve your ability to see coupling and interdependency issues. You should thus plan the order of your design work to provide a logical and coherent order for your reviews. While you need not review in the order you design, you do need to provide a review context for every design you review.

REVIEW THE DESIGN IN STAGES

As you review each design segment, consider the following guidelines:

1. Check to ensure you designed all the required program elements. If you omitted any, you may want to suspend the review until you complete the design.

2. Verify the overall program structure and flow. Doing this can be tricky, particularly when the program has multiple states that involve several objects or procedures. Techniques for verifying such designs are described in Chapter 12.

3. Check the program's logical constructs for correctness. How you do this is a matter of personal preference and experience. Whatever your method, you should check every loop and recursion to ensure it terminates under all conditions and it produces the correct result. Several techniques for doing this are described in Chapter 12.

4. After you are reasonably sure the logic performs properly under normal conditions, check it for robustness. If your program is part of a large system or if it will go into the reusable parts library, it must be robust. At some point, another engineer may improperly use your part and cause an overflow or an exception. You may even do it yourself. Unless you identify every instance when such mistakes could occur and ensure your design can handle every one, you or your user engineers will almost certainly encounter time-consuming problems. These odd conditions are fairly easy to check in design reviews, but some of them can be extraordinarily hard to find in test. It is best to be safe, even if doing so adds a substantial amount of logic.

5. Check the function, method, and procedure calls to ensure all the correct parameters and types are specified and each function is properly used. It is also advisable to check the limits and error conditions for every call.

6. Check all the special variables, parameters, data types, and files. Be particularly careful in checking all the aliases used for the abstraction levels. A careful review can often save a lot of testing time.

Some programmers feel the compiler does name and type checks so efficiently that they should not do them. This is a perfectly valid view if their data show they do not have name and type problems. My preference is to check all the globally declared and state-controlling parameters and all the specially declared types during the design review. I then defer the more local name and type checks until the code review.

A frequent symptom of design problems is when many parameters are passed through multiple objects or procedures. This situation often indicates that the original design concept did not quite fit the problem being solved. This condition is relatively easy to check during the design review, giving you an early indication of design problems. Almost any passing of multiple variables or parameters across several object or procedure levels indicates a troublesome and defect-prone design.

VERIFY THAT THE LOGIC CORRECTLY IMPLEMENTS THE REQUIREMENTS

Verifying that the logic correctly implements the requirements is, in principle, a simple check. It can, however, involve a lot of work. It involves going back to the requirements and verifying that they are completely covered by the design. Oversights and omissions are important defect categories that can be handled almost completely by a careful review of the design against the requirements.

8.7 Review Measures

The four explicit review measures are

- □ the size of the program being reviewed,
- □ the review time in minutes,
- □ the number of defects found, and
- □ the number of defects in the program that were later found. (These are called *escapes*.)

The appropriate size measure for code reviews is LOC. For design reviews, however, you have no LOC count at review time. You could thus use text lines or pages of design as a general size measure. I have found, however, that I generally analyze my reviews later when LOC measures for the design are available. For early analysis, you can then still deal with defects per estimated LOC reviewed per hour. At review time, you can use either estimated LOC or a rule of thumb such as one pseudocode line equals three LOC or some other conversion that is appropriate for your particular design style.

From these basic measures, you can derive several other useful measures. The most important ones are

□ the review yield, that is, the percentage of defects in the program that were found during the review,

□ the defects found per KLOC of design or code reviewed,

□ the defects found per hour of review time,

□ the LOC reviewed per hour, and

□ defect removal leverage (DRL), or the relative rate of defect removal for any two process phases.

These measures are discussed further in the following paragraphs.

REVIEW YIELD

Review yield refers to the percentage of defects in the design or code at the time of the review that were found by that review. This measure cannot be precisely calculated until after the reviewed program has been thoroughly tested and extensively used. Even then, there could be some latent defects still to be discovered. However, you can make useful early approximations of review yield. For example, if you find three defects in design review, one during coding, eight in code review, and six in compile, you know that your maximum review yield is 57.1 percent and can be much lower. If you subsequently find three defects in unit test, clearly there were at least nine you missed and eight you found in code review. Your maximum review yield then declines to 47.1 percent. You may also have historical data that shows that generally one more defect is later found in integration test, system test, or customer use for every three defects found in compile and unit test. The resulting defect profile for this product would then be as shown in Table 8.4.

In this table, the defects found in each phase are listed in the second column. At each process phase in which you find defects, you learn more about when defects were injected. In the Design Review column under Defects Injected, you know only that of the three defects found one was injected in planning and two in design. During coding, you find another defect injected in design, so you now know that the design review found three of the four known defects in the product—a 75 percent yield. During code review, you find eight defects—one injected in design and seven in coding. As far as you know, you have now found all eight of the defects in the code—a 100 percent code review yield; however, you found one more defect the design review missed, bringing its current yield to 60 percent. During compile, you find six more defects, all of which were injected

TABLE 8.4   A YIELD CALCULATION EXAMPLE

Phase	Defects Found	Defects Injected					
		Design Review	Code	Code Review	Compile	Test	Post Development
Planning	0	1	1	1	1	1	1
Detailed Design	0	2	3	4	4	5	6
Design Review	3						
Code	1			7	13	15	17
Code Review	8						
Compile	6						
Test	3						
Post Development	3						
Total	24						
Yield							
Design Review		3/3 = 100%	3/4 = 75%	3/5 = 60%	3/5 = 60%	3/6 = 50%	3/7 = 42.9%
Code Review				8/8 = 100%	8/14 = 57.1%	8/17 = 47.1%	8/20 = 40%
Total Process		3/3 = 100%	4/4 = 100%	12/12 = 100%	12/18 = 66.7%	12/21 = 57.1%	12/24 = 50.0%

$$Yield = \frac{100*Defects\ removed\ before\ compile}{Defects\ injected\ before\ compile}$$

during coding, so you actually found only eight of the 14 defects in the product at code review time, for a yield of 57.1 percent. The way you calculate the number 14 is to note that 18 defects were found through compile and four were removed before code review. None were injected after code review, so all 14 were in the product at the time of code review. The test and post development defect data further refine your design and code review yield numbers. Note that Total Process yield is the percentage of defects found before first compile. It is shown at the bottom of Table 8.4 and is 57.1 percent at test exit and 50.0 percent when you consider the postdevelopment data.

TABLE 8.5   EXAMPLE DEFECT LOG DATA

Defects #	Phase Injected	Phase Removed
1	Design	Design Review
2	Planning	Design Review
3	Design	Design Review
4	Design	Code
5	Code	Code Review
6	Code	Code Review
7	Design	Code Review
8	Code	Code Review
9	Code	Code Review
10	Code	Code Review
11	Code	Code Review
12	Code	Code Review
13	Code	Compile
14	Code	Compile
15	Code	Compile
16	Code	Compile
17	Code	Compile
18	Code	Compile
19	Code	Test
20	Code	Test
21	Design	Test

For yield calculation, the essential data are the process phase at which each defect was injected and the phase in which it was found. The phase escapes are then all those defects injected before or during the phase, not found before or during the phase, and found later. An example of the kind of data you would get from the PSP Defect Recording Log is shown in Table 8.5. Because these data are difficult to analyze in this form, the PSP summarizes them on the Project Plan Summary forms. To show how the yield calculation is done, however, I use these data to construct Table 8.6. Note that the left two columns are precisely the data you have been recording in the Plan and Summary Report Form. You complete these columns by counting the numbers of defects in your defect log that were injected and removed in each phase. The Cumulative Injected and Cumulative Removed columns are then the cumulative sums of these columns up to each phase. The escapes from each phase can now be calculated by subtracting each entry in the Cumulative Removed column from the corresponding entry in the Cumulative Injected column. The yield for any phase or the total process can then be calculated by using the formulas at the bottom of the table. Without the information in Table 8.6, you cannot calculate yield and you cannot accurately judge the effectiveness of your review processes.

It is clear from this that a high yield would be good and a low yield poor. The yield goal should be 100 percent. Some data on C++ code review yield that I achieved with my PSP research are shown in Fig. 8.5. As you can see, despite considerable yield fluctuation there is a gradual, improving trend.

The yield improvements for 12 students in a PSP course are shown in Fig. 8.6. Improvements in review yield take time and the rate of improvement varies widely among individuals. The trend for this class, however, was clearly up.

INSTANT MEASURES

While yield gives the best measure of review quality, it cannot be accurately calculated until well after the review is completed. Thus you must find current or in-

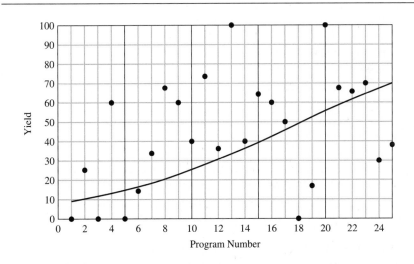

FIGURE 8.5
C++ Code Review Yield

TABLE 8.6   EXAMPLE DEFECT SUMMARY

Phase	Injected	Removed	Cumulative Injected	Cumulative Removed	Net Escapes
Planning	1	0	1	0	1
Detailed Design	5	0	6	0	6
Design Review	0	3	6	3	3
Code	15	1	21	4	17
Code Review	0	8	21	12	9
Compile	0	6	21	18	3
Test	0	3	21	21	0
Total	21	21			

$$\text{Phase\_yield} = 100* \frac{Removed\_in\_phase}{Removed\_in\_phase + Net\_escapes\_for\_phase}$$

$$\text{Design\_review\_yield} = 100* \frac{3}{3 + 3} = 50\%$$

$$\text{Code\_review\_yield} = 100* \frac{8}{8 + 9} = 47.1\%$$

$$\text{Compile\_yield} = 100* \frac{6}{6 + 3} = 66.7\%$$

$$\text{Process\_yield} = 100* \frac{Removed\ before\ compile}{Removed\ before\ compile + escapes\ into\ compile\ and\ test}$$

$$\text{Process\_yield} = 100* \frac{3 + 1 + 8}{3 + 1 + 8 + 9} = 100*\frac{12}{21} = 57.1\%$$

stant measures that correlate with yield so that you can know how good your reviews are likely to be while you are doing them. This knowledge enables you to better manage your review process and thus to get higher yields more consistently.

The defects per KLOC is an instant measure that can be calculated during a code review and used to judge review quality. Because you can also generally judge LOC quite accurately from a completed design, you can view defects per KLOC as an instant measure for both design and code reviews. The defects per KLOC measure presents one problem, however: It is hard to tell whether a low rate means the review was superficial or the program began with few defects. As you can see from Fig. 8.7, high defects per KLOC found in review does seem to indicate high yield, at least for my C++ programs. While the highest defects per KLOC are associated with the highest yield, the correlation is not strong.

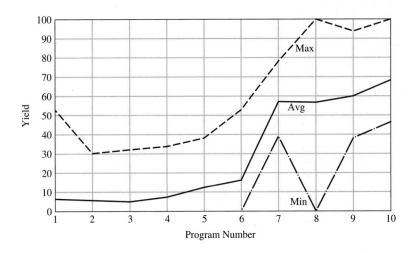

FIGURE 8.6
Yield—12 Students

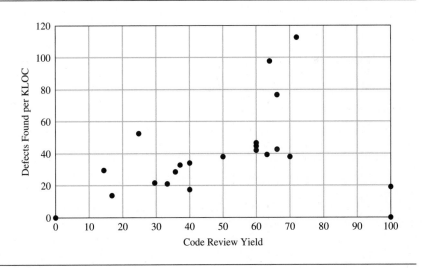

FIGURE 8.7
Defects/KLOC versus Yield
25 C++ Programs

The defects per hour measure shown in Fig. 8.8 indicates the effectiveness of your review time. For example, if your defects per hour has been declining but your yield has not been increasing, you may be spending too much time in unproductive reviews. As long as yield is increasing, a declining defects per hour rate is natural. The data in Fig. 8.8 do not show any strong correlation between defects per hour and yield.

The KLOC per hour measure tells whether you are trying to review too much design or code too quickly. By plotting yield versus LOC reviewed per hour, you can get some idea of the yield consequences of reviewing too quickly. From Fig. 8.9, you can see that the high-yield code reviews tended to be below 200 LOC per hour and many of the low-yield reviews were at higher rates. The composite data on the class of 12 students do not clearly show this because of the wide variations among the students and because most students had only done a few reviews by the end of the course. As shown in Fig. 8.10, however, Student 12 had done code reviews for all 10 programs. The student's data also clearly show that high yields are associated with lower review rates. It appears that rates of 100 to 200 LOC per hour were required to give moderately high yields. This result is consistent with the findings on review rates for code inspections, where 300 LOC per hour is considered an upper limit. [Fagan 86, Gilb, Humphrey 89] While you will get data on only a few of your design and code reviews during the

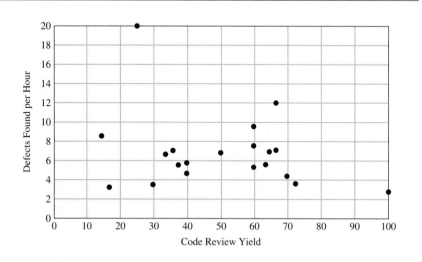

FIGURE 8.8
Defects/Hour versus Yield
25 C++ Programs

should periodically review the yield of your reviews to see how you are doing. For example, on the name/type check see how many of these defects you catch with the review. If your yield is low, watch yourself on your next review to see if you can devise a more effective technique.

You may also have a problem reviewing multiple small routines or procedures. For example, if you review a program with several procedures you should establish a review strategy. Suppose the program had a main routine and three principal procedures. If the main routine and the procedures each had about 50 to 75 lines of source code, you may consider reviewing the entire program in one pass of the checklist. To decide if this would be a sound strategy, look again at Table 8.3 and picture the following review process:

1. Ensure the code covers all the design by reviewing the main routine and each procedure to check that all the required functions are included.

2. Check the main routine and each procedure to ensure the proper includes are entered for each library function.

3. Again think through the logic of the main routine and each procedure as you check initialization.

When you do the review this way, you will likely find yourself jumping back and forth among the main routine and the procedures. You will build a mental context as you examine one procedure that you lose when you switch to another. Because context switches take time and often cause errors, you are increasing the likelihood of a low yield review. When programs are even moderately complex, it pays to review each separable part as a unit. You should thus complete the entire checklist for each part before you go on to the next. If you have any doubt that this is the best approach, do a controlled experiment where you follow one strategy with several programs or parts of programs and another strategy with the rest. The data on defects per hour, LOC per hour, and yield should help you decide which approach is most effective for you.

With a large hierarchical program, your design review strategy will likely follow some top-down pattern. For the code review, however, it is often best to start reviewing at the bottom. For example, consider a main routine that calls various procedures. One of these procedures in turn calls a file-handling routine. Here, you should start your code review with the lowest level procedures that depend on no others, in this case, the file-handling routine. After you have reviewed the code in the lowest level procedures, move up to the procedures that call them. As part of this higher level review, check to ensure every call is consistent with the procedure specifications. You do not need to look further into the procedure, however, since you have just reviewed it. By following this order up to the main routine, you can trust the procedural abstractions when you encounter them during the higher level code reviews. If you don't do this, you will keep tracing through the called procedures just to be sure they do what they are supposed to do.

This strategy applies only when you are reviewing your own code because you will have a context for your reviews. You may remember the overall design or have some design records or notes that explain the program's purpose and structure. When you start at the lowest level and work up, you are looking for local issues and checking that all the coding details are correct. When you are reviewing unfamiliar code, you will likely want to follow more of a top-down strategy.

BUILDING CHECKLISTS

I built the PSP Code Review Guideline and Checklist based on my experiences in writing C++ programs. As I analyzed the defects I found and the ones I missed, I could soon see where I needed to focus my reviews. This checklist thus may not fit your needs. To build your own design or code review checklist that is appropriate for the problems you face, you will need to review your defect data to see where you should focus your review attention.

Start with the PSP defect type standard that was introduced with PSP0. It is shown again in Table 8.9. As you gather defect data, you will soon discover that some of these categories give you a lot of trouble and others are not worth much

TABLE 8.9 SUMMARY DEFECT TYPE STANDARD[1]

Defect Type Number	Type Name	Description
10	Documentation	comments, messages
20	Syntax	spelling, punctuation, typos, instruction formats
30	Build, package	change management, library, version control
40	Assignment	declaration, duplicate names, scope, limits
50	Interface	procedure calls and references, I/O, user formats
60	Checking	error messages, inadequate checks
70	Data	structure, content
80	Function	logic, pointers, loops, recursion, computation, function defects
90	System	configuration, timing, memory
100	Environment	design, compile, test, other support system problems

Source: [1]The main defect types were taken from R. Chillarege, I. Bhandari, J. Chaar, M. Halliday, D. Moebus, B. Ray, and M.-Y Wong: "Orthogonal Defect Classification—A Concept of In-Process Measurements," *IEEE Transactions on Software Engineering*, vol. 18, no. 11 (November 1992): 943–956.

attention. I found that four areas—syntax, function, interface, and assignment—accounted for 97 percent of all my compile and test defects.

I next examined my defect logs to determine the specific defect types I encountered so that I could devise checks to find them. This led me to expand the four principal defect types into four or five subcategories as shown in Table 8.10. Doing this allowed me to focus my reviews more specifically on the types of defects that occurred most frequently in my programs, as indicated by the percentages in the right column. These are the percentages of the defect types that were either found in the review or later found in compile and test.

A sorted defect list is called a *Pareto distribution*. Your defect data are sorted with the most frequent type at the left. The defect type frequency distribution shown in Table 8.10 is shown in Fig. 8.12 in Pareto distribution format. Based on the defect types you choose, you can establish your review checklists to focus on the most prevalent types first.

It is wise to reexamine this Pareto distribution periodically to ensure you are still properly focusing on the most prevalent types you miss in your reviews. As you get more successful at finding one defect type, you may want to increase your priorities in other areas. You must be careful not to drop a defect type from

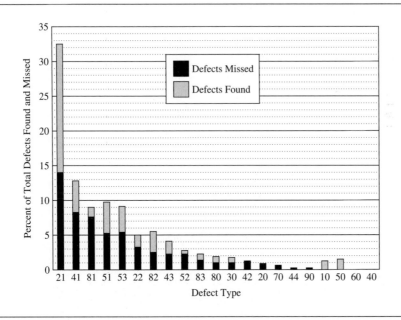

FIGURE 8.12
C++ Code Review Defects
Pareto Distribution (Types, Table 8.10)

TABLE 8.10   DEFECT TYPE STANDARD

Purpose	To facilitate cause analysis and defect prevention		
Note	The types are grouped in ten general categories. • If the detailed category does not apply, use the general category. • The % column lists an example type distribution.		

No.	Name	Description	%
10	Documentation	comments, messages, manuals	1.1
20	Syntax	general syntax problems	0.8
21	Typos	spelling, punctuation	32.1
22	Instruction formats	general format problem	5.0
23	Begin-end	did not properly delimit operation	0
30	Packaging	change management, version control, system build	1.6
40	Assignment	general assignment problem	0
41	Naming	declaration, duplicates	12.6
42	Scope		1.3
43	Initialize and close	variables, objects, and so on	4.0
44	Range	variable limits, array range	0.3
50	Interface	general interface problems	1.3
51	Internal	procedure calls and references	9.5
52	I/O	file, display, printer, communication	2.6
53	User	formats, content	8.9
60	Checking	error messages, inadequate checks	0
70	Data	structure, content	0.5
80	Function	general logic	1.8
81	Pointers	pointers, strings	8.7
82	Loops	off-by-one, incrementing, recursion	5.5
83	Application	computation, algorithmic	2.1
90	System	timing, memory, and so on	0.3
100	Environment	design, compile, test, other support system problems	0

your checklist unless you no longer encounter those types. If you still make a lot of off-by-one errors, for example, but find them all in your code review, you cannot stop reviewing for that defect type. If you did, you would then have to find more of them in test. This is why you should look at the Pareto distribution of both the defects you find and those you miss.

Add items to your checklist based on what you miss in your reviews but keep items on your list based on the total of those you find and miss. This suggests that you not only sort your Pareto distribution in the order of the defects you miss, as in Fig. 8.12, but also by the number of defects you find by type.

REVIEWING AGAINST CODING STANDARDS

Your principal interest in a code review is to ensure all the details are properly handled. Here is where your coding standard can be a big help. It should require that every parameter be initialized before use and that all new pointers be first nulled and later deleted. It should call for robustness checks to ensure all calls have the proper parameter values, overflows are detected, and I/O errors do not disrupt program operation. Each procedure should check for erroneous input and provide clear error messages in the event of problems.

While your defensive programming practices must be influenced by the application and system environment, you should establish a consistent set of personal practices. Once you have decided on your practices, incorporate them in your standards and check them in your reviews. They will help you to prevent problems, to identify problems in test, and to protect your users.

8.9   Reviewing before or after You Compile

One of the more contentious PSP issues is whether to review your code before or after you compile it. Some programmers refuse to consider reviewing their code before they do a first compile. They feel the compiler is designed to find simple syntax errors and that trying to find them by hand is a waste of time.

The issue, however, is not quite that simple. If the compiler caught 100 percent of all syntax errors, you would not have to search for them in code reviews. My PSP research data on 2041 defects show that 8.7 percent of Pascal syntax errors and 9.3 percent of C++ syntax errors are not caught by the compiler. This does not mean that the compiler was faulty, just that random errors occasionally produce valid syntax. The code, however, does not do what was intended. The defect types that were caught and missed by the C++ compiler are shown in Fig. 8.13. Here, the 9.3 percent is composed of all the types 20, 21, 22, 23, 41, and 51 defects. These are the defect types shown in Table 8.10. Compilers can be very effective at finding syntax, naming, and referencing defects, but they will not find them all.

THE ARGUMENTS PRO AND CON

There are valid arguments both for compiling first and for reviewing first. The reasons for compiling before doing a review are the following:

□ As illustrated in Fig. 8.11, for some defect types compiling has about twice the leverage of code reviews.

□ The compiler is highly effective. It will find about 90 percent of syntax and naming defects.

□ Individual effectiveness varies. In spite of your best efforts, you will likely miss between 20 percent and 50 percent of your syntax defects. This result is highly individual, however; some reviewers can catch most syntax problems, while others catch very few.

□ The syntax defects missed by the compiler are generally not difficult to find in test.

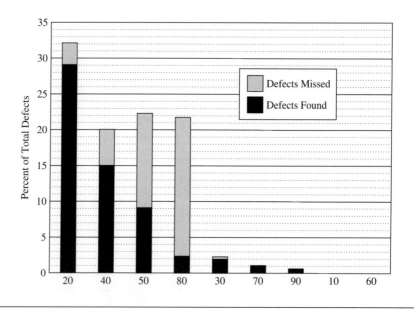

FIGURE 8.13
C++ Compile Total Defects

The points that favor reviewing before compiling are as follows:

- □ The compiler does miss about 9 percent of the syntax defects.
- □ Finding the defects in the review will both save compile time and make it more predictable.
- □ On average, it takes several times longer to fix syntax errors in test than it does in code review. While most syntax defects the compiler misses will be quickly found in test, PSP data show that occasionally one will take much longer.
- □ Unit testing typically finds about half a program's defects. If you count on the compiler to find all syntax problems, about 4 percent of them will likely escape both the compiler and unit test and have to be caught by integration test, system test, or the users.
- □ Typically, subsequent test phases have even lower yields than does unit test. [Thayer]
- □ It is hard to do thorough syntax reviews of compiled code because you find so few syntax problems. Reviewing before compile is more rewarding and thus more effective.
- □ If you are going to review the code for syntax errors, you won't save time by compiling first. However, you will save time by reviewing first.

Personal satisfaction is also important. You will likely get great satisfaction from a clean compile, while a code review that finds nothing seems like a waste of time. Because reviewing compiled code will find only about one tenth as many syntax and naming defects, you may easily get discouraged and stop looking very carefully. After a while, you are likely to stop doing code reviews entirely.

There also is an economical trade-off. If you compile first, your syntax reviews will probably not be as thorough. You thus will be left to find approximately 9 percent of the syntax defects in test. On the other hand, if you do the review first and find from 50 percent to 80 percent of the syntax defects, there will be only about 2 percent of them left to be found in test. Because unit testing is generally only about 50 percent effective, anything you miss could get pretty far through the process. Further, because it typically takes several hours to find each defect in system test you don't want to miss a single defect at the PSP level, almost regardless of the cost.

REVIEW OBJECTIVES

The issue here is your objective. If your objective is to get into test as quickly as possible, there is probably no way to convince you to review before you compile. On the other hand, you should be careful not to confuse speed with progress.

While getting into test often seems like progress, you may be faced with a lot of debugging work. If you try it both ways and measure the results, you will likely find that by reviewing first you take longer to get into test but your total time to finish test is less.

Conversely, if your goal is to remove the maximum number of defects, you will want to do your code reviews when they are most effective. The compiler is equally effective regardless of when it is run, so if you can find any defects it would miss, you are ahead.

My preference is to review the code before compiling and to use the compiler as a statistical check on the quality of my code review. If the compiler finds more than a very few defects, then I may have a quality problem. This can be seen for my PSP programs in Fig. 8.14, where a high number of compile defects per KLOC is associated with a low code review yield. Figure 8.4 showed the relationship between compile defects/KLOC and test defects/KLOC for one student. While this relationship is stronger for some engineers than for others, when the compiler finds more defects than usual, it is likely that testing will as well. If you want to get consistently low defect rates in test, you should strive to get low defect rates in compile. I strongly recommend reviewing your code before you compile, but if you are not convinced try it both ways. The data you gather can then help you to make a rational decision.

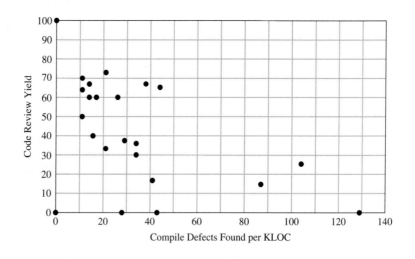

FIGURE 8.14
Compile Defects versus Yield
C++ Code Review

8.10   The Relationship between Reviews and Inspections

In a personal review, you privately review your own program. An inspection is a team review of your program. Inspections are the single most valuable quality technique a software team can use. [Fagan 76, Gilb, Humphrey 89]

As you strive to achieve 100 percent process yield, you should consider incorporating inspections into your PSP process. Even for the exercises in this book, you could ask one or two classmates to inspect your code and offer to inspect theirs in return. If you do this, you should adjust your process to include this step, include your and your reviewers' times in your Time Recording Log, and report all the defects you find. If you do choose to use inspections, you next must decide where in the PSP to put them. The principal questions are whether you should review the code before the inspection and whether to compile before the inspection.

The central issue is one of personal standards. Would you give somebody a rough draft of a technical report to review? You would presumably read it first to eliminate any obvious mistakes. Programs are much the same. Most first-draft programs have obvious defects that stand out in even a cursory review. Do you want each of your reviewers to separately wade through these obvious defects just because you were too lazy to read and correct them first?

This is not just a question of courtesy. Obvious defects are distracting. You are most interested in finding logic problems. When you leave a lot of simple problems in your code, your reviewers are much less likely to see the important ones. To maximize the effectiveness of their time, you should thus make your code as clean as you can before you have it inspected.

Someone who inspects your code is making you a gift of time solely to help you to improve the quality of your product. To show your appreciation, you should treat that time as important by ensuring your code is as clean as you can before submitting it for the inspection.

Whether you compile before the inspection is much more debatable. The issue here concerns where you need help. While you are working to get your defects under control, it might be helpful to have some associates inspect your code before you compile. You objective, however, should be to improve your review skills until you can find most syntax errors yourself. When you can do this, you will then make more effective use of your associates' time by compiling first and having them focus on inspecting design issues.

If the quality of the code entering an inspection is so important, why not also unit test it first? Here, the question regards inspection psychology. When the inspectors know that the code has been tested, they often are not as thorough in their analyses. It could seem pointless, for example, for them to struggle through a complex verification of a while loop when they know it has already been tested. Even though most programmers know that the initial unit test will not find all the defects in a complex program, the fact that the program is known to run can be demotivating. I recommend you not test your programs before the first code inspection. Your inspection target should then be that no defects are subsequently found in test. Your personal review goal, of course, should be that no defects are found in the inspection.

8.11   Summary

The purpose of reviews is to ensure the programs you produce are of the highest quality. Of the many kinds of reviews you can perform, the principal ones are inspections, walk-throughs, and personal reviews. Reviews can be used on the requirements, design, documentation, or any other product element. This chapter deals with design and code reviews.

Many software projects spend almost half their development time in test. This is very inefficient. Design and code reviews are much more efficient ways to find and fix defects. With reviews, you can find the defects directly, while in test you get only symptoms. The crucial difference between these two approaches is called debugging. When you review a program, you know where you are and what the logic is supposed to be doing. Your fixes are then more likely to be complete and correct.

Your PSP reviews will net you a greater return than any other single thing you can do. You should read each program, study it, and understand it. Fix the defects, logic, structure, and clarity. Then learn to rewrite your programs. When areas are unclear or confusing, add comments or, better yet, do a complete rewrite. Make it easy to read and to understand. Produce something you would be proud to publish or to show to your friends and associates.

The three basic principles of personal reviews are to establish review goals, follow a disciplined process, and measure and improve this process. Your decision to do reviews is driven by your desire to be productive and to produce quality products. To tell if your reviews are helping you to achieve these goals, you need to measure them.

This is where you use a Pareto distribution to establish review priorities and to develop a review checklist. It is wise to reexamine this Pareto distribution periodically to ensure you are still properly focusing on the most significant defects for your process.

One of the more contentious PSP issues is whether to review your code before or after you compile. While there are valid arguments for both approaches, my preference is to review the code before compiling. I then use the compiler as a statistical check on the quality of my review. If the compiler finds more than a very few defects, there is likely a quality problem.

While yield gives the best measure of review quality, you cannot calculate it until after you have completed development. It is thus essential to find current or instant measures that correlate with yield, such as LOC reviewed per hour. You can use these control data to improve the quality of your reviews.

8.12 Exercises

The standard course plan for this chapter requires you to produce R4, the mid-term report, at this point. You should also produce a design review checklist and a code review checklist for use with PSP2. Examples of PSP design and code review checklists are shown in Tables C57 and C58 in Appendix C. The specification for report R4 is given in Appendix D.

For other assignment options, consult Appendix D.

References

[Chillarege] Ram Chillarege, Inderpal S. Bhandari, Jarir K. Chaar, Michael J. Halliday, Diane S. Moebus, Bonnie K. Ray, and Man-Yuen Wong, "Orthogonal Defect Classification—A Concept for In-Process Measurements," *IEEE Transactions on Software Engineering,* vol. 18, no. 11 (November 1992): 943–956.

[Fagan 76] Michael Fagan, "Design and Code Inspections to Reduce Errors in Program Development," *IBM Systems Journal,* vol. 15, no. 3 (1976).

[Fagan 86] Michael Fagan, "Advances in Software Inspections," *IEEE Transactions on Software Engineering,* vol. SE-12, no. 7 (July 1986).

[Gilb 94] Tom Gilb and Dorothy Graham, *Software Inspections+*, in press.

[Humphrey 89] W. S. Humphrey, *Managing the Software Process* (Reading, MA: Addison-Wesley, 1989).

[Thayer] T. A. Thayer, M. Lipow, and E. C. Nelson. *Software Reliability, A Study of Large Project Reality,* vol. 2, TRW Series of Software Technology (Amsterdam: North-Holland, 1978).

9

Software Quality Management

If you want a high quality software system, you must ensure each of its parts is of high quality. The PSP strategy focuses on managing the defects in the software you produce. By improving your defect management, you will produce more consistently reliable components. These components, in turn, can then be combined into progressively higher quality systems.

While the quality benefits of this strategy are important, the productivity benefits are even more significant. Software productivity generally declines with increasing product size. [Boehm 81] One reason for this is the increased work entailed by the greater product volume. Another, more important reason is the quality of the product's parts. As products get larger, the increased amount of logic makes debugging much more difficult. More debugging in turn requires much more time in test.

When you produce parts of very high quality, your process will scale up with much less reduction in productivity. This is because as you add new elements to a progressively larger product, your testing need concern only the quality of the new parts. While you could have interface problems, the bulk of your testing will be localized. Hence you will largely retain your small program productivity when you develop larger programs. The PSP3 process introduced in Chapter 11 follows this strategy.

To improve your product, you must improve your process quality. Doing this requires you to measure and track process quality. As you did the exercises in the previous chapters, you gathered a lot of data that you now can use to evaluate the quality of your PSP process. This chapter shows you how process quality relates to product quality and how to use PSP data to measure and track process quality. It first defines software quality and then discusses the economic consequences of poor quality. It next deals with process measurement, process analysis, benchmarking, yield management, and defect management.

9.1   What Is Software Quality?

The principal focus of any software quality definition should be the users' needs. Crosby defines quality as "conformance to requirements." [Crosby] While one can debate the distinction between requirements, needs, and wants, quality definitions must consider the users' perspectives. The key questions then are, who are the users, what is important to them, and how do their priorities relate to the way you build, package, and support your products?

PRODUCT QUALITY

To answer these questions, you must recognize the hierarchical nature of software quality. First, a software product must provide functions of a type and at a time when the user needs them. If it does not, nothing else matters. Second, the product must work. If it has so many defects that it does not perform with reasonable consistency, the users will not use it regardless of its other attributes. This does not mean defects are always the highest priority, but they can be very important. If a minimum defect level has not been achieved, nothing else matters. Beyond this quality threshold, however, the relative importance of defects—as well as of usability, compatibility, functionality, and all the other "ilities"—depends on the user, the application, and the environment.

In a broad sense, the users' views of quality must deal with the product's ease of installation, operational efficiency, and convenience. Will it run on the intended system, will it run the planned applications, and will it handle the required files? Is the product convenient, can the users remember how to use it, and can they easily find out what they do not know? Is the product responsive, does it surprise the users, does it protect them from themselves, does it protect them from others, and does it insulate them from the system's operational mechanics? These and a host of similar questions are important to the users. While priorities will vary among users, quality has many layers, and no universal definition will apply in every case. If your software does not measure up in any single area that is important to your users, they will not judge your product to be of high quality.

While few software people will debate these points, their actions are not consistent with these priorities. Rather than devoting major parts of their development processes to installability, usability, and operational efficiency, they spend them on testing, the largest single cost element in most software organizations. Furthermore, these testing costs are almost exclusively devoted to finding and fixing defects.

When the quality of the parts of a software system is poor, the development process becomes fixated on finding and fixing defects. The magnitude of this fix process is often a surprise. As a result, the entire project becomes so preoccupied with defect repair that more important user concerns are ignored. When a project is struggling to fix defects in system test, it is usually in schedule trouble as well. The pressures to deliver become so intense that all other concerns are forgotten in the drive to fix the last defects. When the system tests finally run, everyone is so relieved that they ship the product. However, by fixing these critical system test defects, the product reached only a bare minimum quality threshold. What has been done to assure the product is usable or installable? What about compatibility or performance? Has anyone checked that the documentation is understandable or that the design is suitable for future enhancement? Because the project's development team has been so obsessed with fixing defects, it has not had the time or resources to address the issues that will ultimately be of greater concern to the users.

By sharply reducing the defect content of your small programs, use of the PSP will permit your projects to address the more important aspects of software quality. The quality of the product and the process thus go hand in hand. When a poor-quality product is put into test it generally means the development process could not be completed on schedule or within the committed costs. Moreover, a poor quality process will generally produce a poor quality product.

Even though software defects are only one facet of software quality, that is the quality focus of this book. It is not that controlling them should be the top priority but that effective defect management provides an essential foundation on which a truly comprehensive quality strategy can be built. While defects can come from many sources, with few exceptions software defects result from errors by individuals. Therefore, to properly address defects and the errors that cause them, you must deal with defects at the individual level. This is where defects are made, and this is where they should be found and fixed.

PROCESS QUALITY

Quality software was previously defined as software that meets the users' needs. A similar definition applies to the software process. Here, the users are the software engineers and, for the PSP, this is you. The definition of a quality PSP is thus a PSP that meets your need to efficiently produce quality products.

Some process requirements are fairly obvious and some are not. The most obvious requirement is that the process consistently produces quality software. Some process measures should thus measure the quality of the finished product. Other less obvious requirements deal with how usable and efficient the process is and how readily you can learn and adapt it.

The list of process requirements can be expanded almost indefinitely. However, the key point is that the definition of a quality PSP is in your hands. The software development process must serve you, and you are the only one who can speak with certainty about how well it does that. You should think about the quality of your process and establish the criteria that will help you to measure it, track it, and consistently improve it.

9.2   The Economics of Software Quality

Software quality can be viewed as an economic issue. You can always run another test or do another inspection. In large systems, every new test generally exposes a host of new defects. It is thus hard to know when to stop testing. While it is important to produce a quality product, each test costs money and takes time. Economics is thus an important quality issue not only because of this test decision but also because of the need to optimize life-cycle quality costs. The key to doing this is to recognize that you must put a quality product into test before you can expect to get one out. The next sections show why this is true.

THE COSTS OF FINDING AND FIXING DEFECTS

The economics of software quality largely concern the costs of defect detection, prevention, and removal. The cost of finding and fixing a defect includes each of the following elements:

- Determining that there is a problem
- Isolating the source of the problem
- Determining exactly what is wrong with the product
- Fixing the requirements as needed
- Fixing the design as needed
- Fixing the implementation as needed
- Inspecting the fix to ensure it is correct

□ Testing the fix to ensure it fixes the identified problem

□ Testing the fix to ensure it doesn't cause other problems

□ Changing the documentation as needed to reflect the fix

While every fix will not involve every cost element, the longer the defect is in the product the larger the number of elements that will likely be involved. Finding a requirements problem in test can thus be very expensive. Finding a coding error during a code review, however, will generally cost much less. Your objective thus should be to remove defects from the requirements, the designs, and the code as soon as possible. Reviewing and inspecting programs soon after they are produced minimizes the number of defects in the product at every stage. Doing this also minimizes the amount of rework and the rework costs. It will also likely reduce the costs of finding the defects in the first place.

Some Fix Time Data.   There are not many published data on the time required to identify software defects. Following are some that are available:

□ IBM: An unpublished IBM rule of thumb for the relative costs to identify software defects: during design, 1.5; prior to coding, 1; during coding, 1.5; prior to test, 10; during test, 60; in field use, 100.

□ TRW: The relative times to identify defects: during requirements, 1; during design, 3 to 6; during coding, 10; in development test, 15 to 40; in acceptance test, 30 to 70; during operation, 40 to 1000. [Boehm 81]

□ IBM: The relative time to identify defects: during design reviews, 1; during code inspections, 20; during machine test, 82. [Remus]

□ JPL: Bush reports an average cost per defect: $90 to $120 in inspections and $10,000 in test. [Bush]

□ Freedman and Weinberg: They report that projects that used reviews and inspections had a tenfold reduction in the number of defects found in test and a 50 percent to 80 percent reduction in test costs, including the costs of the reviews and inspections. [Freedman]

Some other defect data are shown in Table 9.1.

Clearly, defect identification costs are highest during test and use. Thus anyone who seeks to reduce development cost or time should focus on preventing or removing defects before starting test. This conclusion is reinforced by the PSP data on the fix times for the 664 C++ defects and 1377 Pascal defects I found in the development of more than 70 small programs. These data, shown in Figs. 9.1 and 9.2, are for the times to both find and fix these defects. Fix times are clearly much longer during test and use than in the earlier phases. While this pattern varies somewhat between the two languages and by defect type, the principal factor determining defect fix time is the phase in which the defect was found.

TABLE 9.1   HOURS TO FIND A DEFECT

Reference	Inspection	Test	Use
Ackerman	1	2–10	
O'Neill	.26		
Ragland		20	
Russell	1	2–4	33
Shooman	.6	3.05	
vanGenuchten	.25	8	
Weller	.7	6	

A question often raised about these data is, "How do you know that the easy defects are not being found in the inspections with the difficult ones being left for test?" While this question cannot be resolved without substantially more statistical data, there is some evidence that inspections are as good as or better at finding the difficult-to-fix defects than is test.

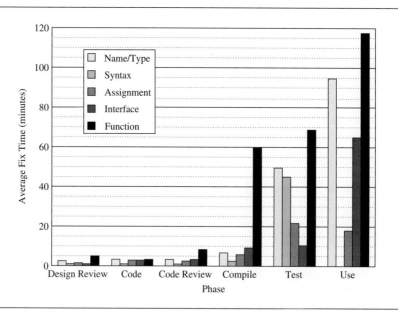

FIGURE 9.1
C++ Average Fix Time

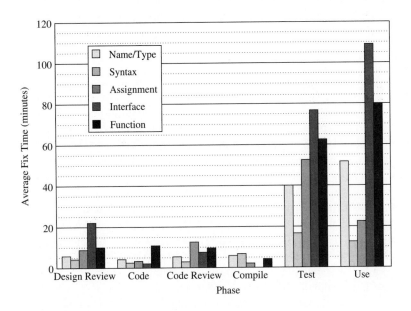

FIGURE 9.2
Pascal Average Fix Time

□ In the PSP, the pattern of fix times between reviews and test time is essentially the same regardless of defect type.

□ Organizations that do inspections report substantial improvements in development productivity and schedule performance. [Dion, Humphrey 91]

□ The PSP data show that reviews are two or more times as efficient as testing at finding and fixing defects. This is true of my own data, students' data, and that of working engineers.

□ The fix advantage of reviews over tests is also true, almost regardless of the phase in which the defect was injected.

While the fix time can often be longer for design defects and much longer for requirements defects, the times to identify the defects appear to be the same. The reason for this appears to be that even trivial typographical defects can cause extraordinarily complex system behavior. Once these symptoms are deciphered, however, the fix is generally trivial. Conversely, very complex logic problems can have relatively obvious system consequences but be quite difficult to fix. It is also likely that the relative costs of finding and fixing sophisticated logic problems is a function of the application. I have seen data suggesting that defects in real-time systems or control programs can average as much as 40 hours each to find and fix in system test. Such data are very important and you need to gather enough to determine the appropriate values for your environment.

TESTING SCHEDULES

The following example is typical of the quality problems in many software organizations. A five-person project team worked for 10 months to define the requirements and build some experimental prototypes. They then spent three months on the high-level design and were about ready to start detailed design and implementation. They were debating whether they could afford to inspect the specification before starting implementation. The product was estimated to be about 50,000 lines of C++ source code. Integration and system test were to start in five months. If they did the inspections, they estimated they would need another three or more months to enter testing. Their plan was to finish testing in about three months, so the inspections appeared to cause a delivery delay.

While this seems like a schedule slippage problem, it is really a scheduling problem. Where did the three-month testing estimate come from? In this case, the test time was not based on a well-defined and estimated plan but on the steadily shrinking time left between implementation and the originally planned delivery date. As Brooks points out, large software projects are about half done when integration starts. [Brooks] This project would thus take about 18 months for the requirements, design, implementation, and unit test and another 18 months in integration and system test. Instead of the original 21-month schedule, a more realistic schedule would have been closer to 36 months. By following the current plan, they would be on schedule up to one or two months from planned completion. They would then face a one-year schedule slip. However, they probably would not fully recognize the problem and would continue to struggle through 12 or more agonizing months of more tests and more delays.

The basic problem is the number of defects in the product at the start of test. While they could either test for another year or ship a poor quality product sooner, the most economical answer is for the software engineers to so manage the quality of their personal processes that they remove most of the defects before test.

THE ECONOMICS OF DEFECT REMOVAL

The issue here is the economics of defect removal. From the data in Table 9.1, the times to find defects in test range from two to 20 hours. I have also seen numbers of 17 hours for an operating system project and 40 hours for a complex military system. The time to find defects in inspections, however, ranges from one quarter of an hour to one hour.

From the PSP data, it is also clear that even experienced software engineers normally inject 100 or more defects per KLOC in their code. Some inject many more. While about half these defects are typically found by the compiler, the rest must be found either by inspections or by testing.

Using these data, you could estimate that a product of 50,000 LOC would enter test with about 50 or more defects per KLOC. This would mean that 2500 or more defects must be found in test. For such a modest-sized product, five to 10 or more programmer hours would be required to find each defect. Hence testing would require 20,000 or more programmer hours. This is about 10 person years. A five-person project working days, nights, and weekends might be able to finish in 18 months.

While there are data on the costs of finding defects with inspections and reviews, there is little data on the effectiveness of inspections and reviews. That is, if you were to inspect a software product that contained 100 defects, how many would you expect to find? We will call the percentage of the defects found the yield of the review or inspection. Again, there are no published data on this, but my experience at IBM was that inspections typically yielded between 60 percent to 80 percent. Data from another organization support this with a reported 68 percent yield for one large operating system. With the PSP, combined design and code reviews can yield up to 80 percent. Typical individual code reviews, however, generally yield between 50 percent and 75 percent. As shown in Fig. 9.3, 12 students who finished the PSP exercises in this book had yields of between 50 percent and 100 percent, with an average of about 70 percent.

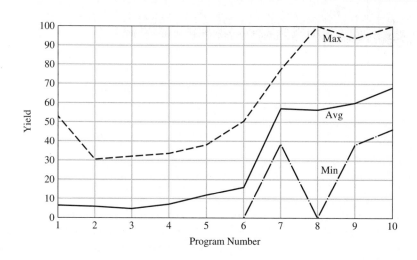

FIGURE 9.3
Yield—12 Students

Returning to the 50,000-LOC product example, assume you could find 70 percent of the defects by using inspections and reviews and your rates would be like those in Table 9.1. Inspections, at an average cost of 0.5 hours, would find 1750 defects and take 875 hours. The remaining 750 defects would have to be found in test at a cost of about 8 hours each. This whole process would take 6000 hours. While it would still take six to eight months of testing by five engineers, they would save a year.

You might ask why organizations do not do more reviews and inspections. There are two reasons why not. First, few organizations have the necessary data to make sound development plans. Their schedules are thus based largely on guesses, and these guesses are often unrealistic. When their plans are treated as accurate projections, the schedule pressure builds so quickly that all the engineers can do is react to the periodic crises. No one has time to think of anything but test, debug, and fix.

Second, yield is not generally managed. Without the discipline of a PSP, the engineers have no data on the number of defects they inject or the cost to find and fix those defects. They thus rarely appreciate the enormous costs that can be avoided by finding and fixing defects before test.

THE COST OF QUALITY

This heading should perhaps more properly be, the cost of poor quality. Juran describes the cost of quality measure as a way to "quantify the size of the quality problem in language that will have impact on upper management." [Juran] While your PSP costs will probably not be visible to your management, it is important that you begin to deal with quality as an economic issue. The cost of quality has three components: failure costs, appraisal costs, and prevention costs. [Crosby 83, Mandeville, Modarress] The definitions for these cost-of-quality components are the following:

- □ Failure costs: the costs of diagnosing a failure, making necessary repairs, and getting back into operation
- □ Appraisal costs: the costs of evaluating the product to determine its quality level
- □ Prevention costs: the costs associated with identifying the causes of the defects and the actions taken to prevent them in the future

For large projects, you should gather detailed data on these cost-of-quality components. For example, appraisal costs should include the costs of running test cases or of compiling when there are no defects. Similarly, the defect repair costs during inspections and reviews should be deducted from appraisal costs and counted as failure costs. For the PSP, a somewhat simpler definition is used as follows:

Failure costs: the total costs spent in compile and test. Because the defect-free compile and test times are typically small compared to the defect-present times, they are included in failure costs.

Appraisal costs: the times spent in design and code reviews plus any inspection times. The defect repair costs are generally a small part of review costs, so the PSP leaves them in appraisal costs.

If the numbers for inspection and review fix times or defect-free compile and test times were excessive, however, you could use the more precise cost-of-quality definition.

Juran categorizes design reviews as prevention costs. For software, it is more appropriate to count both reviews and inspections as appraisal costs. The costs of prototype development, causal analysis meetings, and process improvement action meetings should be classified as prevention costs. The PSP does not specifically include prevention actions because most defect prevention work involves cross-project activities. To be most effective, process improvement actions should be based on the experiences from several projects. Those improvements that are judged to be generally useful are incorporated in the organization's defined processes so that future projects can benefit from them.

Prototypes are typically developed to build a clear understanding of some requirement, function, or software structure. While there are many reasons for developing prototypes, all stem from a desire to avoid making mistakes. For the PSP, developing prototypes can thus be considered defect prevention.

Similarly, a formal specification of a software product is generally not required in order to design and build that product. It has been found, however, that formally defining a specification identifies unclear areas and often produces more complete and unambiguous specifications. Depending on your design practices, you could classify such work as either defect prevention or project performance costs.

The PSP Cost-of-Quality Measures. For the PSP, the cost-of-quality (COQ) measures are defined as follows:

- Failure COQ = 100*(compile time + test time)/(total development time)

- Appraisal COQ = 100*(design review time + code review time)/(total development time)

- Total COQ = Appraisal COQ + Failure COQ

- Appraisal as a % of Total Quality Costs = 100*(Appraisal COQ)/(Total COQ)

- A/FR ratio = Appraisal to failure cost ratio = (Appraisal COQ)/(Failure COQ)

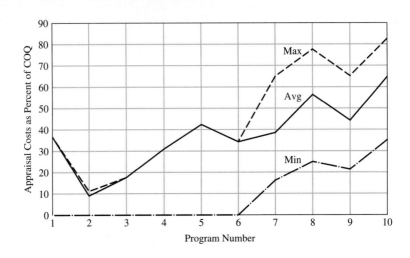

FIGURE 9.4
Appraisal Costs—12 Students

The last two measures are useful for tracking process improvement or for comparing several processes. Figure 9.4 shows the trend of appraisal costs as a percentage of total quality costs for 12 students for the 10 A series exercises in this book. As you can see, appraisal costs generally increase throughout the PSP exercises.

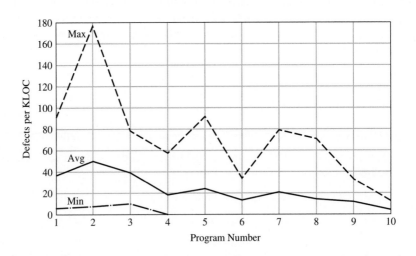

FIGURE 9.5
Defects Found in Test

From Fig. 9.5, you can see that the numbers of test defects are much lower for the later programs. Thus there is a clear association between high appraisal costs and low test defects and a high association between high appraisal costs and improved product quality.

9.3 Developing a Quality Strategy

As you develop a strategy for improving the quality of your programs, you should consider the following issues:

1. Decide how to measure your process.
2. Determine the quality methods that are most effective for you.
3. Periodically reevaluate your strategy and set new goals.

These topics are discussed in the following sections.

MEASURE YOUR PROCESS

It is important to distinguish between measures of product quality and measures of process quality. The quality of the finished product is one important measure of process quality, but it is only one. The other measures discussed in this chapter are defect removal yield, cost of quality, and productivity. Various ratios of these measures also provide interesting insights into the quality of your process.

You should also be careful in using productivity measures because they can easily be misused. The problem is that there are several different ways to achieve high productivity. For example, when management focuses on the numbers of LOC per hour without regard to the quality of the code produced, test costs can grow quite quickly. The typical reaction to such pressures has been to produce lots of new code as quickly as possible without spending much time on requirements, specifications, designs, inspections, or planning. This can cause higher apparent productivity, but it generally leads to later cost, quality, and schedule problems. This strategy often results when management pushes aggressively for simplistic productivity goals. Hence it is wise to couple all productivity measures with broader measures of process and product quality.

As noted in Chapter 8, a useful measure of process quality is total process yield, that is, the percentage of defects removed before the first compile or test. You can also apply this measure to every review, inspection, and test phase. Here, the yield of a phase is defined as follows:

$$\text{Yield(step } n) = \frac{100*(\text{defects removed in step } n)}{(\text{defects removed in } + \text{escaping from step } n)}$$

Overall process yield is calculated as follows:

$$\text{Yield(overall)} = \frac{100*(\text{defects removed before compile})}{(\text{defects injected before compile entry})}$$

The concept of yield management is illustrated in Fig. 9.6. Visualize the various development phases as producing a product that contains some number of defects. The various review, inspection, and test phases then act as filters to remove a percentage of these defects. Your strategy should thus be to

- reduce the number of defects you inject,
- improve the efficiency or yield of the filters,
- ensure the filters inject as few defects as possible, and
- compound the number of filter stages to achieve the desired product quality, cost, and schedule.

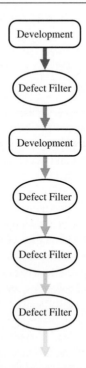

FIGURE 9.6
Yield Management

The cost of quality and the yield measures give you a balanced basis for understanding this strategy's costs and benefits.

DETERMINE THE MOST EFFECTIVE QUALITY METHODS

There are several ways to select a quality strategy. The most common is to focus on improving the product. While you should always strive to produce the highest quality products, a pure product focus will generally not produce significant or sustained results because most errors you make are a direct or indirect consequence of the processes you use. By focusing entirely on product defects, you would not consider their process causes. You thus will keep making and then finding the same types of defects. While this strategy is often essential in the short term, it will not produce significant long-term improvements.

A second way is to strive to improve the way you find and fix defects. This leads you to reviews, inspections, and checklists. While improving the ways you find and fix defects will save you a great deal of cost and time, it also has a certain perpetual motion character. The reason is that you have not addressed the sources of the problems: As long as you follow the same practices, you will make many of the same errors. These, in turn, will result in more defects of just the types you have handled before. You have made an important process improvement by introducing reviews or inspections, but your process is again static.

The problems with this method suggest a third way to select a quality strategy, that of focusing on the causes of the errors that produced the defects. While there is no way to eliminate all defects, there is growing evidence of the effectiveness of software defect prevention. [Gale, Jones CL, Mays] To prevent defects, you must study your process, determine the causes of the most troublesome defects, and work to eliminate them. An appropriate strategy would involve the following actions:

□ Use the best requirements, design, implementation, and testing methods that you can find.

□ Continuously measure the ability of your process to produce quality products.

□ Experiment with and measure the effectiveness of new tools and methods.

□ Incorporate into your process new tools and methods that improve your performance.

□ Start a defect prevention program as your process becomes predictable.

□ Identify the sources of the most troublesome problems, determine their causes, and work to eliminate them.

This last point is important. Defect prevention is effective only if you are motivated to take the required actions to prevent defects. Thus, rather then looking for some blockbuster problem, look for the problems you would most like to address. While these may not look like high-priority items, many such small problems will generally combine to be worth more than any single big item.

Your optimum strategy will probably be a balanced combination of the product, process, and prevention approaches. The product-based quality strategy will keep your focus on the product's objectives. A continuing focus on the effectiveness of your current methods will help you stay on schedule and on plan. The defect prevention strategy will then help you to improve your process to meet the greater challenges you will face in the future.

PERIODICALLY REEVALUATE YOUR STRATEGY

Your process improvement strategy must be dynamic. What is right for you today will not likely be best forever. Not only will you develop new skills, but also the technology will change, you will have a different working environment, and you will be faced with different problems. You thus should continually track your progress and assess your performance. When you find improvement progress has slowed, reevaluate your strategy, set new goals, and start again. You should be aware of new approaches, but the key is to know what works for you and what does not.

This strategy sounds simple; it's not. It requires that you maintain a consistent and long-term focus on process improvement. You will gather data and analyze it. You will study process trends and variations and occasionally restructure your process to incorporate improvements. Your progress will often be slow, and you will have frustrating reverses, but you will no longer be on an endless test-and-fix treadmill. You will be in charge of your process, and you will have a sense of growth and purpose.

9.4 Process Benchmarking

Various benchmarking techniques can be helpful in tracking processes and comparing them with similar processes used by other individuals, groups, or organizations. To use benchmarking, you first seek basic process measures that are independent of the process but that reflect its capability and robustness. If properly done, such comparisons will be valid for very different types of processes.

A useful, general-purpose process benchmark should do the following:

□ Measure the ability of the process to produce high-quality products.

□ Provide a clear ordering of process performance from best to worst.

□ Indicate the ability of the process to withstand perturbations or disruptions.

□ Provide required data that is objectively measurable.

□ Provide data in a timely manner.

BENCHMARKING THE SOFTWARE PROCESS

Unfortunately, no available software process measures meet all these criteria. While better measures may ultimately be developed, for now we must use the data we can get. We must thus devise measures that are as independent as we can make them. One useful approach is to use the combined measures of COQ and yield. For the 10 A series programs in this book, Fig. 9.7 shows data for 12 students on a two-dimensional COQ/yield scale. While higher yields tend to be associated with a lower total cost of quality, the correlation is not strong. Figure 9.8, however, shows the overall COQ as a percentage of development did not fluctuate that much during the 10 programs, although there was a general convergence toward 30 percent.

Another way to look at cost of quality is to consider the ratio of appraisal costs to failure costs. This ratio would indicate the degree to which the process attempts to eliminate defects prior to the compile and test phases. As you can see from Fig. 9.9, the A/FR, or appraisal-to-failure cost ratio, increases with the later programs. Figure 9.10 shows the relationship of process yield to the A/FR ratio. While there is considerable variation, high A/FR values are roughly associated with high yields. Figure 9.11 shows that the number of test defects declines quite sharply with increases in A/FR. A high A/FR value is clearly associated with low test defects and thus is a useful indicator of a quality software process.

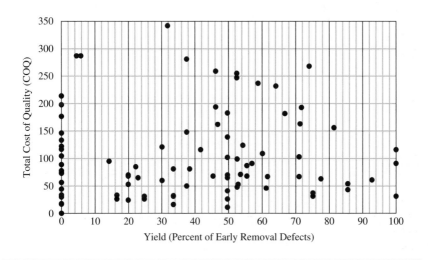

FIGURE 9.7
Yield versus COQ—12 Students

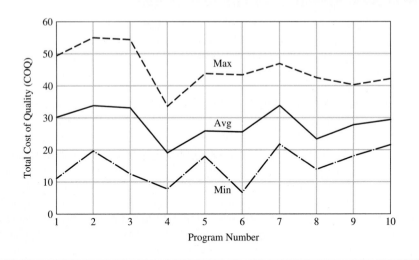

FIGURE 9.8
Total Quality Costs—12 Students

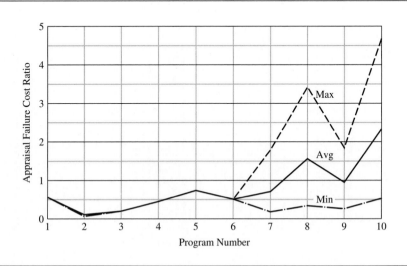

FIGURE 9.9
Appraisal to Failure Ratio—12 Students

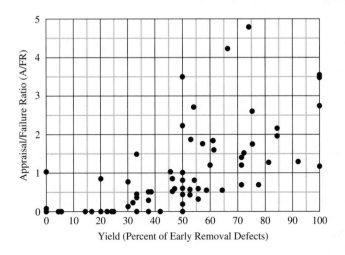

FIGURE 9.10
Yield versus A/FR—12 Students

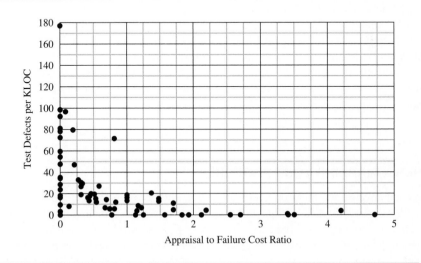

FIGURE 9.11
Test Defects versus A/FR—12 Students

BENCHMARKING CONSIDERATIONS

While the yield and the A/FR ratio appear useful for process benchmarking, they do not fully meet the criteria for a general-purpose benchmark because the COQ and yield measures are not easily standardized. Yield, as used here, is a measure of the fraction of defects removed before compile and test. Such measures are highly sensitive to the definition of a defect and to the specific counting practices used. Few engineers, in fact, count the defects they find in compile or unit test.

Similarly, the COQ measures depend on the process phase definitions. To compare your processes with others, you need comparable practices for counting defects and recording times. Variations in these practices could give quite different benchmark results for otherwise similar processes.

Even with these problems, however, we do need measures. The yield and COQ measures are not perfect, but they can help you to assess changes in your process. As you track and assess your work, tracking the A/FR value, the yield, and their relationships over time will give you a sense of whether and how much your process is improving.

PRODUCTIVITY BENCHMARKS

Another important issue is the degree to which productivity changes with yield. Figure 9.12 shows overall process yield as a function of LOC per hour for 12 students for the 10 A series programs in this book. Again, while there is considerable fluctuation there is no clear relationship. The problem is that there is so much variability among individuals that any relationship between yield and productivity is masked. Figures 9.13 and 9.14 show the yield/productivity relationship for two students. These show a clearer relationship, but there is still considerable variation. On balance, it appears that higher yields are associated with higher productivities. It is also clear, however, that getting high yields need not reduce productivity.

BENCHMARKING YOUR PROCESS

As you develop and measure your PSP, you should occasionally prepare a benchmarking chart like that in Figs. 9.13 or 9.14. The normal statistical fluctuations from one program to the next will often mask process trends, so you should also generate benchmark statistics for groups of several programs that were developed with the same process. You would thus show a total of 20 programs with four points, one each for programs 1 to 5, 6 to 10, 11 to 15, and 16 to 20. You then label each group of programs so that you can see how your process is evolving.

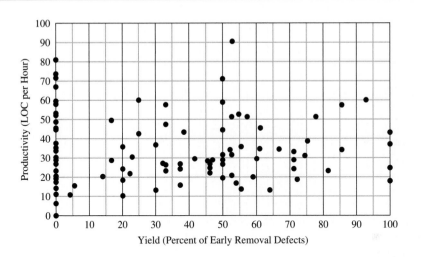

FIGURE 9.12
Yield versus Productivity—12 Students

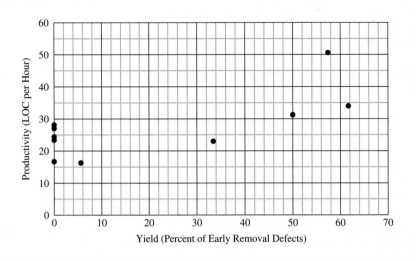

FIGURE 9.13
Yield versus Productivity—Student 1

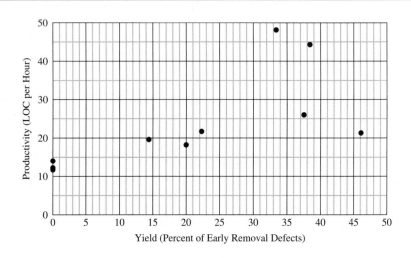

FIGURE 9.14
Yield versus Productivity—Student 4

Doing this has the advantage of more or less smoothing out the program-to-program fluctuations and showing the basic process performance. While comparisons of this sort require considerably more data than you can get from the 10 programs in this book, after you have data on 20 or more programs you should see clear differences between the first and last groups of five.

To see how your process is evolving, you will find it helpful to show the most recent program separately on a benchmarking chart. Doing this could either reveal unique problems or indicate that your process is evolving as you had intended. In either case, it will provide a running basis for you to judge your process status and improvement trends.

9.5   Yield Management

In thinking about the software process from a yield point of view, you should consider a number of factors. First, you can view the software process as the combination of two competing processes: defect injection and defect removal. The defect content of the product comes from the difference between these two processes. Thus relatively small changes in your process yield can cause large changes in the defect content of the finished program.

For example, take the development of a million lines of new and changed code. Because the PSP data show that software engineers inject somewhere between 50 and 150 defects per KLOC, assume 100. This figure requires that the defect removal processes find 100,000 defects. If the inspection processes had a 75 percent yield, 25,000 defects would be left for compile and test. If again, as the PSP data show, about half these defects were found in compile, 12,500 defects would be left to find in test. If you used four levels of test, each with a 50 percent yield, 781 defects would still remain in the final product, a defect level of 0.8 per KLOC. This is a rather good level of quality by current industrial standards. Suppose, however, that the inspection yield fell to 50 percent. Then 50,000 defects would remain for compile and test. If the yields of the other process steps remained the same, the final numbers of defects in the product would double to 1562, or 1.6 defects per KLOC. Thus a 33 percent reduction in yield would double the numbers of defects in the final product.

While this is a significant increase in the number of defects shipped to the customer, the customer impact is modest compared to the impact on testing. As shown in Table 9.1, the average cost to remove defects in test generally runs somewhere between 2 and 20 hours. If the assumed average cost is 10 hours per defect, the 12,500 defects originally left for test would take 125,000 programmer hours, or about 60 programmer years. With the reduced inspection yield of 50 percent, this number would double to 25,000 defects and 120 programmer years—a schedule difference of one year if there were 50 to 60 engineers on the project. What is worse, even with this extra year, the final product would still have twice as many defects as it would have if the inspection process had retained its original 75 percent yield.

The point is that the final numbers of defects, from a yield management point of view, is the residual of the yields of all the process phases. If any single phase degrades, some percentage of the defects it misses will get through the entire process into the final product. This degradation will also impact the cost and schedule of every subsequent phase. In the first case, an injection process produced 100,000 defects and a removal process removed 99,219 of those. A modest change in the yields of these processes could easily result in an increase of several hundred to several thousand defects in the final product.

DEFECT REMOVAL VERSUS DEFECT INJECTION

There is an important difference in process yield between defect removal and defect injection. When making semiconductor chips, engineers attempt to manage defect injection. They start with raw materials and the process progressively introduces defects while producing products. A few of these defects may have been delivered in the raw materials, but the majority are due to environmental contamination or defective process steps. If each process stage has some probability p of introducing a defect, then the probable yield of defect-free product from that stage is $1 - p$. Similarly, if n stages each have the same yield, the defect-free yield of the entire process is $(1 - p)^n$. For example, if there were 10 stages and each had a 1 percent probability of injecting a defect, then the probability of getting a defect-free product would be $(1 - .01)^{10} = 0.904$, or 90.4 percent. If the injection probability in one stage were then to increase to 50 percent, the probability of getting a defect-free result would be $.5*(1 - .01)^9 = 0.457$, or a drop to 45.7 percent. This means that an increase to a 50 percent injection rate in one step cuts overall process yield in half.

In the case of defect removal, you start with a product that contains N defects. You then put it through a multistage process in which each stage has some probability of finding a defect. If the likely fraction of defects found in each stage (the yield) were y, then the number of defects left in the product at exit of the first phase would be $N(1 - y)$. If you used i identical removal stages, then the number of defects remaining would be $N*(1 - y)^i$. For example, if you started with 100,000 defects and used five consecutive phases that each had a process yield of 80 percent, the remaining defects would be $100,000*(1 - .8)^5 = 32$, for an overall yield of $(100,000 - 32)/(100,000) = 0.99968$. If the yield of one stage were to fall to 40 percent, you would end up with $100,000*(1 - .4)*(1 - .8)^4 = 96$ defects, for an overall yield of $(100,000 - 96)/(100,000) = 0.99904$. Yield has fallen, but only by 0.064 percent. A 50 percent reduction in defect removal in one stage tripled the final number of delivered defects, but it had an insignificant effect on overall process yield.

As long as you remove more defects than you inject, you should be able to continue to improve quality by compounding defect removal phases. The problem is that the fix process is highly defect prone, testing is expensive, and product delays impact revenue. This is why economics are so important and why it is so important to have a quantitative basis for determining how much effort to spend on reviews, inspections, and tests.

This is demonstrated by one study of 27 products from one major computer firm. The results are shown in Fig. 9.15. [Krishnan] This figure shows the product cost versus defect levels. Note that the product costs cover the entire product life cycle from development through the usage and maintenance phases. The quality costs are for the numbers of customer reported defects only. In Fig. 9.15, the x-axis is shown as LOC/Defect so that a high value indicates higher quality. Clearly, when total life-cycle costs are included, it costs substantially less to produce high-quality products than to ship lower quality products and fix them later.

THE INJECTION PROCESS

To effectively manage software quality, you need to focus on both the removal and the injection processes. The basic defect causes fall into five categories as follows: [Gale]

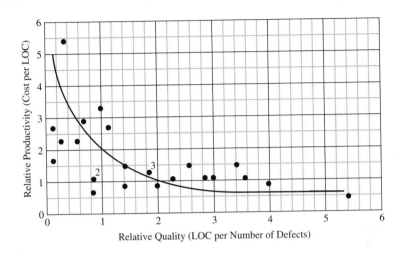

FIGURE 9.15
Industrial Life-cycle Software Costs

1. **Education:** You did not understand how to do something.

2. **Communication:** You were not properly informed about something.

3. **Oversight:** You omitted doing something.

4. **Transcription:** You knew what to do but made a mistake in doing it.

5. **Process:** Your process somehow misdirected your actions.

   In an educational setting, these items are largely under your control. In a software organization, the actions required to prevent these causes could involve many personnel, project, or organizational issues. However, even then, many of the defect causes will involve your PSP. Depending on your role, some of the questions you should consider are the following:

Your personal process management:

   □ Was your PSP sufficiently defined to help you do quality work?

   □ Was your development process supported with adequate tools and methods?

   □ Was your task well enough planned to permit orderly work?

   □ Were you motivated to do a quality job?

Your development methods:

   □ Were the requirements sufficiently defined so you could produce a quality design?

□ Was the design suitably defined to permit you to do a quality implementation?

Your match to the problem:

□ Were you assigned to a task you were capable of performing?

□ Did you have the application knowledge to appreciate the problem requirements?

□ Did you have suitable training and experience for the type of program you were to develop?

□ Were you adequately trained and skilled in using the selected tools, methods, and processes?

□ Did you follow the personal disciplines needed to produce a quality result?

Even if you assume that the answer to every question is yes, there are still many potential sources of problems. You could get sick, have personal problems, or not get enough sleep. Regardless of your training, skill, or motivation, there is a distinct probability that any action you take will produce an error. For example, even when I am extremely careful, close to 5 percent of all my changes contain mistakes that later require correction. This is true whether I am writing programs, doing financial calculations, or editing a manuscript. I have thus learned to expect such errors and to double-check for them.

For software, the change process is probably your most error prone activity. [Levendel] Indications are that the percentage of fixes that generate defects is rarely less than 20 percent; generally it is much higher. When individuals and organizations recognize this problem and address it, they can rapidly bring this percentage down to 5 percent or less. [Bencher]

Some of the most error-prone programming actions involve interpreting requirements and making design decisions. Implementation is also error prone, as is logic design and coding. Some percentage of your fix decisions will be in error, as will a fraction of all your keystrokes. Even expert typists make mistakes, though they have no design decisions to make. Your quality strategy thus must recognize that every action you take has a probability of injecting a defect. Your challenge is then to identify these sources and either prevent them or devise actions to economically and consistently detect and remove them.

9.6 Defect Removal Strategies

It takes an extraordinary amount of discipline just to get a reasonably sized program to run. While the program may contain many defects, the fact that it runs at all is an achievement. And though we may celebrate this feat, society now needs higher quality software than individuals normally produce. We therefore need to devise methods that will enable us to produce high-quality products even though we will inevitably inject many defects.

A yield management strategy should address this problem from several directions. The potential approaches are as follows:

□ Compound multiple defect removal phases so their combined yields produce an acceptable quality product.

□ Evaluate the cost and removal efficiency of these phases to achieve the most economical combination.

□ Measure, analyze, and manage these removal phases to guard against yield busts and to identify and react to them as quickly as possible.

□ Initiate a defect prevention process to gradually reduce the overall defect injection rate.

While we can continue compounding the yields of multiple defect removal processes, doing this is both expensive and time consuming. The yield management strategy should thus identify the highest yield methods and combine them in the most cost-effective way to produce the optimum result.

A YIELD MANAGEMENT APPROACH

As the previous discussion in this chapter makes clear, the yields of the various defect removal phases are interchangeable. That is, from a defect removal point of view, it is just as effective to have an 80 percent inspection yield and a 40 percent test yield as it is to have a 40 percent inspection yield and an 80 percent test yield. However, the economics of these alternatives are quite different. Because test defect correction costs five to 10 times as much as inspection defect correction, several times as much labor is involved. And because every human action is a potential cause of defects, more labor means more opportunities for errors and a higher likelihood of defect injection. Thus, while the yield index may not distinguish between an 80/40 and a 40/80 ratio of test and inspection yield, the A/FR value does.

Undoubtedly it is important to have as high a yield as possible in every phase; however, you must generally choose where to make your maximum effort. Because the benefits of defect removal are greatest early in the process, your defect removal strategy should seek to maximize the yield of the earliest phases. Also, as noted in Chapter 8, it helps to focus each review phase on a particular class of defect type. You are then more likely to get a high yield in that phase. Because it takes time and practice to improve your yield, you will probably have most success if you focus your energy on a few defect types at a time. After you successfully handle the first set of defect types, you can move on to the next.

For example, consider addressing your design and coding problems separately. Assuming you have a reasonably precise way to represent the design, you should review only for design problems during design reviews; you would not look for coding problems. Similarly, in code reviews, you would focus on coding problems. This does not mean you would ignore design problems if you see them, just that you would not make a special effort to find them. As discussed in Chapter 8, this strategy requires that you divide the defects into classes that you can address in each review step. Then if you focus on a particular defect class in each review step, you could establish a special yield measure for that step and that defect class. For example, if you were to pick name and type problems as the first area to address, you would track your yield for that defect type only. With practice, you should be able to find 80 percent to 90 percent of these defects in your code review. At that point, you should identify the next most important defect type and work on that.

YIELD SPECIALIZATION BY PHASE

Your principal guide in selecting review areas for focus should be your own defect data. During each review, however, you should consider the following topics:

High-level design review:

- Completeness of requirements coverage
- System constraints
- The system state machine
- The class and object structures
- The allocation of system functions to high-level objects
- The data structures and data stores
- The reuse of standard components
- System error and exception conditions
- Fast-path performance optimization and synchronization
- Memory management
- File management
- Compatibility, usability, installability, maintainability

Detailed-level design review:

- Completeness of high-level design coverage
- The object state machines
- The logical correctness of the object methods and procedures

☐ Function, method, and procedure calls

☐ Unusual variable and parameter names and types

☐ Unusual variable and parameter scopes

☐ Overflows and exceptions

☐ Cohesion, coupling, logic complexity

☐ Space and packaging

Code reviews:

☐ Complete and proper implementation of the detailed design

☐ Variable and parameter declarations

☐ Includes

☐ Initialization

☐ Instruction formats

☐ Punctuation

☐ Name spelling and consistency

☐ Hardware dependencies and instruction side effects

☐ Dependencies on the fix level or feature content of related programs

Your intent in these reviews is to ensure each program or program element is complete, correct, and defect free. You should explicitly specify and review the interfaces with all the lower-level elements used by each program. You will then be better able to ensure all the functions fit together properly and the total system will work correctly. With this review practice you will find the bulk of the defects and greatly improve the efficiency of your subsequent reviews, inspections, and tests. When you can be reasonably confident that the elemental objects and methods are correct, the identification of system problems is far simpler and their resolution is much more likely to be correct.

UNIT TESTING

It is most desirable to find and fix all defects before you begin testing; however, this is rarely possible. Reviews and inspections are performed by people, and people are error prone. In one example, many people kindly reviewed the manuscript for this book. One bibliography page had four obvious typographical errors that I missed in my personal reviews. Of the several reviewers who noted typographical errors on this page, none found all four. While several found three, the average was only two. That is, the individual yields of the people who had noted typographical defects on that page averaged only 50 percent.

While reviewing code is much different from reviewing a manuscript, it is clear that we cannot expect to reach 100 percent in code reviews or even in inspections. Testing must thus be part of every software quality strategy.

Mills argues that one should strive for complete program correctness without the use of unit testing. [Dyer, Linger] His logic is much like that used previously for doing reviews before compiling. As long as the programmers have the crutch of unit testing, he argues, they will not be as careful with design and implementation. While I agree with this basic objective, I have found that establishing a goal of finding and fixing all defects before unit test provides a similar motivation without sacrificing the benefits of unit testing. This works, however, only as long as you measure and track all your defects.

A principal advantage of doing a unit test is that you can devise comprehensive tests for your program logic. In unit test, some topics to check for each function are:

□ Check all paths and both sides of all branches.

□ Ensure that all instructions execute.

□ Verify operation at normal parameter values.

□ Verify operation at limit parameter values.

□ Verify operation outside of limit parameter values.

□ Check the use of all called objects.

□ Verify the handling of all data structures.

□ Verify the handling of all files.

□ Check normal termination of all loops.

□ Check abnormal termination of all loops.

□ Check normal termination of all recursions.

□ Check abnormal termination of all recursions.

□ Verify the handling of all error conditions.

□ Check timing and synchronization.

□ Verify all hardware dependencies.

This is an enormous amount of work. However, the issue is not how quickly you can get through unit test, but rather what you can do to ensure the product is as nearly defect free as you can make it. [Schulmeyer 90] If your data indicate that you typically do not find all the defects in your product before you exit unit test, then you must adjust your unit test procedures to ensure you find these defects before you pass the product to integration, system testing, and use. Any time you save by not working to find defects in unit test will cost someone a great deal more time and inconvenience later.

9.7 Defect Prevention Strategies

Detecting and fixing defects is critically important, yet it is an inherently defensive strategy. To make significant quality improvements, you should identify the causes of your defects and take steps to eliminate them. By reviewing your PSP data on the defect types you most frequently find in test, you can structure your own defect prevention effort. For example, you may combine any of the following strategies. In each, you focus on certain defect types.

- ☐ Those found in final program test or use.
- ☐ Those that occur most frequently.
- ☐ Those that are most difficult to find and fix.
- ☐ Those for which you can quickly identify effective preventive actions.
- ☐ Those that most annoy you.

There are many possible ways to proceed, but you should establish an explicit strategy and initially focus on a narrow defect class. You will then see what works for you and have a better idea of how to proceed.

DEFECT PREVENTION AT THE PERSONAL LEVEL

In Chapter 8, I introduced review practices that were supported by defect analysis. The principal example was the use of checklists. The checklist structure and content was determined from your defect data. The focus then was on identifying and removing existing defects. For defect prevention, however, you must look at the defects in more detail. You need to visualize what you did or did not do that caused them. You then need to think through what you could have done differently that would have prevented them. Finally, you need to devise means to ensure you consistently take these preventive actions in the future.

The approach to use in personal prevention work is much like that used by software teams in defect prevention reviews, as follows:

1. Select a specific defect type or class for analysis.
2. Summarize the causes of the defect. In team reviews, it is often helpful to use Ishikawa or wishbone diagrams. [Schulmeyer] While I have not found them necessary for the PSP, you may want to try them. An example is shown in Fig. 9.16.
3. Now that you understand the error that caused the defect, determine why you made it. One useful set of cause categories is communications, education, oversight, transcription, and process.

4. Devise ways to prevent the problem in the future.

5. Recycle through steps 1 through 4 until you run out of time or cease to have useful ideas.

6. Look for trends or patterns in your data that might suggest larger or more pervasive problems. An example might be a class of problem that gives you trouble right after an extended period of nonprogramming work.

7. Analyze actions that have worked in the past and ensure you retain them and build on them.

8. Test your defect prevention ideas on at least one PSP-sized program and incorporate those that work in a process update.

While this approach is effective at a team or project level, it is much more difficult to implement by yourself. [Gale, Mays] You may initially have many good ideas. After you have worked on them, you will probably have trouble thinking of anything else you could do. At this point, a brainstorming session with other engineers could give you more ideas. You thus should attempt to form a defect prevention group with your peers or classmates and conduct occasional joint reviews.

Another approach is to do your causal analysis work right after you complete each project. Either as part of your postmortem or shortly after, review your

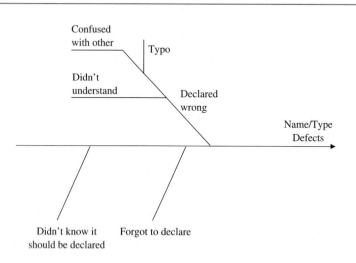

FIGURE 9.16
Ishikawa Diagram—Defect Causes

defects and identify their major causes. Because the project is fresh in your mind, this should not take much time. However, more time will be needed to make a complete enough description of the causes so that you can later remember them. You should also identify the defect numbers you associate with each cause.

Later, you can conduct an action planning study to update your process. You should consider doing this on a set schedule with the frequency controlled in part by how much software development you do. It probably should not be more often than monthly and no less often than quarterly. If you do action planning too often, you will not have enough time to gauge the effectiveness of your previous actions. Conversely, if you wait too long your progress will be slower and you are less likely to remember the defect causes. So do your first defect prevention studies as soon as you have enough data to analyze. After implementing the resulting actions, be guided by your ideas. As soon as you think another session would be productive, even if it is the next day, do it. When you find yourself running out of ideas, establish a schedule for the next review. Initially, set it a month away. When and if the monthly reviews become less productive, you can begin to space them further apart. The point is to avoid wasting time on reviews when you do not have new ideas but not stop doing them entirely. Again, if at any time you can get one or more of your peers or classmates to help, involve them in your prevention review as well.

If you are not sure where to start with defect prevention, examine those defects that caused the most trouble in system test or use. These are the defects that your process is least able to find and fix, so they should get highest priority. However, if you already know the defects you want to tackle first, do so. Those you find most annoying are the ones you are most motivated to fix, so that is not a bad place to start. In either case, next follow these steps:

1. With these data, establish a priority for those defect types that you will initially address. It is wisest to pick a narrow class of problems and establish explicit actions to prevent them in the future.

2. Make specific changes in your process to accomplish these actions. These changes may include changing forms, adding checklist items, or modifying standards. When practical, try to devise automated aids to help with transcription and oversight problems. Other automated defect prevention actions will likely involve too much work to implement by yourself.

3. Conduct a prototype walk-through of these preventive measures to ensure they are convenient, sustainable, and effective. Then make the indicated changes and insert the new methods into your standard process.

A Defect Prevention Example.   Suppose that in a defect prevention review you find that variable initialization was a frequent problem. You could add an entry in your code review checklist, but doing this would be a detection and not a preventive action. You should probably add this checklist item, but you should also devise preventive measures to reduce the total number of such errors.

In devising such measures, first look for likely causes, such as the following:

- □ Education: You may not have known that initialization should be done in some cases.

- □ Communication: You may have thought someone else was going to handle the initialization.

- □ Oversight: You may have just forgotten to initialize some variables.

- □ Transcription: You misspelled the variable name when initializing it.

Next, recognize that each cause requires a different preventive measure. Let's say the problem turned out to be oversight. You could proceed as follows.

You will likely make declaration and initialization decisions during coding, so that is the most promising place to start. Next, you need to figure out what to do. Just telling yourself to be more careful will probably not work, at least not for very long because as you identify additional items you need to be especially careful about, the previous items will get progressively less attention. Soon it is just like a general instruction to try harder; you were probably already trying pretty hard, so this will not improve your process.

You need to find something you can be reasonably confident you will always do. For example, you could establish a special item in your coding standard to require initialization of every variable when it is declared. While doing this will result in some unnecessary code, you could probably train yourself to do this consistently. If you checked this item in your code reviews and counted every such omission as a defect to be corrected, you would soon get in the habit of doing it.

DEFECT PREVENTION IN PRACTICE

Your early PSP defect prevention actions should focus on the quality of your design and code and the actions you can take to ensure you faithfully follow your process. Beyond paying consistent attention to these items, you will probably not see many more items you can handle by yourself. This is where discussions with your teammates and other project members can help. As you discuss what they have done, you may get additional ideas about how to improve your PSP. You may also begin to see where changes in the requirements and specification processes can help you to eliminate problems at their sources.

9.8 Summary

As you work to improve the quality of the software you develop, you should focus on the ability of your process to produce quality products. Seek the most effective methods to find defects as well as the most effective ways to prevent them. Also recognize that the costs of finding and fixing defects escalates rapidly the longer you leave them in the product. Your best strategy is thus to ensure your program is of the highest quality when you first produce it.

Software bugs, defects, and errors are only one small facet of software quality; however, that is the quality focus of this book. Defects are rarely the users' top quality priority, but they are an essential PSP focus because defects are best handled at the individual level. If the elemental programs in a system have many defects, the entire system development will be overwhelmed by the time-consuming and expensive process of finding and fixing defects.

Essentially, software quality is an economic issue. You could always run another test or do another inspection. However, few organizations have the data on which to base sound quality plans. The basic PSP quality measure is yield—the percentage of defects removed before the first compile or test.

Juran describes the cost of quality measure as a way to "quantify the size of the quality problem in language that will have impact on upper management." [Juran] The principal components of the cost of quality are failure costs, appraisal costs, and prevention costs. The cost-of-quality measure is typically used to evaluate the quality performance of organizations. When used on individual projects, it will show considerable variation. A cost-of-quality measure can also be used with the PSP.

Benchmarking techniques are useful for comparing processes. They can be used to track processes over time or to compare processes. To do this, you should define process measures that are independent of the process but that reflect its capability and robustness. Unfortunately, there are no completely adequate benchmark measures for the software process. Process yield, the appraisal-to-failure cost ratio (A/FR), and productivity are useful for software process benchmarking, but they do not fully meet the criteria for a general-purpose benchmark. They are, however, the best we have, and you should use them until better measures are devised.

The software process can be viewed as the combination of two competing processes: defect injection and defect removal. The defect content of the finished product is then governed by the difference between the results of these two processes. As when taking differences of large numbers, relatively small changes in either process can make a large proportionate difference in the final result. To effectively manage software quality, you thus need to focus on both the removal and the injection processes.

While detecting and fixing defects is critically important, it is an inherently defensive strategy. To make significant quality improvements, you should identify the causes of these defects and take steps to eliminate them. Your initial defect prevention actions should address the quality of your design and code and the actions you can take to ensure that you faithfully follow your defined process.

9.9   Exercises

The standard course plan for this chapter uses PSP2 to write program 7A. The specification for this program is given in Appendix D, and the PSP2 process is described in Appendix C. In completing this assignment, you should review and become familiar with PSP2 and faithfully follow the process and the report submission format it specifies.

For other assignment options, consult Appendix D.

References

[Ackerman] A. Frank Ackerman, Lynne S. Buchwald, and Frank H. Lewski, "Software Inspections: An Effective Verification Process," *IEEE Software* (May 1989) 31–36.

[Bencher] D. L. Bencher, "Technical Forum," *IBM Systems Journal*, vol. 33, no. 1, 1994.

[Boehm, 81] Barry W. Boehm, *Software Engineering Economics* (Englewood Cliffs, NJ: Prentice-Hall, 1981).

[Brooks] Frederick P. Brooks, *The Mythical Man-Month* (Reading, MA: Addison-Wesley 1972).

[Bush] Marilyn Bush, "Improving Software Quality: The Use of Formal Inspections at the Jet Propulsion Laboratory," 12th International Conference on Software Engineering, Nice, France (March 26–30, 1990): 196–199.

[Crosby] Philip B. Crosby, *Quality Is Free, The Art of Making Quality Certain* (New York: Mentor, New American Library, 1979).

[Crosby 83] Philip B. Crosby, "Don't Be Defensive about the Cost of Quality," *Quality Progress* (April, 1983).

[Dion] Raymond Dion, "Process Improvement and the Corporate Balance Sheet," *IEEE Software* (July 1993): 28–35.

[Dyer] Michael Dyer, *The Cleanroom Approach to Quality Software Development* (New York: John Wiley & Sons, Inc., 1992).

[Freedman] D. P. Freedman and G. M. Weinberg, *Handbook of Walk-throughs, Inspections, and Technical Reviews: Evaluation Programs, Projects, and Products, Third Edition* (Little, Brown and Company, 1982).

[Gale] J. L. Gale, J. R. Tirso, and C. A. Burchfield, "Implementing the Defect Prevention Process in the MVS Interactive Programming Organization," *IBM Systems Journal,* vol. 29, no. 1 (1990).

[Humphrey 91] W. S. Humphrey, T. R. Snyder, and R. R. Willis, "Software Process Improvement at Hughes Aircraft," *IEEE Software* (July 1991): 11–23.

[Jones] C. L. Jones, "A Process-integrated Approach to Defect Prevention," *IBM Systems Journal,* vol. 24, no. 2 (1985).

[Juran] J. M. Juran and Frank M. Gryna, *Juran's Quality Control Handbook, Fourth Edition* (New York: McGraw-Hill Book Company, 1988).

[Krishnan] M. S. Krishnan, Sunder Kekre, Marc I. Kellner, C. H. Kriebel, T. Mukhopadhyay, and K. Srinivasan, "Cost, Quality, and User Satisfaction of Software Products: A Field Study," *Series on Technology Management*, ed. Kim Clark, Jay Jaikumar, and Uday Kermarker (Cambridge, MA: Harvard Business School Press, 1994).

[Levendel] Ytzhak Levendel, "Reliability Analysis of Large Software Systems: Defect Data Modeling," *IEEE Transactions on Software Engineering*, vol. 16, no. 2 (February 1990): 141–152.

[Linger] R. C. Linger and H. D. Mills, "Case Study in Cleanroom Software Engineering," COMPSAC'88 Proceedings (1988).

[Mandeville] William A. Mandeville, "Software Costs of Quality," *IEEE Journal on Selected Areas in Communications*, vol. 8, no. 2 (February 1990).

[Mays] R. G. Mays, C. L. Jones, G. J. Holloway, and D. P. Studinski, "Experiences with Defect Prevention," *IBM Systems Journal,* vol. 29, no. 1 (1990).

[Modarress] Batoul Modarress and A. Ansari, "Two New Dimensions in the Cost of Quality," *International Journal of Quality and Reliability Management*, vol. 4, no. 4, 9–20, 1987.

[O'Neill] Don O'Neill, personal communication.

[Ragland] Bryce Ragland, "Inspections Are Needed Now More Than Ever," *Journal of Defense Software Engineering #38*, Software Technology Support Center, DoD (November 1992).

[Remus] H. Remus and S. Ziles, "Prediction and Management of Program Quality," Proceedings of the Fourth International Conference on Software Engineering, Munich, Germany (1979): 341–350.

[Russell] Glen W. Russell, "Experience with Inspections in Ultralarge-scale Developments," *IEEE Software* (January 1991): 25–31.

[Schulmeyer] G. Gordon Schulmeyer and James I. McManus, *Handbook of Software Quality Assurance* (New York: Van Nostrand, 198x).

[Schulmeyer 90] G. Gordon Schulmeyer, *Zero Defect Software*, (New York: McGraw-Hill, 1990).

[Shooman] M. L. Shooman and M. I. Bolsky, "Types, Distribution, and Test and Correction Times for Programming Errors," Proceedings 1975 Conference on Reliable Software, IEEE, New York, catalog no. 75 CHO 940-7CSR: 347.

[vanGenuchten] Michiel vanGenuchten, personal communication.

[Weller] E. F. Weller, "Lessons Learned from Two Years of Inspection Data," *IEEE Software* (September, 1993): 38–45.

10

Software Design

A good software design transforms an ill-defined requirement into an implementable product design specification. The quality of this design is important because it is nearly impossible to produce a high quality implementation from a poor quality design. Design quality has two parts: the quality of the design content and the quality of the design representation. While one may view representation as less important, in many ways it is more so. Designs with high quality content likely will be poorly implemented if they are badly represented. A poor representation can also make the design so hard to understand that its problems will not be recognized until implementation or even later.

The PSP addresses design issues from a defect prevention point of view. At this point in PSP evolution, you probably have reduced the number of your coding defects largely because of your increased awareness of the defects you make and the extra care you took during coding. Design defects, however, are more difficult to reduce. To do so, you need to improve your design quality. Because the design methods you use should depend on your product application domain as well as on your skills and experiences, the PSP does not specify a design method. It concentrates instead on the representation quality of your design.

This chapter presents a design framework that is independent of your design methods. While the examples assume an object-oriented design (OOD) methodology, the principles are generally applicable to other methodologies. If you do not use OOD, you can substitute either of the words procedure or function for the words class, method, and object.

The topics covered in this chapter include the design process and the criteria for a quality design. Design templates are used as an aid to meeting these criteria and examples are given of how to use each template. To follow the examples in this and Chapter 12, you should be familiar with Boolean algebra and a notation for describing sets. If you are not, Appendix B briefly describes both.

10. 1   The Design Process

Software design is a creative process that cannot be reduced to a routine procedure. The design process, however, need not be totally unstructured. You generally start a design by defining the product's purpose, gathering relevant data, producing an overview design, and then filling in the details. These steps are not isolated sequential tasks, however; they are cooperative, parallel activities. Design involves discovery and invention, and it frequently requires intuitive leaps from one abstraction level to another.

DESIGN AS A LEARNING PROCESS

For any but the simplest programs, the design process can be quite complex. Fig. 10.1 shows some of the more important elements of this process and one way to relate them. In the simplest case, assuming the requirements information is current and properly communicated this process can proceed in a straight-line manner from top to bottom. Accomplishing this, of course, assumes there are no false starts or changes. In the real world, however, there are many misunderstandings, errors, and omissions. Thus there will likely be many feedback loops and iterative cycles.

As complex as it may seem, Fig. 10.1 is actually a simplification. This entire design process is actually only one element of the much larger process shown in Fig. 10.2. Here, too, only a few of the many possible feedback paths are shown. Clearly, however, changes enormously complicate the design process. The users define new needs, the designers make changes, and the implementers code and fix defects. Everybody introduces defects. As development proceeds, the requirements and the design are progressively refined, leading to new understandings and further changes.

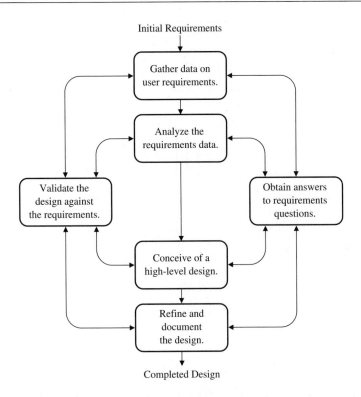

Initial Requirements

Gather data on
user requirements.

Analyze the
requirements data.

Validate the
design against
the requirements.

Obtain answers
to requirements
questions.

Conceive of a
high-level design.

Refine and
document
the design.

Completed Design

FIGURE 10.1
The Design Framework

FREEZING THE DESIGN

This process is so complex because many different people are involved and they are all learning. At the outset, no one really understands either the requirements, the design, or the implementation. As each of these is refined, it sheds further light on the others. This is particularly true when the implementation finally progresses to the point where the users can first try the product. Every new exposure leads to new knowledge, new ideas, and more changes. The tricky problem for the developers is to truncate this learning process at just the right point so that a suitable product can be delivered in a reasonable time and at an affordable cost.

Projects rarely get into trouble because of massive requirements changes. These changes are typically recognized and properly reviewed. The danger is that a host of seemingly trivial enhancements will nibble you to death. If you do not

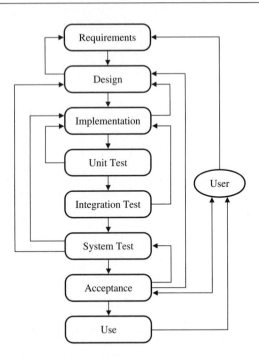

FIGURE 10.2
The Systems Development Framework

have the knowledge, skill, and discipline to analyze the impact of each change, the size of your job can easily double or triple before you know it. The PSP design process can help you to make accurate plans and to produce quality products. You can then estimate the probable impact of proposed changes and provide a rational basis for deciding when to freeze and build and when to make another change.

THE CONCEPTUAL DESIGN

When you first start a software project, you generally have an initial requirement that is both incomplete and imprecise. Your first step thus must be to get enough information so that you can start designing. While this data-gathering task can be quite simple, it also could be very complex, even for relatively modest-sized programs. The complexity of the requirements is determined by the complexity of the problem the potential users want to solve. However, although complex problems often have complex solutions, that need not always be the case. The principal exceptions are when you can identify elements of the problem that have been solved before. In this case, you may be able to reuse part of that previous solution.

Similarly, simple problems do not always have simple solutions. Often, the simple requirements cause the most problems because the simplicity of the requirements is deceptive. Application functions that are very simple for people to conceptualize are often extraordinarily hard to design and to implement.

Another problem with even moderately complex projects is the potentially large volume of information. Here, you face two issues. On the one hand, you must ensure you get all the critical information you need. On the other, you must avoid getting lost in a mass of detail. It is generally wisest to follow an iterative process, as follows:

1. Focus on the high-level issues until you know enough to produce the overall conceptual design.

2. Complete and document the conceptual design.

3. Now make and document your development plan.

4. Once you have the conceptual design, your data gathering process changes. An immediate objective is to test the conceptual design. You thus seek information that will either validate your initial concept or at least define its scope and limits. What are the performance limits and maximum sizes? Are there special peak demands or unusual response needs? What must the users know, and what are their likely skills? To help prevent your getting lost in detail, you should "walk around" the problem and look at it from every angle you can imagine. Try to think like a user and visualize the likely scenarios. Then walk through these scenarios with your conceptual design to ensure it handles them naturally and smoothly. If you find too many exception conditions, your conceptual design may not be a natural fit to the problem.

5. Once you have satisfied yourself that the conceptual design is solid, you can begin to focus on details. The conceptual design now provides the framework for cataloguing the knowledge you gain and ensuring you do not lose important details.

REQUIREMENTS UNCERTAINTIES

This creative design process is complicated by the generally poor state of most requirements descriptions. This is not because the users or the system's designers are incompetent but because of what I call the *requirements uncertainty principle*: For a new software system, the requirements will not be completely known until after the users have used it. The true role of design is thus to create a workable solution to an ill-defined problem. While there is no procedural way to address this task, it is important to establish a rigorous and explicit design process that can identify and help to resolve the requirements uncertainties as early in the development process as possible.

10.2   Design Quality

The software design should contain a sufficiently complete, accurate, and precise solution to a problem in order to ensure its quality implementation.

DESIGN COMPLETENESS

You can waste time over-specifying the design; however, an under-specified design will be expensive and error prone to implement. The complete specification of a software design requires a great deal of information. This includes defining the classes and objects and their relationships, identifying the interactions among them, defining the required data and state transformations, and specifying the system inputs and outputs. The complete and unambiguous definition of all this material generally requires significantly more documentation than the source listing for the finished program. This may seem surprising. The source code must include all the design decisions but in very terse form. A program's uncommented source code is very dense. It has little redundancy, and it precisely defines all aspects of the product's behavior. With the possible exception of the object code, it is the most compact way to completely define the program's design. Unfortunately, unless the source code is extensively commented it is almost unintelligible to anyone but the designers and implementers. Even they can have trouble deciphering it. The questions then are, how much detail must be provided by the designers, and what do the implementers and other design users require?

A fully defined design is expensive and much of its content is not needed by experienced implementers, so you can defer some design decisions to implementation. Even if you are doing both the design and the implementation yourself, over-specifying the design will waste time. To both save time and reduce errors, you should make an explicit design-content trade off. A specification for design completeness will then help you to produce a quality design and to conduct effective design reviews. As long as you meet the design exit criteria, you can use whatever design methods and notations you prefer.

THE USERS' NEEDS

To properly specify the products of the design phase, you should consider the needs of those who will use the design. While there are many potential users, the principal ones are the implementers, the design and code reviewers, the documenters, the test developers, the testers, the maintainers, and the enhancers. With your PSP, you are the principal design user, but you may not be the only one. For the exercises in this book, however, you are the only user of your design.

When you participate in a development project, everyone who works with you will need access to all your design information. When conflicts or questions arise, these people will need to explore related areas. While the design contents must be generally available, they must also be controlled. Each design product must have an author and an owner. The owner should be the only person who can change the design. The various categories of owners and the design products that they should control are the following.

System or Product Management.   Items that should be owned, tracked, and controlled by system or product management are the following:

- □ Issues tracking log: a running list of open issues and questions that must be resolved as the design progresses. These are like defect reports: Anyone can submit one, resolution responsibility must be centrally assigned, the open issues should be tracked, and the resolution must be recorded and communicated.
- □ The specification of any implementation constraints: coding specifications, configuration management standards and procedures
- □ A precise description of the program's intended function
- □ Application notes: descriptions of how the product or system is to be used. They include a statement of how the user will use the products with explanations of special conditions, constraints, or options.
- □ System-level user scenarios: example usage scenarios
- □ System constraints: timing, size, packaging, error handling, security, the hardware and system interface specifications

System Engineers.   Depending on the particular way the design was handled, the following items could be produced and owned at either the system or the product-design level:

- □ A description of all files: the precise specification of all the files to be provided and their structure
- □ A description of system messages: in a communication system, the specification of all message types, including formats, routings, and any relevant performance, security, or integrity specifications

□ Any special error checks or conditions

□ The reasons why the system design choices were made

Software Designers.   The following basic design information is the sole responsibility of the software designers:

□ A picture of where the program fits into the system

□ A logical picture of the program itself

□ A list of all related objects: scope, class structure, functions provided, where
initialized, where destructed

□ A list of all external variables: includes scope, limits, constraints, where declared, where initialized

□ A precise description of all external calls and references

□ A clear statement of the program's logic (pseudocode)

A complete and comprehensive set of design products that meets all these
needs would be large, unwieldy, and confusing. They could also be a major
source of error unless there were some automated way to ensure their self-consistency. In any reasonably large system, there will be many design changes. Thus,
with inadequate change control, design changes will not be completely reflected
in all the design records. These design records will then become inconsistent, and
anyone who uses them could be misled. This problem of change control is vastly
complicated whenever you record the same information in multiple places. It is
therefore essential to specify the absolute minimum of required design information and to ensure it is always kept up to date.

While these design materials must be produced in some form, their content
and format will vary considerably depending on the size of the system you are
building, the application domain, and the product standards. For the PSP, however, some design elements can be more or less standardized—those listed as the
software designers' sole responsibility. They form the base for the PSP design
process. For the PSP, I will thus concentrate on defining standards for this basic
design subset.

DESIGN PRECISION

The lack of a precise design is the source of many implementation errors. Review
your design defects and you will likely find that many were caused by simple errors. The reasons for these errors will vary, but a frequent cause is the lack of a
properly specified design. In some cases, you may have completed the design but
not precisely documented it. In others, you may not even have completed the design. If you don't have a precise specification for what the design must contain,

your decisions on where to stop will generally be spur of the moment and inconsistent. Often, in fact, you will think, "Anyone would know how to do this," and so not bother to document it. When you have not precisely recorded the design, however, you or any other implementer must finish the design during implementation. Doing this can be highly error prone.

DESIGN LEVEL

It helps to think of the design process as an inverted pyramid like that shown in Fig. 10.3. Each level provides a foundation for the next. During high-level design, you deal with structural, performance, and functional decisions. If you do not make and document all the necessary high-level design decisions in high-level design, you will have to reconstruct them again during detailed design. If you don't make and document all the detailed design decisions in detailed design, you will have to reconstruct them in implementation. Even when you are the implementer, the process of reconstructing all your mentally completed but not documented designs can be both time consuming and error prone. During implementation, you are thinking at an implementation level. Without considerable effort and a complete change of mindset, you will have trouble reconstructing all the relevant design details. This is when design errors are most likely. This level problem is a concern during every design stage. For example, when you resolve high-level design issues during detailed design, you are also likely to make errors.

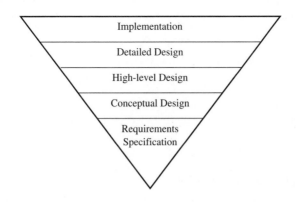

FIGURE 10.3
The Design Pyramid

10.3   Structuring the Design Process

There is considerable evidence that good designers follow a dynamic process in creating complex designs. [Curtis] They may work at a conceptual level for a period and then delve deeply into some issue. Frequently, they may not be sure which of several approaches to take and so may decide to look in detail at the alternatives. Curtis has found that this behavior is normal and often produces the insights needed for high quality designs. This dynamism was, in fact, a trait of all the best designers studied.

Even though the design process is dynamic, it is still helpful to think of it in process terms. However, the purpose in doing this is not to constrain design behavior but to help you to be more precise about the types of design products you produce and how to produce them. A structured design process helps you to manage the dynamics of design work. Because you will mentally jump from one artifact to another and simultaneously consider issues at several design levels, you need a framework in order to maintain control of what you have done and to permit you to readily track your design status.

One way to structure the design task for a large project is shown in Fig. 10.4. Briefly, the design phases required are as follows:

1. Define the need (requirements definition).
2. Define the solution (the system specification).
3. Conceptualize the solution (the system high-level design).
4. Divide up the work (the product specifications).
5. Define the product design (product high-level design).
6. Break the products into components (the component specifications).
7. Define the component design (component high-level design).
8. Break the components into modules (module specifications).
9. Detail the solution (module detailed design).
10. Implement the solution (module implementation and test).

The specifications and high-level designs are progressively refined until the module level is reached. Then the detailed design and implementation can be completed.

REQUIREMENTS DEFINITION

Even when a systems engineering or requirements group is charged with documenting the requirements, what they produce will rarely be adequate for your needs. To produce a competent design, you must ensure that the requirements are accurate and complete and that you understand them. You could argue that you should have a complete requirements statement before you start work, but it is rarely possible to get such a statement. This is for the following reasons:

1. Requirements specification is a specialized skill, and few people have the requisite knowledge and experience.

2. Requirements change. As your design progresses, you will ask questions that will cause the system engineers and/or the customers to think more deeply about the application needs, in turn generating new ideas for even better solutions. Even if you did not stimulate this process with probing questions, the longer you take to do the design the more likely they will think of new needs and enhancements.

3. This reason is much like the second but with a twist. The solution you develop will often change the problem. Most computer-related problems concern new services for people, so the problem solution will change how people work and consequently also probably change their needs. These changing needs will then impact the requirements.

This has major implications for the development process. While you can often hold the customers (or system engineers) responsible for the requirements they produce, your principal concern should be to produce a quality design and not to fix the blame for a poor design. You thus must learn as much as you can about the requirements. Once you have a clear and complete requirements definition, you can proceed with confidence to the design specification. However, if the answers you get are confused or incomplete you should focus on helping the users (or system engineers) to produce a complete and precise requirements statement. While you should not produce the requirements statement for them, often you can propose design solutions, postulate test scenarios, or build prototypes that will help them to better understand their own needs.

THE DESIGN SPECIFICATION

The design specification is a complete and precise statement of what the program must do. The requirements can be viewed as a problem statement without a solution. In fact, if the requirements are properly produced, they should not imply a design solution. The specifications, however, postulate the existence of a solution and state its constraints and invariants. For small products, the specifications can often be a simple extension of the requirements. For larger products, however, the specifications should be completely separate from the requirements.

You want to treat the specifications as a separate phase because you will often deal with multiple product layers. As shown in Fig. 10.4, the requirements definition and system specification are developed at the highest level. As development proceeds, you divide the system into major products, each of which must

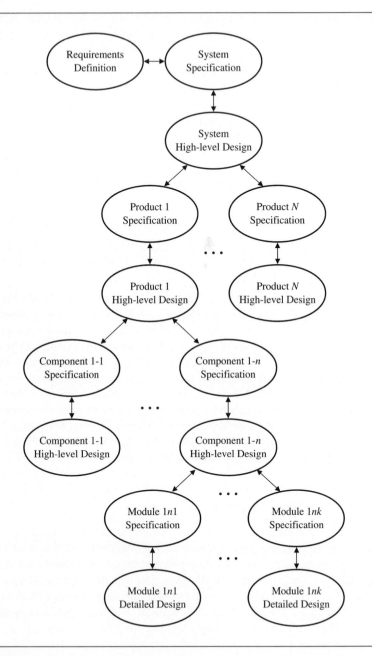

FIGURE 10.4
The Requirements-Specification-Design Cycle

be specified and designed. These products in turn may be composed of several components that also must be specified and designed. The specification thus must be refined for each product level.

The system specification is inextricably linked with the requirements definition. For it takes considerable effort to subdivide the system's functions into coherent products and components and to specify their relationships. If these design decisions are not precisely recorded when initially produced, they must be recreated later, a difficult, error-prone, and time-consuming activity. For example, once you have clarified some requirements aspect you should promptly reduce it to a rigorous specification. You then address and specify the next system aspect. If this specification conflicts with the previously completed specifications, you can make changes before these problems permeate the system design.

The more precise the specifications, the more likely you will identify requirements mistakes, omissions, or inconsistencies. In fact, the precision of the specification is much like the resolving power of a lens. An imprecise specification gives a vague and out-of-focus view of the system, while a precise specification brings requirements mistakes and uncertainties into clear focus. These phases must be so dynamic because of the need to rapidly resolve the issues that the specifications expose. With a clear and explicit specification, you can then proceed to the next design level.

HIGH-LEVEL DESIGN (HLD)

The next design phase is to conceptualize a product solution. In this phase, you create the overall design. You make choices on reusing existing components, defining object classes, and specifying inheritance relationships. During high-level design, you must think about two different systems: the application system and the component asset library. You design the reusable functions as part of a component library and tailor the application-specific functions to the unique needs of the product. To the maximum extent possible, you should design the application-specific functions to use elements from the reuse library.

HLD is where you make the critical design trade-offs. You address feasibility questions and make judgments between product content, development cost, and schedule. A truly elegant design must balance development economics, application needs, and technology. By properly relating these three dimensions, you balance the feasible with the desirable and the affordable. While you may not produce a product that does everything the customers want, you should aim to provide one that neatly and cleanly does what they need and can afford.

During HLD, many questions arise and many redesigns must be considered. You, the customers, and the system engineers must be in close and continuous contact. Earlier trade-offs are largely guesses, while the later ones will often involve time-consuming changes. It is during HLD that you can first settle many of the requirements issues in a businesslike and logical way.

To make proper economic trade-offs during HLD, you must have accurate development estimates. Both development cost and schedule are thus important design considerations. When you present design options, the users must recognize that functional enhancements are expensive. In fact, it is their failure to recognize the consequences of added product complexity that often leads to many development disasters. When you can clearly describe the costs of a proposed enhancement, the users and system designers can make better decisions about what they really need.

DETAILED-LEVEL DESIGN (DLD)

The next design phase is detailed design. In this phase, you reduce the HLD to implementable form. You detail the functions, specify the object state machines, and produce the finished design. Some of your HLD concepts will be unimplementable, while others may have to be changed. You might see reuse opportunities, have performance insights, and think of integration and system test issues. These changes can impact the HLD, so the requirements and HLD cannot be considered firm until you complete the DLD.

IMPLEMENTATION

The final design phase is implementation. While implementation is not design, it must still address design issues. Not only will low level design choices remain but, as you address implementation issues, you will generate many questions about the design. Some will require design changes, some may lead to design improvements. In a sense, then, the implementation phase can be viewed as the first test of the design.

10.4   Design Notation

A principal objective of a software design is to produce a concise and precise statement of exactly what the program is to do and how it is to do it. The English language is not a good vehicle for doing this. It is redundant and imprecise and tends to be voluminous. As a result, many different design approaches have been devised, some graphical and others using various kinds of mathematical notation. This and the next several sections of this chapter describe how to represent designs with a set of templates and a logic notation. The logic notation is based on propositional logic and is easy to learn and to use. If you are not familiar with propositional logic, Appendix B provides sufficient background so you can follow the examples in this and Chapter 12.

Basically, you precisely define the design products because you need to precisely think through your design and to accurately communicate it to others. The PSP does not require that any particular design representation or method be used. However, the representation you choose should meet the following criteria:

- □ It should be capable of precisely and completely representing the design.
- □ It must be understandable and usable to the people who are to use the design.
- □ It should help you to efficiently produce a high quality design.

DESIGN FLUENCY

This last point is particularly critical. In trying new design methods, you will likely find that both your productivity and the quality of your work will suffer. Until you have used a new method enough to achieve basic fluency, you will be unable to think in its terms. You will then mentally translate from your old familiar methods into the new method and back. This is both error prone and time consuming.

As you are determining which design methods and representations to use, consider the following:

- □ Use your PSP to establish a productivity baseline for the design methods you currently use.
- □ Measure your design work on a number of projects. Gather enough data to identify how many design defects you inject and the defect types that cause you the most trouble.
- □ Measure your performance with the new design method. Recognize that your productivity and quality will initially decline, so measure several projects.
- □ Analyze these data to see where and how the new method helps or hurts your performance.
- □ If, as is likely, you find the new method helps in some areas and hurts in others, you may want to use it selectively in combination with your prior techniques or mix it with other methods.

The design method should be your servant. Even though somebody else has found it helpful, it may not address your needs. You should get expert advice on using it properly and you should give it a sufficient trial, but if the numbers do not show that the method helps you, find something that does. A design method that does not help you to do better work is probably not right for you at this time.

IMPLEMENTATION DEPENDENCE

Depending on where you are in the design process, your design description should have varying degrees of implementation dependence. During the earliest requirements phase, you should describe what is wanted with as few implementation constraints as possible. When you get to the detailed design phase, however, be specific. In some cases, you may not want to specify precisely how a function is to be implemented; in others, you will need to be explicit. Your design notation should permit this variability.

Your design notation should also be compatible with the implementation language. Because every transcription is a source of error, you should use implementation constructs and operators wherever possible. While doing this could be inconvenient when you design for two or more different implementation languages, it is a useful general practice and will help you to reduce implementation errors.

The design notation used in the examples in this book is based on the C++ language. If you are not familiar with C++, the basic constructs are shown in Tables 10.1 and 10.2 and described in Appendix B.

10.5   Design Templates

The design representation described in the remainder of this chapter uses a family of four templates to represent an object-oriented design. The templates ensure the required data are clearly defined and concisely represented. If you do not use object-oriented methods, you can use these templates by replacing the words object, class, and method with either of the words function or procedure. As is the case with all PSP elements, you should modify these templates to suit your needs and augment them with flow charts or other graphical aids where helpful.

These templates are designed to provide a complete and precise design representation. They also help to minimize duplication. Each information item is recorded in one place and not copied. Its location is then referenced when needed. This method saves time, reduces the likelihood of errors, and provides reliable reference points. A principle of good design is that its representation should contain minimum duplication.

TABLE 10.1   DESIGN LANGUAGE CONSTRUCTS

Symbol	Function	Examples
Logical Operators		
! or '	not	!A or A'
==	equals	A == B
!= or ≠	not equals	A != B or A ≠ B
>=	greater than or equal	A >= B
<=	less than or equal	A <= B
>	greater than	A > B
<	less than	A < B
ε	member of	D ε CData
!ε	not member of	D !ε CData
true	integer != 0	1
false	integer == 0	0
∀	for all	∀ A ε CData
!∀	not for all	!∀ A ε CData
∃	there exists	∃A ε CData
!∃	there does not exist	!∃A ε CData
∧	intersection, logical and	A ∧ B
∨	union, logical or	A ∨ B
A::B	if A is true then B	if A :: B = 0

TEMPLATE DIMENSIONS

The elements of a complete design can be visualized with the help of the object specification structure described by de Champeaux. [de Champeaux] He suggests that this information be arranged in a two-dimensional box as shown in Table 10.3. Here, the elements of the object's design can be divided into the following four categories:

- Internal-static: contains a static picture of the object, such as its logical design
- Internal-dynamic: the object's dynamic characteristics concerning its behavior. The dynamic behavior of an object can often be described by treating it

TABLE 10.2   DESIGN LANGUAGE CALLS AND DECLARATIONS

Calls and Declarations	Examples
typeA Function(typeB variable)	int AddSet(data D)
passed typeB, returns typeA	function AddSet passes D of type data, returns integer value
type *Function(type &variable)	char *Pop(data &D)
returns pointer passed variable may be modified	function Pop passes D of type data, D may be changed by Pop, returns character string
type Object::method(type variable)	char *ASet::Pop(data &D)
declares method	declares method Pop of object ASet
identifies object method belongs to	
identifies passed variables and types	
defines method's return type	

as a state machine. Other important dynamic characteristics are response times and interrupt behavior.

□ External-static: the static relationship of this object to other objects. An example would be the inheritance hierarchy.

□ External-dynamic: the interactions of this object with other entities. An example would be the call-return behavior of each of the object's methods.

With the four templates described in the following sections, you can specify the main program and all the objects and methods it contains. You can also completely specify the logical design of a small object-oriented program. The four PSP design templates roughly correspond to the quadrants shown in Table 10.4. These templates and the information they contain are described in the following sections, together with examples of how they are used.

TABLE 10.3   OBJECT SPECIFICATION STRUCTURE

Object Specification	Internal	External
Static	Attributes Constraints	Inheritance Class Structure
Dynamic	State Machine	Services Messages

TABLE 10.4 PSP TEMPLATE STRUCTURE

Object Specification Templates	Internal	External
Static	Logic Specification Template	Function Specification Template (Inheritance Class Structure)
Dynamic	State Specification Template	Functional Specification Template (User Interaction) Operational Scenario Template

10.6   The Functional Specification Template

The Functional Specification Template precisely describes the methods provided by an object. As shown in Table 10.5, the class or object name is listed at the top together with the classes from which it directly descends. The object attributes are also listed at the top. In the rows below the object name, you list each method the object includes, such as the method declaration as it is to be included in the source program followed by a precise description of the function it provides. The purpose is to show, in as few lines as possible, exactly what the method does.

In the notation used to describe functional behavior, a logical precondition is stated followed by an action or postcondition. The condition-action pair are linked by '::' as follows:

condition :: action

Multiple conditions and actions can be combined by using standard logical notation as follows:

(condition1 :: action1) $\bigvee$ *(condition2 :: action2)* $\bigvee$ *(condition3 :: action3)*

Your program would take either action1 or action2, or action3 depending on which of the three conditions were satisfied. In fact, if the conditions were all true at the same time this logic could call for your program to take all three actions.

In the following case, if either condition1 or condition2 were true you would take both action1 and action2:

(condition1 $\bigvee$ *condition2) :: action1* $\bigwedge$ *action2*

When a class contains several objects, it is usually convenient to group their templates together as shown in the example in Table 10.6. Doing this provides an accurate and concise reference for the objects' external characteristics. In this ex-

TABLE 10.5 FUNCTIONAL SPECIFICATION TEMPLATE

Student ———————————————————— Date ————————
Program ———————————————————— Program # ————————
Instructor ———————————————————— Language ————————

Object/Class Name	Parent Classes	Attributes
Method declaration	Method external specification	

ample, two of the objects of class CData are described. These objects together provide a basic data structure. CData is indicated as the base class because it has no parent class. It provides the basic functions of a link list. The object ASet adds both the functions of a push-down stack and a set. Additional objects could be added to provide functions for sorting, enqueueing, dequeueing, and so on.

To understand the functions of CData, you should first understand its general behavior. Basically, CData is a linked list that can have zero or some number of members N. It also has a pointer that points to a position in the list. The attribute ListPosition gives the number of the item to which the pointer is pointing, from 0 (for empty) to N. ListState gives the state of CData. The five states of CData are precisely described with the State Specification Template (see Table 10.7) and described in some detail in the next section. In summary, these states are the following:

EmptySet	no members, ListState = 0, ListPosition = 0
First&Only	1 member, ListState = 1, ListPosition = 1
FirstOfSeveral	several members, ListState = 2, ListPosition = 1
MiddleOfSeveral	several members, ListState = 3, $1 <$ ListPosition $< N$
LastOfSeveral	several members, ListState = 4, ListPosition = N

Several of the functions in Table 10.6 can be read as follows:

▢ When the method Empty is called, if CData has no members (ListState = 0) return true, otherwise return false. In this notation, false is indicated by the returned integer 0 and true by a nonzero integer.

TABLE 10.6   EXAMPLE FUNCTIONAL SPECIFICATION TEMPLATE

Student ___WSH_____   Date ____12/2/92_____

Program ___CP025_____   Program # _____

Instructor _____   Language ___C++_____

Object/Class Name	Parent Classes	Attributes
CData	base class	ListState (0 to 4) ListPosition (0 to N)

int Empty()	ListState == 0 :: return(true) $\lor$ ListState $\neq$ 0 :: return(false)
int Clear()	:: set CData pointers to null $\land$ ListState = 0 $\land$ ListPosition = 0 $\land$ return(true)
int Last()	(Empty' $\land$ (ListState == 1 $\lor$ ListState == 4)) :: return (true) $\lor$ (Empty $\lor$ ListState == 2 $\lor$ ListState == 3) :: return (false)
int Reset()	(Empty' $\land$ N = 1) :: ListPosition = 1 $\land$ ListState = 1 $\land$ return(true) $\lor$ (Empty' $\land$ N > 1) :: ListPosition = 1 $\land$ ListState = 2 $\land$ return(true) $\lor$ Empty :: ListPosition = 0 $\land$ ListState = 0 $\land$ return(false)
int StepForward()	(ListState == 2 $\land$ N == 2) :: (step pointers to next position) $\land$ ListPosition = 2 $\land$ ListState = 4 $\land$ return(true) $\lor$ (ListState == 2 $\land$ N > 2) :: (step pointers to next position) $\land$ ListPosition = 2 $\land$ ListState = 3 $\land$ return(true) $\lor$ (ListState == 3 $\land$ ListPosition < N $-$ 1) :: (step pointers to next position) $\land$ ListPosition = ListPosition + 1 $\land$ return(true) $\lor$ (ListState == 3 ListPosition == N $-$ 1) :: (step pointers to next position) $\land$ ListPosition = N $\land$ ListState = 4 $\land$ return(true) $\lor$ (ListState == 0 $\lor$ ListState == 1 $\lor$ ListState == 4) ::return(false)
int StepBackward()	((ListState == 3 $\lor$ ListState == 4) $\land$ ListPosition == 2) :: (step pointers to prior position) $\land$ ListPosition = 1 $\land$ ListState == 2 $\land$ return(true) $\lor$ (ListState == 3 $\land$ ListPosition > 2) :: (step pointers to prior position) $\land$ ListPosition = ListPosition $-$ 1 $\land$ return(true) $\lor$ (ListState == 4 $\land$ ListPosition > 2) :: (step pointers to prior position) $\land$ ListPosition = ListPosition $-$ 1 $\land$ ListState = 3 $\land$

TABLE 10.6   (continued)

Object/Class Name	Parent Classes	Attributes
CData	base class	ListState (0 to 4) List Position (0 to N)
	return(true) $\lor$ (ListState == 0 $\lor$ ListState == 1 $\lor$ ListState == 2) :: return(false)	
int Status()	:: return (ListState)	
int Position()	:: return (ListPosition)	

Object Name	Parent Classes	Attributes
ASet	CData	ListState (0 to 4) ListPosition (0 to N)
void Push(data D)	:: (insert D at position 1) $\land$ Reset	
char *Pop(data &D)	Empty' :: return (D.name) $\land$ (delete first) $\land$ Reset $\lor$ Empty :: return "Empty"	
int AddSet(data D)	D $\notin$ ASet :: Push(D) $\land$ Reset $\land$ return (true) $\lor$ D $\in$ ASet :: Reset $\land$ return (false)	
int SubtractSet(data D)	D $\in$ ASet :: delete D $\land$ Reset $\land$ return (true) $\lor$ D $\notin$ ASet :: Reset $\land$ return (false)	
int MemberSet(data D)	D $\in$ ASet :: return (ListPosition of D) $\lor$ (D $\notin$ ASet $\land$ N == 1) :: ListPosition = 1 $\land$ ListState = 1 $\land$ return (false) $\lor$ (D $\notin$ ASet $\land$ N > 1) :: ListPosition = N $\land$ ListState = 4 $\land$ return (false)	

□ On method Clear, CData is set to the empty state by setting the list pointers to null. The return is always true.

□ When the method Last is called, if Empty is false and the list pointer points to the last member return true

or

if Empty is true or the list pointers are not pointing to the last member return false.

□ When Reset is called, if Empty is false and the list has one member (N==1), set ListPosition to 1 and set ListState to 1 and return true, or

if Empty is false and the list has more than one member (N>1) set ListPosition to 1 and ListState to 2 and return true,

or

if Empty, set ListPosition to 0 and ListState to 0 and return false.

The other items in Table 10.6 can be read in the same way.

When you are dealing with the methods of relatively simple objects, this template format will generally be adequate to describe their external behavior. The class inheritance structures, however, may be too complex to be easily

TABLE 10.7   STATE SPECIFICATION TEMPLATE

Student _____   Date _____

Program _____   Program # _____

Instructor _____   Language _____

Object _____   Routine _____

State #1	Description	Attributes
state #1	Transition conditions	
state #2		
. . .		
. . .		
state #n		

State #2	Description	Attributes
state #1	Transition conditions	
state #2		
. . .		
. . .		
state #n		

. . .

State #n	Description	Attributes
state #1	Transition conditions	
state #2		
. . .		
. . .		
state #n		

TABLE 10.8   EXAMPLE STATE SPECIFICATION TEMPLATE

Student ___WSH_____ Date ____12/2/92_____

Program ___CP025_____ Program # _____

Instructor _____ Language ___C++_____

Object ___CData_____ Routine _____

State		Description	Attributes
EmptySet		the set has no members N == 0	ListState == 0 ListPosition == 0
1	EmptySet	Clear $\vee$ Reset $\vee$ StepForward $\vee$ StepBackward $\vee$ Pop $\vee$ SubtractSet $\vee$ MemberSet $\vee$ Empty $\vee$ Last $\vee$ Status $\vee$ Position	
2	First&Only	Push $\vee$ AddSet	
3	FirstOfSeveral	Impossible	
4	MiddleOfSeveral	Impossible	
5	LastOfSeveral	Impossible	
First&Only		the set has one member N == 1	ListState == 1 ListPosition == 1
6	EmptySet	Clear $\vee$ Pop $\vee$ (SubtractSet(D) $\wedge$ D $\in$ ASet)	
7	First&Only	Reset $\vee$ StepForward $\vee$ StepBackward $\vee$ (AddSet(D) $\wedge$ D $\in$ ASet) $\vee$ (SubtractSet(D) $\wedge$ D ! $\in$ ASet) $\vee$ MemberSet $\vee$ Empty $\vee$ Last $\vee$ Status $\vee$ Position	
8	FirstOfSeveral	Push $\vee$ (AddSet(D) $\wedge$ D ! $\in$ ASet)	
9	MiddleOfSeveral	Impossible	
10	LastOfSeveral	Impossible	
FirstOfSeveral		the set has several members, pointers in first position N >= 2	ListState == 2 ListPosition == 1
11	EmptySet	Clear	
12	First&Only	(N == 2 $\wedge$ SubtractSet(D) $\wedge$ D $\in$ ASet) $\vee$ (N == 2 $\wedge$ Pop) $\vee$ Empty $\vee$ Last $\vee$ Status $\vee$ Position	
13	FirstOfSeveral	Reset $\vee$ StepBackward $\vee$ Push $\vee$ (Pop $\wedge$ N > 2) $\vee$ AddSet $\vee$ (SubtractSet(D) $\wedge$ D ! $\in$ ASet) $\vee$ (N > 2 $\wedge$ SubtractSet) $\vee$ (MemberSet(D) $\wedge$ D in first position) $\vee$ Empty $\vee$ Last $\vee$ Status $\vee$ Position	
14	MiddleOfSeveral	(N > 2 $\wedge$ StepForward) $\vee$ (MemberSet(D) $\wedge$ (D in middle position))	
15	LastOfSeveral	(N == 2 $\wedge$ StepForward) $\vee$!MemberSet(D) $\vee$ (MemberSet(D) $\wedge$ (D in last position))	

TABLE 10.8   (continued)

State		Description	Attributes
MiddleOfSeveral		the set has several members, pointers in nth position $N > 2$	ListState $== 3$ $1 <$ ListPosition $< N$
16	EmptySet	Clear	
17	First&Only	Impossible	
18	FirstOfSeveral	Reset $\lor$ Push $\lor$ Pop $\lor$ (ListPosition $== 2 \land$ StepBackward) $\lor$ AddSet $\lor$ SubtractSet $\lor$ (MemberSet(D) $\land$ (D in first position))	
19	MiddleOfSeveral	(ListPosition $> 2 \land$ StepBackward) $\lor$ (ListPosition $< N - 1 \land$ StepForward) $\lor$ (MemberSet(D) $\land$ (D in middle position)) $\lor$ Empty $\lor$ Last $\lor$ Status $\lor$ Position	
20	LastOfSeveral	(ListPosition $== N - 1 \land$ StepForward) $\lor$!MemberSet $\lor$ (MemberSet(D) $\land$ (D in last position))	
LastOfSeveral		set has $N > 1$ members, pointers in last position $N > 1$	ListState $== 4$ ListPosition $== N$
21	EmptySet	Clear	
22	First&Only	$N == 2 \land$ SubtractSet(D) $\land$ D $\in$ ASet	
23	FirstOfSeveral	Reset $\lor$ Push $\lor$ Pop ($N == 2 \land$ StepBackward) $\lor$ AddSet $\lor$ (SubtractSet $\land$ N > 2) $\lor$ (SubtractSet(D) $\land$ D ! $\in$ ASet) $\lor$ (MemberSet(D) $\land$ D in first position)	
24	MiddleOfSeveral	($N > 2 \land$ StepBackward) $\lor$ (MemberSet(D) $\land$ D in middle position)	
25	LastOfSeveral	StepForward $\lor$!MemberSet $\lor$ (MemberSet(D) $\land$ (D in last position)) $\lor$ Empty $\lor$ Last $\lor$ Status $\lor$ Position	

described in such a simple listing. In these cases, a graphical description is usually desirable. One way to produce such descriptions is described in Coad and Yourdon. [Coad (a), Coad (b)]

10.7   The State Specification Template

The State Specification Template describes the object state behavior. The completed state specification contains a description of each of the object's states and the transitions among them. A blank State Specification Template is shown in Table 10.7. To complete the template, enter in the top space the name of one state and in the spaces to the right of the name a brief word or mathematical description of the state, together with the attribute values for that state. On the next several lines, list each of this state's possible next states, together with the conditions that cause transitions to them. As shown in Table 10.8, you repeat this structure for every state. Thus for an object with five possible states, the structure in Table 10.7 would have five state description sections each with five lines for the next states.

The example State Specification Template shown in Table 10.8 is for the CData class, including the object ASet. As you can see, the class has five states: EmptySet, First&Only, FirstOfSeveral, MiddleOfSeveral, and LastOfSeveral. As described in Section 10.6, these state names refer to both the positions of the pointers and the number of members in the linked list.

The top section of Table 10.8 describes the state EmptySet. Because this state has no members, $N==0$ and the attributes ListState and ListPosition both equal zero. Of the five total states in this state machine, only two are possible next states after EmptySet. First&Only is reached via the Push or AddSet functions, which each add a member to the set. All other functions leave the CData state machine in the empty state.

The transitions for the First&Only state are a bit more complex. Their conditions are defined as shown in lines 6, 7, and 8 of Table 10.8.

GRAPHICALLY REPRESENTING STATE MACHINES

Even relatively simple sequential systems are hard to visualize, so it is often desirable to construct a graphical state diagram, as shown in Fig. 10.5. With the data provided in the State Specification Template, such a figure is relatively easy to produce. If it is not easy, either the state specification is incomplete or the design is too complex.

As you can see from Fig. 10.5, a state machine is a simple way to represent the behavior of a system. The state attribute values and the state transition conditions can be shown on the figure if they are not too complex. In this case, the transitions are indicated by numbers that refer to the conditions in Table 10.8. As you prefer, you may choose to draw the state machine diagram as in Fig. 10.5 and use it to develop the template or to start with the template and then produce the diagram. In either case, by producing the template and drawing a state diagram, you often will spot overlooked states or transitions. It is particularly important to do this during design, since the late discovery of such omissions will often require substantial rework.

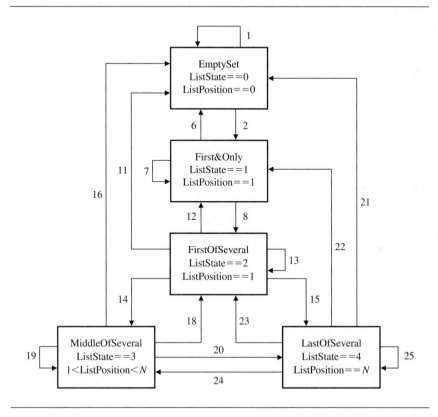

FIGURE 10.5
Example State Machine Transitions

PROPER STATE MACHINES

One way to check a state machine design is to ensure it is proper. Appendix B
gives a fuller description of a proper state machine. In short, a proper state machine has states that are complete and orthogonal, and the transition conditions
among the states are complete and orthogonal. Hence for the entire state machine
the union of all the state attribute values is true. When this is the case, all possible
states have been included. For example, the union of the attribute values in the
example state machine in Table 10.8 is as follows:

$$(ListState == 0 \wedge ListPosition == 0) \vee$$
$$(ListState == 1 \wedge ListPosition == 1) \vee$$
$$(ListState == 2 \wedge ListPosition == 1) \vee$$

$$(\text{ListState} == 3 \land 1 < \text{ListPosition} < N) \lor$$

$$(\text{ListState} == 4 \land \text{ListPosition} == N)$$

In checking this, first note that all the possible values of ListState are given: 0 through 4. Next, for each value of ListState, check to see if all possible values of ListPosition are given. Careful checking reveals that this is the case. Because these attribute combinations represent the state machine states and their union is true, the state completeness condition for a proper state machine is satisfied.

By examining Table 10.8, you can also see that the state machine cannot be in two states at the same time. This is because the values of the attributes List-State and ListPosition are different for each state. Thus the state orthogonality condition is satisfied.

Similarly, in Table 10.8, the union of all the transition conditions from every state should be true. The first state, EmptySet, is easy to check, since its transitions include all the possible method calls. The union of all these conditions is thus true. The second state, First&Only, is a little more complex. In checking the union of all the terms, First&Only includes all the methods as before except for AddSet and SubtractSet. Each of these is included twice: once when D is a member of ASet and once when D is not a member of ASet. Again, because these represent all the possible conditions the union is true. Thus the state transitions are complete, satisfying another condition for a proper state machine.

In checking the transitions from the FirstOfSeveral state, you can see that the set has two or more members and the set pointers are in the first position. This is indicated by N>=2 and ListPosition==1. By examining the possible transitions, you can see that the effect of every method on this state is described. The SubtractSet method is a good illustration. Its conditions are

```
N==2 ∧ D ∈ ASet :: First&Only
D !∈ ASet ∨ N>2 :: FirstOfSeveral
```

A simple truth table demonstrates that this includes all the possibilities for SubtractSet and that each case is uniquely associated with a next state. Note, however, that for the state FirstOfSeveral N>=2, so the cases of N==0 and N==1 need not be considered. The truth table is

	N == 2	N > 2
D ∈ ASet	First&Only	FirstOfSeveral
D !∈ ASet	FirstOfSeveral	FirstOfSeveral

By making similar checks, you can verify that all possible state transitions have been considered and that they are orthogonal, thus satisfying the condition that the state transitions be orthogonal. The only remaining condition for a proper state machine is that it can reach an exit state from every other state. As you can see from Fig. 10.5, the state machine has no unending loops or trap states. It is thus a proper state machine.

STATE TEMPLATE CONSIDERATIONS

It is easy to assume that a state transition is not possible only to later find that it was possible under some unusual conditions. These unusual conditions are often the source of difficult system defects, so you should note during the design the reasons for each impossible transition.

It is also important to precisely describe all the transition conditions. In this example, these conditions are moderately complex. Too complex a state structure, however, is a symptom of an excessively intricate design, which can cause implementation, test, and maintenance problems.

The definition of what is a state is also important. While any reasonably complex program can have many states, you need to identify those that have logical significance. A useful guideline is that a state is characterized by different attribute values and different object behavior. Conversely, if the object's behavior is identical in two different states, those states should be merged, regardless of parameter value differences. This assumes you do not plan to later enhance the object to treat these states differently.

State machines have memory, and their behavior differs depending on their previous history. The current state thus represents the memory of this prior history. So behavior differences result from the previous history of the object rather than from differing combinations of external parameter values. If an object's behavior is completely defined by its externally supplied parameters, then it should not be represented as a state machine. Under these conditions, the Functional Specification Template adequately describes functional behavior and no State Specification Template is needed.

10.8   Logic Specification Template

The Logic Specification Template is shown in Table 10.9 and an example template for SubtractSet is shown in Table 10.10. This logic uses a simple C++-like pseudocode with the design notation described in Appendix B. While this pseudocode is almost a finished source program, instruction details and some variable and parameter declarations and initializations remain to be completed during implementation. The Logic Reference Numbers at the left are used to facilitate the design reviews. To provide maximum help, these numbers should identify every key action and logical decision point in the pseudocode.

TABLE 10.9 LOGIC SPECIFICATION TEMPLATE

Student _____   Date _____
Program _____   Program # _____
Instructor _____   Language _____
Object _____   Function _____

INCLUDES:

TYPE DEFINITIONS:
Declaration: _____
Reference: _____

Logic Reference Numbers	Program Logic (in pseudocode)

TABLE 10.10   EXAMPLE LOGIC SPECIFICATION TEMPLATE

Student	WSH	Date	12/2/92
Program	CP025	Program #	
Instructor		Language	C++
Object	ASet (CData)	Function	SubtractSet

INCLUDES: < iostream.h >
              < stdio.h >
              < string.h >
              "classes\CString.cpp"

TYPE DEFINITIONS: char data[ARRAYSIZE] [STRINGLENGTH + 1]

Declaration: int ASet::SubtractSet(data D)

#define ARRAYSIZE 2

#define STRINGLENGTH 32

typedef char data[ARRAYSIZE] [STRINGLENGTH + 1]

Reference:

Logic Reference Numbers	Program Logic (in pseudocode)
	Done = 0
1	if Empty'
2	if D == first item
	delete first item
	reset set pointer and next item pointer
	Done++
3	while Done' ∧ Last'
	step to next item
4	if D == item
	delete item
	reset prior and next item pointers
	Done++
	Reset
5	return (Done)

10.9   The Operational Scenario Template

The Operational Scenario Template describes the system's operational behavior in one or more scenarios. The purpose is to help you visualize how the program is supposed to react under various typical user scenarios. When faced with a design decision that involves a user action, you should produce a trial scenario to see how it would interact with the user. This scenario will help you to visualize its behavior and to determine the appropriate design choices. While no set of scenarios can cover all usage combinations for even a moderately complex system, you should include examples of the key functions and exception conditions. With careful planning, however, you can often cover a large percentage of the important cases with just a few scenarios. These scenarios then provide a sound basis for program testing. If you don't construct and test such scenarios, you will likely overlook some key actions. Often, these overlooked actions are not even tested and can be a significant source of user annoyance.

As shown in the blank Operational Scenario Template in Table 10.11, space for a scenario number is provided at the top. Numbering scenarios helps when you use several scenarios for one program. In the next space, User's Objective, briefly describe the user's expected purpose in taking these actions. It is often hard for program designers to see the product from the user's perspective. By writing a brief statement of the user's objective, you can better visualize the user's viewpoint. You should also plan to use scenarios to highlight design features or potential problems. You enter this brief statement of your reasons for constructing the scenario in the Scenario Objective space. In the Source column, enter the originator of an action; in Step, enter the action sequence number; in Action, describe the action that is taken; and in Comments, note results, exception conditions, or other useful information.

The example in Table 10.12 is an Operational Scenario Template for a simple file program. It shows the user and system actions to create a new file of one record. The user starts the program at step 1, the program displays a menu at 2, the user enters an improper selection at 3, the program responds with an error message calling for reentry at 4, and so on.

This template provides both the operational view needed for product design and a framework for devising test procedures. A well-thought-out operational specification is thus an important adjunct both to design and to test. It can also help you to see where the user might have problems or where user actions could stress the system.

An example of some of the user actions that could cause system problems is the treatment of erroneous user entries. In the case of the FileManager program in Table 10.12, examples of some error cases that should be considered are the

TABLE 10.11   OPERATIONAL SCENARIO TEMPLATE

Student	_____	Date	_____
Program	_____	Program #	_____
Instructor	_____	Language	_____

Construct operational scenarios to cover the normal and abnormal program uses, including user errors.

Scenario #	User's Objective:		
Scenario Objective:			
Source	Step	Action	Comments

TABLE 10.12   EXAMPLE OPERATIONAL SCENARIO TEMPLATE

Student   WSH _____   Date   10/6/92 _____

Program   FileManager _____   Program # _____

Instructor _____   Language   C++ _____

Construct operational scenarios to cover the normal and abnormal program uses, including user errors.

Scenario #1		User Objective: To create a new file of one record	
Scenario Objective: To identify program response to several incorrect user actions			
Source	Step	Action	Comments
user	1	start program	
program	2	display main menu request selection	
user	3	enter selection	improper value
program	4	display message: "improper selection" display main menu request selection	
user	5	enter selection	proper value
program	6	request file address	
user	7	enter file address	existing file address
program	8	display message "file exists" request file address	
user	9	enter file address	proper address
program	10	display record template request new record	
user	11	enter new record	
program	12	display record display record menu request selection	
user	13	enter selection	correct record
program	14	display field menu request selection	
user	15	enter field number	
program	16	display field correction template request entry	
user	17	enter new field	
program	18	display corrected record	

TABLE 10.12 (continued)

Scenario #1		User Objective: To create a new file of one record	
Scenario Objective: To identify program response to several incorrect user actions			
Source	Step	Action	Comments
		display field menu request entry	
user	19	enter selection	no more corrections
program	20	display record menu request selection	
user	21	select OK	approve and exit
program	22	display main menu request selection	
user	23	select exit	exit
program	24	exit	

following:

- The user enters an impossible menu selection (step 3).
- The user enters an existing file address when creating a new file (step 7).
- The user enters a nonexistent file address when updating a file (not shown).
- The user enters an improper file address format (not shown).
- The user enters any values at any time that are not the proper type, for example, alphabetic characters when an integer menu selection is called for.

You should identify all such cases in the scenarios, produce a robust design that will handle them, and test them. When your reviews or tests show that your design is not sufficiently robust, you should produce a new or modified design that is.

10.10 Using Templates in Design

These design templates provide a basis for establishing design exit criteria. While they do not describe how the program fits into the larger system context, the templates do provide the bulk of the information that the program designer is responsible for producing. In the PSP, completion of the design templates is an important part of design exit criteria.

THE DESIGN HIERARCHY

You can use design templates to progressively refine the specification and the design of a software product. Starting at the highest level, specify the main program functions, including their relationships with the external environment. You do this with the Functional Specification and the Operational Scenario Templates. If the external environment calls for various program states, complete one or more State Specification Templates.

One way to visualize this is shown in Fig. 10.6. Start with a program requirements statement to describe what the user needs. First, translate these requirements into a specification that crisply and concisely describes the program's behavior. As part of this specification, you could complete, for example, an Operational Scenario Template and a Functional Specification Template for the overall program.

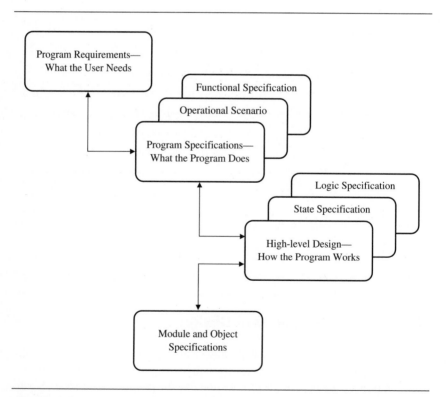

FIGURE 10.6
The Design Hierarchy

Then the high-level design work consists of designing this main routine and precisely specifying the external behavior of all the objects it uses. You can use various flow chart or other design techniques, but you should finish by producing a state specification template and a logic specification template for the main routine. While doing this, you also postulate the services you need from lower-level objects. As you define these needs, you should capture them in a family of functional specification templates for the next lower-level design.

Repeat this process at every successive design level, completing a state specification template and a logic specification template for each module or object. If the program is moderately large, you might continue this iterative process for several additional levels. At the end, as shown in Fig. 10.7, you specify the detailed design for the lowest level program modules.

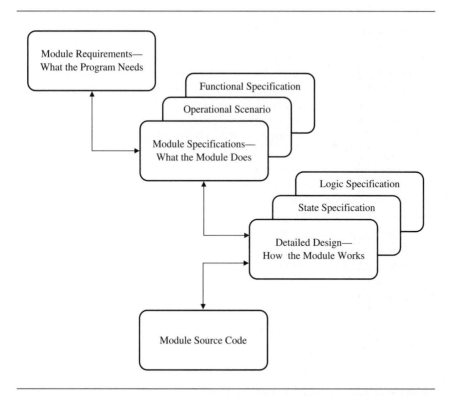

FIGURE 10.7
The Implementation Hierarchy

Note that you first specify the external or system behavior as indicated in Fig. 10.4 on page 320. You then work down this hierarchy alternately specifying and designing until you reach implementable modules. The external behavior at each level is defined with Operational Scenario and Functional Specification Templates and the internal behavior is defined with a State Specification Template and a Logic Specification Template.

DESIGN STRATEGY

You will find that in using these templates to design a small system, one or two passes through them are generally adequate. For a larger system, the first one or two design levels will generally reveal a large number of objects and functions. One design strategy may be to start with the overall specifications and produce the templates for all the top-level objects. While designing each of these objects, you will use lower-level abstractions that must be externally specified. These specifications then serve as the starting point for the next lower-level design. You repeat this alternating specification and design sequence at each program abstraction level until you have specified and designed the entire program.

This top-down design strategy is only one approach. You could, for example, start with a critical module in the heart of the system and design and implement related elements from that level upward. You might even find it desirable to skip from one level to another and back. Regardless of the strategy you use, you should not consider any element's design complete until you fully understand all the logic connecting it to the higher-level program elements that use its services. You should also have specified all the services it requires from lower-level objects.

You should establish a design strategy to help you to develop only what you thoroughly understand and then gradually build on this solid foundation as you design and implement more modules. Chapter 11 describes the PSP3 process as well as several example design strategies.

A logical and orderly design process need not follow a simple pattern. In fact, it is likely you will occasionally need some function that you do not fully understand. To specify it properly, you may then choose to create a prototype for that element or even to complete its detailed design. You could thus bounce from the highest design level down to implementation and back many times during a design. The important point is to try not to constrain this creative process but to ensure you properly capture your growing design knowledge. The design templates will help you to do this.

DISINTEGRATING AND INTEGRATING THE PRODUCT

In essence, design by abstraction consists of successive disintegrations of the system into manageable pieces. Implementation then consists of building and integrating these pieces into a coherent whole. If the design strategy is a poor fit to the problem, you can waste time constructing special test drivers and making multiple program modifications. A poor design strategy is also more likely to produce a confused, hard to understand, and hard to modify system structure that has usability, operational, and performance problems. Because the design strategy must reflect the unique product needs, there is no best design strategy for all systems. Your strategy determines the effectiveness and efficiency of your development process, and you should select it based on the nature of the system you are building.

10.11   Design Guidelines

With the PSP exercises, you can use a simple design strategy. More generally, you will have to define your own design process for each new project. Some of the topics you should then consider are the design level, prototyping, and redesign. These are discussed in the next sections.

DESIGN LEVELS

During the design of a large program, you often cannot specify all the lower-level functions until you know more about them. You could then leave some of the higher-level specifications incomplete until you have done some lower-level design work. You could next do the design in a disconnected series of partial designs. Starting at the top, you would proceed until you hit an unknown abstraction. If this abstraction were particularly difficult or critical, you might design it before proceeding. This abstraction in turn may call others that appear equally critical, and those may lead to others. As a result, you could find yourself delving deeply into the system before you complete the highest-level design. On occasion, you may even find it desirable to work from the bottom up or in some other order. This is acceptable as long as all lower-level work is considered exploratory until all relevant higher-level designs are complete.

When following such a dynamic design strategy, you should consider the following:

- □ Where practical, complete the highest-level designs first.
- □ You should not consider the design of a program or major program element complete until the specifications of all the abstractions it uses are complete.
- □ You should not consider the design of a program element complete until the specification of all the program elements that call it are also complete.

□ If you make assumptions to complete a design, log them so you can later check to ensure they are valid. The Issue Tracking Log (described in Appendix C) provides a convenient place to record outstanding issues, questions, or problems.

□ Resolve the uncertainties that prevent you from specifying an abstraction before you attempt to design it. It may be helpful to use prototype experiments in doing this.

□ Penetrate as many design levels as needed in order to resolve specification uncertainties.

□ Defer resolving lower-level design uncertainties if they do not impact other system elements.

PROTOTYPING

You will find cases in which you cannot externally specify a function before you have fully designed it or even built and tested it. In these cases, develop these functions in prototype form before you complete the higher-level designs. After you have completed the prototypes and resolved the uncertainties, complete the high-level designs.

Prototyping is a powerful tool that can be used in various ways. In some cases, you will want to experiment with reusable program elements to verify how they work. You may seek the most time- or space-efficient way to produce a function or to demonstrate a proposed approach to a user. One practice that can prevent a lot of design defects is to build such prototypes every time you use a new or unfamiliar library function. These prototypes are small throw-away programs developed to answer specific questions. They will not be part of the finished product, so the need for extensive commenting, defect recording, design documentation, or testing is reduced.

A principal benefit of the PSP is that you can see for yourself which parts of the process save you time and which are most costly. You can thus decide how to produce a prototype in the least time. As you do this, however, you should specify the prototype's purpose and define the questions it is to answer. A prototype plan will also help you to manage the prototype work with the same discipline you apply to your project development work. The only difference between a prototype and a project development, is that with the prototype you omit those PSP steps that do not contribute to your current objective.

REDESIGN

A large percentage of industrial software involves redesign. You may modify or enhance an old product or incrementally add functions to a larger, new product.

Whenever your new work can be viewed as a separate development external to the base product, your design process need not differ from that used with the PSP.

More commonly, however, the redesign will require you to delve into some prior product to make fixes or extensions. Doing this will require that you understand this prior product before you change it. If this prior design is fully documented and the documentation is available, your job may not be too different from that of developing a new product. More commonly, however, the prior design is not documented or the documentation is not correct or not available. In these cases, you will have to start with the source code and reconstruct the design. While the methods you use will depend on the product you are developing, you should consider using the PSP design templates to record the design.

10.12 Summary

Many of software development's historic problems have stemmed from a misplaced expectation that development should start with firm and complete requirements. History demonstrates, however, that for a new software system the requirements will not be completely known until after you have a working product. In defining your design process you must therefore recognize that the requirements will likely change. You thus should include steps to identify and resolve requirements uncertainties as early as possible.

One of the more difficult design problems concerns the trade-off between design completeness and development cost and schedule. The complete specification of a software design requires a great deal of information. This includes definitions for the classes and objects that define their relationships, identify the data exchanged among them, define the required data and state transformations, and specify the system inputs and outputs. The complete and unambiguous definition of all this material generally requires a substantial amount of documentation.

As you do software design work, you must consider two different questions: How do you do the design, and what must the design look like when you are done? The PSP does not specify a particular design method. However, it does deal with the exit criteria from the design phases. To properly specify design completeness, you should consider the needs of those who will use the design. You can then determine what the design product should be.

The starting and ending points of the design process can be described with the aid of templates. These templates ensure the required data are clearly defined and concisely represented. The Functional Specification Template describes the functions performed by a program, an object, or a procedure. The State Specification Template describes the program's state model. The Logic Specification Template uses pseudocode to precisely describe the program logic. The Operational Scenario Template describes the program's operational behavior via one or more scenarios.

In essence, design by abstraction consists of successive disintegrations of the system into manageable pieces. Implementation then consists of building and integrating these pieces into a coherent whole. During design, you often cannot precisely define all subsystems until you know more about them. You could then leave some higher-level specifications incomplete until you have done some lower-level design. You could next do the design as a disconnected series of partial designs. You may start at the top and proceed until you hit some unfamiliar abstraction. If that abstraction appeared particularly difficult or critical, you could design it before proceeding. That abstraction in turn may call on others that appear equally critical, and they in turn may call others. As a result, you could find yourself delving deeply into the system before you have completed the highest-level design. On occasion, you may even work from the bottom up or in some other order. This is acceptable as long as all lower-level work is considered exploratory until all relevant, higher-level designs are completed.

You will find cases in which you cannot externally specify an object before you have fully designed it or possibly even built and tested it. In these cases, develop prototypes of these objects before you complete the higher-level designs. After you have completed the prototypes and resolved the uncertainties, complete the high-level designs.

10.13 Exercises

The standard course plan assumes this chapter is covered in two lectures. There are thus two exercises given with this chapter. In the first, use PSP2 to write program 8A and for the second, use PSP2.1 to write program 9A. The specifications for these programs are given in Appendix D and the PSP2 and PSP2.1 processes are described in Appendix C. In completing these assignments, you should faithfully follow the report submission formats specified for PSP2 and PSP2.1.

For other assignment options, consult Appendix D.

References

[Coad a] Peter Coad and Edward Yourdon, *Object-Oriented Analysis* (Englewood Cliffs, NJ: Yourdon Press, 1990).

[Coad b] Peter Coad and Edward Yourdon, *Object-Oriented Design* (Englewood Cliffs, NJ: Yourdon Press, 1991).

[Curtis] Bill Curtis, Herb Krasner, and Neil Iscoe, "A Field Study of the Software Design Process for Large Systems," *Communications of the ACM*, vol. 31, no. 11 (November 1988).

[de Champeaux] D. de Champeaux, Douglas Lea, and Penelope Faure, *Object-Oriented System Development* (Reading, MA: Addison-Wesley, 1993).

11

Scaling Up the Personal Software Process

The size of software products has increased steadily for more than 30 years. While the rate of increase varies among product types, sizes have typically increased by an order of magnitude every five to 10 years. This happens even when essentially the same product is implemented in a new technology. One example is the Hewlett-Packard (HP) laser printer. The initial product used 25,000 LOC, while the next model used 200,000 LOC. HP's third laser printer model uses about 1,000,000 LOC—a 40-fold increase in about 10 years. While this third model printer handles many more fonts, features, and functions, it is still a printer.

Each year, customers demand more sophisticated products. These in turn require more sophisticated software, which takes much more code and a larger-scale process. This is true of both large systems and household products. The newest television sets, for example, now contain over half a million bytes of microcode.

The sizes of the products you develop in the future will be much larger than the product of today. The software in even simple products will soon be larger than individuals can intuitively master. Although individual engineers will still develop software components, their work will increasingly involve large teams and even groups of teams. A process that was optimum for your last project will probably not be optimum for one five to 10 times larger. As the sizes of the products you develop increase, your process must scale up as well. While you should not use a more sophisticated process than you need, you should tailor your process to your project.

The question addressed by this chapter is, how should your PSP change as you work on progressively larger-scale systems? While there is no general answer, a well-defined and practiced PSP will enable you to determine these changes for yourself. This chapter discusses some of the problems of developing large-scale systems and some principles and strategies for dealing with these problems. It outlines how you can relate your PSP to these larger processes, and it describes the PSP3 process as one example of how to do this.

11.1   Using Abstractions

Physicists and engineers make approximations to simplify their work. These are based on known physical laws and verified engineering principles. The software engineer has no Kirkhoff's and Ohm's laws and no grand concepts like Newtonian Mechanics or the Theory of Relativity. We lack basic structural guidelines like strengths of materials or coefficients of friction. We can, of course, defer rarely used functions or temporarily ignore error and recovery procedures, but we cannot separate software procedures by their likely impact on the system's performance. With hardware, you can often determine that the performance of some elements will have a 10 percent impact on the system, while others will have less than a 1 percent impact. In the software business, minor details often make the difference between a convenient and functioning product and an unusable one. Because of the very nature of software, we cannot generally reduce the complexity of our products by making approximations.

THE POWER OF ABSTRACTIONS

We do, however, have some powerful tools at our disposal. We can create abstractions and arbitrarily combine them into larger abstractions. Even if we know nothing about the internal structure of these abstractions, we can name and use them as long as we know all their important external specifications. Hence we have the opportunity essentially to write our own rules. If we conform to the capacities and capabilities of the systems we support, we can create whatever logical structures we choose.

This freedom, however, has its price. We do not face the physical constraints of physicists and hardware engineers, but we do face intellectual ones. As our products become more complex, we are unable to grasp all their critical details.

While we are not constrained by the physical laws of nature, we do need consistent rules and concepts. Because of our human fallibility, however, our rules and concepts are often flawed, incomplete, or inconsistent.

THE ELEMENTS OF INTELLECTUAL WORK

Intellectual work involves three elements: memory, skill, and method. The short-term memory, in fact, is our principal intellectual scratch pad. Miller points out that the range of things we can actively manipulate is only seven chunks, or pieces of information, plus or minus two. [Miller] Without some pictures, notes, or physical reminders, we simply cannot retain much more in our short-term memories.

EXPERT MEMORY

While each of us has different memory capabilities, Simon has identified ways that people can expand their intellectual capacities. [Simon] He found that we remember in chunks. The seven plus or minus two constraint is for chunks, and these chunks may have structure and content. DeGroot did an experiment in which he showed that amateur chess players think of individual chessmen while masters think in patterns. [DeGroot] Simon estimates that an experienced chess master may have built a vocabulary of 50,000 or more of these pattern chunks. The expert thus sees the chessboard as made up of combinations of familiar chunks. In the DeGroot experiment, chess masters and amateurs were tested on their abilities to recall the positions of men on a chessboard. After seeing an in-progress game for a few moments, the amateurs could place only half a dozen or so of the pieces, while the masters could typically reproduce the entire board. When a random set of piece positions was used instead of a game in progress, the amateurs and the experts did about the same. Clearly, the expert's unique abilities applied only to the meaningful patterns of actual games.

EXPERT SKILL

Building chunk vocabularies is just like building word vocabularies. We do it unconsciously as we gain skill and experience. With this chunk vocabulary, we can think in richer terms. This in turn multiplies our abilities to handle complexity. Thus, while beginning programmers think of individual instructions, more experienced professionals think of larger constructs. What may seem complex to a beginner will seem simple to someone with more experience.

With experience, you build a richer collection of larger constructs and can quickly judge where and how to use them. You can thus work with larger systems and still retain intellectual control.

THE POWER OF METHODS

Large-scale processes can also become complex. Like large-scale systems, however, they can be decomposed into subprocesses. As you refine these subprocesses, you ultimately reach the basic methods for doing the technical work. By refining your processes and defining your methods, you will build a vocabulary of process chunks. With this, you get the ability to reason about and to design increasingly sophisticated processes. The limits of our processes are thus affected by our experiences and by the methods we use. As we refine our processes and build families of known and repeatable methods, we can also learn how to scale up our processes.

11.2   The Stages of Product Size

The sizes of software tasks can be divided into the following general ranges:

Stage 0: very small program elements, written by programmers alone

Stage 1: small programs, or modules, designed, implemented, and tested by programmers alone

Stage 2: larger programs, or components, that typically involve teams of developers who develop and integrate multiple Stage-1 modules into larger Stage 2-component programs

Stage 3: very large projects that involve multiple teams controlled and directed by a central project management

Stage 4: massive multisystems that involve many autonomous or loosely federated projects

Within these ranges, the same process will likely be optimum for many projects. A problem arises, however, when you cross a scalability boundary. This changes the nature of the job and presents you with new issues and problems. If you try to use a process that is too low level, you will likely have trouble making good plans and tracking progress against them. The methods you use may not be adequate, and you could overlook important issues. These scalability boundaries are largely determined by your skill and ability, so they will change as you gain experience, use new methods, or work on different applications.

STAGE 0—SIMPLE ROUTINES

At Stage 0, you work with the smallest building blocks. These form a basic alphabet of language constructs like while loops, case statements, if-then-else, and so on. All but beginning programmers construct these elements in their heads and code them without planning or design. Designing or planning such a simple program element would make no more sense to an experienced programmer than planning how to add a string of numbers or designing a long division.

Stage 0 is the beginning stage of scalability, and it is here that programmers reach their peak productivity. While they will occasionally make errors, these are rarely serious and are easily fixed. The principal issue at Stage 0 is skill and ability. If you are not capable of consistently and rapidly producing small programming constructs, you need more training and experience before you attempt larger programs.

STAGE 1—THE PROGRAM OR PROGRAM MODULE

When you combine Stage-0 constructs into a program, you move to Stage 1. Here, you work on simple combinations of your basic alphabet of Stage-0 routines. Stage-1 programs typically range in size from only a few dozen to several hundred LOC. You can generally build them by sitting at your workstation, designing in your head, entering the code, and compiling. You know these Stage-1 abstractions and understand their inner workings. In Mills' terms, they are clear boxes. [Mills 87a] They are what Simon calls chunks. [Simon] As you gain experience, you build a rich vocabulary of these chunks.

These Stage-1 programs are what most programmers learn to write in their initial programming courses. They are what Wulf refers to when he says traditional computer science curricula teach students to "write 300 line programs, from scratch, alone, and in a dead language." [Wulf] Some of the properties of such intuitive Stage-1 processes are the following:

- □ They are not scalable. That is, there is some size beyond which programmers cannot continue to use purely intuitive methods with consistent success.
- □ By exclusively using intuitive methods, programmers do not build the skills and disciplines they will need for larger-scale work.
- □ Because these are the only methods they know, many programmers attempt to use them on projects where they do not apply.

Moving from Stage 1 to Stage 2.   Your principal need in migrating from Stage 1 to Stage 2 is to recognize that you are human and that your intuitive abilities are limited. At Stage 2, you deal with programs that are larger than you can consistently design in your head. These programs generally implement sophisti-cated functions and may involve unfamiliar applications. While you can often still develop such programs by yourself, you should consider getting design help or asking your associates to do an inspection. By exposing your ideas, you will often find problems you didn't expect. The principal benefit of involving your as-sociates is illustrated in Fig. 11.1. With increasingly complicated programs, you can encounter problems you never suspected. By involving others, you can find or at least anticipate some of these problems.

STAGE 2—THE COMPONENT

At Stage 2, experienced programmers start to think of entire programs as abstrac-tions. Now, instead of concentrating on the details of a design you can visualize interconnected collections of Stage-1 modules. Your design is now spread over multiple abstractions, and you can conceive of quite complex structures. You will write some programs with no difficulty, but occasionally one will be a disaster, probably because some of your abstractions will not behave precisely as you thought.

At Stage 2, a process that is beyond its capacity has two symptoms: inade-quate design and overlooked details. As product size increases, the design is both more complex and more voluminous. You then need a more precise and more rigorous design process in order to avoid making mistakes.

Larger programs also involve many more details. Even when the design is completely correct, there are increased opportunities for error. Names and types can be confused, variable scopes can be incorrect, and your design and code changes could be incomplete or inconsistent. The detail problem is aggravated by

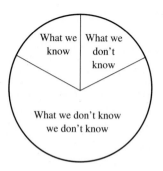

FIGURE 11.1
What We Do and Don't Know

poor program quality. The system's design assumes that each module functions precisely as specified. When these modules contain defects, however, they can produce strange and unpredictable symptoms. As the number of defects increases, system behavior can become so confusing that the development process breaks down.

In this stage, your PSP needs extensive quality controls and your practices must be sufficiently disciplined to consistently use these controls. Here, you also likely work with a team. It may be loosely structured and informal, but you build effective working relationships and learn to trust and support each other. Because your work now must be understood and used by your teammates, your products must be cleanly structured and clearly described. Team coordination is further enhanced if your processes are also cleanly structured and clearly described.

Moving to Stage 3.   The transition from Stage 2 to Stage 3 requires mastery of even larger-sized programs. The quality of the design and its representation are important. The PSP must give maximum priority to defect prevention and early removal, and every professional must know, understand, and adhere to the system standards. Robust design is also important. Such a design requires defensive programming practices that warn of unexpected conditions, protect the system from damage, and provide diagnostic and recovery data. At Stage 3, you must also design for testability. Safety, too, requires attention, so you should consider positive design steps to protect against potentially dangerous system actions. [Leveson]

In moving to Stage 3, the larger project size also requires larger teams or even multiple teams. Team interactions involve more people and thus must become more formal. The informal relationships of Stage 2 are no longer adequate; you need a framework to ensure effective cooperation and support. This calls for better defined team processes and more faithful adherence to these processes.

STAGE 3—THE SYSTEM

At Stage 3, you work with large systems that comprise multiple components. You will know most of their external specifications but will not generally understand their inner workings. The upper size range of Stage-3 systems is very large, and you can now conceive of extraordinarily complex systems. You do this by abstracting the system's essence and relegating much of the complexity to the lower level components. This is the basic approach used for building most large-scale software systems.

While the size of Stage-3 systems theoretically is unlimited, there are two practical problems with such large systems: masking functional complexity and maintaining component quality. Users of sophisticated software systems often have trouble understanding and using them. The technical challenge is to design such systems so that their complexity is masked and the users see these functions in terms that are natural and convenient to them. User manuals should not be required in normal use, and the software system should provide needed information in simple and intuitive form.

Component quality is crucial in stage 3. When components do not consistently perform as they should, integration can be difficult if not impossible. With low-quality components, the test-and-fix cycle can stretch out indefinitely. Because no single person understands the details of the entire system, complex defects are hard to find and hard to fix.

At this stage, your PSP could almost completely change. These systems require many specialties and increased concentration on small parts of the larger process. An entire PSP could thus be devoted, for example, to integration testing or to fixing defects. While quality remains paramount, the quality focus must broaden to encompass every specialty.

Moving toward Stage 4.   The size limit of Stage-3 systems is caused by the problems of central control. As system scale and complexity grows, no central group can control, guide, or direct the work. The principal reasons for this are the following:

1. There are so many activities that no individual or management team could possibly track them all.

2. The system is so complex that no central group could fully understand its design.

3. The organization's communication paths become so extended that it takes too long to communicate the need for action or to get a response.

4. The data available to the central authority is late and incomplete, thus leading to poor decisions.

5. The centrally controlled nature of the system prevents people at the lower levels from being motivated or able to take effective action on their own.

STAGE 4—THE MULTISYSTEM

The managers of very large systems typically divide the principal system responsibilities among the subsystems. Each subsystem can then be given the independence to focus on and manage its designated specialties. While this approach can subdivide system design and development, an interconnection architecture and set of system standards are essential. Process roles are also required to ensure these frameworks remain appropriate and are followed.

Autonomous development groups and self-managed teams will likely be needed to develop Stage-4 systems. These teams must largely define their own roles and often work independently. It is essential, for example, that the requirements for Stage-4 systems be distributed. It would be impractical to centrally gather and communicate requirements information to all the developers.

While the process implications of such massive multisystems will be learned over time, some implications on the PSP are clear. First is the requirement for extraordinary quality. Seemingly minor defects in remote corners of these systems can cause ripple effects that cannot be anticipated. The PSP thus must consider the system implications of all local actions. For example, control actions must be carefully constrained so that errors do not propagate across the system. Overload behavior should gracefully degrade performance, and emergency response must not expose the system to unnecessary shutdowns.

Other potential implications of the PSP are security, privacy, and integrity. All human actions must be checked to ensure authorization and accuracy. The developers can no longer assume that users are authorized and benign, so security provisions are essential and audit trails must be maintained for all transactions. Proper design of such systems requires that all professionals understand the system constraints and know and follow the standards precisely. Semiautonomous, highly disciplined development teams will likely be needed for the large-scale Stage-4 systems of the future.

11.3 Developing Large-scale Programs

Scaling paradigms help you handle larger-sized products. When you face a more complex product, there are several ways you can proceed, depending on your skill and experience. First, if you have built a similar product you can use your prior process. If you know someone who has built such a product, you might copy or tailor his or her process. If the process you select is effective and suitably defined, this process reuse will probably be adequate.

However, you may know how to start the work but not how to complete it. The second way you could proceed is to treat the project as partly exploration. Here you simultaneously seek to understand the product while you search for the best process. After starting the work, you expect to learn how to finish it. This is an iterative development paradigm much like Boehm's spiral model shown in Fig. 11.2. [Boehm 88]

If you don't even know how to start, you have a third way to proceed. You may know how to build some components, but you lack a fundamental understanding of the total problem. One strategy would be to approach this problem much like the second one and assume that once you start you can somehow muddle your way through. This could be a mistake, however. It is unlikely that you can build a fundamental system understanding through an incremental development cycle. By starting on part of the system, you could lose sight of the whole.

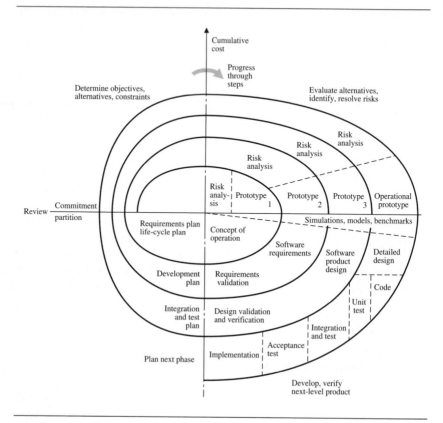

FIGURE 11.2
Spiral Process Model

Brooks suggests one way to address this: Produce a complete system and throw it away. [Brooks] While I am not aware of any case in which this strategy was consciously adopted in advance, a well managed system prototype can produce sufficient insight and knowledge to more than recoup the time spent on the prototype development. It is also an effective way to guard against a total disaster. Such prototypes should be developed with explicit objectives and should concentrate on total system understanding. Once you understand the system, you can start work on the components.

DIVIDE AND CONQUER

All large-scale software development strategies start with a high-level design and then subdivide the system into components. Because these components are each smaller than the total system, they presumably can be developed with smaller-scale methods. The primary concern is that they be divided so that they can be put back together. These steps are often called high-level design and integration, but it helps to think of them as disintegration and reintegration. The methods of disintegration and reintegration then determine the effectiveness of the development strategy.

While this divide and conquer paradigm is generally satisfactory, the principal risk with it is that the development strategy may not be properly designed or managed. It rarely gets the attention it deserves and is almost never even reviewed. Even when you develop an entire system yourself, you need to ensure your development strategy is sound before you start implementation. Where you have made design assumptions, you should build prototypes or hold peer reviews. These invariably turn up problems that would be hard to fix in integration or system test.

THE ESSENCE OF SCALABILITY

A software system is scalable if it can be disintegrated into smaller components, the components separately developed, and the system reintegrated. This does not mean, however, that the system is only the sum of its parts. It does mean that the components are a proper subset of the system. That is, the components live within the system, and, once they have been built, they do not need to be modified during integration. The project thus consists of system design, system disintegration, component development, reintegration, and system test.

A large software system also has an essence that distinguishes it from all other software systems. This essence is not contained in its component parts. It must be created for the system and embodied in the way the parts work together as a coherent whole. Establishing this essence is one principal challenge of scalability: to design large systems that do not look like loosely connected sets of parts.

The systems I know that have met this challenge all had one designer or a small design team that had a clear conceptual view of how the system should behave. This designer or team then either designed the principal system components themselves or had sufficient influence to ensure they were designed consistently with the system concept.

DESIGNING STAGE-4 MULTISYSTEMS

It seems unlikely that many truly massive software systems will be designed in this top-down way. More likely, they will evolve by enhancement and accretion of smaller systems. As their parts are assembled, their incompatibilities are accommodated by interface adapters that make the necessary translations and adjustments. Because these subsystems soon become incomprehensible to anyone but specialists, special user interface systems are needed. These are like shells that interpret the system for a set of users. Because there will be many types of users, there will likely be many interfacing shells.

There are many potential process problems with such laissez faire design strategies. These include all the issues concerning the smaller-scale systems and at least two others: change and intelligence.

Most multisystem development efforts will likely interface with, adapt, or extend some parts of large, existing systems. These existing systems will often be poorly documented and may have a body of users who must not be disrupted. The multisystem development process thus must include methods for modifying existing systems and the disciplines for understanding and controlling changes that span many system elements.

The intelligence problem concerns the need to organize information about these large and dynamic systems. Even if each part's design is fully documented, system behavior likely will not be. Cataloguing problem symptoms and relating them to causes becomes a major need for customer support, design, and test. When an engineer solves a problem or discerns a new behavior, this intelligence should be retained, catalogued, and made generally available.

11.4   A Potential Problem with Abstractions

There are various ways to attack the scalability problem. You could subdivide an entire system into parts and still not have usefully partitioned the work. Suppose, for example, you defined a family of general-purpose, reusable parts that could implement an entire system. While this would likely be helpful, the degree of help would depend on the size and nature of the parts. If the system were to have 1,000,000 LOC and you created 500 parts that each averaged 5 LOC, then the system design task would have been reduced to designing a system of 200,000 parts. While this would seem to be a big help, it would probably not solve the system design problem. In fact it could even make it worse. The designers would now have to learn and become fluent with each of these 500 part types. They would have to both design and develop the parts and then design the system to effectively use them. Essentially, you would have designed a new programming language rather than addressing the system scalability problem. Designers have limitations, and they cannot effectively use large numbers of unfamiliar parts. Merely devising a richer language may help, but doing this does not address the scalability problem.

Object oriented designers can encounter this same part-multiplicity problem unless they are careful. Once they define a comprehensive family of elemental system objects, they could expect to just put these objects together to form the system. While having such objects may help, part definition does not replace the need for system design. To have useful scalability, you must not only meet the requirements of physical scalability but also capture significant system function in the parts.

11.5   The Development Strategy

The development strategy connects your PSP to the overall project and provides the framework for disintegrating and reintegrating the product. A well-founded strategy must consider the logical structure of the ultimate product. That is, if the product has a sequential structure the development strategy could follow a sequence of progressive enhancements. By considering each development in terms of the product's natural structure, you can produce a strategy that naturally fits it.

EXAMPLE DEVELOPMENT STRATEGIES

Suppose you were developing a product with a main program that used a family of application objects. Suppose further that each application object used further objects and they in turn used others. You can visualize all these objects in a tree, with the main routine at the top calling those objects immediately below, and so on. Those objects that are used by several routines would then appear in multiple places on the tree.

After you divide this total program tree into PSP-implementable elements, you must decide on the order in which to develop and integrate them. One approach would be to start with the main program and work toward the bottom of the tree. Another approach would be to start at the bottom and work up. Obviously, a third would be to start in the middle and work in both directions. You could also use hybrid strategies, such as developing multiple top-to-bottom threads or slices of the entire system.

These approaches each have advantages and disadvantages. A top-down strategy ensures each cycle has a clear operational context and well-defined requirements. The reviews and tests are easier to define and can deal realistically with operational issues. The principal problem with the top-down approach is that the lower level abstractions must be stubbed or bypassed. Because some of these functions may be incompletely defined, the higher level functions may misuse them.

Starting from the bottom and working up has the advantage of working with a solid foundation. You first develop those leaf elements that use no undeveloped abstractions. As you add layers, you build on proven designs and are less likely to run into problems with overlooked details. The principal disadvantage of the bottom-up strategy is that you are implementing component specifications that may not do precisely what the system requires. You may, for example, develop a function and then later discover it was improperly specified. Another potential problem is the lack of test drivers. With the bottom-up strategy, the lower level abstractions will not typically form a coherent system. This strategy thus will not provide a natural test environment for most of the abstractions.

The third approach—starting in the middle—could be advantageous when there is some critical function that determines the success of the entire program. An initial focus on that function could be appropriate if it is unusually complex or if you suspect it has special problems.

Some example strategies are given in the following sections. They are the progressive, functional enhancement, fast-path, and dummy strategies.

THE PROGRESSIVE STRATEGY

The progressive strategy is the natural way to develop systems that are composed of a series of sequentially executing functions. You first develop and test the operations that are performed first. You then add and test the next functions, and then the next, and so forth. If this pipeline structure is controlled by a main routine, you develop it in gradually widening vertical slices, each with all its related functions. The routines that are called by that slice are then implemented from top to bottom in that cycle. As each cycle is designed, implemented, and tested, the pipeline is gradually lengthened to include additional functions. The main routine then either is truncated at the end of the last slice or skips over all the unimplemented slices.

This strategy has the principal advantage of being easy to define and to implement. It only needs test scaffolding for special cases, and there is little to rebuild or redesign between cycles. One disadvantage is that there may be no easy way to exhaustively test the behavior of each slice. You thus may need some special test scaffolding to drive functions that are not directly visible to the user. This, however, would likely be a problem for such functions with almost any development strategy.

FUNCTIONAL ENHANCEMENT STRATEGY

The functional enhancement strategy defines an initial stripped-down system version, or kernel, and adds enhancements. This is the common strategy for follow-on enhancement of large systems. A base system kernel is initially defined that need not be functionally useful. The only requirement is that it provide an operational context for subsequent enhancements. It is desirable that this kernel be as small as possible and that it be carefully reviewed and tested. The added functions can then be incorporated in small steps.

The principal advantage of the functional enhancement strategy is that it builds a working system at the earliest point. The initial project focus is to get the system to work, hence this strategy often leads to earlier identification of overall system problems. It also provides an early base for performance measurement and for preliminary user exposure. This strategy has also been the natural fallback for most large system development projects. When engineers attempt to deliver too much function with the first release and then get into trouble, they pare functions and ship a minimum initial system. The principal debates concerning this strategy are which functions to ship with which release.

The main problem with this strategy is that the first step is often quite large.

FAST-PATH ENHANCEMENT STRATEGY

The fast-path strategy is much like functional enhancement except that the initial skeletal system kernel is designed to demonstrate fast-path performance. The critical timing issues are identified and the basic system or control cycle is implemented. The focus is on performance, so this initial fast-path kernel should contain only the minimum logic needed to control the performance-sensitive functions.

The principal advantage of fast-path enhancement is that it exposes timing problems at the earliest point. While the first system kernel may provide no recognizable external functions, performance can be measured and overall system performance estimated. When initial fast-path performance meets the system requirements, functional enhancements can be incrementally added. System performance can be measured with each enhancement and steps taken to ensure it does not deteriorate. If kernel performance does not meet the performance requirements, you will know at the earliest time and have the best chance to fix the problem. For time-critical systems or for the initial release of an operating system, this can be a very attractive development strategy.

Its principal disadvantage, too, is the size of the first step. While it could be smaller than for the functional enhancement strategy, it could still be much larger than can conveniently be handled by a single development team.

THE DUMMY STRATEGY

The dummy strategy follows a top-down sequence. It starts with the high-level system functions and dummies the rest with stubs that provide predefined returns. After the highest level routine is tested, the succeeding cycles gradually fill out the stubs with functions. This is an appropriate strategy for a layered system or for the kernel portion of the fast-path or functional enhancement strategies. It has the advantages that the system is built in small steps and that it provides considerable flexibility in the order in which elements are added. In building the kernel for a fast-path development strategy, for example, the control loop developers would initially need services from multiple servers, all of which would be stubbed with dummy functions. Each of these functions could then be more or less independently developed and incorporated.

The principal disadvantage of the dummy strategy is that development may have to proceed quite far before useful system behavior is visible. This could make it difficult to do comprehensive testing in early development cycles. You can partially alleviate the situation by the judicious choice of abstractions or the use of more sophisticated stubs.

SELECTING A DEVELOPMENT STRATEGY

One potential problem with all these strategies is that some critical function may not be developed until the later development cycles. This in turn has the double problem of delaying exposure to the principal project risks and of testing the most complex element for the first time in the full system context. If the rest of the system has many defects, this could greatly complicate testing of the later slices. It is generally wise to follow a strategy that tests the most difficult components with the smallest amount of untested code. The defects are then more easily identified and fixed.

There is no one best strategy. You must examine the system structure, assess the principal development risks, and select a strategy to fit your situation. Your goals are to have the strategy naturally fit the system structure and to expose the principal risks as soon as possible.

11.6   PSP3

The full PSP3 process is included in Appendix C. The following paragraphs describe its overall logic and structure.

The principal role of PSP3 is to be an example of a personal process foundation for large-scale software development. Hence, your PSP must be capable of handling increased product complexity and must relate to the larger processes of your development team. PSP3 uses the cyclic process shown in Fig. 11.3.

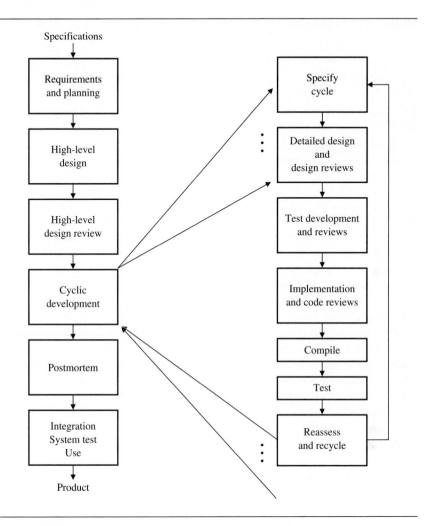

FIGURE 11.3
PSP3 Process

REQUIREMENTS AND PLANNING

PSP3 starts with a requirements and planning step that produces a conceptual design for the overall system, estimates its size, and plans the development work.

HIGH-LEVEL DESIGN

In high-level design, you identify the product's natural divisions and devise a cyclic strategy. If some pieces are much larger than you prefer, you may adopt a special approach for that part. A good rule of thumb is to keep each cycle between 100 and 300 lines of new and changed source code. These cycles often grow much larger than you expect, however, so you should try to keep the cycles small. Combine several functions in a single cycle only if you thoroughly understand them and know they will be simple. After high-level design review, proceed to cyclic development.

CYCLIC DEVELOPMENT

In cyclic development, first establish the specifications for the current cycle. You could develop these specifications during high-level design, but they are not needed before the development cycles. Producing them earlier could also waste your time because they are often affected by subsequent development cycles.

Each cycle is essentially a PSP2.1 process that produces a part of the product. Notice, however, that the planning and postmortem phases are done only once for the complete project. During the cycles, the reviews and tests should be as complete as possible. Each cycle is the foundation for the next, so any defects that are left in one cycle can cause later problems. The cyclic process is effective because it builds and tests new functions on a solid foundation. Scalability is preserved, however, only as long as each incremental development is self-contained and essentially defect free. Thorough design reviews and comprehensive tests are thus critical parts of the cyclic development process.

TEST DEVELOPMENT AND REVIEW

Cyclic development includes a test development step. It is rarely practical to develop the unit tests before detailed design, but they must be developed before unit test. As Beizer points out, test development often reveals as many design problems as testing does, so it is desirable to develop the tests before you write the code. [Beizer]

Test development can reveal design problems as well as operational and user issues. Common problem areas are exception handling, responses to user errors, and out-of-limit conditions. Other issues concern the need for test data, special test modes, user scenarios, and test support facilities. The advantage of early test planning and development is that both force you to think about the product from a testing perspective.

Whether you develop unit tests before or after the detailed design review is a matter of personal preference. Test development done first frequently results in design changes. On the other hand, any design changes made as a result of design reviews could require you to rework the test plan.

In cyclic testing, the first test will generally start with a clean slate. Each subsequent cycle then adds functions and progressively integrates them into the previously tested product. After the final cycle, you have completed a combined unit and integration test of the entire program. It is now ready for system test or for integration into a larger system.

While combining unit and integration testing may seem strange, it is a natural consequence of the cyclic PSP strategy. By progressively integrating each cycle, you avoid the need for special drivers. A separate unit test is usually done to ensure new code debugging is not complicated by defects in the growing base of integrated code. With a high quality PSP, this problem is reduced.

REASSESS AND RECYCLE

After each cycle, you reassess the work to determine status and to reevaluate the plan. If you are working on a project, you should also consider submitting a status report at the end of each cycle. If your data indicate significant deviations from your original plan, adjust the plan and alert project management.

11.7   Summary

The size of software projects has increased rapidly for over 30 years. The products you develop in the future are thus likely to be much larger than today's. Because a process that is optimum for a small program will not likely be so for one five to 10 times larger, you will probably have to change your development process.

The design phase of large-scale software systems typically starts with a high-level system design effort that breaks the product into components. These components are separately developed and then the system is integrated. Because these components are much smaller than the total system, they can presumably be developed with smaller-scale methods.

The sizes of software development projects can be divided into general ranges. These rough scalability boundaries are largely determined by individual skill and ability. At Stage 0, you work with the smallest building blocks. When you combine Stage-0 constructs into a program, you move to Stage 1. At Stage 1, you develop the program modules. At Stage 2, you define component programs that contain several of these modules. Now, instead of focusing on design details you visualize interconnections of these Stage-1 modules. At Stage 3, you work with large systems composed of Stage-1 and Stage-2 abstractions. Truly large-scale software systems at Stage 4 have multiple autonomous subsystems that each handle entire system responsibilities.

The PSP3 is an example of a large-scale personal process. It can support reasonably large individual development or serve as a foundation for large-scale software development. Its strategy is to use a cyclic process. A well-founded development strategy is built on the natural structure of the planned product. This strategy defines cycle contents as bite-sized elements that are separately designed and implemented in development cycles. Each cycle is progressively unit tested and integrated, and, at the end, you have the integrated, complete program ready for system integration or system test.

11.8   Exercises

The standard assignment for this chapter is to use PSP3 to start development of program 10A. Since this will likely be a larger program than those in the previous exercises, it is planned for two assignment periods. The specification for this program is given in Appendix D and the PSP3 process is described in Appendix C. In completing this assignment, you should faithfully follow the report submission format specified for PSP3. For other assignment options, consult Appendix D.

References

[Beizer] B. Beizer, *Software Testing Techniques* (New York: Van Nostrand Reinhold, 1983).

[Boehm, 88] Barry W. Boehm, "A Spiral Model of Software Development and Enhancement," *Computer*, vol. 21 (May 1988): 61–72.

[Brooks] Frederick P. Brooks, *The Mythical Man-Month* (Reading, MA: Addison-Wesley, 1972).

[DeGroot] A. D. DeGroot, *Thought and Choice in Chess* (The Hague: Mouton, 1965).

[Leveson] Nancy G. Leveson and P. R. Harvey, "Analyzing Software Safety," *IEEE Transactions on Software Engineering*, SE-9 (5) (1983): 569–579.

[Miller] George A. Miller, "Magical Number Seven, Plus or Minus Two: Some Limits on Our Capacity for Processing Information," *Psychological Review*, vol. 83, no. 2 (March 1956): 81–97.

[Mills 87a] H. D. Mills, R. C. Linger, and A. R. Hevner, "Box Structured Information Systems," *IBM Systems Journal*, vol. 26, no. 4 (1987): 395–413.

[Simon] H. A. Simon, "Studying Human Intelligence by Creating Artificial Intelligence," *American Scientist*, vol. 69, no. 3 (May-June 1981): 300–309.

[Wulf] Wm. A. Wulf, "Computer Science and Software Engineering: Splitting is the Wrong Solution," *Computer Science Education 3* (1992): 123–134.

12

Design Verification

If you want to develop high-quality programs, you must ensure their designs are correct. This chapter deals with design verification. It briefly introduces the subject and exposes you to some of the more straightforward verification techniques. It also discusses some issues you should consider in deciding how to verify programs.

The question is not whether to verify the correctness of your programs but how. Every review, compilation, test, or analysis is some sort of verification. As you have seen with the PSP, however, some verification methods are more effective than others. The most common verification methods are compiling and testing. These by themselves, however, are not sufficiently effective to produce high-quality programs at reasonable cost. While design and code reviews are more cost effective, they are human intensive and thus error prone and time consuming. The most effective approach is to produce correct designs in the first place. Verification methods can help you to do this, but they are not foolproof, and they take time. To get the best results, you should do program verification as well as review, inspect, compile, and test.

As a program's logic becomes more complex, it is increasingly important for you to verify its correctness. There are various ways to do this, and they each have advantages and disadvantages. Your selection of verification methods should be based on how they work for you. If you are not skilled with a particular method, you are not likely to catch many logic problems with it. However, you may want to practice various verification techniques to see if you can improve your abilities. Several verification methods are described in this chapter, with examples of how they work. You should try them and use your process data to help you decide which are most effective for you.

Formal mathematical methods have been devised for designing correct programs and proving program correctness. They are discussed briefly at the end of this chapter; more complete coverage is beyond the scope of this book. The fact that such formal methods are not discussed more fully does not imply they are not worthwhile. If you have tried them and found them helpful, you should certainly use them. If you have not yet tried them, you should consider doing so. Some of the verification methods described in this chapter have been adapted from these more formal approaches. Many engineers will find these simplified methods helpful.

12.1   Selecting Verification Methods

The verification techniques described in this chapter are shown in Table 12.1, together with suggestions on where you should consider using them. In deciding which verification methods to use, you should consider the following:

- Your defect profile
- The effectiveness of your current verification methods
- The economics of your current verification methods

DEFECT PROFILE

Your first consideration in deciding on verification methods should be your defect experience. If you do not have problems with repeat-until loops, for example, there would be little point in spending additional time verifying them. The key is to examine your defect history and focus on those areas that cause you the most trouble. If you find many design defects in test or if many design defects escape your PSP process, you need to improve your design verification methods.

VERIFICATION EFFECTIVENESS

Whenever you design complex logic, you are likely to make errors. While you should thoroughly verify your designs, this is not the time to introduce unfamiliar methods. The more complex your designs, the more important it is for you to use

TABLE 12.1 USING VERIFICATION METHODS

Method	Application	Comments
Loop Verification	Program Loops	Use on loop logic whenever practical.
Proper State Machines	State Machines Only	Use during design and in reviews and inspections of every state machine.
Symbolic Execution	Algorithmic Logic	Use whenever it applies.
Proof by Induction	Loops and Recursion	Use in conjunction with trace tables.
Trace Tables	Complex Logic	Use for small program elements and with proof by induction and/or symbolic execution whenever possible. Use if other verification methods do not apply.
Execution Tables	Complex Logic	Use for small program elements and, as a last resort, when no other methods apply.
Formal Verification	Entire Program	Use whenever you know how to apply the verification methods, they appear feasible, and they are cost effective.

proven and practiced verification methods. This suggests that you should identify a family of effective verification techniques and make a practice of using them, even on small programs. Verification is a skill that you should develop and practice. Over time, you will become more proficient and much better able to rapidly and accurately verify your programs.

Consider your design experience with small programs. If you never make design mistakes, you probably use effective verification practices. However, if you still make occasional logic mistakes with small programs you must devise better ways to verify your designs. If you do not improve your small-program verification skills, your larger programs will almost certainly contain many design defects. Experiment and practice new verification techniques with small programs and you will be better prepared to develop large programs.

VERIFICATION ECONOMICS

One problem with all current verification methods is that they are time consuming. As programs get larger and more complex, verification methods also get more complex. Thus, as your need to use these methods increases they are progressively less usable. While there is no general solution to this problem, you must learn which verification methods work best for you and the conditions under which they work. You should study the available methods, experiment with them, measure their effectiveness, and decide for yourself where and how to use them.

12.2   Design Standards

Design standards do not fit the common definition of a verification method, but they do provide criteria against which to compare the design. A standard is a norm or a basis for comparison that is established by some authority or by common consent. Because the purpose of verification is to determine if the design is correct, you must have some definition of what would constitute a correct design. Standards provide part of this basis. Some standards that you should use during verification are

- □ product conventions,
- □ product design standards, and
- □ reuse standards.

You should have the appropriate standards available and familiarize yourself with them before you start the design and again when you do verification.

PRODUCT CONVENTIONS

The importance of product conventions is apparent to anyone who has used a system that did not have them. In developing IBM's early BPS/360 system, several programmers were assigned to work on the file-handling routines. Unfortunately, nothing had been standardized except the interfaces between their programs. One programmer specified that the file naming and addressing be in lowercase; another called for uppercase. Because their two programs worked in tandem, the result was total user confusion.

Product conventions are essential if multiple developers are to produce a system that has any external coherence. These conventions should address, for example, the user interfaces, external naming, system error handling, installation procedures, and help facilities. A system must have a clear and consistent appearance to its users, regardless of who designed each element.

PRODUCT DESIGN STANDARDS

Product design standards range from simple conventions to complete system architectures. These standards typically cover calling and naming conventions, header standards, test standards, and documentation formats. While many product design standards are arbitrary, it is a good idea to establish your own personal set. It will help you to produce consistent designs and will make your designs easier to review. This will help you in your PSP work and will make it easier for you to establish a consistent basis for participating on software teams. By establishing consistent design practices with the PSP, you will be better able to adopt and follow the team practices you will later need.

REUSE STANDARDS

Reuse is a powerful technique, but it must be properly managed. It can save time and money and produce higher quality products. Reuse can be at the system design level, the component design level, or the modular part level. To get maximum benefit, you should think about reuse during design and specifically address reuse in your design reviews. When properly managed and implemented, reuse can have a positive impact on both individual and organizational quality and productivity.

I have occasionally had the opportunity to review the development work of a few major Japanese software development groups and have seen the benefits they obtained from a reuse strategy. For example, the Toshiba control-system group had established a standard control-system skeletal design. All new control-system functions were designed as modular components to fit this skeletal structure. At the time of my review, the group had achieved reuse levels approaching 90 percent. Some years later, I toured a major U.S. manufacturer who used a massive Toshiba control system. Its software development people told me the Toshiba system had the lowest defect content of any software they had ever seen.

The effective reuse of component parts requires the absolute integrity of the parts. The group in IBM's German laboratory that develops standard parts for use in IBM's operating systems products distributes and supports standard parts much like a commercial parts supplier. Their catalogue lists the parts and their specifications. The parts are essentially sealed and cannot be modified, but they do have adjustable parameters. This group has product representatives in several major IBM laboratories to help in identifying parts applications, to assist in their use, and to identify new parts needs. When I last visited the laboratory, the catalogue contained over 50 parts. Some parts had been included in IBM's products for up to 10 years. The group was proud to report it had yet to receive its first defect report from a user.

Standard software parts can be developed and will be used, but they must be precisely specified, of the highest quality, and adequately supported. Their acceptance will then depend on their quality, their price, the degree to which they meet their users' needs, the effectiveness of their marketing, and the adequacy of their technical support. A suitably rich variety of available reusable parts can greatly improve development quality and productivity. You should thus thoroughly familiarize yourself with the standard parts that are available to you and consider using them in your designs.

In establishing reuse standards, you primarily want to provide a basis for verifying that you have used the standard components consistently with their specifications. You should also check to ensure you have taken maximum advantage of available reusable components and your new development is producing new reusable parts when practical.

Reuse is important for the PSP both because it can substantially improve your productivity and because it demands extraordinarily high-quality software. One PSP objective is to develop the personal process disciplines needed to produce reuse-quality software.

12.3   Verification Methods

Verification methods include the use of compilers and of the many testing and debugging tools available. In addition to these automated methods, a few nonautomated methods can help you with your logic verification. These nonautomated methods are intended to provide more general proofs than are available with test cases and other single-case verification means. The two methods I discuss next are symbolic execution and proof by induction.

SYMBOLIC EXECUTION

The following logic, due to Mills, shows how symbolic execution works in a simple case [Mills 87]:

```
Procedure Substitution(V1, V2, V3, V4)
BEGIN
      V1  : = V2;
      V2  : = V4;
      V3  : = V1;
      V4  : = V3;
   END
```

Table 12.2 shows the result. This logic looks simple, but seemingly simple logic can become quite complex when it involves sequential processes. The advantage of symbolic verification is that it covers all symbolic values rather than merely a few tested cases.

TABLE 12.2 SYMBOLIC EXECUTION EXAMPLE

Cycle:		Function: Substitution(V1, V2, V3, V4)			
#	*Instruction*	*V1*	*V2*	*V3*	*V4*
	Initial Values	A	B	C	D
1	V1 := V2	B			
2	V2 := V4		D		
3	V3 := V1			B	
4	V4 := V3				B
	Final Values	B	D	B	B

There are no general guidelines for when and how to use symbolic execution. However, you should examine your programs and use it in any case in which it appears practical. One of the great attractions of mathematical verification methods is that they provide a structured and theoretically sound way to logically verify programs. [Gries]

PROOF BY INDUCTION

One objective of logic verification methods is to find general proofs so you do not need to trace out every possible condition. Achieving this generally involves some form of symbolic logic representation and techniques for making logical inferences. One of the most powerful techniques for this purpose is the mathematical method called *proof by induction*. This method applies to logical expressions with integer parameters. It can be stated as follows:

1. If an expression $f(n)$ can be shown to be true for some value n_0
2. and if when $n > n_0$, and when $f(n)$ holds, $f(n + 1)$ can also be shown to hold,
3. then $f(k)$ is true for all $k \geq n_0$.

Using this very powerful concept can save you a lot of time in logic verification. You start by showing that the logic of a program (which is a logical expression) is true for a base case. You then show that if this logic is true for some arbitrary greater value n, it is also true for $n + 1$. This is sufficient proof for all larger values of n, and you need not do any more proofs.

While this is a powerful principle, it must be used with care. Suppose you are examining the performance of the following for loop:

```
for i=1 to 1000
        begin
                do xyz
        end
```

If you checked and verified that the logic behaved properly at values of i=1, i=5, and i=6, you may be tempted to conclude it was valid for all higher values of i. It is obvious, however, that there is a problem when i = 1001. The problem here is with the way the proof was done. After showing that the logic behaved properly at i = 1, you next need to examine an arbitrary case of i = n. You show that if the logic is proper for an arbitrary value of i = n, it is also true for i = n + 1. Note that you are not showing it is true for i = n; you assume this. By examining the problem, you can see that the logic will not work when n = 1000. To avoid this problem, you should make the check with modified logic as follows:

```
for i=1 to Limit
        begin
                do xyz
        end
```

First you verify that the logic functions properly for Limit=1. Next, you show that if it is true for Limit = n, then it is also true for Limit = n + 1. It is then true for all higher values of Limit. Here, n is any arbitrary positive integer value. Again, you need to ensure there are no anomalous numerical values in the function *xyz* that would invalidate these tests. Another way to approach this proof is to see if you can find any value of n where the program would function properly at Limit = n but not at Limit = n + 1. Such problems generally are caused by system memory constraints or the maximum size of the number system.

12.4   Verifying the Object State Machine

When your product includes a state machine, you should prove it is properly designed and used correctly. To determine if a program is a state machine check its external behavior. If it behaves differently with identical inputs, it is likely a state machine. An example would be the behavior of the character reader for a LOC counter. While in the regular portion of the program, the reader will pass all characters to the counter. When it detects the start of a comment, however, it will ignore all subsequent characters until it comes to the end of the comment. Here, the character reader would have two states: `CommentText` and `ProgramText`. With the identical character as input, in one case it will produce no output and in the other it will pass the input character to the output.

When a state machine is properly designed, it is called a proper state machine. To be proper, it must be able to reach a program return state from every other state, all state conditions must be complete and orthogonal, and all the transitions from each state must be complete and orthogonal. You should examine the program's larger context to ensure all the state machines have been identified and consistently used.

As described in Appendix B, a set of functions that is complete means the union of all the members is true. A complete set of functions, for example, would cover every square on a Karnaugh map. A set of functions that is orthogonal means all possible intersections among the members are empty or zero. An orthogonal set of functions has no overlaps on a Karnaugh map. Thus, with an orthogonal set of state transitions every transition is unique and there is no possible confusion about the next state. To check that a state machine is proper, take the following steps:

- □ Check the state machine structure to ensure it has no hidden traps or loops, that is, it cannot get stuck in some endless loop and never reach a return state.

- □ Examine the program design to ensure all the possible states have been identified. That is, is it complete? A program design is complete when a state is defined for every possible combination of the attribute values.

- □ Check for state orthogonality, that is, for every set of conditions there is one and only one possible state.

- □ Verify that the transitions from each state are complete and orthogonal, that is, from every state, a unique next state is defined for every possible combination of state machine input values.

The following two sections give examples of how to check the correctness of state machines. The first is the simple state machine, BSet, shown in Fig. 12.1; the second is the CData state machine defined in Chapter 10.

CHECKING THE BSet STATE MACHINE

The State Specification Template for the `BSet` state machine is shown in Table 12.3. The top row of the template describes the `EmptyState` and the two rows immediately below it give the next states from `EmptyState` and the conditions that cause transitions to them. The first of these next states is `EmptyState` itself, which means that when `BSet` is in `EmptyState` and the Pop or Subtract methods are called, BSet stays in `EmptyState`. The next row,

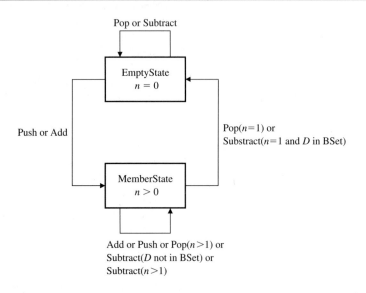

FIGURE 12.1
BSet State Machine Transitions

MemberState, indicates that when in EmptyState BSet will go to the MemberState when either the Push or Add methods are called.

In MemberState, the conditions are a little more complex. Member-State goes to EmptyState when the Pop method is called and there is only one member in BSet(n = 1). It also ends in EmptyState when BSet has a single member D and the Subtract method is called with the argument D. The conditions for MemberState transitioning to MemberState are shown in the bottom row of Table 12.3.

From Table 12.3 and from Fig. 12.1, you can see that BSet has the combined properties of a push-down stack and a simple set. For this example, we do not worry about how many members it contains, the maximum stack capacity, overflow behavior, or other error conditions. We are concerned only with whether it has members. Items can be added to BSet with the Push or Add methods or deleted with the Pop or Subtract methods. These methods behave as follows:

- Push(D): Add dataset D to BSet in the first position, pushing all existing members up one position.

- Pop(&D): Remove the dataset from the first position of BSet, place it in D, and move all other members of BSet down one position.

TABLE 12.3 EXAMPLE BSET STATE SPECIFICATION TEMPLATE

EmptyState	The set has no members.	n = 0
EmptyState	Pop(&D) $\vee$ Subtract(D)	
MemberState	Push(D) $\vee$ Add(D)	
MemberState	The set has one or more members.	n >= 1
EmptyState	[Pop(&D) $\wedge$ (n = 1)] $\vee$ [Subtract(D) $\wedge$ (n = 1) $\wedge$ (D $\in$ BSet)]	
MemberState	Push(D) $\vee$ Add(D) $\vee$ [Pop(&D) $\wedge$ (n > 1)] $\vee$ [Subtract(D) $\wedge$ D $\notin$ BSet] $\vee$ [Subtract(D) $\wedge$ (n > 1)]	

□ Add(D): If D is not a member of BSet, Push(D).

□ Subtract(D): If D is a member of BSet, delete it and reduce by one the position of all higher members of BSet.

To check if this is a proper state machine, ask the following questions:

1. Does BSet have any hidden traps or loops? From Fig. 12.1, BSet clearly can always transition from either state to the other.

2. Is the BSet state machine complete? You need to see if all the possible combinations of state machine attributes are described by states. For BSet, there is only one attribute of interest: n, the number of members in BSet. The two states of BSet are for n = 0 and n >= 1. Because n stands for the number of members in BSet, it can only be 0 or a positive integer. Thus all possible states are covered.

3. Are the BSet states orthogonal? Here, there should be only one possible state for each state machine attribute value. Clearly, these states are orthogonal, since n cannot be 0 and >= 1 at the same time.

4. Are the transitions from each state complete and orthogonal? It is usually best to follow an orderly procedure with this check to ensure you don't make a mistake. One approach is shown in Table 12.4. Here, the current

state is shown across the top and the BSet methods down the left column. Thus, when BSet is in the EmptyState Push will cause transition to MemberState, as will Add. Reading down the column under Empty State, you can see which next state results from the method in the left-most column.

To check for completeness using this table, first ensure all the combinations are filled in and that they cover all possible conditions. The only conditions in which there is any question are MemberState-Pop and MemberState-Subtract. MemberState-Pop goes to EmptyState if $n = 1$ and to MemberState if $n > 1$. Because n must be greater than or equal to 1 to be in MemberState, these cover all possible conditions.

For MemberState-Subtract, the next state is EmptyState when $n = 1$ and D is a member of BSet. The negative of this condition is $n \neq 1 \lor D \notin$ BSet. Because in MemberSet $n >= 1$, $n \neq 1$ is equivalent to $n > 1$. Thus the negative of the conditions for transition to EmptyState causes transition to MemberState. These transitions are thus complete and orthogonal.

THE CData STATE MACHINE EXAMPLE

The CData state machine defined in Chapter 10 and shown in Fig. 12.2 is somewhat more complex. The State Specification Template for this machine is shown

TABLE 12.4 BSET TRANSITION VERIFICATION

Method	Current state	
	EmptyState	MemberState
Push(D)	MemberState	MemberState
Add(D)	MemberState	MemberState
Pop(&D)	EmptyState	$n = 1$ :: EmptyState $\lor$ $n > 1$ :: MemberState
Subtract(D)	EmptyState	$(n = 1 \land D \in BSet)$:: EmptyState $\lor$ $(n > 1 \lor D \notin BSet)$ :: MemberState

in Table 12.5. This state machine has five states that are identified by the values of ListState from 0 to 4.

CHECKING FOR HIDDEN TRAPS OR LOOPS

You can generally check for hidden traps or loops most simply by drawing a diagram of the state transitions as shown in Fig. 12.2. This figure is constructed from the state template and shows every transition among the states. For example, EmptySet transitions to First&Only under condition 2. Condition 2 occurs when either the Push or AddSet methods are called. Figure 12.2 also shows that this state machine has no traps or hidden loops and that it can get from any one state to any other. For example, from the LastOfSeveral state,

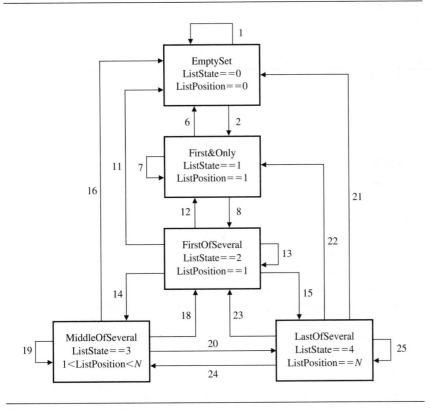

FIGURE 12.2
CData State Machine Transitions

the machine can get to `EmptySet` by condition 21. Similarly, the `EmptySet` state could transition to `LastOfSeveral` by the input sequence 2, 8, and 15.

CHECKING FOR ALL POSSIBLE STATES

Checking for all possible states involves identifying all the possible conditions of the system the state machine represents and ensuring they are complete. The example state machine involves a dataset that contains some number of members and a pointer to one of these members. The question of which combination of these parameters should be considered as separate states is a design decision. For example, in Table 12.6 the values of ListState are shown for various values of `ListPosition` and for various numbers of members in the set. Note, for example, that you could define as many distinct states as there are filled-in spaces in Table 12.6. The numbers 2, 3, and 4 appear in multiple places, which means this state machine is not sensitive to differences among states that have the same ListState value. With eight members in CData, you could thus define such a state machine so it had 37 distinct states.

In the example state machine, only five of the states were useful for the program being designed. These states are that the system have none, one, or some larger number of members and that the pointer point to nothing, the first member, a middle member, or the last member. These states are as follows:

`EmptySet, ListState = 0`: The pointer has nothing to point at, so `ListPosition = 0`.

`First&Only, ListState = 1`: With only one member, the pointer must point to it, so `ListPosition = 1`.

`FirstOfSeveral, ListState = 2`: There are several members with the pointer pointing to the first, so `ListPosition = 1`.

`MiddleOfSeveral, ListState = 3`: When the pointer is addressing a middle member, there must be at least three members in the set. Thus `ListPosition` is greater than 1 and less than N, where N is the number of members in the list.

`LastOfSeveral, ListState = 4`: There must be two or more set members with the pointer pointing to the last one, so `ListPosition = N`.

To verify that all the states are considered, first check to determine the parameter values for each state. The parameters are `ListPosition`, for the position of the pointer, and `ListState`. `ListPosition` is the number of the set

TABLE 12.5   EXAMPLE CDATA STATE SPECIFICATION TEMPLATE

EmptySet	The set has no members. N == 0	ListState == 0 List Position == 0
1	EmptySet	Clear ∨ Reset ∨ StepForward ∨ StepBackward ∨ Pop ∨ SubtractSet ∨ MemberSet ∨ Empty ∨ Last ∨ Status ∨ Position
2	First&Only	Push ∨ AddSet
3	FirstOfSeveral	Impossible
4	MiddleOfSeveral	Impossible
5	LastOfSeveral	Impossible

First&Only	The set has one member. N == 1	ListState == 1 ListPosition == 1
6	EmptySet	Clear ∨ Pop ∨ (SubtractSet(D) ∧ D ∈ ASet)
7	First&Only	Reset ∨ StepForward ∨ StepBackward ∨ (AddSet(D) ∧ D ∈ ASet) ∨ (SubtractSet(D) ∧ D ! ∈ ASet) ∨ MemberSet ∨ Empty ∨ Last ∨ Status ∨ Position
8	FirstOfSeveral	Push ∨ (AddSet(D) ∧ D ! ∈ ASet)
9	MiddleOfSeveral	Impossible
10	LastOfSeveral	Impossible

TABLE 12.5 (continued)

FirstOfSeveral	The set has several members, pointers in first position. N >= 2	ListState == 2 ListPosition == 1
11	EmptySet	Clear
12	First&Only	$(N == 2 \wedge \text{SubtractSet(D)} \wedge D \in \text{ASet}) \vee (N == 2 \wedge \text{Pop}) \vee$ Empty $\vee$ Last $\vee$ Status $\vee$ Position
13	FirstOfSeveral	Reset $\vee$ StepBackward $\vee$ Push $\vee$ (Pop $\wedge N > 2$) $\vee$ AddSet $\vee$ (SubtractSet(D) $\wedge D\ ! \in$ ASet) $\vee$ ($N > 2 \wedge$ SubtractSet) $\vee$ (MemberSet(D) $\wedge$ D in first position) $\vee$ Empty $\vee$ Last $\vee$ Status $\vee$ Position
14	MiddleOfSeveral	($N > 2 \wedge$ StepForward) $\vee$ (MemberSet(D) $\vee$ (D in middle position))
15	LastOfSeveral	($N == 2 \wedge$ StepForward) $\vee$!MemberSet(D) $\vee$ (MemberSet(D) $\wedge$ (D in last position))
MiddleOfSeveral	The set has several members, pointers in nth position N > 2	ListState == 3 1 < ListPosition < N
16	EmptySet	Clear
17	First&Only	Impossible
18	FirstOfSeveral	Reset $\vee$ Push $\vee$ Pop $\vee$ (ListPosition == 2 $\wedge$ StepBackward) $\vee$ AddSet $\vee$ SubtractSet $\vee$ (MemberSet(D) $\wedge$ (D in first position))

TABLE 12.5 (continued)

19	MiddleOfSeveral	(ListPosition $>$ 2 $\wedge$ StepBackward) $\vee$ (ListPosition $<$ N $-$ 1 $\wedge$ StepForward) $\vee$ (MemberSet(D) $\vee$ (D in middle position)) $\vee$ Empty $\vee$ Last $\vee$ Status $\vee$ Position
20	LastOfSeveral	(ListPosition $==$ N $-$ 1 $\wedge$ StepForward) $\vee$!MemberSet $\vee$ (MemberSet(D) $\wedge$ (D in last position))
	LastOfSeveral	Set has N $>$ 1 members, pointers in last position. N $>$ 1 ListState $==$ 4 ListPosition $==$ N
21	EmptySet	Clear
22	First&Only	N $==$ 2 $\wedge$ SubtractSet(D) $\wedge$ D $\in$ ASet
23	FirstOfSeveral	Reset $\vee$ Push $\vee$ Pop $\vee$ (N $==$ 2 $\wedge$ StepBackward) $\vee$ AddSet $\vee$ (SubtractSet $\wedge$ N $>$ 2) $\vee$ (SubtractSet(D) $\wedge$ D ! $\in$ ASet) $\vee$ (MemberSet(D) $\wedge$ D in first position)
24	MiddleOfSeveral	(N $>$ 2 $\wedge$ StepBackward) $\vee$ (MemberSet(D) $\wedge$ D in middle position)
25	LastOfSeveral	StepForward $\vee$!MemberSet $\vee$ (MemberSet(D) $\wedge$ (D in last position)) $\vee$ Empty $\vee$ Last $\vee$ Status $\vee$ Position

TABLE 12.6 POSSIBLE VALUES OF LISTSTATE FOR EXAMPLE STATE MACHINE

Members	ListPosition								
	0	1	2	3	4	5	6	7	8
0	0								
1		1							
2		2	4						
3		2	3	4					
4		2	3	3	4				
5		2	3	3	3	4			
6		2	3	3	3	3	4		
7		2	3	3	3	3	3	4	
8		2	3	3	3	3	3	3	4

item, starting with one, to which the pointer points. When the set is empty, ListPosition is thus 0. These parameter values were shown in Table 12.6. While this appears to be all the possible states, it is sometimes helpful to show all these possibilities in a tabular format like that in Table 12.7a and b. In Table 12.7a, when there are no members, the pointer position (ListPosition) and the number of members (N) must be zero. With one member in the set, $N=1$ and the pointer can only point to it. With two members, $N=2$ and the pointer can point to 1 or 2 and there is no middle member. Finally, with three or more members there is a middle position where ListPosition is greater than 1 and less than N.

You should also check to verify that no empty square in Table 12.7a represents a possible condition. In the $N=0$ row, ListPosition has a value of zero when the set is empty. Because the set has no members, the pointer cannot be in any of the other positions in this row, so they should be empty. Under the None column, when there are members in the set, the pointer must point to one of them. Thus all the positions in the None column must be empty except the top one. Next, in the $N=1$ row there is 1 member and the pointer can only point to it. Thus the Middle and Last columns must be empty. Finally, in the $N=2$ row with 2 members, ListPosition can have only the value 1 or 2. There is thus no middle position, so the middle cell should be blank. Clearly, these are all the possible states, and they are properly represented by the parameter values. The states are therefore complete.

TABLE 12.7   POSSIBLE EXAMPLE STATE MACHINE STATES

a) States for various parameter values

Number of members (N)	ListPosition = 0 None	ListPosition = 1 First	ListPosition > 1 ListPosition < N Middle	ListPosition = N Last
N = 0	EmptySet			
N = 1		First&Only		
N = 2		FirstOfSeveral		LastOfSeveral
N >= 3		FirstOfSeveral	MiddleOfSeveral	LastOfSeveral

b) Parameter values for various states

State	Number of members (N)			
	N = 0	N = 1	N >= 2	N >= 3
EmptySet	ListPosition = 0 ListState = 0			
First&Only		ListPosition = 1 ListState = 1		
FirstOfSeveral			ListPosition = 1 ListState = 2	ListPosition = 1 ListState = 2
MiddleOf Several				ListPosition>1 ListPosition < N ListState = 3
LastOfSeveral			ListPosition = N ListState = 4	ListPosition = N ListState = 4

CHECKING FOR STATE ORTHOGONALITY

To determine if the state definitions are orthogonal, you need to determine if any two states can exist under the same parameter conditions. By examining the values of ListState and ListPosition in Table 12.7b, you can see that the value of ListState is uniquely determined for every combination of the N and ListPosition parameters. That is, for every combination of N and ListPosition there is one and only one value of ListState. These states are thus orthogonal.

VERIFYING TRANSITIONS FROM EACH STATE ARE COMPLETE AND ORTHOGONAL

This check can become complex, so it is important to do it carefully. One approach is to use a tabular listing of all possible conditions, as shown in Table 12.8. This check ensures there is one and only one state transition from each state for each possible instruction and parameter combination.

An examination of Table 12.8 shows how such a transition verification table is constructed. The Call column lists all the methods that could be called. The top row lists the current states, and below each current state are listed the states to which the machine transitions for each method call. The EmptySet column, for example, describes the transitions from the EmptySet state. Note that from EmptySet, every method call will cause a transition either back to EmptySet or to First&Only. If you scan down the EmptySet column to the Push method, you will see that when the object is in the EmptySet state and Push is called the next state will be First&Only. This is also true for AddSet.

In the First&Only column, all but the last two methods cause unconditional transitions. The AddSet method has two conditions: The new item D is already a member of the set, or it is not. The state machine is left in the First&Only state if the item being added is already a member of the set. If it is a new item, however, a new member is added to the set and the transition is to the FirstOfSeveral state. For the AddSet instruction, either D is a member of the set or it is not. Because these are the only possible conditions, this case is complete. The SubtractSet transitions have a similar logic. When D is a member of the set, SubtractSet removes it, leaving the EmptySet state. If D is not a member, the state is left unchanged. These are the only possible cases, so this transition condition is also complete.

Some of the later transitions are a bit more complex. For example, the MemberSet instruction is designed to leave the pointer at the matching member if one of that value is in ASet. If the last member is the match or if there is no match, the pointer is left at the last member in the set. This happens in the three states FirstOfSeveral, MiddleOfSeveral, and LastOfSeveral.

TABLE 12.8 TRANSITION VERIFICATION—EXAMPLE STATE MACHINE

Call	EmptySet	First&Only	FirstOfSeveral	MiddleOfSeveral	LastOfSeveral
Reset	EmptySet	First&Only	FirstOf Several	FirstOf Several	FirstOf Several
Clear	EmptySet	EmptySet	EmptySet	EmptySet	EmptySet
Empty	EmptySet	First&Only	FirstOf Several	MiddleOf Several	LastOf Several
Last	EmptySet	First&Only	FirstOf Several	MiddleOf Several	LastOf Several
Status	EmptySet	First&Only	FirstOf Several	MiddleOf Several	LastOf Several
Position	EmptySet	First&Only	FirstOf Several	MiddleOf Several	LastOf Several
MemberSet	EmptySet	First&Only	D in first position: FirstOf Several > D in middle position: MiddleOf Several	D in first position: FirstOf Several > D in middle position: MiddleOf Several	D in first position: FirstOf Several > D in middle position: MiddleOf Several

Chapter 12   Design Verification

TABLE 12.8 (continued)

Call	EmptySet	First&Only	FirstOfSeveral	MiddleOfSeveral	LastOfSeveral
MemberSet	EmptySet	First&Only	∨ (D in last position ∨ !member): LastOf Several	∨ (D in last position ∨ !member): LastOf Several	∨ (D in last position ∨ !member): LastOf Several
StepForward	EmptySet	First&Only	N > 2: MiddleOf Several ∨ N = 2: LastOf Several	ListPosition < N − 1: MiddleOf Several ∨ ListPosition = N − 1: LastOf Several	LastOf Several
StepBackward	EmptySet	First&Only	FirstOf Several	ListPosition = 2: FirstOf Several ∨ ListPosition > 2: MiddleOf Several	N = 2: FirstOf Several ∨ N > 2: MiddleOf Several

TABLE 12.8 (continued)

Call	EmptySet	First&Only	FirstOfSeveral	MiddleOfSeveral	LastOfSeveral
Push	First&Only	FirstOf Several	FirstOf Several	FirstOf Several	FirstOf Several
Pop	EmptySet	EmptySet	N = 2: First&Only ∨ N > 2: FirstOf Several	FirstOf Several	FirstOf Several
AddSet	First&Only	D member: First&Only ∨ D !member: FirstOf Several	FirstOf Several	FirstOf Several	FirstOf Several
SubtractSet	EmptySet	D member: EmptySet ∨ D !member: First&Only	D member and N = 2: First&Only ∨ (D !member ∨ N > 2): FirstOf Several	FirstOf Several	D member and N = 2: First&Only ∨ (D !member ∨ N > 2): FirstOf Several

TABLE 12.9 CLEARSPACES LOGIC SPECIFICATION TEMPLATE

```
ClearSpaces(Input; State)
  1   Length = length(Input)
      State = 0

  2   repeat until (State = 3 or Length = 0)

  3       if Input[Length] = ' '   {a space character at
          the end of the input string}

  4           Length = Length - 1

  5           if State < 2
                  State = State + 1

  6       else State = 3
      until (State = 3 or Length = 0)

  7   if Length > 0

  8      for N = 1 to Length do

  9         if (Input[N] <> ' ' or First)

 10             Output = Output + Input[N]

                First = true

 11   Input = Output
```

Similarly, the StepForward and StepBackward instructions have qualifying conditions. Here, in the FirstOfSeveral and LastOfSeveral states N >= 2 and in MiddleOfSeveral, N > 2. Thus all the possible conditions are covered. In the FirstOfSeveral case, when N > 2, StepForward would take the pointer to MiddleOfSeveral. If, however, N = 2, then StepForward would take the state to LastOfSeveral. A similar analysis shows that the StepBackward method is also completely covered. Thus the transitions from the states are complete and orthogonal.

For even fairly simple state machines, if you have not produced the state machine specifications there is a high likelihood that you will have design problems. State machine problems are often immediately obvious from the State Specification Template or the state transition diagram. When the problems do not show up here, a transition verification table will generally reveal them. While such proofs may seem complex and time consuming, with a little practice you will be able to do them quite quickly even for moderately complex state machines. From your PSP data on test defects, you can see how frequently you make state machine specification errors and how long it takes you to find and fix them with these verification methods. You will then be more willing to do a complete state machine review. Your only alternative is to spend much more time to find these problems in test.

12.5   Program Tracing

There are various ways to verify a Logic Specification Template before you implement or test a program. Examples of such methods are execution tables, trace tables, and mathematical verification. [Mills 87] This section and the next describe these approaches and illustrate how they work.

EXECUTION TABLES

An execution table provides an orderly way to check the logic flow in a Logic Specification Template. This method can be time consuming, particularly for long or complex programs, but it is a reliable and simple verification method. An example would be a routine, `ClearSpaces`, to clear the leading and trailing spaces from a character string. You pass the routine a character string, and the one it passes back has no leading or trailing spaces. The routine also returns an integer value `State` that provides information about the string.

The `ClearSpaces` Logic Specification Template is shown in Table 12.9, its State Specification Template in Table 12.10, and its state diagram in Fig. 12.3. Note that the 1 condition for transition from state 3 to itself in Table 12.10 means

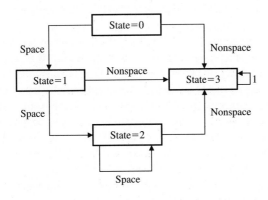

FIGURE 12.3
ClearSpaces State Machine

this transition always occurs, regardless of the character input. State 3 is an exit state, however, so this is still a proper state machine.

While this simple routine removes the leading and trailing spaces from a character string, it must leave any spaces imbedded within the character string. The calling program also needs to know if the input was an empty string, if it contained a string of exactly one space, if it contained a string of two or more spaces, or if it contained some nonspace characters. The Functional Specification Template in Table 12.11 shows the returns from this function. Some example cases for how this routine behaves are the following:

□ When the input is an empty string, the empty string is passed back with State=0.

□ When the input is a single-space character, an empty string is passed back with the returned State=1.

□ When the input is a string of two or more spaces with no nonspace characters, an empty string is passed back with the return State=2.

□ When the input is a character string containing nonspace characters, say '_ab___', the string 'ab' is passed back with the return State=3.

In building an execution table, you list the logic steps in order together with the variable and parameter values for each case to be examined. When loops are encountered, their instructions are repeated until the cycle is completed. The example execution table in Table 12.12 steps through the first six logic steps for the five-character input string '_ab___'. That is, the characters 'ab' are preceded by one space and followed by two spaces. In the following discussion, the characters in the final string are referred to as message characters. In this example, the message characters would be 'ab' without the leading or trailing spaces.

For cycle 1 in Table 12.12, the logic runs through program steps 1 through 6. These are the same program steps given in the Logic Specification Template in Table 12.9. They examine the trailing end of the string to see if it contains any spaces. Here, there is a problem at step 3 of cycle 1. Input[Length] refers to the character after the last one in the string. The logic should have referred to Input[Length-1], since an N character string actually has characters in positions 0 ... N-1. Also, with this change, a 0 length string would cause instruction 3 to refer to Input[-1]. A check for similar errors elsewhere shows that the logic has the same problem at steps 9 and 10. The logic should be corrected to refer to the proper character in the string and to handle the case of a 0 length string. The newly modified logic is shown in Table 12.13.

After making this change, you have the execution tables given in Table 12.14. The first steps examine the trailing end of the string to see if it contains spaces. If it does, the length of the string is reduced until the first nonspace char-

TABLE 12.10 CLEARSPACES STATE SPECIFICATION TEMPLATE

0		Empty String	State = 0
	0		
	1	space	
	2		
	3	nonspace	
1		1 Space	State = 1
	0		
	1		
	2	space	
	3	nonspace	
2		2 Spaces	State = 2
	0		
	1		
	2	space	
	3	nonspace	
3		Nonspace Characters	State = 3
	0		
	1		
	2		
	3	1	

acter is encountered where State is set to 3. Reading then starts from the front of the string in cycle 3. Now, the intent is to skip initial spaces and to pass the first nonspace characters and all succeeding message characters to the output. At step 10 of cycle 3, however, the value of First is not explicitly defined. It thus must be initialized to false. After this defect is corrected, this program produces the correct output 'ab' and State=3.

While it may seem that this simple logic design has been completely checked, it has not been. For example, behavior has not been verified when the input string is empty, when it contains a single character, or when it contains only spaces. These cases could all be checked with more copies of the execution table. Just like a test case, the execution table checks only logical correctness for the single tested combination of inputs and parameters.

TABLE 12.11 CLEARSPACES FUNCTIONAL SPECIFICATION TEMPLATE

Name	Base Class	State (0-3)
ClearSpaces (Input; State)	Input empty :: (return = empty) $\land$ State = 0 $\lor$ Input == 1 space :: (return = empty) $\land$ State = 1 $\lor$ Input >= 2 spaces :: (return = empty) $\land$ State = 2 $\lor$ Input has nonspace characters :: [return = Input (without leading and trailing spaces)] $\land$ State = 3	

TRACE TABLES

Trace tables often are more efficient for verifying logic correctness than are execution tables. The trace table proof method involves three complementary techniques that should be used in combination when possible:

1. Symbolic execution
2. Trace table examination of all possible cases
3. Proof by induction

Trace tables can produce a fairly general verification from relatively few cases. To the maximum extent practical, you should use symbolic execution and proof by induction to support your trace table verifications.

Checking Logic Cases with a Trace Table. In trace table checking, you identify all possible logic cases and separately verify each. For the Clear-Spaces routine you do this by defining an input string of total length k, and examining all the possible cases as follows:

1. 0, 1, or m message characters in the string, where a message is a contiguous character string that starts and ends with a nonspace character
2. 0, 1, or j leading spaces in the string
3. 0, 1, or n trailing spaces in the string

TABLE 12.12 EXECUTION TABLE FOR CLEARSPACES

Cycle: 1		Function : ClearSpaces(Input; State)						
#	Instruction	Condition	Input	Output	Length	State	First	N
1	Length = length(Input), State = 0		'_ab_'		5	0		
2	repeat until (State = 3 or Length = 0)							
3	if input[Length] = ' '	??						
4	Length = Length − 1							
5	if State < 2 State = State + 1							
6	else State = 3							
	until (State = 3 or Length = 0)							

TABLE 12.13 CLEARSPACES LOGIC SPECIFICATION TEMPLATE (WITH FIX)

```
ClearSpaces(Input; State)
 1  Length = length(Input)
    State = 0
 2  if Length > 0
 3    repeat until (State = 3 or Length = 0)
 4      if Input[Length - 1] = ' ' {a space character
        at the end of the input string}
 5        Length = Length - 1
 6        if State < 2
              State = State + 1
 7      else State = 3
    until (State = 3 or Length = 0)
 8  if Length > 0
 9    for N = 1 to Length do
10      if (Input[N - 1] <> ' ' or First)
11          Output = Output + Input[N - 1]
            First = true
12  Input = Output
```

Here, j, m, and n can have any positive integer values, as long as k = j + m + n. These cases are shown in Table 12.15. Here, by induction, you need to check with the 0 and 1 cases and then verify the logic for some number q and q+1 cases. If you can show the logic is correct for all these cases, you can be confident the logic is correct. Note, however, that it is not necessary to check all these combinations if some behave identically.

In doing the trace table checks in Table 12.16, steps 1 through 7 examine the trailing spaces. Clearly this portion of the program operates properly when the string is empty (case 1 in Table 12.15). It will leave Length=0 and State=0. Also, program steps 1 through 11 will be skipped when Length=0 and the final result returns the value of Input=Output. This, however, raises a question: What is the value of Output when there is a 0 length input? This suggests that the Output value should be initialized to empty. This logic defect should have been caught by the execution table but was not as obvious with the single case that was checked. With this fix the logic, when called with an empty string, will return an empty string with State=0. Program behavior with any number of trailing spaces is also clearly correct, including case 7.

TABLE 12.14   SECOND EXECUTION TABLE FOR CLEARSPACES

Cycle: 1 — Function : ClearSpaces(Input; State)

#	Instruction	Condition	Input	Output	Length	State	First	N
1	Length = length(Input), State = 0		'_ab_'		5	0		
2	if Length > 0	true						
3	repeat until (State = 3 or Length = 0)							
4	if Input[Length − 1] = ' '	true						
5	Length = Length − 1				4			
6	if State < 2 State = State + 1	true				1		
7	else State = 3							
	until (State = 3 or Length = 0)	false						

Cycle: 2 — Function : ClearSpaces(Input; State)

#	Instruction	Condition	Input	Output	Length	State	First	N
3	repeat until (State=3 or Length=0)							
4	if input[Length − 1] = ' '	true						
5	Length=Length − 1				3			
6	if State < 2 State = State + 1	true				2		

TABLE 12.14 (continued)

Cycle: 2	Function : ClearSpaces(Input; State)		
7	else State = 3		
	until (State = 3 or Length = 0)	false	

Cycle: 3	Function : ClearSpaces(Input; State)			
3	repeat until (State = 3 or Length = 0)			
4	if Input[Length − 1] = ' '	false		
5	Length = Length − 1			
6	if State < 2 State = State = State + 1			
7	else State = 3			3
	until (State = 3 or Length = 0)	true		
8	if Length > 0	true	3	
9	for N = 1 to Length do			1
10	if (Input[N − 1] <> ' ' or First)	false??		??
11	Output = + Input[N − 1] First = true			

TABLE 12.14 (continued)

Cycle: 4		Function : ClearSpaces(Input; State)						
#	Instruction	Condition	Input	Output	Length	State	First	N
9	for N = 1 to Length do							2
10	if (Input[N – 1] <> ' ' or First)	true						
11	Output = + Input[N – 1] First = true			a			true	

Cycle: 5		Function : ClearSpaces(Input; State)						
9	for N = 1 to Length do							3
10	if (Input[N – 1] <> ' ' or First)	true						
11	Output = + Input[N – 1] First = true			ab			true	
12	Input = Output		ab					

TABLE 12.15   CLEARSPACES TRACE TABLE CASES

Case number	Case	Number of leading spaces	Number of message characters, m	Number of trailing spaces
1	000	0	0	0
2	010	0	1	0
3	0m0	0	k	0
4	001	0	0	1
5	011	0	1	1
6	0m1	0	$k - 1$	1
7	00n	0	0	n
8	01n	0	1	n
9	0mn	0	$k - n$	n
10	100	1	0	0
11	110	1	1	0
12	1m0	1	$k - 1$	0
13	101	1	0	1
14	111	1	1	1
15	1m1	1	$k - 2$	1
16	10n	1	0	n
17	11n	1	1	n
18	1mn	1	$k - 1 - n$	n
19	j00	j	0	0
20	j10	j	1	0
21	jm0	j	$k - j$	0
22	j01	j	0	1
23	j11	j	1	1
24	jm1	j	$k - j - 1$	1
25	j0n	j	0	n
26	j1n	j	1	n
27	jmn	j	$k - j - n$	n

TABLE 12.16 CLEARSPACES TRACE TABLE—CASE 0-0-0

Cycle: 1	Function : ClearSpaces(Input; State)							
#	Instruction	Condition	Input	Output	Length	State	First	N
1	Length = length(Input), State = 0		"		0	0		
	First = false						false	
2	if Length > 0	false						
3	repeat until (State = 3 or Length = 0)							
4	if Input[Length − 1] = ' '							
5	Length = Length − 1							
6	if State < 2 State = State + 1							
7	else State = 3							
	until (State = 3 or Length = 0)	true						
8	if Length > 0	false						
9	for N = 1 to Length do							
10	if (Input[N − 1] <> ' ' or First)							
11	Output = + Input[N − 1] First = true							
12	Input = Output			??				

TABLE 12.17 CLEARSPACES TRACE TABLE—CASE 0-K-0

Cycle: 1; k = 2

Function : ClearSpaces(Input; State)

#	Instruction	Condition	Input	Output	Length	State	First	N
1	Length = length(Input), State = 0		'ab'		2	0		
	Output = ' ', First = false			''			false	
2	if Length > 0	true						
3	repeat until (State = 3 or Length = 0)							
4	if Input[Length − 1] = ' '	false						
5	Length = Length − 1							
6	if State < 2 State = State + 1							
7	else State = 3					3		
	until (State = 3 or Length = 0)	true						

TABLE 12.17 (continued)

Cycle: 2

		Function : ClearSpaces(Input; State)						
#	Instruction	Condition	Input	Output	Length	State	First	N
8	if Length > 0	true						
9	for N = 1 to Length do							1
10	if (Input[N - 1] <> ' ' or First)	true						
11	Output = + Input[N - 1] First = true			a			true	

Cycle: 3

		Function : ClearSpaces(Input; State)						
9	for N = 1 to Length do							2
10	if (Input[N - 1] <> ' ' or First)	true						
11	Output = + Input[N - 1] First = true			ab			true	
12	Input = Output		ab					

Next, in Table 12.17, check the case of 0 trailing spaces when there are 0 leading spaces and a total of k input characters (cases 2 and 3). This case works properly when k=1. To check the remaining values with proof by induction, assume that program behavior is correct for some value $k = q$ and see if there are any values of n where program behavior would not be correct at $k = q+1$. An examination of the logic shows there is no such value. Since varying numbers of trailing spaces were previously checked, this check also verifies cases 5, 6, 8, and 9.

The reasoning for this proof by induction logic is as follows:

1. Demonstrate the logic is correct for some value k_0. Here, this is done with k=2, so $k_0 = 2$.

2. Assume the program logic is correct for some value of k larger than k_0.

3. Knowing that the logic is correct for $k = q$, show it is also correct for $k = q + 1$. From Table 12.17, it is clear that the $q + 1$ case would merely add one more cycle to the prior trace table and would produce the proper output.

In Table 12.18, the case is checked in which there are no trailing spaces, j leading spaces, and k-j message characters (cases 11, 12, 20, and 21). As you can see, this case works properly, returning State=3 and the message string. Again, the proof-by-induction logic shows that there is no value of q when program logic is correct at $j = q$ and incorrect at $j = q + 1$. This program is thus correct for this case and for all larger values of j and k−j. In a real implementation, there will always be some upper size limit imposed by system capacity. This limit should be determined whenever it could be pertinent and steps taken to ensure the logic handles that situation properly. Because varying numbers of trailing spaces have already been verified, this check covers cases 17 and 18.

One case that was not explicitly checked is that of ensuring the internal spaces within the message are not disturbed. As you can see in step 11 in cycle 4 (Table 12.18), the condition *First* takes care of this. After the first nonspace character is encountered at the beginning of the string, any later spaces are copied from the input to the output. If there were any doubt about this function, this condition could be checked in another trace table.

In Table 12.19, the case is checked in which there is one trailing space with no other spaces or characters (case 4). As you can see, this case works properly, returning an empty string and State=1. This case also checks case 7.

The case with one trailing space, j leading spaces, and k-j-1 intervening characters, is shown in Table 12.20 (cases 23 and 24). This case is also correct with no identified defects. The verification of the remaining cases follow the same procedure as those just given. Rather than doing each verification separately, you can save time by examining each of the verifications you have done to see if it can be easily extended to cover some of the remaining cases.

TABLE 12.18 CLEARSPACES TRACE TABLE—CASE J-(K-J)-0

Cycle: 1; j = 3, k − j = 2			Function : ClearSpaces(Input; State)					
#	Instruction	Condition	Input	Output	Length	State	First	N
1	Length = length(Input), State = 0		'ab'		5	0		
	Output = ' ', First = false			' '			false	
2	if Length > 0	true						
3	repeat until (State = 3 or Length = 0)							
4	if Input[Length − 1] = ' '	false						
5	Length = Length − 1							
6	if State < 2 State = State + 1							
7	else State = 3					3		
	until (State = 3 or Length = 0)	true						
8	if Length > 0	true						
9	for N = 1 to Length do							1
10	if (Input[N − 1] <> ' ' or First)	false						
11	Output = + Input[N − 1] First = true							

TABLE 12.18 (Continued)

Cycle: 2:

Function : ClearSpaces(Input; State)

#	Instruction	Condition	Input	Output	Length	State	First	N
9	for N = 1 to Length do							2
10	if (Input[N - 1] <> ' ' or First)	false						
11	Output = + Input[N - 1] First = true							

Cycle: 3

Function : ClearSpaces(Input; State)

#	Instruction	Condition	Input	Output	Length	State	First	N
9	for N = 1 to Length do							3
10	if (Input[N - 1] <> ' ' or First)	false						
11	Output = + Input[N - 1] First = true							

TABLE 12.18 (continued)

Cycle: 4

Function : ClearSpaces(Input; State)							
#	Instruction	Condition	Input	Output	Length	State	First	N
								4
9	for N = 1 to Length do							
10	if (Input[N - 1] <> ' ' or First)	true						
11	Output = + Input[N - 1] First = true			a			true	

Cycle: 5

Function : ClearSpaces(Input; State)							
#	Instruction	Condition	Input	Output	Length	State	First	N
								5
9	for N = 1 to Length do							
10	if (Input[N - 1] <> ' ' or First)	true						
11	Output = + Input[N - 1] First = true			ab			true	
12	Input = Output		ab					

TABLE 12.19 CLEARSPACES TRACE TABLE—CASE 0-0-1

Function : ClearSpaces(Input; State)

Cycle: 1

#	Instruction	Condition	Input	Output	Length	State	First	N
1	Length = length(Input), State = 0		' '		1	0		
	Output = ' ', First = false			' '			false	
2	if Length > 0	true						
3	repeat until (State = 3 or Length = 0)							
4	if Input[Length - 1] = ' '	true						
5	Length = Length - 1				0			
6	if State < 2 State = State + 1	true				1		
7	else State = 3							
	until (State = 3 or Length = 0)	true						
8	if Length > 0	false						
9	for N = 1 to Length do							
10	if (Input[N - 1] <> ' ' or First)							
11	Output = + Input[N - 1] First = true							
12	Input = Output		' '					

TABLE 12.20 CLEARSPACES TRACE TABLE—CASE J-(K-J-1)-1

Cycle: 1 — Function : ClearSpaces(Input; State)

#	Instruction	Condition	Input	Output	Length	State	First	N
1	Length = length(Input), State = 0		'ab'		k	0		
	Output = ' ', First = false			''			false	
2	if Length > 0	true						
3	repeat until (State = 3 or Length = 0)							
4	if Input[Length $-$ 1] = ' '	true						
5	Length = Length $-$ 1				k $-$ 1			
6	if State < 2 State = State + 1	true				1		
7	else State = 3							
	until (State = 3 or Length = 0)	false						

Cycle: 2 — Function : ClearSpaces(Input; State)

#	Instruction	Condition			
3	repeat until (State = 3 or Length = 0)				
4	if Input[Length-1] = ' '	false			
5	Length = Length $-$ 1				

TABLE 12.20   (continued)

Function : ClearSpaces(Input; State)

Cycle: 2

#	Instruction	Condition	Input	Output	Length	State	First	N
6	if State < 2 State = State + 1							
7	else State = 3					3		
	until (State = 3 or Length = 0)	true						
8	if Length > 0	true						
9	for N = 1 to Length do							
10	if (Input[N − 1] <> ' ' or First)	false						1
11	Output = + Input[N − 1] First = true							

Function : ClearSpaces(Input; State)

Cycle: 3

#	Instruction	Condition	Input	Output	Length	State	First	N
9	for N = 1 to Length do							
10	if (Input[N − 1] <> ' ' or First)	false						2
11	Output = + Input[N − 1] First = true							

TABLE 12.20 (Continued)

Cycle: 4

		Function : ClearSpaces(Input; State)						
#	Instruction	Condition	Input	Output	Length	State	First	N
9	for N = 1 to Length do							3
10	if (Input[N – 1] <> ' ' or First)	true						
11	Output = + Input[N – 1] First = true			a			true	

Cycle: 5 (k = 5)

		Function : ClearSpaces(Input; State)						
#	Instruction	Condition	Input	Output	Length	State	First	N
9	for N = 1 to Length do							4
10	if (Input[N – 1] <> ' ' or First)	true						
11	Output = + Input[N – 1] First = true			ab			true	
12	Input = Output		ab					

Using Trace Tables.   Although trace-table verification can be quite time consuming, it is no more so than identifying all the cases needed for a comprehensive unit test of a program's logic. If you plan to develop and run such tests, you may as well capitalize on that effort to verify the program's correctness. However, if you do not intend to run such tests you must either check the logic very carefully during the design review or resign yourself to a lot of debugging.

12.6   Verifying Program Correctness

A considerable body of literature deals with mathematically proving program correctness. [Gries, Mills 87, Spivey] The methods described here borrow some ideas from these formal techniques, but they are not as rigorous and could not be described as proofs. They can be very helpful, however, particularly when you are attempting to verify the logic of an existing program before modifying or correcting it. Even in new program development, there are often cases for which formal specifications are not available. In all these, you must infer the specifications as best you can and then verify the logic against them. That is essentially the technique followed here.

TESTING LOOPS

Mills and Dyer have described methods for verifying the correctness of various logical structures. [Dyer, Mills 87] The methods that are most generally useful are for the for loop, the while loop, and the repeat-until loop.

For-loop Verification.   Before doing the `for-loop` verification, identify the `for-loop` preconditions and verify that these preconditions are always met. The for-loop verification is as follows:

Does `ForLoop` = `FirstPart` + `SecondPart` + ... `LastPart`?

Here, `ForLoop` is assumed to have the following form:

```
ForLoop
  for n=First to Last
    begin
      nPart
    end
```

where nPart takes the values FirstPart, SecondPart, ThirdPart, through LastPart. If you were to lay out the execution of this program through all the loops, it would then be as follows:

```
ForLoop
 begin
   FirstPart
   SecondPart
   ThirdPart
   . . .
   LastPart
 end
```

While this test may seem obvious, the actual verification is not trivial.

To answer the question, construct a trace table for each side of the equality and show that the two trace tables always produce the identical result. In this case, you would produce one trace table for ForLoop and another for FirstPart + SecondPart + . . . + LastPart. If the two trace tables then produce the identical results, the answer to the question is yes and the for loop is validated.

Example of the For-loop Verification. To demonstrate this verification, consider the ClearSpaces example where the for loop ran from instructions 9 through 11:

```
9  for N = 1 to Length do
10    if (Input[N-1] <> '' or First)
11       Output = Output + Input[N − 1]
         First = true
```

Here, as before, you must examine all the cases. These start with the program preconditions, which are established by the program inputs and the logic up until the for loop. The preconditions are as follows:

1. First is always false.
2. Length may be any positive integer, not including 0.
3. The input string must include one or more nonspace characters, thus State=3.
4. The string starts with j spaces, where j may be 0 or any positive integer.
5. There may be spaces imbedded in the string after the first nonspace character.
6. The last character is always a nonspace character.
7. The Output string is initially empty.

By examining the logic for steps 1 through 8 in Table 12.19, you can verify that these conditions are satisfied. In determining the possible cases, let k represent the total number of characters in the message and j the number of leading spaces. Thus $k - j > 0$. Looking again at Table 12.15 on page 406, you can see that the cases to test are the following:

- A single message character with no leading spaces: $j = 0, k = 1$ (case 2)
- Several message characters and no leading spaces: $j = 0, k > 1$ (case 3)
- A single message character with one leading space: $j = 1, k = 2$ (case 11)
- Several message characters with one leading space: $j = 1, k > 2$ (case 12)
- A single message character with several leading spaces: $j > 1, k = j + 1$ (case 20)
- Several message characters with several leading spaces: $j > 1, k > j + 1$ (case 21)

If you check these cases against Table 12.15, you will see that these six conditions include all the cases except those with zero message characters and those with trailing spaces; by preconditions 3 and 6, these two classes of cases are excluded. Thus, if you can verify these six cases and by induction show they are true for all values of j and k, then you have verified all cases.

The verification in these cases consists of determining the value of FirstPart + SecondPart + ... + LastPart to see if the result is what the for loop is supposed to produce. In these cases, the trace table is a good way to do this. These six verifications are constructed in the manner described in the previous section and are shown in Tables 12.21 to 12.26. You then check each table to ensure the result produced is the result desired. Because all these cases produce correct results and the general cases of j leading spaces and k characters has also been demonstrated, this design clearly is correct.

While-loop Verification.   Before doing the `while-loop` verification, identify the `while-loop` preconditions and verify that they are always met. This while loop is in the following form:

```
WhileLoop
  begin
    while WhileTest
      LoopPart
  end
```

The while-loop verification involves your answering the following questions:

1. Is loop termination guaranteed for any argument of `WhileTest`?
2. When `WhileTest` is true, does `WhileLoop = LoopPart` followed by `WhileLoop`?
3. When `WhileTest` is false, does `WhileLoop = identity`?

TABLE 12.21 FOR-LOOP TRACE TABLE VERIFICATION—CASE 2 (0-1-0)

Case 1: j = 0, k = 1

		Input: 0(spaces), 1(nonspace)						
#	Instruction	Condition	Input	Output	Length	State	First	N
9	for N = 1 to Length do		'a'	"	1	3	false	1
10	if (Input[N − 1] <> ' ' or First)	true						
11	Output = + Input[N − 1] First = true			'a'			true	

TABLE 12.22 FOR-LOOP TRACE TABLE VERIFICATION—CASE 3 (0-K-0)

Case 2: j = 0, k > 1

		Input: 0(spaces), 1(nonspace), k − 2(characters), 1(nonspace)						
#	Instruction	Condition	Input	Output	Length	State	First	N
9	for N = 1 to Length do		'ab..k'	"	k	3	false	1
10	if (Input[N − 1] <> ' ' or First)	true						
11	Output = + Input[N − 1] First = true			'a'			true	
	...			'ab..j'			true	.k − 1
9	for N = 1 to Length do							..k
10	if (Input[N − 1] <> ' ' or First)	true						
11	Output = + Input[N − 1] First = true			'a..k'			true	

TABLE 12.23 FOR-LOOP TRACE TABLE VERIFICATION—CASE 11 (1-1-0)

Case 3: j = 1, k = 2

Input: 1(space), 1(nonspace)

#	Instruction	Condition	Input	Output	Length	State	First	N
9	for N = 1 to Length do		'b'	"	2	3	false	1
10	if (Input[N − 1] <> ' ' or First)	false						
11	Output = + Input[N − 1] First = true							
9	for N = 1 to Length do							2
10	if (Input[N − 1] <> ' ' or First)	true						
11	Output = + Input[N − 1] First = true			'b'			true	

TABLE 12.24 FOR-LOOP TRACE TABLE VERIFICATION—CASE 12 (J-1-0)

Case 4: j > 1, k = j + 1		Input: j(spaces), 1(nonspace)						
#	Instruction	Condition	Input	Output	Length	State	First	N
9	for N = 1 to Length do		' k'	"	j + 1	3	false	1
10	if (Input[N − 1] <> ' ' or First)	false						
11	Output = + Input[N − 1] First = true							
	. . .							j − 1
9	for N = 1 to Length do							2. j
10	if (Input[N − 1] <> ' ' or First)	false						
11	Output = + Input[N − 1] First = true							
9	for N = 1 to Length do							j + 1
10	if (Input[N − 1] <> ' ' or First)	true						
11	Output = + Input[N − 1] First = true		'k'	'k'			true	

TABLE 12.25 FOR-LOOP TRACE TABLE VERIFICATION—CASE 20 (1-(K-1)-0)

Case 5: j = 1, k > 2		Input: 1(space), 1(nonspace), k − 3(characters), 1(nonspace)						
#	Instruction	Condition	Input	Output	Length	State	First	N
9	for N = 1 to Length do		'b...k'	''	k	3	false	1
10	if (Input[N − 1] <> ' ' or First)	false						
11	Output = +Input[N − 1] First = true							
9	for N = 1 to Length do							2
10	if (Input[N − 1] <> ' ' or First)	true						
11	Output = +Input[N − 1] First = true			'b'			true	
...								
9	for N = 1 to Length do							k − 1
10	if (Input[N − 1] <> ' ' or First)	true						k
11	Output = +Input[N − 1] First = true			'b..k'			true	

Case 6: $j > 1$, $k > j + 1$ | **Input: j(spaces), 1(nonspace), k − j − 2(characters), 1(nonspace)**

#	Instruction	Condition	Input	Output	Length	State	First	N
9	for N = 1 to Length do		' j ..k'	"	k	3	false	1
10	if (Input[N − 1] <> ' ' or First)	false						
11	Output = + Input[N − 1] First = true							
	...							
9	for N = 1 to Length do							j
10	if (Input[N − 1] <> ' ' or First)	false						
11	Output = + Input[N − 1] First = true							
9	for N = 1 to Length do	true						j + 1
10	if (Input[N − 1] <> ' ' or First)							
11	Output = + Input[N − 1] First = true			'j'			true	
	...							
9	for N = 1 to Length do							k
10	if (Input[N − 1] <> ' ' or First)	true						
11	Output = + Input[N − 1] First = true			'j..k'			true	

The first question is crucial: Is loop termination guaranteed for any argument of WhileTest? If loop termination is not guaranteed, this logic could possibly cause an endless loop. This is obviously to be avoided. Proving that this condition is either true or false can sometimes be difficult, but it can be demonstrated by identifying every possible case and using trace tables to prove them if necessary. Often, however, this condition can be verified by inspection. It is essential when doing such checks informally to ensure all possible cases have been considered.

The second question is somewhat trickier. To determine if the WhileTest is true, it asks if the function WhileLoop is identical to a function that consists of LoopPart followed by WhileLoop. If this is not true, then WhileLoop has a defect. To understand why this is true, consult the Mills or Dyer references. [Dyer, Mills 87] As before, you answer the second question by constructing a trace table for WhileLoop and a trace table for LoopPart followed by WhileLoop and showing that they produce equal results.

The final question asks whether, when WhileTest is false the logic continues through WhileLoop with no changes. If it does not, there is a defect.

Example of While-loop Verification.   For the while-loop example, use the following pseudocode logic:

NormalizeReal(Mant, Exp, NegEx)

```
1    while Mant > 10 do
2      Mant  := Mant / 10
3        if NegEx then Exp := Exp − 1
4          else Exp := Exp + 1
5      while Mant < 1 do
6        Mant := Mant*10
7          if NegEx then Exp := Exp + 1
8            else Exp := Exp − 1
```

This logic is to reduce a nonzero real number in the form *Mantissa** $10^{Exponent}$ to a standard form in which the Mantissa has a single nonzero digit before the decimal point. In this problem, Mant = abs(Mantissa) and Exp = abs(Exponent). Thus Exp is a nonnegative integer and Mant is a positive real number. Two Boolean variables, NegMant and NegEx, indicate whether the Mantissa and/or the Exponent are negative. It is assumed that the values of these numbers are within the range of the number systems for the compiler and language being used.

To verify this logic, you must verify both while loops. Both loops are examined for question 1, but only the first loop is used to illustrate questions 2 and 3. First examine the while tests to see if they terminate. The cases to examine are for Mant $>$ 10, Mant $<$ 1, and 1 $=<$ Mant $<=$ 10. The first case is Mant $>$ 10. Here, when Mant $>$ 10 the first loop is executed and successive divisions by 10 ultimately reduce Mant to less than 10. The while test is then not satisfied and the first while loop terminates. Now, Mant is less than 10 and greater than 1 so the second while loop will not be invoked and the loop will terminate.

The second case is Mant $<$ 1. The first while loop is skipped and the second is invoked. Now Mant is progressively multiplied by 10 until its absolute value exceeds 1 and the second while test fails. This also terminates the loop.

Even though these two while loops terminate in these cases, this examination raises the questions of what happens when Mant $=$ 10 or Mant $=$ 1. In the first case, both loops fail with the incorrect result of Mant $=$ 10. The program thus has a defect, and line 1 should be changed as follows:

```
NormalizeReal(Mant, Exp, NegEx)
1    while Mant >= 10 do
2      Mant := Mant/10
3        if NegEx then Exp := Exp − 1
4          else Exp := Exp + 1
5      while Mant < 1 do
6        Mant := Mant*10
7          if NegEx then Exp := Exp + 1
8            else Exp := Exp − 1
```

When Mant $=$ 1, both loops are skipped and the number is unchanged. Because it is already in the correct form, this is the correct result. Both while loops in this procedure now satisfy question 1 of while-loop verification. The second question is, When WhileTest is true, does WhileLoop $=$ LoopPart followed by WhileLoop?

Answering this requires you to examine all cases of WhileTest and WhileLoop. To invoke the first while loop, the cases must all have Mant $>=$ 10. Because Mant must be a nonnegative number, this then involves only two conditions as follows:

1. Mant $>=$ 10, NegExp

2. Mant $>=$ 10, not NegExp

For the first case, the test consists of substituting the Mant and NegExp values into the program to see if the equality is correct or not. Thus you test to see if WhileLoop:

```
1    while Mant >= 10 do
2      Mant := Mant/10
3        if NegEx then Exp := Exp − 1
4          else Exp := Exp + 1
```

equals LoopPart followed by WhileLoop:

```
2    Mant := Mant / 10
3      if NegEx then Exp := Exp − 1
4        else Exp := Exp + 1
5    while Mant >= 10 do
6      Mant := Mant / 10
7        if NegEx then Exp := Exp − 1
8          else Exp := Exp + 1
```

This equality can be demonstrated with the trace table in Table 12.27. The first part of this equality in the top table cycles through the while test until the value of Mant is less than 10. If it started with Mant >= 10 and less than 100, for example, there would be one cycle of the while loop and the final result would be Mant/10 and Exp-1. Mant is now equal to or greater than 1 and less than 10.

Under these same conditions, with Mant between 10 and 100, the second part of the equality in the lower part of Table 12.27 would take one pass through LoopPart in steps 2 through 4, leaving the result of Mant/10 and Exp-1. In this case, the while test fails and steps 5 through 8 are not executed. In the general case, the while loop in the second part of the equality would be performed one less time than the first while loop, leaving the identical result. The equality is thus true.

The second verification case is identical except with not NegExp. Here, the results are identical except that the resulting Exp values are increased to Exp+1 when Mant starts between 10 and 100.

The cases for the second while loop, with Mant < 1, are handled the same way, so their verification is not repeated.

The third question for the while test is, When WhileTest is false, does WhileLoop = identity?

This condition can be demonstrated by inspection. The first while loop is

```
1    while Mant >= 10 do
2      Mant := Mant / 10
3        if NegEx then Exp := Exp − 1
4          else Exp := Exp + 1
```

Here, when Mant < 10 the entire loop is skipped and the step at 5 is next executed. This means that nothing is changed, and this logic is equivalent to identity. This same reasoning can be used with the second while loop.

The program with the change made to correct the defect when Mant = 10 thus passes these tests and is correct.

Repeat-until verification.   The repeat-until verification is similar to that for the while test. Before doing the repeat-until verification, identify the repeat-until preconditions and verify that they are always met. These tests assume repeat-until has the following form:

```
RepeatUntil
  begin
    LoopPart
    UntilTest
  end
```

The repeat-until verification questions are as follows:

1. Is loop termination guaranteed for any argument of `UntilTest`?

2. When `UntilTest` after `LoopPart` is false, does `RepeatUntil = LoopPart` followed by `RepeatUntil`?

3. When `UntilTest` after `LoopPart` is true, does `RepeatUntil = LoopPart`?

As before, you answer the second question by constructing a trace table for `RepeatUntil` and another trace table for `LoopPart` followed by `Repeat-Until`. The third question can be similarly answered with the aid of a trace table if needed.

Example of Repeat-until Verification. The verification for this case can be demonstrated with the repeat-until loop from the `ClearSpaces` logic specification template shown again in Table 12.28. The repeat-until loop is on lines 3 through 7. The preconditions require that `Length>0` and `State=0`. These are clearly satisfied by the earlier logic steps.

The first condition, that loop termination is guaranteed for all arguments of `UntilTest`, is obviously satisfied for all finite-length strings. String length is reduced by one for every trailing space until a nonspace is encountered. If such a character is encountered, State is set to 3 and the loop terminates. If the string has no such character, all the spaces will ultimately be tested and `Length` will be reduced to zero. Again, the loop will terminate.

The second question is, When `UntilTest` after `LoopPart` is false, does `LoopUntil = LoopPart` followed by `LoopUntil`?

Here, for `UntilTest` to be false, you are concerned only with the cases in which `Length > 0` and `State <> 3`. This condition can occur only when there are initially some number of spaces at the end of the string and they have not all yet been examined. This means that at least for the first pass from steps 3 to 7, a space was found in step 4, `Length` was reduced by 1, but not to 0, and `State` was increased from 0 to 1 or 1 to 2 but not to 3. The until test will then fail and the loop will be repeated. To demonstrate that the answer to this second question is yes under these conditions, compare the two situations in the trace table in Table 12.29. Start with the initial condition that `UntilTest` is false and see if both programs produce the identical result. In this case, it is clear from the trace table that they do, so the answer to the second question is yes.

TABLE 12.27 WHILE-LOOP TRACE TABLE VERIFICATION—CASE 1

#	Instruction	Condition	Input	Exp=E	NegExp	Mant=M
	Case: Mant >= 10	**NegExp = true**				
1	while Mant >= 10 do	true			true	M >= 10
2	Mant := Mant/10					M/10
3	if NegEx then Exp = Exp - 1	true		E - 1		
4	else Exp := Exp + 1					
	...k times			E - k - 1		M/10^{k+1}
1	while Mant >= 10 do	false				
2	Mant := Mant/10					
3	if NegEx then Exp = Exp - 1					
4	else Exp := Exp + 1					

TABLE 12.27 (continued)

Case: Mant >= 10		NegExp = true				
#	Instruction	Condition	Input	Exp=E	NegExp	Mant=M
2	`Mant := Mant/10`					M/10
3	`if NegEx then Exp = Exp - 1`	true		E − 1	true	
4	`else Exp := Exp + 1`					
5	`while Mant >= 10 do`	true				M >= 10
6	`Mant := Mant/10`					M/100
7	`if NegEx then Exp = Exp - 1`	true		E − 2		
8	`else Exp := Exp + 1`					
	`... k - 1 times`			E − k − 1		$M/10^{k+1}$
5	`while Mant >= 10 do`	false				
6	`Mant := Mant/10`					
7	`if NegEx then Exp = Exp - 1`					
8	`else Exp := Exp + 1`					

TABLE 12.28 CLEARSPACES LOGIC SPECIFICATION TEMPLATE (WITH SECOND FIX)

ClearSpaces(Input; State)

```
 1  Length = length(Input)
    State = 0
    Output = '', First=false

 2  if Length > 0

 3      repeat until (State = 3 or Length = 0)

 4          if Input[Length − 1] = ' ' {a space character
            at the end of the input string}

 5              Length = Length − 1

 6              if State < 2
                    State = State + 1

 7      else State = 3
        until (State = 3 or Length = 0)

 8  if Length > 0

 9      for N = 1 to Length do

10          if (Input[N − 1] <> ' ' or First)

11              Output = Output + Input[N − 1]
                First = true

12  Input = Output
```

The third question is, When UntilTest after LoopPart is true, does RepeatUntil = LoopPart?

For this test, we are concerned with cases where the UntilTest is passed when first encountered. This can only happen in two cases. Either the string is of length 1 with one space, or there are no spaces trailing some number of non-space characters. For these cases, RepeatUntil is identical to the LoopPart followed by RepeatUntil because the LoopPart will only be executed once. It will either pass the if test at step 4 and reduce length to 0 or it will fail the if test and set State to 3. RepeatUntil will then start with State=3 and no trailing spaces or with a one space message. In the first case, it will fail the if test on the first pass and then satisfy the UntilTest and terminate. In the second case, it will pass the if test, set Length to 0, satisfying the UntilTest, and terminate. Thus the same result is produced in both cases and the answer to question 3 is yes. The until loop has thus been demonstrated to be correct.

TABLE 12.29 REPEAT-UNTIL TRACE TABLE

Cycle: LoopUntil

#	Instruction	Condition	Input	Output	Length	State	First	N
3	repeat until (State = 3 or Length = 0)		'a..k'		k + n	0	false	
4	if Input[Length − 1] = ' '	true						
5	Length = Length − 1				k + n − 1			
6	if State < 2 State = State + 1	true				1		
7	else State = 3							
	until (State = 3 or Length = 0)	false						
...								
3	repeat until (State = 3 or Length = 0)		'a..k'		k	2		
4	if Input[Length − 1] = ' '	false						
5	Length = Length − 1							
6	if State < 2 State = State + 1							
7	else State = 3					3		
	until (State = 3 or Length = 0)	true						

TABLE 12.29 (Continued)

Cycle:		LoopPart followed by LoopUntil						
#	Instruction	Condition	Input	Output	Length	State	First	N
4	if Input[Length - 1] = ' '	true	'a..k'		k + n	0	false	
5	Length = Length - 1				k + n - 1			
6	if State < 2 State = State + 1	true				1		
7	else State = 3							
3	repeat until (State = 3 or Length = 0)		'a..k'					
4	if Input[Length - 1] = ' '	true						
5	Length = Length - 1				k + n - 2			
6	if State < 2 State = State + 1	true				2		
7	else State = 3 until (State = 3 or Length = 0)	false						

TABLE 12.29 (Continued)

Cycle:		LoopPart followed by LoopUntil						
#	Instruction	Condition	Input	Output	Length	State	First	N
	...				k			
3	repeat until (State = 3 or Length = 0)		'a.k'					
4	if Input[Length - 1] = ' '	false						
5	Length = Length - 1							
6	if State < 2 State = State + 1							
7	else State = 3					3		
	until (State = 3 or Length = 0)	true						

12.7   Comments on Verification Methods

While program verification can take time, with practice you can learn to work through these steps quite quickly. Often, it is unnecessary to use trace tables for simple cases. Since you should be absolutely certain that you have precisely verified all cases, however, you should use a trace table when you have any doubt about the logic's behavior. Even when you are confident the program is correct, it is a good idea to test one case. If you find a problem, you had best then do a complete verification.

In each of these examples, the verification was relatively simple and could be done quite quickly. While these steps are simple, their principal benefit is that they make you work through every possible case and ensure the design will handle each one properly. If an hour or so spent on such a proof reveals even a single defect, the time you spend will generally be more than repaid by the test time you save.

DESIGN VERIFICATION STRATEGY

One observation frequently raised about these verification methods is that they look more like verifying code than verifying design. Design logic must be represented precisely. For small programs like those in these examples, the pseudocode logic is thus quite close to the finished code. For more complex programs, the pseudocode logic will involve many higher level constructs and procedures. The logic for the various loop constructs, however, must be completely represented. As long as the intended behavior of all the high level constructs and procedures is known, the verification process is exactly as described in this chapter.

These comments, however, suggest a more general verification strategy. To ensure you don't waste verification time, you should design down and verify up, that is, as you design each routine, you specify the functions to be provided by each called object and method. If you verify your designs as you produce them, you should review the way you did the verification in your design reviews and inspections. If you have not already verified your designs, then you should start your design reviews at the bottom and verify each object or method before you verify the routines that use them. You can then be confident of the performance of each object or method before you encounter it in a higher level verification.

VERIFICATION THAT A PROGRAM CONFORMS
TO A SPECIFICATION

Whenever possible, you should have a precise specification for the design's intended function. This specification permits you to define the preconditions and ensure the logic properly handles every case. In many cases, however, you may not be able to get a precise specification and so will have to work with your less formal understanding of what the program is intended to do.

Regardless of the methods and notations you use, consider all possible logic cases and verify that they are correctly handled. Use whatever method you find most effective, but be sure to comprehensively review all possible conditions.

VERIFICATION COMPLEXITY

You do design reviews both to save time and to improve product quality. You thus need to be concerned with the time these methods take and the degree to which they produce high-quality results. Track the time verification takes and the degree to which it helps you to find design defects. Try whatever methods seem potentially most useful, but be guided by your data. After you have tried a method enough to build reasonable competence, if your data do not show that it works for you don't use it. You should, however, use some orderly and reliable method to verify all your program's logic.

FORMAL VERIFICATION METHODS

A number of mathematical methods have been developed for proving program correctness. [Baber, Gries, Spivey] Like the methods just discussed, these methods are also best used during program design. They can also be used during design reviews and inspections. When you verify your designs as you produce them, your design verification data can greatly accelerate your design reviews.

While the concept of reviewing designs for correctness seems attractive, it is appropriate to question the costs of these methods versus their benefits. These verification methods are human-intensive, so they are also subject to error. Unless you are sufficiently well versed in these methods to make fewer verification errors than design errors, they will be only marginally useful. To properly evaluate this question, you must thus practice each method until you are reasonably proficient. Then you should analyze your data and decide if the method helps you to do better work. As new verification methods are developed, you should also explore them and adopt those that are most effective for you.

12.8   Summary

When your designs are complete, clear, and correct, you can produce a quality implementation more efficiently. You verify your designs to determine if they meet the requirements and are correct. In addition to the program specifications, standards are an important part of verification. The pertinent standards concern product conventions, product design, and reuse.

When your product includes a state machine, you should verify that the machine is properly designed and consistently used. The conditions for a proper state machine are that all state conditions be complete and orthogonal, all the transitions from each state be complete and orthogonal, and the machine be able to reach a program return state from every other state. It is also important to examine the program's larger context to ensure all the state machines have been identified and consistently used.

There are several ways to determine the correctness of a design's logic before you implement and test it. Examples are execution tables, trace tables, and mathematical verification. While trace table verification can be time consuming, it is no more so than is identifying all the cases needed for a comprehensive logic test. If you plan to develop and run comprehensive tests, you may as well capitalize on that effort to verify the program's correctness. However, if you do not intend to run such tests then you certainly should do a very thorough design verification.

A growing body of literature deals with mathematical methods for proving program correctness. This chapter applied some of these concepts but in a simplified and less rigorous manner. Except for execution tables, formal mathematical methods are sophisticated and require considerable knowledge and skill. Until you become sufficiently versed in these methods to make fewer verification errors than you do design errors, they will not likely help you very much. Verifying design correctness is simple in concept, but it takes time to build sufficient skill to be confident that your verifications are complete and correct.

Because no single verification method has gained general acceptance, you should try various ones and decide which are best for you. Regardless of those you select, use them to validate your designs before you implement them. Since new verification methods will likely be introduced, you should track your validation effectiveness and experiment with any new methods that appear helpful. If you consistently verify your programs, you should ultimately learn to produce designs that have essentially no defects.

12.9 Exercises

The standard assignment for this chapter is to use PSP3 to finish developing program 10A. This program will likely be larger than those you have previously developed, so it is planned for two assignment periods. Its specifications are given in Appendix D, and the PSP3 process is described in Appendix C. In completing this assignment, you should faithfully follow the report submission format specified for PSP3.

For other assignment options, consult Appendix D.

References

[Baber] Robert L. Baber, *Error-Free Software, Know-how and Know-why of Program Correctness* (New York, John Wiley & Sons, 1991).

[Dyer] Michael Dyer, *The Cleanroom Approach to Quality Software Development* (New York: John Wiley & Sons, 1992).

[Gries] David Gries, *The Science of Programming* (New York: Springer-Verlag, 1981).

[Mills 87] Harlan D. Mills, Victor R. Basili, John D. Gannon, and Richard G. Hamlet, *Principles of Computer Programming, A Mathematical Approach* (Newton, MA: Allyn and Bacon, 1987).

[Spivey] J. M. Spivey, *The Z Notation: a Reference Manual* (Englewood Cliffs, NJ: Prentice Hall, 1992).

13

Defining the Software Process

So far in this book, you have used processes without worrying about where they came from. Processes, however, must be developed. Even for a simple PSP, this can take a lot of work. When you develop one to meet your own needs, however, the process development process can be simpler. You are, after all, the leading expert on what you want and what you will find most convenient and understandable.

Now that you have used the PSP to develop a number of small programs, you probably want to expand and adapt it to meet your future needs. For example, if you plan to develop a program of several thousand LOC, you may not feel the PSPs in this book are fully adequate. Alternatively, you may be working on a larger project or as part of a team and need to adapt the PSP to relate to other people's work. You could even develop a new process to perform a totally different task such as writing a report, building a database, conducting tests, or modifying an existing program.

This chapter covers process development concepts and outlines a procedure for defining personal processes. Several related topics are discussed to provide the background you will need to address the many new issues involved in moving beyond the predefined processes in this book.

13.1   Why Define Processes

You should consider defining a process when those you have are not adequate for the tasks you want to perform. This means that the process definition work must be intimately connected to what you want to do. If you don't have a clear idea of your objectives, it is hard to develop a process to meet them.

In general, you will want to use a process when your end objective is to perform some repetitive activity like writing a program, producing a report, analyzing a requirement, or running a test. In addition to producing products, however, you should also have process objectives, such as

□ to help you to plan and track your work,

□ to guide you in performing tasks, and

□ to help you to evaluate and improve the way you do your job.

The PSP has addressed these objectives for writing small programs. As you look beyond the exercises in this book, however, your process needs will change. And as you start to define or refine your processes, you need to be clear about your objectives.

13.2   Software Process Basics

Before I address process development issues, it is important to introduce some basic definitions. As in most technical fields, the process community has developed terms to describe its work. [Feiler] A brief summary of key process terms is given in Table 13.1. Read these definitions now and then refer to them as you encounter the terms in this chapter.

PROCESS ELEMENTS

A personal process contains the following items:

□ Scripts to describe how the process is enacted and to refer you to the pertinent standards, forms, guidelines, and measures.

□ Forms to provide a convenient and consistent framework for gathering and retaining data. They specify which data are required and where to record them.

TABLE 13.1 PROCESS TERMS

Term	Definition
Accuracy	The degree to which the product produced by the process matches the intended result
Agent	An entity that enacts a process definition. This entity may be a person following a process script or a machine executing a process program.
Development	The act of creating enactable processes. It may include planning, architecture, design, instantiation, and validation.
Enactable process	A process definition that includes all the elements required for enactment. An enactable process consists of a process definition, required process inputs, and assigned agents and resources.
Fidelity	The faithfulness with which a defined process is followed. Fidelity concerns the degree with which the agents performing the process exactly follow the defined actions.
Fitness	The degree to which the agents enacting the process can faithfully follow actions it specifies. A fit process is thus designed so that the enacting agent can faithfully follow it, while an unfit process may be so poorly represented as to be impractical, inconvenient, or unintelligible.
Precision	The degree to which the process definition specifies all the actions needed to produce accurate results, that is, a precisely defined process executed with fidelity produces an accurate result.
Process	A set of partially ordered steps intended to reach a goal
Process architecture	A conceptual framework for consistently incorporating, relating, and tailoring process elements into enactable processes
Process design (noun)	An embodiment of a process architecture that establishes the architectural options and parameters, the existing elements to be reused, the structure and behavior of the new elements, and the relationships among these elements. A process design may be for a specific project, an entire organization, or possibly for larger classes of projects or organizations.
Process definition	An implementation of a process design in the form of a partially ordered set of process steps that is enactable. At a lower level of abstraction, any process step may be further refined into more detailed process steps.
Process element	A component of a process. Process elements range from individual process steps to very large parts of processes.

TABLE 13.1   (continued)

Term	Definition
Process enactment	The performance of the process by the agent
Process script	A process definition that is suitably designed and instantiated for human enactment and including the steps needed to enact it
Process step	An atomic action of a process that has no externally visible substructure. A process step is a discrete, bounded activity of finite duration with a level of abstraction that depends on the enacting context.
Scalability	The breadth of activities for which the process definition is designed. This may include the ranges in numbers of people, size of product, time duration, product life cycle, or development environment for which the process is fit and precise.
Tailoring	The act of adapting process designs and process definitions to support the enactment of a process for a particular purpose

- Standards to guide your work and to provide a basis for verifying product and process quality. The PSP provides example coding and defect type standards as well as design review and code review checklists. While these are adequate for the example programs in this book, you should enhance them or develop new ones to fit your future needs.

- Process improvement provisions to help ensure your process will continue to meet your evolving needs. The Process Improvement Proposal (PIP) is an example of a process defect reporting procedure. It is a key part of the process improvement process, and you should include similar forms in every process you develop. A multi-person process should also include means for receiving, evaluating, and responding to PIPs as well as a periodic procedure for assessing and updating the process.

For the PSP, you are the process agent and when you develop software you are enacting your PSP process. These process elements are designed to help you to be more effective in doing your software work. Because it is your process, you can change it to better fit your needs. This chapter addresses some of the issues you should consider when you develop new processes or enhance existing ones.

PROCESS FORMATS

The purpose of a process is to provide a clear and succinct description of what you intend to do. Several language and modeling methods have been proposed for representing processes. [Kellner, Sutton] As this technology evolves, we will likely see many more tools and techniques for analyzing and defining processes. As your processes grow larger and more complex, you should be aware of these more advanced techniques and consider using them where they apply.

Sophisticated techniques are sometimes appropriate, but remember that programs are enacted by machines, while processes are principally enacted by people. Your primary objective is thus to make your processes understandable and usable. Remember your objectives and do not use some advanced method unless it clearly supports your needs. As you have seen with the PSP, you do not need to use fancy tools to produce useful processes. The methods used in this book are based on the techniques that Robert E. Horn calls information mapping. [Horn] The principles of information mapping are shown in Table 13.2. Initially use simple methods and adopt new techniques only when they will clearly help you. Focus on the process content and don't let the technology become too important.

Much like software development, process definition is a skill that you can learn and practice. As you gain experience in defining and using processes, you will soon see what tools and methods work best for you.

TABLE 13.2 PRINCIPLES OF INFORMATION MAPPING®[1] [HORN]

Chunking	Group information into manageable chunks.
Relevance	• Place "like things" together. • Exclude unrelated items from each chunk.
Labeling	Provide the reader with a label for each chunk of information.
Consistency	Use consistent • terms within each chunk of information, • terms in the chunk and label, • organization, and • formats.
Integrated graphics	Use tables, illustrations, and diagrams as an integral part of the writing.
Accessible detail	Write at the level of detail that will make the document usable for all readers.
Hierarchy of chunking and labeling	• Group small chunks around a single relevant topic. • Provide the group with a label.

[1]Information Mapping® is a registered trademark of Information Mapping, Inc., Waltham, MA.

13.3   Process Definition

You define a software process in much the way you develop a software product. You start with the users' needs and end with final test and release. For a personal process, the cycle is similar. The process is for your personal use, however, so the normal negotiation and support activities of most software projects are unnecessary. The steps for defining a personal process are as follows:

1. Determine your needs and priorities.
2. Define the process objectives, goals, and quality criteria.
3. Characterize your current process.
4. Characterize your target process.
5. Establish a process development strategy.
6. Define your initial process.
7. Validate your initial process.
8. Enhance your process.

Although these steps are listed in an order, they need not be done sequentially. It is likely, for example, that the needs, goals, and criteria steps will affect each other. Do them in whatever order is most appropriate for your situation; just make sure you address them all. The following sections discuss these steps in more detail.

DETERMINE YOUR NEEDS AND PRIORITIES

A software development process exists principally to produce software products. These, in turn, must satisfy some users' needs. Hence, your process definition should consider both your product and your process objectives. To ensure you do a complete and accurate job of addressing all these needs, you should follow an orderly procedure. While there are many ways to do this, the quality function deployment method (QFD) provides a consistent framework for relating your process characteristics to your users' product needs. [King, Zultner] In simple terms, the approach is as follows:

- Determine the nature of the products your process is to produce.
- Identify the principal product attributes.
- Determine the relative priorities of these product attributes.
- Determine the process features needed to produce these product attributes.
- Note whether the relationships between the process features and product attributes are strong, medium, or weak (S, M, W).

□ Categorize these process features into highest priority (HP), priority (P), needed (N), and not needed (NN).

Depending on your situation, you may follow these steps precisely or you may find that a less formal procedure is adequate. You should, however, think through each step.

The QFD method was devised to help engineers establish process improvement priorities for the design and manufacture of products. It has been widely used in the automobile industry, for example, to help engineers balance conflicting functional priorities. In the PSP, the process is much less complex and you seek somewhat different guidance. Your objective is to identify those improvements that will currently help you the most. This is important because you should limit yourself to a very few process changes at any one time.

The QFD method helps you to ensure your process priorities are sound. Starting with the highest priority product attributes, you include process actions to ensure these priority attributes are built into the product during its development. With well-defined product priorities, you are more likely to develop a process that is capable of producing quality products.

With the PSP, the product priorities are as follows:

Highest priority

□ Meet functional objectives.

□ Keep the number of defects to a minimum.

Priority

□ Require the minimum development time.

□ Complete development within the planned costs.

Needed

□ Produce easy-to-use products.

□ Provide reusable end products.

You next determine the process features needed to produce these product attributes. Here, a process feature may strongly influence the product attribute or may have a weak influence on the attribute. For the PSP, the process features included to meet the product priorities are shown in Table 13.3.

It is useful to use a mapping system to relate these process features to the product attributes. One approach is shown in Table 13.4. This is similar to, but simpler than, the House of Quality method used in QFD. [Zells] Here, an arbitrary weighting of 10, 4, and 2 is given to the Highest Priority, Priority, and Needed product features. Similarly, weightings of 10, 4, and 2 are given to the strong, moderate, and weak couplings among process features and product attributes. The entries in the table are then obtained by multiplying the priority by the coupling, giving you the relative rankings of several process features from a product requirements perspective as follows:

224: Design reviews

164: Code reviews

120: User scenarios

120: Test scenarios

40: Planning

20: Design documentation

20: Commenting practices

You now have a list of the process features you need to produce the kinds of products you desire. However, this is not the entire story. You should also have goals and priorities for your process.

DEFINE PROCESS OBJECTIVES, GOALS, AND QUALITY CRITERIA

Product attributes are critically important. However, they concern how the process meets business needs. Your process should also meet your needs. What

TABLE 13.3 MAP OF PROCESS FEATURES TO PRODUCT NEEDS

Highest Priority: Functional objectives met • Produce user scenarios to characterize the users' functional requirements (S). • Review the design for coverage of the requirements (S). • Review the code for coverage of the design (M). • Test the product against the user scenarios (S).
Highest Priority: Minimum number of defects • Strive for maximum process yield (S).
Priority: Minimize development time • Strive for maximum process yield (M).
Priority: Development cost within plan • Incorporate a defined project planning and tracking procedure (S).
Needed: Easy-to-use product • Consider principal user scenarios during the design (S). • Test the product against the user scenarios (S).
Needed: Reusable end product • Provide comprehensive design documentation (S). • Establish commenting practices (S). • Review to ensure the design and commenting practices are followed (M). • Strive for maximum process yield (M).

Note: The relationships among the process steps and the product features are as follows:
S—Strong
M—Medium
W—Weak

TABLE 13.4 MAPPING PROCESS FEATURES TO PRODUCT ATTRIBUTES

	Meet Functional Objectives (HP)	Minimum Defects (HP)	Minimum Development Time (P)	Cost within 10 percent of Plan (P)	Easy-to-Use Product (N)	Reuseable Product (N)	Totals
Values	10	10	4	4	2	2	
User Scenarios	S/100				S/20		120
Design Reviews	S/100	S/100	M/16			M/8	224
Code Reviews	M/40	S/100	M/16			M/8	164
Test Scenarios	S/100				S/20		120
Planning				S/40			40
Design Documentation						S/20	20
Commenting Practices						S/20	20

do you want from your process? Do you have personal improvement goals? Can you characterize what a good or bad process would look like? To define your process priorities, you first define process quality criteria. For the PSP, these are to develop quality software, to be measurable, and to be predictable.

If you do not have criteria for a quality process, you can now use the PSP quality criteria and your data to set up some. Establish preliminary objectives and consider what data you will need to define measurable long-term objectives and short-term goals. To incorporate these into your process improvement, produce process improvement priorities like those shown in Table 13.5. With these, you can construct another house of quality as shown in Table 13.6. Now, with Tables 13.4 and 13.6, you have two sets of process priorities: one mapping process features to product attributes and the other mapping process features to process attributes.

Depending on your preferences, you can combine these in various ways. If you consider the process attributes as more important than the product attributes, you could give them more weight in combining them. Conversely, you could weight the product attributes more heavily. In Table 13.7, the process and product priorities are simply added.

With a simple process like the PSP, you will not generally need to use sophisticated quality methods to determine improvement priorities. The advantage of the QFD method, however, is that it forces you to think of those process steps needed to accomplish each process and product objective.

Now that you have identified the principal process features, you next need to decide how to improve your process. To do this, you need to consider what you know about your process and where you feel you can make improvements. You can then establish measurable process criteria, establish long-term improvement objectives, and postulate short-term goals.

The PSP goals and objectives are shown in Table 13.8. Measurable criteria are given for each goal. While some of these measurements are simplistic, it is helpful to have goals that can be explicitly verified. A simple yes or no is often adequate, as with the goals for objectives 1 and 2. However, you should try to establish measurable criteria for every goal.

Following the goal-question-metric paradigm described in Chapter 7, you next define measures for these goals. Then, check the process to ensure it gathers the desired data. The PSP does this by providing a space on some form for each desired data element.

CHARACTERIZE YOUR CURRENT PROCESS

If you don't know where you are, a map won't help. [Humphrey 89] To improve human-intensive processes, you need to understand how they work currently. While the PSP provides a baseline for your software work, you need a clear picture of both where you are and where you want to go before you can sensibly establish a plan to get there.

TABLE 13.5 PSP PROCESS PRIORITY NEEDS

Highest Priority: Process improvement feedback
   • Time measurements (S)
   • Defect measurements (S)
   • PIP process (S)

Highest Priority: A planned and tracked process   • Incorporate comprehensive project planning and tracking (S).

Highest Priority: Maximum process yield
   • Use measured and managed design reviews (S).
   • Use measured and managed code reviews (S).

Priority: Minimize test and rework costs   • Maximize process yield (S).
Priority: Maximize process predictability   • Incorporate comprehensive project planning and tracking (S).

Needed: Minimum development resource
   • Use a defined design process (S).
   • Maximize process yield (S).
   • Incorporate comprehensive project planning and tracking (S).

Note: The relationships among the process steps and the product features are as follows:
    S—Strong
    M—Medium
    W—Weak

In general, your process improvement efforts will be most successful when you plan for multiple incremental improvements rather than a single drastic change. Hence you should not attempt to completely define a new process. If the task the process is to implement is one you currently perform, start with a simple definition of your current work and ask some questions about it:

1. How well do you understand the current process? Can you describe its principal steps, how they relate, and the time you spend on each?

2. Do you have serious problems with your current process? If so, list them and decide on their relative priorities.

3. Do the steps in your current process have explicit entry and exit criteria? Make these as specific as you can. If they are unstated or general, the process measurements will be poorly defined and not very helpful.

4. Is your current process planned and tracked? If you do not now consistently make project plans and track performance against them, this should be your initial improvement priority.

5. Is your current process sufficiently well measured to permit quantitative improvement plans? After introducing planning and defining entry and exit criteria, you should next incorporate time and quality measures in your current process.

TABLE 13.6 MAPPING PROCESS FEATURES TO PROCESS ATTRIBUTES

	Improvement Feedback (HP)	Planned and Tracked (HP)	Maximum Process Yield (HP)	Minimum Test and Rework (P)	Maximum Predictability (P)	Minimum Development Resource (N)	Totals
Values	10	10	10	4	4	2	
Time Measurements	S/100						100
Defect Measurements	S/100						100
PIP Process	S/100						100
Planning		S/100			S/40		160
Design Reviews			S/100	S/40		S/20	160
Code Reviews			S/100	S/40		S/20	160
Defined Design Process						S/20	20

TABLE 13.7 COMBINING PRODUCT AND PROCESS PRIORITIES

Process Feature	Product Priority	Process Priority	Total = Product + Process
Time Measurements		100	100
Defect Measurements		100	100
PIP Process		100	100
Planning	40	160	200
Design Reviews	224	160	384
Code Reviews	164	160	324
Design Documentation	20		20
Defined Design Process		20	20
User Scenarios	120		120
Test Scenarios	120		120
Commenting Practices	20		20

6. Do you have a current process baseline? For the PSP, you now have productivity, quality, and planning data. If you do not have such data on your new process, get some as quickly as you can.

Even if you do not have historical data, you can often find some with modest effort. You can generally estimate your past performance by reconstructing the dates when you did the work and measuring or estimating the sizes of the products produced. Such rough numbers will not be very accurate, but they will give you a sense for general performance magnitudes. These are a poor substitute for precise data, but they are better than nothing.

CHARACTERIZE YOUR TARGET PROCESS

"If you don't know where you are going, any road will do." [Humphrey 89] The target process is your ideal. It is the goal to which you seek to evolve. You characterize your target process as a basis for setting improvement priorities. You then relate your process goals and objectives to this target. If minimum cycle time is the highest priority, for example, you will try to establish parallel activities, perhaps even at additional cost. On the other hand, a goal to minimize late requirements changes would suggest early steps to validate the requirements with selected users.

TABLE 13.8 EXAMPLE PSP GOALS AND OBJECTIVES

Objective 1: Learn how to produce an effective PSP.
Goal 1.1: PIPs submitted for all improvement suggestions
Goal 1.2: A process development process in use
Goal 1.3: Process development data gathered and being used
Objective 2: Obtain comprehensive process data.
Goal 2.1: A final report on each project
Goal 2.2: A database for all defect data
Goal 2.3: A database for all plan and actual project data
Objective 3: Achieve high process and product quality.
Goal 3.1: Overall inspection yield better than 80 percent
Goal 3.2: Test defects below 5/KLOC
Goal 3.3: Compile time less than 2% of development time
Objective 4: Produce a highly predictable process.
Goal 4.1: Average estimate to actual error of under 25 percent

Next, postulate the target process structure and identify its principal elements. Here, your focus should be on characterization. You seek measurable criteria for the major process elements. At the outset, you may establish only very general criteria. An example might be that your target process be fully defined, that it predictably produce quality products, and that every process phase be characterized and measured. To be most helpful, at least some of these measurements should be available for your current process. This will help you to decide on an improvement strategy and to set achievable intermediate milestones.

Don't be too concerned if you have trouble defining a target process. You will likely find that the only way to learn how to characterize a process is to start to characterize it. Initially, you may not know how to start. You could examine other processes or see what I did for the PSP. As you gain process development experience, however, this will change. When you have defined a baseline process, used it, measured it, and analyzed its behavior, you will then see how to set measurable long-term objectives. You will also have the data with which to establish suitably challenging short-term goals.

When you have characterized your target process, ask some questions about it:

□ Which steps are new and which do you currently perform?

□ Which steps do you now understand and which are ill-defined?

□ Which steps will you frequently repeat and which will be single shots?

□ Which steps will consume the most time?

□ Where do you expect the most problems?

Use the answers to guide your prototype studies and improvement priorities.

ESTABLISH A PROCESS DEVELOPMENT STRATEGY

Now that you know where you are and where you want to go, establish the route. Even simple processes have many steps, and they are not all equally important. Start by defining those things you generally know how to do. If some steps are vague or confusing, observe them or talk to people who might better understand them. One approach is to pick steps that someone has performed successfully. If you have no one to learn from, produce a simple definition and prototype it. If that isn't possible, find the most knowledgeable people on the subject and hold a technical review. Or observe someone doing the process and record what they do and how long they take. You can, of course, even observe yourself. Remember that defining some general conceptual process that no one understands will not likely be of much help when you are doing the work.

To set your improvement priorities, ask some new questions and repeat some of the same questions you asked about your target process:

- Which steps do you understand and which are ill defined?
- Which steps are frequently repeated and which are single shots?
- Which steps take the most time?
- Which steps are the source of the most quality problems?
- Which steps are the source of the most planning and tracking problems?
- Which steps are the source of the most technical problems?

To provide the data you need for continuing process improvement, include the following initial priorities in your process development strategy:

- Start with a project planning phase. This is an essential first step because it helps to make your process predictable. You cannot consistently manage or improve an unpredictable process.
- Include basic resource and product measures such as time spent by phase, LOC produced, pages of documentation produced, and so on.
- If practical, include quality measures such as defects by phase or user reported problems.
- Include in the project plans documented estimates for all measured items.
- Define planning and reporting forms for these items.
- Define a final report to summarize project results, report key process findings, and suggest process improvements.
- Define a postmortem phase for recording and analyzing the data, producing a final report, and submitting process improvement proposals.

DEFINE YOUR INITIAL PROCESS

Now that you have characterized your current and target processes and established your objectives, goals, and strategy, you next produce the scripts, standards, and forms for the initial process. This initial process should be relatively close to your current process but should include a few changes that will move you towards your target. While you should establish aggressive improvement plans, it is almost impossible to make more than a very few changes at any time.

In defining your initial process, you will find it helps to follow an abstraction procedure. Start by defining the entire process as a single step that includes multiple tasks. Next, define a subprocess for each task. Continue this refinement procedure until you reach a refinement level that is reasonably consistent with your current process knowledge and needs.

There would be little point, for example, in defining a process step if it is not a current problem area. On the other hand, if you do not understand some process area you cannot define it in much detail. The appropriate definition level is as deep as you can knowledgeably go in the areas that cause you the most trouble. Define what you know and then carry the definition a little further. This helps you to learn about this step when you next perform it. This will give you ideas about how to further refine it the next time.

For example, with the PSP you started with only general planning, development, and postmortem steps. The first enhancements focused on planning. Measures were introduced to ensure the appropriate data were gathered and measurement and estimating techniques were introduced. The postmortem step then ensured the data were retained and analyzed.

The next PSP improvement refined the design, design review, code, and code review steps. While the PSP evolution stopped at this point, you could further refine any or all of these steps as you learn more about them. You could, for example, extend the design process to cover a particular design method. This could help you match the design templates to your design methods and provide you data on how you spend your time or where you make errors.

VALIDATE YOUR INITIAL PROCESS

Next, test your process. First, walk through a simulated enactment using data from a project you have recently completed. If you do not have all the needed data, assume some and do a walk-through. Next, try the process on a small project or a prototype. The better the test, the more likely you are to flush out problems.

13.4   Defining Process Phases

The definition of a process phase includes the following items:

Purpose: Why is this phase performed?

Responsible agent: Who enacts this process phase? For the PSP, this is you.

Entry criteria: Which inputs are needed and what conditions must be satisfied before starting the phase and who is responsible for each? Also, what process elements are needed and where do they come from?

Tasks: Which subprocess tasks are performed and where are they described?

Exit criteria: Which conditions must be satisfied at phase exit, what outputs are produced, and where do those outputs go?

Next phase: Which steps come next and what are the conditions or selection criteria among them?

You can answer these questions in any convenient way, but you must know the answers before you can fully define a process phase. A standardized format such as that shown in Table 13.9 can help in answering them. When an answer is too voluminous, expand the form or add references. The Phase Definition Template is a convenient place to record information about a process phase while you are developing it. It is a design document, however, and is not used in enacting the process.

You start the definition process by completing a phase definition template for the entire process. Assuming you want to make further refinements, complete another template for one or more of the tasks in this highest level template. Once you have reached the desired refinement level, you can produce the process scripts. Finally, you produce and validate the necessary forms, templates, and standards.

This top-down phase definition sequence is the easiest to explain, but it is not the only way to define processes. For example, you may want to start with some low-level subprocess and then connect it to the higher level processes. This could be appropriate when your work is part of some larger ill-defined process. Rather than trying to define the entire operation, you could choose to first define the part of the process that you control. Another reason to start at the bottom and work up is when one phase is particularly troublesome and you want to improve it. Whatever approach you follow, set up an overall process context as soon as you can. This provides the framework for establishing entry and exit criteria, goals, and measurements. Until these are all in place, you will not have an adequate foundation for continued process improvement.

An example of a completed PSP Phase Definition Template is shown in Table 13.10.

TABLE 13.9 PHASE DEFINITION TEMPLATE

Author _____   Date _____

Process _____   Phase _____

Purpose _____

Responsible Agent _____

Entry

Condition	Responsibility

Input Items	Sources

Tasks

Name	References

Exit

Condition

Product Names	Destinations

Next

Name	Conditions

TABLE 13.10 PSP3 DESIGN REVIEW PHASE DEFINITION

Author   W. S. Humphrey   Date   July 30, 1993

Process   PSP2   Phase   Design Review

Purpose   To define the design review phase of the PSP2 process

Responsible Agent   The development programmer

Entry

Condition	Responsibility
Complete design specifications	Programmer
Complete program design	Programmer

Input Items	Sources
Design standards	Process
Defect type standard	Process
Design review checklist	Process
Design review script	Process
Time and defect logs	Process

Tasks

Name	References
Follow checklist.	DLDR Checklist—C57
Correct all defects.	
Check the corrections.	DLDR Checklist—C57
Record defect data.	Defect Type Standard—C20

Exit

Condition	
Completed checklist	
Corrected design	
Corrected specifications (if needed)	
Completed time and defect logs	
Product Names:	Destinations:
Corrected design	Next phase
Completed checklist	Next phase
Product Names:	Destinations:
Defect log	Postmortem
Time log	Postmortem

Next

Name	Conditions
Implementation phase	All exit criteria

13.5   Process Development Considerations

There is nothing more annoying than a process definition that prescribes some complex procedure that you can't understand or remember. At the time you wrote it, you may have known exactly what you intended, but if you did not explain it in terms that will later be clear, it is not a fit process. You can also go too far in the other direction. There is no value in defining steps in great detail if a simple summary provides all the information you need for the task.

Design the process at just the level you need to guide your work. If it provides helpful reminders and useful guidance, you are more likely to use it. People get careless when they follow routine procedures. They want simple directions and checklists to remind them of all the steps. Remember, you are defining the process to help you follow it more faithfully. You thus must decide where you need guidance, where reminders are adequate, and where you need no help. You will quickly become proficient at any repetitive process, so make sure it is convenient during intense use but also helpful when you need guidance and reminders.

Start with a simple process and gradually enhance it. If you make the process too comprehensive, you will do a lot of unnecessary work. When you first use the process, you will find it went into detail where you didn't need it and that it didn't help where it should have. In defining processes, you will unconsciously describe steps you understand and skip over those you do not. Your needs, however, are the reverse. Until you make trial definitions, you will not know enough to provide detail where it will be of most help.

One example is the code review checklist. Without historical data, you would not know what to include. While you could start with the checklist in the text, it may not fit your needs. From reviewing your PSP data, you can set preliminary review priorities and make a first draft checklist. After using the checklist, you can then see where to refine it. You could initially call for a general punctuation review and then later list specific punctuation marks.

Forms are more difficult to design than you may expect. To be convenient, a form must capture the essence of the task being performed. If you do not understand the task, you cannot design a good form. Forms design takes time, and your first pass will rarely be complete or convenient. The best advice is to produce a simplified form and then to elaborate, revise, and enhance it as you use it.

This evolutionary principle applies to the entire process. Produce a simple initial process, then elaborate, revise, and enhance it as you gain experience. View every process enactment as a test. Record all your improvement ideas in PIPs and use these PIPs to guide your next process update.

You define a process to help you to understand it. Process definition is an experiment in which you almost know the answer. You should generally know how the job should be done, but you should not have defined the precise steps. You start with an experimental definition that extends the process in a direction you think would improve it. When you perform it, you may find that some ideas worked as expected and that others need to be changed. Such learning is an inherent part of process definition. As you evolve your process, focus on your current needs. When your knowledge and skills improve, you must improve your process.

13.6   Process Evolution

It is practically impossible to produce a usable process the first time you try. The problem is that the work required to define a process changes that process. This concept is best explained by thinking of the four processes shown in Fig. 13.1. The perceived process is what you think you do. If you have not defined your process, you will have an idealized perception of it. In any complex activity, we often know what we should do. In doing it, however, we always encounter complications. You may be rushed and skip a review, or you may defer a design update. If someone were to ask you what you did, you would probably not mention all these "exceptions."

The actual process is what you do, with all its omissions, mistakes, and oversights. The official process is what the book says you are supposed to do. That process may be out of date or totally impractical, but it is what your management would describe as your process. The fourth process is your target process. This is your objective—the ideal you would like to reach.

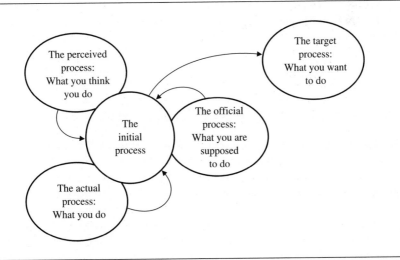

FIGURE 13.1
The Four Processes

When you first define your process, your objective should be an initial one that both represents reality and moves you in the direction of your target process. Generally, however, it will be close to your perceived process. But when you try it, the shortcuts and omissions will stand out. This realization will change what you do. You will recognize areas that lack discipline and resolve to do better next time. When you adjust the first definition, you thus will again define what you should do rather than what you actually did. After repeating this cycle several times, your process and your actions will converge on a realistic initial process.

While you will not likely converge on either your perceived or your actual process, your initial process will be a more disciplined and stable starting point. This is one reason why defined processes are of higher quality than are undefined ones. The act of defining them makes the oversights and omissions more obvious. This raises process fidelity and improves performance. The principal reason our processes are so poor is that we often don't do what we know we should.

You cannot usefully evolve your process definition until it reasonably represents what you do. When it does, you can measure your performance, identify areas for improvement, and make useful process changes. When your actual, official, and perceived processes converge on your initial process, you will find your process improvements most successful.

13.7 The Process Development Process

Process development is a task that can be defined, planned, measured, tracked, and improved. Just as with software, defining the process definition tasks helps you to be more efficient and to better plan and manage your work. The principles that helped in software process development also help in defining process development. Even for a personal process, there is a lot to do. A defined process development process helps you in both planning and doing this work.

A SIMPLE PROCESS DEVELOPMENT PROCESS

A simple process development process is shown in Fig. 13.2. It follows the steps just described for improving the software process. Its key feature is the Process Improvement Proposal (PIP) that was introduced with PSP0.1 to record process problems and improvement suggestions. Many process problems concern minor details. Such details, however, make the difference between an inconvenient process and an efficient one. While you may remember that some form or step was a problem, you will forget the details if you do not promptly record them. Keep blank PIP forms at hand and promptly record each of your process

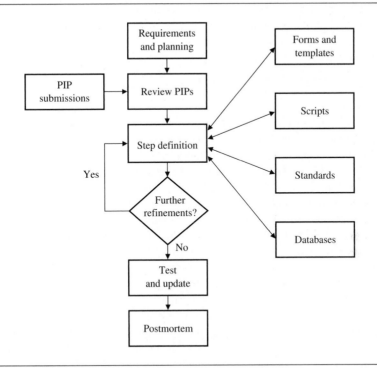

FIGURE 13.2
A Process Development Process

improvement ideas. Surprisingly, if you even wait a few minutes, the idea will be hard to remember. With a personal process, details are important. To fix the details, you must religiously complete PIPs. PIPs provide an invaluable source of improvement ideas, even for a personal process.

PROCESS DEVELOPMENT GUIDELINES

The guidelines for producing an effective process development process are the same as for the software process:

- ☐ Start with a simplified process definition.
- ☐ Include a planning step.
- ☐ Record the development time for each major step and product category.
- ☐ Keep track of the numbers of product items produced in each category.
- ☐ Define productivity measures. Examples are minutes per form, script, or standard.

□ Keep a record of each process development.

□ Produce a summary report for each process development.

PROCESS DEVELOPMENT DATA

An example of the summary data I have gathered in developing my latest PSP process version is given in Table 13.11, which shows the numbers of process elements produced and the amount of time planned and actually spent. A total of 42 items were developed. The total development time was 63.12 hours. These totals are within 10 percent of the estimated 40 items and 67 hours.

In making process development plans, you will find it most convenient to base estimates on overall rates that include all process phases. These measurements are for the time you spend on the requirements, design, test, update, and postmortem. For development, however, you should separately record your design time for forms, scripts, and standards. When you test the process or do a postmortem, however, it is not practical to split your time among the forms, scripts, and standards. You thus record design, definition, and review time by process item but record only total time for the rest of the process phases.

To provide an actual rate for making process development plans, you must allocate the overhead time for these other phases proportionately to each product item. The following steps show one way to make a process development time allocation. This description uses the data in Table 13.11:

1. Estimate the number of items to be produced in each of the following categories:

   □ Forms and templates—17

   □ Scripts—20

   □ Standards—3

2. Using historical data, estimate the number of minutes each item definition will likely take.

   □ Forms and templates—120

   □ Scripts—90

   □ Standards—60

3. Calculate the total estimated time in minutes for each item.

   □ Forms and templates—17*120 = 2040

   □ Scripts—20*90 = 1800

   □ Standards—3*60 = 180.

4. Total these item times to give the total estimated process development time: 2040 + 1800 + 180 = 4020

TABLE 13.11   PROCESS DEVELOPMENT PLAN DATA

Process: PSP7 _____   Author: WSH _____

Date: 1/4/93 _____   Job#:   113 _____

Resource Estimate:	Estimated	Actual
Requirements Definition and Plan	120	229
Design, Definition, and Review	3400	2687
Instantiation and Test	200	502
Update and Review	200	273
Postmortem	100	96
Total Time—minutes	4020	3787
hours	67	63.12

Number of Items:	Estimated			Actual Direct		
	Number	Rate	Total Time	Number	Rate	Total Time
Forms, Templates	17	120	2040	13	98.3	1278
Scripts	20	90	1800	19	41.8	794
Standards	3	60	180	10	61.5	615
Total Items	40		4020	42		2687

Allocation:	Direct Minutes	Allocated Minutes	Total Minutes	Total Items	Total Rate
Forms, Templates	1278	523	1801	13	138.5
Scripts	794	325	1119	19	58.9
Standards	615	252	867	10	86.7
Databases					
Total Time (minutes)	2687	1100	3787		

PIPs Used:				
Author:	PIP #	Items	Date	Project
WSH		17		
PS		21		
CS		3		
JM		26		
RS		7		
Total:		74		

5. Based on historical data, divide this total time among the various process development phases.

6. Develop the process and record the total time you spent on each step. For the Design, Definition, and Review step only, measure the time by item type.

At this point, you have the actual and estimated data shown in Table 13.12. The problem is that these actual rates for the product items include only the time spent in the Design, Definition, and Review step and not all the other times. Because you will need overall rates in order to plan future process developments, you must allocate the requirements, test, update, and postmortem costs to each process item. You can do this as shown in the allocation section of Table 13.11 as follows:

1. Enter the direct times for each item type in the allocation section in the spaces under direct minutes.
   - Forms and templates—1278
   - Scripts—794
   - Standards—615
   - Total—2687

2. Enter the total actual time you spent in process development in the allocation section under total minutes: 3787.

3. Find the difference between the total direct minutes and the total minutes and enter this amount in the total time space under allocated minutes: $3787 - 2887 = 1100$.

4. Divide this allocated time among the process items in the same proportion as for the direct time.
   - Forms and templates—$1100*1278/2687 = 523$
   - Scripts—$1100*794/2687 = 325$
   - Standards—$1100*615/2687 = 252$

5. Add together the direct and allocated minutes to give the total minutes for each process item.
   - Forms and templates—$1278 + 523 = 1801$
   - Scripts—$794 + 325 = 1119$
   - Standards—$615 + 252 = 867$

6. Enter the actual total number of items produced in each category under total items.
   - Forms and templates—13
   - Scripts—19
   - Standards—10

TABLE 13.12 PROCESS DEVELOPMENT PLAN

Process: PSP7   Author: WSH

Date: 1/4/93   Job#: 113

Resource Estimate:	Estimated	Actual
Requirements Definition and Plan	120	229
Design, Definition, and Review	3400	2687
Instantiation and Test	200	502
Update and Review	200	273
Postmortem	100	96
Total Time—minutes	4020	3787
hours	67	63.12

Number of Items:	Estimated			Actual Direct		
	Number	Rate	Total Time	Number	Rate	Total Time
Forms, Templates	17	120	2040	13	98.3	1278
Scripts	20	90	1800	19	41.8	794
Standards	3	60	180	10	61.5	615
Total Items	40		4020	42		2687

Allocation:	Direct Minutes	Allocated Minutes	Total Minutes	Total Items	Total Rate
Forms, Templates					
Scripts					
Standards					
Databases					
Total Time (minutes)					

PIPs Used:

Author:	PIP #	Items	Date	Project
WSH		17		
PS		21		
CS		3		
JM		26		
RS		7		
Total:		74		

7. For each item, divide the total minutes by the total items to give the total rate:

- ☐ Forms and templates—1801/13 = 138.5
- ☐ Scripts—1119/19 = 58.9
- ☐ Standards—867/10 = 86.7.

8. These are the actual rates you spent on this process development. You next combine these with your data on prior process developments to arrive at new rates for the next project. For example, if your prior time for each form and template was 120 minutes, you may decide to average this with the actual rate of 138.5 minutes and select a new planning rate of about 130 minutes.

This allocation process may seem complex, but it takes only a few minutes once you have the data and a properly designed form. It is also more convenient than tracking the planning, test, review, and postmortem times by process item. Further, it is more accurate than doing a multiple regression of the times for several completed process development projects to determine development rates for each process element type.

As you do more process development work, you will soon find that you will more often modify forms, scripts, and standards than develop new ones. In the example shown in Table 13.11, all the times were for modification, not for new development. Modifying existing process elements is generally easier than producing new ones, so it is helpful to separately measure these development times. If you track your time this way, you can then use separate rates for new development and modification. Doing this will also help to make your process development plans more accurate.

13.8   Summary

Software process development is much like software development. It has similar artifacts and requires many of the same disciplines and methods. The steps for designing a process are to define the needs, establish goals, and define quality criteria. You next characterize the current and target processes and establish a development strategy. Finally, you define and validate the initial process and establish means for its enhancement.

It is practically impossible to produce a usable process the first time you try. The problem is that the work you do to define a process changes the process. This concept is best explained by thinking of the following four processes: the perceived process is what you think you do, the actual process is what you actually do, the official process is what management thinks you do, and the target process is the process to which you are evolving. A principal reason the quality of our processes is so poor is that we often don't do what we know we should. This point is important because you cannot evolve your process until it reasonably represents what you are doing.

Process development should be planned, measured, tracked, and improved. Guidelines for an effective process development process include planning and measuring your work, tracking the products you produce, and recording the time you spend by each major product type and development category. To plan your process development, you must define productivity measures, use these measures to plan your work, and keep a development record. Finally, you should produce a summary report for each process development.

13.9 Exercises

The standard assignment for this chapter requires that you produce a final report on your process. This work includes three tasks: to update the process you developed for the midterm report R4, to plan the effort to produce the final report, and to produce the report. For the details of the assignment, consult the specifications for report R5 in Appendix D.

For other assignment options, consult Appendix D.

References

[Feiler 92] P. H. Feiler and W. S. Humphrey, "Software Process Development and Enactment: Concepts and Definitions," *SEI Technical Report* CMU/SEI-92-TR-04 (September 1992).

[Horn] Robert E. Horn, *Developing Procedures, Policies, and Documentation* (Waltham, MA: Information Mapping, Inc., 1990).

[Humphrey 89] W. S. Humphrey, *Managing the Software Process* (Reading, MA: Addison-Wesley, 1989).

[Kellner] M. I. Kellner, "Representation Formalisms for Software Process Modeling," Proceedings of the 4th International Software Process Workshop, *ACM Press* (1988): 93–96.

[King] Bob King, *Better Design in Half the Time, Implementing QFD Quality Function Deployment in America, Third Edition* (Methuen, MA: GOAL/QPC, 1989).

[Sutton] S. M. Sutton, Jr., D. Heimbigner, and L. J. Osterweil, "Language constructs for managing change in process-centered environments," *SIGSOFT Software Engineering Notes*, vol. 15, no. 6 (Dec. 1990): 206–217.

[Zells 92] Lois Zells, "Learning from Japanese TQM Applications to Software Engineering," *Total Quality Management for Software*, Ed. by G. Gordon Schulmeyer and James I. McManus (New York: van Nostrand Reinhold, 1992).

[Zultner] Richard E. Zultner, "Software QFD, The First Five Years, Lessons Learned," ASQC Annual Quality Congress, Las Vegas, NV (May 1994).

14

Using the Personal
Software Process

Now that you have learned how to manage your personal software process, your next step is deciding how to use it. In considering this question, weigh the costs involved in using a PSP and use it where the expected benefits are more than the likely costs. By consciously making this cost-benefit trade-off, you will be better prepared to stick with your new process until it is fully effective. With such conviction, you will also be better able to maintain the discipline to follow your process. This chapter discusses the costs and benefits of using a PSP and some of the issues you will likely face in using it in a software organization.

14.1 Making Personal Commitments

In a software organization, you will often be pressured into schedule commitments that you think are unreasonable. The problem is that management wants products *now* at zero cost. It knows this is unrealistic, but it will push until either you agree to a plan it feels is reasonable or you convince these managers your plan is the best they can expect. Some managers believe that heavy pressure is always required to make engineers produce realistic plans. While most managers will be reasonable, few will have a sound basis for deciding what is a good plan.

They may ask for a few expert opinions, but they will primarily depend on how you act when you present your plan.

MAKING PLANS

The only way most managers know to get good plans is to ask the best people they can find to produce them. Thus when they asked you to make a plan, they must have thought you could do a good job. Regardless of your plan, however, they will aggressively push until you convince them it is as tight a plan as they can realistically expect. So you should prepare yourself to handle the pressure.

Today, few software professionals know how to deal with unreasonable schedule demands. By following disciplined personal practices, however, you can assess a new task and make a realistic plan to address it. If your plan does not meet management's objectives, you have a fully documented plan and historical data to support it. While these details will help, what will convince management is your conviction that this is what the job will take. You should willingly accept aggressive challenges, but you must draw a line between a feasible challenge and a ridiculous one. The knowledge of what the job will take gives you the strength to stand up for your convictions and the authority to be convincing.

HANDLING PRESSURE

The proper approach to handling pressure depends on the situation. Often you will be given a cost or schedule target. You might be told something like, "This is a critical project, and we must deliver in under a year." While this guidance will not help you to make an objective plan, management really does believe that a tight plan is needed and they might even believe that delivery in less than 12 months is essential. Often, the engineer who is charged with making this plan will be so cowed that he or she will come back in a few days with a flimsy plan to deliver the product in 12 months. The manager's actions at this point are critical. Some managers will be so relieved to get what they wanted that they will buy the plan. Often, however, the manager will shoot the plan so full of holes that the engineer will have to start over, but with a lot less time to do it right.

The managers don't know what schedule is right. If they knew, they would not waste time having you produce a plan. They want the tightest plan that will actually deliver the product. They also need a competent authority (you) who says this is what the job will take. And regardless of the quality of your plan, your name will be tied to that plan from then on.

Only the dumbest managers want a flimsy plan that can't be met. They have business commitments, and timely delivery is important. Product schedules are the foundation for revenue and expense projections. The managers may blame you for the fiasco. However, if there are too many fiascos, they will lose their jobs. Your most successful course is to strive to produce a good plan, regardless of the pressure. Then defend it.

A STRATEGY FOR DEFENDING YOUR PLAN

In defending your plan, you might make statements like this:

- ☐ This is the best plan I can make to meet the requirements I was given. I can review the plan assumptions and the historical data on which this plan is based and show you comparisons with similar projects. I think you will then agree that this is a tight but reasonable plan.

- ☐ If you want to change the requirements or the assumptions, I will reexamine the plan to see how such changes could alter the result.

- ☐ This is a minimum cost plan. If you are more concerned about schedule, we could save time but at added cost. I could develop some schedule options if you could tell me what cost premium you would consider.

You might even have an alternative plan prepared in advance. One manager, on being presented the plan for a proposed contract was convinced that the schedule was too long. He asked the planners to go back to work to see what it would take to reduce it by 25 percent. When the planners later returned to the manager, they proposed several technical, administrative, and requirements changes. The manager agreed to the changes, the proposal was submitted, and they won the contract. He then made the agreed upon changes, and the project was completed ahead of the accelerated schedule.

The key point is to do your utmost to be responsive. You have done a thorough job, but you are unwilling to commit to a plan that you cannot meet. You will examine any alternatives and do whatever you can to help solve the problem, but you will resist any edicted cuts that are not based on changes in the job. Remember that in the long run, a disaster will be blamed on you. If you must, dig in your heels and refuse to commit. Remember, however, that you are paid to do what management directs, so don't refuse to do the job. Just refuse to commit to an unreasonable schedule.

14.2   Using the PSP in an Organization

You will find it easier and more rewarding to use the PSP when your associates are similarly disciplined. If you work in an organization that supports your effort to improve, you are more likely to find similarly motivated associates. Even when you work alone, you can still use the PSP to help you manage your own performance and to provide the historical data you need to handle management pressure.

THE SOLO PSP PERFORMER

When you are the only person using a PSP, your biggest problem will be maintaining a consistent discipline. This is hard to do under the best conditions, and it is particularly difficult to do by yourself. While your peers will likely be interested in what you are doing, they also will be skeptical. Normal statistical fluctuations will take on greater significance and the occasional poor result, instead of being a learning experience, will seem like a major reverse. Your friends may laugh at your discomfort and you will likely regret ever discussing the PSP. If you are not sure of the PSP's benefits, you could have trouble continuing to use it without support. Hence your initial focus should be on building a performance record. Don't worry about convincing anybody else of the value of the PSP until you have convinced yourself.

With an experience record, you have something to discuss. While your data will still fluctuate, you will have enough of a record to put these variations in perspective. But try not to seem critical of anyone else. If you suggest that your methods are better than someone else's, you are implying that their methods are worse. Be open with your results, but concentrate on what works for you. You invite problems when you argue that your results will apply to others. Urge them to gather their own data and to see for themselves. Once they do, then you can debate the facts.

When your performance is better than someone else's, your data then become threatening. However, if your associates think they now do better than you do, they will not be impressed. They probably don't know their performance, and they are likely to compare your routine performance with their best. Even if you are a star, your data may not look that convincing. Such a static comparison misses the point. You are not trying to show that you are better or worse than anybody else. The power of the PSP is that it teaches you about yourself. Your work is more consistent and predictable, and you can demonstrate sustained improvement.

One strategy for interesting your peers in the PSP is to ask them to help you. Get them to review your plans, your designs, or your code. Show them that the PSP is a continuous learning process. While you would be happy to advise them or to share your findings, they are the experts on what works for them. After you have established your own credibility, you can consider discussing such PSP facets as estimating methods, defect management, and process benchmarking.

Software professionals are just starting to learn about disciplined engineering behavior. Intuitive planning and ad hoc development have seemed normal.

With luck, and a little persistence on your part, you may be able to convince one or two members of your team to try some PSP techniques. As they define and measure their work, they may see some benefits. Emphasize, however, that the PSP is not a simple tool or technique. It is a discipline that takes time to learn and practice to perfect. Your improvement took several months. Theirs likely will as well. While you should interest them in learning the PSP, you should not mislead them about the work involved.

Once you have peers who use the PSP, it will be easier to sustain your personal discipline. A cheering section is enormously helpful, and supportive peers can put your reverses in perspective. It is personally rewarding to perform with skill, but you need to share your results. Your family can help, but it is not the same as supportive and involved associates.

OBTAINING ORGANIZATIONAL SUPPORT FOR THE PSP

The PSP is not something people can pick up casually. Unless there is a strong motivation to do the work, few will be able to do it. For example, in one PSP course of 18 students, 12 took it for credit and six were auditing. The 12 were all in a degree program and needed the course to graduate. The six were working engineers who sought to improve their skills. On the first day of class, they all committed to doing all the work. Of the 12 taking the course for credit, 11 did all the assignments and completed the course. Of the six auditors, only one finished on time.

If there is interest in your organization in introducing the PSP, insist it be done as part of the job. It should be a team commitment with an instructor, allocated time, assigned support, and an established schedule. The managers must be involved and the PSP must be treated as an important job commitment. Engineers quickly learn to concentrate their energies on what their managers are interested in and they judge their managers, interests by what they ask about. To motivate the engineers to do the PSP work, the managers should ask them about it at least once a week.

14.3   The Personal Costs of a PSP

There are three potential personal costs of using a PSP, as follows:

1. The time required to learn and use it
2. The emotional cost of maintaining the needed discipline
3. The potential risk to your ego

THE TIME REQUIRED

The time required to learn and use the PSP can be substantial. Even though I have years of process development experience, many reusable process elements, and mountains of data, process updates still take me a lot of time. It took me 63.1 hours to upgrade my PSP6.2 version to PSP7.0. This figure did not surprise me, however, since I had planned for 67 hours. For example, I actually averaged over two hours to define each form and template. This time did not include producing process improvement proposals (PIPs), but it did include planning, PIP analysis, the generation and editing of text, the organization of the forms, and a simulated process test. While 63.1 hours is a lot of time, PSP7 is a sophisticated personal process.

Even after you have a defined process, there are still time commitments. The time it takes to follow the process should be balanced by your increased efficiency. You will, however, have a process to maintain and data to enter and analyze. Try to promptly enter your process data. The longer you wait, the harder it will be to reconstruct missing or incorrect items and the bigger the data entry job will become. It is also important to analyze your data periodically. Doing this will keep your progress visible and show which process changes helped your performance. When you used this book as a text, you examined your historical data for each exercise. When you use these methods on the job, however, you may find it more practical to do the analyses less frequently, particularly after your performance has stabilized. Every few weeks, however, you should analyze your data.

THE EMOTIONAL COST

Personal process improvement can have substantial emotional consequences. It takes work to define a process and a lot of discipline to use it. The first time you use a process you have defined, you will learn a great deal about how you work. You will then make some changes and try again. You will sometimes find you got worse instead of better. The temptation is to feel guilty and to resolve to try harder next time. The next time, if you again find that things haven't improved, you may begin to get frustrated.

The problem is that merely defining and measuring your process will not improve it. While there is often a one time gain from the measurement program, consistent improvement requires you to change your methods, tools, or procedures. You probably tried pretty hard the first time and are merely dissatisfied with the fact that you are human. While there will be statistical variations, merely trying harder will produce more frustration than improvement. Instead, study your results, postulate how behavior changes could produce improvements, and change your process accordingly.

People are often capable of far more than they realize. There are many examples of people performing tasks they or no one else imagined they could accomplish. Such achievements, however, are preceded by a lot of hard work. People do make breakthroughs but generally only when they are fully prepared.

Most professional careers are built on a succession of capability improvements. There are, however, easy improvements and difficult ones. For example, while building basic programming skills you likely experienced fairly rapid improvement. At some point, however, you probably hit a plateau. From there on, improvement was more difficult to achieve. A PSP can help you recognize these plateaus and identify likely areas for improvement. By better understanding the details of your work, you can deal more objectively with your personal process improvement.

THE RISK TO YOUR EGO

In addition to the emotional effort of self-improvement, there is the issue of personal worth. We each have a personal image of ourselves. Sometimes it is realistic, sometimes it is not. For example, you may have seen that your friend was a better baseball pitcher than you were. No matter how important being a good pitcher was to you and no matter how hard you tried, you just could not pitch as well as your friend could. Although it took a while to come to terms with the unfairness of it all, sooner or later you did, and life went on. By the time most of us have finished our formal education, we are resigned to the fact that we will not be world champions. World-class runners, baseball players, and concert pianists have unique talents. Regardless of our childhood dreams, many of us have learned how to lead happy and productive lives by using the assets *we* possess.

Programming is no different. The present intuitive state of the software profession provides few professionals a clear appreciation of their limitations or abilities. While you may be upset to learn that someone is better at debugging or reviewing code than you are, you would probably not be too concerned. After all, these functions are just modest parts of the software job. However, if you find that someone consistently produces better designs than you do, you may be pretty upset. Somehow, design ability is more important to our self-images.

Software development takes various talents, skills, and abilities. Although we can all improve with experience, some people are inherently better at some tasks than are others. The key to ego management is to recognize your unique strengths and to compensate for and deal realistically with your weaknesses. Find and capitalize on the talents you have and don't dwell on those you don't.

CONSCIOUS AND UNCONSCIOUS COMPETENCE

William F. Hayes, president of Texas Instruments Defense Systems Group, has described the four stages of learning, as shown in Fig. 14.1. [Hayes] In

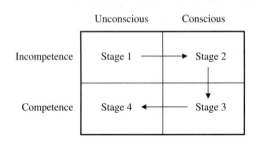

FIGURE 14.1
The Four Stages of Learning

stage 1, our incompetence is unknown, ill defined, and unconscious. Through observation, measurement, and analysis, we gradually learn how we currently perform. Once we have reached conscious incompetence, stage 2, we are in a position to make changes. Through trials and experiments, by learning from others, or by applying improved tools and methods, we learn how to make the improvements that advance us to stage 3. Conscious competence is effective, but transient. It takes constant effort to guard against backsliding. After practice, competent performance becomes natural. Now competence takes little effort to sustain, so it becomes so normal that it is unconscious. This is stage 4.

In a static world, unconscious competence would be the end of the improvement cycle. Fortunately, however, technology advances, jobs change, and we develop new skills and abilities. What was leading-edge performance becomes normal, then routine, and ultimately barely adequate. While we seek to internalize our processes so that we can naturally do superior work, we must continue to measure, analyze, and improve our performance. Even world champions will tell you there is always room for improvement.

14.4   The Personal Benefits of a PSP

In addition to providing the data you need to handle management pressure, the PSP offers many other potential benefits as follows:

- ☐ The insight you gain into your talents and abilities
- ☐ The stimulation of an almost unlimited stream of improvement ideas
- ☐ The framework it provides for personal improvement
- ☐ The degree of control you gain over your work

□ The feeling of pride and personal accomplishment

□ An improved basis for effective teamwork

□ The conviction to do the job the way you know you should

INSIGHT

Defining, measuring, and tracking your work gives you remarkable insight into how you perform, as the following illustrates:

□ It helps you to know your performance. When you measure your work and analyze these data, you see what works best for you.

□ Knowing what works best for you helps you to understand variation and to see what is repeatable and controllable. You can learn from the extremes, both good and bad.

□ You then incorporate these lessons into a growing body of documented personal practices.

As you identify your strengths, your weaknesses will come into better focus. You can then maximize your assets and deal more objectively with your weaknesses. This knowledge will guide you in selecting tasks and defining roles that best fit your talents.

IDEAS

The use of a personal process stimulates an almost unlimited stream of ideas about how to improve. This occurs for several reasons. By defining your process, you assert control over it. You now own the process, and you can change and improve it. You begin to act like two people at once: one does the job, and the other observes. The observer is your process self constantly seeking better approaches. Your critical faculties are in gear, searching for ways to improve each task as you perform it. Not surprisingly, lots of improvement ideas show up.

IMPROVEMENT FRAMEWORK

A personal process provides a framework for improvement. As you define your process, you think in its terms. Abstract globs of work take on a structure and become subject to rational analysis and revision. For example, a design that is one big monolithic activity is difficult to reason about and almost impossible to change. However, once you separate the design task into elements you can see how each part relates to the others and how they relate to the larger process. You now have a basis for measurement and a context for improvement. As I pointed out in Chapter 2, professional body builders don't think about building muscle; they think in terms of arms, legs, and torsos. As they gain more experience, they think of building specific muscles: the biceps, the triceps, and the deltoids. The clearer the focus, the better you can improve in each area and the better you can take advantage of the knowledge and experience of others. Until you define your tasks in sufficient detail, you will have difficulty improving the way you do them.

PERSONAL CONTROL

Personal control means consistently doing what you intend. This depends to a great extent on your ability to plan. Planning involves relating the job you face with something you have already done. You may do this at a gross level or in considerable detail. It soon becomes clear, however, that detailed planning produces more accurate results than gross planning. This is particularly true when you get feedback in the same level of detail. By gathering data on your personal process, you can see how long each process step takes. These data improve your ability to make accurate plans and to track your progress against them. When you need to make a commitment, you will no longer need to guess how long the job will take. You will know.

PERSONAL ACCOMPLISHMENT

Whether it is painting a building, carving a statue, or writing a program, a successful accomplishment is personally rewarding. Your personal satisfaction with this accomplishment will be heightened by an understanding of the task and an appreciation of the work involved. With experience, you will recognize your personal bests and know what it takes to achieve peak performance and to do so more often. While your performance may not be world class, you are entitled to feel proud of your improvement.

TEAMWORK

Most software work is done by teams. When each team member has a defined and disciplined personal process, the team behaves differently. Their mutual confidence enables them to have superior combined performance. They understand each others' abilities and do not need to protect themselves from their teammates' mistakes. They can focus on doing their best and on supporting each other. Their synergy comes from the intuitive precision with which they interact and support each other.

14.5 Coaching

We have not yet developed a coaching ethic in software development. It could certainly help if we did. Sports and the performing arts have learned the value of coaching. Coaches help professionals to maximize their talents. They observe and study each practice and each performance. They are constantly looking for improvement opportunities. They push you to your known limits and then a little more. They can even drive you beyond what you thought was possible. They make the practice sessions so tough that the performance seems easy. Your coach is your greatest fan and your most demanding audience.

Accomplished coaches recognize talent and see the possibilities for excellence. Their charges must start with the essential ingredients: basic skills and a commitment to perform with distinction. The coach is continually testing the performer's ability to produce superior results. The objective is to make these occasional achievements seem normal and natural.

Superior coaches experiment. They watch each session and seek new ways to train and to motivate. They strive to help you improve your performance while looking for ways to improve their own. They view every training session as a practice coaching session.

It seems unlikely that truly superior software development performance will be achieved without the help of skilled coaches. The software coach will have three objectives:

1. Motivate superior performance.
2. Insist on a dedication to excellence.
3. Support and guide individual development.

MOTIVATE SUPERIOR PERFORMANCE

Motivation is crucial. Most professionals want to perform, and motivated professionals strive for superior performance. As Martin says, [Martin 93]

> "Improved performance comes from motivation, from arousing and maintaining the will to work effectively—not because the individual is coerced, but because he is committed."

Without motivation, professionals do not excel; with motivation, they will tackle and surmount unbelievable challenges. While there are many keys to motivation, the coach's first task is to find these keys and devise the mix of goals, rewards, and demands that will achieve consistently high performance.

INSIST ON DEDICATION TO EXCELLENCE

The coach must know excellence in order to demand it. In sports, there are world records and national champions. We have great singers and actors and world-renowned dancers. They provide constant benchmarks and highly visible ideals. While some performers know they can never reach such pinnacles, they get satisfaction from striving for excellence and occasionally performing with distinction.

In software, we don't have world records or even renowned performers. However, with a coach to help you measure and track your PSP, you will better understand what excellence means for you. You will begin to establish the kind of personal benchmarks that professional athletes take for granted. You will know your personal bests and be able to judge how each performance compares. With such benchmarks, coaching becomes possible. Both you and your coach can define excellence and measure every practice and every performance against it.

SUPPORT AND GUIDE INDIVIDUAL DEVELOPMENT

Practice makes perfect. In software, as in life, we rarely do well the first time we try something. The coach makes your practice more than repetition. The focus is on objectives and goals. You start with high standards and then strive to surpass them. Your coach will help you to set standards that are near enough to seem achievable but far away enough to be challenging. Every performance is a practice, and every practice is part performance. You learn to put your heart and soul into every task, whether for real or just for practice.

Industrial organizations are beginning to see the value of manager-coaches. Flat organizations, flexible work groups, and self-managed teams are the new management credo. Managers will no longer direct and control their people. They must learn to support and to guide them and to count on them to manage their own work. We are beginning to see the wisdom of Drucker's words: [Drucker]

> "The purpose of an organization is to enable common men to do uncommon things. No organization can depend on genius; the supply is always scarce and unreliable. It is the test of an organization to make ordinary men perform better than they seem capable of, . . . The focus must be on the strengths of a man—on what he can do rather than on what he cannot do."

There are many cases in which seemingly incapable teams have achieved far more than they or anyone else thought possible. [Humphrey 87] While basic talents are always required, surprisingly, championship teams often are built from seemingly ordinary materials.

FINDING A COACH

The odds are that your current instructor or manager will not know how to act like a coach. Either may be willing to try, but coaching is a skill. Without training and practice, few people make good coaches. While each of us could certainly benefit from professional coaching, we are not likely to find it in today's organizations. Perhaps your best strategy is to focus on the goals of coaching and to see how you can fulfill them for yourself. If you have supportive classmates or teammates or a willing manager, so much the better.

Talk to your classmates or teammates. See if you can get others interested in the idea of coaching. When you do, discuss some approaches and work out a strategy. Take turns coaching each other. Analyze the results and see what worked and what didn't. Then try again. Over time, you could learn how to coach others and you could get valuable help and support as well.

14.6   The Responsible Software Professional

Professional behavior is demanding. It can also be rewarding. To take full advantage of the PSP, however, you must act like a professional by doing the following:

- ☐ Use effective methods in your work.
- ☐ Recognize your strengths and weaknesses.
- ☐ Practice, practice, practice.
- ☐ Learn from history.
- ☐ Find and learn new methods.

USE EFFECTIVE METHODS IN YOUR WORK

The tragedy of modern software engineering is that almost all disasters are avoidable. Good software practices are straightforward, but few people consistently use them. Often, in fact, the appropriate methods were known but not used. The people were too busy to consider them. They may rationalize that there is no evidence that these methods help. But there is plenty of evidence. As a dedicated professional, you must find the methods that work and use them. Finding them can take a little work, but the really challenging part is using them once you find them.

RECOGNIZE YOUR STRENGTHS AND WEAKNESSES

This is the role of the postmortem. As you build understanding of your abilities, you will find tasks you are good at and areas for improvement. Strengths and weaknesses are relative. Balance your capabilities with those of your associates. Capitalize on your strengths and seek support where you are weak.

Treat every project as a chance to learn. Measure your work, analyze the data, and see what works. Learn from variation. When things go well, try to figure out why. Practice what you did and attempt to reproduce it. Perhaps you will develop a new trick or technique. Above all, focus on the small improvements. If you can regularly make small improvements, the major changes will take care of themselves.

PRACTICE, PRACTICE, PRACTICE

If you want to improve your skills, get in the habit of practicing. Try out new methods and work on your personal problem areas. You may not have time for practice projects, but there are usually practice opportunities in everyday work. You may need a prototype to prove a design or to resolve an interface. Prototypes are not always appropriate, but experiment as often as you can. While you should use proven methods on product code, you should learn from your prototypes.

You can also practice on your projects, particularly those parts that are not on critical schedules. When learning a new method, practice it to build skill. Using new measurements, new process forms, or new analyses or verification methods is acceptable as long as the project's quality and schedule are not exposed. Practice is an essential part of personal improvement and you should make practicing a normal part of your daily work.

LEARN FROM HISTORY

The difference between a tragedy and a fiasco is that in a tragedy, you have not learned from the fiasco. We do few things for the first time. Invariably, somebody has produced a program just like the one you are now developing. They have made the mistakes you will make, and they know the traps and pitfalls. A little exploration can save you a lot of grief. Look for relevant experience and check the literature. There will often be pertinent books and articles.

As Harry Truman once said, "The only thing new in the world is the history you have not learned." [Miller 73] Observe and learn from others, and as you build your knowledge, make it known. You can then be part of building a more structured software engineering discipline. The power of science comes from the accumulating wealth of knowledge. Take advantage of what you find and contribute what you learn.

FIND AND LEARN NEW METHODS

This book has introduced a number of methods and techniques, but they are only examples. Many tools and methods are now available, and new ones are constantly being developed. You cannot expect to learn everything, but you can watch for innovations that are pertinent to your personal needs. Keep a list and select those that are most important to you now. Allocate time for skill building and spend a few hours a week learning something new. If you do this consistently, you will learn the equivalent of one graduate course a year. With the current pace of technology, this is the bare minimum to keep up.

The rate of technical change is accelerating, and new tools and methods are being developed faster than ever before. While there is a vast amount of literature to monitor, there are now many tools that can help do this. Most libraries will run keyword searches and quickly provide lists of pertinent articles. Think of it this way: Suppose you had a serious medical problem and wanted a competent doctor. Would you pick one who never cracked a journal or attended a conference? Or would you seek someone who was skilled and current? When you trust your life to someone, you want them to behave professionally.

Now consider your professional life. Should you entrust it to someone who is out of date? If you were looking for career guidance, would you ask someone who had not cracked a technical book since college? Probably not. The skill, knowledge, and ability you bring to your job will determine your future. Your future is in your hands.

14.7   Your Future in Software Engineering

As you look to the future, you will face many questions. How will your field evolve, and what can you do to meet the mounting challenges? While no one can know, your progress probably will be limited by your ability to build your personal skills. Make practice a part of every project and measure and observe your own work. You cannot stand still, so you should treat every project as a way to build talent rather than merely treating your talent as a way to build projects.

Deciding what you want from your chosen field is like asking what you want from life. Surprisingly often, people achieve their objectives, but in ways they did not expect. Life rarely turns out the way we plan. While our carefully developed strategies may go down in flames, a new and more rewarding opportunity shows up in the ashes. The key is to keep an open mind and to keep looking. In life, we all reach the same end, so we need to concentrate on the trip. Just as with a process, once you decide how you want to live, the rest will follow. Devote yourself to excellence, and you just might achieve it. That would be worth the trip.

References

[Drucker] Peter F. Drucker, *Management* (New York: Harper & Row, 1974).

[Hayes] William F. Hayes, "Quality and Leadership," talk at the Software Engineering Institute (November 11, 1993).

[Humphrey 87] W. S. Humphrey, *Managing for Innovation, Leading Technical People* (Englewood Cliffs, NJ: Prentice Hall, 1987).

[Martin 93] Don Martin, *Team Think, Using the Sports Connection to Develop, Motivate and Manage a Winning Business Team* (New York: Dutton, 1993).

[Miller 73] Merle Miller, *Plain Speaking: An Oral Biography of Harry S Truman* (New York: The Putnam Publishing Group, Berkley Publishing Group, 1973).

A

APPENDIX
Statistical Methods for the Personal Software Process

This appendix describes the statistical and mathematical methods used in this book. While these methods are briefly described in Chapters 5 and 6 and in Appendix D, they are discussed more fully here. This appendix also combines these separate treatments in one place for a more convenient reference. The methods described here can be used in various ways to help you to be a more effective software engineer. Statistics is a large field, however, so these topics represent only a small fraction of it.

OBJECTIVE

This section is intended to show you how to use several useful statistical methods. The focus is on how you can use these methods, not on why they work. There is a risk, however, in using any method without fully understanding it. I have thus included some cautions and guidelines. If you use these methods for problems that are not similar to those described here, you should check with a statistician or consult a statistics text. [DeGroot, Box]

This appendix has been formatted for easy reference. Each section includes a procedural description of how to use the method, a brief summary of the conditions for its use, and guidance on interpreting the results. The text also briefly explains key points about each method and its use. For your convenience, Tables A1, A2, and A3 give selected values of the normal, t, and χ^2 distributions.

Because statistics deals with data, it is important that you establish good practices for gathering and managing data. This subject is discussed at length in Chapter 7. It is particularly important to observe your data and see if you can understand what it has to tell you. It is thus always a good idea to look at your data graphically before you spend a lot of time doing calculations.

TABLE A1   SELECTED VALUES OF THE STANDARD NORMAL
DISTRIBUTION

x	$\Phi(x)$	x	$\Phi(x)$
−4.0	0.0000	0.0	0.5000
−3.9	0.0000	0.1	0.5398
−3.8	0.0001	0.2	0.5793
−3.7	0.0001	0.3	0.6179
−3.6	0.0002	0.4	0.6554
−3.5	0.0002	0.5	0.6915
−3.4	0.0003	0.6	0.7257
−3.3	0.0005	0.7	0.7580
−3.2	0.0007	0.8	0.7881
−3.1	0.0010	0.9	0.8159
−3.0	0.0013	1.0	0.8413
−2.9	0.0019	1.1	0.8643
−2.8	0.0026	1.2	0.8849
−2.7	0.0035	1.3	0.9032
−2.6	0.0047	1.4	0.9192
−2.5	0.0062	1.5	0.9332
−2.4	0.0082	1.6	0.9452
−2.3	0.0107	1.7	0.9554
−2.2	0.0139	1.8	0.9641
−2.1	0.0179	1.9	0.9713
−2.0	0.0227	2.0	0.9773
−1.9	0.0287	2.1	0.9821
−1.8	0.0359	2.2	0.9861
−1.7	0.0446	2.3	0.9893
−1.6	0.0548	2.4	0.9918
−1.5	0.0668	2.5	0.9938
−1.4	0.0808	2.6	0.9953
−1.3	0.0968	2.7	0.9965
−1.2	0.1151	2.8	0.9974
−1.1	0.1357	2.9	0.9981
−1.0	0.1587	3.0	0.9987
−0.9	0.1841	3.1	0.9990
−0.8	0.2119	3.2	0.9993
−0.7	0.2420	3.3	0.9995
−0.6	0.2743	3.4	0.9997
−0.5	0.3085	3.5	0.9998
−0.4	0.3446	3.6	0.9998
−0.3	0.3821	3.7	0.9999
−0.2	0.4207	3.8	0.9999
−0.1	0.4602	3.9	1.0000
−0.0	0.5000	4.0	1.0000

TABLE A2   A TABLE OF SELECTED VALUES OF THE t DISTRIBUTION

Degrees of Freedom	$p(\alpha) = 0.60$ $p(\alpha/2) = 0.20$	0.70 0.40	0.85 0.70	0.90 0.80	0.95 0.90	0.975 0.95	0.99 0.98	0.995 0.99
1	.325	.727	1.963	3.078	6.314	12.706	31.821	63.657
2	.289	.617	1.386	1.886	2.920	4.303	6.965	9.925
3	.277	.584	1.250	1.638	2.353	3.182	4.541	5.841
4	.271	.569	1.190	1.533	2.132	2.776	3.747	4.604
5	.267	.559	1.156	1.476	2.015	2.571	3.365	4.032
6	.265	.553	1.134	1.440	1.943	2.447	3.143	3.707
7	.263	.549	1.119	1.415	1.895	2.365	2.998	3.499
8	.262	.546	1.108	1.397	1.860	2.306	2.896	3.355
9	.261	.543	1.100	1.383	1.833	2.262	2.821	3.250
10	.260	.542	1.093	1.372	1.812	2.228	2.764	3.169
15	.258	.536	1.074	1.341	1.753	2.131	2.602	2.947
20	.257	.533	1.064	1.325	1.725	2.086	2.528	2.845
30	.256	.530	1.055	1.310	1.697	2.042	2.457	2.750
∞	.253	.524	1.036	1.282	1.645	1.960	2.326	2.576

TABLE A3 A TABLE OF SELECTED VALUES OF THE χ^2 DISTRIBUTION

Degrees of Freedom	p = 0.25	0.50	0.75	0.90	0.95	0.975	0.99	0.995
1	0.102	0.455	1.323	2.706	3.841	5.024	6.635	7.879
2	0.575	1.386	2.773	4.605	5.991	7.378	9.210	10.60
3	1.213	2.366	4.108	6.251	7.815	9.348	11.34	12.84
4	1.923	3.357	5.385	7.779	9.488	11.14	13.28	14.86
5	2.675	4.351	6.626	9.236	11.07	12.83	15.09	16.75
6	3.455	5.348	7.841	10.64	12.59	14.45	16.81	18.55
7	4.255	6.346	9.037	12.02	14.07	16.01	18.48	20.28
8	5.071	7.344	10.22	13.36	15.51	17.53	20.09	21.95
9	5.899	8.343	11.39	14.68	16.92	19.02	21.67	23.59
10	6.737	9.342	12.55	15.99	18.31	20.48	23.21	25.19
15	11.04	14.34	18.25	22.31	25.00	27.49	30.58	32.80
20	15.45	19.34	23.83	28.41	31.41	34.17	37.57	40.00
30	24.48	29.34	34.80	40.26	43.77	46.98	50.89	53.67

THE ORGANIZATION AND STRUCTURE OF APPENDIX A

The topics covered in this appendix are shown in Table A4. These methods can be used in various ways. For example, Fig. A1 shows several key software engineering activities involved in planning and managing software projects. At the top of the figure, various statistical and mathematical tools are shown, together with their relationships to several software planning and management methods. The next few sections discuss the application of these statistical methods.

FINDING PRIORITY DEFECT TYPES

This topic is discussed in Chapters 8 and 9. Here, you are interested in establishing action priorities. An example would be to determine the highest priority defect types so that you could focus on finding them early in your process or eliminating their causes. The Pareto distribution provides a way to do this.

DECISION TO USE SIZED-BASED ESTIMATING

This topic is treated in Chapters 4, 5, and 6. When the sizes of development projects can be shown to closely relate to the time required to develop them, a size-based estimating method can help you to make more accurate plans. One way to measure the relationship between size and development time is called correlation. A correlation that is close to 1 indicates that the size and development time are closely related. Because you can get high correlations with small amounts of data, it is also wise to check to see if the correlation is meaningful. The significance test is used for this purpose.

CATEGORIZING SOFTWARE SIZE

This topic is discussed in Chapter 5. Dividing the size data for a number of software objects into size ranges helps you to judge the size of a new program. The technique for establishing these categories involves checking the data to see if they are normally distributed and then using the standard deviation to calculate the size ranges. This use of the standard deviation requires that the data be approximately normally distributed. If they are not, adjustments are required before the data can be used in these analyses.

PROJECTING SOFTWARE SIZE AND DEVELOPMENT TIME

This topic is discussed in Chapters 5 and 6. If the historical relationship between the size of previously developed programs and the resources required to develop

TABLE A4 THE CONTENTS OF APPENDIX A

Section Topic	Description
A1—Statistical Distributions	This section describes how statistical distributions are represented and some common distributions.
A2—Variance and Standard Deviation	These common properties of statistical distributions are described, together with the formulas for calculating them.
A3—Correlation	Correlation measures the strength of the relationship between two sets of data. This section shows how to calculate the correlation coefficient r.
A4—Significance of a Correlation	Relationships may occur by chance or result from some cause. The significance measure helps you to distinguish between these cases.
A5—Numerical Integration	You will often want to use the values of various statistical distributions in your programs. You will need to use numerical integration to do so.
A6—Tests for Normality	Many statistical calculations require the data be normally distributed. You will need to test them for normality.
A7—Linear Regression	The linear regression method calculates the numerical relationships between two sets of data. The resulting regression parameters can then be used to make estimates and projections based on these data.
A8—Linear Regression Prediction Interval	The prediction interval provides a measure of the quality of an estimate using the linear regression parameters.
A9—Multiple Regression	The multiple regression method calculates the numerical relationships among three or more sets of data. The resulting regression parameters can then be used to make estimates or projections based on these data.
A10—Multiple Regression Prediction Interval	The multiple regression prediction interval provides a measure of the quality of an estimate made with the multiple regression parameters.
A11—Gauss's Method	Gauss's method is used in multiple regression to calculate the parameter values.
A12—The Pareto Distribution	The Pareto distribution provides a way to rank the relative importance of various categories of data.

them is approximately linear, you can use linear regression techniques to obtain a projection formula. Because size estimation is an essential element of the methods discussed in this text, you will make regression calculations for many of the exercises. When a product development involves multiple size parameters, such as newly developed LOC, reused LOC, and modified LOC, multiple re-

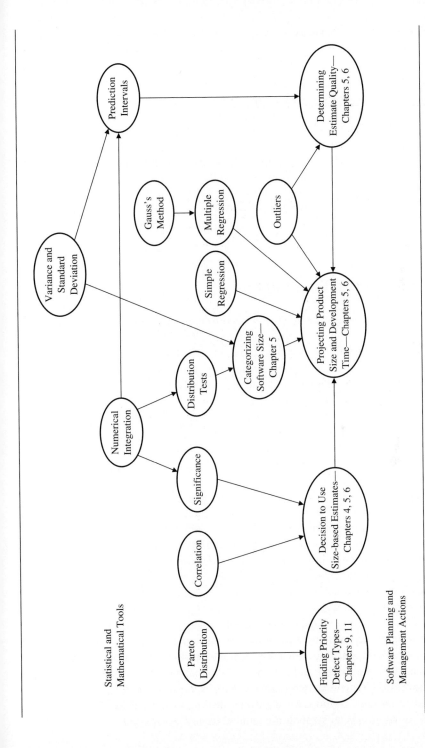

FIGURE A1
Some Uses of Statistics in Software Engineering

gression can be used. Multiple regression is also used in one of the programming exercises.

DETERMINING ESTIMATE QUALITY

Prediction accuracy is discussed in Chapters 5 and 6. Here, you are interested in an indication of your estimate accuracy. By calculating the prediction intervals and using a parameter from the t distribution, you can determine the range within which the actual result will likely fall. Note, however, that this calculation describes the likely variation of your estimate based on the historical data you used in making the estimate. It is not a forecast.

A1   Statistical Distributions

When using statistical methods, you need to understand the nature of statistical distributions, their analysis, and their interpretation. First, all distributions have two basic parameters: the variance and the mean. The mean, μ, is what is called the expected value of the distribution and can generally be viewed as the average of the values of its members. The variance, σ^2, is a measure of the distribution's "spread," or "tightness," around the mean. Figure A2 shows a distribution with a low variance that is tightly clustered about the mean. Figure A3 shows a distribution that is rather widely spread around the mean; this distribution would have a high variance. The positive square root of the variance is called the standard deviation, σ. The mean, μ, the variance, σ^2, and the standard deviation, σ, are used in the statistical analyses of distributions.

Usually, instead of dealing with distributions you are dealing with a number of numerical values that you believe are generated by some common process. You thus can consider them as coming from a distribution. By analyzing these numerical values, you can infer things about this underlying distribution and the process that generated it. However, you are dealing not with the actual values of the distribution parameters but with estimates of them. Thus, when you take the mean, or the average, of all the data values, you get some $\mu_{estimate}$—not the mean of the distribution but an estimate of it.

This distinction is important because when you have limited amounts of data, your approximations of μ and σ^2 can be seriously in error. You should thus remember that throughout this book, you are dealing with estimates of the various statistical parameters and not with their actual values. In a statistics text, this point would be emphasized through the use of special symbols with all these estimated parameters. Because we are always dealing with the estimated parameters, however, these special symbols are omitted throughout this text.

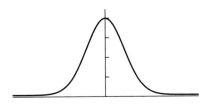

FIGURE A2
Probability Distribution, Low Variance

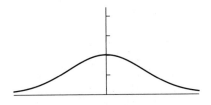

FIGURE A3
Probability Distribution, High Variance

A1.1   REPRESENTATIONS OF DISTRIBUTIONS

Distributions can be represented in many ways. The two most common are the cumulative distribution, shown in Fig. A4, and the density distribution, shown in Fig. A5. In a cumulative distribution, the height of the curve at any point x represents the fraction of the members of the distribution that are smaller than the value of x. Thus the height of a cumulative distribution at the median value of x is always 0.5. Note that in a symmetrical density distribution like that in Fig. A5, the mean value equals the median and is always at the center.

The density distribution, shown in Fig. A5, is the derivative of the cumulative distribution. That is, the height of its curve at any point is equal to the slope of the cumulative distribution at that point. Another way to think about this is that the height of the curve represents the density of the data at that point. To see how such a density distribution can be drawn, consider the data in Table A5. This distribution is shown in Fig. A6. As you can see, the total area under such a density distribution curve is always equal to 1.0.

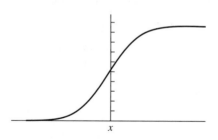

FIGURE A4
A Cumulative Distribution

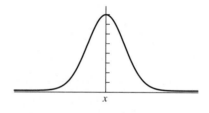

FIGURE A5
Density Distribution

As the number of points increases and the width of the units is made narrower, the shape of such density distributions can be made to approach a smoother curve, as in Fig. A5. The precise shape of the curve depends, of course, on the nature of the distribution.

A1.2   THE NORMAL DISTRIBUTION

The normal distribution is a mathematical way to describe how many things, such as women's heights, are distributed. The distribution of women's heights can be drawn as shown in Fig. A7. The likelihood that a woman of some height, say 64 inches, is taller than another woman is shown by the height of the curve. As you can see, a 64-inch woman would be taller than about half the population. The height of the curve at 64 inches is thus at 50 percent. Clearly, with a 64-inch median height, half the women are shorter and half are taller.

TABLE A5 EXAMPLE OF A DENSITY DISTRIBUTION

a) Data Values

Data Item Rank	Data Value—x
1	1.3
2	2.1
3	2.4
4	2.8
5	3.2
6	3.2
7	3.6
8	3.7
9	4.0
10	4.2
11	4.3
12	4.4
13	4.6
14	4.8
15	5.2
16	5.2
17	5.3
18	5.4
19	5.7
20	6.4
21	6.7
22	6.9
23	7.4
24	7.7
25	8.8
Mean	4.772
Standard Deviation	1.848

b) Data Density

From $x =$	To $x <$	Number	Fraction
0	1	0	0.00
1	2	1	0.04
2	3	3	0.12
3	4	4	0.16
4	5	6	0.24
5	6	5	0.20
6	7	3	0.12
7	8	2	0.08
8	9	1	0.04
9	10	0	0.00
Totals		25	1.00

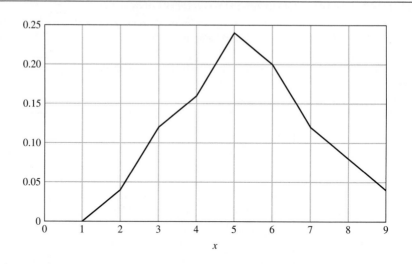

FIGURE A6
A Density Distribution Example

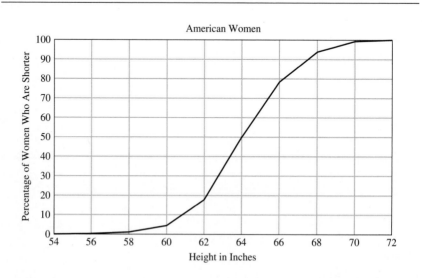

FIGURE A7
Height Distribution—American Women

A mathematically exact normal distribution looks like that in Fig. A8. In this figure, the x axis is in numbers of standard deviations above or below the mean. Based on the data on women's heights, the standard deviation is about 2.5 inches. Hence, if Fig. A8 represented women's heights, zero would be equivalent to 64 inches, -1 standard deviation would represent a height of 61.5 inches, -2 standard deviations would be 59 inches, and so on.

This same curve can be drawn as the more traditional bell-shaped distribution as shown in Fig. A9. Here, you have the probability density—the fraction of the population that is in a given height range—say, between 60 and 61 inches. Many natural phenomena are normally distributed, so the standard deviation actually coincides fairly closely with our intuitions. At 59 inches, a woman's height would be two standard deviations below the mean. Most people would consider such a woman to be quite short and, in fact, only about 2 percent of women are shorter. Similarly at 69 inches, a woman would be two standard deviations above the mean and would be considered quite tall. Only about 2 percent of the population is taller.

A1.3 THE STANDARD NORMAL DISTRIBUTION

Actually, your data will generally be in the form of Table A5 or look like Fig. A7. This is not at all like what you find in the statistical tables shown in Tables A1,

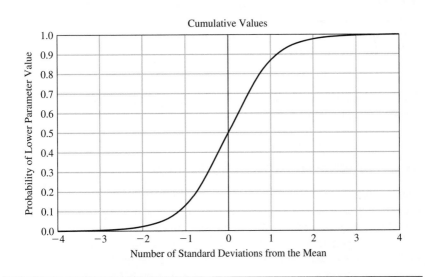

FIGURE A8
Normal Distribution–Cumulative

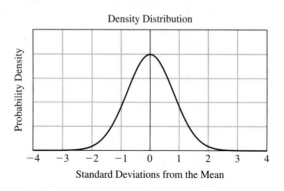

FIGURE A9
Normal Distribution–Density

A2, or A3. The problem is that distributions have all kinds of means and variances, so in order to represent them in statistical tables you would need some standard form. Otherwise, you would need a different statistical table for every possible combination of the mean and variance of each distribution. This clearly would be impractical.

To put a distribution into standard form, you first need to find its mean, μ, and standard deviation, σ. The mean is the average of all the items; the standard deviation is calculated as described in Section A2. You first obtain the values of μ and σ, and then adjust the value of each term, x_i, in your dataset to some standard value, z_i, using Eq. A1:

$$z_i = (x_i - \mu)/\sigma. \tag{A1}$$

The z_i values are shown along with the original x_i values for the example of the density distribution in Table A6.

A1.4   LOG-NORMALLY DISTRIBUTED DATA

Often in the software process, you are dealing with physical phenomena that cannot have negative values, such as the hours spent on a development project or the size of the product produced. In some cases, a limitation of the data to nonnegative values may actually affect the shape of the distribution you are working with. In the case of women's heights, the fact that women do not have negative heights is not very important to the shape of the distribution because the zero value is quite far away from the mean. That is, the zero value is more than three standard

TABLE A6 EXAMPLE OF STANDARD VALUES

Data Item Number	Data Value—x_i	Standard Value—z_i
1	1.3	-1.87847
2	2.1	-1.44564
3	2.4	-1.28333
4	2.8	-1.06692
5	3.2	-0.85050
6	3.2	-0.85050
7	3.6	-0.63409
8	3.7	-0.57999
9	4.0	-0.41768
10	4.2	-0.30947
11	4.3	-0.25537
12	4.4	-0.20126
13	4.6	-0.09306
14	4.8	0.01515
15	5.2	0.23156
16	5.2	0.23156
17	5.3	0.28567
18	5.4	0.33977
19	5.7	0.50208
20	6.4	0.88080
21	6.7	1.04311
22	6.9	1.15132
23	7.4	1.42184
24	7.7	1.58415
25	8.8	2.17928
Mean (μ)	4.772	0.00000
Standard Deviation (σ)	1.848	1.00000

deviations below the mean. In other cases, such as program sizes or the time spent in test, the zero value may not be that far from the smaller data points. Often in these cases, the data tend to bunch up at the smaller positive values and the distribution no longer has a long tail at the left of a bell-shaped curve, as shown in Fig. A9. An example of a log-normal distribution is shown in Fig. A10. Here, the data values may approach zero, but they never actually reach it.

Data distributed in this way can cause problems. Many of the common statistical techniques assume the data are normally distributed. One trick you can use when data have this characteristic is to perform what is called a log-normal transformation. To do this, you take the natural logarithm of all the data, perform all the statistical analyses on these natural-log values, and then convert these results to the original form by taking the anti-logarithm (that is, by taking e to the power of the log value).

For example, suppose you had the six data points given in Table A7 and concluded they were from a log-normal distribution. Assuming you were interested in the mean (or average) of the data, if you merely took the average of the points you would get 35.83. In looking at the data, you can see that 35.83 is above most of the points and could not be said to be anywhere near their "middle," or median. A mean and median that differ widely is one indication you are not dealing with a normal distribution.

By making a log-normal transformation, as also shown in Table A7, you obtain the natural logarithm of each data value, as shown. The average of these values is 3.33, or the log-average, which can be converted to the original form taking the exponential value, or $e^{3.33} = 27.93$. This new average now seems much closer to the middle of the data. This trick is used in many places in this book.

There are also cases with such nonnegative distributions where zero is a valid data value, such as with time measures or defect counts. Zero, although a rare value, is possible. Here, you cannot take the log-normal distribution because it would give values of negative infinity. A standard statistical technique in these

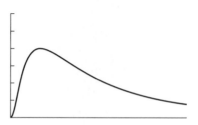

FIGURE A10
The Log-Normal Distribution

TABLE A7 LOG-NORMAL PROGRAM SIZE MEASURES

Program Number	Size (LOC)	ln(Size)
1	86	4.45
2	12	2.48
3	15	2.71
4	28	3.33
5	53	3.97
6	21	3.04
Totals	215	19.98
Average	35.83	3.33
ln-normal Mean	27.93	

cases is essentially to replace the zeros by a small constant, such as $\frac{1}{2}$. You do this by taking the log transform as $y = \log(x + \frac{1}{2})$. If your variables have a very narrow range, however, such as between zero and 1, you could apply a constant scaling factor to give a transformation such as $y = \log(100x + \frac{1}{2})$. When you are finished with the statistical calculations, you take the following inverse transformations: $x = e^y - \frac{1}{2}$ or $x = (e^y - \frac{1}{2})/100$.

A1.5   DEGREES OF FREEDOM

The number of degrees of freedom in a calculation are very important for statistical purposes. For example, if you have n independent variables or data points, you will generally have n degrees of freedom. When working with these data, however, you often do calculations that reduce the degrees of freedom. For example, if you convert such a distribution to its standard form you use the average of all the data points in the conversion. The reason this reduces the number of degrees of freedom can best be understood by recognizing that if you knew the average value and $n - 1$ of the points, you could calculate the value of the nth point. To use many of the statistical tables, you must know the degrees of freedom. In the calculations in this book, the degree of freedom is typically $n - 1$ or $n - 2$. There are exceptions, however, that are pointed out when they occur.

More generally, when you are using your data to calculate various parameters the number of degrees of freedom is reduced by every added parameter. With n data points and p parameters, the number of degrees of freedom would then be $n - p$.

A1.6   THE t DISTRIBUTION

The t distribution, sometimes called Student's t, is a very important statistical tool. It is used instead of the normal distribution when the true value of the population variance is not known and must be estimated from a sample. The reason it is important to use the t distribution can be visualized by considering the nature of your software data. Every process measurement you make can be considered to be a sample. For example, when you write one program you have one data point on program size and the time it took you to produce that program. If you wrote a second program, you would have a second data point. Because your performance fluctuates, your productivity in each case will probably differ. If your productivity in the first case was 12 LOC per hour and in the second case, 16 LOC per hour, you would likely judge that your average productivity was around 14 LOC per hour.

Over time, if you wrote many dozens of programs and you continued to do programming in the same way, you would get a progressively more accurate understanding of your average productivity. The point is, when you take the average of your measurements you are calculating the average productivity of your data sample. This is not your actual productivity but rather an estimate of your productivity. The larger the number of samples you gather, the better the estimate. The t distribution provides a way to correct for the sample size of the estimated variance.

Several t distributions are shown in Fig. A11 for various values of n, the number of points in your dataset. As n gets very large, the t distribution approaches the normal distribution, but for lower values it has a lower central "hump" and fatter "tails."

A1.7   SINGLE-SIDED AND DOUBLE-SIDED t DISTRIBUTIONS

The t distribution is used in two ways in this book: single-sided and double-sided. In the single-sided case, you are interested in whether some event occurred by coincidence or whether it is a truly significant result of your measurements. Such significance tests are discussed in Section A4. In these tests, you are concerned with the size of the tail of the t distribution, as shown in Fig. A12. This value is actually found by looking in a standard table of the t distribution, like Table A2. Here, if you had 10 items ($n = 10$) and a value of t of 1.833, you would look in Table A2 in the row for 9 degrees of freedom. For this test, you typically use $n - 1$ degrees of freedom. Looking across the row $n = 9$, you find the value $t = 1.833$ under probability $p(\alpha) = 0.95$. Because such statistical tables are generally cumulative distributions, the 0.95 represents the entire area under the t distribution curve up to the $t = 1.833$ point. In Fig. A12, this is the unshaded area on the left of the figure. Your interest, however, is in the tail of the distribution,

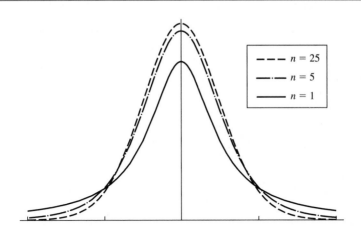

FIGURE A11
The t Distribution

that is, those points that are above the $t = 1.833$ point in the shaded area. As a result, you subtract the 0.95 value from 1.0, the area of the total curve. This gives
the area of the shaded tail as 0.05. In significance calculations, you will use various formulas to determine the value of t and then look it up in this way. You write
such single-sided expressions as $t(\alpha, n - 1)$, where α refers to the probability
value and $n - 1$ to the degrees of freedom. Here, single-sided means you are
talking only about one tail of the distribution, or the shaded area in Fig. A12.

In the double-sided case, you use the t distribution in calculating prediction
intervals. Here you are concerned with the likelihood that some projection is
within or outside of some range. For example, if you have estimated a job at 100

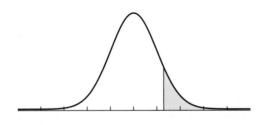

FIGURE A12
The Single-Sided t Distribution

hours, you would be interested in the likelihood that it will actually take between 90 and 110 hours. So you would use a two-sided t distribution as shown in Fig. A13. If you were interested in a 90 percent prediction interval you would want the value of t for which 90 percent of the distribution is under the curve and only 10 percent is in the tails. Hence you would have an upper tail of 0.05 and a lower tail of 0.05, giving 0.10 in the tails and 0.90 under the distribution. For $n = 10$, or 9 degrees of freedom, this is the same value of $t = 1.833$ that you had before for a 95 percent probability.

In this book, you use tables of the single-sided t distribution. These are referred to as $t(\alpha, n - 1)$, or simply t. The double-sided t distribution is referred to as $t(\alpha/2, n - 1)$. To look up the double-sided t distribution value in a table, note that $t(\alpha/2, n - 1)$ refers to two tails, while $t(\alpha, n - 1)$ refers to one. Thus if you sought the $t(\alpha/2, n - 1)$ value for $n = 10$ and 70 percent, the area of the two tails would be equal to 0.30. Thus a single tail would have an area of 0.15 and you would look in the single-sided table under 0.85 in the row for nine degrees of freedom. From Table A2, $t = 1.100$. Similarly, for the two-sided distribution at $p = 0.95$ you would look under 0.975 to get $t = 2.262$ and for $p = 0.99$, you would look under 0.995 to get $t = 3.250$.

A1.8   THE χ^2 DISTRIBUTION

The χ^2, or Chi-squared, distribution is used for analyzing distributions of discrete data. For continuous data, you would use a t test, which I do not discuss in this book. You can use the χ^2 test, for example, to compare two distributions and calculate the likelihood that data come from particular distributions. In this book, the χ^2 distribution is used for testing data to see if they are normally distributed. This test is described in Section A6.

Other uses of the χ^2 distribution include determining the likelihood that a distribution mean is greater than some value or the chance that two sets of data

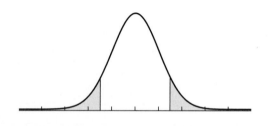

FIGURE A13
The Double-Sided t Distribution

come from the same distribution. While such tests are not used in this book, they are described in standard statistical texts. [Box, DeGroot]

Various cumulative plots of the χ^2 distribution are shown in Fig. A14. As you can see from the figure, this distribution's behavior varies substantially depending on the value of n.

A1.9   OUTLIERS

Regression analyses are sensitive to extreme data values because they involve the use of the variance. The variance calculation computes the square of the distance of each point from some estimated value or trend line. Linear regression (which is used for estimating) is based on minimizing the value of the variance. Thus an unusual data point that significantly effected the variance would impact the accuracy of all your estimates.

A principal lesson of process management is that occasionally some extraordinary event will disrupt a project. The process data for such an unusual event could distort the statistical parameters to such a degree that they no longer represent normal process performance. To effectively use the regression method, you must remove such unusual values, or outliers, from the dataset before you do the

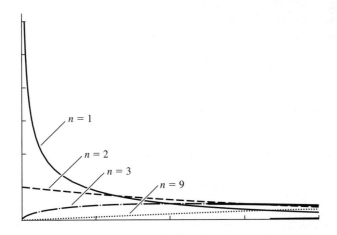

FIGURE A14
The χ^2 Distribution

analysis. Contrary to common opinion, this is not cheating; it is sound statistical practice. The following approaches can help you to identify outliers:

- □ Control charts: Control charts were explicitly designed to identify unusual process events and to help separate special causes from general causes. You can then safely treat the special cause situations as outliers and remove them from your analysis dataset. Control charts are not used in this text, but they are widely applied in other fields, and the techniques for using them are well known. [Montgomery]

- □ You may know that this particular process enaction was unusual and should thus be viewed as an outlier.

- □ The particular process instance may be at an extreme of the process measurement values. Although extreme points should not be eliminated just because they are extreme, if a point is substantially beyond the previous process limits and has one or more other characteristics that appear unusual, it is generally appropriate to consider it an outlier.

In removing outliers, you should observe the following cautions:

- □ With datasets of fewer than 10 points, you should establish clear and objective criteria for including items in the dataset and not remove any outliers if they fit these criteria.

- □ With 10 to 20 points, you may remove at most one outlier.

- □ With larger datasets, those having 20 or more points, watch the percentage of outliers. If they consistently represent more than 1 percent to 5 percent of the data points, you should reexamine the special cause categories. Of course, you should also examine your control values to see if they are still appropriate. For a further discussion of these issues, consult a reference on control charts. [Montgomery]

A2   Variance and Standard Deviation

The variance of a distribution measures the spread of that distribution about its mean (or average). When the variance is small, the points are clustered closely around the mean, as in Fig. A2; when larger, the distribution would be much more widespread, as in Fig. A3. The variance can also be taken about other values than the mean. The linear regression method discussed in Sections A7 and A9 determines the line through the data that will minimize the variance of the data about that line. It is referred to as the estimated mean response.

The variance is the square of the standard deviation. The common symbol for the standard deviation is σ and the symbol for variance is σ^2. The standard deviation and variance are always positive numbers.

A2.1   THE VARIANCE CALCULATION

The procedure for calculating the variance is shown in Table A8. The standard deviation is found by taking the positive square root of the variance. Note that in step 4, the value of the sum is divided by $n - 1$, where n is the number of points in the dataset. Some formulas for the variance divide by n and others by $n - 1$, so there is often confusion on which should be used. If you were dealing with a complete population, you would know all the values and could thus calculate the variance exactly. In this case, use n. For PSP data, however, you are generally using sample data to make estimates and should thus generally use $n - 1$.

An Example Variance Calculation.   The variance calculation is shown in Table A9 and uses Eq. A2.

$$\text{Variance} = \sigma^2 = \frac{1}{n - 1} \sum_{i=1}^{n} \left(x_i - x_{avg}\right)^2$$

$$(\text{A2})$$

$$\text{StdDeviation} = \sigma = \sqrt{Variance}$$

TABLE A8   THE VARIANCE CALCULATION PROCEDURE

Purpose	To determine the degree of spread of a dataset about its mean
Conditions	None
Inputs	• The values, x_i, of the data points for which the variance is desired • The number of data items, n.
Steps	1. Calculate the dataset mean (or average)—x_{avg}: $$x_{avg} = \frac{1}{n} \sum_{i=1}^{n} x_i.$$ 2. Calculate the square of the distance of each point x_i from the mean value: $\left(x_i - x_{avg}\right)^2.$ 3. Sum these values: $\sum_{i=1}^{n} \left(x_i - x_{avg}\right)^2.$ 4. Divide by $n - 1$: Variance $= \sigma^2 = \dfrac{1}{n - 1} \sum_{i=1}^{n} \left(x_i - x_{avg}\right)^2.$
Interpretation	A large variance indicates a wide degree of variation in the data.

The result is

$$\sigma^2 = \frac{1}{9} * 3{,}522{,}761.0 = 391{,}417.89,$$

$$\sigma = \sqrt{391{,}417.89} = 625.63.$$

A3   Correlation

Correlation is a measure of the degree to which two variables are related. If the two are highly correlated and if they have a cause-and-effect relationship, you can use one variable's value to predict or control the other. This section describes what a correlation is, how to take the correlation between two variables, and how to test the significance of that result. To take the correlation of two variables, however, they must be paired. That is, for every value x_i of variable x there must be a matching value y_i for variable y.

TABLE A9   VARIANCE CALCULATION FOR THE SIZES OF 10 PROGRAMS

Item Number	Total (LOC)	
n	x	$(x_i - x_{avg})^2$
1	186	205,118.40
2	699	3,612.01
3	132	256,947.60
4	272	134,615.60
5	291	121,034.40
6	331	94,802.40
7	199	193,512.00
8	1890	1,565,251.00
9	788	22,230.80
10	1601	925,636.40
Totals	6389	3,522,761.00
Average	638.9	
Variance		391,417.89
Standard Deviation		625.63

Correlations can be tricky. Two variables may be highly correlated by pure coincidence, one may influence the other, or they may both result from some common cause. When you observe a strong correlation between two sets of data like stock prices and baseball scores and this relationship has been unbroken for many years, you could believe there was a hidden causal relationship. However, any sophisticated process contains an almost infinite variety of data. Thus if you look hard enough, you can often find a near match for any given historical dataset. In such situations, however, this relationship has no predictive value. Consider the example of a relationship that survived unbroken for over 120 years. From 1840 through 1960, no U.S. president elected in a year ending in a zero survived his presidency. As compelling as this record may be, it had no special significance and in fact was broken in 1989 when George Bush replaced a living Ronald Reagan.

While looking through such historical correlations, you may actually stumble across some new causal relationship. However, it is probably just a coincidence. Thus even very high correlations do not imply causality. For that, you need to understand the actual processes at work.

A3.1 GRAPHICAL TEST FOR CORRELATION

Suppose you had the data shown in Table A10 and wanted to determine the degree to which the number of LOC were related to the development hours required to write these programs. Although there are several ways to attack this problem, it is wise to first examine a plot of the data. Fig. A15 shows a scatter plot of these data with program size plotted on the x-axis and development hours on the y-axis. As you can see, the LOC and hours appear to be closely related. When data are linearly related, the quality of this relationship is indicated by the relative closeness of the data points to a straight line. This quality is measured by the value of the correlation. Note, however, that the correlation measures only the quality of linear relationships. If the data have a strong quadratic or exponential relationship, for example, the correlation may not be a good measure of the strength of this relationship.

A3.2 CORRELATION CALCULATION

The correlation of x with y is found from the formula

$$r(x,y) = \frac{n\sum_{i=1}^{n} x_i y_i - \sum_{i=1}^{n} x_i \sum_{i=1}^{n} y_i}{\sqrt{\left[n\sum_{i=1}^{n} x_i^2 - \left(\sum_{i=1}^{n} x_i\right)^2\right]\left[n\sum_{i=1}^{n} y_i^2 - \left(\sum_{i=1}^{n} y_i\right)^2\right]}}, \tag{A3}$$

where n is the number of members in each dataset and i is the index to the individual items. The value of r can vary from -1 to $+1$. A procedure for making this calculation is given in Table A11.

TABLE A10 TOTAL LOC AND DEVELOPMENT HOURS FOR 10
               PASCAL PROGRAMS

Item Number	Total LOC	Development Hours
n	x	y
1	186	15.0
2	699	69.9
3	132	6.5
4	272	22.4
5	291	28.4
6	331	65.9
7	199	19.4
8	1890	198.7
9	788	38.8
10	1601	138.2
Totals	6389	603.2

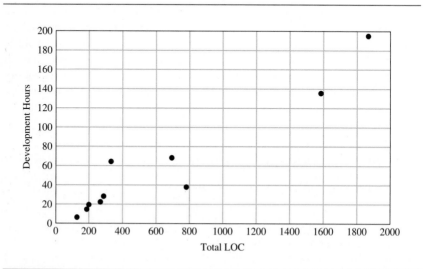

FIGURE A15
Pascal Total LOC versus Hours

A Correlation Example.   An example of these calculations is shown in Table A12. Here, $n = 10$ and the correlation calculation is done as follows:

$$r(x,y) = \frac{10 * 719{,}914.4 - 6{,}389 * 603.2}{\sqrt{\left(10 * 7{,}604{,}693 - 6389^2\right) * \left(10 * 71{,}267.12 - 603.2^2\right)}} =$$

0.9543158

$$\left[r(x,y)\right]^2 = 0.9107.$$

This is a high positive correlation. Because r^2 is greater than 0.9, LOC is a good predictor of development hours, at least for these data.

TABLE A11 THE CORRELATION CALCULATION PROCEDURE

Purpose	To determine the degree to which two variables are linearly related
Conditions	The variables must be paired and have the same number of members.
Inputs	• The two sets of data, x and y • The number of their members, n.
Steps	1. Evaluate the following formula for r: $$r(x,y) = \frac{n\sum_{i=1}^{n} x_i y_i - \sum_{i=1}^{n} x_i \sum_{i=1}^{n} y_i}{\sqrt{\left[n\sum_{i=1}^{n} x_i^2 - \left(\sum_{i=1}^{n} x_i\right)^2\right]\left[n\sum_{i=1}^{n} y_i^2 - \left(\sum_{i=1}^{n} y_i\right)^2\right]}}.$$ 2. Determine r^2, the square of the correlation.
Interpretation	• An r value near 1 implies a high positive linear relationship. That is, increases in x are associated with increases in y. • An r value near -1 implies a high negative linear relationship. That is, increases in x are associated with decreases in y. • An r value near 0 implies little linear relationship between the two sets of data.
Uses	• When $0.9 <= r^2$, the relationship is considered predictive and you can use it with high confidence. • When $0.7 <= r^2 < 0.9$, there is a strong correlation. The relationship is adequate for planning purposes. • When $0.5 <= r^2 < 0.7$, there is an adequate correlation for many purposes. Use the relationship for planning, but with caution. • When $r^2 < 0.5$, the relationship is not reliable for planning purposes.

TABLE A12 CORRELATION CALCULATION FOR 10 PASCAL PROGRAMS

Item Number	Total LOC	Development Hours			
n	x	y	x^2	xy	y^2
1	186	15.0	34,596	2,790.0	225.00
2	699	69.9	488,601	48,860.1	4,886.01
3	132	6.5	17,424	858.0	42.25
4	272	22.4	73,984	6,092.8	501.76
5	291	28.4	84,681	8,264.4	806.56
6	331	65.9	109,561	21,812.9	4,342.81
7	199	19.4	39,601	3,860.6	376.36
8	1890	198.7	3,572,100	375,543.0	39,481.69
9	788	38.8	620,944	30,574.4	1,505.44
10	1601	138.2	2,563,201	221,258.2	19,099.24
Totals	6389	603.2	7,604,693	719,914.4	71,267.12

A4   The Significance of a Correlation

The strength of a relationship between two sets of data is determined by r^2, the square of the correlation. If you find a strong relationship, however, you also need to know whether it is of practical significance to you. This is the purpose of the significance test. For example, there is some likelihood that two random sets of data will be highly correlated. The significance of a correlation determines this likelihood. It is thus possible to have a high correlation that is not very significant. For example, you can always get a correlation of $r = 1$ with two datasets that each have two data points. However, this correlation has no significance. As the number of points in the dataset increases above two, the significance of the correlation increases.

A4.1   THE SIGNIFICANCE CALCULATION

The significance calculation procedure is shown in Table A13. In this calculation, the value of t is computed with the following formula:

$$t = \frac{|r(x,y)|\sqrt{n-2}}{\sqrt{1 - r(x,y)^2}}, \tag{A4}$$

where r is calculated as described in Section A3. The absolute value of r is used because correlations near -1 can also be highly significant. Once the t value is calculated, its corresponding probability value is obtained from Table A2 for the single-sided t distribution with $n - 1$ degrees of freedom.

Note also that just as high correlations can be misleading, so can high levels of significance. The reason is that for a given value of r, an increase in the number of items in the dataset will increase the value of t. When the correlation is low, say 0.1, four hundred items will give a value of $t = 2.005$ and a respectable significance of about 0.025. The rule is that when the number of items is large, watch the correlation, and when small, pay more attention to the significance. Thus, to use a relationship such as that between LOC and hours for planning purposes, you want both high correlation and high significance.

Significance Calculation Example.   Using the data from the example in Section A3, you got a correlation of $r = 0.9543158$, with $n = 10$ items. The t calculation is thus

$$t = \frac{0.9543158\sqrt{8}}{\sqrt{1 - 0.9543158^2}} = 9.0335.$$

Looking in Table A2 under nine degrees of freedom ($n - 1$), the largest value in the table is 3.25, with a probability of 0.995, so $p > 0.995$. Hence, the likelihood of finding this correlation by chance is $1 - p$, or less than 0.005. The correlation between total LOC and development hours is therefore highly significant, implying that if you knew the total number of LOC to be developed for a program, you should be able to accurately project the required development hours.

Note, however, that a correlation is not a prediction. So if your process changed or there was some important difference between this project and those in the historical database, this projection may not be very accurate despite the high values of correlation and significance.

A5   Numerical Integration

For most purposes, you should look in standard statistical tables for the values of the various statistical distributions. Doing this is often inconvenient, however, when you want to use these values in a program. For example, in writing many of the exercise programs in this book you must calculate the values of the various

TABLE A13 THE SIGNIFICANCE CALCULATION PROCEDURE

Purpose	To determine the statistical significance of a correlation
Conditions	• Generally most useful where there is a high positive or negative correlation from a sample of 15 or more observations. • Significance tests with large numbers of items (50 or more) are often misleading.
Inputs	• The correlation value, r • The number of items, n • The values of the t-distribution (see Table A2)
Steps	1. Calculate the value of t from the following formula: $$t = \frac{\left|r(x,y)\right|\sqrt{n-2}}{\sqrt{1 - r(x,y)^2}}.$$ 2. Look for the single-sided probability p with this value of t in Table A2 for $n-1$ degrees of freedom. 3. Alternatively, calculate the probability p by numerically integrating the t distribution for $n-1$ degrees of freedom from $-\infty$ to t (see Section A5). 4. Calculate the distribution tail, $1-p$.
Interpretation	• A tail area of ≤ 0.05 means there is a small likelihood of finding this correlation by chance. This is considered strong evidence that there is a relationship between the variables. • A tail area of ≥ 0.20 means there is a good likelihood of finding this relationship by chance. This is considered strong evidence that there is not a relationship. • Intermediate tail areas indicate intermediate degrees of significance between these extremes.

statistical distributions. This means you must numerically integrate the appropriate statistical functions.

A5.1 SIMPSON'S RULE

Simpson's rule provides a simple way to integrate complex functions within finite limits. The procedure for evaluating Simpson's rule is shown in Table A14. The following function is evaluated by Simpson's rule: [Cohen]

TABLE A14 SIMPSON'S RULE CALCULATION PROCEDURE

Purpose	To evaluate the integral of a known function $F(x)$ between two given points
Conditions	• $F(x)$ must return a finite value for all x values in the integration range. • $F(x)$ may be computable from a formula or obtainable from a table look-up mechanism.
Inputs and Parameters	• x_{low}, x_{high}: real—the integration limits • E: real—the acceptable error of the result • N: int—the number of segments in the integration • `OldResult` = 0: real—the previous answer • `Result`: real—the answer
Steps	1. Identify the upper and lower limits of the numerical integration. 2. Select the initial number of segments, N, an even number. 3. Divide the range, $x_{high} - x_{low}$, into N segments of width W: $$W = \left(x_{high} - x_{low}\right) / N.$$ 4. Compute the integral value with the following equation: $$\int_{x_{low}}^{x_{high}} F(u)du = \frac{W}{3}\left[F(x_{low}) + 4F(x_{low} + W) + 2F(x_{low} + \right.$$ $$2W) + 4F(x_{low} + 3W)$$ $$\left. \ldots 2F(x_{high} - 2W) + 4F(x_{high} - W) + F(x_{high})\right].$$ 5. Compare the result: ``` if abs{(Result - OldResult)/Result} <=E return Result else, continue ``` 6. Adjust the parameter values: ``` OldResult = Result; N = 2*N ``` 7. Recycle at step 3

$$\int_{x_{low}}^{x_{high}} F(u)du = \frac{W}{3}\Big[F\big(x_{low}\big) + 4F\big(x_{low} + W\big) + 2F\big(x_{low} + 2W\big) +$$

$$4F\big(x_{low} + 3W\big) \ldots 2F\big(x_{high} - 2W\big) + 4F\big(x_{high} - W\big) + F\big(x_{high}\big)\Big]. \qquad \text{(A5)}$$

In integrating such statistical functions as the normal distribution, you should select the integration range with care. For example, the integration required for many statistical tables is from $-\infty$ to x. Simpson's rule, however, works only for a finite integration range. In the case of the normal distribution, the approach is first to recognize that the value of its integral from $-\infty$ to zero is 0.5. The reason for this can be seen in Fig. A16. Suppose the integral of interest is over the left shaded area from $-\infty$ to -1.1. Note, however, that the curve is symmetrical, so this area exactly equals the shaded area on the right side of Fig. A16. The curve has a total area of 1, however, because there is a probability of 1 that a value will fall between $-\infty$ and $+\infty$, meaning the total area on the right side of the curve is 0.5. Therefore, if you were to integrate from 0 to $+1.1$, you would get the **unshaded** area on the right half of the curve. You then subtract this result from 0.5 to get your answer. The general rule for integrating from $-\infty$ to x is the following:

> For positive values of x, integrate from 0 to x and add the result to 0.5 to get the answer.
>
> For negative values of x, integrate from 0 to the absolute value of x and subtract the result from 0.5 to get the answer.

In this book, the integrals of the statistical distributions you will need are the following:

☐ The Standard Normal Distribution:

$$\Phi(x) = \int_{-\infty}^{x} \frac{1}{(2\pi)^{1/2}} e^{-u^2/2} \, du \qquad \text{(A6)}$$

☐ The χ^2 distribution for $x > 0$

$$f(x) = \frac{1}{2^{n/2}\Gamma(n/2)} \int_{0}^{x} u^{(n/2) - 1} e^{-u/2} \, du \qquad \text{(A7)}$$

☐ The t distribution

$$g(x) = \frac{\Gamma\left(\dfrac{n+1}{2}\right)}{(n\pi)^{1/2}\Gamma\left(\dfrac{n}{2}\right)} \int_{-\infty}^{x} \left(1 + \frac{u^2}{n}\right)^{-(n+1)/2} \, du \qquad \text{(A8)}$$

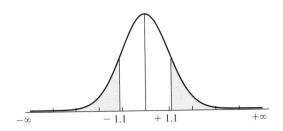

FIGURE A16
The Standard Normal Distribution

The t distribution is symmetrical and its integration range is handled in the same way as the normal distribution. Note that if the t distribution integral is from $-\infty$ to t, the distribution is single-sided. However, if the integral is from $-t$ to t, it is two-sided.

The function $\Gamma(x)$ is the Gamma function, where $\Gamma(x) = (x - 1)\Gamma(x - 1)$. For integer values of x, $\Gamma(x) = (x - 1)!$. Also, $\Gamma(1) = 1$ and $\Gamma(1/2) = \pi^{1/2}$.

A5.2 INTEGRATING THE NORMAL DISTRIBUTION WITH SIMPSON'S RULE

To calculate the value of the normal distribution for one case, say $x = -1.1$, you do the following, using the data in Table A15. The numbers are keyed to the procedure in Table A14.

1. Note from Eq. A6 that the integral is from $-\infty$ to -1.1. Thus, using the above rule for integrating negative values of x, pick $x_{low} = 0$ and $x_{high} = 1.1$. You then subtract the integration result from 0.5 to get the answer.

2. Select an initial number N. For this example, use $N = 20$. While you may need larger numbers to get an accurate result, a low initial value is often helpful in debugging programs. Thus you may even want to initially start with $N = 10$, for example.

3. Divide the range from 0 to 1.1 by 20 to give an initial segment width of $W = 0.055$.

4. Calculate the value of Eq. A5. The sum, 0.364334, is obtained by summing the values of each of the 21 terms in the equation, as illustrated in Table A15 and described in later paragraphs.

5. Compare this result with the value obtained in the previous iteration. The error is thus (Result − OldResult)/Result. If this error is larger than the per-

**TABLE A15   NUMERICAL INTEGRATION EXAMPLE—
NORMAL DISTRIBUTION**

$x_{low} = 0$ Term $(0) = F(x_0)*w/3$

$x_{high} = 1.1$ Term $(20) = F(x_{20})*w/3$

$N = 20$ Term $(i = \text{odd}) = 4*F(x_i)*w/3$

$W = 0.055$ Term $(i = \text{even}) = 2*F(x_i)*w/3$

$(1/\sqrt{2\pi} = 0.39894$

Term Number i	x_i	$x_i{}^2/2$	$e^{-x_i^2/2}$	$F(x_i)$	Term (i)
0	0.000	0.000000	1.00000	0.39894	0.007314
1	0.055	0.001513	0.99849	0.39834	0.029212
2	0.110	0.006050	0.99397	0.39654	0.014540
3	0.165	0.013613	0.98648	0.39355	0.028860
4	0.220	0.024200	0.97609	0.38940	0.014278
5	0.275	0.037813	0.96289	0.38414	0.028170
6	0.330	0.054450	0.94701	0.37780	0.013853
7	0.385	0.074113	0.92857	0.37045	0.027166
8	0.440	0.096800	0.90774	0.36214	0.013278
9	0.495	0.122513	0.88470	0.35294	0.025882
10	0.550	0.151250	0.85963	0.34294	0.012575
11	0.605	0.183013	0.83276	0.33222	0.024363
12	0.660	0.217800	0.80429	0.32086	0.011765
13	0.715	0.255613	0.77444	0.30896	0.022657
14	0.770	0.296450	0.74345	0.29660	0.010875
15	0.825	0.340313	0.71155	0.28387	0.020817
16	0.880	0.387200	0.67896	0.27086	0.009932
17	0.935	0.437113	0.64590	0.25768	0.018896
18	0.990	0.490050	0.61260	0.24439	0.008961
19	1.045	0.546013	0.57926	0.23109	0.016947
20	1.100	0.605000	0.54607	0.21785	0.003994
Total					0.364334

$$F(x_i) = \frac{1}{\sqrt{2\pi}} e^{-\frac{1}{2}x_i^2}$$

missible value E, you continue the integration to improve its accuracy. This was the first pass, so the previous value of OldResult was initialized to 0, hence, the error is 1.0. This error is larger than your permissible error value, you iterate again. Note that in the next iteration, with $N = 40$, the result will be 0.364334, or the same value, so you have zero error. If after the first trial, the absolute value of the error were larger than you wanted you would iterate again.

6. Double N. The example here started with $N = 20$, so the second cycle would be with $N = 40$.

7. Repeat the calculations starting at step 3.

The calculation of the value of Eq. A5 is done as shown in Table A15. The terms are obtained as follows:

1. Evaluate the function $F(x)$ at x_{low}, $x_{low} + W$, $x_{low} + 2W$, and so on, all the way up to x_{high}. $W = \left(x_{high} - x_{low}\right) / N$, so it takes N terms from x_{low} to reach x_{high}. Counting x_{low}, there are $N + 1$ terms to evaluate.

2. The x values are shown in the x_i column in Table A15. Starting with x_{low}, which is 0, the second x value is $x_{low} + W = 0 + 0.055 = 0.055$. Obtain all the 21 x_i terms in this way.

3. Evaluate the terms for $F(x_i)$:

$$F(x_i) = \frac{1}{\sqrt{2\pi}} e^{(-x^2/2)}.$$

The value of $1/\sqrt{2\pi} = 0.39894$ and the values of the exponential for each x_i term are also shown in Table A15.

4. Multiply this exponential value by $1/\sqrt{2\pi}$ to give the value of the $F(x_i)$ function.

5. Calculate the final terms by multiplying each by $W/3$ and by the constant 1, 2, or 4, depending on which term it is in Eq. A5.

6. Add these term values to give the result of 0.364334.

Of course, this procedure computes the value for this function only for a single value of N. You must repeat this calculation with progressively larger values of N until the error is low enough to be acceptable. Note also that when you are done, you will have the value for Eq. A5. You still need to adjust this value to account for the fact that your integral was from $x_{low} = 0$ instead of from $-\infty$. In this case, you adjust by subtracting this value from 0.5, giving a final result of 0.135666. Because the value of the normal distribution for -1.1 in Table A1 is 0.1357, clearly only 20 terms give a very accurate result. Note that with 40 terms, the result is 0.135666, which is the same as the value with 20 terms.

A5.3 INTEGRATING THE χ^2 DISTRIBUTION WITH SIMPSON'S RULE

The calculations for the χ^2 numerical integration follow the same procedure described in Section A5.2 for the normal distribution, except for the calculation of the $F(x)$ terms. The terms in the χ^2 $F(x)$ calculation use Eq. A7 and are shown in Table A16.

As before, $N = 20$, $n = 9$, and $W = \left(x_{high} - x_{low}\right) / N$. Here, n is the number of degrees of freedom and N is the number of segments in the numerical integra-

TABLE A16 NUMERICAL INTEGRATION EXAMPLE—
χ^2 DISTRIBUTION

$x_{low} = 0$

$x_{high} = 11.39$

$N = 20$

$W = 0.5695$

$n = 9$

$\Gamma(n/2) = 11.6317$

$2^{n/2} = 22.6274$

Term Number i	x_i	$x^{\left(\frac{n}{2}-1\right)}$	$e^{-(x/2)}$	$F(x_i)$	Term (i)
0	0.0000	0.000000	1.000000	0.000000	0.000000
1	0.5695	0.139389	0.752202	0.000398	0.000302
2	1.1390	1.577005	0.565808	0.003390	0.001287
3	1.7085	6.518572	0.425602	0.010541	0.008004
4	2.2780	17.84177	0.320139	0.021702	0.008239
5	2.8475	38.96037	0.240809	0.035647	0.027068
6	3.4170	73.74922	0.181137	0.050756	0.019270
7	3.9865	126.4944	0.136252	0.065484	0.049724
8	4.5560	201.8566	0.102489	0.078603	0.029843
9	5.1255	304.8434	0.077092	0.089291	0.067802
10	5.6950	440.7863	0.057989	0.097117	0.036872
11	6.2645	615.3220	0.043620	0.101977	0.077435
12	6.8340	834.3772	0.032811	0.104016	0.039491
13	7.4035	1,104.154	0.024680	0.103538	0.078620
14	7.9730	1,431.120	0.018565	0.100944	0.038325
15	8.5425	1,821.996	0.013964	0.096669	0.073404
16	9.1120	2,283.747	0.010504	0.091143	0.034604
17	9.6815	2,823.575	0.007901	0.084764	0.064364
18	10.2510	3,448.910	0.005943	0.077880	0.029568
19	10.8205	4,167.404	0.004471	0.070786	0.053750
20	11.3900	4,986.927	0.003363	0.063716	0.012095
Total					0.750067

$$F(x_i) = \frac{1}{2^{n/2}\Gamma(n/2)}\, x_i^{(n/2)-1} e^{-x_i/2}$$

tion range. For this example, $x_{low} = 0$ and $x_{high} = 11.39$, so $W = 0.5695$. You can visualize the procedure from Fig. A14, in which integration is along the x-axis from $x = 0$ to $x = 11.39$. Visualize the area under the $n = 9$ curve as cut into 21 slices; this integration is essentially adding up their areas. Obviously, in a real program you would use whatever values for the integration limits the application required. From Eq. A7, you also need the values of $2^{n/2} = 2^{9/2} = 22.6274$ and $\Gamma(n/2) = \Gamma(9/2) = 11.6317$. You obtain this Gamma function value as follows:

$$\Gamma(9/2) = \frac{7}{2}*\Gamma(7/2) = \frac{7}{2}*\frac{5}{2}*\frac{3}{2}*\frac{1}{2}*\sqrt{\pi} = 11.6317.$$

In Table A16, the first term in the $F(x_i)$ column is zero and the next 20 are calculated by multiplying each $F(x_i)$ alternately by $4W/3$ or $2W/3$, depending on the term in Eq. A5. For example, the last term is

$$\text{Term}_{20} = \frac{W}{3}*F\left(x_{20}\right) = \frac{0.5695}{3}*0.0637 = 0.012095.$$

The final answer, 0.750067, is obtained by summing up all the terms and is quite close to the table value of 0.75 given for row $n = 9$ of Table A3. To check this, look across row 9 until you come to the value 11.39 and then look up to find the probability value of 0.75. Note that because the χ^2 integral is from 0 to the desired value, this is the final answer and no adjustments are needed to correct for $-\infty$ or negative values.

A5.4   INTEGRATING THE t DISTRIBUTION WITH SIMPSON'S RULE

In this example, evaluate the t distribution for $x = +1.1$ and $n = 9$. The t distribution is symmetrical and the integral is from $-\infty$ to the desired value, so you must make the same corrections as with the normal distribution as follows:

For positive values of x, integrate from 0 to x and add the result to 0.5 to get the answer.

For negative values of x, integrate from 0 to the absolute value of x and subtract the result from 0.5 to get the answer.

The t distribution integral follows the procedure described in Section A5.2 and Table A14 for the normal distribution, except for the evaluation of the $F(x_i)$ terms. Here, $x_{low} = 0$, $x_{high} = 1.1$, $N = 20$, $n = 9$, and $W = 0.055$. Again, n is the number of degrees of freedom and N is the number of segments in the numerical integration range. From Eq. A8, calculate the terms as shown in Table A17 and add the result to 0.5 to get the answer.

To show how the calculations are done, the third and fourth columns in Table A17 show the values of $1 + \dfrac{x^2}{n} = 1 + \dfrac{x^2}{9}$ and $\left(1 + x^2 / n\right)^{-(n+1)/2} = \left(1 + x^2 / 9\right)^{-5}$, respectively. The various constants used are

$$\Gamma\left(n/2\right) = \Gamma\left(9/2\right) = 11.6317,$$

$$\Gamma\left(\frac{n+1}{2}\right) = \Gamma\left(5\right) = 4! = 24, \text{ and}$$

$$\sqrt{n\pi} = \sqrt{9\pi} = 5.3174.$$

**TABLE A17   NUMERICAL INTEGRATION EXAMPLE—
            t DISTRIBUTION**

$x_{low} = 0$
$x_{high} = 1.1$
$n = 9$
$N = 20$
$W = 0.055$
$\Gamma(n/2) = 11.6317$
$\Gamma\left(\dfrac{n+1}{2}\right) = 24$
$\sqrt{n\pi} = 5.3174$

Term Number i	x_i	$1 + x^2/n$	$(1 + x^2/n)^{-(n+1)/2}$	$F(x_i)$	Terms
0	0.000	1.00000	1.00000	0.3880	0.007114
1	0.055	1.00034	0.99832	0.3874	0.028408
2	0.110	1.00134	0.99331	0.3854	0.014133
3	0.165	1.00303	0.98501	0.3822	0.028029
4	0.220	1.00538	0.97354	0.3778	0.013851
5	0.275	1.00840	0.95903	0.3721	0.027290
6	0.330	1.01210	0.94164	0.3654	0.013398
7	0.385	1.01647	0.92157	0.3576	0.026224
8	0.440	1.02151	0.89905	0.3489	0.012792
9	0.495	1.02723	0.87432	0.3393	0.024880
10	0.550	1.03361	0.84765	0.3289	0.012060
11	0.605	1.04067	0.81929	0.3179	0.023314
12	0.660	1.04840	0.78952	0.3064	0.011233
13	0.715	1.05680	0.75863	0.2944	0.021588
14	0.770	1.06588	0.72688	0.2821	0.010342
15	0.825	1.07563	0.69454	0.2695	0.019764
16	0.880	1.08604	0.66185	0.2568	0.009417
17	0.935	1.09714	0.62907	0.2441	0.017901
18	0.990	1.10890	0.59640	0.2314	0.008486
19	1.045	1.12134	0.56405	0.2189	0.016051
20	1.100	1.13444	0.53221	0.2065	0.003786
Total					0.350059

$$F(x_i) = \frac{\Gamma\left(\dfrac{n+1}{2}\right)}{\sqrt{n\pi}\,\Gamma(n/2)}\left(1 + \frac{x_i^2}{n}\right)^{-(n+1)/2}$$

The function terms are then obtained by evaluating $\left(1 + x^2/9\right)^{-5}$ for each value of x_i and multiplying and dividing by the appropriate constants, as in Eq. A8. The first and last terms are obtained by multiplying the $F\!\left(x_0\right)$ and $F\!\left(x_{20}\right)$ terms by $W/3$. All the others are obtained by alternately multiplying $F\!\left(x_i\right)$ by $4W/3$ and $2W/3$. The sum of the terms is 0.350059, and the answer is this value plus 0.5, or 0.850059. This is very close to the Table A2 value of the t distribution for $t = 1.1$ and $n = 9$, which is 0.85. To check this, look across row 9 of Table A2 until you come to the value 1.1 and then look up to find the probability $p(\alpha)$ value of 0.85.

A6   Tests for Normality

Because much of the statistical work done in software estimating and quality management requires that the data be normally distributed, it is generally wise to ensure they are. If they are not, there are usually corrective measures you can take. The distribution of a dataset can be tested graphically or with the χ^2 test. The first step should be to examine the data graphically. It is then often relatively easy to see special groupings or unexpected associations. Next, examine the dataset with the χ^2 test to see how well it corresponds to a particular distribution. The test can be used to test any one discrete dataset against any other or against a statistical distribution.

A6.1   THE GRAPHICAL TEST FOR NORMALITY

In plotting statistical data, you must convert them to a standard form so that they can be compared to normal or other distributions. In doing this, you replace each data value, x_i with a value z_i as follows:

$$z_i = \frac{\left(x_i - \mu\right)}{\sigma} = \frac{\left(x_i - x_{avg}\right)}{\sigma}. \tag{A9}$$

The μ, or x_{avg}, term is the average value of all the x's and the σ term is the standard deviation of the x's. As before, the variance of the x data (the square of the standard deviation) is calculated as follows:

$$\text{Variance} = \sigma^2 = \frac{1}{n-1}\sum_{i=1}^{n}\left(x_i - x_{avg}\right)^2, \tag{A10}$$

$$\text{StdDeviation} = \sqrt{Variance} = \sigma.$$

Note that here you get the variance by dividing by n if you are testing a full population or $n - 1$ if you are testing a sample. By using this transformation, you plot the distribution in units of standard deviation above and below the mean.

A6.2 THE PROCEDURE FOR GRAPHICALLY TESTING FOR NORMALITY

Table A18 shows the procedure for graphically testing a dataset to see if it is normally distributed.

Example of a Graphical Test for Normality.   The results of the graphical test of the size data in Table A19 are shown in Fig. A17. The following comments track the numbered steps in the procedure in Table A18:

Note that this test is made against only one variable and it is that variable that must be used as the sort key. In Table A19, the key variable is object LOC/method.

1. Calculate the average value of the object LOC/method in the data table (Table A19) to get 18.336.

2. This is a full population, so calculate the variance using $n = 58$: 166.13.

3. Calculate the standard deviation of the object LOC/method data as $\sqrt{166.13} = 12.889$.

4. Calculate the normal form as shown in the Normal Form columns of Table A19. For example, for item 32, this calculation is

$$z_i = \frac{\left(x_i - x_{avg}\right)}{\sigma} = \frac{14.5 - 18.336}{12.889} = -0.298.$$

5. Construct the data table (see Table A19). In the i columns, list the data items in ascending order, and in the i/n columns, list the fraction of the items up to that point. For item 18, for example, $i/n = 18/58 = 0.310$, meaning 31 percent of the items have been included to that point.

6. Construct the normal table (see Table A20). From Table A1, copy the appropriate $\Phi(x)$ numbers to Table A20. For example, under $x = -1.8$ in Table A1, $\Phi(x) = 0.0359$. Enter this value in Table A20 beside $z = -1.8$.

7. Starting at $z = -4$ in the normal table, look for an equal or lower z value in the data table. All the way to $z = -1.0$ in the normal table (Table A20), there are no lower z values in the data table (Table A19). You thus enter 0 in the Data-Cumulative Fraction column of the normal table. The next term, -0.8, has lower terms. The nearest lower term, -0.810 is the fourteenth item. List its cumulative fraction, 0.241, in the Data-Cumulative Fraction column opposite -0.8 in the normal table. At -0.6 in the normal table, the nearest lower item is 24 with a cumulative fraction of 0.414.

TABLE A18 PROCEDURE FOR GRAPHICALLY TESTING FOR NORMALITY

Purpose	To graphically examine a dataset to see if it is normally distributed
Conditions	None
Inputs	• The dataset to be tested, sorted in increasing order • The number of items in the dataset, n • A table of the normal distribution

Steps	1. Calculate the average of the data values to be tested, x_{avg}:
	
	$$x_{avg} = \mu = \frac{1}{n} \sum_{i=1}^{n} x_i.$$
	
	2. If these data are a full population, calculate the variance of the data using the following formula
	
	$$\sigma^2 = \frac{1}{n} \sum_{i=1}^{n} \left(x_i - x_{avg}\right)^2.$$
	
	If these data are a sample of a population, calculate the variance of the data, using the following formula:
	
	$$\sigma^2 = \frac{1}{n-1} \sum_{i=1}^{n} \left(x_i - x_{avg}\right)^2.$$
	
	3. Take the positive square root of the variance to give the standard deviation, σ.
	
	4. Convert the distribution terms to normal form by calculating for each data term x_i the normal form term z_i using the following formula:
	
	$$z_i = \frac{\left(x_i - x_{avg}\right)}{\sigma}.$$
	
	5. Construct a data table of the data to be tested as follows (see Table A19):
	   a. List the item number i, from 1 to n.
	   b. For each item, calculate its cumulative fraction of the total number of items, i/n.
	   c. List the data in ascending order.
	   d. List the normal form of the data in ascending order.
	
	6. Construct a normal distribution table as follows (see Table A20):
	   a. List z values from -4.0 to $+4.0$ in increments of 0.2 in the z value column.
	   b. Take the normal distribution $\Phi(x)$ values from Table A1 for each z value and list them in the Normal-Cumulative Fraction column.
	   c. Make a blank column for the cumulative fraction of the data.

TABLE A18 (continued)

Steps	7. For each z value in Table A20, find the nearest lower value z_i in Table A19 and enter its cumulative fraction in Table A20 under Data—Cumulative Fraction. If there is no lower value, enter 0. 8. From Table A20, plot the normal cumulative fraction and the data cumulative faction data as functions of z.
Interpretation	• Visually examine the quality of the fit. • This test is appropriate for comparing the fit quality between two datasets or between one dataset and a standard distribution.

8. After completing the normal table in step 7, plot both the Normal-Cumulative Fraction and Data-Cumulative fraction columns against z as shown in Fig. A17.

As you can see from Fig. A17, the normal distribution is quite smooth, while the object distribution is much less even and cuts off at -1. The absence of a tail at negative values is one indication that these object data are not normally distributed.

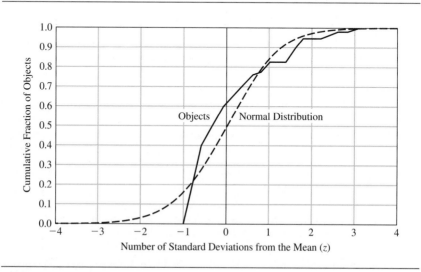

FIGURE A17
Object LOC versus Normal Distribution

When your graphical test shows that a fit is as poor as this, it is wise to seek some transformation to make it more closely fit the normal pattern. Often, when data sharply cut off like this they may have a log-normal distribution (see Section A1.4). This is frequently the case with a data distribution that does not have a reasonably long negative tail. To determine the fit to a log-normal distribution, you would first take the log of the data and then repeat the entire test, substituting the log values for the x values. Plots of this comparison are produced in the same way and are shown in Fig. A18. This appears to be a better fit.

A6.3   THE χ^2 TEST FOR NORMALITY

The χ^2 test for normality determines the likelihood that a dataset is from a normal distribution. It is done by comparing the structure of the dataset with that of an ideal normal distribution, as shown in Fig. A19. Here, the normal distribution has been divided into 10 equal-area segments. For example, if you had a dataset with 50 randomly distributed values, you would expect that about five of them would fall into each of these segments.

In doing the χ^2 test, you divide the normal distribution into some number of segments, determine how many items would normally fall into each segment, determine the number that actually fall into each segment, and then calculate the value of Q. You then look up Q in a table for the χ^2 distribution to determine

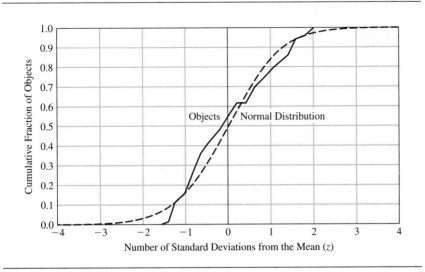

FIGURE A18
Object LnLOC versus Normal Distribution

TABLE A19 PASCAL OBJECT LOC/METHOD—DATA TABLE

Item	Cumulative Fraction	Object LOC/Method	Normal Form	Item	Cumulative Fraction	Object LOC/Method	Normal Form
i	i/n	x	$z_i = (x_i - x_{avg})/\sigma$	i	i/n	x	$z_i = (x_i - x_{avg})/\sigma$
1	.017	5.67	−0.983	30	.517	13.75	−0.356
2	.034	5.75	−0.976	31	.534	14.00	−0.336
3	.052	5.80	−0.973	32	.552	14.50	−0.298
4	.069	6.00	−0.957	33	.569	14.67	−0.285
5	.086	6.00	−0.957	34	.586	16.40	−0.150
6	.103	6.00	−0.957	35	.603	16.40	−0.150
7	.121	6.33	−0.931	36	.621	16.40	−0.150
8	.138	7.00	−0.880	37	.638	19.20	0.067
9	.155	7.33	−0.854	38	.655	19.33	0.077
10	.172	7.50	−0.841	39	.672	20.50	0.168
11	.190	7.57	−0.835	40	.690	21.75	0.265
12	.207	7.67	−0.828	41	.707	22.25	0.304
13	.224	7.80	−0.817	42	.724	23.00	0.362
14	.241	7.90	−0.810	43	.741	24.17	0.452
15	.259	8.33	−0.776	44	.759	25.42	0.549
16	.276	8.33	−0.776	45	.776	28.33	0.776

TABLE A19 (continued)

Item	Cumulative Fraction	Object LOC/Method	Normal Form	Item	Cumulative Fraction	Object LOC/Method	Normal Form
i	i/n	x	z_i	i	i/n	x	z_i
17	.293	8.67	−0.750	46	.793	29.00	0.827
18	.310	8.67	−0.750	47	.810	29.67	0.879
19	.328	8.67	−0.750	48	.828	30.14	0.916
20	.345	8.83	−0.737	49	.845	36.50	1.409
21	.362	9.00	−0.724	50	.862	36.80	1.432
22	.379	9.00	−0.724	51	.879	37.33	1.474
23	.397	10.00	−0.647	52	.897	38.00	1.526
24	.414	10.33	−0.621	53	.914	39.00	1.603
25	.431	10.67	−0.595	54	.931	40.25	1.700
26	.448	11.75	−0.511	55	.948	41.00	1.758
27	.466	12.00	−0.492	56	.966	48.17	2.314
28	.483	12.33	−0.466	57	.983	50.63	2.505
29	.500	13.25	−0.395	58	1.00	52.80	2.674
Average: x_{avg}						18.336	

Standard Deviation: $\sigma = \sqrt{\dfrac{1}{n}\sum\left(x_i - x_{avg}\right)^2} = 12.889$

TABLE A20 NORMAL DISTRIBUTION VERSUS DATA—NORMAL TABLE

z value	Normal-Cumulative Fraction	Data-Cumulative Fraction
−4.0	0	0
−3.8	.0001	0
−3.6	.0002	0
−3.4	.0003	0
−3.2	.0007	0
−3.0	.0013	0
−2.8	.0026	0
−2.6	.0047	0
−2.4	.0082	0
−2.2	.0139	0
−2.0	.0227	0
−1.8	.0359	0
−1.6	.0548	0
−1.4	.0808	0
−1.2	.1151	0
−1.0	.1587	0
−.8	.2119	.241
−.6	.2743	.414
−.4	.3446	.483
−.2	.4207	.569
0	.5000	.621
.2	.5793	.672
.4	.6554	.724
.6	.7257	.759
.8	.7881	.776
1.0	.8413	.828
1.2	.8849	.828
1.4	.9192	.828
1.6	.9452	.897

TABLE A20   (continued)

z value	Normal- Cumulative Fraction	Data- Cumulative Fraction
1.8	.9641	.948
2.0	.9773	.948
2.2	.9861	.948
2.4	.9918	.966
2.6	.9953	.983
2.8	.9974	1.000
3.0	.9987	1.000
3.2	.9993	1.000
3.4	.9997	1.000
3.6	.9998	1.000
3.8	.9999	1.000
4.0	1.0000	1.000

how well these data fit the normal distribution. The only limitation for the χ^2 test is that you have 15 or more data values. The more data items, the more reliable the test.

A6.4   THE χ^2 TEST PROCEDURE

The procedure for conducting the χ^2 test is shown in Table A21.

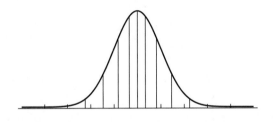

FIGURE A19
The χ^2 Test for Normality

534   Appendix A   Statistical Methods for the Personal Software Process

TABLE A21 THE χ^2 TEST PROCEDURE

Purpose	To determine the quality of fit between a dataset and a normal distribution
Conditions	• The quality of this test depends on the quantity of data. It is generally desirable to have about 30 or more data items. • You should not use a four-cell χ^2 test with 15 or fewer data items.
Inputs	• The dataset, sorted in increasing order • The number of items in the test distribution, n • A table of the normal distribution

Steps	1. Calculate the average of the data values to be tested, x_{avg}:
	
	$$x_{avg} = \frac{1}{n}\sum_{i=1}^{n} x_i.$$
	
	2. If these data are a full population, calculate the variance of the data, using the following formula:
	
	$$\sigma^2 = \frac{1}{n}\sum_{i=1}^{n}\left(x_i - x_{avg}\right)^2.$$
	
	If these data are a sample of a population, calculate the variance of the data, using the following formula:
	
	$$\sigma^2 = \frac{1}{n-1}\sum_{i=1}^{n}\left(x_i - x_{avg}\right)^2.$$
	
	3. Take the positive square root of the variance to give the standard deviation, σ.
	
	4. Convert the distribution terms to normal form by calculating for each term x_i the term z_i, using the following formula:
	
	$$z_i = \frac{\left(x_i - x_{avg}\right)}{\sigma}.$$
	
	5. Construct a data table of the data to be tested as follows (see Table A22):
	   a. List the item number i, from 1 to n.
	   b. For each item, calculate its cumulative fraction of the total number of items, i/n.
	   c. List the data in ascending order.
	   d. List the normal form of the data in ascending order.
	
	6. Determine the maximum number of segments S so that, if possible, n/S is an integer equal to or greater than 5, S is greater than three, and $S^2 \geq n$. If necessary, pick S so that n/S is not an integer. When you have two or more choices, select the one where the values of n and S^2 are most nearly equal.

TABLE A21 (continued)

Steps	7. Divide the probability range of the normal distribution into S equal segments (if step 6 did not produce an integer value for n/S, see the second following example). Do this by dividing the normal distribution into S equal segments that each have a probability of $1/S$.
	
	8. Construct a normal table as follows (see Table A23):
	   a. List the upper and lower bounds for each segment of the normal distribution.
	   b. In the Normal Items column, list the expected number of items, N_i, in each segment. For equal-sized segments, all the N_i equal n/S.
	   c. In the Data Items column, list the number of items in the dataset with z_i values that fall within that segment's range, are above the lower limit and less than or equal to the upper limit. This number is k_i.
	   d. Find k_i by counting the items in Table A22 with z_i values between the limits for that segment.
	
	9. Calculate the value of Q as follows:
	
	$$Q = \sum_{i=1}^{S} \frac{(N_i - k_i)^2}{N_i}.$$
	
	10. Look up the probability value p for this value of Q in Table A3 for the χ^2 distribution under $S - 1$ degrees of freedom.
	
	Alternatively, calculate the probability value p of the χ^2 distribution for $S - 1$ degrees of freedom by integrating from 0 to Q.
	
	11. Calculate the distribution tail as $1 - p$.

Interpretation	• Tail areas < 0.05 are generally considered sufficient to reject a fit. • Tail areas > 0.2 are generally considered sufficient to accept a fit. • Intermediate values indicate intermediate degrees of fit.

Example of the χ^2 Test with Equal Segments.   The χ^2 test of the Object LOC/method data from Table A22 is done as shown in the procedure in Table A21. The following comments track the numbered steps in this procedure:

1. Calculate the average value of the Object LOC/method in the data table (Table A22) as 18.0776.

2. We will consider this a sample population, so calculate the variance using $n - 1 = 49$: 163.49.

3. Obtain the standard deviation of the object LOC/method data by taking the square root of the variance: 12.7864.

TABLE A22 PASCAL OBJECT LOC/METHOD—DATA TABLE FOR 50 OBJECTS

Item	Cumulative Fraction	Object LOC/Method	Normal Form	Item	Cumulative Fraction	Object LOC/Method	Normal Form
	i/n	x	z		i/n	x	z
1	.02	5.67	-0.9704	26	.52	13.75	-0.3385
2	.04	5.75	-0.9641	27	.54	14.00	-0.3189
3	.06	5.80	-0.9602	28	.56	14.50	-0.2798
4	.08	6.00	-0.9446	29	.58	14.67	-0.2665
5	.10	6.00	-0.9446	30	.60	16.40	-0.1312
6	.12	6.00	-0.9446	31	.62	16.40	-0.1312
7	.14	7.00	-0.8664	32	.64	19.20	0.0878
8	.16	7.33	-0.8406	33	.66	19.33	0.0979
9	.18	7.50	-0.8273	34	.68	20.50	0.1895
10	.20	7.57	-0.8218	35	.70	21.75	0.2872
11	.22	7.67	-0.8140	36	.72	22.25	0.3263
12	.24	7.80	-0.8038	37	.74	24.17	0.4765
13	.26	8.33	-0.7623	38	.76	25.42	0.5742
14	.28	8.33	-0.7623	39	.78	28.33	0.8018
15	.30	8.67	-0.7358	40	.80	29.00	0.8542
16	.32	8.67	-0.7358	41	.82	29.67	0.9066

TABLE A22 (continued)

Item	Cumulative Fraction	Object LOC/Method	Normal Form	Item	Cumulative Fraction	Object LOC/Method	Normal Form
	i/n	x	z		i/n	x	z
17	.34	8.67	-0.7358	42	.84	30.14	0.9434
18	.36	8.83	-0.7232	43	.86	36.80	1.4642
19	.38	9.00	-0.7099	44	.88	37.33	1.5057
20	.40	10.00	-0.6317	45	.90	38.00	1.5581
21	.42	10.33	-0.6059	46	.92	39.00	1.6363
22	.44	10.67	-0.5793	47	.94	40.25	1.7341
23	.46	11.75	-0.4949	48	.96	41.00	1.7927
24	.48	12.00	-0.4753	49	.98	50.63	2.5459
25	.50	13.25	-0.3776	50	1.00	52.80	2.7156
Average: x_{avg}						18.0776	

Standard Deviation: $\sigma = \sqrt{\dfrac{1}{n-1}\sum(x_i - x_{avg})^2} = 12.7864$

4. Convert the data to normal form.

5. Construct the data table as shown in Table A22. In the i columns, list the data items in ascending order, and in the i/n columns, list the fractions of the items up to that point. For example, for item 18, $i/n = 18/50 = 0.36$, meaning 36 percent of the items have been included to that point.

6. Follow the ground rules for this step: with 50 items, $S = 10$ meets the criteria.

7. Divide the normal distribution into 10 equal area segments, as shown in Fig. A19.

8. Construct the normal table as shown in Table A23. With 10 segments, there is a probability of 0.1 that a data item will fall in any one. Table A24 shows these values for various values of S. From Table A1, for example, the first cell will be bounded by $-\infty$ and about -1.3. You get the actual value of -1.282 by interpolating between -1.2 and -1.3. The second cell will have a lower limit of -1.282 and an upper limit of -0.842.

□ The normal number of items to fall in each segment is $n/S = 50/10 = 5$, so enter 5 in the Normal Items column for each segment.

□ To count the items, first get the segment limits from Table A23 and then find the number of items in Table A22 that have z values between these limits. For cell 6, for example, the lower limit is 0 and the upper limit is 0.253. In Table A22, items 32, 33, and 34 have z values of 0.0878,

TABLE A23 χ^2 TEST FOR EQUAL SEGMENTS—NORMAL TABLE

Segment	Lower Limit	Upper Limit	Normal Items N_i	Data Items k_i	$(N_i - k_i)^2$	$(N_i - k_i)^2 / N_i$
1	$-\infty$	-1.282	5	0	25	5.0
2	-1.282	$-.842$	5	7	4	0.8
3	$-.842$	$-.524$	5	15	100	20.0
4	$-.524$	$-.253$	5	7	4	0.8
5	$-.253$	0	5	2	9	1.8
6	0	.253	5	3	4	0.8
7	.253	.524	5	3	4	0.8
8	.524	.842	5	2	9	1.8
9	.842	1.282	5	3	4	0.8
10	1.282	∞	5	8	9	1.8
Q						34.4

TABLE A24 NORMAL DISTRIBUTION SEGMENTS

Note: The values are the bottom and top bounds for *n* equal-sized segments.

Segment	Number of Equal-sized Segments (*S*) in the Normal Distribution						
Number n	*4*	*5*	*6*	*7*	*8*	*10*	*12*
1 - lower	$-\infty$	$-\infty$	$-\infty$	$-\infty$	$-\infty$	$-\infty$	$-\infty$
1 - upper	−.766	−.842	−.967	−1.067	−1.150	−1.282	−1.383
2 - lower	−.766	−.842	−.967	−1.067	−1.150	−1.282	−1.383
2 - upper	0	−.253	−.431	−.566	−.675	−.842	−.867
3 - lower	0	−.253	−.431	−.566	−.675	−.842	−.867
3 - upper	.766	.253	0	−.180	−.312	−.524	−.675
4 - lower	.766	.253	0	−.180	−.312	−.524	−.675
4 - upper	∞	.842	.431	.180	0	−.253	−.431
5 - lower		.842	.431	.180	0	−.253	−.431
5 - upper		∞	.967	.566	.312	0	−.210
6 - lower			.967	.566	.312	0	−.210
6 - upper			∞	1.067	.675	.253	0
7 - lower				1.067	.675	.253	0
7 - upper				∞	1.150	.524	.210
8 - lower					1.150	.524	.210
8 - upper					∞	.842	.431
9 - lower						.842	.431
9 - upper						1.282	.675
10 - lower						1.282	.675
10 - upper						∞	.967
11 - lower							.967
11 - upper							1.383
12 - lower							1.383
12 - upper							∞

0.0979, and 0.1895, respectively. Because these are the only items between 0 and 0.253, these are the only three that are counted. You thus enter 3 in the k_i column for cell 6 in Table A23.

9. To obtain Q, calculate the values in the two right columns in Table A23. The sum of the rightmost column then gives the value of 34.4 for Q.

10. In looking in Table A3 for 34.4, look under $S - 1$ degrees of freedom. In the 9 row, you look across and find that the largest value is 23.59. Because this value is under $p = 0.995$, it means that $p > 0.995$.

11. Calculate the significance: because $p > 0.995$, $1 - p < 0.005$.

This says that there is a less than 0.005 chance that these data could be normally distributed, sufficient reason to reject the fit of these data to a normal distribution.

Example of a χ^2 Test with Unequal Segments. When the number of items in your dataset do not divide neatly into S equal segments, you need to establish unequal size ranges. To do this, you must allocate the total probability range of 1.00 proportionately among these unequal segments. For example, if there were 58 members you could assign two segments with five members each and eight segments with six members each, as shown in Table A25. To calculate the values of the upper and lower limits, first divide 1.00 into 58 parts, giving a unit member value of 0.01724138. This is the area under the normal curve that is to be allocated to each of the 58 items.

Next, allocate unit values to each segment based on the number of its members. For example, the first segment, with five members, would get five unit values, so it is bounded by the probabilities 0.0 and 5*0.01724, or 0.0862. Hence, this segment should have 8.62 percent of the area of the normal curve. Calculate the cumulative areas of all the segments in this way and enter the values in the Cumulative Segment Area column of Table A25.

Then, with the areas for the segments established, find the z values that bound each segment. Do this by looking in the normal distribution table in Table A1 to find the z values that most nearly correspond to each area.

The probability of 0 for the lower limit of the first segment is for $x = -\infty$, so $-\infty$ is entered in Table A25 as the lower limit of segment 1. The probability value for the upper limit of segment 1 is 0.0862. Look in Table A1 to find the values of x for this segment, where you find that the probability of 0.0862 is between probabilities 0.0808 and 0.0968. You thus have to interpolate between the x values of -1.3 and -1.4. To do this, use the general interpolation procedure as follows:

1. To find the value of some term x_k, given some probability value p_k, look in the normal distribution table in the $\Phi(x)$ column to find the p values nearest to p_k.

TABLE A25 NORMAL DISTRIBUTION TEST FOR UNEQUAL SEGMENTS

Segment	Cumulative Segment Area	Lower Limit	Upper Limit	Normal Items N_i	Data Items k_i	$(N_i - k_i)^2$	$(N_i - k_i)^2 / N_i$
1	0.0862	$-\infty$	-1.3663	5	0	25	5.0000
2	0.1897	-1.3663	-.8800	6	8	4	0.6667
3	0.2931	-.8800	-.5450	6	17	121	20.1667
4	0.3966	-.5450	-.2626	6	8	4	0.6667
5	0.5000	-.2626	0	6	3	9	1.5000
6	0.6035	0	.2626	6	3	9	1.5000
7	0.7069	.2626	.5450	6	4	4	0.6667
8	0.8103	.5450	.8800	6	4	4	0.6667
9	0.9138	.8800	1.3663	6	1	25	4.1667
10	1.0000	1.3663	∞	5	10	25	5.0000
Q							40.0002

2. a) If you find an exact match, take the corresponding value of x as x_k.

b) If you do not find an exact match, find the nearest p values that bound p_k. Call them P_{above} and P_{below}. Also find the x values corresponding to these p values and label them x_{above} and x_{below}.

3. Calculate the value of x_k as follows:

$$x_k = x_{below} + \frac{\left(P_k - P_{below}\right)}{\left(P_{above} - P_{below}\right)} * (x_{above} - x_{below}). \qquad \text{(A11)}$$

This interpolation procedure results in $p_k = 0.0862$ (the upper probability limit of segment 1 calculated above), $p_{above} = 0.0968$, and $p_{below} = 0.0808$. The value of x_{above} is -1.3 and x_{below} is -1.4. Using these values, obtain the value of x_k as follows:

$$x_k = (-1.4) + \frac{(0.0862 - 0.0808)}{(0.0968 - 0.0808)} * \left(-1.3 - (-1.4)\right) = -1.3663.$$

The corresponding x values for this first segment are thus $-\infty$ and -1.3663. The next segment would be bounded by 0.0862 and 0.1896. Here, the lower limit of segment 2 equals the upper limit of segment 1 and the upper limit is increased by six units. The lower x limit for this segment is thus -1.3663, corresponding to the probability of 0.0862. For the probability of 0.1897, you again need to interpolate from Table A1. The above and below probabilities are now 0.2119 and 0.1841, and the x values are $x_{above} = -0.8$ and $x_{below} = -0.9$. The interpolation formula is thus

$$x_k = (-0.9) + \frac{(0.1897 - 0.1841)}{(0.2119 - 0.1841)} * \left(-0.8 - (-0.9)\right) = -0.8800.$$

So segment 2 is bounded by $x = -1.3663$ and $x = -0.8800$. The remaining entries in the table are completed in the same way. Note, however, that with a symmetrical table like this, when you have calculated the ranges for the five segments with negative limits the entries for the positive segments are their mirror images. With these values, you count the numbers of data items in each segment in Table A19 as before and calculate the Q value, also as before. The value of Q in this case is 40.0002.

The probability for this Q value is obtained from Table A3 for the χ^2 distribution with $S - 1$ degrees of freedom. Again, with nine degrees of freedom, the greatest value in the table is 23.59, so the p values are > 0.995. The tail of the distribution is $1 - p$, or less than 0.005. Because a number less than 0.05 is considered poor enough to reject the fit, this case is clearly rejected as a fit to the normal distribution.

A7   Linear Regression

When you calculate the correlation of two variables, you are determining the degree to which the variations of one coincide with the variations of the other. Linear regression estimates the (presumed) relationship between one variable and another by expressing one in terms of a linear (or more complex) function of the other. This function can then be used to predict the value of one variable based on the value of the other.

Linear regression is a way of optimally fitting a line to a set of data. For example, if you had the data in Table A26 and you estimated a new program would have 386 object LOC, you could use these historical data to determine the most likely number of new and changed LOC in the new program. The linear regression method provides a way to do this.

A7.1   THE LINEAR REGRESSION METHOD

For example, to use the linear regression method for a program size estimate assume the number of new and changed LOC can be represented as a function of

TABLE A26   EXAMPLE SIZE DATA—10 PASCAL PROGRAMS

Program Number i	Estimated Object LOC: x_i	Actual New and Changed LOC: y_i
1	130	186
2	650	699
3	99	132
4	150	272
5	128	291
6	302	331
7	95	199
8	945	1890
9	368	788
10	961	1601
Sum	3828	6389
Average	382.8	638.9

the number of the program's estimated object LOC. Where x_k is the estimated object LOC and y_k is the total program LOC,

$$y_k = \beta_0 + \beta_1 x_k. \tag{A12}$$

Note that linear regression refers to a linear relationship in the parameters β_0 and β_1. The relationship between x and y need not be linear, however. In this book a linear relationship is assumed. For Eq. A12 to be appropriate, a reasonably good linear relationship between the x and y variables must exist. This can be checked with the correlation method described in Sections A3 and A4. The calculations to find the β_0 and β_1 parameters are performed as follows:

$$\beta_1 = \frac{\sum\limits_{i=1}^{n} x_i y_i - n x_{avg} y_{avg}}{\sum\limits_{i=1}^{n} x_i^2 - n x_{avg}^2} \tag{A13}$$

$$\beta_0 = y_{avg} - \beta_1 x_{avg} \tag{A14}$$

A7.2   THE LINEAR REGRESSION PROCEDURE

The linear regression procedure is shown in Table A27.

A Linear Regression Example.   This example of the linear regression method follows the procedure in Table A27 and uses the data in Table A26 to calculate the expected new and changed LOC in a program for which you have an estimated 386 object LOC. To evaluate Eq. A13, you first calculate several terms as shown in Table A28. Using these data, you find the value of β_1 as follows:

$$\beta_1 = \frac{\sum\limits_{i=1}^{n} x_i y_i - n x_{avg} y_{avg}}{\sum\limits_{i=1}^{n} x_i^2 - n x_{avg}^2} = \frac{4,303,108 - 10*382.8*638.9}{2,540,284 - 10*382.8^2} = 1.7279.$$

You can now calculate β_0 from Eq. A14:

$$\beta_0 = y_{avg} - \beta_1 x_{avg} = 638.9 - 1.7279*382.8 = -22.54.$$

As you can see from Fig. A20, this regression line is a reasonably good fit to these data.

Using the values of the β_0 and β_1 parameters, you can now calculate the expected value of the program's total new and changed LOC, given the estimated object size of 386 LOC:

$$Size_{total} = y_k = \beta_0 + \beta_1 * Size_{object} = \beta_0 + \beta_1 * x_k =$$
$$-22.54 + 1.7279*386 = 644.$$

TABLE A27 THE LINEAR REGRESSION PROCEDURE

Purpose	• Given a set of historical data for variables x and y, you want to determine a likely value y_k based on a known or estimated new value x_k. An example would be the relationship between the estimated object LOC in a program and the ultimate actual total program LOC.
	• After determining the β_0 and β_1 parameters that best represent the relationship between these x and y data, you can calculate y_k as follows:
	$$y_k = \beta_0 + \beta_1 x_k.$$
Conditions	• The historical x and y data must demonstrate a relationship.
	• For example, there should be an historical relationship between estimated object LOC and actual total LOC, as demonstrated by a significant correlation (see Sections A3 and A4).
	• There must be sufficient data to produce a statistically significant result (at least three items and preferably five or more).
Inputs	n sets of historical data for x and y. For example, sets of data on n programs, giving estimated object LOC (x) and actual total LOC (y) for each
Steps	1. Eliminate the possibly one or two outlier points from the dataset (see discussion in Section A1.9).
	2. Using the following formula and the available data, calculate β_1:
	$$\beta_1 = \frac{\sum_{i=1}^{n} x_i y_i - n x_{avg} y_{avg}}{\sum_{i=1}^{n} x_i^2 - n x_{avg}^2}.$$
	3. Calculate β_0 as follows:
	$$\beta_0 = y_{avg} - \beta_1 x_{avg}.$$
	4. Calculate $y_k = \beta_0 + \beta_1 x_k.$

A7.3   THE LIMITATIONS OF LINEAR REGRESSION

In principle, all the regression method does is provide the best least squares fit of a linear function to some data. Note that the linear restriction on this method applies only to the β parameters and not to the variables. For example, if you knew that x^2 and y were more highly correlated, you could use the linear regression procedure to calculate the β_0 and β_1 values for the equation

$$y_k = \beta_0 + \beta_1 x_k^2.$$

TABLE A28 LINEAR REGRESSION EXAMPLE

Program Number i	Estimated Object LOC: x_i	Total Actual LOC: y_i	$x_i y_i$	x_i^2
1	130	186	24,180	16,900
2	650	699	454,350	422,500
3	99	132	13,068	9,801
4	150	272	40,800	22,500
5	128	291	37,248	16,384
6	302	331	99,962	91,204
7	95	199	18,905	9,025
8	945	1890	1,786,050	893,025
9	368	788	289,984	135,424
10	961	1601	1,538,561	923,521
Sum	3828	6389	4,303,108	2,540,284
Average	382.8	638.9		

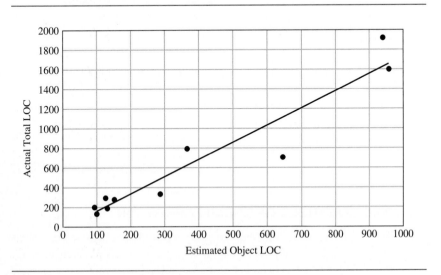

FIGURE A20
Object LOC Data versus the Regression Line

While linear regression is very useful, it is only a mathematical procedure and using it poses potential problems. First, the data must be linearly related for the least squares fit to provide useful projections. Second, a good fit does not necessarily mean the resulting equation will be useful for making projections beyond the range of the data. An examination of the β values will often indicate a third problem. If the relationship were completely proportional, for example, β_0 would be zero. Because β_0 is equivalent to a fixed adjustment, it should be small in comparison to the size of the values you are computing. If β_0 is equal to or larger than many of the x items, you should be careful about using the regression equation and should avoid using it near either end of the dataset range.

Another caution concerns the spread of the data. For example, if all the points are clustered rather close together, the linear relationship could easily be masked by the random fluctuations in the data. This could happen if you used a large number of projects that were all clustered around 300 to 400 LOC. With no cases at much larger or smaller values, the value of β_1 could easily turn out to be negative, resulting in negative productivity projections. Hence, larger programs would be estimated to take less time to develop than would smaller ones. This is clearly unrealistic. So you should not use such values for planning purposes. It is also important not to use data from projects that use different processes from that planned for the project being estimated.

In using linear regression, you should consider the following general guidelines:

- When the value of β_0 is large, either positive or negative, be cautious about using the method for small valued cases, particularly when the results are likely to be smaller than or of the same magnitude as the value of β_0.

- If your process is evolving, use only relatively recent data for your regression calculations. Generally the most recent 10 or so projects are adequate.

- Recognize that using an outlier can distort the values of the β parameters and also result in excessively large prediction intervals (see Section A8). The smaller the dataset, the more serious this distortion can be. If the error is truly an exception that you understand and do not expect to repeat, exclude this case from the data. For more discussion of outliers, see Section A1.9.

Linear regression is very useful, but it is only a tool. You should always check the linear regression results with a simple calculation using your average productivity or average scale-up factors from object to total program LOC. If the regression results do not seem reasonable, use the average values. When you are using linear regression to calculate the development hours from estimated object LOC, you would then check with historical averages of estimated object LOC and actual hours.

A8   Linear Regression Prediction Interval

When estimating, you will find it useful to know the likely size of the prediction error. With the linear regression method, you can use your historical data to calculate both the β_0 and β_1 regression parameters as well as the likely error of your estimate. You determine this error by calculating the degree to which the line defined by the regression parameters fits the historical data. The prediction interval then uses the variance of the data around the regression line to calculate the likely error of the estimate.

The prediction interval, however, is not a forecast. For example, if you calculate a 90 percent prediction interval, then roughly 90 percent of the time the true result would be in the interval. If the projected event does not behave in the same way as the events used to generate the regression data, the prediction interval would not apply. For example, if all your historical data were for programs written in C and the new estimate were for C++, the linear regression and prediction interval calculations would not likely give very good results. While they may be the best you could use at the time, you should use them with caution.

A8.1   THE PREDICTION INTERVAL

The prediction interval is calculated by using the t distribution and the data used for the linear regression calculations. The formula for the interval is

$$\text{Range} = t(\alpha/2, n-2)\sigma \sqrt{1 + \frac{1}{n} + \frac{(x_k - x_{avg})^2}{\sum_{i=1}^{n}(x_i - x_{avg})^2}}. \tag{A15}$$

where t is a value for the double-sided t distribution for the probability $\alpha/2$ and $n-2$ degrees of freedom. Also, σ is the standard deviation of the regression function (calculated below), n is the number of terms in the dataset used for the linear regression calculation, x_k is the new estimate term, and x_i is the value of each term in the dataset. The variance of the data is taken from the regression line instead of from the average value of the data as before.

$$\text{Variance} = \sigma^2 = \left(\frac{1}{n-2}\right) \sum_{i=1}^{n}(y_i - \beta_0 - \beta_1 x_i)^2, \tag{A16}$$

$$\text{StdDeviation} = \sigma = \sqrt{\text{Variance}}.$$

The y_i's are the y data values in the regression dataset. The variance is thus the mean square deviation of the linear regression line from the data in this dataset.

The $\alpha/2$ indicates that you use the two-sided t distribution. For a 90 percent prediction interval with 10 data points, you would use $n - 2$, or eight degrees of freedom, and look under 0.95 (the two-sided p value for an $\alpha/2$ of 0.9). In Table A2, $t = 1.860$. This is the value you would use in the calculations with Eq. A15. For a 70 percent prediction interval, you would use $t = 1.108$.

A8.2   THE PREDICTION INTERVAL PROCEDURE

The procedure for calculating the prediction interval is shown in Table A29.

A Prediction Interval Example.   The data used in the linear regression example in Section A7 are shown again in Table A30 with some additional terms. The numbers in this example the procedure in Table A29.

1. Calculate the value of σ using the data from Table A30:

$$\text{Variance} = \sigma^2 = \frac{1}{n-2} \sum_{i=1}^{n} \left(y_i - \beta_0 - \beta_1 x_i\right)^2 = \frac{313,301.3}{8} =$$

39,162.66,

$$\text{StdDeviation} = \sigma = \sqrt{39,162.66} = 197.896.$$

2. To find the $\alpha/2$ or two-sided value of t for $\alpha/2 = 90$, look in Table A2 under $p(\alpha) = 0.95$. With 10 data points, you use $n - 2$ or eight degrees of freedom. From Table A2, this gives a value of $t = 1.860$.

3. Using Eq. A15 and the original object LOC estimate of 386, calculate the range as follows:

$$\text{Range} = t(\alpha/2, n-2)\sigma \sqrt{1 + \frac{1}{n} + \frac{\left(x_k - x_{avg}\right)^2}{\sum_{i=1}^{n}\left(x_i - x_{avg}\right)^2}},$$

$$\text{Range} = 1.86 * 197.896 * \sqrt{1 + \frac{1}{10} + \frac{\left(386 - 382.8\right)^2}{1,074,925.6}} = 386.05.$$

4. Combine this result with the 644 LOC projection obtained in Section A7 to get a 90 percent prediction interval of 258 to 1030 LOC.

If you sought a 70 percent interval instead of a 90% prediction interval, the value of t would be 1.108 instead of 1.860 and all the other terms would remain unchanged. The result would be a range value of 230.0, an estimate of 644 LOC, and a 70 percent prediction interval of 414 to 874 LOC.

TABLE A29 THE PREDICTION INTERVAL PROCEDURE

Purpose	To determine the prediction interval for a projection
Conditions	• The project being estimated will be performed under conditions similar to those in effect when the historical data were gathered. • The possibly one or two outlier points are excluded from the data set (see Section A1.9).
Inputs	• The historical dataset • The number of items in the dataset, n • The percentage confidence desired, $\alpha/2$, say 70 percent or 90 percent • The estimated object LOC for the new program, x_k • A table for the t distribution (see Table A2)
Steps	1. Calculate the value of σ using the following formula: $$\text{Variance} = \sigma^2 = \left(\frac{1}{n-2}\right)\sum_{i=1}^{n}\left(y_i - \beta_0 - \beta_1 x_i\right)^2,$$ $$\text{StdDeviation} = \sigma = \sqrt{Variance}.$$ 2. Using probability $\alpha/2$ and $n-2$, look up the t value in a table of the t distribution. Note that for a 70 percent probability, look under 0.85 and for a 90 percent probability, under 0.95. 3. Calculate the range using the following formula: $$\text{Range} = t(\alpha/2, n-2)\sigma\sqrt{1 + \frac{1}{n} + \frac{\left(x_k - x_{avg}\right)^2}{\sum_{i=1}^{n}\left(x_i - x_{avg}\right)^2}}.$$ 4. Calculate the upper prediction interval (UPI) and lower prediction interval (LPI) as follows: LPI = y_k − Range UPI = y_k + Range
Interpretation	• The prediction interval gives the range around the estimate within which the actual result will likely fall. • This is not a forecast. • If the new project is statistically similar to the projects in the historical dataset, this is what you can expect.

A8.3 COMBINING MULTIPLE ESTIMATES

It is common to estimate large projects in parts. When you are developing a larger program in multiple development cycles and separately estimate each, you generally cannot treat them as independent projects. Because you will typically

TABLE A30 PREDICTION INTERVAL EXAMPLE

Program Number i	Estimated Object LOC: x_i	Total Actual LOC: y_i	$\beta_0 + \beta_1 x_i$	$(y_i - \beta_0 - \beta_1 x_i)^2$	$(x_i - x_{avg})^2$
1	130	186	202.1	258.5	63,907.84
2	650	699	1100.6	161,285.4	71,395.84
3	99	132	148.5	272.7	80,542.44
4	150	272	236.6	1,250.5	54,195.84
5	128	291	198.6	8,533.5	64,923.04
6	302	331	499.3	28,319.2	6,528.64
7	95	199	141.6	3,294.6	82,828.84
8	945	1890	1610.3	78,207.7	316,068.84
9	368	788	613.3	30,510.8	219.04
10	961	1601	1638.0	1,368.3	334,315.24
Sum	3828	6389	6389.0	313,301.3	1,074,925.60
Average	382.8	638.9			

make these multiple cycle estimates from the same regression data, you will use the same regression parameters for each. In this case, you obtain the total estimate by adding together the individual estimates. You then calculate the prediction interval by using this total estimate value as the y_k term.

For example, suppose you planned to use PSP3 to develop a program in six cycles. You separately estimated the object LOC of the cycles as 113, 153, 69, 197, 135, and 58 LOC. Using the previously calculated linear regression factors of $\beta_0 = -22.54$ and $\beta_1 = 1.7279$, you estimate the sizes of the cycles to be 173, 242, 97, 318, 211, and 78 LOC. Your total LOC estimate is thus the sum of these individual estimates, or 1119 LOC, but what is the prediction interval? Using the data from the previous example, you find that σ is still 197.896 and the 90 percent value of t is 1.860. In this case, the new value of y_k is 1119 and the value of x_k is 725, or the sum of the object LOC estimates. The range calculation is thus

$$\text{Range} = 1.860*197.896* \sqrt{1 + \frac{1}{10} + \frac{(725 - 382.8)^2}{1,074,925.6}} = 404.7.$$

So the 90 percent UPI = 1119 + 405 = 1524 LOC and the LPI = 1119 − 405 = 714 LOC. For a 70 percent range, t would be 1.108, the range would be 241, and the UPI and LPI would be 1360 and 878 LOC, respectively.

Three comments should be made about this result. First, because of the high variance the 70 percent range will be at least 230 LOC or more for any estimate, regardless of its size. This is calculated as follows:

$$\text{Range(min.)} = 1.108*197.896* \sqrt{1 + 1/10} = 230.0.$$

Hence, your small estimates will always have a wide range of likely error. Second, the errors of the larger estimates will tend to be smaller on a percentage basis. Because of the added knowledge you used in making the estimate in parts, you are likely to get greater accuracy when you total several separate smaller estimates. Note that in this case, however, you would get the same small prediction interval if you made a single estimate of 725 object LOC. So the prediction interval will tend to underestimate the error for large estimates and overestimate it for small ones. This means that for most representative prediction intervals, you should attempt to make your individual estimates near the mean or average of your dataset. Third, if there are consistent biases with these estimates, these biases will not offset each other when the estimates are combined. The additive nature of such consistent biases could lead to significant overall estimate errors regardless of the prediction interval. The regression method should help you to compensate for this problem, but it is important to recognize that some of these biases could be unique to a particular project and thus not consistent with the regression data and not addressed by the regression method.

A9   Multiple Regression

Multiple regression is necessary when you have combined data for several different categories of work and cannot separate them. An example would be when you had the time and size data for developing a number of programs that each involved both new development, reuse of standard programs, and program modification. You have the total development times for each program but no way to determine how many hours were spent on new development, reuse, or modification. This is a common problem because it is generally impractical to separately measure the time spent in each such category of development work.

As you attempt to make accurate estimates for larger projects, you will want to consider using this method. Your productivity will likely vary substantially depending on whether you develop new programs, reuse existing programs, or modify existing programs. Thus, if you were to use some average productivity number your estimates could have serious errors whenever the mix of new, reused, and modified code differed from that on which your historical average was based.

A9.1   THE MULTIPLE REGRESSION METHOD

Suppose that in planning a new project you had several variables that all related to development hours. In this case, you would have an equation like the following:

$$z_k = \beta_0 + w_k\beta_1 + x_k\beta_2 + y_k\beta_3, \tag{A17}$$

where, for example, the variables w, x, and y might stand for the numbers of newly developed LOC, the unmodified LOC of reused programs, and the numbers of modified LOC, respectively. Depending on the variables used, and assuming you had sufficient historical data, the multiple linear regression method could be used to find the appropriate estimating parameters. In this case, the β parameters would be found by solving the following linear equations:

$$\beta_0 n + \beta_1 \sum_{i=1}^{n} w_i + \beta_2 \sum_{i=1}^{n} x_i + \beta_3 \sum_{i=1}^{n} y_i = \sum_{i=1}^{n} z_i$$

$$\beta_0 \sum_{i=1}^{n} w_i + \beta_1 \sum_{i=1}^{n} w_i^2 + \beta_2 \sum_{i=1}^{n} w_i x_i + \beta_3 \sum_{i=1}^{n} w_i y_i = \sum_{i=1}^{n} w_i z_i$$

$$\beta_0 \sum_{i=1}^{n} x_i + \beta_1 \sum_{i=1}^{n} w_i x_i + \beta_2 \sum_{i=1}^{n} x_i^2 + \beta_3 \sum_{i=1}^{n} x_i y_i = \sum_{i=1}^{n} x_i z_i \tag{A18}$$

$$\beta_0 \sum_{i=1}^{n} y_i + \beta_1 \sum_{i=1}^{n} w_i y_i + \beta_2 \sum_{i=1}^{n} x_i y_i + \beta_3 \sum_{i=1}^{n} y_i^2 = \sum_{i=1}^{n} y_i z_i$$

The equations for four variables involving five β parameters are

$$\beta_0 n + \beta_1 \sum v_i + \beta_2 \sum w_i + \beta_3 \sum x_i + \beta_4 \sum y_i = \sum z_i$$

$$\beta_0 \sum v_i + \beta_1 \sum v_i^2 + \beta_2 \sum v_i w_i + \beta_3 \sum v_i x_i + \beta_4 \sum v_i y_i = \sum v_i z_i$$

$$\beta_0 \sum w_i + \beta_1 \sum v_i w_i + \beta_2 \sum w_i^2 + \beta_3 \sum w_i x_i + \beta_4 \sum w_i y_i = \sum w_i z_i \tag{A19}$$

$$\beta_0 \sum x_i + \beta_1 \sum v_i x_i + \beta_2 \sum w_i x_i + \beta_3 \sum x_i^2 + \beta_4 \sum x_i y_i = \sum x_i z_i$$

$$\beta_0 \sum y_i + \beta_1 \sum v_i y_i + \beta_2 \sum w_i y_i + \beta_3 \sum x_i y_i + \beta_4 \sum y_i^2 = \sum y_i z_i$$

These equations are solved using a standard algebraic technique for simultaneous linear equations either by successive variable elimination or with determinants. Gauss's method, described in Section A11, is helpful when you want to write a program to solve such equations.

The structure of the Eqs. A18 and A19 is quite regular, so they can be readily extended to any number of variables. Note, for example, that in Eq. A19 the second equation is obtained from the first by dropping the n and multiplying every term by v_i. The third equation drops n and multiplies by w_i, the fourth by

x_i, and the fifth by y_i. Similarly, the first column in every equation has β_0, the second $\beta_1 v_i$, the third $\beta_2 w_i$, and so on.

These equations assume you do not have separate data on the hours required for each of the separate parameter categories. If you do, you should estimate each category separately and combine them as described in Section A8.3. Further, in using multiple regression you also must have sufficient historical data to provide significant results. With only limited data, you may get very good parameter fits, but the projections could be useless. With four variables, for example, you will get exact fits to any five data points, but such a fit would have no significance and no prediction value. This is why you should be cautious about using any estimating method that has a large number of "complexity" adjustments. Each adjustment to improve the fit of your estimating equation to the historical data reduces the significance of the result.

A9.2   THE MULTIPLE REGRESSION PROCEDURE

With the procedure in Table A31, you are seeking to determine the relationship between a dependent variable, say hours, and several independent variables. An example would be the relationship between the estimated new LOC, reused LOC, and modified LOC in several programs and the total hours required to develop these programs. However, there should be an historical relationship between estimated new LOC, the estimated reused LOC, the estimated modified LOC, and the actual hours required to develop these programs. The multiple regression procedure uses the historical data to calculate the terms in Eq. A18 and then uses Gauss's method to solve these equations.

A Multiple Regression Example.   Suppose you are working on a large program and estimate it will have about 650 LOC of new code. You plan to reuse about 3000 LOC of unmodified reused code and to modify an additional 155 LOC of base code. You also have the historical data in Table A32. Unfortunately, however, this is all the detail available. You thus have no way to figure out how much time you will spend developing new code, reusing previous code, or making the modifications. You must use the multiple regression method.

Following the procedure in Table A31, you first check for outliers. Unfortunately, multiple parameters make it difficult to tell when some point is seriously out of line. In the prediction interval calculation, however, you will see a more reliable way to make this check.

Next, evaluate the terms for Eqs. A18. Using the values in Tables A32 and A33, you can calculate the values for the terms in these simultaneous linear equations as follows:

$$6\beta_0 + 4,863\beta_1 + 8,761\beta_2 + 654\beta_3 = 714$$
$$4,863\beta_0 + 4,521,899\beta_1 + 8,519,938\beta_2 + 620,707\beta_3 = 667,832$$

TABLE A31 THE MULTIPLE REGRESSION PROCEDURE

Purpose	• Given a set of data relating multiple variables, say w, x, y, and z, you want to determine the likely value of z_k based on the known or estimated values of w_k, x_k, and y_k.
	• By determining the β_0, β_1, β_2, and β_3 parameters that best represent the relationship among these w, x, y, and z data, you can calculate z_k as follows:
	$$z_k = \beta_0 + \beta_1 w_k + \beta_2 x_k + \beta_3 y_k.$$
Conditions	• The historical w, x, y, and z data must demonstrate a relationship.
	• There must be sufficient data to produce a statistically significant result.
	• As a rule, the required minimum number of datasets is two more than the number of unknown β parameters.
Inputs	Historical data for n sets of w, x, y, and z data.
Steps	1. Eliminate the possibly one or two outlier points from the dataset (see discussion in Section A1.9).
	2. Use the available data to calculate the values of the β parameters in the following formulae:
	$$\beta_0 n + \beta_1 \sum_{i=1}^{n} w_i + \beta_2 \sum_{i=1}^{n} x_i + \beta_3 \sum_{i=1}^{n} y_i = \sum_{i=1}^{n} z_i,$$
	$$\beta_0 \sum_{i=1}^{n} w_i + \beta_1 \sum_{i=1}^{n} w_i^2 + \beta_2 \sum_{i=1}^{n} w_i x_i + \beta_3 \sum_{i=1}^{n} w_i y_i = \sum_{i=1}^{n} w_i z_i,$$
	$$\beta_0 \sum_{i=1}^{n} x_i + \beta_1 \sum_{i=1}^{n} w_i x_i + \beta_2 \sum_{i=1}^{n} x_i^2 + \beta_3 \sum_{i=1}^{n} x_i y_i = \sum_{i=1}^{n} x_i z_i,$$
	$$\beta_0 \sum_{i=1}^{n} y_i + \beta_1 \sum_{i=1}^{n} w_i y_i + \beta_2 \sum_{i=1}^{n} x_i y_i + \beta_3 \sum_{i=1}^{n} y_i^2 = \sum_{i=1}^{n} y_i z_i.$$
	3. Use Gauss's method to determine the values of these β parameters. Note that there is always one more parameter than independent variable in these equations.
	4. Calculate $z_k = \beta_0 + \beta_1 w_k + \beta_2 x_k + \beta_3 y_k.$

TABLE A32 MULTIPLE REGRESSION EXAMPLE DATA

Program Number	New LOC	Reused LOC	Modified LOC	Hours
	w	x	y	z
1	1142	1060	325	201
2	863	995	98	98
3	1065	3205	23	162
4	554	120	0	54
5	983	2896	120	138
6	256	485	88	61
Totals	4863	8761	654	714

$$8{,}761\beta_0 + 8{,}519{,}938\beta_1 + 21{,}022{,}091\beta_2 + 905{,}925\beta_3 = 1{,}265{,}493$$
$$654\beta_0 + 620{,}707\beta_1 + 905{,}925\beta_2 + 137{,}902\beta_3 = 100{,}583$$

Next, solve these equations with standard algebraic methods. A procedure for using Gauss's method to solve such equations is described in Section A11, along with the solution to this example. The resulting values for the β parameters are as follows:

$$\beta_0 = 6.7013$$
$$\beta_1 = 0.0784$$
$$\beta_2 = 0.0150$$
$$\beta_3 = 0.2461$$

Using these values in the original equation, you calculate the estimated hours for the new project as follows:

Hours $= 6.71 + 0.0784{*}650 + 0.0150{*}3000 + 0.2461{*}155 = 140.902$.

You can interpret the β parameters as follows:

- Every project has a constant overhead of 6.7 hours.
- It takes 0.0784 hours to develop a LOC, or 12.76 LOC per hour.
- It takes 0.015 hours to reuse a line of previously developed code, or 66.48 LOC per hour.
- It takes 0.2461 hours to modify a LOC, or 4.06 LOC per hour.

These numbers are hypothetical. In a real case, you should examine these parameters to see if they make sense. If they do not, read the cautions about the regression method in Section A7.3 and take appropriate corrective actions.

TABLE A33 MULTIPLE REGRESSION EXAMPLE CALCULATIONS

Program Number	New²	New*Reuse	New*Modified	New*Hours
	w^2	w^*x	w^*y	w^*z
1	1,304,164	1,210,520	371,150	229,542
2	744,769	858,685	84,574	84,574
3	1,134,225	3,413,325	24,495	172,530
4	306,916	66,480	0	29,916
5	966,289	2,846,768	117,960	135,654
6	65,536	124,160	22,528	15,616
Totals	4,521,899	8,519,938	620,707	667,832

Program Number	Reuse²	ReUse*Modified	ReUse*Hours	Modified²	Modified*Hours
	x^2	x^*y	x^*z	y^2	y^*z
1	1,123,600	344,500	213,060	105,625	65,325
2	990,025	97,510	97,510	9,604	9,604
3	10,272,025	73,715	519,210	529	3,726
4	14,400	0	6,480	0	0
5	8,386,816	347,520	399,648	14,400	16,560
6	235,225	42,680	29,585	7,744	5,368
Totals	21,022,091	905,925	1,265,493	137,902	100,583

A10   Multiple Regression Prediction Interval

The multiple regression prediction interval is calculated in much the same way as the linear regression interval, except it uses a few more terms. For three variables and four parameters, the variance term is calculated as follows:

$$\sigma^2 = \left(\frac{1}{n-4}\right) \sum_{i=1}^{n} (z_i - \beta_0 - \beta_1 w_i - \beta_2 x_i - \beta_3 y_i)^2, \qquad \text{(A20)}$$

where n is the number of terms in the historical dataset used to evaluate the β terms. This equation gives the mean square deviation of the linear regression line for z from the actual z_i values. Clearly, a larger value of σ indicates a poorer multiple regression fit to the actual data and thus a larger prediction interval.

Note also that outliers can best be identified by examining the mean-square deviation of the points from the regression line. If one is much larger than the others, it should be examined as a possible outlier.

The calculation of the range is then made using the following equation:

$$\text{Range} = t(\alpha/2, n - 4)*$$

$$\sigma \sqrt{1 + \frac{1}{n} + \frac{(w_k - w_{avg})^2}{\sum(w_i - w_{avg})^2} + \frac{(x_k - x_{avg})^2}{\sum(x_i - x_{avg})^2} + \frac{(y_k - y_{avg})^2}{\sum(y_i - y_{avg})^2}}. \quad \text{(A21)}$$

Here, with four β parameters you use $n - 4$ degrees of freedom, with five, you would use $n - 5$. For linear regression, you had two β parameters so you used $n - 2$ when finding the value of the t distribution. As before, you obtain the two-sided value of t from Table A2. Again, for a 70 percent prediction interval look under probability $p(\alpha) = 0.85$ and for a 90 percent interval, look under $p(\alpha) = 0.95$.

A10.1   MULTIPLE REGRESSION PREDICTION INTERVAL PROCEDURE

The procedure for the multiple regression prediction interval is identical to that described in Section A8 and shown in Table A29, except there are more terms in the equation.

Example of the Multiple Regression Prediction Interval.   Using the same example as in Section A9, you first calculate the multiple regression prediction interval from Eq. A21. The values needed for these calculations are given in Table A34. The variance and standard deviation are as follows:

$$\sigma^2 = \left(\frac{1}{n - 4}\right)\sum_{i=1}^{n}(z_i - \beta_0 - \beta_1 w_i - \beta_2 x_i - \beta_3 y_i)^2 = 1026.115/2 = 513.058,$$

$$\sigma = \sqrt{\sigma^2} = \sqrt{513.058} = 22.651$$

Second, determine the value of t. There are four β parameters, so look in Table A2 under $n - 4$. In this case, $n = 6$, so look in the row for two degrees of freedom. For a 70 percent prediction interval, look under the 0.85 percent column. The resulting value for t is 1.386.

Third, evaluate the term under the square root. Note, the k subscripted terms are the values for the desired estimate, which means the three numerator terms are as follows:

$$(New_k - New_{avg})^2 = (w_k - w_{avg})^2 = (650 - 810.5)^2 = 25,760.25$$
$$(Reuse_k - Reuse_{avg})^2 = (x_k - x_{avg})^2 = (3,000 - 1,460.17)^2 = 2,371,076.43$$
$$(Modify_k - Modify_{avg})^2 = (y_k - y_{avg})^2 = (155 - 109)^2 = 2,116$$

TABLE A34   MULTIPLE REGRESSION PREDICTION INTERVAL
CALCULATIONS

Program Number	$(Hours_i - \beta_0 - \beta_1 New_i - \beta_2 Reuse_i - \beta_3 Modify_i)^2$ $(z_i - \beta_0 - \beta_1 w_i - \beta_2 x_i - \beta_3 y_i)^2$	$(New_i - New_{avg})^2$ $(w_i - w_{avg})^2$	$(Reuse_i - Reuse_{avg})^2$ $(x_i - x_{avg})^2$	$(Modified_i - Modified_{avg})^2$ $(y_i - y_{avg})^2$
1	79.077	109,892.25	160,133.4	46,656
2	237.495	2,756.25	216,380	121
3	322.995	64,770.25	3,044,443	7,396
4	4.322	65,792.25	1,796,047	11,881
5	354.253	29,756.25	2,061,617	121
6	27.973	307,470.25	950,950	441
Totals	1,026.115	580,437.50	8,229,571	66,616

$New_{avg} = w_{avg} = 810.5$ $New_k = w_k = 650$

$Reuse_{avg} = x_{avg} = 1460.17$ $Reuse_k = x_k = 3000$

$Modify_{avg} = y_{avg} = 109$ $Modify_k = y_k = 155$

$\beta_0 = 6.70134$

$\beta_1 = 0.07837$

$\beta_2 = 0.01504$

$\beta_3 = 0.24606$

The range calculation is then done as follows:

$$\text{Range} = t(\alpha/2, n - 4)*$$

$$\sigma \sqrt{1 + \frac{1}{n} + \frac{(w_k - w_{avg})^2}{\sum(w_i - w_{avg})^2} + \frac{(x_k - x_{avg})^2}{\sum(x_i - x_{avg})^2} + \frac{(y_k - y_{avg})^2}{\sum(y_i - y_{avg})^2}},$$

$$\text{Range} = 1.386*22.651*$$

$$\sqrt{1 + (1/6) + \frac{25,760.25}{580,437.5} + \frac{2,371,076.43}{8,229,571} + \frac{2,116}{66,616}} = 38.846.$$

The final answer is the original estimate of 140.902 hours plus or minus 38.846 hours, or a 70 percent prediction interval from 102.1 to 179.7 hours.

A11   Gauss's Method

Simultaneous linear equations can be solved by using standard algebraic techniques. Gauss's method is an orderly procedure for doing these algebraic steps, and thus is helpful when you are writing a program to solve such equations.

A11.1   A PROCEDURE FOR USING GAUSS'S METHOD

Table A35 shows a procedure for using Gauss's method for solving a set of simultaneous linear equations with three variables and four unknown parameters. You can extend this procedure to handle more parameters by inserting new parameter evaluation sections at the front of it. Each new parameter evaluation section would then have steps to eliminate additional parameters. Also, if you wanted to solve a smaller set of equations with fewer variables and parameters, you would drop parameter elimination steps from the front of this procedure.

An Example of Gauss's Method for Determining the Regression Parameters.   This example solves the equations in Section A9 for the β parameters. These equations are shown again as follows:

$$6\beta_0 + 4,863\beta_1 + 8,761\beta_2 + 654\beta_3 = 714$$
$$4,863\beta_0 + 4,521,899\beta_1 + 8,519,938\beta_2 + 620,707\beta_3 = 667,832$$
$$8,761\beta_0 + 8,519,938\beta_1 + 21,022,091\beta_2 + 905,925\beta_3 = 1,265,493$$
$$654\beta_0 + 620,707\beta_1 + 905,925\beta_2 + 137,902\beta_3 = 100,583$$

TABLE A35 PROCEDURE FOR GAUSS'S METHOD

Purpose	To solve for the unknown parameters given a set of four simultaneous linear equations with three variables and four unknown parameters
Conditions	• There must be the same number of equations as unknown parameters. • The equations must have the following forms: $A_0\beta_0 + A_1\beta_1 + A_2\beta_2 + A_3\beta_3 = A_4$ $B_0\beta_0 + B_1\beta_1 + B_2\beta_2 + B_3\beta_3 = B_4$ $C_0\beta_0 + C_1\beta_1 + C_2\beta_2 + C_3\beta_3 = C_4$ $D_0\beta_0 + D_1\beta_1 + D_2\beta_2 + D_3\beta_3 = D_4$
Inputs	Historical data for a sufficient number of cases involving variables A, B, C, and D so that the values of the parameters can be calculated.
First Parameter Elimination	Eliminate the first parameter. Typically select it as the parameter with the lowest alphabetic or numerical label: 1. Multiply each constant in the A equation by B_0/A_0, giving $\quad B_0\beta_0 + A_1\beta_1 B_0/A_0 + A_2\beta_2 B_0/A_0 + A_3\beta_3 B_0/A_0 = A_4 B_0/A_0$ 2. Subtract this new A equation from the original B equation, giving $\quad 0^*\beta_0 + (B_1 - A_1 B_0/A_0)\beta_1 + (B_2 - A_2 B_0/A_0)\beta_2 +$ $\quad (B_3 - A_3 B_0/A_0)\beta_3 = B_4 - A_4 B_0/A_0.$ 3. Eliminate the first parameter from the third equation by multiplying each term in the A equation by C_0/A_0. 4. Subtract this new A equation from the original third equation, yielding a result like that in step 2, but with a C replacing each B. 5. Eliminate the first parameter from the fourth equation by multiplying each term in the A equation by D_0/A_0. 6. Subtract this new A equation from the original fourth equation, yielding a result like that in step 2, but with a D replacing each B. 7. You now have three new equations with three parameters. Relabel their terms as follows: $\quad E_1\beta_1 + E_2\beta_2 + E_3\beta_3 = E_4$ $\quad F_1\beta_1 + F_2\beta_2 + F_3\beta_3 = F_4$ $\quad G_1\beta_1 + G_2\beta_2 + G_3\beta_3 = G_4$

TABLE A35 (continued)

	These new terms have the following values: $E_1 = B_1 - A_1 B_0 / A_0$ $E_2 = B_2 - A_2 B_0 / A_0$ $E_3 = B_3 - A_3 B_0 / A_0$ $E_4 = B_4 - A_4 B_0 / A_0$ The F and G equations have the identical form, except the B's are replaced by C's and D's, respectively.
Second Parameter Elimination	Eliminate the second parameter, β_1, from these new equations by following the same procedure. This yields two new equations as follows: $H_2 \beta_2 + H_3 \beta_3 = H_4$, $I_2 \beta_2 + I_3 \beta_3 = I_4$. The new H and I terms have the following values: $H_2 = F_2 - E_2 F_1 / E_1$, $H_3 = F_3 - E_3 F_1 / E_1$, $H_4 = F_4 - E_4 F_1 / E_1$. The I terms are identical, except the F's are replaced by G's.
Third Parameter Elimination	Eliminate the third parameter, β_2, from these new equations by following the same procedure. This yields one new equation as follows: $J_3 \beta_3 = J_4$. The new J terms have the following values: $J_3 = I_3 - H_3 I_2 / H_2$, $J_4 = I_4 - H_4 I_2 / H_2$.
Solve for the Parameters	Solve the diagonalized equations for the parameters as follows: 1. Construct the diagonalized equations from the original A equation, the E equation, the H equation, and the J equation as follows: $A_0 \beta_0 + A_1 \beta_1 + A_2 \beta_2 + A_3 \beta_3 = A_4$, $E_1 \beta_1 + E_2 \beta_2 + E_3 \beta_3 = E_4$, $H_2 \beta_2 + H_3 \beta_3 = H_4$, $J_3 \beta_3 = J_4$.

TABLE A35 (continued)

Solve for the Parameters	2. Solve the J equation for β_3.
	3. Replace β_3 in the A, E, and H equations.
	4. Solve the new H equation for β_2.
	5. Replace β_2 in the A and E equations with this value.
	6. Solve the new E equation for β_1.
	7. Replace β_1 in the A equation with this value.
	8. Solve this final A equation for β_0.

To eliminate one parameter at a time, the Gauss's method procedure in Table A35 does what is called *diagonalizing*, where the first equation is used to eliminate the β_0 terms from the second, third, and fourth equations. The first elimination is done by multiplying every term of the first equation by the ratio 4863/6. This new equation is then subtracted, term by term, from the second equation, giving the following new equation:

$$0\beta_0 + 580{,}437.5\beta_1 + 1{,}419{,}148\beta_2 + 90{,}640\beta_3 = 89{,}135.$$

The same procedure is followed to eliminate β_0 from the third equation, except in this case the multiplier is 8761/6 and for the fourth equation, 654/6. The resulting three equations all have 0 as the multiplier for β_0, as follows:

$$0\beta_0 + 580{,}437.5\beta_1 + 1{,}419{,}148\beta_2 + 90{,}640\beta_3 = 89{,}135$$
$$0\beta_0 + 1{,}419{,}148\beta_1 + 8{,}229{,}571\beta_2 - 49{,}024\beta_3 = 222{,}934$$
$$0\beta_0 + 90{,}640\beta_1 - 49{,}024\beta_2 + 66{,}616\beta_3 = 22{,}757$$

With these three equations with three unknowns, you next eliminate the β_1 term from the new second and third equations. The multiplier for the second is $1{,}419{,}148/580{,}437.5 = 2.44496$ and that for the third, $90{,}640/580{,}437.5 = 0.156158$. After the β_1 elimination, you have two equations in two unknowns and can use the first to eliminate β_2 from the second, leaving one equation in one unknown. By selecting the first equation from each set, you have the following diagonalized set of equations:

$$6\beta_0 + 4{,}863\beta_1 + 8{,}761\beta_2 + 654\beta_3 = 714$$
$$0\beta_0 + 580{,}437.5\beta_1 + 1{,}419{,}148\beta_2 + 90{,}640\beta_3 = 89{,}135$$
$$0\beta_0 + 0\beta_1 + 4{,}759{,}809\beta_2 - 270{,}635\beta_3 = 5{,}002.332$$
$$0\beta_0 + 0\beta_1 + 0\beta_2 + 37{,}073.93\beta_3 = 9{,}122.275$$

Now the unknowns can be obtained by first solving for β_3 in the last equation. For example, $\beta_3 = 9{,}122.275/37{,}073.93 = 0.2461$. This value is then substituted into the other three equations and the next β parameter is calculated. By repeating this for all the equations, you find the parameter values as follows:

$$\beta_0 = 6.7013$$
$$\beta_1 = 0.0784$$

$\beta_2 = 0.0150$
$\beta_3 = 0.2461$

These parameters can now be used in Eq. A17 to calculate the value of the multiple regression estimate.

A12   The Pareto Distribution

When working on process improvement, you often seek to rank issues by priority. Doing this can help you decide which problems to attack first. For example, defects are ranked primarily by frequency of occurrence. Such a ranking is called a Pareto distribution.

A12.1   THE PARETO DISTRIBUTION PROCEDURE

The procedure for constructing a Pareto distribution is shown in Table A36.

TABLE A36   PROCEDURE FOR CONSTRUCTING A PARETO
             DISTRIBUTION TABLE

Purpose	To rank data items in priority order
Conditions	The data should all belong to the same general class. For example, a listing of major defect categories should not be combined with more detailed data on several types of syntax defects.
Inputs	A listing of the data items and their pertinent parameters
Steps	1. Select the parameter to be used as the sorting key, for example, the number of defects in each type.
	2. Count the number of items in each category.
	3. Calculate the percentage of the total items that each category represents.
	4. Sort these categories in descending order by their percentage frequency of occurrence.
	5. Plot these sorted data in a bar chart.
Interpretation	• The interpretation of a Pareto distribution depends on the types of data shown.
	• Generally, the leftmost items on the chart should receive the highest priority attention.

A Pareto Distribution Example.   An example of a Pareto distribution is shown in Fig. A21 for the defect data in Table A37. These data are for PSP C++ defects that were missed in code reviews and found either in compile or in test. The pattern of the distribution seems relatively clear: Syntax defects are the most prevalent, with assignment, interface, and function defects nearly tied for second place.

It is important to ensure all the items being examined in a Pareto distribution are at the same level of detail. For example, if the function defect types were subdivided into subcategories, such as loops, pointers, recursion, and so on, the percentages in each subcategory would be smaller in comparison to the other broader categories, thus reducing their priority. If you were particularly concerned about the function defects, you could use a finer categorization to examine them in more detail. When doing this, however, you should restrict the study to function defects and not include other categories that are at different levels of detail.

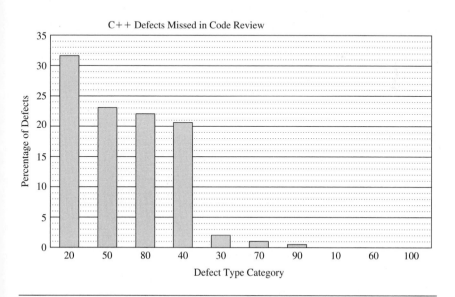

FIGURE A21
Pareto Distribution

TABLE A37 C++ DEFECT TYPES MISSED IN CODE REVIEW

Defect Type Name	Defect Type Number	Percentage of Total Defects
Documentation	10	0
Syntax	20	31.4
Build, package, etc.	30	1.9
Assignment	40	20.5
Interface	50	22.9
Checking	60	0
Data	70	1.0
Function	80	21.9
System	90	0.5
Environment	100	0

References

[Box] George E. P. Box, William G. Hunter, and J. Stuart Hunter, *Statistics for Experimenters* (New York: John Wiley & Sons, 1978).

[Cohen] Harold Cohen, *Mathematics for Scientists and Engineers* (Englewood Cliffs, NJ: Prentice-Hall, 1992).

[DeGroot] Morris H. DeGroot, *Probability and Statistics* (Reading, MA: Addison-Wesley, 1989).

[Montgomery] D. C. Montgomery, *Introduction to Statistical Quality Control* (New York: John Wiley & Sons, 1991).

APPENDIX
Software Design Notation

In designing a software product, you need to produce clear and concise descriptions that the implementer will understand. Although everyday language would be most natural, it is not very good for this purpose. Commonly used languages are redundant, imprecise, and often quite voluminous. Fortunately, mathematical notation can help with this problem. Boolean algebra, or the algebra of sets, is the principal mathematical tool for describing logical constructs. Other mathematical terms and symbols can also be useful in describing designs. This appendix provides a brief overview of these notations and illustrates how they can be used in program design. For a more complete treatment of this topic, consult the references listed at the back of this appendix.

B1   The Algebra of Sets

Sets can be described symbolically. By using Boolean algebra, you can manipulate sets as mathematical variables. [Gill] Examples of symbolic ways to represent operations in Boolean algebra are shown in Table B1. For example, the negation symbol is '. Thus x' means "not x." Negation can also be represented by !, so !x also means "not x." While these different representations all behave identically, it is important to select a particular notation and use it consistently. In this book, I use the notation in the left column in Table B1. While this notation may not initially be as easy for you to use as the computer notations, there are good reasons for using it:

1. It is the common notation used in the mathematical analysis of programs, so it is important that you become familiar with it.

2. By using this notation, you can clearly distinguish your logical expressions from your mathematical ones.

Because these notations are all correct, you can use any of them.

The laws of Boolean algebra and some properties of sets are shown in Tables B2 and B3. Set operations are similar to ordinary arithmetic. For example, if you used the computer notation in Table B1, the distributive law would be

$$x*(y + z) = x*y + x*z.$$

In this case, for arithmetic, if you substituted $x = 4$, $y = 8$, and $z = 3$, you would get

$$4*(8 + 3) = 4*8 + 4*3 = 32 + 12 = 44,$$

which is correct, but the second half of the distributive law for sets is

$$x + (y*z) = (x + y)*(x + z).$$

If you make the same arithmetic substitution, you get

$$4 + 8*3 \neq (4 + 8)*(4 + 3),$$

which is not true for arithmetic. The first expression equals 28, while the second equals 84. Similarly, the reflexive, antisymmetric, transitive, commutative, identity, involution, and associative relationships all hold for the arithmetic operations on numbers. The relationships that do not hold are the idempotent, null, consistency, absorption, and DeMorgan's Theorem. In each of these cases, if you still use $x = 4$, $y = 8$, and $z = 3$ you get the following:

Idempotent: $4*4 \neq 4$ and $4 + 4 \neq 4$

Complement: $4*(-4) \neq 0$ and $4 + (-4) \neq 1$

Null: $4*0 = 0$ but $4 + 1 \neq 1$

TABLE B1   NOTATIONS FOR BOOLEAN ALGEBRA

This text	Computer notation	Mathematical notation	Set notation	Examples	English
$\vee$	+	$\vee$	$\cup$	A or B	join, or, sum, union
$\wedge$	*	$\wedge$	$\cap$	A and B	meet, and, product, intersection
$'$	$-$	$!$	c	not A	complement, not, negation
1				all	true, universal set
0				none	false, empty set

TABLE B2 THE LAWS OF BOOLEAN ALGEBRA

Commutative	$x \wedge y = y \wedge x$ $x \vee y = y \vee x$
Associative	$x \wedge (y \wedge z) = (x \wedge y) \wedge z$ $(x \vee y) \vee z = x \vee (y \vee z)$
Distributive	$x \wedge (y \vee z) = (x \wedge y) \vee (x \wedge z)$ $x \vee (y \wedge z) = (x \vee y) \wedge (x \vee z)$
Identity	$x \vee 0 = x$ $x \wedge 1 = x$
Complement	$x \wedge x' = 0$ $x \vee x' = 1$
Idempotent	$x \wedge x = x$ $x \vee x = x$
Null	$x \wedge 0 = 0$ $x \vee 1 = 1$
Absorption	$x \wedge (x \vee y) = x \vee (x \wedge y) = x$
DeMorgan's theorem	$(x \wedge y)' = x' \vee y'$ $(x \vee y)' = x' \wedge y'$
Involution	$(x')' = x$

TABLE B3 PROPERTIES OF SETS

Reflexive	for every x, $x <= x$
Antisymmetric	if $x <= y$ and $y <= x$, then $x = y$
Transitive	if $x <= y$ and $y <= z$, then $x <= z$
Consistency	$x <= y$, $x \wedge y = x$, $x \vee y = y$ are equivalent

Absorption: $4*(4 + 8) \neq 4 + (4*8) \neq 4$

Consistency: $4 \leq 8$, but $4*8 \neq 4$, and $4 + 8 \neq 8$

DeMorgan's: $-(4*8) \neq -4 + (-8)$ and $-(4 + 8) \neq (-4)*(-8)$

Using the mathematical or computer notation could thus cause confusion. Sets have different properties than numbers, and it is wisest to use a special notation for them.

B1.1   USING BOOLEAN ALGEBRA

Consider the set of all humans. As shown in the Venn diagram in Fig. B1, this set is composed of two subsets: men and women. In Fig. B2, the set of adults can be added, giving a total of four subsets: nonadult women, adult women, nonadult men, and adult men. With each new characteristic, the number of subsets is doubled. Looking at Fig. B3 and using ' to represent negation, you can represent the characteristics A, B, and C, with a total of eight subsets: $A' \wedge B' \wedge C'$, $A' \wedge B' \wedge C$, $A' \wedge B \wedge C'$, $A' \wedge B \wedge C$, $A \wedge B' \wedge C'$, $A \wedge B' \wedge C$, $A \wedge B \wedge C'$, and $A \wedge B \wedge C$. Here, for example, $A \wedge B' \wedge C'$ can be read as A and not B and not C.

Boolean algebra can be used to examine various logical propositions. For example, the statement that all men are adults would mean the subset of nonadult men, or boys, was empty. Hence, men would be a subclass of adults, as shown in Fig. B4. While this assertion does not represent reality, it is consistent with the conditions of this Venn diagram. It is important to realize the distinction between truth and consistency. In Boolean algebra, you are seeking to determine the consistency of a set of logical statements. Thus saying a statement is logically correct is a little like saying a program can be mathematically correct even though it does not do what the user wants. This would happen when the program was consistent with its requirements, but the requirements did not represent the users' needs.

Boolean algebra can also be used to define the conditions for an action. Given three switches, A, B, and C, suppose you want a bulb to light when A is on, or when B is on, or when C is on, but not when A and B are on or when A and C are on. The fact that this statement is hard to interpret is a good example of the problems of expressing logical statements in ordinary language. To describe these switch conditions in Boolean algebra, give the conditions for the bulb to light as follows:

$$On = (A \vee B \vee C) \wedge [(A \wedge B) \vee (A \wedge C)]'.$$

This is now a precise statement of the above conditions. In ordinary language, this can be read as saying precisely what the above sentence says.

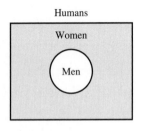

FIGURE B1
Venn Diagrams

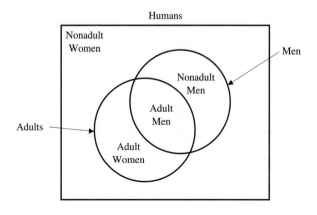

FIGURE B2
Venn Diagrams

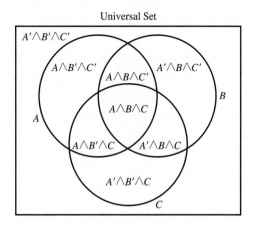

FIGURE B3
Venn Diagrams

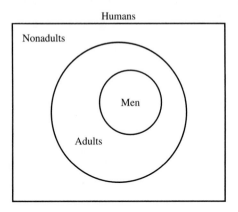

FIGURE B4
Men as a subset of Adults

B2   Simplifying Boolean Expressions

By manipulating set expressions according to the laws of Boolean algebra, you can simplify them, compare them, and demonstrate their consistency. Because programs themselves are logical statements, Boolean algebra can thus be used to describe and to analyze program behavior.

Logical expressions can become extraordinarily complex, so it is important to know how to simplify them. While there are no general rules for doing this, a few guidelines can help:

1. If there are any complemented (or primed) parenthetical expressions, use DeMorgan's theorem to remove them.
2. Look for common terms that can be factored with the distributive law.
3. Make substitutions to reduce complexity and to make relationships more apparent.
4. Attempt to reduce the expression to a union of intersections.

Step 4 is purely for convenience. It suggests that you seek expressions of the form

$$x = (A' \wedge B) \vee (A \wedge B')$$

rather than in the form:

$$x = (A \vee B) \wedge (A' \vee B').$$

The first expression reads, "x equals not A and B or A and not B." The second expression reads, "x equals A or B and not A or not B." While these two expressions are exactly equivalent, expressions like the first are generally easier to understand than are the second.

B2.1 The light bulb example. The light bulb and switch example from section B1 can demonstrate simplification. The bulb is on when

$$\text{On} = (A \vee B \vee C) \wedge [(A \wedge B) \vee (A \wedge C)]'.$$

Following step 1 of the simplification guidelines, apply DeMorgan's theorem:

$$(A \vee B \vee C) \wedge [(A' \vee B') \wedge (A' \vee C')].$$

Now, by step 2, A' is common to the last two terms, so it can be factored out with the distributive law as follows:

$$(A \vee B \vee C) \wedge [A' \vee (B' \wedge C')].$$

It may not be obvious how to reduce this further. However, you could replace $B \vee C$ with some new variable x. Thus $B' \wedge C'$ would be replaced by x'. This substitution yields

$$(A \vee x) \wedge (A' \vee x').$$

While this expression is fully simplified, it is an intersection of two unions. By applying the distributive and null laws, this can be changed as follows:

$$
\begin{aligned}
\text{On} = (A \vee x) \wedge (A' \vee x') &= [(A \vee x) \wedge A'] \vee [(A \vee x) \wedge x'] \\
&= [(A \wedge A') \vee (x \wedge A')] \vee [(A \wedge x') \vee (x \wedge x')] \\
&= [0 \vee (x \wedge A')] \vee [(A \wedge x') \vee 0] \\
&= (x \wedge A') \vee (A \wedge x')
\end{aligned}
$$

Now, replacing x with $B \vee C$ you get

$$
\begin{aligned}
\text{On} = [(B \vee C) \wedge A'] \vee [A \wedge (B' \wedge C')] \\
= [A' \wedge (B \vee C)] \vee [A \wedge B' \wedge C'] \\
= [A \wedge B' \wedge C'] \vee [A' \wedge (B \vee C)].
\end{aligned}
$$

You can now read this as "the bulb is on when A is on and B and C are both off or when A is off and B or C are on." The Venn diagram for this expression is shown in Fig. B5.

B2.2 Another simplification example. Next, simplify the following logical expression:

$$F = [(A \vee B) \wedge (A' \vee C') \wedge (A \vee B')] \vee (A' \wedge B).$$

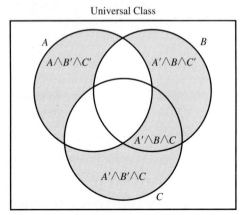

Universal Class

On $= (A \wedge B' \wedge C') \vee (A' \wedge (B \vee C))$

FIGURE B5
Switch Venn Diagram

Take the following steps:

1. Using the associate law, rearrange the terms to group the A terms together as follows:

   $F = [(A \vee B) \wedge (A \vee B') \wedge (A' \vee C')] \vee (A' \wedge B).$

2. You can simplify part of this, $(A \vee B) \wedge (A \vee B') = A$, as follows:
   By the distributive law:

   $[(A \vee B) \wedge (A \vee B')] = A \vee (B \wedge B')$

   By the property of the empty class:

   $A \vee (B \wedge B') = A \vee 0 = A$

3. You now have the following partially simplified equation:

   $F = [(A \wedge (A' \vee C')] \vee (A' \wedge B).$

4. Again using the distributive law, simplify the first bracketed expression:

   $A \wedge (A' \vee C') = (A \wedge A') \vee (A \wedge C') = 0 \vee (A \wedge C') = (A \wedge C').$

5. The total expression is now reduced to

   $F = (A \wedge C') \vee (A' \wedge B),$

which is the final answer.

B2.3   EXERCISES

Simplify the following expressions (the answers are at the back of Appendix B):

1. $F = X \vee (X' \wedge Y)$

2. $F = (X \vee Y) \vee [(X \wedge Z) \vee Y]$

3. $F = (X' \wedge Y' \wedge Z') \vee (X \wedge Y \wedge Z') \vee (X \wedge Y' \wedge Z')$

4. $F = [X' \wedge (Y \vee Z')]' \wedge (X \vee Y' \vee Z) \wedge (X' \wedge Y' \wedge Z')'$

5. $F = [(A \wedge B') \vee C]' \vee [(A' \vee B) \wedge (A' \vee C) \wedge D \wedge (A \vee B') \wedge C']$

6. $F = [(A \vee B') \wedge B]' \vee [A' \wedge D \wedge (B \vee C)]$

7. $F = (A' \wedge B) \vee \{D' \wedge B \wedge [(C \wedge E) \vee (A' \wedge E')]\} \vee \{C \wedge [A \vee [B \wedge (A \vee (D' \wedge E'))]]\}$

8. $F = \{W' \wedge [(X \vee Y' \vee Z')' \vee [X \wedge ((Y \wedge Z \wedge U' \wedge V) \vee (W \wedge V'))]]\} \vee \{X' \wedge [(W' \wedge Y') \vee [W \wedge (U \vee V)]]\} \vee \{Y \wedge [(W \wedge Z) \vee (X' \wedge (W \vee Z))]\}$

B3   Karnaugh Maps

Karnaugh maps are a graphical way to represent logical functions. They can be used for two-, three-, and four-variable expressions, but beyond that their use requires some special techniques.

B3.1   MINTERMS AND MAXTERMS

Karnaugh maps divide the universal set into squares that each represent a minterm. A minterm is a term that contains the intersection (or $\wedge$) of all the variables, either primed or not. Thus two variables, X and Y, would have the following four minterms:

$X' \wedge Y'$
$X' \wedge Y$
$X \wedge Y'$
$X \wedge Y$

For the three variables X, Y, and Z, the eight minterms would be the following:

$X' \wedge Y' \wedge Z'$
$X' \wedge Y' \wedge Z$
$X' \wedge Y \wedge Z'$
$X' \wedge Y \wedge Z$
$X \wedge Y' \wedge Z'$
$X \wedge Y' \wedge Z$
$X \wedge Y \wedge Z'$
$X \wedge Y \wedge Z$

With n variables, there are 2^n possible minterms. Three three-variable Karnaugh maps are shown in Fig. B6 for the functions x, y, and z.

While minterms are generally used in Karnaugh maps, you can also construct dual maps using maxterms. Maxterms are the unions (or $\lor$) of all the possible variable combinations. Thus, for the two variables X and Y, the maxterms would be as follows:

$X' \lor Y'$
$X' \lor Y$
$X \lor Y'$
$X \lor Y$

Again, for n variables, there are 2^n maxterms.

B3.2   CONSTRUCTING KARNAUGH MAPS

To construct a Karnaugh map, you represent those conditions under which an expression is true. Thus the expression $X \land Y$ is true only when X and Y are true, that is, when $X = 1$ and $Y = 1$. Similarly, the expression $X \land Y'$ is true when $X = 1$ and $Y = 0$. Figure B7 shows how to construct Karnaugh maps with three variables. The map in Fig. B7(a) represents the expression

$$(X \land Y' \land Z') \lor (X \land Y' \land Z).$$

Notice that in Fig. B7(b), the 1s can be grouped together to eliminate the variable Z. Enclosing these two 1s in this way is exactly equivalent to the factoring $X \land Y'$. Thus

$$(X \land Y' \land Z') \lor (X \land Y' \land Z) = X \land Y'.$$

Figure B7(c) shows the expression

$$(X \land Y' \land Z') \lor (X' \land Y' \land Z).$$

Here, however, there is no way to cover these 1s with a factoring to eliminate any variables. Thus the expression cannot be further reduced on the Karnaugh map.

Figure B8 shows how to construct the expression $(X \land Y') \lor (X' \land Z)$. Figure B8(a) shows that $X \land Y'$ is represented with a 1 in those squares in which $X = 1$ and $Y = 0$, and Fig. B8(b) has 1s only where $X = 0$ and $Z = 1$, or $X' \land Z$. The union of these two maps then produces the map in Fig. B8(c). Here, the function has 1s where either of the two maps had 1s, giving $(X \land Y') \lor (X' \land Z)$.

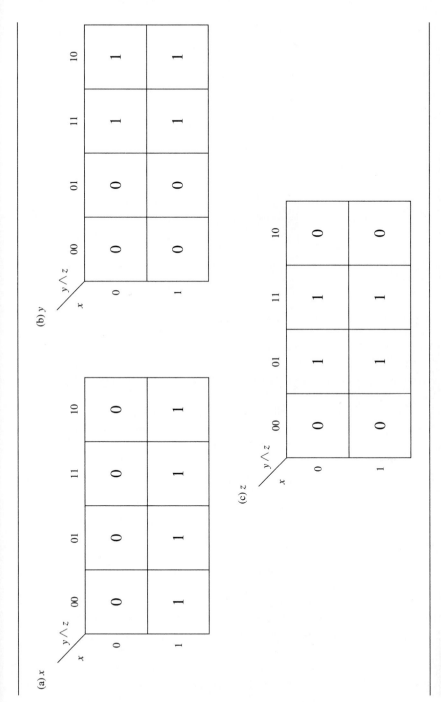

FIGURE B6
Karnaugh Maps

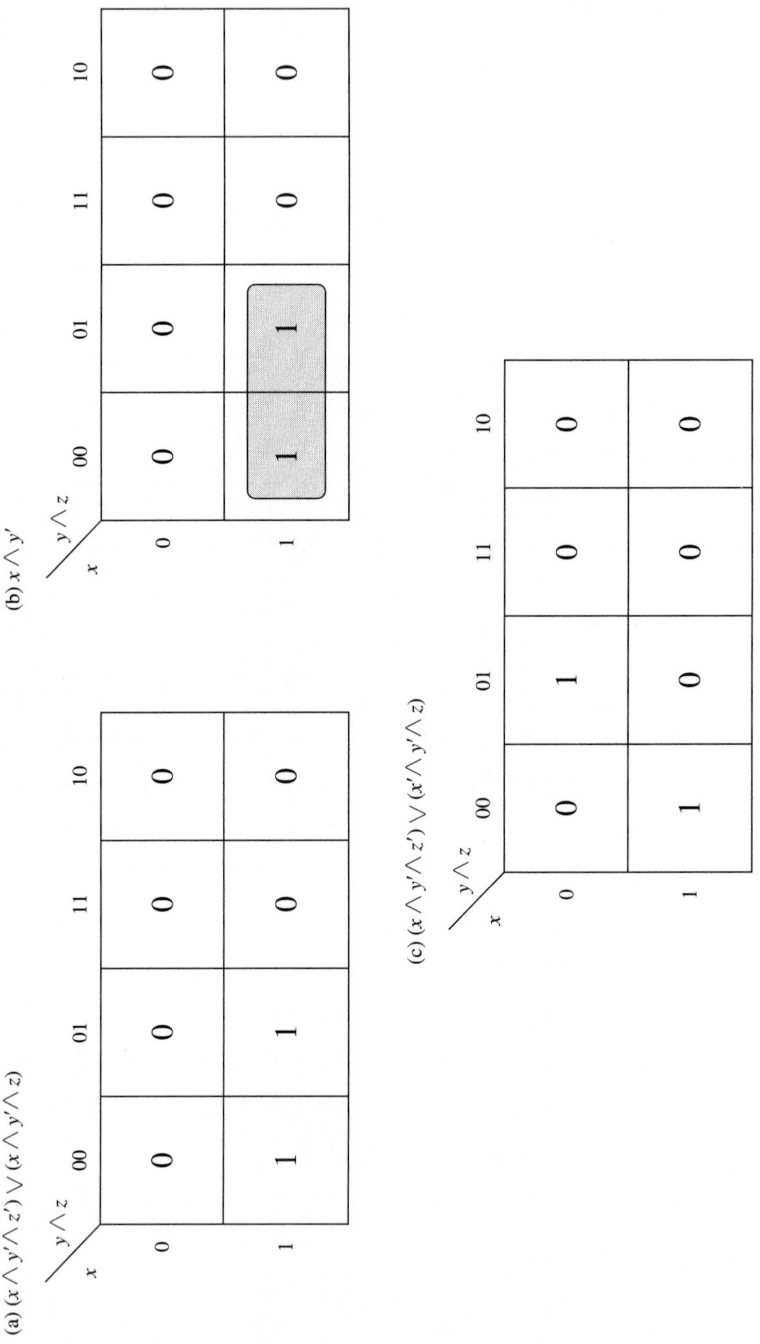

FIGURE B7
Karnaugh Maps

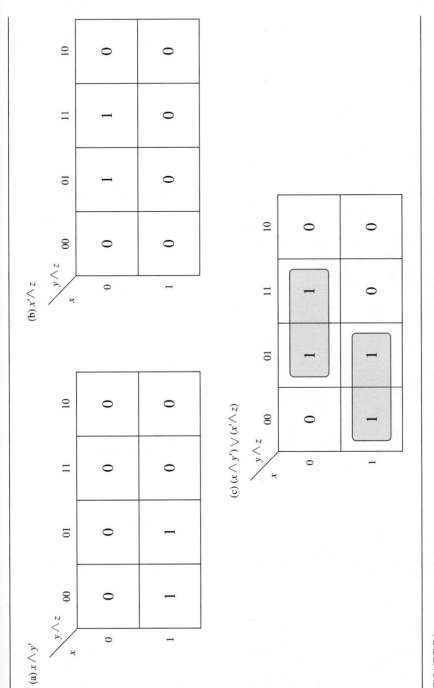

FIGURE B8
Karnaugh Maps

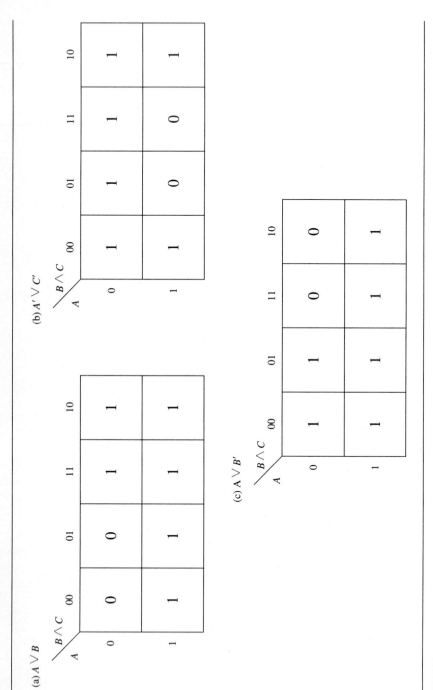

FIGURE B9
Karnaugh Maps

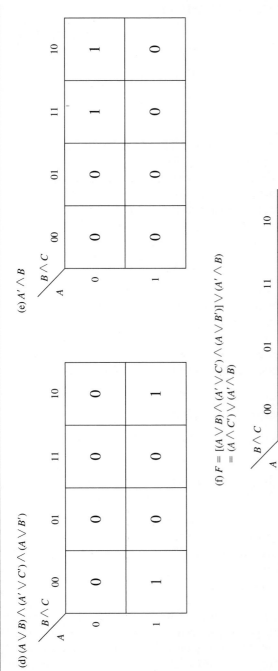

(d) $(A \vee B) \wedge (A' \vee C') \wedge (A \vee B')$

(e) $A' \wedge B$

(f) $F = [(A \vee B) \wedge (A' \vee C') \wedge (A \vee B')] \vee (A' \wedge B)$
$= (A \wedge C') \vee (A' \wedge B)$

FIGURE B9 (continued)

B3.3   DEMONSTRATING EQUALITY WITH MAPS

You can use a Karnaugh map to demonstrate the equality or inequality of two logical expressions. For example, the expression

$$F = [(A \vee B) \wedge (A' \vee C') \wedge (A \vee B')] \vee (A' \wedge B)$$

can be shown to equal the expression

$$G = (A \wedge C') \vee (A' \wedge B).$$

To do this, construct the Karnaugh map of the full expression in steps as in Fig. B9. Figure B9(a) shows the leftmost term of F, $A \vee B$. The second term is in Fig. B9(b) and the third in Fig. B9(c). The intersection of these terms is contained in the left parenthesis and is shown in Fig. B9(d). The intersection of these three functions is obtained by producing a map that has a 1 only where the separate terms in Figs. B9(a), (b), and (c) all have 1s.

Now, from the original equation, you have one remaining term, $A' \wedge B$, shown in Fig. B9(e). The final answer is the union of this last term with the function represented by the map in Fig. B9(d). This is shown in Fig. B9(f). The union of two maps results in a map with a 1 where either of the term maps had 1s. As before, the remaining map spaces are filled with 0s. The simplified result is $(A \wedge C') \vee (A' \wedge B)$, which is the same as expression G. The two expressions are thus equal.

Note that Karnaugh maps can be extended to a square to cover four variables but that five and more variables are more difficult to represent.

B3.4   FACTORING ON KARNAUGH MAPS

Fig. B10 shows how Karnaugh maps can be factored. This figure is a map of the expression

$$F = (W' \wedge X' \wedge Y \wedge Z) \vee (W' \wedge X \wedge Y' \wedge Z') \vee (W' \wedge X \wedge Y' \wedge Z) \vee$$
$$(W' \wedge X \wedge Y \wedge Z) \vee (W \wedge X \wedge Y' \wedge Z) \vee (W \wedge X \wedge Y \wedge Z).$$

This map is factored by seeing where the 1s can be clustered in groups of two, four, or eight. Each two-group eliminates one variable and each four-group eliminates two variables. As you can see, the 1s are all covered by these three factorings, giving the final result of

$$F = (W' \wedge Y \wedge Z) \vee (W' \wedge X \wedge Y') \vee (X \wedge Z).$$

In factoring on a Karnaugh map, your objective is to find the minimum number of square or rectangular coverings that will include all the 1s. As shown in Fig. B11, for example, a map can quickly show redundancies. The coverings in Fig. B11(a) give the function $(X \wedge Y') \vee (Y' \wedge Z) \vee (X' \wedge Z)$. Note, however, that the $Y' \wedge Z$ term is unnecessary, since the function can be completely covered as in Fig. B11(b), to give the simplest answer $(X \wedge Y') \vee (X' \wedge Z)$.

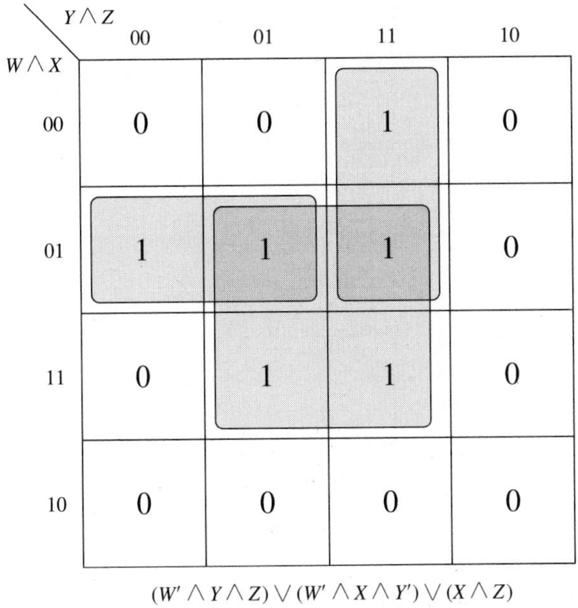

$$(W' \wedge Y \wedge Z) \vee (W' \wedge X \wedge Y') \vee (X \wedge Z)$$

FIGURE B10
A Four-variable Karnaugh Map

B3.5 INVERSE FACTORING

Often, it is not obvious how to best cover the 1s on a Karnaugh map, while the 0s may seem easier. When covering zeros, you get the negative of the desired function. You then use DeMorgan's theorem to get the final result.

For example, suppose you had a light that was controlled by four switches and you wanted the light to be on whenever two or more switches were on. By labeling the switches A, B, C, and D, the on conditions are:

On = $AB + AC + AD + BC + BD + CD + ABC + ABD + ACD +$
     $BCD + ABCD$.

This function is shown in the Karnaugh map in Fig. B12. Because there are relatively fewer 0s than 1s, a simpler factoring will likely result from covering the 0s, as in Fig. B13. This gives the conditions under which the light would be off as

On' = $(A' \wedge B' \wedge C') \vee (A' \wedge B' \wedge D') \vee (A' \wedge C' \wedge D') \vee (B' \wedge C' \wedge D')$.

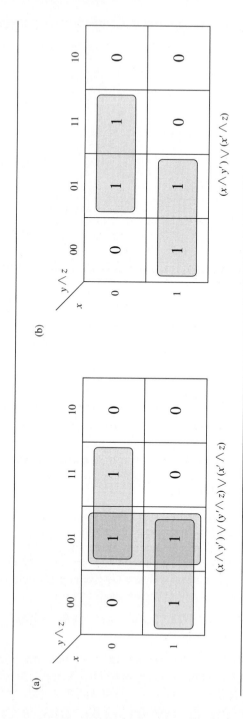

FIGURE B11
Karnaugh Maps

Note that the $A' \wedge B' \wedge D'$ and $B' \wedge C' \wedge D'$ factors each wrap around to cover the 0000 cell of the map. This expression can be further factored as

$$\text{On}' = [A' \wedge B' \wedge (C' \vee D')] \vee [C' \wedge D' \wedge (A' \vee B')].$$

Now, by using DeMorgan's theorem you get the most simplified form for the answer as follows:

$$\text{On} = [A \vee B \vee (C \wedge D)] \wedge [C \vee D \vee (A \wedge B)].$$

B3.6 FACTORING TECHNIQUES

A number of techniques can be used with Karnaugh maps to get minimum factorings. One approach is to factor out zeros. When you have a map that has a big block of 1s and one or two inconvenient 0s in the middle, you first factor the 1s, ignoring the inconvenient 0s. Then you factor out the 0s. An example of such a factoring is shown in Fig. B14. Here, the top factoring would represent $A' \wedge B'$ and not $C \wedge D$. This can be written as

$$A' \wedge B' \wedge (C \wedge D)' = A' \wedge B' \wedge (C' \vee D').$$

Similarly, the factoring on the left would be

$$C' \wedge D' \wedge (A' \vee B').$$

This now gives the answer as

$$[A' \wedge B' \wedge (C' \vee D')] \vee [C' \wedge D' \wedge (A' \vee B')].$$

Here, you describe the 0 by using the variables not included in the larger factoring to identify where in this factoring the 0 appears. Thus the top row factoring in Fig. B14 is $A' \wedge B'$, so the remaining variables are C and D. You can look at this as using the factoring as a kind of mini map for the remaining variables. You then identify the zeros within this smaller map.

B3.7 EXCEPTION FACTORING

Factoring with exceptions can also be used to simplify expressions that have more than four variables. Suppose, for example, you wanted to simplify the following expression:

$$F = (A' \wedge B) \vee (A \wedge B \wedge C \wedge D) \vee \{D' \wedge B \wedge [(C \wedge E) \vee (A' \wedge E')]\}$$
$$\vee \{C \wedge [(A \wedge B') \vee (B \wedge D' \wedge E)]\}.$$

The first two terms are shown on one map in Fig. B15(a). The third term is a bit more tricky. Fig. B15(b) shows this term as the union of the two terms as follows:

$$\{D' \wedge B \wedge [(C \wedge E) \vee (A' \wedge E')]\} = (D' \wedge B \wedge C \wedge E) \vee (D' \wedge B \wedge A' \wedge E').$$

$C \wedge D$		00	01	11	10
$A \wedge B$	00	0	0	1	0
	01	0	1	1	1
	11	1	1	1	1
	10	0	1	1	1

FIGURE B12
Karnaugh Map of the Switch Problem

If it were not for the E terms, you could now plot the terms $B \wedge C \wedge D'$ and $A' \wedge B \wedge D'$ with 1s on the map in Fig. B15(b). The fact that these two terms have E and E' in them, however, means that instead of 1s, you plot E or E'. Once you do this, notice also that the square at $A' \wedge B \wedge C \wedge D'$ has both an E and an E'. Because $E \vee E' = 1$, you can enter a 1 in this square.

The fourth term is shown in Fig. B15(c). It, too, is the union of two terms as follows:

$$(C \wedge A \wedge B') \vee (C \wedge B \wedge D' \wedge E).$$

Taking the union of all the maps in Fig. B15 (a), (b), and (c) gives the map in Fig. B15(d). The factoring of this is

$$F = (A' \wedge B) \vee \{A \wedge C \wedge [E \vee (B \wedge D')']\} =$$
$$(A' \wedge B) \vee [A \wedge C \wedge (E \vee B' \vee D)],$$

which is the final answer.

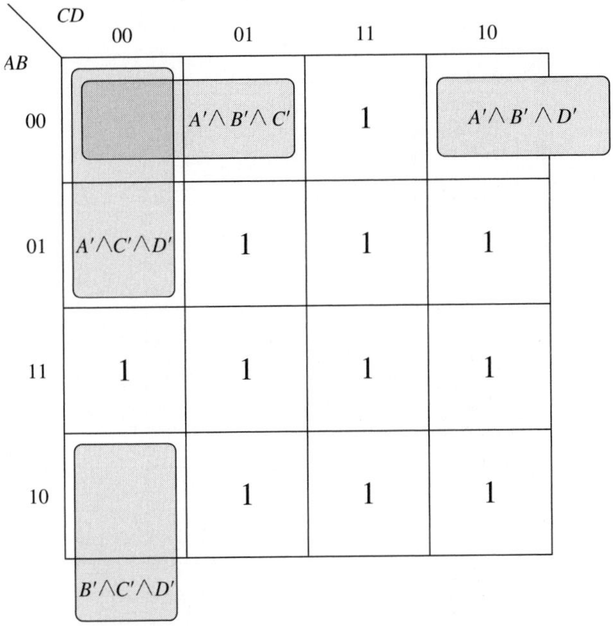

CD \ AB	00	01	11	10
00		$A' \wedge B' \wedge C'$	1	$A' \wedge B' \wedge D'$
01	$A' \wedge C' \wedge D'$	1	1	1
11	1	1	1	1
10		1	1	1

$B' \wedge C' \wedge D'$

$$\text{On}' = (A' \wedge B' \wedge C') \vee (A' \wedge B' \wedge D') \vee (A' \wedge C' \wedge D') \vee (B' \wedge C' /$$
$$= [A' \wedge B' \wedge (C' \vee D')] \vee [C' \wedge D' \wedge (A' \vee B')]$$

FIGURE B13
Factoring the Four-switch Problem

Note that when you take the factor that contains the variable E, you treat it as $0 \vee E$.

You can use this approach to factor expressions with large numbers of variables, as long as most of them appear in only a few of the terms.

Example of exception factoring. Exercise 8 from Section B2 provides a good demonstration of how to do exception factoring. The function was

$$F = \{W' \wedge [(X \vee Y' \vee Z')' \vee [X \wedge ((Y \wedge Z \wedge U' \wedge V) \vee (W \wedge V'))]]\} \vee \{X' \wedge [(W' \wedge Y') \vee [W \wedge (U \vee V)]]\} \vee \{Y \wedge [(W \wedge Z) \vee (X' \wedge (W \vee Z))]\}.$$

To draw the Karnaugh map, first apply DeMorgan's theorem to the first term, giving

$$F = \{W' \wedge [(X' \wedge Y \wedge Z) \vee [X \wedge ((Y \wedge Z \wedge U' \wedge V) \vee (W \wedge V'))]]\} \vee \{X' \wedge [(W' \wedge Y') \vee [W \wedge (U \vee V)]]\} \vee \{Y \wedge [(W \wedge Z) \vee (X' \wedge (W \vee Z))]\}.$$

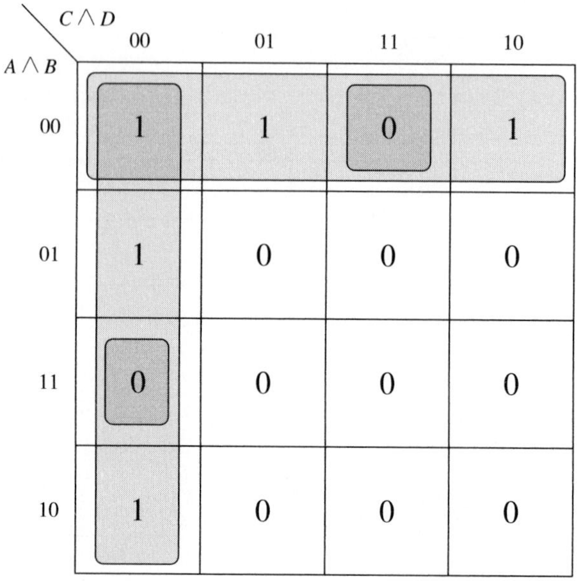

FIGURE B14
Factoring Out Zeros

Next, by applying the distributive law, reduce this to the union of minterms or partial minterms as follows:

$$F = (W' \wedge X' \wedge Y \wedge Z) \vee (W' \wedge X \wedge Y \wedge Z \wedge U' \wedge V) \vee (X' \wedge W' \wedge Y') \vee (X' \wedge W \wedge U) \vee (X' \wedge W \wedge V) \vee (Y \wedge W \wedge Z) \vee (Y \wedge X' \wedge W) \vee (Y \wedge X' \wedge Z)$$

From this, construct the Karnaugh map in Fig. B16. It is generally simplest first to construct a map for the terms that do not involve exceptions. These are the terms that contain only the variables W, X, Y, and Z. This is done in Fig. B16(a) and includes the first, third, sixth, seventh, and eighth terms.

Next, in Fig. B16(b), the exception terms are shown. These are the terms with variables in addition to W, X, Y, and Z, such as U or V. Here, for example, the second term refers to the 0111 square in the map. Because the full term is the intersection of $W' \wedge X \wedge Y \wedge Z$ with $U' \wedge V$, $U' \wedge V$ is entered in the 0111 square instead of a 1. The fourth term, $X' \wedge W \wedge U$, calls for a U in every square across the bottom row of the map in Fig. B16(b). Note, however, that the fifth term also calls for a V in every square across the bottom row. Thus these two terms require a $U \vee V$ in every square across the bottom row.

(a) First two terms $(A' \wedge B) \vee (A \wedge B \wedge C \wedge D)$

$A \wedge B$ / $C \wedge D$	00	01	11	10
00	0	0	0	0
01	1	1	1	1
11	0	0	1	0
10	0	0	0	0

(b) Third term $\{D' \wedge B \wedge [(C \wedge E) \vee (A' \wedge E')]\}$

$A \wedge B$ / $C \wedge D$	00	01	11	10
00	0	0	0	0
01	E'	0	0	$E \vee E'$
11	0	0	0	E
10	0	0	0	0

FIGURE B15
Exception Factoring

(c) Fourth term $\{C \wedge [(A \wedge B') \vee (B \wedge D' \wedge E)]\}$

$A \wedge B$ \ $C \wedge D$	00	01	11	10
00	0	0	0	0
01	0	0	0	*E*
11	0	0	0	*E*
10	0	0	1	1

(d) All terms

$A \wedge B$ \ $C \wedge D$	00	01	11	10
00	0	0	0	0
01	1	1	1	1
11	0	0	1	*E*
10	0	0	1	1

$$F = (A' \wedge B) \vee \{A \wedge C \wedge [E \vee (B \wedge D')']\}$$
$$= (A' \wedge B) \vee [A \wedge C \wedge (E \vee B' \vee D)]$$

FIGURE B15 (continued)

Next, to produce the map for F in Fig. B16(c), take the square-by-square union of the (a) and (b) maps. Because the union of 1 with anything equals 1, the F map will have 1s wherever either of the (a) or (b) maps do. Similarly, because the union of 0 with any function always equals that function, the exception U and V terms will appear wherever the (a) map has zeros and the (b) map has U or V terms. The factoring of this map is shown in Fig. B16(d). The top row is

$$W' \wedge X' \wedge (Y \wedge Z')' = W' \wedge X' \wedge (Y' \vee Z).$$

The third column factoring is

$$Y \wedge Z \wedge [(U' \wedge V) \vee (W' \wedge X)'] = Y \wedge Z \wedge [(U' \wedge V) \vee W \vee X'].$$

The bottom row factoring is

$$W \wedge X' \wedge [(U \vee V \vee (Y')'] = W \wedge X' \wedge (U \vee V \vee Y).$$

The union of these terms is the same as the answer given in Section B2.

B3.8   EXCEPTION FACTORING OF ZEROS

If you want to factor the zeros on a map with exception conditions, it is best to first invert the map to give the F' map and then factor that as before. In factoring a map with exceptions, however, you must remember to invert all the functions that appear in the squares of the map.

Fig. B17 shows the F' map for exercise 8 from Section B2.3. Here, all the 0s are replaced by 1s and all the 1s by 0s. Those squares that hold functions, however, now hold the inverses of those functions. Thus $U \vee V$ is entered in the F' map as $U' \wedge V'$.

Now you can factor the map exactly as before. When you are through, you apply DeMorgan's theorem to the final expression to get the answer.

B3.9   FACTORING PROGRAMMING EXPRESSIONS

While it is important to know how to reduce logical expressions to their simplest form, programming logic is rarely very complex. It is usually wise to check logical constructs to ensure they contain no redundancies or inconsistencies. Further, to completely understand the complex expressions you should always analyze them. Often, however, you should not factor programming logical expressions to their absolute minimum form. These minimum forms could be harder to understand or more difficult to modify. However, the minimum factors can be helpful in checking the correctness of your logic and in defining comprehensive test conditions.

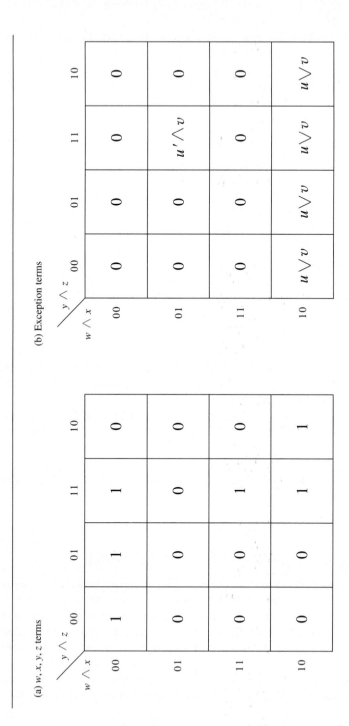

(a) w, x, y, z terms

(b) Exception terms

FIGURE B16
Karnaugh Map for Exercise 8

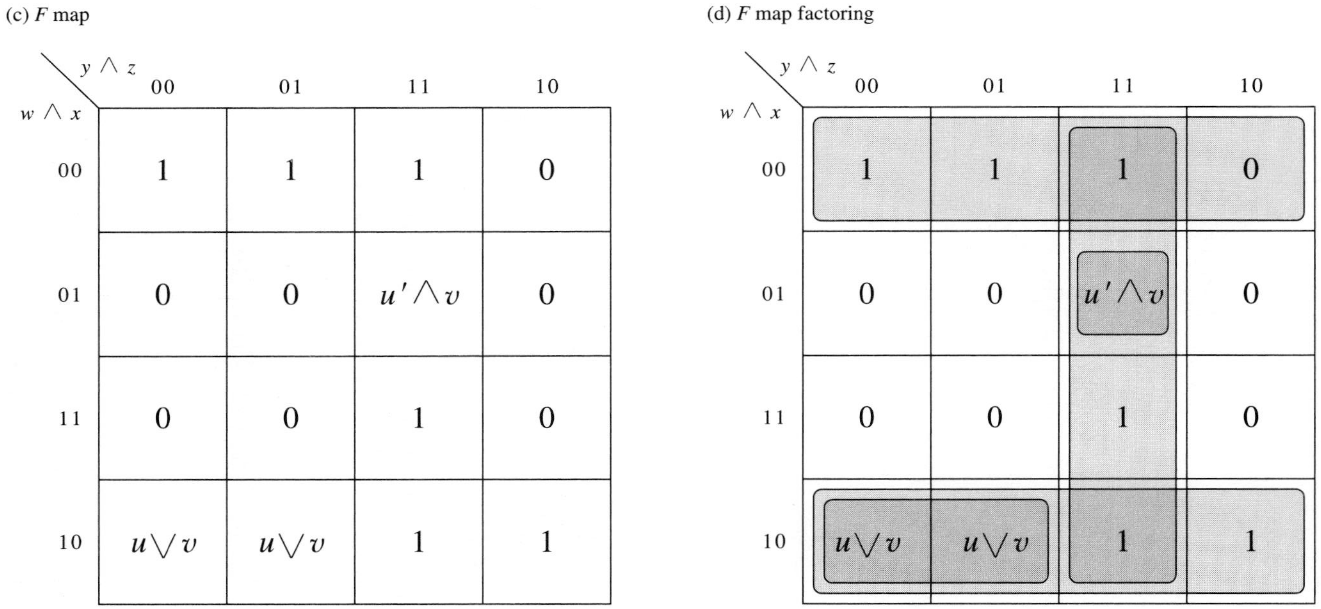

(c) F map

$w \wedge x$ \ $z \wedge y$	00	01	11	10
00	1	1	1	0
01	0	0	$u' \vee v$	0
11	0	0	1	0
10	$u \vee v$	$u \vee v$	1	1

(d) F map factoring

$w \wedge x$ \ $z \wedge y$	00	01	11	10
00	1	1	1	0
01	0	0	$u' \vee v$	0
11	0	0	1	0
10	$u \vee v$	$u \vee v$	1	1

FIGURE B16 (continued)

$y \wedge z$ $w \wedge x$	00	01	11	10
00	0	0	0	1
01	1	1	$u' \vee v'$	1
11	1	1	0	1
10	$u' \wedge v'$	$u' \wedge v'$	0	0

FIGURE B17
Inverted Map for Exercise 8

B3.10 EXERCISES

Using Karnaugh maps, simplify the expressions in the exercises in Section B2.3.

B4 Describing Program Functions

In using the algebra of sets to describe programming functions, some additional symbols are required. Following are a few of the most important:

   $\in$ means "is a member of the set."

   $\notin$ means "is not a member of the set."

   $\forall$ means "for all members of the set."

   $\exists$ means "there exists a member of the set."

These symbols can help you to represent a variety of programming functions both precisely and succinctly. While many more symbols are often used by those versed in formal design methods, these are sufficient for expressing many simple functions. For sophisticated operations, however, you may have to revert to ordinary language expressions. For example, if you wanted to represent all the even-numbered members of a set you could use a parenthetical expression in your formula, such as (the even-numbered members), rather than inventing some special symbol. While this is not mathematically elegant, it will often be adequate to represent simple program functions. However, if you expect to spend a great deal of time using formal design methods, you should become familiar with some common methods and notations. [Baber, Gries, Spivey, Woodcock]

B4.1 PROGRAM FUNCTIONAL STATEMENTS

When you describe program functions, it is also important to separate the condition from the action. The symbols used for this are

```
Condition :: Action
```

This reads, "When *Condition* is true, do *Action*." Several condition/action pairs would then be written as follows:

```
Condition1 :: Action1
  ∨
Condition2 :: Action2
  ∨
  ...
ConditionN :: ActionN
```

B4.2 USING MATHEMATICAL SYMBOLS

If you have some dataset and a name D and want to take an action if D is the name of any dataset in a file, you could write the logic as follows:

```
(D ∈ File) :: Action
```

This reads, "If *D* is a member of *File*, take *Action*." The expression (D ∈ File) is now a logical statement that you can manipulate in expressions just as you did with the variables w, x, and so on. Similarly, if you wanted to take some other action whenever D was not in the file you would use the expression

```
D ∉ File or D ! ∈ File or (D ∈ File)' :: Action
```

This reads, "When *D* is not a member of *File*, take *Action*."

The 'for all' symbol can be used to take some action when every member of a set meets some condition. For example, the following conditions would call for some action when every character in a string was alphabetic:

$$\forall \text{ Character } \bullet \text{ (Character } \in \text{ Alpha) } :: \text{ Action}$$

This reads, "For all *Character*, such that *Character* is in the set *Alpha*, take *Action*." Note that the symbol ● should be read "such that." Similarly, if you wanted to take some action when any character was not in *Alpha*, use

$$\exists \text{ Character } \bullet \text{ (Character } \notin \text{ Alpha) } :: \text{ Action}$$

This reads, "When there is any *Character* such that *Character* is not in *Alpha*, take *Action*."

B4.3   THE CDATA FUNCTIONS

Table B4 shows the Function Specification Template for the class *CData* used in Chapter 10. This template uses a notation much like that of C++. The *Pop* function, for example, is

```
char *Pop(data &D)

    Empty' :: return (D.first name)∧(D = first element)
    ∧(delete first)∧reset
    ∨
    Empty :: return "Empty"
```

This reads as follows:

- □ The function *Pop* passes a variable *D* of type data.
- □ The return is a character string, as indicated by the char *.
- □ The variable *D* may be modified by the function, as indicated by the &*D* in the declaration.
- □ When the class *CData* is not *Empty*, *D* is set equal to the first element, the return is the name field of *D*, the first element is deleted, and *CData* is reset.

  or
- □ When the class *CData* is *Empty*, return the string "*Empty*."

TABLE B4 CDATA FUNCTION SPECIFICATION TEMPLATE

CData	Base class	ListState (0 to 4) ListPosition (0 to N)
int Empty()		ListState == 0 :: return(true) $\lor$ ListState $\neq$ 0 :: return(false)
int Clear()		:: Set CData pointers to null $\land$ ListState = 0 $\land$ List Position = 0 $\land$ return(true)
int Last()		(Empty' $\land$ (ListState == 1 $\lor$ ListState == 4)) :: return (true) $\lor$ (Empty $\lor$ (ListState == 2 $\lor$ ListState == 3) :: return (false)
int Reset()		(Empty' $\land$ N = 1) :: ListPosition = 1 $\land$ ListState = 1 $\land$ return(true) $\lor$ (Empty' $\land$ N > 1) :: ListPosition = 1 $\land$ ListState = 2 $\land$ return(true) $\lor$ Empty :: ListPosition = 0 $\land$ ListState = 0 $\land$ return(false)
int StepForward()		(ListState == 2 $\land$ N == 2) :: (step pointers to next position) $\land$ ListPosition = 2 $\land$ ListState = 4 $\land$ return(true) $\lor$ (ListState == 2 $\land$ N > 2) :: (step pointers to next position) $\land$ ListPosition = 2 $\land$ ListState = 3 $\land$ return(true) $\lor$ (ListState == 3 $\land$ ListPosition < N $-$ 1) :: (step pointers to next position) $\land$ ListPosition = ListPosition + 1 $\land$ return(true) $\lor$ (ListState == 3 $\land$ ListPosition == N $-$ 1) :: (step pointers to next position) $\land$ ListPosition = N $\land$ ListState = 4 $\land$ return(true) $\lor$ (ListState == 0 $\lor$ ListState == 1 $\lor$ ListState == 4) :: return(false)
int StepBackward()		((ListState == 3 $\lor$ ListState == 4) $\land$ ListPosition == 2) :: (step pointers to prior position) $\land$ ListPosition = 1 $\land$ ListState = 2 $\land$ return(true) $\lor$ (ListState == 3 $\land$ ListPosition > 2) :: (step pointers to prior position) $\land$ ListPosition = ListPosition $-$ 1 $\land$ return(true) $\lor$ (ListState == 4 $\land$ ListPosition > 2) :: (step pointers to prior position) $\land$ ListPosition = ListPosition $-$ 1 $\land$ ListState = 3 $\land$ return(true)

TABLE B4 (continued)

CData	base class	ListState (0 to 4) ListPosition (0 to N)
int StepBackward()	$\bigvee$ (ListState == 0 $\bigvee$ ListState == 1 $\bigvee$ ListState == 2) :: return(false)	
int Status()	:: return (ListState)	
int Position()	:: return (ListPosition)	

ASet (CData)	CData	ListState (0 to 4) ListPosition (0 to N)
void Push(dataD)	:: (insert D at position 1) $\wedge$ Reset	
char *Pop(data &D)	Empty' :: return (D.first name) $\wedge$ (D = first element) $\wedge$ (delete first) $\wedge$ Reset $\bigvee$ Empty :: return "Empty"	
Int AddSet(data D)	D $\notin$ ASet :: Push(D) $\wedge$ Reset $\wedge$ return (true) $\bigvee$ D $\in$ ASet :: return (false)	
Int SubtractSet (data D)	D $\in$ ASet :: delete D $\wedge$ Reset $\wedge$ return (true) $\bigvee$ D $\notin$ ASet :: return (false)	
Int MemberSet (data D)	D $\in$ ASet :: return (ListPosition of D) $\bigvee$ (D $\notin$ ASet $\wedge$ N == 1) :: ListPosition = 1 $\wedge$ ListState = 1 $\wedge$ return (false) $\bigvee$ (D $\notin$ ASet $\wedge$ N > 1) :: LlstPosition = N $\wedge$ ListState = 4 $\wedge$ return (false)	

B5   The Elevator Example

As an example of this notation, suppose you wanted to precisely state the conditions under which an elevator were to go up, to go down, or to hold its door open. The inputs are the current floor, the previous elevator direction, the set of buttons on the various floors, the set of floor buttons inside the elevator, and the door open button. While this is a very simplified statement of a potentially complex set of conditions, it illustrates the point.

B5.1   THE LANGUAGE DESCRIPTION OF THE ELEVATOR PROBLEM

The language description of this problem is as follows:

- Hold the door open when the Door Open button is pushed inside the elevator or when the floor button on the elevator's current floor is pushed.

- Go up when the door is not held open and when the current floor is less than *TOP* and when the elevator was previously going up and when either an elevator button or a floor button for a floor higher than the current floor is pushed, or when the elevator had previously been going down and there are no lower buttons pushed in the elevator or on the floors and there are higher buttons pushed in the elevator or on the floors.

- Go down when the door is not held open and when the current floor is greater than *BOTTOM* and the elevator was previously going down and when an elevator button or a floor button for a floor lower than the current floor is pushed or when the elevator had previously been going up and there are no higher buttons pushed in the elevator or on the floors and there are lower buttons pushed.

As you can see, what appears to be simple logic can become seemingly quite complex and confusing when expressed in ordinary language.

B5.2   MATHEMATICALLY DESCRIBING THE ELEVATOR PROBLEM

Using mathematical notation, you can express these elevator conditions more precisely with the following variables:

x: The current floor

u: The elevator was previously going up

u':   The elevator was previously going down

F: The set of pushed floor buttons that call the elevator

E: The set of pushed elevator buttons that indicate the desired floor

D: The Door Open button in the elevator

TOP: The top floor

BOTTOM: The bottom floor

b, c: Positive integers that represent the floor numbers of pushed elevator or floor buttons

Now, the various elevator commands can be expressed as follows:

```
Open Door: D∨[∃b●(b∈F∧b==x)] :: Open Door
```

This can be read as follows:

> Open door when D (Door Open button) is true or when there exists some pushed button b that is a member of F (the floor call buttons) and $b==x$ (b equals the current floor x).

Up

$\{x<TOP \wedge u \wedge (Open\ Door)' \wedge [\exists b \bullet (b \in F \vee b \in E) \wedge b>x]\}$

$\vee$

$\{x<TOP \wedge u' \wedge (Open\ Door)' \wedge [!\exists c \bullet (c \in F \vee c \in E) \wedge c<x] \wedge [\exists b \bullet (b \in F \vee b \in E) \wedge b>x]\}$

:: Up

This up condition can be read as follows:

> x (the current floor) is less than TOP and u (the elevator was going up) and the door open conditions are not met and there exists a b such that b is a member of F or b is a member of E (the floor button in the elevator) and b is greater than x (a higher button is pushed).
>
> or
>
> x is less than TOP and the elevator was going down and the door open conditions are not met and there does not exist a c such that c is in F or c is in E and c is less than x and there does exist a b such that b is in F or b is in E and b is greater than x.

Down

$\{x>BOTTOM \wedge u' \wedge (Open\ Door)' \wedge [\exists b \bullet (b \in F \vee b \in E) \wedge b<x]\}$

$\vee$

$\{x>BOTTOM \wedge u \wedge (Open\ Door)' \wedge [!\exists c \bullet (c \in F \vee c \in E) \wedge c>x] \wedge [\exists b \bullet (b \in F \vee b \in E) \wedge b<x]\}$

:: Down

The down condition reads much like the up condition.

These expressions could be simplified somewhat by factoring the common expressions from both terms. This would give the Up condition in most simplified form as follows:

$\{x<TOP \wedge (OpenDoor)' \wedge [\exists b \bullet (b \in F \vee b \in E) \wedge b>x] \wedge \{u \vee [!\exists c \bullet (c \in F \vee c \in E) \wedge c<x]\}$ :: Up

This is mathematically simpler and it would likely be simpler to program. Depending on the types of modifications and extensions planned, however, it may not lead to a better design.

In spite of the seeming complexity of these functions, they omit many conditions that would normally be involved in a real elevator case. For example, these expressions assume the elevator is at a floor and is never between floors. There are no provisions for door obstructions or elevator overload, and there is no emergency stop. Presumably, the elevator would also return to the first floor when no other actions were called for. Also, if there were multiple elevators, there would be logical dependencies among them.

B6   Function Completeness and Orthogonality

As described in Chapter 10, state machines can be helpful in describing program behavior. It is important, however, to ensure the state machine description is correct. While there is no general way to prove that a state machine is properly designed, various conditions can often cause design problems with state machines, for example, when some states have been overlooked or when there are conflicting conditions leading to uncertainty or even overlapping conditions for several state transitions. The likelihood of these problems can be reduced if you are careful to design only proper state machines.

A state machine is proper when it can reach a program return state from every other state, when all state conditions are complete and orthogonal, and when all the transitions from each state are complete and orthogonal. The properties of completeness and orthogonality are thus important in proving that a state machine is proper.

B6.1   COMPLETE FUNCTIONS

A set of functions is complete when it covers all possible logical conditions. This would be shown in a Karnaugh map when a set of functions filled all the spaces on the map. Suppose, for example, you had three variables, x, y, and z, and wanted to perform the functions f, g, and h under the following conditions:

$$x \lor y' \; :: \; f$$
$$\lor$$
$$z \; :: \; g$$
$$\lor$$
$$y \; :: \; h$$

The composite map of these functional conditions is shown in Fig. B18(a). There is at least one function in every square of this map, hence the sum of these functions equals the universal set. This means all possible conditions are represented by the functions. These functions are thus said to be complete. Complete sets of functions are important in state machines because an incomplete map could mean some logical condition has been overlooked.

B6.2   ORTHOGONAL FUNCTIONS

A set of functions is orthogonal if none of its members have any conditions in common. The products of all possible function combinations then equal zero, or the empty set. This is the case for the functions in the map in Fig. B18(b). Here, the functions are to be invoked as follows:

```
z :: i
y∧z' :: j
```

With orthogonal functions, there is no confusion about what happens in any condition. For example, under condition $x \wedge y \wedge z$, only function i is performed. Note that in the case in Fig. B18(a), where the functions are complete, all the functions f, g, and h are performed under condition $x \wedge y \wedge z$. While this may be satisfactory in many cases, it is not usually desirable for the states or the state transitions in state machines.

B6.3   COMPLETE AND ORTHOGONAL FUNCTIONS

In Fig. B18(c), a complete and orthogonal set of functions uniquely covers all cells in the Karnaugh map. Here, the functions are defined as follows:

```
x∧(y∨z') :: k
y'∧(x'∨z) :: l
x'∧y :: m
```

From this map it is clear that $k \vee l \vee m = 1$, so these functions are complete. It is also clear that $k \wedge l = k \wedge m = m \wedge l = 0$, so the functions are also orthogonal.

When the state conditions of a state machine are complete and orthogonal, all the possible states have been specified and each is unique. That is, the machine can be in one and only one state at any point in time. Similarly, when the transition conditions from each state to all other states in the state machine are complete and orthogonal, it means that for every logical condition, there is always a next state and that next state is always unique.

This is important for software design because program loops involve state changes. If such a state machine is not complete it means there is some combination of conditions that has not been defined. Similarly, a state machine that is not orthogonal means there is some set of conditions where more than one next state is defined. When such conditions are encountered, programs are likely to go into endless loops, hang up, or do something unexpected.

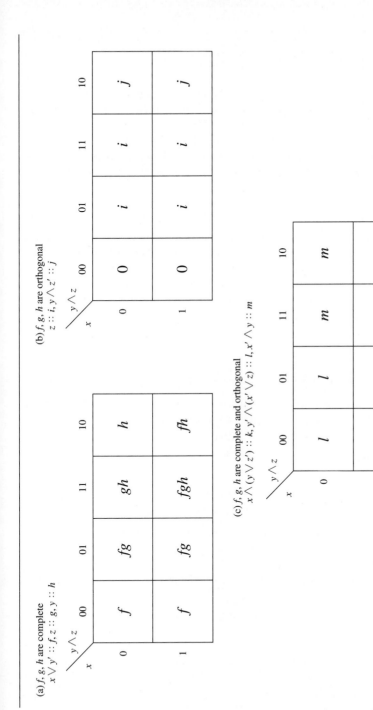

(a) f, g, h are complete
$x \lor y' :: f, z :: g, y :: h$

(b) f, g, h are orthogonal
$z :: i, y \land z' :: j$

(c) f, g, h are complete and orthogonal
$x \land (y \lor z) :: k, y' \land (x' \lor z) :: l, x' \land y :: m$

FIGURE B18
Complete and Orthogonal Functions

B7   Formally Describing Designs

Formal design methods describe the program's intended result rather than the manner in which it is produced. It is always a good practice to define program requirements and specifications in this way because you want to retain as much design flexibility as you can. Once the problem is fully defined, you can examine alternative designs to see which best meets the overall needs of the job. For further information on formal specification and design methods, consult the references.

While mathematical notation can be used to describe the logical design of programming procedures using such notation, this way does not take full advantage of their conceptual power. An attempt to use these notations this way would also require provisions for all the loop and conditional constructs of traditional programming languages. To see this difference, consider the procedural description of the up elevator command:

```
if x<TOP
  then
      if not Open Door
       then
         if higher floor or elevator button pushed
           then
              if u
                then command=up
                elseif not lower floor or elevator
                button pushed
                  then command=up
```

While this program follows the same logic as before, it describes only one way to implement the up function. It is wise to avoid such descriptions, however, because they generally constrain program design and implementation.

B8   Answers to B2 Exercises

1. $F = X \vee Y$
2. $F = X \vee Y$
3. $F = Z' \wedge (Y' \vee X)$
4. $F = X \vee (Y' \wedge Z)$

5. $F = (A' \vee B) \wedge C'$

6. $F = B' \vee A'$

7. $F = (A' \wedge B) \vee (A \wedge C)$

8. $F = [W' \wedge X' \wedge (Y' \vee Z)] \vee [W \wedge X' \wedge (U \vee V \vee Y)]$
   $\vee [Y \wedge Z \wedge ((U' \wedge V) \vee W \vee X')]$

References

[Baber] Robert L. Baber, *Error-Free Software, Know-how and Know-why of Program Correctness* (New York: John Wiley & Sons, 1991).

[Gill] Arthur Gill, *Applied Algebra for the Computer Sciences* (Englewood Cliffs, NJ: Prentice-Hall, 1976).

[Gries] David Gries, *The Science of Programming* (New York: Springer Verlag, 1981).

[Spivey] J. M. Spivey, *The Z Notation: a Reference Manual* (Englewood Cliffs, NJ: Prentice Hall, 1992).

[Woodcock] Jim Woodcock and Martin Loomes, *Software Engineering Mathematics* (Reading, MA: Addison-Wesley, 1989).

C

APPENDIX
The Personal Software
Process (PSP) Contents

This appendix contains all the scripts, forms, templates, and standards for the PSP versions used in this book. It has two principal sections:

☐ PSP process contents
Sections C1 through C7 describe all the PSP process versions and their elements and include examples of completed Project Plan Summary forms. The data in these examples are from students' assignments done for a course I taught at Carnegie Mellon University in spring 1994.

☐ Tables containing the PSP process elements
The tables are a complete set of the PSP process scripts, forms, templates, and standards.

The PSP cross-reference in Table C9 on page 650, gives the process version contents, the chapter prerequisites, and the table number for each element. Each process version is a prerequisite to all subsequent process versions.

To read Table C9, look at the top for the process version and down the left for the process element. For example, the PSP0 contents are in the column under PSP0 and PSP0.1 contents are under PSP0.1. The PSP0 Process Script is given in Table C10 and the PSP0 Planning Script in Table C11. Similarly, the PSP0.1 Process Script is given in Table C21. Most of the elements in the section under Process Scripts and Summaries change from one process version to the next. With the exception of the Design Review Checklist, all the forms, templates, and standards are introduced once and used in every subsequent process version without change. The table numbers for these unchanging elements are given in the Table Number column with an X indicating the process versions that use them. For example, the Code Review Checklist is given in Table C58 and is used in

PSP2, PSP2.1, and PSP3. Similarly, the Size Estimating Template is shown in Table C39, its instructions are in Table C40, and it is used in PSP1, PSP1.1, PSP2, PSP2.1, and PSP3.

To help you identify the items added as the process scripts and project planning forms are enhanced, the additions from the prior process versions are shown in ***bold italics***.

THE PSP PROCESS CONTENTS

The following seven sections describe all the PSP versions. Each description contains the following parts:

- The opening paragraph
  A brief overview of the process version and its new elements
- Objectives
  A brief description of the process objectives and prerequisites
- Process scripts, forms, templates, and standards
  A list of all the process elements used in the process version
- New process elements
  The new elements for the given process version and an example of a completed Project Plan Summary form.
- Process reporting specifications
  The form and content of the reports to be submitted for the exercises done with this PSP version

Before you use a process version, review its elements to ensure you understand their purpose and use.

C1 PSP0 Process Contents

PSP0 introduces you to the PSP process family and its forms, scripts, and standards. By providing you with an orderly structure for planning your work and reporting your results, these process elements can save you a substantial amount of time. Without standard forms, for example, you would have to decide how to produce a plan, what data to gather, and how to record it.

As shown in the PSP0 script in Table C10, you

1. ensure you have all the required inputs,
2. ensure you understand the requirements for the job,
3. estimate the time in minutes you expect a program development to take

4. record this time under Plan in the Project Plan Summary, including the time the planning took

5. do the development

6. enter the actual data from your Time Recording and Defect Recording Logs in the Actual column in the Project Plan Summary.

In development, you design, implement, compile, and test the program, using your current development methods. You also record the defects you find in the Defect Recording Log and the time you spent in the Time Recording Log. Each process phase is further described in the Planning, Development, and Post-mortem Scripts in Tables C11, C12, and C13, respectively.

C1.1   OBJECTIVES AND PREREQUISITES

The PSP0 objectives are

- □ to incorporate basic measurements in your software development process,
- □ to require minimal changes in your personal practices,
- □ to demonstrate the use of a defined process in writing small programs, and
- □ to use your current process as an introductory process framework.

The prerequisites for PSP0 are that you be reasonably fluent with at least one programming language and that you have read Chapter 2. The PSP0 process and its scripts, forms, templates, standards, and instructions are described in general terms in that chapter. You should review these elements before starting to write your first program.

C1.2   SCRIPTS, FORMS, TEMPLATES, AND STANDARDS

The scripts, forms, templates, and standards are the items used in the PSP0 process. The scripts and the Project Plan Summary change with every process, but the Time Recording Log, Defect Recording Log, and Defect Type Standard are used without change in every subsequent process version. All these items are included at the back of this appendix at the table numbers indicated.

PSP0 Process Script	Table C10
PSP0 Planning Script	Table C11
PSP0 Development Script	Table C12
PSP0 Postmortem Script	Table C13
PSP0 Project Plan Summary and Instructions	Tables C14 and C15
Time Recording Log and Instructions	Tables C16 and C17
Defect Recording Log and Instructions	Tables C18 and C19
Defect Type Standard	Table C20

C1.3   PSP0 PROCESS ELEMENTS

Because PSP0 is the first PSP process, all its elements are new. The scripts, Time Recording Log, Defect Recording Log, and Defect Type Standard are described in Chapter 2. The Project Plan Summary is described with the aid of the following example.

C1.4   PROJECT PLAN SUMMARY EXAMPLE

An example of a completed PSP0 Project Plan Summary is shown in Table C1. The items in this form are as follows:

- ☐ Student
  This form was completed by Student 1.

- ☐ Date
  The student completed the form on 1/18/94.

- ☐ Program
  This summary is for the first program in the textbook, calculating the standard deviation.

- ☐ Program #
  This is program 1A.

- ☐ Instructor
  This summary was for the course I taught at Carnegie Mellon University in spring 1994.

- ☐ Language
  The student used C++.

- ☐ Time in Phase—Plan
  Before starting development, Student 1 estimated 195 minutes to develop program 1A.

- ☐ Time in Phase (min.)—Actual
  After completing development and during the postmortem phase, Student 1 examined the Time Recording Log and determined how much time was actually spent in each project phase. These times were entered in the phase spaces under Actual. For example, 44 minutes were spent in design. These times were added and equaled 356 minutes. As you can see, the original time estimate was not very close to the actual time. You will find that this is not unusual.

- ☐ Time in Phase (min.)—To Date
  This column contains the sums of all the times spent in each phase for all the PSP projects developed to date. If, as in this case, only one program has been developed the To Date column will contain the same numbers as the Actual column. When two or more programs have been developed, how-

TABLE C1 PSP0 PROJECT PLAN SUMMARY EXAMPLE

Student __Student 1__   Date __1/18/94__
Program __Standard Deviation__   Program # __1A__
Instructor __Humphrey__   Language __C++__

Time in Phase (min.)	Plan	Actual	To Date	To Date %
Planning		7	7	2.0
Design		44	44	12.4
Code		97	97	27.2
Compile		67	67	18.8
Test		111	111	31.2
Postmortem		30	30	8.4
Total	195	356	356	100.0

Defects Injected		Actual	To Date	To Date %
Planning		0	0	0
Design		4	4	16.7
Code		13	13	54.2
Compile		2	2	8.3
Test		5	5	20.8
Total Development		24	24	100.0

Defects Removed		Actual	To Date	To Date %
Planning		0	0	0
Design		0	0	0
Code		0	0	0
Compile		16	16	66.7
Test		8	8	33.3
Total Development		24	24	100.0
After Development		0	0	

ever, the To Date column is the sum of the Actual column for this program and the To Date column on the Project Plan Summary of the most recent prior program development.

□ Time in Phase (min.)—To Date %
This column holds the percentage distribution of the data in the To Date column. For this example, the To Date total is 356 minutes. Of this, the student spent 7 minutes in planning, or 2.0 percent of the total To Date development

time. The percentage values for the other phases are also calculated and entered in the same way.

The To Date % entries help you to plan future projects by providing an historical record of the time you have spent in each process phase.

☐ Defects Injected—Actual
During the postmortem phase, the student reviewed the Defect Recording Log and determined that four defects were injected in design, 13 in code, two in compile, and five in test. The student entered these values in the appropriate phase spaces and entered the total of 24 defects in the Total Development row.

☐ Defects Injected—To Date
This column holds the total of the defects injected in each phase for all the programs developed to date. If, as in this case, only one program has been developed the To Date column will hold the same numbers as the Actual column.

☐ Defects Injected—To Date %
This column holds the percentage distribution of the data in the To Date column. Here, for example, Student 1 injected 54.2 percent of the defects during coding. These To Date % data provide an historical record of the percentage of total defects injected in each phase.

You use these data in later process versions to make defect projections.

☐ Defects Removed—Actual
The defects removed are similarly entered in the spaces provided and totaled to get the total number of defects. The total number of defects removed should equal the total number injected. In this case, these numbers are both 24, so there is no problem. Another useful self-consistency check is to ensure the numbers of defects removed up to any phase is always less than or equal to the number injected to that point. Here, for example, 19 defects have been injected up to the end of the compile phase. Only 16 defects have been removed up to that point, so there is no problem. If, however, 14 were injected and 16 removed you should check your data to see where you made a mistake. Defects cannot be removed before they are injected.

☐ Defects Removed—To Date
This column holds the total of the defects removed in each phase for all the programs developed to date.

☐ Defects Removed—To Date %
This column holds the percentage distribution of the data in the To Date column.

☐ Defects Removed—After Development
In this space, you record defects found in later use or enhancement of the program. Suppose, for example, you found a defect in part of program 1A while you were enhancing it for use with program 6A. You would record all

the data on this defect in the Defect Recording Log for program 6A, noting that it was injected in program 1A. Determine the phase injected if possible. The defect, however, should be entered in the Project Plan Summary for program 1A under Defects Removed—Actual—After Development. You should also note on this form where the defect was found. If you later want to examine the after development defect data, you can then find the logs in which they are recorded.

C1.5   PROCESS REPORTING SPECIFICATION

A principal objective of the PSP0 exercises is to provide you with experience in using a disciplined process. While it is important to produce a working program, the criteria for evaluating the PSP0 exercises are as follows:

- ☐ The process data are complete.
- ☐ The data are accurate and self-consistent.
- ☐ The process report is submitted in the proper order and format.

The use of a standard format and order makes it easier both for you to ensure your results are complete and for your instructor to ensure they are correct. The items to be included in PSP0 exercise reports and the order in which they are to be submitted are as follows:

- ☐ PSP0 Project Plan Summary
- ☐ Time Recording Log
- ☐ Defect Recording Log
- ☐ Source program listing
- ☐ Any other requested materials

Your results must be neat and legible, but they need not be typed. You should provide only the requested materials; no cover sheets, binders, or written reports are needed other than those called for. Concentrate on providing the required materials as quickly and efficiently as you can. You will need all your PSP data for subsequent assignments, so you should retain a complete copy of everything you submit.

C2   PSP0.1 Process Contents

The PSP0.1 process introduces size measurements, the Process Improvement Proposal (PIP), and coding standards. Otherwise, it is identical to PSP0. Before you use PSP0.1 to develop a program, you make a size estimate and a complete time estimate. At development completion, you measure the completed program's size and count or calculate the reused, deleted, modified, added, total new and changed, and total new reused LOC.

C2.1 OBJECTIVES AND PREREQUISITES

In addition to the objectives for PSP0, this process has the further objective of helping you to measure and estimate the sizes of the programs you produce. The prerequisites for PSP0.1 are Chapter 4, PSP0, and the LOC counting and coding standards produced with assignments R1 and R2.

C2.2 SCRIPTS, FORMS, TEMPLATES, AND STANDARDS

PSP0.1 Process Script	*Table C21*
PSP0.1 Planning Script	*Table C22*
PSP0.1 Development Script	*Table C23*
PSP0.1 Postmortem Script	*Table C24*
PSP0.1 Project Plan Summary and Instructions	*Tables C25 and C26*
Process Improvement Proposal (PIP)	
and Instructions	*Tables C27 and C28*
Coding Standard	*Table C29*
Time Recording Log and Instructions	Tables C16 and C17
Defect Recording Log and Instructions	Tables C18 and C19
Defect Type Standard	Table C20

C2.3 NEW PROCESS ELEMENTS

New elements to PSP0.1 include not only scripts and the summary report but also the Process Improvement Proposal (PIP) and coding standards. While these are each briefly described in Chapter 4, the following sections give a more complete description.

Process Improvement Proposal.   The PIP is used to record any problems or improvement suggestions that occur to you while you use a process. Many process definition problems concern seemingly minor details. It is such details, however, that make the difference between an annoying and inconvenient process and a comfortable and efficient one. While you may later remember that some form or step was a problem, you will likely forget the details if you do not promptly record them. Keep blank PIP forms at hand and promptly record any improvement ideas. Surprisingly, if you wait even a few minutes, the idea can be hard to reconstruct. Details are important to a personal process, and to fix the details, you must regularly complete and retain your PIPs.

In this course, you should also use PIPs to record comments or to make notes on what you learned from writing each program. Describe anything you found that was particularly interesting or helpful or any unusual problems you had with the development. This will later help you when you try to remember what happened on a project. While doing the assignments in this book, you should submit PIPs with your process reports.

The PIP form is shown in Table C27 and its instructions are in Table C28. Retain copies of all your completed PIPs for use when you later adjust or enhance your PSP.

Coding Standards.   While programs must be correct, the source code should also be understandable. Writing readable code will help you to think more clearly about your design and to test, modify, and reuse it. Clear and accurate comments also help others who work with your programs. Even when you do not expect your program to be used by anyone else, you should get in the habit of writing readable code. This requires that it be well structured and clearly commented.

The PSP coding standard is shown in Table C29. It was largely drawn from a standard developed by Jim Murphy of the University of Massachusetts in Lowell, Massachusetts. I am also indebted to Brian Milnes for his suggestion to include a table of contents at the beginning of each listing. This table is particularly helpful with large listings and can be convenient with small ones.

I have found it helpful to include reuse instructions in the comments near the top of each program listing. You describe precisely how the program is called, the types and ranges of every variable, constraints on the calling parameters, the meanings of the returns, and any special warnings or conditions. Almost every time I have looked for something in the listing of a previously developed program, this section has contained the answer. It is so useful, in fact, that I now religiously include it in every listing whether or not I expect to reuse it. It is simple to produce while you are writing the program, but it can be difficult to reconstruct later.

To be most useful, your coding standard should be designed for the language and working environment you use. You should thus tailor the PSP coding standard to your particular needs. While learning the PSP, you may add steps or make other language-specific adjustments, but you should retain all the items this standard includes. You should then use this standard while completing the exercises in this text.

C2.4   PROJECT PLAN SUMMARY EXAMPLE

An example of a completed PSP0.1 Project Plan Summary is shown in Table C2. The bulk of this form was described with PSP0, so only the new sections are described here.

TABLE C2 PSP0.1 PROJECT PLAN SUMMARY EXAMPLE

Student ___Student 11_____   Date ___2/1/94_____

Program ___Object LOC Counter_____   Program # ___3A___

Instructor___Humphrey_____   Language ___C___

Program Size (LOC)	Plan	Actual	To Date
Base(B)		87	
		(Measured)	
Deleted (D)		0	
		(Counted)	
Modified (M)		6	
		(Counted)	
Added (A)		113	
		(T − B + D − R)	
Reused (R)		0	0
		(Counted)	
Total New and Changed (N)	90	119	315
		(A + M)	
Total LOC (T)		200	396
		(Measured)	
Total New Reused		0	0

Time in Phase (min.)	Plan	Actual	To Date	To Date %
Planning	10	11	36	6.4
Design	25	21	63	11.2
Code	75	97	249	44.2
Compile	20	4	35	6.2
Test	45	39	105	18.7
Postmortem	20	33	75	13.3
Total	195	205	563	100.0

Defects Injected		Actual	To Date	To Date %
Planning		0	0	0
Design		1	3	11.5
Code		8	23	88.5
Compile		0	0	0
Test		0	0	0
Total Development		9	26	100.0

Defects Removed		Actual	To Date	To Date %
Planning		0	0	0
Design		0	0	0
Code		0	0	0
Compile		2	13	50.0
Test		7	13	50.0
Total Development		9	26	100.0
After Development		0	0	

☐ Program Size (LOC)—Plan

Before starting development, you estimate how many LOC of new and changed code this program will likely require and enter it at Total New and Changed (N). Here, Student 11 estimated 90 LOC for program 3A.

☐ Program Size (LOC)—Actual

Before enhancing program 2A to make program 3A, Student 11 measured program 2A's size as 87 LOC. This was the Actual Base LOC for program 3A. At project completion, the student then used program 3A to count program 3A's total size as 200 LOC. The result was two measurements: 87 LOC for the base program and 200 LOC for the total size of the finished program. The student also counted by hand that no LOC were deleted, six LOC were modified, and none were reused. Thus the data to complete the Actual Added and New and Changed entries are as follows:

Added (A) = T − B + D − R = 200 − 87 + 0 − 0 = 113

Total New and Changed (N) = A + M = 113 + 6 = 119

The added calculation can best be understood by recognizing that the base LOC remaining in the total program after deletions are B − D. To find the LOC added, you must thus subtract B − D from the total. You must, of course, also subtract the reused LOC(R) as well.

At this point, you should also count by hand the number of newly developed LOC that were intended to be reusable on later projects. This is that portion of the added LOC that will be entered in the reuse library.

In the example, even though program 2A was enhanced to produce program 3A its LOC provided the base for the next development. While that is a form of reuse, PSP counts such prior-version code as base LOC and not reused LOC.

☐ Program Size (LOC)—To Date

For the reused, total LOC, total new and changed LOC, and total new reused, add the actual value for this program to the total to-date value for the most recently developed prior program and enter that number in the To Date column. In the Table C2 example, Student 11 had no reused or new reused LOC on programs 1A through 3A and so he entered zero in these To Date spaces. The new and changed LOC for programs 1A and 2A totaled 196, so adding the 119 LOC for program 3A gave the 315 To Date value for program 3A. Similarly, the total LOC for programs 1A and 2A was 196, so adding 200 gives the To Date value of 396 LOC.

When your prior programs were developed with PSP0, you will need first to measure and calculate the size data for those programs and then complete this section of the Project Plan Summary. It would also be a good idea to complete the Program Size—Actual portion of the PSP0.1 Project Plan Summary for all the programs you developed with PSP0. This will provide you the data you will later need for making more accurate development plans.

□ Time in Phase (min.)—Plan

In planning a new development, you first estimate the total development time. You can then use the To Date percentage data from your most recent previously developed program to judge how much of this total time you will spend in each phase of the new project. You can either use these numbers as your plan or adjust them to what you think the new project will require. Student 11, for example, had previously spent about 5 percent of total development time in planning. This would be about 10 minutes out of the estimated 195 minutes, so that is what was used.

The remaining entries in this summary form were described with the previous process versions.

C2.5   PROCESS REPORTING SPECIFICATIONS

The criteria for evaluating the PSP0.1 exercises in this text are the same as those for the PSP0 exercises, as follows:

□ The process data are complete.

□ The data are accurate and self-consistent.

□ The process report is submitted in the proper order and format.

The items to be included in PSP0.1 exercise reports and the order in which they are to be submitted are as follows:

□ *PSP0.1 Project Plan Summary*

□ *The PIP forms, including a brief statement of lessons learned*

□ Time Recording Log

□ Defect Recording Log

□ Source program listing

□ Any other requested materials

Your results must be neat and legible, but they need not be typed. You should provide only the requested materials; no cover sheets, binders, or written reports are needed other than those called for. Concentrate on providing the required materials as quickly and efficiently as you can. Because you will need all your PSP data for subsequent assignments, you should retain a complete copy of everything you submit.

C3   PSP1 Process Contents

PSP1 introduces size estimation to the PSP. Before starting a PSP1 software development, you should use the PROBE size estimating method to estimate the size of the new and changed LOC in the new program. You should also estimate the base, reused, deleted, modified, added, total, and total new and changed LOC. Note that when you first use PSP1 you will not have historical data for making size estimates. You should thus estimate the object LOC and use your judgment on the factor to use to get the total new and changed LOC. For the second and third programs you write with PSP1, you can use the data from the first and second to guide your estimates. After this point, you can follow the PROBE Estimating Script in Table C36.

C3.1   OBJECTIVES AND PREREQUISITES

In addition to the objectives of PSP0.1, PSP1 is intended to establish an orderly and repeatable procedure for developing software size estimates. As you use this process to estimate your program developments, you will build a growing base of estimating data that should help you to make progressively more accurate size estimates.

The prerequisites for PSP1 are Chapter 5, PSP0.1, and program 3A. You must also have actual size data on at least three previously developed programs.

C3.2   SCRIPTS, FORMS, TEMPLATES, AND STANDARDS

PSP1 Process Script	*Table C30*
PSP1 Planning Script	*Table C31*
PSP1 Development Script	*Table C32*
PSP1 Postmortem Script	*Table C33*
PSP1 Project Plan Summary and Instructions	*Tables C34 and C35*
PROBE Estimating Script	*Table C36*
Test Report Template and Instructions	*Tables C37 and C38*
Size Estimating Template and Instructions	*Tables C39 and C40*
Process Improvement Proposal (PIP) and Instructions	Tables C27 and C28
Coding Standard	Table C29
Time Recording Log and Instructions	Tables C16 and C17
Defect Recording Log and Instructions	Tables C18 and C19
Defect Type Standard	Table C20

C3.3   NEW PROCESS ELEMENTS

The size estimating method and Size Estimating Template are fully described in Chapter 5 along with an example. The Test Report Template, however, is not covered elsewhere in this text.

TABLE C3 PSP1 PROJECT PLAN SUMMARY EXAMPLE

Student	Student 2	Date	2/21/94
Program	Linear Regression	Program #	4A
Instructor	Humphrey	Language	C

Summary	Plan	Actual	To Date
LOC/Hour	26.7	20.2	17.8

Program Size (LOC)	Plan	Actual	To Date
Base(B)	30	20	
	(Measured)	(Measured)	
Deleted (D)	0	0	
	(Estimated)	(Counted)	
Modified (M)	20	2	
	(Estimated)	(Counted)	
Added (A)	149	77	
	(N − M)	(T − B + D − R)	
Reused (R)	72	81	81
	(Estimated)	(Counted)	
Total New and Changed (N)	169	79	492
	(Estimated)	(A + M)	
Total LOC (T)	251	178	628
	(N + B − M − D + R)	(Measured)	
Total New Reused	144	50	50

Time in Phase (min.)	Plan	Actual	To Date	To Date %
Planning	60	50	93	5.6
Design	60	30	305	18.3
Code	120	80	575	34.6
Compile	20	20	95	5.7
Test	60	40	415	25.0
Postmortem	60	15	180	10.8
Total	380	235	1663	100.0

Defects Injected	Actual	To Date	To Date %
Planning	0	0	0
Design	0	3	6.8
Code	6	33	75.0
Compile	0	0	0.0
Test	0	8	18.2
Total Development	6	44	100.0

Defects Removed	Actual	To Date	To Date %
Planning	0	0	0
Design	0	0	0
Code	0	0	0
Compile	2	13	50.0
Test	7	13	50.0
Total Development	9	26	100.0
After Development	0	0	

Test Report Template.   The Test Report Template is shown in Table C37 and its instructions are shown in Table C38. It is used to record data on each of your tests. While recording test conditions and results may not seem important for small programs, when you incorporate small programs into larger programs, make later modifications, fix problems, or otherwise reuse your programs, you will often find it helpful to rerun previously completed tests. To do this, you must know which tests were run, which test data were used, and the results that were obtained.

Doing this typically could be useful when you are modifying a program to incorporate a new function. As part of testing, you will want to ensure your changes have not caused problems with functions that previously worked. Such problems are called regressions. Regression problems are common when many changes are made in large multi-version programs. A regression test is most easily and effectively done by rerunning tests that previously worked. This is difficult, however, if adequate test data were not saved. These data are simple to record when you first do the tests but are often hard to reconstruct later.

One way to ensure your test reports are adequate is to complete them in advance and to use them to guide your initial testing. If they are inaccurate or incomplete, you will be able to correct them quickly.

With a complete test record, you can also quickly detect and address the problem of multiple defective fixes. When in a hurry, engineers often think they understand a problem and make a quick fix. In doing so, they make a simple mistake, so then they make another quick patch. If you do not stop and carefully check the correctness of your fixes, these test-and-fix-and-test cycles can stretch out to several hours. By recording each of your tests and their results, you will quickly detect this problem and be able to address it more logically. Since the proper format for a test report will depend on your personal preferences, the data to be recorded, and the types of tests that were run, you may not find the test report in Table C37 very convenient. I suggest you use it first and then experiment with various modifications until you find a format that meets your personal needs. Then you can use that report format for the remainder of the exercises. It is important, however, that you complete and submit a test report with every PSP1 and later assignment.

C3.4   PROJECT PLAN SUMMARY EXAMPLE

An example of a completed PSP1 Project Plan Summary is shown in Table C3. The bulk of this form was described with the previous PSP versions, so only the new sections are described here.

□ Summary—LOC/Hour
   This entry holds the numbers of new and changed LOC developed divided by the total development time. The planned number is

   LOC/Hour—Plan = 60 * 169/380 = 26.7.

This is computed from the planned number of new and changed LOC, 169, and the planned development time, 380 minutes. The actual and previous To Date numbers are similarly calculated as follows:

LOC/Hour—Actual = 60 * 79/235 = 20.2
LOC/Hour—To Date = 60 * 492/1,663 = 17.8

You calculate these data in order to easily check the reasonableness of your plans. If your planned LOC/hour rate significantly differs from your To Date experience, your plan is probably unrealistic.

□ Program Size(LOC)—Plan
The program size plan entries involve a number of calculations using data from the Size Estimating Template. Here, Student 2 started with 30 base LOC and an estimated 169 new and changed LOC. The student also estimated 20 LOC for modified and 72 LOC for reused and so could then calculate the estimated total and estimated added LOC as follows:

Total (T) = New and Changed (N) + Base (B) − Modified(M) −
Deleted(D) + Reused(R)
= 169 + 30 − 20 − 0 + 72 = 251
Added (A) = New and Changed (N) − Modified (M) = 169 − 20 = 149

The total is obtained by adding the new and changed estimate (N) to the base (B) less any deleted code (D). You also add any reused code (R). Note, however, that the LOC of modified code (M) are subtracted because the new and changed LOC number N includes the modified LOC. Modifying a LOC does not change the total LOC count, so M must be subtracted to produce the proper result.

□ Program Size (LOC)—Plan—Reused (R)
In making the plan, Student 11 expected to reuse 72 LOC of unmodified code from the library of reusable programs.

□ Program Size (LOC)—Total New Reused
Student 11 expected that 144 LOC of the newly developed routines would go in the reuse library and so entered 144 in the total new reuse space. This is a portion of the 169 total new and changed LOC.

It is important to recognize that the actual new and changed LOC will equal the sum of the added and modified LOC. With the PROBE size estimating method, however, the number of new and changed LOC is calculated as follows:

New and Changed LOC = β_0 + β_1*(Projected LOC + Modified LOC).

Thus, in calculating the total LOC you should properly subtract β_1*(Modified LOC) rather than the modified LOC alone. Doing this is typically not worth the trouble, however, unless your estimating is very accurate and you need an exact number for the total LOC.

Your size estimating process always starts with the number of new and changed LOC. In estimating the total size of the first version of a new program, you start with zero under Base and enter the LOC of new code in the Added line. Assuming there is no reused code, the total LOC and total new and changed LOC would then be the same. However, if the new development is a modification of an existing program you would enter the size of the existing program under Base and then estimate how the new and changed LOC are divided between added and modified LOC and how many base LOC will be deleted. You can then calculate the estimated total LOC as shown in this example. To ensure the numbers total properly, you can also calculate the added LOC as new and changed (N) minus modified (M).

The remaining entries in this form were described with the previous process versions.

C3.5   PROCESS REPORTING SPECIFICATION

For exercises done with PSP1 and higher level processes, you must meet the evaluation criteria used for PSP0.1, as follows:

- ☐ The process data are complete.
- ☐ The data are accurate and self-consistent.
- ☐ The process report is submitted in the proper order and format.

If these criteria are not met, the data will not be suitable for the analyses required in the later exercises. With PSP1, a fourth evaluation criterion is that you effectively use your historical data to guide your work. For example, your planned defect and time distributions should relate to your historical experience. If you have some reason for not following this historical pattern, you should describe why in your PIP or Project Plan Summary.

The items to be included in the PSP1 exercise reports and the order in which they are to be submitted are as follows:

- ☐ **PSP1 Project Plan Summary**
- ☐ **Test Report Template**
- ☐ The PIP forms, including a brief statement of lessons learned
- ☐ **The Size Estimating Template**
- ☐ Time Recording Log
- ☐ Defect Recording Log
- ☐ Source program listing
- ☐ Any other requested materials

Your results must be neat and legible, but they need not be typed. You should provide only the requested materials; no cover sheets, binders, or written reports are needed other than those called for. Concentrate on providing the required materials as quickly and efficiently as you can. You will need all your PSP data for subsequent assignments, so you should retain a complete copy of everything you submit.

C4   PSP1.1 Process Contents

The PSP1.1 process introduces resource and schedule estimating and planning. When combined with the PROBE size estimating method introduced with PSP1, and when you have gathered sufficient size and cost data, you will be able to make better development plans. You will also know how to judge their accuracy.

C4.1   OBJECTIVES AND PREREQUISITES

In addition to the objectives for PSP1, the objectives of PSP1.1 are to introduce and practice methods for:

- making resource and schedule plans,
- tracking your performance against these plans, and
- judging likely project completion dates.

The prerequisites for the PSP1.1 process are PSP1 and Chapter 6.

C4.2   FORMS, TEMPLATES, AND STANDARDS

PSP1.1 Process Script	*Table C41*
PSP1.1 Planning Script	*Table C42*
PSP1.1 Development Script	*Table C43*
PSP1.1 Postmortem Script	*Table C44*
PSP1.1 Project Plan Summary and Instructions	*Tables C45 and C46*
Task Planning Template and Instructions	*Tables C47 and C48*
Schedule Planning Template and Instructions	*Tables C49 and C50*
PROBE Estimating Script	Table C36
Test Report Template and Instructions	Tables C37 and C38
Size Estimating Template and Instructions	Tables C39 and C40
Process Improvement Proposal (PIP) and Instructions	Tables C27 and C28

Coding Standard	Table C29
Time Recording Log and Instructions	Tables C16 and C17
Defect Recording Log and Instructions	Tables C18 and C19
Defect Type Standard	Table C20

C4.3   NEW PROCESS ELEMENTS

The two new process elements included with PSP1.1 are the Task Planning Template and the Schedule Planning Template. These are typically used for projects that will take several days or weeks to complete. Both of these forms have been described in Chapter 6.

The summary section of the Project Plan Summary has been expanded to include basic process statistics for this program and for the development work to date. Hence you can compare your recent performance with your historical averages and judge the reasonableness of your plans.

C4.4   PROJECT PLAN SUMMARY EXAMPLE

An example of a completed PSP1.1 Project Plan Summary is shown in Table C4. The bulk of the items in this form have been described with the previous processes, so the only items discussed here are those shown in bold italics in the form. These are all in the summary section at the top of the form. Their purpose is to give you a brief overview of process performance and quality. These new items are as follows:

☐ Planned Time
The plan time is the entry from the Time In Phase—Total—Plan column from a later section of the form. In this example, the plan time is 260 minutes. The To Date entry is the sum of all the plan times from all the PSP projects to date. Student 14 had planned a total of 1100 minutes for projects 1A through 5A, so the To Date total is 1100 + 260, or 1360 minutes. On future projects, the To Date figure is calculated by adding the plan figure on this form to the to-date figure for the most recent previous project.

☐ Actual Time
The actual time entry is taken from the Time In Phase—Total—Actual column later in the form. Here, the actual time is 271 minutes and the To Date time is 1420 minutes.

☐ CPI (Cost Performance Index)—To Date
This is the ratio of the planned time to date divided by the actual time to date, in this case, 1360/1420, or 0.96. This ratio indicates the degree to which you are meeting your cost commitments. Ideally, the CPI should be

TABLE C4 PSP1.1 PROJECT PLAN SUMMARY EXAMPLE

Student __Student 14__   Date __2/25/94__
Program __Prediction Interval__   Program # __6A__
Instructor __Humphrey__   Language __C__

Summary	Plan	Actual	To Date
LOC/Hour	26.5	29.7	26.3
Planned Time	260		1360
Actual Time		271	1420
CPI(Cost-Performance Index)			0.96
			(Planned/Actual)
% Reused	19.9	19.0	16.7
% New Reused	40.0	36.6	25.7

Program Size (LOC)	Plan	Actual	To Date
Base(B)	64	64	
	(Measured)	(Measured)	
Deleted (D)	6	11	
	(Estimated)	(Counted)	
Modified (M)	0	4	
	(Estimated)	(Counted)	
Added (A)	115	130	
	(N − M)	(T − B + D − R)	
Reused (R)	43	43	142
	(Estimated)	(Counted)	
Total New and Changed (N)	115	134	626
	(Estimated)	(A + M)	
Total LOC (T)	216	226	850
	(N + B − M − D + R)	(Measured)	
Total New Reused	46	49	161

Time in Phase (min.)	Plan	Actual	To Date	To Date %
Planning	44	50	243	17.1
Design	84	62	434	30.6
Code	47	67	276	19.4
Compile	23	4	105	7.4
Test	49	71	288	20.3
Postmortem	13	17	74	5.2
Total	260	271	1420	100.0

Defects Injected	Actual	To Date	To Date %
Planning	0	0	0.0
Design	1	9	18.8
Code	4	34	70.8
Compile	0	2	4.2
Test	0	3	6.2
Total Development	5	48	100.0

TABLE C4 (continued)

Defects Removed	Actual	To Date	To Date %
Planning	0	0	0
Design	0	0	0
Code	0	1	2.1
Compile	2	24	50.0
Test	3	23	47.9
Total Development	5	48	100.0
After Development	0	0	

slightly greater than 1.0. If it is less than 1.0, you are spending more time than planned on your projects. If it is substantially more than 1.0, your plans are too conservative.

□ % Reused
This is the percentage of the total LOC that were taken from the reuse library. Because reusing existing code typically takes less time than developing new code, a high reused percentage is desirable. For the plan entry, the percentage reused is $100*43/216 = 19.9$ percent. The Actual and To Date entries are similarly calculated as follows:

Reused—Actual = $100*43/226 = 19.0$ percent
Reused—To Date = $100*142/850 = 16.7$ percent

□ % New Reused
This number indicates the degree to which your new development effort is contributing to building a larger reuse library. It is the percentage of new and changed LOC that are planned for the reuse library. A high number is generally good. Here, the planned percentage of new reused equals $100*46/115 = 40.0$. The Actual and To Date entries are similarly calculated as follows:

New Reused—Actual = $100*49/134 = 36.6\%$
New Reused—To Date = $100*161/626 = 25.8\%$

C4.5   PROCESS REPORTING SPECIFICATIONS

The PSP1.1 process uses the same evaluation criteria used for PSP1, as follows:

□ The process data are complete.
□ The data are accurate and self-consistent.

□ The process report is submitted in the proper order and format.

□ The historical data are used in planning the work.

The items to be included in PSP1.1 exercise reports and the order in which they are to be submitted are as follows:

□ *PSP1.1 Project Plan Summary*

□ Test Report Template

□ The PIP forms, including a brief lessons learned statement

□ The Size Estimating Template

□ *The Task Planning Template*

□ *The Schedule Planning Template*

□ Time Recording Log

□ Defect Recording Log

□ Source program listing

□ Any other requested materials

Your results must be neat and legible, but they need not be typed. You should provide only the requested materials; no cover sheets, binders, or written reports are needed other than those called for. Concentrate on providing the required materials as quickly and efficiently as you can. You will need all your PSP data for subsequent assignments, so you should retain a complete copy of everything you submit.

C5   PSP2 Process Contents

The PSP2 process introduces design and code reviews. These will both improve your productivity and the quality of the products you produce. With PSP2, you also start to calculate prediction intervals for the size and time estimates.

C5.1   OBJECTIVES AND PREREQUISITES

In addition to the objectives for PSP1.1, those for PSP2 are

□ to introduce design and code reviews, and

□ to introduce methods for evaluating and improving the quality of your reviews.

The prerequisites for PSP2 are PSP1.1, Chapter 8, and the Design Review and Code Review Checklists produced by assignment R4.

C5.2   SCRIPTS, FORMS, TEMPLATES, AND STANDARDS

PSP2 Process Script	*Table C51*
PSP2 Planning Script	*Table C52*
PSP2 Development Script	*Table C53*
PSP2 Postmortem Script	*Table C54*
PSP2 Project Plan Summary and Instructions	*Tables C55 and C56*
PSP2 Design Review Checklist	*Table C57*
Code Review Checklist	*Table C58*
Task Planning Template and Instructions	Tables C47 and C48
Schedule Planning Template and Instructions	Tables C49 and C50
PROBE Estimating Script	Table C36
Test Report Template and Instructions	Tables C37 and C38
Size Estimating Template and Instructions	Tables C39 and C40
Process Improvement Proposal (PIP) and Instructions	Tables C27 and C28
Coding Standard	Table C29
Time Recording Log and Instructions	Tables C16 and C17
Defect Recording Log and Instructions	Tables C18 and C19
Defect Type Standard	Table C20

The new process elements included with PSP2 are the Design Review and Code Review Checklists, which were thoroughly described in Chapter 8. As noted there, you should modify these checklists so that they properly reflect the language you use and the defects you have found in your PSP work to date.

C5.3   PROJECT PLAN SUMMARY EXAMPLE

Table C5 shows an example of a completed PSP2 Project Plan Summary. Most of these items have been described for the earlier process versions, so only the new items are described here.

☐ Test Defects/KLOC
This number indicates the quality of the program you put into test. Because testing typically finds only some of the defects in a program, test defects/KLOC is an indicator of the quality of the program that will exit test. Test defects/KLOC is calculated as 1000*(Defects Removed in Test)/(Total New and Changed LOC). For Student 14, these numbers are as follows:

Test Defects/KLOC—Plan = 1000*4/112 = 35.7
Test Defects/KLOC—Actual = 1000*2/137 = 14.6
Test Defects/KLOC—To Date = 1000*25/759 = 32.9

☐ Total Defects/KLOC
This is the total number of defects injected during the process. Because defect removal is expensive regardless of the method you use, it is most desirable to reduce the total number you inject. Your defect prevention methods include the improved care you take as a result of measuring your defects as well as any improvements you make in your design and coding methods. Total defects/KLOC is calculated as 1000*(Total Defects Removed)/(Total New and Changed LOC). For Student 14, this was as follows:

Total Defects/KLOC—Plan = 1000*8/112 = 71.4
Total Defects/KLOC—Actual = 1000*7/137 = 51.1
Total Defects/KLOC—To Date = 1000*55/759 = 72.5

☐ Yield
Yield, when calculated for a full development process, refers to the percentage of the defects injected before the first compile that have been removed before that compile. For this example, Student 14's yield calculations were made as follows:

Yield—Plan = 100*0/8 = 0%
Yield—Actual = 100*5/7 = 71.4%
Yield—To Date = 100*6/50 = 12.0%

In the To Date yield calculation, for example, the total number of defects removed in all PSP projects before compile is 6 and the total number injected before compile is 50.

☐ Program Size—Prediction Intervals
The 70 percent upper and lower prediction intervals of 126 and 98 LOC are calculated using the method described in Section A8. The size prediction interval is taken from the Size Estimating Template. Note that this prediction interval can be calculated only if the linear regression method has been used. It is also not likely to be very accurate without at least three prior data points; you should generally have five or more. Consult Section A7 for further guidance on using linear regression. Note that in this example, the actual new and changed LOC value of 137 was somewhat above the 70 percent UPI value of 126. This is not surprising as the result should fall within the 70 percent prediction interval only about 70 percent of the time.

☐ Total Development Time—Prediction Interval
This prediction interval, too, is calculated using the method described in Section A8. The same guidelines also apply to using linear regression as in the size estimating case. Here, the actual time of 247 minutes is almost at the midpoint of the prediction interval range of 227 to 273 minutes.

☐ Time In Phase—Design and Code Review
The planned and actual times for the design and code reviews are entered at plan time and during the postmortem. Note that Student 14 had no prior data

TABLE C5 PSP2 PROJECT PLAN SUMMARY EXAMPLE

Student __Student 14__   Date __3/4/94__

Program __Correlation__   Program # __7A__

Instructor __Humphrey__   Language __C__

Summary	Plan	Actual	To Date
LOC/Hour	26.9	33.3	27.3
Planned Time	250		1610
Actual Time		247	1667
CPI(Cost-Performance Index)			0.97
			(Planned/Actual)
% Reused	60.8	55.9	27.2
% New Reused	0	0	43.0
Test Defects/KLOC	35.7	14.6	32.9
Total Defects/KLOC	71.4	51.1	72.5
Yield%	0	71.4	12.0

Program Size (LOC):	Plan	Actual	To Date
Base(B)	0	0	
	(Measured)	(Measured)	
Deleted (D)	0	0	
	(Estimated)	(Counted)	
Modified (M)	0	0	
	(Estimated)	(Counted)	
Added (A)	112	137	
	(N − M)	(T − B + D − R)	
Reused (R)	174	174	316
	(Estimated)	(Counted)	
Total New and Changed (N)	112	137	759
	(Estimated)	(A + M)	
Total LOC (T)	286	311	1161
	(N + B − M − D + R)	(Measured)	
Total New Reused	0	0	326
Upper Prediction Interval (70%)	126		
Lower Prediction Interval (70%)	98		

Time in Phase (min.)	Plan	Actual	To Date	To Date %
Planning	42	44	287	17.2
Design	76	56	490	29.4
Design Review				
Code	48	61	337	20.2
Code Review	30	27	27	1.6
Compile	15	1	106	6.4

TABLE C5 (continued)

Time in Phase (min.)	Plan	Actual	To Date	To Date %
Test	26	38	326	19.6
Postmortem	13	20	94	5.6
Total	250	247	1667	100.0
Total Time UPI (70%)	273			
Total Time LPI (70%)	227			

Defects Injected	Plan	Actual	To Date	To Date %
Planning	0	0	0	0.0
Design	2	1	10	18.2
Design Review	0	0	0	0.0
Code	6	6	40	72.7
Code Review	0	0	0	0.0
Compile	0	0	2	3.6
Test	0	0	3	5.5
Total Development	8	7	55	100.0

Defects Removed	Plan	Actual	To Date	To Date %
Planning	0	0	0	0.0
Design	0	0	0	0.0
Design Review	0	0	0	0.0
Code	0	0	1	1.8
Code Review	0	5	5	9.1
Compile	4	0	24	43.6
Test	4	2	25	45.5
Total Development	8	7	55	100.0
After Development	0	0	0	

Defect Removal Efficiency	Plan	Actual	To Date
Defects/Hour—Design Review	0	0	0
Defects/Hour—Code Review	0	11.1	11.1
Defects/Hour—Compile	16	0	13.6
Defects/Hour—Test	9.2	3.2	4.6
DRL(DLDR/UT)	0	0	0
DRL(CodeReview/UT)	0	3.5	2.4
DRL(Compile/UT)	1.7	0	3.0

on how to estimate the time effects of design and code reviews and so had to make an informed guess. From the To Date percentage data for program 6A, shown in Table C4, the student calculated how the 250 minutes of planned development time would likely be distributed and used those numbers for the new plan for planning, design, code, and postmortem. For code review, the student arbitrarily used a figure of 30 minutes and reduced the projected compile time of 18.5 minutes to 15 and the projected test time of 50.75 minutes to 26. The total planned time thus remained at 250 minutes. Due to round-off error, the amount of reduction for compile and test is slightly less than 30 minutes. Note that when the student wrote program 7A, design reviews were not included in the PSP until PSP3. The actual design review time was thus zero.

□ Time In Phase—To Date and To Date %

Because the introduction of design and code reviews substantially changed the distribution of Student 14's development time, the student could have adjusted the To Date and To Date % calculations to start over with programs that use PSP2 and higher version processes. Had the student done so, the time and percentage distributions would have been as follows:

	To Date	To Date %
Planning	44	17.8
Design	56	22.7
Design Review	0	0
Code	61	24.7
Code Review	27	10.9
Compile	1	0.4
Test	38	15.4
Postmortem	20	8.1
Total	247	100.0

Had Student 14 decided to start the To Date calculations over with this program, this should have been done for the summary, size, time, defect, and defect removal efficiency data.

In judging the time distribution of your projects, you should use data from prior projects that use processes resembling the one you plan to use. It would thus be a good idea to start accumulating new To Date and To Date % time data with PSP2.

□ Defects Injected/Removed—Plan
As you can calculate from the data in Table C4, Student 14's total defects per KLOC to date from the most recent prior project were 76.7. For the estimated 112 LOC for this project, this would mean a probable total of 8.59 found defects; the student projected 8. Based on the To Date % distribution from program 6A, this would suggest the following defect injection and removal distributions:

Phase	Defects Injected	Defects Removed
Planning	8*0 = 0	8*0 = 0
Design	8*0.188 = 1.5	8*0 = 0
Design Review	8*0 = 0	8*0 = 0
Code	8*0.708 = 5.7	8*0.021 = 0.2
Code Review	8*0 = 0	8*0 = 0
Compile	8*0.042 = 0.3	8*0.5 = 4
Test	8*0.062 = 0.5	8*0.479 = 3.8
Total Development	8	8
After Development	0	0

As you can see, Student 14 assumed that the historical defect injection and removal patterns would apply to this new project. While true for the injected defects, the code reviews were much more successful than expected, yielding over 70 percent of the defects before the first compile. With no prior experience with reviews, however, Student 14 had no data from which to make a more accurate projection.

□ Defects Injected/Removed—To Date and To Date %
Because the introduction of design and code reviews will also change the defect-removal distribution, the To Date and To Date % figures could also be shown as only using data from the PSP2 process. In this example, if Stu-

dent 14's injection and removal To Date and To Date % numbers had been shown this way, they would have been as follows:

Phase	Injected		Removed	
	To Date	To Date %	To Date	To Date %
Planning	0	0	0	0
Design	1	14.3	0	0
Design Review	0	0	0	0
Code	6	85.7	0	0
Code Review	0	0	5	71.4
Compile	0	0	0	0
Test	0	0	2	28.6
Total	7	100.0	7	100.0

With data on a few more programs, the new To Date % defect removal distribution would likely become quite accurate for projection purposes. Even these limited data provide a more accurate basis for planning the next project than do the To Date data for all the projects completed so far. Your defect removal distribution is likely to change significantly with PSP2, so it would be a good idea to start accumulating new To Date and To Date % figures for defects injected and removed starting with PSP2.

□ Defect Removal Efficiency
These figures show the number of defects removed per hour in each defect removal phase. These data are useful in gauging the relative efficiency of your defect removal methods and in tracking their improvement. Student 14 calculated these rates as follows:

Code Review Defects/Hour—Planned = 60*0/30 = 0
Code Review Defects/Hour—Actual = 60*5/27 = 11.1
Code Review Defects/Hour—To Date = 60*5/27 = 11.1
Compile Defects/Hour—Planned = 60*4/15 = 16.0
Compile Defects/Hour—Actual = 60*0/1 = 0
Compile Defects/Hour—To Date = 60*24/106 = 13.6
Test Defects/Hour—Planned = 60*4/26 = 9.2
Test Defects/Hour—Actual = 60*2/38 = 3.2
Test Defects/Hour—To Date = 60*25/326 = 4.6

Note that design reviews were not part of PSP2 at the time Student 14 did this work.

☐ Defect Removal Leverage (DRL)

To calculate the relative defect-removal leverage of any two phases A versus B, you divide the defects per hour for A by the defects per hour for B. In this example, the DRL's for code review and compile versus test are as follows:

DRL(Code Review/UT)—Plan = 0/9.2 = 0
DRL(Code Review/UT)—Actual = 11.1/3.2 = 3.47
DRL(Code Review/UT)—To Date = 11.1/4.6 = 2.41
DRL(Compile/UT)—Plan = 16.0/9.2 = 1.74
DRL(Compile/UT)—Actual = 0/3.2 = 0
DRL(Compile/UT)—To Date = 13.6/4.6 = 2.96

Note that when the testing process finds no defects, you should calculate DRL with the latest available To Date value for test defects per hour. Also, for the PSP, unit test (UT) and test are the same.

C5.4 PROCESS REPORTING SPECIFICATIONS

The PSP2 process evaluation criteria includes all the evaluation items for PSP1, as follows:

☐ The process data are complete.

☐ The data are accurate and self-consistent.

☐ The process report is submitted in the proper order and format.

☐ The historical data are used in planning the work.

A fifth evaluation criterion for PSP2 is that the historical data be consistently used to improve the process, for example, to update your Design and Code Review Checklists. To meet this criterion, you should examine your recent defect data before each new project to see if your checklists should be modified. If so, make the indicated changes and use the new checklists on the next project. Also note this change in the notes and comments section of the PIPs you submit with the assignment and include the new checklists with the assignment report.

The items to be included in PSP2 exercise reports and the order in which they are to be submitted are as follows:

☐ *PSP2 Project Plan Summary*

☐ Test Report Template

☐ *PSP2 Design Review Checklist*

☐ *Code Review Checklist*

☐ The PIP forms, including a brief lessons learned statement

☐ The Size Estimating Template

- The Task Planning Template
- The Schedule Planning Template
- Time Recording Log
- Defect Recording Log
- Source program listing
- Any other requested materials

Your results must be neat and legible, but they need not be typed. You should provide only the requested materials; no cover sheets, binders, or written reports are needed other than those called for. Concentrate on providing the required materials as quickly and efficiently as you can. You will need all your PSP data for subsequent assignments, so you should retain a complete copy of everything you submit.

C6   PSP2.1 Process Contents

The PSP2.1 process introduces four design templates that provide an orderly framework and format for recording your designs. While they will not tell you how to do the design, they can help you to properly record the design when you are done.

C6.1   OBJECTIVES AND PREREQUISITES

In addition to the objectives for PSP2, the objectives for PSP2.1 are

- to help you to reduce the number of defects in your designs,
- to provide criteria for determining if a design is complete, and
- to provide a consistent framework for verifying the quality of your designs.

The prerequisites for PSP2.1 are PSP2 and Chapter 10.

C6.2   SCRIPTS, FORMS, TEMPLATES, AND STANDARDS

PSP2.1 Process Script	*Table C59*
PSP2.1 Planning Script	*Table C60*
PSP2.1 Development Script	*Table C61*
PSP2.1 Postmortem Script	*Table C62*
PSP2.1 Project Plan Summary and Instructions	*Tables C63 and C64*

Operational Scenario Template and Instructions   *Tables C66 and C67*
Functional Specification Template and Instructions *Tables C68 and C69*
State Specification Template and Instructions   *Tables C70 and C71*
Logic Specification Template and Instructions   *Tables C72 and C73*
PSP2.1 Design Review Checklist   *Table C65*
Code Review Checklist   Table C58
Task Planning Template and Instructions   Tables C47 and C48
Schedule Planning Template and Instructions   Tables C49 and C50
PROBE Estimating Script   Table C36
Test Report Template and Instructions   Tables C37 and C38
Size Estimating Template and Instructions   Tables C39 and C40
Process Improvement Proposal (PIP) and Instructions   Tables C27 and C28
Coding Standard   Table C29
Time Recording Log and Instructions   Tables C16 and C17
Defect Recording Log and Instructions   Tables C18 and C19
Defect Type Standard   Table C20

C6.3   NEW PROCESS ELEMENTS

The design templates introduced with PSP2.1 were described in Chapter 10. The only change in the PSP2.1 Design Review Checklist is an addition that refers to those templates.

C6.4   PROJECT PLAN SUMMARY EXAMPLE

Table C6 shows an example of a completed PSP2.1 Project Plan Summary. Most of these items have been described for the earlier process versions, so only the new items are described here.

☐ Summary—% Appraisal COQ
   This is the percentage of total development time spent in design and code reviews. For Student 20, this was calculated as follows:

   % Appraisal COQ—Plan = 100*(0 + 40)/340 = 11.8%
   % Appraisal COQ—Actual = 100*(0 + 11)/165 = 6.7%
   % Appraisal COQ—To Date = 100*(0 + 48)/2684 = 1.8%

☐ Summary—% Failure COQ
   This is the percentage of total development time spent in compile and test, calculated as follows:

   % Failure COQ—Plan = 100*(17 + 58)/340 = 22.1%
   % Failure COQ—Actual = 100*(6 + 8)/165 = 8.5%
   % Failure COQ—To Date = 100*(202 + 500)/2684 = 26.2%

TABLE C6 PSP2.1 PROJECT PLAN SUMMARY EXAMPLE

Student   Student 20   Date   3/25/94

Program   Sort   Program # 8A

Instructor Humphrey   Language Pascal

Summary	Plan	Actual	To Date
LOC/Hour	17.1	26.2	18.7
Planned Time	340		3085
Actual Time		165	2684
CPI(Cost-Performance Index)			1.15
			(Planned/Actual)
% Reused	5.2	0	13.8
% New Reused	0	0	13.4
Test Defects/KLOC	30.9	0	21.6
Total Defects/KLOC	123.7	55.6	143.7
Yield %	50.0	50.0	12.5
% Appraisal COQ	11.8	6.7	1.8
% Failure COQ	22.1	8.5	26.2
COQ A/F Ratio	0.53	0.79	0.07

Program Size (LOC):	Plan	Actual	To Date
Base(B)	43	52	
	(Measured)	(Measured)	
Deleted (D)	0	0	
	(Estimated)	(Counted)	
Modified (M)	13	22	
	(Estimated)	(Counted)	
Added (A)	84	50	
	(N − M)	(T − B + D − R)	
Reused (R)	7	0	133
	(Estimated)	(Counted)	
Total New and Changed (N)	97	72	835
	(Estimated)	(A + M)	
Total LOC (T)	134	102	996
	(N + B − M − D + R)	(Measured)	
Total New Reused	0	0	112
Upper Prediction Interval (70%)	112		
Lower Prediction Interval (70%)	82		

Time in Phase (min.)	Plan	Actual	To Date	To Date %
Planning	27	33	227	8.5
Design	82	55	666	24.8
Design Review	0	0	0	0.0

TABLE C6   (continued)

Time in Phase (min.)	Plan	Actual	To Date	To Date %
Code	92	21	822	30.6
Code Review	40	11	48	1.8
Compile	17	6	202	7.5
Test	58	8	500	18.6
Postmortem	24	31	219	8.2
Total	340	165	2684	100.0
Total Time UPI (70%)	778			
Total Time LPI (70%)	0			

Defects Injected	Plan	Actual	To Date	To Date %
Planning	0	0	0	0.0
Design	2	0	18	15.0
Design Review	0	0	0	0.0
Code	10	4	102	85.0
Code Review	0	0	0	0.0
Compile	0	0	0	0.0
Test	0	0	0	0.0
Total Development	12	4	120	100.0

Defects Removed	Plan	Actual	To Date	To Date %
Planning	0	0	0	0.0
Design	0	0	1	0.8
Design Review	0	0	0	0.0
Code	0	0	0	0.0
Code Review	6	2	14	11.7
Compile	3	2	87	72.5
Test	3	0	18	15.0
Total Development	12	4	120	100.0
After Development	0	0	0	

Defect Removal Efficiency	Plan	Actual	To Date
Defects/Hour—Design Review	0	0	0
Defects/Hour—Code Review	9.0	10.9	17.5
Defects/Hour—Compile	10.6	20.0	25.8
Defects/Hour—Test	3.1	0	2.2
DRL(DLDR/UT)	0	0	0
DRL(CodeReview/UT)	2.9	5.0	8.0
DRL(Compile/UT)	3.4	9.1	11.7

Note that in this example, design reviews were not conducted with either PSP2 or PSP2.1.

□ COQ A/F Ratio
This is the ratio of appraisal to failure costs, in this example calculated as follows:

COQ A/F Ratio—Plan = $(0 + 40)/(17 + 58) = 11.8/22.1 = 0.53$
COQ A/F Ratio—Actual = $(0 + 11)/(6 + 8) = 6.7/8.5 = 0.79$
COQ A/F Ratio—To Date = $(0 + 48)/(202 + 500) = 1.8/26.2 = 0.07$

C6.5   PROCESS REPORTING SPECIFICATIONS

The PSP2.1 process evaluation criteria are the same as those for PSP2, as follows:

□ The process data are complete.

□ The data are accurate and self-consistent.

□ The process report is submitted in the proper order and format.

□ The historical data are used in planning the work.

□ Historical data are consistently used to improve the process.

The items to be included in PSP2.1 exercise reports and the order in which they are to be submitted are as follows:

□ *PSP2.1 Project Plan Summary*

□ Test Report Template

□ *PSP2.1 Design Review Checklist*

□ Code Review Checklist

□ The PIP forms, including a brief lessons learned statement

□ The Size Estimating Template

□ The Task Planning Template

□ The Schedule Planning Template

□ *Operational Scenario Template*

□ *Functional Specification Template*

□ *State Specification Template*

□ *Logic Specification Template*

□ Time Recording Log

□ Defect Recording Log

□ Source program listing

□ Any other requested materials

Your results must be neat and legible, but they need not be typed. You should provide only the requested materials; no cover sheets, binders, or written reports are needed other than those called for. Concentrate on providing the required materials as quickly and efficiently as you can. You will need all your PSP data for subsequent assignments, so you should retain a complete copy of everything you submit.

C7   PSP3 Process Contents

PSP3 introduces a cyclic process designed to help you to develop larger programs. The conceptual flow of the PSP3 process is shown in Fig. C1. The process starts with planning and high-level design followed by a series of development cycles. The principal concerns of the high-level design phase are to produce an overall design and a development strategy. This strategy addresses testing, reuse, and the structuring of product development into increments that are each suitable for development with PSP2.1-like process cycles. The PSP3 process is more completely described in Chapter 11.

C7.1   OBJECTIVES AND PREREQUISITES

The PSP3 objectives include the PSP2.1 objectives plus one other: to extend personal process capability to develop programs of up to several thousand LOC. The prerequisites for PSP3 are PSP2.1 and Chapter 11.

C7.2   SCRIPTS, FORMS, TEMPLATES, AND STANDARDS

PSP3 Process Script	*Table C74*
PSP3 Planning Script	*Table C75*
PSP3 High-level Design Script	*Table C76*
PSP3 High-level Design Review Script	*Table C77*
PSP3 Development Script	*Table C78*
PSP3 Postmortem Script	*Table C79*
PSP3 Project Plan Summary and Instructions	*Tables C80 and C81*
Cycle Summary and Instructions	*Tables C82 and C83*
Issue Tracking Log and Instructions	*Tables C85 and C86*
Operational Scenario Template and Instructions	Tables C66 and C67
Functional Specification Template and Instructions	Tables C68 and C69
State Specification Template and Instructions	Tables C70 and C71
Logic Specification Template and Instructions	Tables C72 and C73

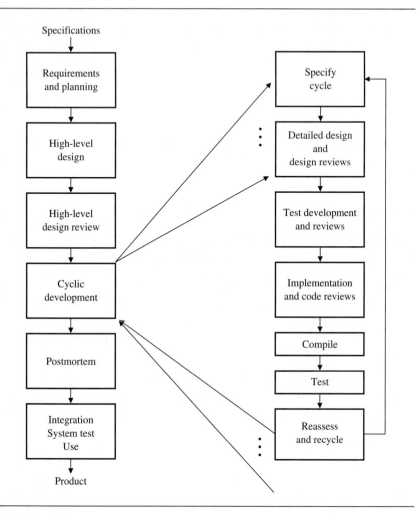

FIGURE C1
PSP3 Process

PSP3 Design Review Checklist	*Table C84*
Code Review Checklist	Table C58
Task Planning Template and Instructions	Tables C47 and C48
Schedule Planning Template and Instructions	Tables C49 and C50
PROBE Estimating Script	Table C36
Test Report Template and Instructions	Tables C37 and C38
Size Estimating Template and Instructions	Tables C39 and C40
Process Improvement Proposal (PIP) and Instructions	Tables C27 and C28

C7.3 NEW PSP3 PROCESS ELEMENTS

In addition to the PSP3 scripts, which are described in Chapter 11, the new process elements introduced with PSP3 are the Issue Tracking Log and the Cycle Summary.

The Issue Tracking Log.   The Issue Tracking Log (ITL) provides a convenient place to record issues, problems, and open questions. While in the middle of a design, for example, you might decide to change a variable name to better represent its purpose. Rather than stopping at that point to ensure every occurrence of this name is changed throughout the program, you could note this item in the ITL for later attention.

While an ITL is not usually needed for developing small programs, it will be increasingly helpful as the sizes of your programs increase. When you work on larger projects or with other developers, you will likely find an ITL to be invaluable.

The Cycle Summary.   When using PSP3, you should plan to implement larger programs in incremental modules of about 100 LOC. This figure is arbitrary; you will soon see which cycle sizes are most effective for you. Use one copy of the Cycle Summary to record your cycle plans and another to enter the actual cycle results. The cycle data are easy to obtain at the end of each cycle but are generally difficult to reconstruct later. Even if you defer cycle recording only until program completion, you will find it takes time to decipher items that would have been obvious at the time you completed the development cycle. In size recording, for example, you can count total program LOC at the end of each cycle and determine which lines were reused, added, deleted, or modified. Later, this could be much more difficult. Even if you had separately saved the code for every cycle, you would probably have trouble remembering just which lines were added, deleted, and reused with each. The time and defect data are easier to reconstruct than the size data, but they are also simple to record at cycle completion.

You want to save the plan and actual size, time, and defect data because each PSP3 cycle is essentially a small project. By gathering these data and tracking your performance, you can better plan and manage your work. When you consider each cyclic step as a task and use the earned value method to track your development progress, you can get a surprisingly accurate picture of your status and the likely completion schedule.

C7.4   PROJECT PLAN SUMMARY EXAMPLE

A complete PSP3 Project Plan Summary is shown in Table C7. The only new items in this form are the high-level design and high-level design review steps. These are discussed in Chapter 11 and covered in the scripts in Tables C76 and C77. Note also that Student 17 did not expect program 10A to be very large, hence the student did not use the high-level design phase or the design review phase.

C7.5   CYCLE SUMMARY EXAMPLE

Student 17's completed PSP3 Cycle Summary for the actual data is shown in Table C8. The size data in this table are a good example of the use of LOC accounting for program enhancement. The cycle LOC changes are as follows:

- □ Cycle 1
  Starting with a base of 0, 95 LOC are added in cycle 1, giving a total of 95 LOC.
- □ Cycle 2
  The 95 LOC total from cycle 1 are the base for cycle 2. Of this, 20 are deleted and 8 are modified. A total of 113 LOC are added along with 65 LOC of reused code. The Cycle 2 totals are thus calculated the same way as are the actual size totals in the Project Plan Summary. The total and reused LOC are measured as 253 and 65, respectively. The deleted and modified are then counted as 20 and 8 LOC, respectively, and the added can be calculated as follows:

$$\text{Added} = \text{Total (T)} - \text{Base (B)} + \text{Deleted (D)} - \text{Reused (R)}$$
$$= 253 - 95 + 20 - 65 = 113$$

  Now the total new and changed is found as the sum of M (modified) and A (added) code, or $8 + 113 = 121$ LOC.
- □ Cycle 3
  Starting with a base of 253 LOC, the student added 48 LOC and reused 143, for a total of 444 LOC for the size of the finished program.

For the cycle totals, the deleted, modified, added, reused, new and changed, and new reused LOC are all added across all the cycles to give the final results. The base and total LOC numbers are cumulative, however, so they are not added across the cycles. The final base LOC is the total from the first cycle, and the final total LOC is the total from the last cycle.

These cycle totals are transferred to the PSP3 Project Plan Summary in Table C7. The development time and defect data are similarly copied over. While the cycle defects injected and removed are the same in this case, they may not be in some cases. The reason is that some defects could be injected or removed in the high-level design and high-level design review phases. If fewer are removed than injected, the cycle inject and remove totals would differ by the same amounts. The totals of the defects injected and removed will differ also whenever you enter phase data for defects found after completing PSP development. In this case, you would add to the phase-injected totals and note the phase removed in the after-development space. The totals in the Project Plan Summary would thus balance as long as the after-development numbers were included. If you could not determine the cycle in which the defect was injected, the cycle and project summary defect data would then differ.

C7.6   PROCESS REPORTING SPECIFICATIONS

The PSP3 process evaluation criteria include all those for PSP2.1, as follows:

- □ The process data are complete.
- □ The data are accurate and self-consistent.
- □ The process report is submitted in the proper order and format.
- □ The historical data are used in planning the work.
- □ Historical data are consistently used to improve the process.

   In addition, PSP3 has a sixth criteria: that historical data and experience be used to establish goals for future process improvement. Short term derivatives of these goals should then be used to establish suitably challenging objectives for each project. Merely establishing goals, however, would not be adequate. To meet this criteria, you must identify process actions to meet the goals.
   The items to be included in PSP3 exercise reports and the order in which they are to be submitted are as follows:

- □ *PSP3 Project Plan Summary*
- □ *Cycle Summary*
- □ Test Report Template
- □ *PSP3 Design Review Checklist*
- □ Code Review Checklist
- □ *Issue Tracking Log*
- □ The PIP forms, including a brief lessons learned statement
- □ The Size Estimating Template
- □ The Task Planning Template
- □ The Schedule Planning Template
- □ Operational Scenario Template
- □ Functional Specification Template

TABLE C7 PSP3 PROJECT PLAN SUMMARY EXAMPLE

Student	Student 17	Date	5/1/94
Program	Multiple Regression	Program #	10A
Instructor	Humphrey	Language	Ada

Summary	Plan	Actual	To Date
LOC/Hour	26.7	28.5	20.5
Planned Time	571		3770
Actual Time		556	3386
CPI(Cost-Performance Index)			1.11
			(Planned/Actual)
% Reused	47.5	46.8	41.1
% New Reused	42.5	80.3	60.4
Test Defects/KLOC	31.5	3.8	25.9
Total Defects/KLOC	137.8	79.5	123.5
Yield %	34.4	71.4	39.7
% Appraisal COQ	8.2	15.6	9.5
% Failure COQ	25.2	13.5	23.2
COQ A/F Ratio	0.33	1.16	0.41

Program Size (LOC):	Plan	Actual	To Date
Base(B)	0	0	
	(Measured)	(Measured)	
Deleted (D)	0	20	
	(Estimated)	(Counted)	
Modified (M)	0	8	
	(Estimated)	(Counted)	
Added (A)	254	256	
	(N − M)	(T − B + D − R)	
Reused (R)	230	208	849
	(Estimated)	(Counted)	
Total New and Changed (N)	254	264	1158
	(Estimated)	(A + M)	
Total LOC (T)	484	444	2067
	(N + B − M − D + R)	(Measured)	
Total New Reused	108	212	699
Upper Prediction Interval (70%)	293		
Lower Prediction Interval (70%)	264		

Time in Phase (min.)	Plan	Actual	To Date	To Date %
Planning	104	98	618	18.3
High-level Design	0	0	0	0.0
High-level Design Review	0	0	0	0.0
Detailed Design	63	124	435	12.8
Detailed Design Review	0	30	30	0.9
Code	139	100	788	23.3

TABLE C7 (continued)

Code Review	47	57	292	8.6
Compile	37	10	191	5.6
Test	107	65	595	17.6
Postmortem	74	72	437	12.9
Total	571	556	3386	100.0
Total Time UPI (70%)	702			
Total Time LPI (70%)	441			

Defects Injected	Plan	Actual	To Date	To Date %
Planning	0	0	1	0.7
High-level Design	0	0	0	0.0
High-level Design Review	0	0	0	0.0
Detailed Design	4	5	17	11.9
Detailed Design Review	0	0	0	0.0
Code	28	16	112	78.3
Code Review	0	0	1	0.7
Compile	1	0	4	2.8
Test	2	0	8	5.6
Total Development	35	21	143	100.0

Defects Removed	Plan	Actual	To Date	To Date %
Planning	0	0	0	0.0
High-level Design	0	0	0	0.0
High-level Design Review	0	0	0	0.0
Detailed Design	0	0	0	0.0
Detailed Design Review	0	3	3	2.1
Code	0	0	0	0.0
Code Review	11	12	49	34.3
Compile	16	5	61	42.6
Test	8	1	30	21.0
Total Development	35	21	143	100.0
After Development	0	0	0	

Defect Removal Efficiency	Plan	Actual	To Date
Defects/Hour— Design Review	0	6.0	6.0
Defects/Hour— Code Review	14.0	12.6	10.1
Defects/Hour—Compile	25.9	30.0	19.2
Defects/Hour—Test	4.5	0.9	3.0
DRL(DLDR/UT)	0.0	6.7	2.0
DRL(CodeReview/UT)	3.1	14.0	3.4
DRL(Compile/UT)	5.8	33.3	6.4

- ☐ State Specification Template
- ☐ Logic Specification Template
- ☐ Time Recording Log
- ☐ Defect Recording Log
- ☐ Source program listing
- ☐ Any other requested materials

Your results must be neat and legible, but they need not be typed. You should provide only the requested materials; no cover sheets, binders, or written reports are needed other than those called for. Concentrate on providing the required materials as quickly and efficiently as you can. You should retain a complete copy of everything you submit.

TABLE C8 CYCLE SUMMARY EXAMPLE
PLAN _____ ACTUAL __X____

Student __Student 17_____ Date ____5/1/94____
Program __Multiple Regression_____ Program # ___10A____
Instructor __Humphrey_____ Language __Ada____

Cycles	To Date	1	2	3	4	5	Total
Program Size (LOC):							
Base(B)		0	95	253			0
Deleted (D)		0	20	0			20
Modified (M)		0	8	0			8
Added (A)		95	113	48			256
Reused (R)		0	65	143			208
Total New and Changed (N)		95	121	48			264
Total LOC (T)		95	253	444			444
Total New Reused		81	90	41			212
Time in Phase (min.)							
Design		66	47	11			124
Design Review		13	13	4			30
Code		43	43	14			100
Code Review		10	40	7			57
Compile		3	5	2			10
Test		38	22	5			65
Total		173	170	43			386
Defects Injected							
Design		2	3	0			5
Design Review		0	0	0			0
Code		4	9	3			16
Code Review		0	0	0			0
Compile		0	0	0			0
Test		0	0	0			0
Total		6	12	3			21
Defects Removed							
Design		0	0	0			0
Design Review		1	2	0			3
Code		0	0	0			0
Code Review		3	7	2			12
Compile		1	3	1			5
Test		1	0	0			1
Total		6	12	3			21

TABLE C9 PSP CROSS-REFERENCE

Heading	Table Number	PSP0	PSP0.1	PSP1	PSP1.1	PSP2	PSP2.1	PSP3
Process Version		PSP0	PSP0.1	PSP1	PSP1.1	PSP2	PSP2.1	PSP3
Prerequisite Chapters		2	4	5	6	8	10	11
Process Scripts and Summaries								
PSP Process Script		C10	C21	C30	C41	C51	C59	C74
PSP Planning Script		C11	C22	C31	C42	C52	C60	C75
PSP High-level Design Script								C76
High-level Design Review Script								C77
PSP Development Script		C12	C23	C32	C43	C53	C61	C78
PSP Postmortem Script		C13	C24	C33	C44	C54	C62	C79
Project Plan Summary and Instructions		C14 C15	C25 C26	C34 C35	C45 C46	C55 C56	C63 C64	C80 C81
PROBE Estimating Script	C36			X	X	X	X	X
Cyclic Summary and Instructions								C82 C83
Forms, Templates, Standards, and Instructions								
Time Recording Log	C16, C17	X	X	X	X	X	X	X
Defect Recording Log	C18, C19	X	X	X	X	X	X	X
Defect Type Standard	C20	X	X	X	X	X	X	X

TABLE C9 (continued)

Heading	Table Number	PSP0	PSP0.1	PSP1	PSP1.1	PSP2	PSP2.1	PSP3
Process Version								
Forms, Templates, Standards, and Instructions								
PIP	C27, C28		X	X	X	X	X	X
Coding Standard	C29		X	X	X	X	X	X
Test Report Template	C37, C38			X	X	X	X	X
Size Estimating Template	C39, C40			X	X	X	X	X
Task Planning Template	C47, C48				X	X	X	X
Schedule Planning Template	C49, C50				X	X	X	X
Design Review Checklist						C57	C65	C84
Code Review Checklist	C58					X	X	X
Operational Scenario Template	C66, C67						X	X
Function Specification Template	C68, C69						X	X
State Specification Template	C70, C71						X	X
Logic Specification Template	C72, C73						X	X
Issue Tracking Log	C85, C86						X	X

TABLE C10 PSP0 PROCESS SCRIPT

Phase Number	Purpose	To guide you in developing module-level programs
	Inputs Required	• Problem description • PSP0 Project Plan Summary form • Time and Defect Recording Logs • Defect Type Standard • Stop watch (optional)
1	Planning	• Produce or obtain a requirements statement. • Estimate the required development time. • Enter the plan data in the Project Plan Summary form. • Complete the Time Recording Log.
2	Development	• Design the program. • Implement the design. • Compile the program and fix and log all defects found. • Test the program and fix and log all defects found. • Complete the Time Recording Log.
3	Postmortem	Complete the Project Plan Summary form with actual time, defect, and size data.
	Exit Criteria	• A thoroughly tested program • Completed Project Plan Summary with estimated and actual data • Completed Defect and Time Recording Logs

TABLE C11 PSP0 PLANNING SCRIPT

Phase Number	Purpose	To guide the PSP planning process
	Entry Criteria	• Problem description • Project Plan Summary form • Time Recording Log
1	Program Requirements	• Produce or obtain a requirements statement for the program. • Ensure the requirements statement is clear and unambiguous. • Resolve any questions.
2	Estimate Resources	• Make your best estimate of the time required to develop this program.
	Exit Criteria	• A documented requirements statement • A completed Project Plan Summary with estimated development time data • Completed Time Recording Log

TABLE C12 PSP0 DEVELOPMENT SCRIPT

Phase Number	Purpose	To guide the development of small programs
	Entry Criteria	• Requirements statement • Project Plan Summary with planned development time • Time and Defect Recording Logs • Defect Type Standard
1	Design	• Review the requirements and produce a design to meet them. • Record time in Time Recording Log.
2	Code	• Implement the design. • Record in the Defect Recording Log any requirements or design defects found. • Record time in Time Recording Log.
3	Compile	• Compile the program until error free. • Fix all defects found. • Record defects in Defect Recording Log. • Record time in Time Recording Log.
4	Test	• Test until all tests run without error. • Fix all defects found. • Record defects in Defect Recording Log. • Record time in Time Recording Log.
	Exit Criteria	• A thoroughly tested program • Completed Defect Recording Log • Completed Time Recording Log

TABLE C13 PSP0 POSTMORTEM SCRIPT

Phase Number	Purpose	To guide the PSP postmortem process
	Entry Criteria	• Problem description and requirements statement • Project Plan Summary with planned development time • Completed Time Recording Log • Completed Defect Recording Log • A tested and running program
1	Defects Injected	• Determine from the Defect Recording Log the number of defects injected in each PSP0 phase. • Enter this number under Defects Injected—Actual on the Project Plan Summary.
2	Defects Removed	• Determine from the Defect Recording Log the number of defects removed in each PSP0 phase. • Enter this number under Defects Removed—Actual on the Project Plan Summary.
3	Time	• Review the completed Time Recording Log. • Enter the total time spent in each PSP0 phase under Actual on the Project Plan Summary form.
	Exit Criteria	• A fully tested program • Completed Project Plan Summary form • Completed Defect and Time Recording Logs

TABLE C14 PSP0 PROJECT PLAN SUMMARY

Student _____ Date _____

Program _____ Program # _____

Instructor _____ Language _____

Time in Phase (min.)	Plan	Actual	To Date	To Date %
Planning		_____	_____	_____
Design		_____	_____	_____
Code		_____	_____	_____
Compile		_____	_____	_____
Test		_____	_____	_____
Postmortem		_____	_____	_____
Total	_____	_____	_____	_____

Defects Injected		Actual	To Date	To Date %
Planning		_____	_____	_____
Design		_____	_____	_____
Code		_____	_____	_____
Compile		_____	_____	_____
Test		_____	_____	_____
Total Development		_____	_____	_____

Defects Removed		Actual	To Date	To Date %
Planning		_____	_____	_____
Design		_____	_____	_____
Code		_____	_____	_____
Compile		_____	_____	_____
Test		_____	_____	_____
Total Development		_____	_____	_____
After Development		_____	_____	

TABLE C15 PSP0 PROJECT PLAN SUMMARY INSTRUCTIONS

Purpose	This form holds the estimated and actual project data in a convenient and readily retrievable form
Header	Enter the following: • Your name and today's date • The program name and number • The instructor's name • The language you used to write the program
Time in Phase	• Under Plan, enter your original estimate of the total development time. • Under Actual, enter the actual time in minutes spent in each development phase. • Under To Date, enter the sum of the actual time and the To Date time from your most recently developed program. • Under To Date %, enter the percentage of To Date time in each phase.
Defects Injected	• Under Actual, enter the number of defects injected in each phase. • Under To Date, enter the sum of the actual numbers of defects injected in each phase and the To Date values from the most recently developed program. • Under To Date %, enter the percentage of To Date defects injected by phase.
Defects Removed	• Under Actual, enter the number of defects removed in each phase. • Under To Date, enter the sum of the actual number of defects removed in each phase and the To Date value from the most recently developed program. • Under To Date %, enter the percentage of To Date defects removed by phase. • After development, record any defects later found during program use, reuse, or modification.

TABLE C16 TIME RECORDING LOG

Student _____   Date   _____

Instructor _____   Program # _____

Date	Start	Stop	Interruption Time	Delta Time	Phase	Comments

TABLE C17 TIME RECORDING LOG INSTRUCTIONS

Purpose	This form is for recording the time spent in each project phase. These data are used to complete the Project Plan Summary.
General	• Record all the time you spend on the project. • Record the time in minutes. • Be as accurate as possible. If you need additional space, use another copy of the form.
Header	Enter the following: • Your name • Today's date • The instructor's name • The number of the program If you are working on a nonprogramming task, also enter a job description in the Program # field.
Date	Enter the date when the entry is made.
Example	10/18/93
Start	Enter the time when you start working on a task.
Example	8:20
Stop	Enter the time when you stop working on that task.
Example	10:56
Interruption Time	Record any interruption time that was not spent on the task and the reason for the interruption. If you have several interruptions, enter their total time.
Example	37 – took a break
Delta Time	Enter the clock time you actually spent working on the task, less the interruption time.
Example	From 8:20 to 10:56, less 37 minutes, or 119 minutes.
Phase	Enter the name or other designation of the phase or step being worked on.
Example	Planning, code, test, and so on
Comments	Enter any other pertinent comments that may later remind you of any unusual circumstances regarding this activity.
Example	Had a compiler problem and had to get help.
Important	It is important to record all worked time. If you forget to record the starting, stopping, or interruption time for a task, promptly enter your best estimate of the time.

Defect Types
10	Documentation	60	Checking
20	Syntax	70	Data
30	Build, Package	80	Function
40	Assignment	90	System
50	Interface	100	Environment

TABLE C18 DEFECT RECORDING LOG

Student _____ Date _____

Instructor_____ Program # _____

Date	Number	Type	Inject	Remove	Fix Time	Fix Defect
[ ]	[ ]	[ ]	[ ]	[ ]	[ ]	[ ]

Description: _____

_____

Date	Number	Type	Inject	Remove	Fix Time	Fix Defect
[ ]	[ ]	[ ]	[ ]	[ ]	[ ]	[ ]

Description: _____

_____

Date	Number	Type	Inject	Remove	Fix Time	Fix Defect
[ ]	[ ]	[ ]	[ ]	[ ]	[ ]	[ ]

Description: _____

_____

Date	Number	Type	Inject	Remove	Fix Time	Fix Defect
[ ]	[ ]	[ ]	[ ]	[ ]	[ ]	[ ]

Description: _____

_____

Date	Number	Type	Inject	Remove	Fix Time	Fix Defect
[ ]	[ ]	[ ]	[ ]	[ ]	[ ]	[ ]

Description: _____

_____

Date	Number	Type	Inject	Remove	Fix Time	Fix Defect
[ ]	[ ]	[ ]	[ ]	[ ]	[ ]	[ ]

Description: _____

_____

Date	Number	Type	Inject	Remove	Fix Time	Fix Defect
[ ]	[ ]	[ ]	[ ]	[ ]	[ ]	[ ]

Description: _____

_____

Date	Number	Type	Inject	Remove	Fix Time	Fix Defect
[ ]	[ ]	[ ]	[ ]	[ ]	[ ]	[ ]

Description: _____

_____

Date	Number	Type	Inject	Remove	Fix Time	Fix Defect
[ ]	[ ]	[ ]	[ ]	[ ]	[ ]	[ ]

Description: _____

_____

TABLE C19   DEFECT RECORDING LOG INSTRUCTIONS

Purpose	To hold the data on each defect as you find and correct it. You use these data to complete the Project Plan Summary.
General	• Record in this log all defects found in review, compile, and test. • Record each defect separately and completely. If you need additional space, use another copy of the form.
Header	Enter the following: • Your name • Today's date • The instructor's name • The number of the program
Date	Enter the date when the defect was found.
Number	Enter the defect number. For each program, this should be a sequential number starting with, for example, 1 or 001.
Type	Enter the defect type from the defect type standard in Table C20 (also summarized at the top of the log form). Use your best judgment in selecting which type applies.
Inject	Enter the phase during which this defect was injected. Use your best judgment.
Remove	Enter the phase during which the defect was removed. This will generally be the phase during which you found the defect.
Fix Time	Enter your best judgment of the time you took to fix the defect. This time can be determined by using a stop watch or your judgment.
Fix Defect	• If you injected this defect while fixing another defect, record the number of the improperly fixed defect. • If you cannot identify the defect number, enter an X in the Fix Defect box.
Description	Write a succinct description of the defect that is clear enough to later remind you about the error and help you to remember why you made it.

TABLE C20 DEFECT TYPE STANDARD

Type Number	Type Name	Description
10	Documentation	comments, messages
20	Syntax	spelling, punctuation, typos, instruction formats
30	Build, package	change management, library, version control
40	Assignment	declaration, duplicate names, scope, limits
50	Interface	procedure calls and references, I/O, user formats
60	Checking	error messages, inadequate checks
70	Data	structure, content
80	Function	logic, pointers, loops, recursion, computation, function defects
90	System	configuration, timing, memory
100	Environment	design, compile, test, or other support system problems

TABLE C21 PSP0.1 PROCESS SCRIPT

Phase Number	Purpose	
	Purpose	To guide you in developing module-level programs
	Inputs Required	• Problem description • PSP0.1 Project Plan Summary form • Time and Defect Recording Logs • Defect Type Standard • Stop watch (optional)
1	Planning	• Produce or obtain a requirements statement. • ***Estimate the total new and changed LOC required.*** • Estimate the required development time. • Enter the plan data on the Project Plan Summary. • Complete the Time Recording Log.
2	Development	• Design the program. • Implement the design. • Compile the program and fix and log all defects found. • Test the program and fix and log all defects found. • Complete the Time Recording Log.
3	Postmortem	Complete the Project Plan Summary with actual time, defect, and size data.
	Exit Criteria	• A thoroughly tested program • Completed Project Plan Summary with estimated and actual data • ***Completed PIP forms*** • Completed Defect and Time Recording Logs

TABLE C22 PSP0.1 PLANNING SCRIPT

Phase Number	Purpose	To guide the PSP planning process
	Inputs Required	• Problem description • PSP0.1 Project Plan Summary form • Time Recording Log
1	Program Requirements	• Produce or obtain a requirements statement for the program. • Ensure the requirements statement is clear and unambiguous. • Resolve any questions.
2	Size Estimate	***Make your best estimate of the total new and changed LOC required to develop this program.***
3	Resource Estimate	• Make your best estimate of the time required to develop this program. • ***Using the To Date % from the most recently developed program as a guide, distribute the development time over the planned project phases.***
	Exit Criteria	• Documented requirements statement • Project Plan Summary with estimated ***program size and*** development time data • Completed Time Recording Log

TABLE C23 PSP0.1 DEVELOPMENT SCRIPT

Phase Number	Purpose	To guide the development of small programs
	Entry Criteria	• Requirements statement • Project Plan Summary with estimated program *size and* development time • Time and Defect Recording Logs • Defect Type Standard *and Coding Standard*
1	Design	• Review the requirements and produce a design to meet them. • Record time in Time Recording Log.
2	Code	• Implement the design *following the Coding Standard.* • Record in the Defect Recording Log any requirements or design defects found. • Record time in Time Recording Log.
3	Compile	• Compile the program until error free. • Fix all defects found. • Record defects in Defect Recording Log. • Record time in Time Recording Log.
4	Test	• Test until all tests run without error. • Fix all defects found. • Record defects in Defect Recording Log. • Record time in Time Recording Log.
	Exit Criteria	• A thoroughly tested program *that conforms to the Coding Standard* • Completed Defect Recording Log • Completed Time Recording Log

TABLE C24 PSP0.1 POSTMORTEM SCRIPT

Phase Number	Purpose	To guide the PSP postmortem process
	Entry Criteria	• Problem description and requirements statement • Project Plan Summary with planned **program size and** development time • Completed Time Recording Log • Completed Defect Recording Log • A tested and running program **that conforms to the Coding Standard**
1	Defects Injected	• Determine from the Defect Recording Log the number of defects injected in each PSP0.1 phase. • Enter this number under Defects Injected—Actual on the Project Plan Summary.
2	Defects Removed	• Determine from the Defect Recording Log the number of defects removed in each PSP0.1 phase. • Enter this number under Defects Removed—Actual on the Project Plan Summary.
3	*Size*	• **Count the LOC in the completed program.** • **Determine the base, reused, deleted, modified, added, total, total new and changed, and new reused LOC.** • **Enter these data on the Project Plan Summary.**
4	Time	• Review the completed Time Recording Log. • Enter the total time spent in each PSP0.1 phase in the Actual column of the Project Plan Summary.
	Exit Criteria	• A fully tested program **that conforms to the Coding Standard** • Completed Project Plan Summary • **Completed PIP forms describing process problems, improvement suggestions, and lessons learned** • Completed Defect Recording Log and Time Recording Log

TABLE C25 PSP0.1 PROJECT PLAN SUMMARY

Student _____ Date _____

Program _____ Program # _____

Instructor _____ Language _____

Program Size (LOC)	Plan	Actual	To Date
Base(B)		_____ (Measured)	
Deleted (D)		_____ (Counted)	
Modified (M)		_____ (Counted)	
Added (A)		_____ $(T - B + D - R)$	
Reused (R)		_____ (Counted)	_____
Total New and Changed (N)	_____	_____ $(A + M)$	_____
Total LOC (T)		_____ (Measured)	_____
Total New Reused		_____	_____

Time in Phase (min.)	Plan	Actual	To Date	To Date %
Planning	_____	_____	_____	_____
Design	_____	_____	_____	_____
Code	_____	_____	_____	_____
Compile	_____	_____	_____	_____
Test	_____	_____	_____	_____
Postmortem	_____	_____	_____	_____
Total	_____	_____	_____	_____

Defects Injected		Actual	To Date	To Date %
Planning		_____	_____	_____
Design		_____	_____	_____
Code		_____	_____	_____
Compile		_____	_____	_____
Test		_____	_____	_____
Total Development		_____	_____	_____

Defects Removed		Actual	To Date	To Date %
Planning		_____	_____	_____
Design		_____	_____	_____
Code		_____	_____	_____
Compile		_____	_____	_____
Test		_____	_____	_____
Total Development		_____	_____	_____
After Development		_____	_____	

TABLE C26 PSP0.1 PROJECT PLAN SUMMARY INSTRUCTIONS

Purpose	This form holds the estimated and actual project data in a convenient and readily retrievable form
Header	Enter the following: • Your name and today's date • The program name and number • The instructor's name • The language you will use to write the program
Program Size (LOC)	*Prior to Development:* • *If you are modifying or enhancing an existing program, count that program's LOC and enter it under Base—Actual.* • *Using your best judgment, estimate the new and changed LOC you expect to develop.* *After Development:* • *If the base LOC (B) has changed, enter the new value.* • *Measure the total program size and enter it under Total LOC (T)—Actual.* • *Review your source code and, with the help of program 3A, determine the actual LOC that were deleted (D), modified (M), or reused (R).* • *Calculate the LOC of added code as $A = T - B + D - R$.* • *Calculate the total new and changed LOC as $N = A + M$.*
Time in Phase	• Under Plan, enter your original estimate of the total development time *and the time required by phase*. • Under Actual, enter the actual time in minutes spent in each development phase. • Under To Date, enter the sum of the actual time and the To Date time from your most recently developed program. • Under To Date %, enter the percentage of To Date time in each phase.
Defects Injected	• Under Actual, enter the number of defects injected in each phase. • Under To Date, enter the sum of the actual numbers of defects injected in each phase and the To Date values from the most recently developed program. • Under To Date %, enter the percentage of To Date defects injected by phase.
Defects Removed	• Under Actual, enter the number of defects removed in each phase. • Under To Date, enter the sum of the actual numbers of defects removed in each phase and the To Date values from the most recently developed program. • Under To Date %, enter the percentage of To Date defects removed by phase. • After development, record any defects later found during program use, reuse, or modification.

TABLE C27 PROCESS IMPROVEMENT PROPOSAL (PIP)

Student _____   Date _____

Instructor _____   Program # _____

Process _____   Elements _____

PIP Number   **Problem Description**

_____   _____
_____   _____
_____   _____
_____   _____
_____   _____
_____   _____
_____   _____
_____   _____

Proposal   **Proposal Description**
PIP Number

_____   _____
_____   _____
_____   _____
_____   _____
_____   _____
_____   _____

Notes and Comments

_____
_____
_____
_____
_____
_____
_____
_____
_____
_____
_____
_____
_____
_____
_____
_____
_____
_____
_____

TABLE C28 PROCESS IMPROVEMENT PROPOSAL (PIP) INSTRUCTIONS

Purpose	• To provide a way to record process problems and improvement ideas • To provide an orderly record of your process improvement ideas for use in later process improvement
General	Use the PIP form as follows: • To record process improvement ideas as they occur to you • To establish priorities for your improvement plans • To record lessons learned and unusual conditions Keep PIP forms on hand while using the PSP. • Record process problems even without proposed solutions. • Retain the PIPs for use in process improvement.
PIP Form Identification	Use the date and program number to identify the PIP form.
Header	• Enter your name, the date, the instructor's name, and the program number or other project designation. • Enter the name of the process you are using, such as PSP0.1. • If the PIP concerns a particular process element, note the element name, such as PSP0.1 Plan Summary.
Problem	Describe the problem as clearly as possible: • The difficulty encountered • The impact on the product, the process, and you Number the problems in each form in the left column: • Use a convenient sequence number. • Start with 1 on each PIP.
Proposal	• Describe your proposed process improvement as explicitly as possible. • Where possible, reference the specific process element and the words or entries to be changed. • Where appropriate, reference the problem description numbers in the left column. • If you feel a proposed improvement is particularly important, describe its priority and explain why.
Notes and Comments	For each project, complete at least one PIP form with overall comments about the process: • Record the process lessons learned. • Note any conditions you need to remember to later determine why the process worked particularly well or poorly.

TABLE C29 C++ CODING STANDARD

Purpose	To guide the development of C++ programs
Program Headers	Begin all programs with a descriptive header.
Header Format	(see below)

```
/*********************************************************/
/* Program Assignment: the program number               */
/* Name:                your name                        */
/* Date:                the date program development started */
/* Description:         a short description of the program */
/*                      function                         */
/*********************************************************/
```

Listing Contents	Provide a summary of the listing contents.
Contents Example	(see below)

```
/*********************************************************/
/* Listing Contents:                                     */
/*      Reuse instructions                               */
/*      Modification instructions                        */
/*      Compilation instructions                         */
/*      Includes                                         */
/*      Class declarations:                              */
/*          CData                                        */
/*          ASet                                         */
/*      Source code in c:\classes\CData.cpp:             */
/*          CData                                        */
/*          CData()                                      */
/*          Empty()                                      */
/*********************************************************/
```

TABLE C29 (continued)

Reuse Instructions	• Describe how the program is used. Provide the declaration format, parameter values and types, and parameter limits. • Provide warnings of illegal values, overflow conditions, or other conditions that could potentially result in improper operation.
Reuse Example	```/*** */
/* Reuse Instructions   */
/*   int PrintLine(char *line_of_character)   */
/*   Purpose: to print string, 'line_of_character', on one print */
/*   line   */
/*   Limitations: the maximum line length is LINE_LENGTH */
/*   Return: 0 if printer not ready to print, else 1 */
/*** */```
Identifiers	Use descriptive names for all variables, function names, constants, and other identifiers. Avoid abbreviations or single-letter variables.
Identifier Example	```int number_of_students; /* This is GOOD */
float x4, j, ftave;   /* These are BAD */```
Comments	• Document the code so that the reader can understand its operation. • Comments should explain both the purpose and behavior of the code. • Comment variable declarations to indicate their purpose.
Good Comment	```if(record_count > limit)/* have all the records been processed? */
limit */```
Bad Comment	```if(record_count > limit)/* check if record_count greater than */
limit */```
Major Sections	Precede major program sections by a block comment that describes the processing that is done in the next section.

TABLE C29 (continued)

| Example | ```
/*******************************************
/* This program section will examine the contents of the array   */
/* "grades" and will calculate the average grade for the class.   */
/*******************************************
``` |
| --- | --- |
| Blank Spaces | • Write programs with sufficient spacing so that they do not appear crowded.
• Separate every program construct with at least one space. |
| Indenting | • Indent every level of brace from the previous one.
• Open and close braces should be on lines by themselves and aligned with each other. |
| Indenting<br>Example | ```
while (miss_distance > threshold)
{
    success_code = move_robot (target_location);
    if (success_code == MOVE_FAILED)
    {
        printf("The robot move has failed.\n");
    }
}
``` |
| Capitalization | • Capitalize all defines.
• Lowercase all other identifiers and reserved words.
Messages being output to the user can be mixed-case so as to make a clean user presentation. |
| Capitalization<br>Example | ```
#define DEFAULT-NUMBER-OF-STUDENTS 15
int class-size = DEFAULT-NUMBER-OF-STUDENTS;
``` |
```

TABLE C30 PSP1 PROCESS SCRIPT

Phase Number	Purpose	To guide you in developing module-level programs
	Inputs Required	• Problem description • PSP1 Project Plan Summary form • **Size Estimating Template** • **Historical estimate and actual size data** • TIme and Defect Recording Logs • Defect Type Standard • Stop watch (optional)
1	Planning	• Produce or obtain a requirements statement. • **Use the PROBE method** to estimate the total new and changed LOC required. • **Complete the Size Estimating Template**. • Estimate the required development time. • Enter the plan data in the Project Plan Summary. • Complete the Time Recording Log.
2	Development	• Design the program. • Implement the design. • Compile the program and fix and log all defects found. • Test the program and fix and log all defects found. • Complete the Time Recording Log.
3	Postmortem	Complete the Project Plan Summary with actual time, defect, and size data.
	Exit Criteria	• A thoroughly tested program • Completed Project Plan Summary with estimated and actual data • **Completed Size Estimating Template** • **Completed Test Report Template** • Completed PIP forms • Completed Defect and Time Recording Logs

TABLE C31   PSP1 PLANNING SCRIPT

Phase Number	Purpose	To guide the PSP planning process
	Inputs Required	• Problem description • PSP1 Project Plan Summary form • *Size Estimating Template* • *Historical estimated and actual size data* • TIme Recording Log
1	Program Requirements	• Produce or obtain a requirements statement for the program. • Ensure the requirements statement is clear and unambiguous. • Resolve any questions.
2	Size Estimate	• *Produce a program conceptual design.* • *Use the PROBE method* to estimate the new and changed LOC required to develop this program. • *Estimate the base, added, deleted, modified, and reused LOC.* • *Complete the Size Estimating Template and Project Plan Summary.*
3	Resource Estimate	• *Based on the time required per LOC on previous programs*, make your best estimate of the time required to develop this program. • Using the To Date % from the most recently developed program as a guide, distribute the development time over the planned project phases.
	Exit Criteria	• A documented requirements statement • *The program conceptual design* • *Completed Size Estimating Template* • Completed Project Plan Summary with estimated program size and development time data • Completed Time Recording Log

TABLE C32 PSP1 DEVELOPMENT SCRIPT

Phase Number	Purpose	To guide the development of small programs
	Entry Criteria	• Requirements statement • Project Plan Summary with estimated program size and development time • Time and Defect Recording Logs • Defect Type Standard and Coding Standard
1	Design	• Review the requirements and produce a design to meet them. • Record time in Time Recording Log.
2	Code	• Implement the design, following the Coding Standard. • Record in the Defect Recording Log any requirements or design defects found. • Record time in Time Recording Log.
3	Compile	• Compile the program until error free. • Fix all defects found. • Record defects in Defect Recording Log. • Record time in Time Recording Log.
4	Test	• Test until all tests run without error. • Fix all defects found. • Record defects in Defect Recording Log. • Record time in Time Recording Log. • ***Complete a Test Report Template on the tests conducted and results obtained.***
	Exit Criteria	• A thoroughly tested program that conforms to the Coding Standard • ***Completed Test Report Template*** • Completed Defect Recording Log • Completed Time Recording Log

TABLE C33 PSP1 POSTMORTEM SCRIPT

Phase Number	Purpose	To guide the PSP postmortem process
	Entry Criteria	• Problem description and requirements statement • Project Plan Summary with program size and development time data • **_Completed Test Report Template_** • Completed Time Recording Log • Completed Defect Recording Log • A tested and running program that conforms to the Coding Standard
1	Defects Injected	• Determine from the Defect Recording Log the number of defects injected in each PSP1 phase. • Enter this number under Defects Injected—Actual on the Project Plan Summary.
2	Defects Removed	• Determine from the Defect Recording Log the number of defects removed in each PSP1 phase. • Enter this number under Defects Removed—Actual on the Project Plan Summary.
3	Size	• Count the LOC in the completed program. • Determine the base, reused, deleted, modified, added, total, total new and changed, and new reused LOC. • Enter these data in the Project Plan Summary.
4	Time	• Review the completed Time Recording Log. • Enter the total time spent in each PSP1 phase in the Actual column of the Project Plan Summary.
	Exit Criteria	• A fully tested program that conforms to the Coding Standard • **_A completed Test Report Template_** • Completed Project Plan Summary • Completed PIP forms describing process problems, improvement suggestions, and lessons learned • Completed Defect and Time Recording Logs

TABLE C34 PSP1 PROJECT PLAN SUMMARY

Student _____ Date _____

Program _____ Program # _____

Instructor_____ Language _____

Summary	Plan	Actual	To Date
LOC/Hour			
Program Size (LOC)	*Plan*	**Actual**	**To Date**
Base(B)			
	(Measured)	(Measured)	
Deleted (D)			
	(Estimated)	(Counted)	
Modified (M)			
	(Estimated)	(Counted)	
Added (A)			
	(N − M)	(T − B + D − R)	
Reused (R)			
	(Estimated)	(Counted)	
Total New and Changed (N)			
	(Estimated)	(A + M)	
Total LOC (T)			
	(N + B − M − D + R)	(Measured)	
Total New Reused			

Time in Phase (min.)	Plan	Actual	To Date	To Date %
Planning				
Design				
Code				
Compile				
Test				
Postmortem				
Total				

Defects Injected		Actual	To Date	To Date %
Planning				
Design				
Code				
Compile				
Test				
Total Development				

Defects Removed		Actual	To Date	To Date %
Planning				
Design				
Code				
Compile				
Test				
Total Development				
After Development				

TABLE C35 PSP1 PROJECT PLAN SUMMARY INSTRUCTIONS

Purpose	To hold the estimated and actual project data in a convenient and readily retrievable form
Header	Enter the following: • Your name and today's date • The program name and number • The instructor's name • The language you will use to write the program
Summary	*Enter the new and changed LOC per hour planned and actual for this program and for all programs developed to date.*
Program Size (LOC)	Prior to Development: • If you are modifying or enhancing an existing program, count that program's LOC and enter it under Base—***Plan***. • *Enter the estimated new and changed LOC (N) from the Size Estimating Template.* • *Estimate the numbers of added (A) and modified (M) LOC so that N = A + M.* • *Estimate the numbers of deleted (D) and reused (R) LOC and combine with the measured base (B) LOC so that T = N + B − M − D + R.* After Development: • If the base LOC (B) has changed, enter the new value. • Measure the total program size and enter it under Total LOC (T)—Actual • Review your source code and, with the help of program 3A, determine the actual LOC that were deleted (D), modified (M), or reused. • Calculate the LOC of added code as A = T − B + D − R. • Calculate the total new and changed LOC as N = A + M.
Time in Phase	• Under Plan, enter your original estimate of the total development time and the time required by phase. • Under Actual, enter the actual time in minutes spent in each development phase. • Under To Date, enter the sum of the actual time and the To Date time from your most recently developed program. • Under To Date %, enter the percentage of To Date time in each phase.
Defects Injected	• Under Actual, enter the number of defects injected in each phase. • Under To Date, enter the sum of the actual numbers of defects injected in each phase and the To Date values from the most recently developed program. • Under To Date %, enter the percentage of To Date defects injected by phase.
Defects Removed	• Under Actual, enter the number of defects removed in each phase. • Under To Date, enter the sum of the actual numbers of defects removed in each phase and the to-date numbers from the most recently developed program. • Under To Date %, enter the percentage of the To Date defects removed by phase. • After development, record any defects later found during program use, reuse, or modification.

TABLE C36 PROBE ESTIMATING SCRIPT

Phase Number	Purpose	To guide the PROBE estimation process
	Entry Criteria	• Requirements statement • Size Estimating Template and instructions • LOC per method data for object types • Time Recording Log
1	Conceptual Design	Review the requirements and produce a conceptual design to meet them.
2	Object Identification	• Identify and name the objects needed to implement this design. • Judge the number of methods in each object. • Determine the type category for each object (L = Logic, I = I/O, C = Calculation, T = Text, D = Data, S = Set-up). • Estimate the relative size of the object's methods (VS = very small, S = small, M = medium, L = large, VL = very large). • Find the LOC per method from the object database for that object type. • Calculate the estimated object size as the number of methods times the LOC per method. • Judge which of these objects will likely be entered in the reuse library and note them with an * in the LOC (New Reused*) column.
3	Other Program LOC	Follow the Size Estimating Template instructions to estimate the base, deleted, modified, added, reused, and new reused LOC.
4	Estimating Basis	A—If you have no historical data, use your judgment to estimate the new and changed LOC and the required development time per new and changedLOC. B—If you have sufficient actual data on development time and program size, estimate the new and changed LOC for the new program and multiply it by your historical new and changed LOC per hour productivity rate. C—If you have sufficient actual development time and actual object LOC data, calculate the β_0 and β_1 regression factors from these actual object LOC and actual hours data. D—If you have sufficient estimated object LOC data, calculate two sets of β_0 and β_1 regression parameters. One for the estimated object LOC versus actual new and changed LOC and use these parameters to calculate the estimated new and changed LOC on the Size Estimating Template. Calculate the second set of β_0 and β_1 regression parameters for estimated object LOC and actual hours. Use these parameters to estimate total planned development time.

5	Sufficient Data	• To use the averaging method, you need only historical data on actual new and changed LOC and actual development hours for one project. • To use the regression method, you must have at least three sets of historical development data. To be useful for estimating purposes, the correlation between LOC (estimated or actual) and development time should give an r value such that $r^2 \geq 0.50$.
6	Regression Method	• Use the linear regression procedure described in Appendix A, Table A27, to calculate the β_0 and β_1 regression parameters. • Select the size data as actual object LOC (case C in step 4 above) or estimated object LOC (case D in step 4 above). *Note*: The regression parameters in the Size Estimating Template relate the base program additions (BA), new objects (NO), and base program modifications (M) to total new and changed LOC (N). Your regression dataset should include these same items.
7	Regression Parameter Test	The absolute magnitude of β_0 should be substantially less than the expected size (for size estimates) or development time (for hour estimates) of the program you are estimating. • For size estimates, the value of β_1 should be positive and relatively near to 1.0. • For development time estimates, the value of $1/\beta_1$ should be relatively near historical LOC/hour. If these conditions are not met, use the averaging method.
8	Averaging Method	• Set the value of $\beta_0 = 0$. • Set β_1 as follows: $$\beta_1 = \sum_{i=1}^{n}\left(Time_i\right)\Big/\sum_{i=1}^{n}\left(Size_i\right).$$ Time: the development time for each program in the database Size: the actual object LOC (case B in step 4) for each program in the database *Note*: The size data in the size estimating database should include the same items included in the new program estimate.
9	Estimate	Estimate the projected LOC in the Size Estimating Template and calculate the development time: Hours = $\beta_0 + \beta_1$*(projected plus modified LOC).
10	Prediction Interval	If you used the regression method, calculate the prediction interval for the estimate as described in Appendix A, section A8. *Note*: The use of actual new and changed LOC and actual development time in the regression calculations is equivalent to assuming that the size estimate was exactly correct. This will generally give an unrealistically small prediction interval.

TABLE C37 TEST REPORT TEMPLATE

Student _____   Date _____

Instructor _____   Program # _____

Test Name/Number	_____
Test Objective	_____
Test Description	_____
	_____
	_____
	_____
Test Conditions	_____
	_____
	_____
	_____
Expected Results	_____
	_____
	_____
Actual Results	_____
	_____
	_____
	_____
	_____

Test Name/Number	_____
Test Objective	_____
Test Description	_____
	_____
	_____
	_____
Test Conditions	_____
	_____
	_____
	_____
Expected Results	_____
	_____
	_____
Actual Results	_____
	_____
	_____
	_____

TABLE C38 TEST REPORT TEMPLATE INSTRUCTIONS

Purpose	• To maintain a record of the tests run and the results obtained • To be sufficiently complete so you can later repeat the same tests and get the same results Proper use of this report will simplify the regression testing of modified programs.
General	• Expand this table or use multiple copies as needed. • Report every test performed. • Be as brief and concise as possible.
Header	Enter the following: • Your name • Today's date • The instructor's name • The number of the program
Test Name/ Number	Uniquely identify each test execution for each program: • The same tests with different data • The same data with different tests • Rerun the test with the fix applied
Test Objective	Briefly describe the test objective.
Test Description	Describe each test's data and procedures in sufficient detail to permit it to later be rerun.
Test Conditions	• List any special configuration, timing, fix, or other conditions of the test. • When multiple tests are run with different fixes, separately list each, for example, Initial, Fix A, Fix B, and so on.
Expected Results	List the results that the test should produce if it runs properly.
Actual Results	• List the results that were actually produced. • When the same test is run multiple times while fixing multiple defects, note the results of each test, for example, Initial result, Result A, Result B, and so on.

TABLE C39 SIZE ESTIMATING TEMPLATE

Student _____ Date _____

Instructor_____ Program # _____

BASE PROGRAM

BASE SIZE (B)   => => => => => => => => => =>   _____

LOC DELETED (D)   => => => => => => => => => =>   _____

LOC MODIFIED (M) => => => => => => => => => =>   _____

PROJECTED LOC (P)

BASE ADDITIONS	TYPE	METHODS	RELATIVE SIZE	LOC
_____	_____	_____	_____	_____
_____	_____	_____	_____	_____
_____	_____	_____	_____	_____
_____	_____	_____	_____	_____

TOTAL BASE ADDITIONS (BA)=> => => => => => => =>   _____

NEW OBJECTS (NO)	TYPE[1]	METHODS	RELATIVE SIZE	LOC (New Reused*)
_____	_____	_____	_____	_____
_____	_____	_____	_____	_____
_____	_____	_____	_____	_____
_____	_____	_____	_____	_____
_____	_____	_____	_____	_____

TOTAL NEW OBJECTS (NO)=> => => => => => => =>   _____

REUSED OBJECTS   LOC

_____   _____

_____   _____

_____   _____

_____   _____

REUSED TOTAL (R) => => => => => => => => =>   _____

Projected LOC (P):	$P = BA + NO$	_____
Regression Parameter:	β_0	_____
Regression Parameter:	β_1	_____
Estimated New and Changed LOC (N):	$N = \beta_0 + \beta_1{}^*(P + M)$	_____
Estimated Total LOC (T):	$T = N + B - D - M + R$	_____
Estimated Total New Reused (sum of * LOC):		_____
Prediction Range:	Range	_____
Upper Prediction Interval:	$UPI = N + Range$	_____
Lower Prediction Interval:	$LPI = N - Range$	_____

[1]L=Logic, I=I/O, C=Calculation, T=Text, D=Data, S=Set-up

TABLE C40 SIZE ESTIMATING TEMPLATE INSTRUCTIONS

Purpose	To guide the size estimating process and to hold the estimate data
Header	Enter the following: • Your name • Today's date • The instructor's name • The program number If you need additional space in any category, use separate sheets and include the totals on this form.
Application Note	While the PROBE method is described for object-oriented languages, it can be used with other languages with the following changes: • If your language uses procedures, substitute the word *procedure* for the word *object*. • If your language uses functions, substitute the word *function* for the word *object*. • With these changes, use PROBE to estimate for your language, using one method per procedure or function.
Base Program	If this development is a modification or enhancement of an existing program, do the following: • Count and enter the base program size at B. • Enter the base program LOC to be deleted at D. • Enter the base program LOC to be modified at M.
Projected LOC—Base Additions (BA)	If you plan to add LOC to the base program, do the following: • Identify the functions to be added. • Estimate the LOC for each additional function. • If appropriate, estimate this function as if it were a new object, using the type categories that apply. • Enter the total base additions at BA.
Projected LOC—New Objects (NO)	• Assign a name to each planned new object. • Estimate the object type (see footnote on template). • Estimate the number of methods the object will likely contain. • Estimate the relative size of the object: very small (VS), small (S), medium (M), large (L), very large (VL). • Obtain the LOC per method for the object type and relative size from Table 5.7 or your size database. • To determine the estimated LOC for each object type, multiply the method LOC by the estimated number of methods. • Note each new object planned for the reuse library with an *. • Total the estimated New Object LOC and enter at NO. • Total the LOC for the new reused objects (those with an *) and enter on the Project Plan Summary.

TABLE C40   (continued)

Reused Objects	• Enter the name of each unmodified reused object.
	• Enter the LOC of each unmodified reused object under Size.
	• Sum these LOC and enter at REUSED TOTAL (R).
	If any reused objects are to be modified or enhanced, include the object LOC in the base program size numbers along with any deletions and modifications. Include their additions with base additions.
Calculations	Projected LOC:
	• Sum the LOC for the base additions (BA) and new objects (NO).
	• Enter this total as projected LOC (P).
	Estimated New and Changed LOC (N):
	• Using the regression parameters and the projected (P) and modified (M) LOC for the new program, calculate N.
	• Calculate the regression parameters from your historical data using the procedure described in Appendix A, Table A27.
	Estimated Total LOC (T):
	• $T = N + B - D - M + R$
	Estimated Total New Reused:
	• The sum of the New Reused * items
	The Prediction Range:
	• Calculate the Range using the procedure described in Appendix A, Table A29.
	The upper (UPI) and lower (LPI) prediction intervals:
	• UPI = N + Range
	• LPI = N − Range
	If the LPI is negative, use zero.
	Prediction Interval Percentage:
	• List the probability percentage used to calculate the prediction interval (70 percent or 90 percent).

TABLE C41   PSP1.1 PROCESS SCRIPT

Phase Number	Purpose	To guide you in developing module-level programs
	Inputs Required	• Problem description • PSP1.1 Project Plan Summary form • Size Estimating Template • Historical estimate and actual size **and time** data • TIme and Defect Recording Logs • Defect Type Standard • Stop watch (optional)
1	Planning	• Produce or obtain a requirements statement. • Use the PROBE method to estimate the total new and changed LOC required. • Complete the Size Estimating Template • **Use the PROBE method** to estimate the required development time. • **Complete a Task Planning Template.** • **Complete a Schedule Planning Template.** • Enter the plan data in the Project Plan Summary. • Complete the Time Recording Log.
2	Development	• Design the program. • Implement the design. • Compile the program and fix and log all defects found. • Test the program and fix and log all defects found. • Complete the Time Recording Log.
3	Postmortem	Complete the Project Plan Summary with actual time, defect, and size data.
	Exit Criteria	• A thoroughly tested program • Completed Project Plan Summary with estimated and actual data • Completed estimating and planning templates • Completed Test Report Template • Completed PIP forms • Completed Defect and Time Recording Logs

TABLE C42 PSP1.1 PLANNING SCRIPT

Phase Number	Purpose	To guide the PSP planning process
	Inputs Required	• Problem description • PSP1.1 Project Plan Summary form • Size Estimating, **Task Planning, and Schedule Planning Templates** • Historical estimated and actual size **and time** data • TIme Recording Log
1	Program Requirements	• Produce or obtain a requirements statement for the program. • Ensure the requirements statement is clear and unambiguous. • Resolve any questions.
2	Size Estimate	• Produce a program conceptual design. • Use the PROBE method to estimate the new and changed LOC required to develop this program. • Estimate the base, added, deleted, modified, and reused LOC. • Complete the Size Estimating Template and Project Plan Summary.
3	Resource Estimate	• **Use the PROBE method** to estimate the time required to develop this program. • Using the To Date % from the most recently developed program as a guide, distribute the development time over the planned project phases.
4	**Task and Schedule Planning**	**For projects requiring several days or more of work, complete the Task Planning and Schedule Planning Templates.**
	Exit Criteria	• A documented requirements statement • The program conceptual design • A completed Size Estimating Template • **For projects of several days' duration, completed Task Planning and Schedule Planning Templates** • Completed Project Plan Summary with estimated program size and development time data • Completed Time Recording Log

TABLE C43 PSP1.1 DEVELOPMENT SCRIPT

Phase Number	Purpose	
	Purpose	To guide the development of small programs
	Entry Criteria	• Requirements statement • Project Plan Summary with estimated program size and development time • ***For projects of several days' duration, completed Task Planning and Schedule Planning Templates*** • Time and Defect Recording Logs • Defect Type Standard and Coding Standard
1	Design	• Review the requirements and produce a design to meet them. • Record time in Time Recording Log.
2	Code	• Implement the design, following the Coding Standard. • Record in the Defect Recording Log any requirements or design defects found. • Record time in Time Recording Log.
3	Compile	• Compile the program until error free. • Fix all defects found. • Record defects in Defect Recording Log. • Record time in Time Recording Log.
4	Test	• Test until all tests run without error. • Fix all defects found. • Record defects in Defect Recording Log. • Record time in Time Recording Log. • Complete a Test Report Template on the tests conducted and results obtained.
	Exit Criteria	• A thoroughly tested program that conforms to the Coding Standard • Completed Test Report Template • Completed Defect Recording Log • Completed Time Recording Log

TABLE C44 PSP1.1 POSTMORTEM SCRIPT

Phase Number	Purpose	To guide the PSP postmortem process
	Entry Criteria	• Problem description and requirements statement • Project Plan Summary with program size and development time data • *For projects of several days' duration, completed Task Planning and Schedule Planning Templates* • Completed Test Report Template • Completed Time Recording Log • Completed Defect Recording Log • A tested and running program that conforms to the Coding Standard
1	Defects Injected	• Determine from the Defect Recording Log the number of defects injected in each PSP1.1 phase. • Enter this number under Defects Injected—Actual on the Project Plan Summary.
2	Defects Removed	• Determine from the Defect Recording Log the number of defects removed in each PSP1.1 phase. • Enter this number under Defects Removed—Actual on the Project Plan Summary.
3	Size	• Count the LOC in the completed program. • Determine the base, reused, deleted, modified, added, total, total new and changed, and new reused LOC. • Enter these data in the Project Plan Summary.
4	Time	• Review the completed Time Recording Log. • Enter the total time spent in each PSP1.1 phase in the Actual column of the Project Plan Summary.
	Exit Criteria	• A fully tested program that conforms to the Coding Standard • A completed Test Report Template • Completed Project Plan Summary • Completed PIP forms describing process problems, improvement suggestions, and lessons learned • Completed Defect Recording Log and Time Recording Log

TABLE C45 PSP1.1 PROJECT PLAN SUMMARY

Student	_____	Date	_____
Program	_____	Program #	_____
Instructor	_____	Language	_____

Summary	Plan	Actual	To Date
LOC/Hour	_____	_____	_____
Planned Time	_____		_____
Actual Time		_____	_____
CPI(Cost-Performance Index)			_____ (Planned/Actual)
% Reused	_____	_____	_____
% New Reused	_____	_____	_____

Program Size (LOC)	Plan	Actual	To Date
Base(B)	_____ (Measured)	_____ (Measured)	
Deleted (D)	_____ (Estimated)	_____ (Counted)	
Modified (M)	_____ (Estimated)	_____ (Counted)	
Added (A)	_____ (N − M)	_____ (T − B + D − R)	
Reused (R)	_____ (Estimated)	_____ (Counted)	_____
Total New and Changed (N)	_____ (Estimated)	_____ (A + M)	_____
Total LOC (T)	_____ (N + B − M − D + R)	_____ (Measured)	_____
Total New Reused	_____	_____	_____

Time in Phase (min.)	Plan	Actual	To Date	To Date %
Planning	_____	_____	_____	_____
Design	_____	_____	_____	_____
Code	_____	_____	_____	_____
Compile	_____	_____	_____	_____
Test	_____	_____	_____	_____
Postmortem	_____	_____	_____	_____
Total	_____	_____	_____	_____

Defects Injected		Actual	To Date	To Date %
Planning		_____	_____	_____
Design		_____	_____	_____
Code		_____	_____	_____
Compile		_____	_____	_____
Test		_____	_____	_____
Total Development		_____	_____	_____

Defects Removed		Actual	To Date	To Date %
Planning		_____	_____	_____
Design		_____	_____	_____
Code		_____	_____	_____
Compile		_____	_____	_____
Test		_____	_____	_____
Total Development		_____	_____	_____
After Development		_____	_____	

TABLE C46 PSP1.1 PROJECT PLAN SUMMARY INSTRUCTIONS

Purpose	To hold the estimated and actual project data in a convenient and readily retrievable form
Header	Enter the specified data.
Summary	• Enter the new and changed LOC per hour planned and actual for this program and for all programs developed to date. • *Enter the planned and actual times for this program and the sums of the planned and actual times for all the exercises to date.* • *CPI = (To Date Planned Time)/(To Date Actual Time)* • *Enter the planned, actual, and To Date reuse data.*
Program Size (LOC)	Prior to Development: • If you are modifying or enhancing an existing program, count that program's LOC and enter it under Base—Plan. • Enter the estimated new and changed LOC (N) from the Size Estimating Template. • Estimate the numbers of added (A) and modified (M) LOC so that $N = A + M$. • Estimate the numbers of deleted (D) and reused (R) LOC and combine with the measured base (B) LOC so that $T = N + B - M - D + R$. After Development: • If the base LOC (B) has changed, enter the new value. • Measure the total program size and enter it under Total LOC (T) —Actual. • Review your source code and, with the help of program 3A, determine the actual LOC that were deleted (D), modified (M), or reused (R). • Calculate the LOC of added code as $A = T - B + D - R$. • Calculate the total new and changed LOC as $N = A + M$.
Time in Phase	• Under Plan, enter your original estimate of the total development time and the time required by phase. • Under Actual, enter the actual time in minutes spent in each development phase. • Under To Date, enter the sum of the actual time and the To Date time from your most recently developed program. • Under To Date %, enter the percentage of To Date time in each phase.

TABLE C46 (continued)

Defects Injected	• Under Actual, enter the number of defects injected in each phase.
	• Under To Date, enter the sum of the actual numbers of defects injected in each phase and the To Date values from the most recently developed program.
	• Under To Date %, enter the percentage of To Date defects injected by phase.
Defects Removed	• Under Actual, enter the number of defects removed in each phase.
	• Under To Date, enter the sum of the actual numbers of defects removed in each phase and the To Date values from the most recently developed program.
	• Under To Date %, enter the percentage of To Date defects removed by phase.
	• After development, record any defects later found during program use, reuse, or modification.

TABLE C47 TASK PLANNING TEMPLATE

Student —————— Date ——————
Project —————— Instructor ——————

Task		Plan					Actual		
Number	Name	Hours	Planned Value	Cumulative Hours	Cumulative Planned Value	Date Monday	Date	Earned Value	Cumulative Earned Value

Totals

TABLE C48 TASK PLANNING TEMPLATE INSTRUCTIONS

Purpose	• To estimate the development time for each project task • To compute the planned value for each project task • To estimate the planned completion date for each task • To provide a basis for tracking schedule progress even when the tasks are not completed in the planned order
General	• Expand this template or use multiple pages as needed. • Include every significant task. • Use task names and numbers that support the activity and are consistent with the project work breakdown structure.
Header	Enter the following: • Your name • Today's date • The project name • The instructor's name
Task	• Enter a task number and name. List the tasks in the order in which you expect to complete them. • Select tasks that have explicit completion criteria, for example, planning completed, program compiled and all defects corrected, testing completed and all defects corrected, and so on.
Plan—Hours	Enter the planned hours for each task.
Plan—Planned Value	• Total the planned hours for all the tasks. • For each task, calculate the percentage its planned hours are of total hours. • Enter this percentage as the planned value for that task. • The total planned value should equal 100.
Plan—Cumulative Hours	Enter the cumulative sum of the planned hours down through each task.
Plan—Cumulative Value	• Sum the planned values through each task. • Before proceeding, complete the Schedule Planning Template down through Plan—Cumulative Hours. • Then complete the Schedule Planning and Task Planning templates together.
Plan Date—Monday	• For each cumulative hours entry, find the planned cumulative hours entry on the Schedule Planning Template that equals or just exceeds it. • Enter the date from that row (of the Schedule Planning Template) as the plan date on the Task Planning Template. • If several weeks on the Schedule Planning Template have the same cumulative value, enter the earliest date. • Unless you made daily plans, pick the plan date as the Monday of the week during which completion for that task is planned.
Actual Date	As each task is completed, enter the completion date.
Earned Value	For each completed task, enter the planned value.
Cumulative Earned Value	As each task is completed, total all the earned value entries and enter that total beside the latest task that was completed.

TABLE C49 SCHEDULE PLANNING TEMPLATE

Student _____ Date _____

Project _____ Instructor _____

Week Number	Date Monday	Plan			Actual			
		Direct Hours	Cumulative Hours	Cumulative Planned Value	Direct Hours	Cumulative Hours	Cumulative Earned Value	Adjusted Earned Value

TABLE C50 SCHEDULE PLANNING TEMPLATE INSTRUCTIONS

Purpose	• To record the estimated and actual hours expended by calendar period • To relate the task planned value to the calendar schedule • To calculate adjusted planned and earned values when tasks change
General	• Expand this template or use multiple pages as needed. • Complete it in conjunction with the Task Planning Template.
Header	Enter the following: • Your name • Today's date • The project name • The instructor's name
Week Number	• From the project start, enter a week number, typically starting with 1. • For very small projects, it may be more convenient to use days instead of weeks.
Date (Monday)	• Enter the calendar date for each week. • Pick a standard day in the week, for example, Monday.
Plan—Direct Hours	• Enter the planned number of direct project hours you expect to spend each week. • Consider nonwork time such as vacations, holidays, and so on. • Consider other committed activities such as classes, meetings, and other projects.
Plan—Cumulative Hours	Enter the cumulative planned hours through each week.
Plan—Cumulative Planned Value	For each week do the following: • Take the plan cumulative hours from the Schedule Planning Template. • On the task Planning Template, find the task with the nearest equal or lower plan cumulative hours and note its plan cumulative value. • Enter this cumulative value in the Schedule Planning Template for that week. • If the cumulative value for the prior week still applies, enter it again.
Actual	• During development, enter the actual direct hours, cumulative hours, and cumulative earned value for each week. • Determine status against plan by comparing the cumulative planned value and the actual cumulative earned value.
Adjusted Earned Value	Proportionately adjust the earned value up or down as tasks are added or deleted. The adjusted earned value compensates for these changes without requiring a complete new plan.

TABLE C51 PSP2 PROCESS SCRIPT

Phase Number	Purpose	To guide you in developing module-level programs
	Inputs Required	• Problem description • PSP2 Project Plan Summary form • Size Estimating Template • Historical estimated and actual size and time data • TIme and Defect Recording Logs • Defect Type Standard • Stop watch (optional)
1	Planning	• Produce or obtain a requirements statement. • Use the PROBE method to estimate the total new and changed LOC required **and the prediction interval**. • Complete the Size Estimating Template. • Use the PROBE method to estimate the development time required **and the prediction interval**. • Complete a Task Planning Template. • Complete a Schedule Planning Template. • Enter the plan data in the Project Plan Summary. • Complete the Time Recording Log.
2	Development	• Design the program. • **Review the design and fix and log all defects found.** • Implement the design. • **Review the code and fix and log all defects found.** • Compile the program and fix and log all defects found. • Test the program and fix and log all defects found. • Complete the Time Recording Log.
3	Postmortem	Complete the Project Plan Summary with actual time, defect, and size data.
	Exit Criteria	• A thoroughly tested program • Completed Project Plan Summary with estimated and actual data • Completed estimating and planning templates • **Completed Design Review Checklist and Code Review Checklist** • Completed Test Report Template • Completed PIP forms • Completed Defect and Time Recording Logs

TABLE C52 PSP2 PLANNING SCRIPT

Phase Number	Purpose	To guide the PSP planning process
	Inputs Required	• Problem description • PSP2 Project Plan Summary form • Size Estimating, Task Planning, and Schedule Planning Templates • Historical estimated and actual size and time data • TIme Recording Log
1	Program Requirements	• Produce or obtain a requirements statement for the program. • Ensure the requirements statement is clear and unambiguous. • Resolve any questions.
2	Size Estimate	• Produce a program conceptual design. • Use the PROBE method to estimate the new and changed LOC required to develop this program. • Estimate the base, added, deleted, modified, and reused LOC. • Complete the Size Estimating Template and Project Plan Summary. • *Calculate the 70 percent size prediction interval (you may use a spreadsheet).*
3	Resource Estimate	• Use the PROBE method to estimate the time required to develop the new program. • *Calculate the 70 percent time prediction interval (you may use a spreadsheet).* • Using the To Date % from the most recently developed program as a guide, distribute the development time over the planned project phases.
4	Task and Schedule Planning	For projects requiring several days or more of work, complete the Task Planning and Schedule Planning Templates.
5	**Defect Estimate**	• *Based on your To Date data on defects per new and changed LOC, estimate the total defects to be found in this program.* • *Based on your To Date % data, estimate the numbers of defects to be injected and removed by phase.*
	Exit Criteria	• A documented requirements statement • The program conceptual design • A Completed Size Estimating Template • For projects of several days duration, completed Task and Schedule Planning Templates • A Project Plan Summary with estimated program size, development time, and 70 percent prediction intervals • Completed Time Recording Log

TABLE C53 PSP2 DEVELOPMENT SCRIPT

Phase Number	Purpose	To guide the development of small programs
	Entry Criteria	• Requirements statement • Project Plan Summary with estimated program size and development time • For projects of several days' duration, completed Task Planning and Schedule Planning Templates • Time and Defect Recording Logs • Defect Type Standard and Coding Standard
1	Design	• Review the requirements and produce a design to meet them. • Record time in Time Recording Log.
2	*Design Review*	• *Follow the Design Review Checklist and review the design.* • *Fix all defects found.* • *Record defects in Defect Recording Log.* • *Record time in Time Recording Log.*
3	Code	• Implement the design, following the Coding Standard. • Record in the Defect Recording Log any requirements or design defects found. • Record time in Time Recording Log.
4	*Code Review*	• *Follow the Code Review Checklist and review the code.* • *Fix all defects found.* • *Record defects in Defect Recording Log.* • *Record time in Time Recording Log.*
5	Compile	• Compile the program until error free. • Fix all defects found. • Record defects in Defect Recording Log. • Record time in Time Recording Log.
6	Test	• Test until all tests run without error. • Fix all defects found. • Record defects in Defect Recording Log. • Record time in Time Recording Log. • Complete a Test Report Template on the tests conducted and results obtained.
	Exit Criteria	• A thoroughly tested program that conforms to the Coding Standard • *Completed design Review and Code Review Checklists* • Completed Test Report Template • Complete Defect Recording Log • Complete Time Recording Log

TABLE C54 PSP2 POSTMORTEM SCRIPT

Phase Number	Purpose	To guide the PSP postmortem process
	Entry Criteria	• Problem description and requirements statement • Project Plan Summary with program size, development time, **and defect** data • For projects of several days' duration, completed Task Planning and Schedule Planning Templates • Completed Test Report Template • **Completed Design Review and Code Review Checklists** • Completed Time Recording Log • Completed Defect Recording Log • A tested and running program that conforms to the Coding Standard
1	Defects Injected	• Determine from the Defect Recording Log the number of defects injected in each PSP2 phase. • Enter this number under Defects Injected—Actual on the Project Plan Summary.
2	Defects Removed	• Determine from the Defect Recording Log the number of defects removed in each PSP2 phase. • Enter this number under Defects Removed—Actual on the Project Plan Summary. • **Calculate the actual overall process yield and enter it in the Project Plan Summary.**
3	Size	• Count the LOC in the completed program. • Determine the base, reused, deleted, modified, added, total, total new and changed, and new reused LOC. • Enter these data on the Project Plan Summary.
4	Time	• Review the completed Time Recording Log. • Enter the total time spent in each PSP2 phase in the Actual column of the Project Plan Summary.
	Exit Criteria	• A fully tested program that conforms to the Coding Standard • **Completed Design Review and Code Review Checklists** • A completed Test Report Template • Completed Project Plan Summary • Completed PIP forms describing process problems, improvement suggestions, and lessons learned • Completed Defect and Time Recording Logs

TABLE C55 PSP2 PROJECT PLAN SUMMARY

Student _____ Date _____

Program _____ Program # _____

Instructor _____ Language _____

Summary	Plan	Actual	To Date
LOC/Hour	_____	_____	_____
Planned Time	_____		_____
Actual Time		_____	_____
CPI(Cost-Performance Index)			_____
			(Planned/Actual)
% Reused	_____	_____	_____
% New Reused	_____	_____	_____
Test Defects/KLOC	_____	_____	_____
Total Defects/KLOC	_____	_____	_____
Yield %	_____	_____	_____

Program Size (LOC)	Plan	Actual	To Date
Base(B)	_____ (Measured)	_____ (Measured)	
Deleted (D)	_____ (Estimated)	_____ (Counted)	
Modified (M)	_____ (Estimated)	_____ (Counted)	
Added (A)	_____ $(N - M)$	_____ $(T - B + D - R)$	
Reused (R)	_____ (Estimated)	_____ (Counted)	_____
Total New and Changed (N)	_____ (Estimated)	_____ $(A + M)$	_____
Total LOC (T)	_____ $(N + B - M - D + R)$	_____ (Measured)	_____
Total New Reused	_____	_____	_____
Upper Prediction Interval (70%)	_____		
Lower Prediction Interval (70%)	_____		

Time in Phase (min.)	Plan	Actual	To Date	To Date %
Planning	_____	_____	_____	_____
Design	_____	_____	_____	_____
Design Review	_____	_____	_____	_____
Code	_____	_____	_____	_____
Code Review	_____	_____	_____	_____
Compile	_____	_____	_____	_____
Test	_____	_____	_____	_____
Postmortem	_____	_____	_____	_____
Total	_____	_____	_____	_____
Total Time UPI (70%)	_____			
Total Time LPI (70%)	_____			

TABLE C55 (continued)

Defects Injected	Plan	Actual	To Date	To Date %
Planning				
Design				
Design Review				
Code				
Code Review				
Compile				
Test				
Total Development				

Defects Removed	Plan	Actual	To Date	To Date %
Planning				
Design				
Design Review				
Code				
Code Review				
Compile				
Test				
Total Development				
After Development				

Defect Removal Efficiency	Plan	Actual	To Date
Defects/Hour—Design Review			
Defects/Hour—Code Review			
Defects/Hour—Compile			
Defects/Hour—Test			
DRL(DLDR/UT)			
DRL(CodeReview/UT)			
DRL(Compile/UT)			

TABLE C56 PSP2 PROJECT PLAN SUMMARY INSTRUCTIONS

Purpose	To hold the estimated and actual project data in a convenient and readily retrievable form
Header	Enter the specified data.
Summary	• Enter the new and changed LOC per hour planned and actual for this program and for all programs developed to date. • Enter the planned and actual times for this program and the sums of the planned and actual times for all the exercises to date. • CPI = (To Date Planned Time)/(To Date Actual Time) • Enter the planned, actual, and To Date reuse data. • *Enter the planned, actual, and To Date defect data.* • *Enter the planned and actual yield.*
Program Size (LOC)	Prior to Development: • If you are modifying or enhancing an existing program, count that program's LOC and enter it under Base—Plan. • Enter the estimated new and changed LOC (N) from the Size Estimating Template. • Estimate the numbers of added (A) and modified (M) LOC so that N = A + M. • Estimate the numbers of deleted (D) and reused (R) LOC and combine with the measured base (B) LOC so that T = N + B − M − D + R. After Development: • If the base LOC (B) has changed, enter the new value. • Measure the total program size and enter it under Total LOC (T) —Actual. • Review your source code and, with the help of program 3A, determine the actual LOC that were deleted (D), modified (M), or reused (R). • Calculate the LOC of added code as A = T − B + D − R. • Calculate the total new and changed LOC as N = A + M.
Time in Phase	• Under Plan, enter your original estimate of the total development time and the time required by phase. • Under Actual, enter the actual time in minutes spent in each development phase. • Under To Date, enter the sum of the actual time and the To Date time from your most recently developed program. • Under To Date %, enter the percentage of To Date time in each phase.

TABLE C56 (continued)

Defects Injected	• Under Actual, enter the number of defects injected in each phase. • Under To Date, enter the sum of the actual numbers of defects injected in each phase and the To Date values from the most recently developed program. • Under To Date %, enter the percentage of To Date defects injected by phase.
Defects Removed	• Under Actual, enter the numbers of defects removed in each phase. • Under To Date, enter the sum of the actual numbers of defects removed in each phase and the To Date values from the most recently developed program. • Under To Date %, enter the percentage of the To Date defects removed by phase. • After development, record any defects later found during program use, reuse, or modification.
Defect Removal Efficiency	• *Under Plan, enter the planned efficiencies for this project.* • *Under Actual, enter the actual efficiencies achieved.* • *Under To Date, enter the actual efficiencies for all the projects to date.*

TABLE C57 C++ PSP2 DESIGN REVIEW CHECKLIST

PROGRAM NAME AND #:

Purpose	To guide you in conducting an effective design review				
General	• As you complete each review step, check off that item in the box to the right. • Complete the checklist for one program unit before you start to review the next.				
Complete	Ensure that the requirements, specifications, and high-level design are completely covered by the design: • All specified outputs are produced. • All needed inputs are furnished. • All required includes are stated.				
Logic	• Verify that program sequencing is proper: ☐ Stacks, lists, and so on are in the proper order. ☐ Recursion unwinds properly. • Verify that all loops are properly initiated, incremented, and terminated.				
Special Cases	Check all special cases: • Ensure proper operation with empty, full, minimum, maximum, negative, zero values for all variables. • Protect against out-of-limits, overflow, underflow conditions. • Ensure "impossible" conditions are absolutely impossible. • Handle all incorrect input conditions.				
Functional Use	• Verify that all functions, procedures, or objects are fully understood and properly used. • Verify that all externally referenced abstractions are precisely defined.				
Names	Verify the following: • All special names and types are clear or specifically defined. • The scopes of all variables and parameters are self-evident or defined. • All named objects are used within their declared scopes.				
Standards	Review the design for conformance to all applicable design standards.				

TABLE C58 C++ CODE REVIEW CHECKLIST

PROGRAM NAME AND #:

Purpose	To guide you in conducting an effective code review				
General	• As you complete each review step, check off that item in the box to the right. • Complete the checklist for one program unit before you start to review the next unit.				
Complete	Verify that the code covers all the design.				
Includes	Verify that includes are complete.				
Initialization	Check variable and parameter initialization: • At program initiation • At start of every loop • At function/procedure entry				
Calls	Check function call formats: • Pointers • Parameters • Use of '&'				
Names	Check name spelling and use: • Is it consistent? • Is it within the declared scope? • Do all structures and classes use '.' reference?				
Strings	Check that all strings are • identified by pointers and • terminated in NULL.				
Pointers	Check that • pointers are initialized NULL • pointers are deleted only after new, and • new pointers always deleted after use.				
Output Format	Check the output format: • Line stepping is proper. • Spacing is proper.				
{} Pairs	Ensure the {} are proper and matched.				
Logic Operators	• Verify the proper use of ==, =, //, and so on. • Check every logic function for proper ().				
Line-by-line Check	Check every LOC for • instruction syntax and • proper punctuation.				
Standards	Ensure the code conforms to the coding standards.				
File Open and Close	Verify that all files are • properly declared, • opened, and • closed.				

TABLE C59 PSP2.1 PROCESS SCRIPT

Phase Number	Purpose	To guide you in developing module-level programs
	Inputs Required	• Problem description • PSP2.1 Project Plan Summary form • Size Estimating Template • Historical estimated and actual size and time data • TIme and Defect Recording Logs • Defect Type Standard • Stop watch (optional)
1	Planning	• Produce or obtain a requirements statement. • Use the PROBE method to estimate the total new and changed LOC required and the prediction interval. • Complete the Size Estimating Template. • Use the PROBE method to estimate the required development time and the prediction interval. • Complete a Task Planning Template. • Complete a Schedule Planning Template. • Enter the plan data in the Project Plan Summary • Complete the Time Recording Log.
2	Development	• Design the program. • Review the design and fix and log all defects found. • Implement the design, **using design templates where appropriate**. • Review the code and fix and log all defects found. • Compile the program and fix and log all defects found. • Test the program and fix and log all defects found. • Complete the Time Recording Log.
3	Postmortem	Complete the Project Plan Summary with actual time, defect, and size data.
	Exit Criteria	• A thoroughly tested program • Completed Project Plan Summary with estimated and actual data • Completed estimating and planning templates • **Completed design templates** • Completed Design Review Checklist and Code Review Checklist • Completed Test Report Template • Completed PIP forms • Completed Defect and Time Recording Logs

TABLE C60 PSP2.1 PLANNING SCRIPT

Phase Number	Purpose	To guide the PSP planning process
	Inputs Required	• Problem description • PSP2.1 Project Plan Summary form • Size Estimating, Task Planning, and Schedule Planning Templates • Historical estimated and actual size and time data • TIme Recording Log
1	Program Requirements	• Produce or obtain a requirements statement for the program. • Ensure the requirements statement is clear and unambiguous. • Resolve any questions.
2	Size Estimate	• Produce a program conceptual design. • Use the PROBE method to estimate the new and changed LOC required to develop this program. • Estimate the base, added, deleted, modified, and reused LOC. • Complete the Size Estimating Template and Project Plan Summary. • Calculate the 70 percent size prediction interval (you may use a spreadsheet).
3	Resource Estimate	• Use the PROBE method to estimate the time required to develop the new program. • Calculate the 70 percent size prediction interval (you may use a spreadsheet). • Using the To Date % from the most recently developed program as a guide, distribute the development time over the planned project phases.
4	Task and Schedule Planning	For projects requiring several days or more of work, complete the Task Planning and Schedule Planning Templates.
5	Defect Estimate	• Based on your To Date data on defects per new and changed LOC, estimate the total defects to be found in this program. • Based on your To Date % data, estimate the numbers of defects to be injected and removed by phase.
	Exit Criteria	• A documented requirements statement • The program conceptual design • A completed Size Estimating Template • For projects of several days duration, completed Task and Schedule Planning Templates • A Project Plan Summary with estimated program size, development time, and 70 percent prediction intervals • Completed Time Recording Log

TABLE C61 PSP2.1 DEVELOPMENT SCRIPT

Phase Number	Purpose	To guide the development of small programs
	Entry Criteria	• Requirements statement
		• Project Plan Summary with estimated program size and development time
		• For projects of several days' duration, completed Task Planning and Schedule Planning Templates
		• Time and Defect Recording Logs
		• Defect Type Standard and Coding Standard
1	Design	• Review the requirements and produce *an external specification to meet them.*
		• *Complete Function Specification and Operational Scenario Templates to record this specification.*
		• *Produce a design to meet this specification.*
		• *Record the design in Functional Specification, Operational Scenario, State Specification, and Logic Specification Templates as required.*
		• *Record in the Defect Recording Log any requirements defects found.*
		• Record time in Time Recording Log.
2	Design Review	• Follow the Design Review Checklist and review the design.
		• Fix all defects found.
		• Record defects in Defect Recording Log.
		• Record time in Time Recording Log.
3	Code	• Follow the Coding Standard and implement the design.
		• Record in the Defect Recording Log any requirements or design defects found.
		• Record time in Time Recording Log.
4	Code Review	• Follow the Code Review Checklist and review the code.
		• Fix all defects found.
		• Record defects in Defect Recording Log.
		• Record time in Time Recording Log.
5	Compile	• Compile the program until error free.
		• Fix all defects found.
		• Record defects in Defect Recording Log.
		• Record time in Time Recording Log.

TABLE C61   (continued)

6	Test	• Test until all tests run without error. • Fix all defects found. • Record defects in Defect Recording Log. • Record time in Time Recording Log. • Complete a Test Report Template on the tests conducted and results obtained.
	Exit Criteria	• A thoroughly tested program that conforms to the Coding Standard • ***Completed Design Templates*** • Completed Design Review and Code Review Checklists • Completed Test Report Template • Completed Defect Recording Log

TABLE C62 PSP2.1 POSTMORTEM SCRIPT

Phase Number	Purpose	To guide the PSP postmortem process
	Entry Criteria	• Problem description and requirements statement • Project Plan Summary with program size, development time, defect, **and prediction interval** data • For projects of several days' duration, completed Task Planning and Schedule Planning Templates • Completed Test Report Template • **Completed Design Templates** • Completed Design Review and Code Review Checklists • Completed Time Recording Log • Completed Defect Recording Log • A tested and running program that conforms to the Coding Standard
1	Defects Injected	• Determine from the Defect Recording Log the number of defects injected in each PSP2.1 phase. • Enter this number under Defects Injected—Actual on the Project Plan Summary.
2	Defects Removed	• Determine from the Defect Recording Log the number of defects removed in each PSP2.1 phase. • Enter this number under Defects Removed—Actual on the Project Plan Summary. • Calculate the actual overall process yield and enter it in the Project Plan Summary.
3	Size	• Count the LOC in the completed program. • Determine the base, reused, deleted, modified, added, total, total new and changed, and new reused LOC. • Enter these data in the Project Plan Summary.
4	Time	• Review the completed Time Recording Log. • Enter the total time spent in each PSP2.1 phase in the Actual column of the Project Plan Summary.
	Exit Criteria	• A fully tested program that conforms to the Coding Standard • **Completed Design Templates** • Completed Design Review and Code Review Checklists • A completed Test Report Template • Completed Project Plan Summary • Completed PIP forms describing process problems, improvement suggestions, and lessons learned • Completed Defect and Time Recording Logs

TABLE C63 PSP2.1 PROJECT PLAN SUMMARY

Student _____   Date _____

Program _____   Program # _____

Instructor _____   Language _____

Summary	Plan	Actual	To Date
LOC/Hour	_____	_____	_____
Planned Time	_____		_____
Actual Time		_____	_____
CPI(Cost-Performance Index)			_____
			(Planned/Actual)
% Reused	_____	_____	_____
% New Reused	_____	_____	_____
Test Defects/KLOC	_____	_____	_____
Total Defects/KLOC	_____	_____	_____
Yield %	_____	_____	_____
% Appraisal COQ	_____	_____	_____
% Failure COQ	_____	_____	_____
COQ A/F Ratio	_____	_____	_____

Program Size (LOC)	Plan	Actual	To Date
Base(B)	_____ (Measured)	_____ (Measured)	
Deleted (D)	_____ (Estimated)	_____ (Counted)	
Modified (M)	_____ (Estimated)	_____ (Counted)	
Added (A)	_____ (N − M)	_____ (T − B + D − R)	
Reused (R)	_____ (Estimated)	_____ (Counted)	_____
Total New and Changed (N)	_____ (Estimated)	_____ (A + M)	
Total LOC (T)	_____ (N + B − M − D + R)	_____ (Measured)	_____
Total New Reused	_____	_____	_____
Upper Prediction Interval (70%)	_____		
Lower Prediction Interval (70%)	_____		

TABLE C63   (continued)

Time in Phase (min.)	Plan	Actual	To Date	To Date %
Planning				
Design				
Design Review				
Code				
Code Review				
Compile				
Test				
Postmortem				
Total				
Total Time UPI (70%)				
Total Time LPI (70%)				

Defects Injected	Plan	Actual	To Date	To Date %
Planning				
Design				
Design Review				
Code				
Code Review				
Compile				
Test				
Total Development				

Defects Removed	Plan	Actual	To Date	To Date %
Planning				
Design				
Design Review				
Code				
Code Review				
Compile				
Test				
Total Development				
After Development				

Defect Removal Efficiency	Plan	Actual	To Date
Defects/Hour—Design Review			
Defects/Hour—Code Review			
Defects/Hour—Compile			
Defects/Hour—Test			
DRL(DLDR/UT)			
DRL(CodeReview/UT)			
DRL(Compile/UT)			

TABLE C64 PSP2.1 PROJECT PLAN SUMMARY INSTRUCTIONS

Purpose	To hold the estimated and actual project data in a convenient and readily retrievable form
Header	Enter the specified data.
Summary	• Enter the new and changed LOC per hour planned and actual for this program and for all programs developed to date. • Enter the planned and actual times for this program and the sums of the planned and actual times for all the exercises to date. • CPI = (To Date Planned Time)/(To Date Actual Time) • Enter the planned, actual, and To Date reuse data. • Enter the planned, actual, and To Date defect data. • Enter the planned and actual yields.
Cost of Quality	*Enter the % Appraisal COQ: the percentage of development time spent in design and code reviews.* *Enter the % Failure COQ: the percentage of development time spent in compile and test.* *Enter the A/F Ratio: the ratio of Appraisal COQ divided by Failure COQ.*
Program Size (LOC)	Prior to Development: • If you are modifying or enhancing an existing program, count that program's LOC and enter it under Base—Plan. • Enter the estimated new and changed LOC (N) from the Size Estimating Template. • Estimate the numbers of added (A) and modified (M) LOC so that N = A + M. • Estimate the numbers of deleted (D) and reused (R) LOC and combine with the measured base (B) LOC so that T = N + B − M − D + R. After Development: • If the base LOC (B) has changed, enter the new value. • Measure the total program size and enter it under Total LOC (T) —Actual. • Review your source code and, with the help of program 3A, determine the actual LOC that were deleted (D), modified (M), or reused (R). • Calculate the LOC of added code as A = T − B + D − R. • Calculate the total new and changed LOC as N = A + M.

TABLE C64 (continued)

Time in Phase	• Under Plan, enter your original estimate of the total development time and the time required by phase. • Under Actual, enter the actual time in minutes spent in each development phase. • Under To Date, enter the sum of the actual time and the To Date time from your most recently developed program. • Under To Date %, enter the percentage of To Date time in each phase.
Defects Injected	• Under Actual, enter the number of defects injected in each phase. • Under To Date, enter the sum of the actual numbers of defects injected in each phase and the To Date values from the most recently developed program. • Under To Date %, enter the percentage of the To Date defects injected by phase.
Defects Removed	• Under Actual, enter the number of defects removed in each phase. • Under To Date, enter the sum of the actual numbers of defects removed in each phase and the To Date values from the most recently developed program. • Under To Date %, enter the percentage of the To Date defects removed by phase. • After development, record any defects later found during program use, reuse, or modification.
Defect Removal Efficiency	• Under Plan, enter the planned efficiencies for this project. • Under Actual, enter the actual efficiencies achieved. • Under To Date, enter the actual efficiencies for all the projects to date.

TABLE C65 C++ PSP2.1 DESIGN REVIEW CHECKLIST

PROGRAM NAME AND #:

Purpose	To guide you in conducting an effective design review				
General	• As you complete each review step, check off that item in the box to the right. • Complete the checklist for one program unit before you start to review the next unit.				
Complete	Ensure the requirements, specifications, and high-level design are completely covered by the design: • All specified outputs are produced. • All needed inputs are furnished. • All required includes are stated.				
State Machine	*Verify the state machine design:* • *The structure has no hidden traps or loops.* • *It is complete; that is, all possible states have been identified.* • *It is orthogonal; that is, for every set of conditions there is one and only one possible next state.* • *The transitions from each state are complete and orthogonal. That is, from every state a unique next state is defined for every possible combination of state machine input values.*				

Logic	• Verify that program sequencing is proper:
	  ☐ Stacks, lists, and so on are in the proper order.
	  ☐ Recursion unwinds properly.
	• Verify that all loops are properly initiated, incremented, and terminated.				

Special Cases	Check all special cases: • Ensure proper operation with empty, full, minimum, maximum, negative, zero values for all variables. • Protect against out-of-limits, overflow, underflow conditions. • Ensure "impossible" conditions are absolutely impossible. • Handle all incorrect input conditions.				
Functional Use	• Verify that all functions, procedures, or objects are fully understood and properly used. • Verify that all externally referenced abstractions are precisely defined.				
Names	Verify the following • All special names and types are clear or specifically defined. • The scopes of all variables and parameters are self-evident or defined. • All named objects are used within their declared scopes.				
Standards	Review the design for conformance to all applicable design standards.				

TABLE C66 OPERATIONAL SCENARIO TEMPLATE

Student _____ Date _____

Program _____ Program # _____

Instructor _____ Language _____

Construct operational scenarios to cover the normal and abnormal program uses,
including user errors.

Scenario Number:		User Objective:	
Scenario Objective:			
Source	Step	Action	Comments

TABLE C67 OPERATIONAL SCENARIO TEMPLATE INSTRUCTIONS

Purpose	• This template holds descriptions of likely operational scenarios to be followed in using the program. • The template is used to ensure the designers consider all significant usage issues. • It is also used to specify test scenarios.
Header	Enter the following: • Your name and today's date • The program name and number • The instructor's name • The language you will use to write the program
General	• This template should be used for complete programs, subsystems, or systems. • Multiple scenarios may be grouped on a single template as long as they are clearly distinguished and have related objectives.
Scenario Number	When several scenarios are involved, reference numbers are required.
User Objective	List the users' likely purpose for the scenario, for example, to start the system and select the operational mode.
Scenario Objective	List the designer's purpose for the scenario, for example, to define the common errors that users can make when selecting operational modes.
Source	The source of the scenario action; for example, three sources could be user, program, and system.
Step	Provide sequence numbers for the scenario steps. These are needed when the scenario recycles, branches, or repeats.
Action	Describe the action the source takes, such as the following: • Enter incorrect mode selection. • Provide error message.
Comments	List significant information relating to the action, such as the following: • User enters an alphabetical rather than a numerical mode selection. • System message: "Incorrect selection, try again."

TABLE C68 FUNCTIONAL SPECIFICATION TEMPLATE

Student _____   Date _____

Program _____   Program # _____

Instructor _____   Language _____

Object/Class Name	Parent Classes	Attributes

Method Declaration	Method External Specification

TABLE C69 FUNCTIONAL SPECIFICATION TEMPLATE INSTRUCTIONS

Purpose	To hold an object's functional specifications You can use this template to describe functions and procedures when you do not use object-oriented methods. If you do, replace the word *object* with either of the words *function* or *procedure* as appropriate.
Header	Enter the following: • Your name and today's date • The program name and number • The instructor's name • The language you will use to write the program
General	If several objects belong to the same class, group these multiple, related specification templates together.
Object/Class Name	• Enter the object name and the classes from which it inherits. • List the class names starting with the most immediate. • Where practical, list the full inheritance hierarchy.
Attributes	Enter any parameters whose values are externally visible and impact object behavior.
Method Declaration	• List the declaration for each object method. • Include all the required variables and parameters. • Include the required type designations. • Use the format used to declare the method in the program.
Method External Specification	• Describe the operation performed by each method. • Where possible, use a formal or a mathematical specification. • Include all returns and exception conditions.

TABLE C70 STATE SPECIFICATION TEMPLATE

Student _____   Date _____

Program _____   Program # _____

Instructor_____   Language _____

Object _____   Routine _____

State #1	Description	Attributes
state #1	Transition Conditions	
state #2		
. . .		
. . .		
state #n		

State #2	Description	Attributes
state #1	Transition Conditions	
state #2		
. . .		
. . .		
state #n		

. . .

State #n	Description	Attributes
state #1	Transition Conditions	
state #2		
. . .		
. . .		
state #n		

TABLE C71 STATE SPECIFICATION TEMPLATE INSTRUCTIONS

Purpose	To hold the state specifications for each object or program module Even if the design does not use object-oriented methods, this template should be useful for specifying program state behavior.
Header	Enter the following: • Your name and today's date • The program name and number • The instructor's name • The language you will use to write the program • Object/Routine: List the name of the object and routine whose state behavior is being described.
General	Complete a segment of this template for each state. For example, with four states, the value of n would be 4. There would then be four complete sections and for each section, there would be four rows of next states. Use additional space as needed.
State #1	While states could merely be numbered, it is helpful to give each state a descriptive name. For example, a state machine with three states could use names such as Empty, Partial, Full.
Description	• This section holds a text description of the state.
Attributes	List the variable values that characterize the state. For example, if the full state is characterized by $K == 10$ and $n == 3$, then the attribute entry would be $K == 10, n == 3$. • Be as precise as possible.
Next State #1	• Enter here the name of state #1. • Under every state, list the names of all the other states. For example, under State Empty, the rows would be Empty, Partial, Full.
Transition Conditions	• For each next state, list the conditions under which a transition is made from the current state to this state. • Be as precise as possible. • If the transition is impossible, enter impossible.
Transition Condition Examples	For the state Empty, the transition conditions might be as follows: • Empty: no input • Partial: any input • Full: impossible

TABLE C72 LOGIC SPECIFICATION TEMPLATE

Student _____ Date _____

Program _____ Program # _____

Instructor_____ Language _____

Object _____ Function _____

INCLUDES:

TYPE DEFINITIONS:

Declaration: _____

Reference: _____

Logic reference numbers	Program logic, in pseudocode

TABLE C73 LOGIC SPECIFICATION TEMPLATE INSTRUCTIONS

Purpose	To hold the pseudocode logic for each object or modular program element A separate copy of this template should be used for each program. • If the program design does not fit on a single template page, either it is too large and should be partitioned into several smaller programs or the pseudocode is at too detailed a level. • If object-oriented design methods are not used, this template can still be used for specifying function, procedure, and main routine logic.
Header	Enter the following: • Your name and today's date • The program name and number • The instructor's name • The language you will use to write the program • Object/Function: List the name of the function being specified together with the object to which it belongs.
Includes	• List all the new or unusual includes required by this program. • Project standard includes should not be separately listed. • Where standard includes are used, the statement "PROJECT STANDARD INCLUDES" should be entered. • Includes for abstractions should be included with their design and implementation descriptions.
Type Definitions	• When unusual or special types are used, they should be defined or a reference given to the definition. • To save implementation time, define all or most of the special types in this template.
Declaration	• Give the function declaration exactly as it is to be written in the program. • Except where noted, all declarations, initializations, and terminations are defined during implementation.
Reference	When a clear understanding of this function requires information not in the design, identify where that information can be found.
Logic Reference Numbers	• Give a standard reference number for each significant logic statement. • Number every procedure call, loop, and conditional statement. • These reference numbers are useful during design reviews and inspections.
Program Logic	• List the pseudocode for the program. • Use a separate line for each significant function. • Use mathematical or common language statements where needed for clarity. • Include comments where needed to explain the logic.

TABLE C74 PSP3 PROCESS SCRIPT

Phase Number	Purpose	To guide you in developing component-level programs
	Inputs Required	• Problem description *or component specifications* • Process forms and standards • Historical estimated and actual size and time data • Stop watch (optional)

1	*Requirements and Planning*	• *Produce the requirements and development plan:*
		  ☐ *Requirements document*
		  ☐ *Design concept*
		  ☐ *Size, quality, resource, and schedule plans*
		• *Produce a master Issue Tracking Log.*

2	*High-level Design (HLD)*	*Produce the design and implementation strategy:* • *Functional specifications* • *State specifications* • *Operational scenarios* • *Reuse specifications* • *Development strategy* • *Test strategy*
3	*High-level Design Review (HLDR)*	• *Review the high-level design.* • *Review the development and test strategy.* • *Fix and log all defects found.* • *Note outstanding issues in the Issue Tracking Log.* • *Record in the Defect Recording Log all defects found.*
4	Development	• Design the program. • Review the design and fix and log all defects found. • Implement the design, using design templates where appropriate. • Review the code and fix and log all defects found. • Compile the program and fix and log all defects found. • Test the program and fix and log all defects found. • Complete the Time Recording Log. • *Reassess and recycle as needed.*

TABLE C74 (continued)

5	Postmortem	• Complete the Project Plan Summary form with actual time, defect, and size data. • ***Completed Cycle Summary form with actual cycle data.***
	Exit Criteria	• A thoroughly tested program • Completed Project Plan Summary with estimated and actual data • Completed estimating and planning templates • Completed Design Templates • Completed Design Review Checklist and Code Review Checklist • Completed Test Report Template • ***Completed Issue Tracking Log*** • Completed PIP forms • Completed Defect and Time Recording Logs

TABLE C75 PSP3 PLANNING SCRIPT

Phase Number	Purpose	To guide the PSP planning process
	Inputs Required	• Problem description • PSP3 Project Plan Summary **and Cycle** Summary • Size Estimating, Task Planning, and Schedule Planning Templates • Historical estimated and actual size and time data • TIme Recording Log
1	Program Requirements	• Produce or obtain a requirements statement for the program. • Ensure the requirements statement is clear and unambiguous. • Resolve any questions.
2	Size Estimate	• Produce a program conceptual design. • Use the PROBE method to estimate the new and changed LOC required to develop this program. • Estimate the base, added, deleted, modified, and reused LOC. • Complete the Size Estimating Template and Project Plan Summary. • Calculate the 70 percent size prediction interval for the total project (you may use a spreadsheet).
3	*Cyclic Development Strategy*	*Subdivide the program development into modules of about 100 and no more than 250 new and changed LOC.* • *Allocate the LOC to be developed among the cycles.* • *Enter the size data in the Cycle Summary—Plan.*
4	Resource Estimate	• Use the PROBE method to estimate the time required to develop the new program. • Calculate the 70 percent prediction interval for the total project (you may use a spreadsheet). • *Subdivide this total development time among the development cycles.* • Using the To Date % from the most recently developed program as a guide, distribute the development time over the planned project phases *of each development cycle*. • Enter the time data in the Cycle Summary Plan.
5	Task and Schedule Planning	For projects requiring several days or more of work, complete the Task Planning and Schedule Planning Templates.

TABLE C75 (continued)

6	Defect Estimate	• Based on your To Date data on defects per new and changed LOC, estimate the total defects to be found in this program.
		• Based on your To Date % data, estimate the numbers of defects to be injected and removed by cycle and by phase.
	Exit Criteria	• A documented requirements statement
		• The program conceptual design
		• A completed Size Estimating Template
		• For projects of several days' duration, completed Task Planning and Schedule Planning Templates
		• Project Plan Summary **and Cycle Plan Summary** forms with estimated program size and development time
		• 70 percent prediction intervals for the total project
		• Completed Time Recording Log

TABLE C76 PSP3 HIGH-LEVEL DESIGN SCRIPT

Phase Number	Purpose	To guide the PSP3 High-level design process
	Entry Criteria	Check that the following are on hand: • The requirements statement • The conceptual design • Size and time estimates • The Issue Tracking Log
1	External Specifications	• Complete Operational Scenario Templates for all normal and abnormal uses of external functions. • Complete a State Specification Template for the complete program. • Complete a Function Specification Template for the overall program.
2	Module Design	• Subdivide the program into several modular units. • Specify the external characteristics of each of these modules with Operational Scenario and Functional Specification Templates. • Complete Logic and State Specification Templates for the highest level main or control routine. • Record key issues or concerns in the Issue Tracking Log.
3	Prototypes	Identify, plan for, and perform needed prototype experiments.
4	Development Strategy	Decide on a strategy for developing and testing the program in cycles. Where possible • keep each cycle to about 100 LOC of new and changed code, • develop complete modules in one cycle. • minimize the amount of test scaffolding required, and • expose major development risks as early as possible.
5	Development Strategy Documentation	Produce the development strategy: • Define the program functions and/or modules to be produced in each development cycle. • Specify the testing approach to progressively integrate the modules in each cycle.
6	Issue Tracking Log	Review the Issue Tracking Log during design and make appropriate additions or changes.

	Exit Criteria	• The overall program design, including the specification templates for the main or control routine
		• The design specification for all the planned program component modules:
		  ☐ Function Specification Templates
		  ☐ Operational Scenario Templates
		• The cycle development and test strategy
		• Also:
		  ☐ A completed Cycle Summary with plan data
		  ☐ An updated Issue Tracking Log

TABLE C77 PSP3 HIGH-LEVEL DESIGN REVIEW SCRIPT

Phase Number	Purpose	To guide the PSP3 High-level design review process
	Entry Criteria	Check that the following are on hand: • The requirements statement • The design specifications for all the planned component modules, including the Function Specification and Operational Scenario Templates • All Design Specification Templates for the total program and main routine • The cycle development strategy • The Issue Tracking Log
1	Design Coverage	Verify that the requirements are covered by the design: • All the required functions are specified. • The high-level design topics in the Issue Tracking Log have been addressed. • The required design materials have been produced.
2	State Machine Verification	Verify the state machine designs: • The states are complete and orthogonal. • The transition conditions from each state are complete and orthogonal.
3	Logic Verification	Verify the high-level design logic. Use a defined method such as the following: • Execution tables • Trace tables • Verification proofs
4	Design Consistency Verification	Verify that all special names and types are clear, consistent, and according to established standards.
5	Reuse Verification	Verify that the reused functions are available and that their planned use is proper.
6	Development Strategy Verification	Review the development strategy to ensure that • all required functions are provided, • the necessary functions are available consistent with the testing strategy, and • the test strategy covers all the required functions and the key program states.
7	Defect Fixes	• Fix all defects found. • Record defects in the Defect Recording Log.
	Exit Criteria	At completion you must have the following: • The completed high-level design • Updated Issue Tracking Log • Completed Time Recording Log • Completed Defect Recording Log

TABLE C78 PSP3 DEVELOPMENT SCRIPT

Phase Number	Purpose	To guide the development of component-level programs
	Entry Criteria	• ***Module functional and operational specifications*** • ***Development and test strategy*** • ***Completed high-level design review*** • ***Updated Issue Tracking Log*** • Time Recording Log and Defect Recording Log • Defect Type Standard and Coding Standard
1	***Module* Design**	• Review the ***module*** requirements and produce an external specification to meet them. • Complete Function Specification and Operational Scenario Templates to record this specification. • Produce a design to meet these specifications. • Record the design in Functional Specification, Operational Specification, State Specification, and Logic Specification Templates as required. • ***Complete the design for the module test materials and facilities.*** • Record in the Defect Recording Log any defects found. • Record time in Time Recording Log.
2	Design Review	• Follow the Design Review Checklist and review the ***module and test materials*** designs. • Fix all defects found. • Record defects in Defect Recording Log. • Record time in Time Recording Log.
3	Code	• Follow the Coding Standard and implement the design. • Record in the Defect Recording Log any defects found. • Record time in Time Recording Log.
4	Code Review	• Follow the Code Review Checklist and review the ***module and test*** code. • Fix all defects found. • Record defects in Defect Recording Log. • Record time in Time Recording Log.
5	Compile	• Compile the program ***and test materials*** until error free. • Fix all defects found. • Record defects in Defect Recording Log. • Record time in Time Recording Log.

TABLE C78   (continued)

6	Test	• Test *the modules* until all tests run without error.
		• Fix all defects found.
		• Record defects in Defect Recording Log.
		• Record time in Time Recording Log.
		• Complete a Test Report Template on the tests conducted and results obtained.
7	*Reassessment and Recycling*	• *Record data on the development cycle.*
		• *Reassess the status against plan and decide to continue as planned or make changes.*
	Exit Criteria	• Thoroughly tested *modules* that conform to the Coding Standard
		• Completed Design Templates
		• Completed Design Review and Code Review Checklists
		• *Updated Cycle Summary form with actual data*
		• Completed Test Report Template
		• Completed Defect Recording Log
		• Completed Time Recording Log
		• *Updated Issue Tracking Log*

TABLE C79 PSP3 POSTMORTEM SCRIPT

Phase Number	Purpose	To guide the PSP postmortem process
	Entry Criteria	• Problem description and requirements statement • Project Plan Summary with program size, development time, defect, and prediction interval data • ***Completed Cycle Summary*** • For projects of several days' duration, completed Task Planning and Schedule Planning Templates • Completed Test Report Template • Completed Design Templates • Completed Design Review and Code Review Checklists • Completed Time Recording Log • Completed Defect Recording Log • A tested and running program that conforms to the Coding Standard • ***Updated Issue Tracking Log***
1	Defects Injected	• Determine from the Defect Recording Log the number of defects injected in each PSP3 phase. • Enter this number under Defects Injected—Actual on the Project Plan Summary.
2	Defects Removed	• Determine from the Defect Recording Log the number of defects removed in each PSP3 phase. • Enter this number under Defects Removed—Actual on the Project Plan Summary. • Calculate the actual overall process yield and enter it in the Project Plan Summary.
3	Size	• Count the LOC in the completed program. • Determine the base, reused, deleted, modified, added, total, total new and changed, and new reused LOC. • Enter these data in the Project Plan Summary.
4	Time	• Review the completed Time Recording Log. • Enter the total time spent in each PSP3 phase in the Actual column of the Project Plan Summary.
	Exit Criteria	• A fully tested program that conforms to the Coding Standard • Completed Design Templates • Completed Design Review and Code Review Checklists • A completed Test Report Template • Completed Project Plan and Cycle Summary forms • Completed PIP forms describing process problems, improvement suggestions, and lessons learned • Completed Defect and Time Recording Logs • ***Updated Issue Tracking Log***

TABLE C80   PSP3 PROJECT PLAN SUMMARY

Student _____   Date _____

Program _____   Program # _____

Instructor _____   Language _____

Summary	Plan	Actual	To Date
LOC/Hour	_____	_____	_____
Planned Time	_____		_____
Actual Time		_____	_____
CPI(Cost-Performance Index)			_____
			(Planned/Actual)
% Reused	_____	_____	_____
% New Reused	_____	_____	_____
Test Defects/KLOC	_____	_____	_____
Total Defects/KLOC	_____	_____	_____
Yield	_____	_____	_____
% Appraisal COQ	_____	_____	_____
% Failure COQ	_____	_____	_____
COQ A/F Ratio	_____	_____	_____

Program Size (LOC)	Plan	Actual	To Date
Base(B)	_____ (Measured)	_____ (Measured)	
Deleted (D)	_____ (Estimated)	_____ (Counted)	
Modified (M)	_____ (Estimated)	_____ (Counted)	
Added (A)	_____ (N − M)	_____ (T − B + D − R)	
Reused (R)	_____ (Estimated)	_____ (Counted)	_____
Total New and Changed (N)	_____ (Estimated)	_____ (A + M)	
Total LOC (T)	_____ (N + B − M − D + R)	_____ (Measured)	_____
Total New Reused	_____	_____	_____
Upper Prediction Interval (70%)	_____		
Lower Prediction Interval (70%)	_____		

Time in Phase (min.)	Plan	Actual	To Date	To Date %
Planning	_____	_____	_____	_____
High-level Design	_____	_____	_____	_____
High-level Design Review	_____	_____	_____	_____
Detailed Design	_____	_____	_____	
Detailed Design Review	_____	_____	_____	_____
Code	_____	_____	_____	_____
Code Review	_____	_____	_____	_____
Compile	_____	_____	_____	_____
Test	_____	_____	_____	_____
Postmortem	_____	_____	_____	_____
Total	_____	_____	_____	_____
Total Time UPI (70%)	_____			
Total Time LPI (70%)	_____			

TABLE C80 (continued)

Defects Injected	Plan	Actual	To Date	To Date %
Planning				
High-level Design				
High-level Design Review				
Detailed Design				
Detailed Design Review				
Code				
Code Review				
Compile				
Test				
Total Development				

Defects Removed	Plan	Actual	To Date	To Date %
Planning				
High-level Design				
High-level Design Review				
Detailed Design				
Detailed Design Review				
Code				
Code Review				
Compile				
Test				
Total Development				
After Development				

Defect Removal Efficiency	Plan	Actual	To Date
Defects/Hour—Design Review			
Defects/Hour—Code Review			
Defects/Hour—Compile			
Defects/Hour—Test			
DRL(DLDR/UT)			
DRL(CodeReview/UT)			
DRL(Compile/UT)			

TABLE C81 PSP3 PROJECT PLAN SUMMARY INSTRUCTIONS

Purpose	To hold the estimated and actual project data in a convenient and readily retrievable form
Header	Enter the specified data.
Summary	• Enter the new and changed LOC per hour planned and actual for this program and for all programs developed to date. • Enter the planned and actual times for this program and the sums of the planned and actual times for all the exercises to date. • CPI = (To Date Planned Time)/(To Date Actual Time) • Enter the planned, actual, and To Date reuse data. • Enter the planned, actual, and To Date defect data. • Enter the planned and actual yield.
Cost of Quality	• Enter the % Appraisal COQ: the percentage of development time spent in design and code reviews. • Enter the % Failure COQ: the percentage of development time spent in compile and test. • Enter the A/F Ratio: the ratio of Appraisal COQ divided by Failure COQ.
Program Size (LOC)	Prior to Development: • If you are modifying or enhancing an existing program, count that program's LOC and enter it under Base—Plan. • Enter the estimated new and changed LOC (N) from the Size Estimating Template. • Estimate the numbers of added (A) and modified (M) LOC so that $N = A + M$. • Estimate the numbers of deleted (D) and reused (R) LOC and combine with the measured base (B) LOC so that $T = N + B - M - D + R$. After Development: • If the base LOC (B) has changed, enter the new value. • Measure the total program size and enter it under Total LOC (T)—Actual. • Review your source code and, with the help of program 3A, determine the actual LOC that were deleted (D), modified (M), or reused (R). • Calculate the LOC of added code as $A = T - B + D - R$. • Calculate the total new and changed LOC as $N = A + M$.

TABLE C81   (continued)

Time in Phase	• Under Plan, enter your original estimate of the total development time and the time required by phase. • Under Actual, enter the actual time in minutes spent in each development phase. • Under To Date, enter the sum of the actual time and the To Date time from your most recently developed program. • Under To Date %, enter the percentage of To Date time in each phase.
Defects Injected	• Under Actual, enter the number of defects injected in each phase. • Under To Date, enter the sum of the actual numbers of defects injected in each phase and the To Date values from the most recently developed program. • Under To Date %, enter the percentage of the To Date defects injected by phase.
Defects Removed	• Under Actual, enter the number of defects removed in each phase. • Under To Date, enter the sum of the actual numbers of defects removed in each phase and the To Date values from the most recently developed program. • Under To Date %, enter the percentage of To Date defects removed by phase. • After development, record any defects later found during program use, reuse, or modification.
Defect Removal Efficiency	• Under Plan, enter the planned efficiencies for this project. • Under Actual, enter the actual efficiencies achieved. • Under To Date, enter the actual efficiencies for all the projects to date.

TABLE C82 CYCLE SUMMARY

PLAN _____ ACTUAL _____

Student _____ Date _____

Program _____ Program # _____

Instructor _____ Language _____

Cycles	To Date	1	2	3	4	5	Total
Program Size (LOC):							
Base(B)							
Deleted (D)							
Modified (M)							
Added (A)							
Reused (R)							
Total New and Changed (N)							
Total LOC (T)							
Total New Reused							
Time in Phase (min.)							
Design							
Design Review							
Code							
Code Review							
Compile							
Test							
Total							
Defects Injected							
Design							
Design Review							
Code							
Code Review							
Compile							
Test							
Total							
Defects Removed							
Design							
Design Review							
Code							
Code Review							
Compile							
Test							
Total							

TABLE C83 CYCLE SUMMARY INSTRUCTIONS

Purpose	To hold the estimated and actual cycle development data in a convenient and readily retrievable form Unless such data are promptly recorded when the cycle is planned and again when completed, they will be hard to reconstruct. An historical record of such data provides a sound basis for planning and tracking larger projects.
Planned/Actual	This form can be used to hold planned or actual cyclic data. Check which is the case.
Header	Enter the specified data.
General	If more than five cycles are used, use multiple copies of this form and replace the cycle numbers.
To Date	• This column will typically be empty unless previous cycles have been recorded on another form. • When this is a second or later sheet, enter here the total column from the Cycle Summary for the previous cycles.
1,2,3,4,5	Enter the actual or planned data for each cycle.
Total	Total the numbers for all the cycles, including the To Date column.
Program Size	These data are particularly difficult to reconstruct after the fact. It is thus wise to measure and to record the actual values during or immediately after completing each cycle.
TIme in Phase	• These data are relatively simple to reconstruct, as long as the time log entries include a notation for the development cycle involved. • This notation can be made in the comments space.
Defects	• The defect data can be readily reconstructed if the phase entries include a cycle number. • The cycle of the phase removed can be readily determined at the time of removal. • The cycle of the phase injected may be difficult to determine.

TABLE C84 C++ PSP3 DESIGN REVIEW CHECKLIST

PROGRAM NAME AND #:

Purpose	To guide you in conducting an effective design review				
General	• As you complete each review step, check off that item in the box to the right. • Complete the checklist for one program unit before you start to review the next unit. • *As you encounter issues whose resolution must be deferred, record them in the Issue Tracking Log.*				
Complete	Ensure the requirements, specifications, and high-level design are completely covered by the design: • All specified outputs are produced. • All needed inputs are furnished. • All required includes are stated.				
State Machine	Verify the state machine design: • The structure has no hidden traps or loops. • It is complete; that is, all possible states have been identified. • It is orthogonal; that is, for every set of conditions there is one and only one possible next state. • The transitions from each state are complete and orthogonal. That is, from every state, a unique next state is defined for every possible combination of state machine input values.				
Logic	• Verify that program sequencing is proper: ☐ Stacks, lists, and so on are in the proper order. ☐ Recursion unwinds properly. • Verify that all loops are properly initiated, incremented, and terminated. • *Use defined verification methods such as execution tables, trace tables, or mathematical verification.*				

TABLE C84 (continued)

Special Cases	Check all special cases: • Ensure proper operation with empty, full, minimum, maximum, negative, zero values for all variables. • Protect against out of limits, overflow, underflow conditions. • Ensure "impossible" conditions are absolutely impossible • Handle all incorrect input conditions				
Functional Use	• Verify that all functions, procedures, or objects are fully understood and properly used. • Verify that all externally referenced abstractions are precisely defined.				
Names	Verify the following: • All special names and types are clear or specifically defined. • The scopes of all variables and parameters are self-evident or defined. • All named objects are used within their declared scopes.				
Standards	Review the design for conformance to all applicable design standards.				

ITL No. _____

TABLE C85 PSP ISSUE TRACKING LOG

Student _____   Date   _____
Program _____   Program # _____
Instructor _____   Language _____

Issue #: _____ Date: _____ Phase: _____		
Description: _____		
Resolution: _____		
Date:		
Issue #: _____ Date: _____ Phase: _____		
Description: _____		
Resolution: _____		
Date:		
Issue #: _____ Date: _____ Phase: _____		
Description: _____		
Resolution: _____		
Date:		
Issue #: _____ Date: _____ Phase: _____		
Description: _____		
Resolution: _____		
Date:		
Issue #: _____ Date: _____ Phase: _____		
Description: _____		
Resolution: _____		
Date:		
Issue #: _____ Date: _____ Phase: _____		
Description: _____		
Resolution: _____		
Date:		

TABLE C86 ISSUE TRACKING LOG INSTRUCTIONS

Purpose	• To provide an orderly way to record, trace, and manage project issues. • On large projects, issues are often lost or forgotten because there is no orderly way to record them. • When developers defer issues for later handling, they need to ensure they are not forgotten.
General	Use the Issue Tracking Log as follows: • To record issues that are deferred for later handling • To record potential problems that should be checked • To record issues that may have been overlooked • To prioritize the issues to be addressed in each phase • To track issue handling Keep an Issue Tracking Log form on hand while using PSP3 and record all problems that need future attention.
ITL Number	If multiple pages are required, enter a unique number to identify each Issue Tracking Log page.
Issue Number	• Number each issue. • To avoid confusion, these numbers should be unique. • Where several people are involved in a common project, each should be assigned a number series such as 1001, 2001, etc.

Description	• Describe the issue as clearly as possible for example:
	  ☐ The change that must be made
	  ☐ The issue that must be checked
	  ☐ The test that must be run
	  ☐ The phase in which it was encountered
	• Describe the issue in enough detail so that you can later take the suggested action.

Date	Enter the date on which you identified and recorded the issue.
Resolution	Describe how the issue was resolved.
Date	Enter the date the issue was resolved.
Tracking	Keep the Issue Tracking Log in a central place for consultation at the beginning of and during each development phase.

D

APPENDIX
The Personal Software
Process Exercises

This book contains 19 PSP exercise programs (1A to 10A and 1B to 9B) and five report assignments (R1 to R5). There is some flexibility regarding the order in which you can do these exercises. However, some constraints apply to the relationships of the programs to the PSP process levels, textbook chapters, and other programs. This appendix describes the exercise programs and shows how they are related so you can take advantage of their reuse possibilities.

This appendix has the following parts:

1. A description of the 19 exercise programs
2. The specifications for those exercises
3. A description of the five report assignments
4. The standard relationships among the textbook chapters, process levels, and program exercises

Table D1 contains a brief description of the program and report exercises; Table D2 shows the standard assignment pattern given in the textbook chapters. This appendix describes the various prerequisites and dependencies among the programs and chapters so that you can design other assignment patterns to better fit your needs. I suggest, however, that you start with the 10 A series programs as a basic set and add B series programs where appropriate if time permits. (Depending on the number of programs your schedule allows, the suggested programs are shown in Table D3.) For example, if you have time to develop only eight programs, do programs 1A through 6A, program 8A, and program 10A.

The exercises in this book are listed separately from the textbook chapters and process versions so you can easily modify them or add new ones. For

TABLE D1 THE PSP EXERCISES

a) Program Exercises

Program #	Brief Program Description
1A	Using a linked list, write a program to calculate the mean and standard deviation of a set of data.
2A	Write a program to count program LOC.
3A	Enhance program 2A to count total program and object LOC.
4A	Using a linked list, write a program to calculate the linear regression parameters.
5A	Write a program to perform a numerical integration.
6A	Enhance program 4A to calculate the linear regression parameters and the prediction interval.
7A	Using a linked list, write a program to calculate the correlation of two sets of data.
8A	Write a program to sort a linked list.
9A	Using a linked list, write a program to do a χ^2 test for a normal distribution.
10A	Using a linked list, write a program to calculate the 3-parameter multiple regression parameters and the prediction interval.
1B	Write a program to store and retrieve numbers in a file.
2B	Enhance program 1B to modify records in a file.
3B	Enhance program 2B to handle common user errors.
4B	Enhance program 3B to handle further user error types.
5B	Enhance program 4B to handle arrays of real numbers.
6B	Enhance program 5B to calculate the linear regression parameters from a file.
7B	Enhance program 6B to calculate the linear regression parameters and the prediction interval.
8B	Enhance program 5B to sort a file.
9B	Write a program to do a χ^2 test for a normal distribution from data stored in a file.

b) Report Exercises

Program #	Brief Report Description
R1	LOC counting standard: Count logical LOC in the language you use to develop the PSP exercises.
R2	Coding standard: Provide one logical LOC per physical LOC.
R3	Defect analysis report: Analyze the defects for programs 1A through 3A.
R4	Midterm analysis report of process progress
R5	Final report of process progress, quality, and lessons learned

example, if you wanted to use the COBOL language to write the exercises, you could pattern a new C series of programs on the A and B series in the text, as follows:

Program 1C: Write program 1B, as described in the text.

Program 2C: Write program 2A, as described in the text.

Program 3C through 7C: Write programs 2B through 6B, as described in the text.

Program 8C: Write program 7B, but instead of using program 5A to do the numerical integration, call for the program user to enter the 70% and 90% $p(\alpha/2)$ values for the t distribution.

Program 9C: Write program 8B, as described in the text.

Program 10C: Write program 9B, but instead of using program 5A to do the numerical integration, call for the program user to enter the nearest values of the normal distribution for each cell and do the interpolation in the program. Also, produce the value of Q as the answer and leave the program user to look up the p value in Table A3 for the χ^2 distribution.

D1   Guidelines for Doing the Exercises

The exercises in this book are designed to provide you with experience and with data on your use of disciplined software methods. This experience and data will help you to decide which methods to use and to establish an orderly program of personal improvement. Large-scale software development is not a solo activity, so it is perfectly acceptable for you to get help from your classmates and associates. The ground rules for getting such assistance are as follows:

1. Your principal goal should be to turn in work that is correct. If you are not sure how to do something, find out and do it correctly. If you have completed the program and are not sure about some entries in the Project Plan Summary, complete the summary as best you can but find out how to complete it properly and correct it before you turn it in. **Do not turn in incorrect homework**. While it is important that you turn in your work on time, it is much more important that it be correct.

2. If you have a technical question, you may ask your associates for help. You must also record the point in the process where you got this assistance and the time you and your associates spent on the question.

3. You must make your own conceptual designs, size estimates, and resource estimates. Once you have completed them, you may ask that your associates review and comment on them. You may also change your estimates as a result of the reviews. If you do, submit a copy of your original estimate

TABLE D2 THE STANDARD ASSIGNMENT PLAN

Lecture Number	Chapter	Number of Lectures	Program Number	Process Number	Other Assignments
1	1	1/2			
1	2	1/2	1A	PSP0	
2	3	1/2			
2	4	1/2	2A	PSP0.1	R1 LOC Counting Standard R2 Coding Standard
3	5	1	3A	PSP0.1	R3 Defect Analysis Report
4	5	1	4A	PSP1	
5	6	1	5A	PSP1.1	
6	7	1	6A	PSP1.1	
7	8	1			R4 Midterm Report, including design and code-review checklists
8	9	1	7A	PSP2	Read Appendix B
9	10	1	8A	PSP2	
10	10	1	9A	PSP2.1	
11	11	1	10A	PSP3	
12	12	1			
13	12	1			R5 Final report
14	13	1			
15	14	1			

together with the revised one. You must also record the point in the process where you got this assistance and the time you and your associates spent in this review.

4. You must design the program yourself, but you may ask your associates to review your design when you are through. You may change the design as a result of this review, and you must record all defects found in the defect log, noting that they were found during this peer review. You must also record the time you and your associates spent in this review.

5. You must produce the source code for the program yourself, but you may ask your associates to review your code when you are through. You may change the code as a result, and you must record all defects found in the de-

TABLE D3 SUGGESTED PROGRAM ASSIGNMENTS

Program Number	Total Number of Programs for Course												
	7	8	9	10	11	12	13	14	15	16	17	18	19
1A	X	X	X	X	X	X	X	X	X	X	X	X	X
2A	X	X	X	X	X	X	X	X	X	X	X	X	X
3A	X	X	X	X	X	X	X	X	X	X	X	X	X
4A	X	X	X	X	X	X	X	X	X	X	X	X	X
5A	X	X	X	X	X	X	X	X	X	X	X	X	X
6A	X	X	X	X	X	X	X	X	X	X	X	X	X
7A				X	X	X	X	X	X	X	X	X	X
8A		X	X	X	X	X	X	X	X	X	X	X	X
9A			X	X	X	X	X	X	X	X	X	X	X
10A	X	X	X	X	X	X	X	X	X	X	X	X	X
1B					X	X	X	X	X	X	X	X	X
2B						X	X	X	X	X	X	X	X
3B							X	X	X	X	X	X	X
4B								X	X	X	X	X	X
5B									X	X	X	X	X
6B										X	X	X	X
7B											X	X	X
8B												X	X
9B													X

fect log, noting that they were found during this peer review. You must also record the time you and your associates spent in this review.

6. You are expected to compile and test the programs yourself; however, you may request assistance where needed. You must also record the defects found, the point in the process where you got this assistance, and the time you and your associates spent on this process.

While there is nothing wrong with getting help, it does take time. You should thus monitor the amount of help you get to ensure the results are worth the time.

D2   The Programming Exercises

The specifications for the 19 exercise programs are given in Section D3. Table D4(a) shows the prerequisite relationships among the program exercises and the textbook chapters. Table D4(b) shows the chapter and exercise prerequisites for the process levels. For each program exercise, you should use the highest level process for which you are qualified.

   As Table D1 shows, several of the programs are enhancements of other exercise programs. There are several ways to reuse prior design and code in developing these programs. Figure D1 shows the relationships among the A series programs. The degree to which you can actually achieve the potential levels of reuse is determined by how you design the programs. If you consider their possible future reuse in the design, you are more likely to be successful. Accidental reuse is rarely successful, even when the desired function is identical to the one you have previously developed. This is because successful reuse is more than a functional problem. You must also assure compatibility of the variable and parameter types, error handling, and packaging. While you need not completely design the subsequent application to ensure reuse, you must use a common set of standards and conventions.

   From Fig. D1, the following patterns are clear for the A series programs:

- The linked list used in program 1A can potentially be adopted for reuse in programs 4A and 7A. When these programs are further enhanced to produce programs 6A, 8A, 9A, and 10A, the linked list capability is potentially reused again. Thus the linked list produced with program 1A is potentially reused with six other A series programs.

- Program 2A is enhanced to make program 3A but is not further changed. These programs are used to count the size of every program developed with these exercises.

- Program 5A, numerical integration, is used in programs 6A, 7A, 9A, and 10A.

- Programs 4A, 6A, and 10A form a linear regression sequence. These programs reuse the linked list and numerical integration functions of programs 1A and 5A.

- Program 8A provides sort capabilities for the linked list. This function is used only in program 9A.

- The χ^2 test in program 9A uses both the linked list, sort, and numerical integration.

   The relationships of the B series programs with each other and with the A series are shown in Fig. D2. The following reuse patterns are clear from this figure:

- Programs 1B through 5B are used to build and progressively enhance a simple file-handling system.
- Program 6B does linear regression from the data in the file system. If you had previously written program 4A, you could consider reusing some of its functions.
- Program 7B calculates the prediction interval from a file. If you had previously written program 6A, you could reuse some of its functions.
- Program 8B further enhances the file system by adding a sort capability.
- Program 9B performs a χ^2 test from data in the file. If you had previously written program 9A, you could reuse some of its functions.

You may choose not to take full advantage of all these reuse possibilities; however, you should attempt to do so. There are potentially important savings for

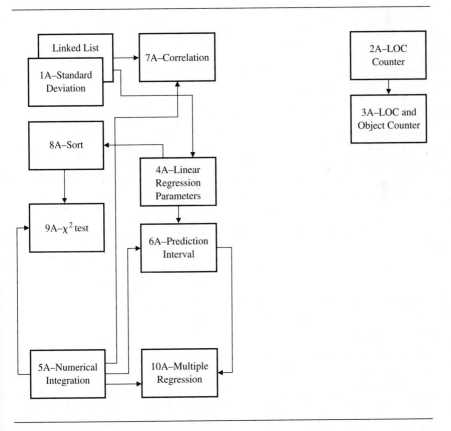

FIGURE D1
Program Evolution and Reuse—A Series Programs

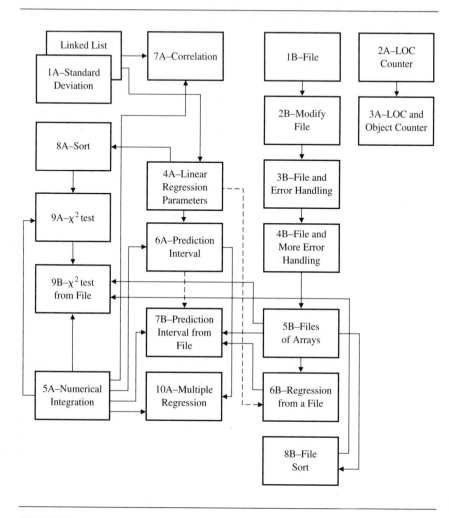

FIGURE D2
Program Evolution and Reuse—A and B Series Programs

many of the programs. In particular, the development of programs 9A, 9B, and 10A can be significantly reduced by effectively reusing the previously developed programs.

While the exercises in this book require that you write programs and gather data on this work, you will learn about as much from writing a 100-LOC program as from writing a 300-LOC program. By reusing previously developed code, you will not significantly reduce the value of the process data and you will save time and gain valuable reuse experience.

TABLE D4 ASSIGNMENT PREREQUISITES

a) Exercise Program Prerequisites

Program/ Exercise Number	Prerequisite Exercises	Reference
1A		Section A2
2A	R1, R2	Chapter 4
3A	2A	Chapter 5
4A	1A	Section A7
5A		Section A5
6A	4A, 5A	Section A8
7A	R4, 1A, 5A	Sections A3 and A4
8A	4A	
9A	5A, 8A	Section A6
10A	4A, 5A, 6A	Sections A9, A10, A11
1B		
2B	1B	
3B	2B	
4B	3B	
5B	4B	
6B	5B	Section A7
7B	5A, 5B, 6B	Section A8
8B	5B	
9B	5A, 5B, 8B	Section A6
R1		Chapter 4
R2	R1	
R3	1A, 2A, 3A	
R4	R3	
R5	R4	Chapter 9

TABLE D4 (continued)

b) Process Prerequisites

Process Level	Prerequisite Process	Reference Chapters	Prerequisite Assignments
PSP0		Chapter 2	
PSP0.1	PSP0	Chapter 4	R1, R2
PSP1	PSP0.1	Chapter 5	3A
PSP1.1	PSP1	Chapter 6	
PSP2	PSP1.1	Chapter 8	R4
PSP2.1	PSP2	Chapter 10	
PSP3	PSP2.1	Chapter 11	

D3   Program Development Specifications

This section describes each programming assignment, its objectives and prerequisites, and in many cases one or more sets of test data.

PROGRAM 1A

Program 1A Prerequisites and References: Section A2

    Program 1A Requirements: Write a program to calculate the mean and standard deviation of a series of n real numbers. The mean is the average of the numbers. The formula for standard deviation is

$$\sigma(x_1, \ldots, x_n) = \sqrt{\frac{\sum_{i=1}^{n}(x_i - x_{avg})^2}{n - 1}},$$

where $\sigma(x_1, \ldots, x_n)$ is the standard deviation of the x values and x_{avg} is the average of these n values. The standard deviation calculation is described in Section A2.

    Use a linked list to hold the n numbers for the calculations.

    Program 1A Testing: Thoroughly test the program. At least three of the tests should use the data in each of the three columns on the right of Table D5. The standard deviations for the columns in this table are Object LOC: 572.03; New and Changed LOC: 625.63; and Development Hours: 62.26. The standard deviation for the total LOC case is worked out in Section A2.1.

TABLE D5   PASCAL OBJECT SIZE AND DEVELOPMENT HOURS

Program Number	Object LOC	New and Changed LOC	Development Hours
1	160	186	15.0
2	591	699	69.9
3	114	132	6.5
4	229	272	22.4
5	230	291	28.4
6	270	331	65.9
7	128	199	19.4
8	1657	1890	198.7
9	624	788	38.8
10	1503	1601	138.2

PROGRAM 2A

Program 2A Prerequisites and References: Chapter 4 and exercises R1 and R2
   Program 2A Requirements: Write a program to count the logical lines in a program, omitting comments and blank lines. Use the counting standard produced by report exercise R1 to place one logical line on each physical line and count physical lines. Produce a single count for the entire program source file.
   Program 2A Testing: Thoroughly test the program. As one test, count the LOC in programs 1A, 1B (if written), and 2A. Submit these data with your homework results, using the format in Table D6.

TABLE D6   TEST RESULTS FORMAT—PROGRAM 2A

Program Number	LOC
1A	
1B (if written)	
2A	

PROGRAM 3A

Program 3A Prerequisites and References: Chapter 5 and program 2A

   Program 3A Requirements: Write a program to count the total program LOC, the total LOC in each object the program contains, and the number of methods in each object. Produce a single LOC count for an entire source program file and separate LOC and method counts for each object. Print out each object name together with its LOC and method count. Also print out the total program LOC count. If an object-oriented language is not used, count the procedure and function LOC and print out the procedure and function names and LOC counts. Use the counting standard produced by report exercise R1. It is acceptable to enhance program 2A or to reuse some of its methods, procedures, or functions in developing program 3A.

   Program 3A Testing: Thoroughly test the program. At a minimum, test the program by counting the total program and object LOC in programs 1A, 1B (if written), 2A, 2B (if written), and 3A. Include in your test report a table giving the counts obtained with program 2A and 3A for all the programs written to date. Use the format in the example in Table D7(a).

TABLE D7 TEST RESULTS FORMAT—PROGRAM 3A

a) Format for object-oriented program designs

Program Number	Object Name	Number of Methods	Object LOC	Total Program LOC
1A	ABC	3	86	
	DEF	2	8	
	GHI	4	92	
				212
2A	. . .			

b) Format for non object-oriented designs

Program Number	Procedure/ Function Name	Number of Methods	Procedure/ Function LOC	Total Program LOC
1A	ABC	1	86	
	DEF	1	8	
	GHI	1	92	
				212
2A	. . .			

If you do not use object-oriented programming, use the reporting format in Table D7(b).

PROGRAM 4A

Program 4A Prerequisites and References: Section A7 and program 1A

Program 4A Requirements: Write a program to calculate the linear regression size-estimating parameters for a set of n programs where historical object LOC and new and changed LOC data are available. Linear regression and the required formulas are explained in Section A7. Enhance the linked list of program 1A to hold the n data records, where each record holds two real numbers.

Program 4A Testing: Thoroughly test the program. At a minimum, use this program to calculate the β parameters for three cases. For the first, use the data in Table D8 for estimated object LOC and actual new and changed LOC. The resulting values should be $\beta_0 = -22.54$ and $\beta_1 = 1.7279$. This example is worked out in Section A7.2. Second, calculate the β_0 and β_1 parameters for the regression fit of estimated new and changed LOC to actual new and changed LOC columns in Table D8. The answer in this case should be $\beta_0 = -23.92$ and $\beta1 = 1.4310$. Third, calculate the β_0 and β_1 parameters for the estimated new and changed LOC and the actual new and changed LOC for the programs 2A, 3A, and 4A that you have developed. Prepare a report of your tests that includes a table of the planned and actual results from these tests in the format in Table D9.

PROGRAM 5A

Program 5A Prerequisites and References: Section A5

Program 5A Requirements: Write a program to numerically integrate a function using Simpson's rule and write the function for the normal distribution. The program should be designed to integrate using various supplied functions. This rule and several example calculations are given in Section A5. You will need this program to calculate the values of the various statistical distributions used in later program assignments and in the analysis of your PSP data. This program is used in several subsequent exercises where programs are used to calculate values of the normal distribution, the t distribution, and the χ^2 distribution.

Program 5A Testing: Thoroughly test the program. Include a test to calculate the probability values of the normal distribution integral from $-\infty$ to $x = 2.5$, from $-\infty$ to $x = 0.2$ and from $-\infty$ to $x = -1.1$. The results should be approximately 0.9938, 0.5793, and 0.1357, respectively. Include in your test report a table of results in the format in Table D10.

TABLE D8 SIZE ESTIMATING REGRESSION DATA

Program Number	Estimated Object LOC	Estimated New and Changed LOC	Actual New and Changed LOC
1	130	163	186
2	650	765	699
3	99	141	132
4	150	166	272
5	128	137	291
6	302	355	331
7	95	136	199
8	945	1206	1890
9	368	433	788
10	961	1130	1601
Sum	3828	4632	6389
Average	382.8	463.2	638.9

TABLE D9 TEST RESULTS FORMAT—PROGRAM 4A

Test	Expected Results		Actual Results	
	β_0	β_1	β_0	β_1
Table D8: Estimated Object versus Actual New and Changed LOC	−22.54	1.7279		
Table D8: Estimated New and Changed LOC versus Actual New and Changed LOC	−23.92	1.4310		
Programs 2A, 3A, 4A: Estimated New and Changed LOC versus Actual New and Changed LOC	NA	NA		

TABLE D10   TEST RESULTS FORMAT—PROGRAM 5A

Test Value—x	Expected Results	Actual Results
2.5	0.9938	
0.2	0.5793	
−1.1	0.1357	

PROGRAM 6A

Program 6A Prerequisites and References: Section A8 and programs 4A and 5A

Program 6A Requirements: Write a program to calculate an LOC estimate and the 90 percent and 70 percent prediction intervals for this estimate. The formula for calculating the prediction interval is given in Section A8. Use program 5A to calculate the value of the t distribution and use a linked list for the data. You may enhance program 4A to develop this program. Note that to calculate the value of t, you integrate from 0 to a trial value of t. You find the correct value by successively adjusting the trial value of t up or down until the p value is within an acceptable error of 0.85 (for a 70 percent prediction interval) or 0.95 (for a 90 percent prediction interval).

Program 6A Testing: Thoroughly test the program. As one test, use the data for estimated object LOC and actual new and changed LOC in Table D8 and the β_0 and β_1 values found from testing program 4A. Also assume an estimated object LOC value of 386. Under these conditions, the estimated LOC values and the parameter values obtained should be as follows:

$\beta_0 = -22.54$

$\beta_1 = 1.7279$

$\sigma = 197.8956$

Projection $= 644.429$

$t(70 \text{ percent}) = 1.108$

$t(90 \text{ percent}) = 1.860$

Range(70 percent) $= 229.9715$, UPI $= 874.401$, LPI $= 414.4579$

Range(90 percent) $= 386.0533$, UPI $= 1030.483$, LPI $= 258.3761$

This example is worked out in Section A8.2. Using the object LOC estimate you developed while planning program 6A, calculate the projected new and changed LOC and prediction interval for program 6A. Compare this interval with the actual new and change LOC that resulted. Include these data in the test report using the format in Table D11.

TABLE D11 TEST RESULTS FORMAT—PROGRAM 6A

Test	Parameter	Expected Value	Actual Value
Table D8	β_0	−22.54	
	β_1	1.7279	
	UPI(70%)	874	
	LPI(70%)	414	
	UPI(90%)	1030	
	LPI(90%)	258	
Program 6A, using Historical Data for Programs 2A through 6A	Estimated New and Changed LOC	NA	
	UPI(70 percent)	NA	
	LPI(70 percent)	NA	
	UPI(90 percent)	NA	
	LPI(90 percent)	NA	
	Actual New and Changed LOC	NA	

PROGRAM 7A

Program 7A Prerequisites and References: Report R4, Sections A3 and A4, and programs 1A and 5A.

Program 7A Requirements: Write a program to calculate the correlation between two series of numbers and determine the significance of this correlation. The formula for making the correlation calculation is given in Section A3. Use the numerical integration function from program 5A to calculate the value of the t distribution and hold the data in a linked list.

Program 7A Testing: Thoroughly test the program. As one test, use the data in Table D12. Here, the results for the correlation between x and y should be $r = 0.9543157$, $t = 9.0335$, with $1 - p = 3.93*10^{-6}$. This is a significance of substantially better than (less than) 0.005. This example is worked out in Sections A3.2 and A4.1. Also use program 7A to analyze the data on your programming exercises to date to determine the correlation between the actual new and changed LOC and the actual development time, the correlation between the estimated new and changed LOC and the actual development time, and the significance of these correlations. Prepare and submit a test report that includes these data and uses the format in Table D13.

TABLE D12   TOTAL LOC AND DEVELOPMENT HOURS FOR
10 PASCAL PROGRAMS

Item Number	Actual New and Changed LOC	Development Hours
n	x	y
1	186	15.0
2	699	69.9
3	132	6.5
4	272	22.4
5	291	28.4
6	331	65.9
7	199	19.4
8	1890	198.7
9	788	38.8
10	1601	138.2
Totals	6389	603.2

TABLE D13   TEST RESULTS FORMAT—PROGRAM 7A

Test	Expected Value			Actual Value		
	r	t	$1 - p$	r	t	$1 - p$
Table D12:	0.9543	9.0335	$3.93*10^{-6}$			
Actual LOC versus Development Time	NA	NA	NA			
Estimated LOC versus Development Time	NA	NA	NA			

PROGRAM 8A

Program 8A Prerequisites and References: Program 4A

   Program 8A Requirements: Write program 8A to sort a linked list of n real numbers in ascending order. Where the list items have multiple fields, provide the capability to sort on any field. Assume that the list is short enough to fit in computer memory.

Program 8A Testing: Thoroughly test the program. As one test, sort the data in the right two columns of Table D14. Do two sorts, one on each field, and submit a test report describing both results. Note, your program need not print the results.

PROGRAM 9A

Program 9A Prerequisites and References: Section A6 and programs 5A and 8A

Program 9A Requirements: Write program 9A to calculate the degree to which a string of n real numbers is normally distributed. The methods and formulas used in this calculation are explained in Section A6. Use program 5A to calculate the values of the normal and χ^2 distributions. Assume that n is > 20 and an even multiple of 5. Use program 8A to sort the numbers in ascending order.

Program 9A Testing: Thoroughly test the program. As one test, use the LOC/Method data in Table D14 as a test case. Here, the result should be $Q = 34.4$ with a probability value < 0.005 that the data are normally distributed. The solution to this case is shown in Appendix A, Section A6.4. Submit a test report that includes the test results and uses the format in Table D15.

PROGRAM 10A

Program 10A Prerequisites and References: Programs 4A, 5A, and 6A and Sections A9, A10, and A11

Program 10A Requirements: Write a program to calculate the three-variable multiple regression estimating parameters, make an estimate from user-supplied inputs, and determine the 70 percent and 90 percent prediction intervals. The formulas and methods for doing this calculation are described in Sections A9, A10, and A11. Further enhance the linked list from program 4A.

Program 10A Testing: Thoroughly test the program. As one test, use the data in Table D16. For the estimated values, use 185 LOC of new code, 150 LOC of reused code, and 45 LOC of modified code. The projected hours should be 20.76 hours, the 90 percent UPI is 33.67 hours, and the 90 percent LPI is 7.84 hours. The 70 percent prediction interval is from 14.63 to 26.89 hours. The values of the beta parameters are $\beta_0 = 0.56645$, $\beta_1 = 0.06533$, $\beta_2 = 0.008719$, and $\beta_3 = 0.15105$. These are equivalent to productivities of 15.3 new and changed LOC per hour, reuse of 114.7 LOC per hour, and modification of 6.6 LOC per hour. As a further test case you should also verify that your program produces the same results given in the examples in Sections A9 and A10. Submit a test report giving your results in the format in Table D17.

TABLE D14 PASCAL OBJECT LOC

Object Number	Object LOC	LOC/Method
1	26	8.67
2	39	7.80
3	26	8.67
4	53	7.57
5	17	5.67
6	26	8.67
7	22	7.33
8	53	8.83
9	31	10.33
10	18	6.00
11	25	8.33
12	30	7.50
13	42	14.00
14	45	9.00
15	40	10.00
16	195	39.00
17	114	38.00
18	87	21.75
19	87	29.00
20	25	8.33
21	53	13.25
22	47	11.75
23	58	5.80
24	49	7.00
25	88	14.67
26	82	16.40
27	46	5.75
28	55	13.75
29	32	10.67
30	18	6.00
31	89	29.67
32	18	6.00
33	36	12.00
34	161	40.25
35	112	37.33
36	89	22.25

TABLE D14 (continued)

Object Number	Object LOC	LOC/Method
37	85	28.33
38	82	20.50
39	82	16.40
40	46	7.67
41	184	36.80
42	145	24.17
43	96	19.20
44	123	41.00
45	211	30.14
46	405	50.63
47	58	14.50
48	264	52.80
49	58	19.33
50	305	25.42

TABLE D15 TEST RESULTS FORMAT—PROGRAM 9A

Test	Expected Result	Actual Result
Table D14		
Q	34.4	
$1-p$	$7.60*10^{-5}$	

PROGRAM 1B

Program 1B Prerequisites and References: None

    Program 1B Requirements: Store and retrieve a series of *n* real numbers into and from a file. On entry, the program should accept integer or real numbers and store them as real numbers. The user functions to be provided by this program are as follows:

□ The user enters the file name.

□ The user selects either the read or write mode.

□ For read, the program displays the numbers in the file, one per line.

□ For write, the user enters the quantity of numbers to be recorded followed by entry of all the numbers, one at a time.

TABLE D16 MULTIPLE REGRESSION EXERCISE DATA

Program Number	New LOC w	Reused LOC x	Modified LOC y	Hours z
1	345	65	23	31.4
2	168	18	18	14.6
3	94	0	0	6.4
4	187	185	98	28.3
5	621	87	10	42.1
6	255	0	0	15.3
Sum	1670	355	149	138.1
Average	278.33	59.17	24.83	23.02
Estimate	185	150	45	?

Program 1B Testing: Thoroughly test the program. As one test, enter and read one or more columns of the data in Table D5 on page 753.

PROGRAM 2B

Program 2B Prerequisites and References: Program 1B

Program 2B Requirements: Enhance program 1B to permit modification or addition of data for the files handled by program 1B. When the user selects the modify mode, this program is to provide the following functions:

☐ The program reads one data item (number) from the file.

☐ The user may either accept, replace, or delete this number.

☐ The user may insert a new number after the current number and before any following numbers.

☐ The user may instruct the program to accept the remainder of the numbers in the file.

☐ The user may store the modified file with a new file name, leaving the original file undisturbed.

Program 2B Testing: Thoroughly test the program. As one test, use the Object LOC, New and Changed LOC, and Development Hours columns in Table D5 as datasets A, B, and C and use the following test procedure:

1. Enter all the values of dataset A.
2. Replace all values of dataset A with the values from dataset B.

TABLE D17 TEST RESULTS FORMAT—PROGRAM 10A

Test	Parameter	Expected Value	Actual Value
Table D16			
	β_0	0.56645	
	β_1	0.06533	
	β_2	0.008719	
	β_3	0.015105	
	Projected Hours	20.76	
	UPI(70%)	26.89	
	LPI(70%)	14.63	
	UPI(90%)	33.67	
	LPI(90%)	7.84	
Appendix A			
	β_0	6.7013	
	β_1	0.0784	
	β_2	0.0150	
	β_3	0.2461	
	Projected Hours	140.9	
	UPI(70%)	179.7	
	LPI(70%)	102.1	
	UPI(90%)	222.74	
	LPI(90%)	59.06	

3. Insert each item of dataset C after the corresponding item of dataset B. Thus the first B item (186) is followed by the first C item (15.0), the second B item (699) is followed by the second C item (69.6), and so on.

4. Delete the dataset B items.

5. Check to ensure the file now only holds the dataset C items.

Submit a report on the tests conducted and the results obtained.

PROGRAM 3B

Program 3B Prerequisites and References: Program 2B

Program 3B Requirements: Enhance program 2B to handle the following two common user errors without terminating:

1. The user enters an improper mode selection.
2. The user enters an improper data character.

In each case, inform the user of the error and provide the user the opportunity to make a correct entry or to terminate program execution. *Note:* The handling of additional user error types is called for in program 4B.

Program 3B Testing: Thoroughly test the program. At a minimum, test the program for operation with correct and incorrect user entries in each of the anticipated error cases. Prepare a test report describing the tests conducted and the results obtained.

PROGRAM 4B

Program 4B Prerequisites and References: Program 3B

Program 4B Requirements: Modify program 3B to handle the following additional user errors without terminating:

- The user enters an improperly formatted file name or address.
- The user enters an existing file name/address when creating a new file.
- The user enters a non existing file name/address when reading or modifying a file.

In each case, inform the user of the error and provide the user the opportunity to make a correct entry or to terminate program execution.

Program 4B Testing: Test the program for operation with correct and incorrect user entries in each of these cases. Prepare a test report describing the tests conducted and the results obtained.

PROGRAM 5B

Program 5B Prerequisites and References: Program 4B

Program 5B Requirements: Enhance program 4B to handle arrays of real numbers. That is, each record will be an array of K real numbers, where K is a parameter that can be set prior to compilation. A single change of parameter K should be sufficient to permit this program to handle arrays of from 1 to N real numbers, where N is at least equal to 10.

Program 5B Testing: Thoroughly test the program. Include a test to record and read the program numbers, the estimated and actual program sizes in LOC, and the estimated and actual hours expended in developing each programming exercise written to date. The program numbers should be entered as real numbers, where program number 5A is represented as 5.1, program 5B as 5.2, and so on. In particular, show how you tested operation with the maximum array size covered by your design and what happens when you exceed this size. Prepare a test report describing the tests conducted and the results obtained.

PROGRAM 6B

Program 6B Prerequisites and References: Program 5B and Section A7

Program 6B Requirements: Using program 5B, calculate the linear regression size and resource estimating parameters from process data stored in a file. Use the requirements statement for program 4A as a guide.

Program 6B Testing: Thoroughly test the program. As one test, repeat the tests specified for program 4A and show that the same results are obtained. Prepare a test report describing the tests conducted and the results obtained. For this report, use the format of Table D9.

PROGRAM 7B

Program 7B Prerequisites and References: Programs 5A, 5B, and 6B and Section A8

Program 7B Requirements: Write a program to calculate the regression parameters and prediction interval from historical process data stored in a file. You may enhance program 6B. Use the requirements for program 6A as a guide.

Program 7B Testing: Thoroughly test the program. As one test, repeat the tests specified for programs 4A and 6A and show that the same results are obtained with program 7B. Prepare a test report describing the tests conducted and the results obtained. For this report, use the format of Table D11.

PROGRAM 8B

Program 8B Prerequisites and References: Program 5B

Program 8B Requirements: Modify program 5B to sort the data in a file. Provide the user the option of selecting which term in the array of real numbers to use as the sort key. Use a merge sort.

Program 8B Testing: Thoroughly test the program. As one test, repeat the two tests specified for program 8A and show that the same results are obtained. Prepare a test report describing the tests conducted and the results obtained.

PROGRAM 9B

Program 9B Prerequisites and References: Programs 5A, 5B, and 8B, and Section A6

   Program 9B Requirements: Write a program to calculate the degree to which a string of n real numbers stored in a file is normally distributed. Use program 5A to calculate the values of the normal and χ^2 distributions. Assume n is > 20. Assume that n does not divide into segments that are equal in size. One approach is to allocate the excess elements to the distribution segments, one at a time, starting alternately with the center segments and working out. For example, with 20 elements, the segments would contain 5, 5, 5, and 5 elements. With 21 elements, the segments would contain 5, 6, 5, and 5 elements. With 22, they would have 5, 6, 6, and 5. After 24 elements are allocated to four segments with six elements each, the program should use five segments with five elements each. The χ^2 test is described in Section A6 with an example of unequal segments. Use Program 8B to sort the file of n numbers into ascending order.

   Program 9B Testing: Thoroughly test the program. For one test, use the 58 Object LOC/Method data given in Table D18. Using the same allocation procedure as in Appendix A, the result should be $Q = 40.0002$ with a probability value of less than 0.005. A second test should be for the 50 elements from Table D14. The result should be the same as found by program 9A. Submit a test report that includes the test results and uses the format in Table D19.

D4   Report Exercises

This book calls for five report exercises. These reports involve various kinds of analyses of the data you have gathered on the PSP exercise programs. Depending on the particular exercise, you then produce various reports or standards. These report exercises are described in the following sections.

R1 LINE-OF-CODE COUNTING STANDARD

Assignment Overview: Produce a standard specifying how you will count LOC.
   Assignment Objectives:

- To define the LOC counting standards that are appropriate for the programming language you use
- To provide a basis for developing a coding standard
- To prepare for developing a program to count LOC

TABLE D18 PASCAL OBJECT DATA

Object Number	Object LOC	LOC/ Method	Object Number	Object LOC	LOC/ Method
1	26	8.67	30	18	6.00
2	39	7.80	31	89	29.67
3	26	8.67	32	18	6.00
4	53	7.57	33	36	12.00
5	17	5.67	34	161	40.25
6	26	8.67	35	112	37.33
7	22	7.33	36	89	22.25
8	53	8.83	37	85	28.33
9	31	10.33	38	37	12.33
10	18	6.00	39	82	16.40
11	25	8.33	40	46	7.67
12	30	7.50	41	184	36.80
13	42	14.00	42	145	24.17
14	45	9.00	43	96	19.20
15	40	10.00	44	123	41.00
16	195	39.00	45	19	6.33
17	114	38.00	46	54	9.00
18	87	21.75	47	58	14.50
19	87	29.00	48	264	52.80
20	25	8.33	49	58	19.33
21	53	13.25	50	305	25.42
22	47	11.75	51	578	48.17
23	58	5.80	52	82	20.50
24	49	7.00	53	88	14.67
25	79	7.90	54	82	16.40
26	82	16.40	55	230	23.00
27	46	5.75	56	219	36.50
28	55	13.75	57	405	50.63
29	32	10.67	58	211	30.14

Task: Exercise R1—Develop and submit a standard for counting logical LOC for the programming language you use to write the PSP exercise programs.

Result: Produce, document, and submit the completed standard, using the format in Tables 4.1, 4.2, and 4.3 in Chapter 4.

Assignment Timing: You should do this assignment after reviewing Chapter 4 and either before or in conjunction with writing program 2A.

TABLE D19 TEST RESULTS FORMAT—PROGRAM 9B

Test	Expected Result	Actual Result
Table D18		
Q	40.0	
$1-p$	$7.60*10^{-6}$	
Table D14		
Q	34.4	
$1-p$	$7.60*10^{-5}$	

R2   CODING STANDARD

Assignment Overview: Produce a coding standard for use in writing the PSP exercise programs.

Assignment Objectives:

- To establish a consistent set of coding practices
- To provide criteria for judging the quality of the code you produce
- To facilitate LOC counting by ensuring your programs are written with a separate physical line for each logical line of code

Task: Exercise R2—Produce a coding standard that calls for quality coding practices. Use the PSP coding standard in Table C29 (page 670) and the discussion in Chapter 4 as a guide. Also ensure a separate physical source line is used for each logical line of code, as defined in exercise R1. Submit this standard with your assignment package.

Result: Produce, document, and submit the completed coding standard.

Assignment Timing: You should do this assignment after reviewing Chapter 4 and producing report R1 and either before or in conjunction with writing program 2A.

R3   THE DEFECT ANALYSIS REPORT

Assignment Objectives:

- To understand the density and types of defects introduced and found while developing the initial programs in this book
- To demonstrate the importance of carefully gathering, recording, and reporting process data

Task: Analyze the defects found in developing the initial programs in this book and produce a report that includes the following:

1. A table giving
   - □ the total numbers of defects found,
   - □ the new and changed LOC, and
   - □ the defects per KLOC.

   Give these data for each program and for the total of the programs written to date. Use the format in Table D20.

2. A table giving
   - □ the number of defects found in compile,
   - □ the number of defects found in test,
   - □ the number of defects per KLOC found in compile, and
   - □ the number of defects per KLOC found in test.

   Give these data for each program and for the total of the programs written to date. Use the format in Table D21.

3. Produce a table showing the average fix times for defects found in compile, defects found in test, defects injected in design, and defects injected in coding. Produce a table in the format shown in Table D22.

Result: Complete and submit the required tables.

Assignment Timing: You should do this assignment in conjunction with or immediately following completion of program 3A. Because an assignment objective is to demonstrate the importance of gathering quality process data, this assignment should not be delayed beyond that point. Its prerequisites are Chapter 4 and at least three completed programs.

TABLE D20 DEFECT DENSITIES

Program Number	New and Changed LOC	Number of Defects	Defects/KLOC
1A			
2A			
3A			
Totals			

TABLE D21   COMPILE AND TEST DEFECTS

Program Number	New and Changed LOC	Defects found in compile	Defects found in test	Compile defects per KLOC	Test defects per KLOC
1A					
2A					
3A					
Totals					

TABLE D22   DEFECT FIX TIMES

	Defects found in compiling	Defects found in testing	Total defects found
Defects injected in designing	For defects injected in design and found in compile: total fix time: total number of defects: average fix time:	For defects injected in design and found in test: total fix time: total number of defects: average fix time:	For all defects injected in design: total fix time: total number of defects: average fix time:
Defects injected in coding	For defects injected in code and found in compile: total fix time: total number of defects: average fix time:	For defects injected in code and found in test: total fix time: total number of defects: average fix time:	For all defects injected in code: total fix time: total number of defects: average fix time:
Total defects injected	For all defects found in compile: total fix time: total number of defects: average fix time:	For all defects found in test: total fix time: total number of defects: average fix time:	For all defects: total fix time: total number of defects: average fix time:

R4   THE MIDTERM ANALYSIS REPORT

Assignment Overview: Define a process for analyzing your PSP data and producing a report. Use this process to produce report R4. You will update this process to produce the final report at the end of the course.

Assignment Objectives:

☐ To get early experience in defining and using a process

□ To understand your baseline personal software process and how it has changed so far in the course

□ To provide design and code review checklists

Tasks:

Task 1—Develop a process for analyzing the data and creating a report on programs 1A through 6A. This should include the results listed below under Task 3. This process must include a planning phase, the task performance phases, and a postmortem phase. Produce and submit a process script and planning forms for enacting this process.

Task 2—Plan and enact the process defined in Task 1. Use the planning form to record the planned time for this work and track and record the actual time you spend. Submit the planned and actual process data together with the analysis report.

Task 3—Analyze the data for programs 1 through 6. Spreadsheet analyses are suggested and graphical summaries and presentations are encouraged. At a minimum, produce the following:

□ An analysis of LOC and development time estimating accuracy and how it has evolved during the programs developed to date

□ An analysis of the defect types injected and removed for the programs developed to date. These data should be shown in a format similar to that in Table D23

□ An analysis of the defect types found by the compiler. These data should be shown in a format similar to that in Table D24

□ An analysis of the defect fix times, using the format used in report R3 (Table D22)

□ Develop a design review checklist to find the most-frequent design defects in a design review

□ Develop a code-review checklist to find the most-frequent coding defects in a code review.

Result: Use the GQM method to draw conclusions and set personal improvement goals. Submit the required analyses, tables, and checklists, together with a brief written report. Use graphs wherever possible.

Assignment Timing: You should do this assignment in conjunction with program 6A or shortly after its completion. It should precede the development of any programs using the PSP2 or later processes.

R5 FINAL REPORT

Overview: Produce a report on what you have learned from doing the exercises in this book. The assignment is to provide you with a thorough understanding of

TABLE D23 PERCENTAGE OF DEFECTS INJECTED AND REMOVED
BY PHASE

	Number Injected		Percentage Injected		Number Removed		Percentage Removed	
Type	Design	Code	Design	Code	Compile	Test	Compile	Test
10								
20								
30								
40								
50								
60								
70								
80								
90								
100								
Total								

TABLE D24 PERCENTAGE OF DEFECTS FOUND IN COMPILE

Defect Type	Number of defects at Compile Entry	Number of defects found in Compile	Percentage of Defects Found by the Compiler
10			
20			
30			
40			
50			
60			
70			
80			
90			
100			
Total			

your current software development performance and your highest-priority areas for improvement. Update the process you used to develop the midterm report and use this updated process to produce this final report.

Tasks:

Task 1—Update the process you developed for the midterm report. Submit an updated copy of the process and note the changes you made and why. Note particularly if you used PIPs and what changes you made as a result.

Task 2—Plan and enact the process defined in Task 1 to do the work defined in Task 3. Use the planning form to record the planned time for this work and track and record the actual time you spend. Submit the planned and actual data on the process together with the final report.

Task 3—Analyze the data for the programs you have developed with the PSP. Spreadsheet analyses are suggested and graphical summaries and presentations are encouraged. At a minimum, produce the following:

- Analyze your size-estimating accuracy and determine the degree to which your estimates were within the 70 percent and 90 percent statistical prediction intervals. Also show how your size-estimating accuracy evolved during the assignments.

- Analyze your time-estimating accuracy and determine the degree to which your estimates were within the 70 percent and 90 percent statistical prediction intervals. Also show how your time-estimating accuracy evolved during the assignments.

- Analyze the types of defects you injected in design and in coding. Include a Pareto analysis of these defect types (see Section A12).

- Determine your trends for defects per KLOC found in design review, code review, compile, and test. Also, show your trends for total defects per KLOC throughout the course.

- Analyze your defect-removal rates for design reviews, code reviews, compile, and test and show the defect-removal leverage for design reviews, code reviews, and compile versus unit test. In those cases in which you had no test defects, use the average unit test defect-removal rate for the programs developed to date.

- Produce an analysis of yield versus LOC reviewed per hour in your code reviews.

- Produce an analysis of design-review yield versus LOC reviewed per hour. Note that design-review yield is calculated as follows:
  Yield(DR) = 100*(defects removed in design review)/
  (defects removed in design review + defects escaping design review).

- Produce an analysis of the yield versus the A/FR ratio for programs 7 through 10.

☐ Produce a brief write-up describing your highest-priority areas for personal process improvement and why. Briefly summarize your current performance, your desired future performance, and your improvement goals. Describe how and roughly when you intend to meet these goals.

Result: Submit the required analyses and a brief written report describing your findings and conclusions. Use graphs wherever possible. Note particularly how you will use these results to manage and improve your software and other work in the future.

D5 ASSIGNMENT PLANS—SUGGESTIONS FOR THE INSTRUCTOR

The standard assignment plan included in the text is shown in Table D2. This assignment plan represents a fairly heavy one-semester workload which should not be augmented unless you expect the students to spend substantially more than 10 hours per week on the assignments. Note in particular that the various chapters take from one half to two lectures. Also, warn the students to start program 10A as soon as they complete program 9A, since it is substantially larger than the other programs. Allow them about one week to develop report R4 and one to two weeks for report R5. Also allow one week to develop each of programs 1A through 8A, one to two weeks for program 9A, and two to three weeks for program 10A. You should not plan to assign any of the B series programs unless you plan a course that runs longer than 16 weeks or allows for more than 10 hours per week of preparation.

INDEX

absolute measures, 208
absorption law, 569
abstractions, 354
  level of, 138
  potential problems with, 364
  power of, 354
accuracy
  estimating 222
  process, 443
  versus precision, 73
Ackerman, A. Frank, 276, 306
action planning for defect prevention, 303
actual time per phase, 224
added LOC, 92
adjusted earned value, 183
  see also earned value
A/FR, *see* appraisal to failure ratio
after-development defects, 218
agent, process, 443
AIS Corporation, 17
Albrecht, A. J., 101, 106, 142, 210, 230
alerting management to changes, 195
algebra of sets, 567
Amsden, R. T., 16, 27
antisymmetric property of sets, 569

application notes, 315
appraisal costs, 280, 637
  formula for, 281
  12 students, 282
appraisal to failure ratio, 281, 287, 640
  formula, 281
  versus test defects, 289
  versus yield, 289
Armour, Jody, 3, 27
assessing program quality, 83
assignment plan, 746, 747
  instructor suggestions, 775
assignment prerequisites, 751
associative law, 569
autonomous development groups, 360
available work hours, 169, 172
  calculating, 172
  see also productive time

Baber, Robert L., 437, 439, 595, 605
Bannister, Roger, 8
base program LOC, 121
baseline, personal process, 227
Basili, V., 207, 211, 230
Beizer, B., 12, 27, 370, 372

objectives, PSP, 214
O'Neill, Don, 276, 307
OOD (object-oriented design), 309, 364
Operational Scenario Template, 340, 341, 717
  example, 342
  instructions, 718
optimizing process level, 6
orthogonal functions, 601, 602
  see also proper state machine
OS/360, 60
outliers, 150, 507
  cautions regarding, 508
overcompensation, 199, 203
overestimating, 203

packaging, 82
parameters
  linear regression, 122, 544
  multiple regression, 162, 553
Pareto distribution, 261, 491, 492, 564
  example, 565
  procedure, 564
Park, Robert E., 63, 68, 74, 95, 100, 142
Pascal LOC counting standard, 77
Paulk, M. C., 6, 28
percent new reused, 626
percent reused, 626
performance, 273
personal
  goals, 240
  process baseline, 227
  reviews, 232, 238
  standards 267
  software process, *see* PSP
PERT, 63, 180
phase
  definition, 34
  Definition Template, 457, 458
physical LOC, 75, 90, 92
PIP, *see* Process Improvement Proposal
Pirsig, Robert M., 12, 28
planning, 57, 59
  accuracy, 146
  development time, 149
  error formula, 197
  errors, 67, 196
  essential issues of, 58
  framework, 64
  phase of PSP, 34
  resource, 145
  role of, 58

software planning steps, 62
  tools, 63
  why planning is the first PSP step, 57
plans, 61
  and commitments, 59, 472
  accessibility of, 66
  accuracy of, 67, 146
  clarity of, 66
  completeness of, 66
  customer needs from a plan, 61
  making plans, 472
  minimum cost, 473
  precision of, 67
  project, 59
  quality of, 64, 197
  specificity of, 67
  strategy for defending, 473
  what you need from a plan, 61
  why plans are needed, 11, 60
postmortem phase, 34
precision, 73, 81
  of a process, 443
prediction interval, 123, 152, 160, 492, 548
  calculation example, 154
  combining, 158, 159
  development time, 629
  example, 549
  lower (LPI), 160, 162, 168
  meaning of, 124
  multiple regression, 558
  multiple regression example, 166, 557
  procedure, 549
  range formula, 548
  size, 629
  upper (UPI), 160, 162, 168
  variance formula, 548
  see also range
predictive measures, 208
prerequisites, assignment, 751
pressure, handling, 472
prevention costs, 280
PriceS, 63, 99
PROBE, 97, 101, 121, 150, 157
  estimating script, 679
  method, 117
  method flow chart, 118
  philosophy behind, 136
process
  architecture, 443
  benchmarking, 286, 290
  definition, 443
  definition of, 443

tracking, 181, 195
transitive property, 569
Truman, Harry S., 484
TRW, 275
TSP, 13, 14

underestimating, 203
unit testing, 299, 300, 370
unplanned time, 170
  cushion, 170
unprecedented products, 140
UPI, *see* upper prediction interval
Upp, Gregg, 17
upper prediction interval (UPI), 160
  example, 162
  multiple regression, 168
  see also prediction interval
usability, 273
user scenarios, 315
using limited data, 137
utilization factor, 172

van Genuchten, Michiel, 276, 307
variance (σ), 135, 161, 492, 508
  calculation, 507, 509,
  calculation example, 509
  calculation procedure, 509
  formula, 124, 161, 509
  linear regression, 548
  multiple regression, 557
Venn diagrams, 570
verification
  comments on methods, 436
  complexity, 437
  design, 373
  economics, 375
  effectiveness, 374
  ForLoop, 418
  ForLoop example, 419
  formal methods, 437
  loops, 418
  methods, 373, 378
  objectives, 379
  program correctness, 418
  RepeatUntil, 428

RepeatUntil example, 429
selecting methods for, 374
state machine, 380
strategy, 436
using verification methods, 375
WhileLoop, 420
WhileLoop example, 426

walk-through, 232
Weinberg, Gerald M., 275
Weller, E. F., 276, 307
WhileLoop verification, 420
  example, 426
Wideband Delphi, 101, 102
Wirfs-Brock, R., 113, 143
wishbone diagrams, 301
Wohlwend, Harvey, 4, 28
women's height distribution, 496
Woodcock, Jim, 595, 605
Wulf, Wm. A., 357, 372

yield, 225, 240, 279, 629
  calculation, essential data for, 250
  calculation example, 249, 252
  formula, 249, 284
  management of, 284, 292
  management strategy, 297
  review, 279
  specialization by phase, 298
  total process, 283
  twelve students, 253, 279
  versus A/FR, 289
  versus COQ, 287
  versus defects/hour, 254
  versus defects/KLOC, 253
  versus LOC per hour, 255
  versus productivity, 12 students, 291
  versus productivity, student 1, 291
  versus test defects, 289
Yourdon, Edward, 333

Zells, Lois, 60, 68, 180, 205, 447, 470
Zultner, Richard E., 446, 470
Zwanzig, K., 109, 143

PSP Support Materials Available on Diskette

In *A Discipline for Software Engineering*, Watts S. Humphrey provides seven versions of personal software process (PSP) and exercises to demonstrate their use. To assist individual rea in doing these exercises and in producing the required analyses and reports, a **Support Diskett** available for purchase. This diskette contains copies of the forms illustrated in the book, as we data analysis spreadsheets for the exercises. You will find these materials to be a practical addi to the book itself.

Both an **Instructor's Guide** and an **Instructor's Diskette** are available free of charge for use instructors in courses where *A Discipline for Software Engineering* has been adopted as a requ text. The Instructor's Guide includes lecture and grading suggestions, as well as forms that car copied for student use. The Instructor's Diskette contains electronic copies of the forms, lec overheads, and spreadsheets to review and analyze student data.

Requirements: The Support Diskette requires an IBM PC or PC-compatible that can use f from Microsoft Windows 3.1 versions of Word 2.0 and Excel 4.0. An A Macintosh version is also available. The Instructor's Diskette requires an IBM or PC-compatible that can use files from Microsoft Windows 3.1 version Word 2.0, Excel 4.0, and PowerPoint 3.0 and has 8.0 MB of available disk sp. No Macintosh version is available.

Ordering Information
Copies of the Support Diskette may be purchased from Addison-Wesley $14.95 per copy (price includes shipping and handling). To order, you n photocopy and complete the form below, enclose a check for the appropr amount made out to Addison-Wesley Publishing Company, Inc., and mail to:

> Addison-Wesley Publishing Company, Inc.
> CS Marketing
> One Jacob Way
> Reading, MA 01867-9984

Instructors should contact their local Addison-Wesley representative to request Instructor's Guide and Instructor's Diskette or call Addison-Wesley's Comp Science Marketing Department at 1-617-944-3700, extension 2575.

More Information
To receive future information about this book, the diskettes, and other work interest to software-engineering educators and practitioners, be sure to incl your e-mail address on the order form. Also, please take a look at our electr catalog on the Internet: Type **gopher@aw.com** and follow the instructions.

Please send me _____ copy/copies of the Support Diskette that supplements *A Discipline Software Engineering*. I enclose a check for $14.95 per copy, including shipping and hand [Mass. residents add 5% sales tax]. Please specify which version:

PC _____(#83485)   Macintosh _____(#83998)

Name _____

Company/School _____ E-mail address _____

Title _____

Address _____

City _____ State _____ Zip _____

*The ordering information described here is valid only in the United States. Contact your Addis Wesley office for ordering information in other countries.

Terms introduced with PSP1 (continued)

Linear Regression	
Linear Regression Parameters	$$\beta_1 = \dfrac{\displaystyle\sum_{i=1}^{n} x_i y_i - n x_{avg} y_{avg}}{\displaystyle\sum_{i=1}^{n} x_i^2 - n(x_{avg})^2}$$ $$\beta_0 = y_{avg} - \beta_1 x_{avg}$$
x_i, x_{avg}	For size and time estimates, the estimated object LOC for each previous developed program and the average of these values
y_i, y_{avg}	For size estimates, the actual new and changed LOC for each previously developed program and the average of these values; for time estimates, the actual total time spent developing each previously developed program and the average of these values
Range	$$Range = t(\alpha/2, n-2)\sigma \sqrt{1 + \dfrac{1}{n} + \dfrac{(x_k - x_{avg})^2}{\displaystyle\sum_{i=1}^{n}(x_i - x_{avg})^2}}$$
Variance	$$Variance = \sigma^2 = \left(\dfrac{1}{n-2}\right)\sum_{i=1}^{n}(y_i - \beta_0 - \beta_1 x_i)^2$$
x_k	For size and time estimates, the estimated object LOC for the new program
t	the double-sided value of the t distribution for $n-2$ degrees of freedom and the percentage desired for the prediction range
n	the number of items in the historical dataset
Standard Deviation	$Standard\ Deviation = \sqrt{Variance} = \sigma$

Terms introduced with PSP1.1

PSP1.1 Project Plan Summary	
Cost Performance Index	CPI = planned total development time to date divided by Time in Phase Total To Date
% Reused	The percentage of total program LOC taken from the reuse library
% New Reused	The percent of new and changed LOC planned for addition to the reuse library

Task and Schedule Planning Templates	
Planned Value	The percentage of the total planned project time that the planned task represents.
Cumulative Planned Value	The running cumulative sum of the planned values
Earned Value	The planned value for a task is earned when the task is completed. There is no partial credit for partially completed tasks.
Cumulative Earned Value	The running cumulative sum of the earned values for the completed task
Adjusted Earned Value	The earned value, after adjustment for plan changes